Yamaha XVS V-Twins
Service and Repair Manual

by Phil Mather

(4195 - 5AO1 - 304)

Models covered

Europe

Yamaha XVS650 Drag Star. 649cc. 1997 to 2005
Yamaha XVS650A Drag Star Classic. 649cc. 1998 to 2008
Yamaha XVS1100 Drag Star. 1063cc. 1999 to 2006
Yamaha XVS1100A Drag Star Classic. 1063cc. 2000 to 2008

US

Yamaha XVS650 V-Star Custom. 649cc. 1998 to 2011
Yamaha XVS650A V-Star Classic. 649cc. 1998 to 2010
Yamaha XVS650S V-Star Silverado. 649cc. 2003 to 2010
Yamaha XVS1100 V-Star Custom. 1063cc. 1999 to 2009
Yamaha XVS1100A V-Star Classic. 1063cc. 2000 to 2009
Yamaha XVS1100S V-Star Silverado. 1063cc. 2002 to 2009

ABCDE
FGHI

© Haynes Publishing 2015

A book in the **Haynes Service and Repair Manual Series**

ISBN 978 1 78521 269 7

British Library Cataloguing in Publication Data
A catalogue record for this book is available from the British Library

Library of Congress Control Number 2015941206

Printed in Malaysia

Haynes Publishing
Sparkford, Yeovil, Somerset BA22 7JJ, England

Haynes North America, Inc
859 Lawrence Drive, Newbury Park, California 91320, USA

Printed using NORBRITE BOOK 48.8gsm (CODE: 40N6533) from NORPAC; procurement system certified under Sustainable Forestry Initiative standard. Paper produced is certified to the SFI Certified Fiber Sourcing Standard (CERT - 0094271)

Contents

Contents

Yamaha
Musical instruments to motorcycles

**The FS1E -
first bike of many sixteen year olds in the UK**

The Yamaha Motor Company

The Yamaha name can be traced back to 1889, when Torakusu Yamaha founded the Yamaha Organ Manufacturing Company. Such was the success of the company, that in 1897 it became Nippon Gakki Limited and manufactured a wide range of reed organs and pianos.

During World War II, Nippon Gakki's manufacturing base was utilised by the Japanese authorities to produce propellers and fuel tanks for their aviation industry. The end of the war brought about a huge public demand for low cost transport and many firms decided to utilise their obsolete aircraft tooling for the production of motorcycles. Nippon Gakki's first motorcycle went on sale in February 1955 and was named the 125 YA-1 Red Dragonfly. This machine was a copy of the German DKW RT125 motorcycle, featuring a single cylinder two-stroke engine with a four-speed gearbox. Due to the outstanding success of this model the motorcycle operation was separated from Nippon Gakki in July 1955 and the Yamaha Motor Company was formed.

The YA-1 also received acclaim by winning two of Japan's biggest road races, the Mount Fuji Climbing race and the Asama Volcano race. The high level of public demand for the YA-1 led to the development of a whole series of two-stroke singles and twins.

Having made a large impact on their home market, Yamahas were exported to the USA in 1958 and to the UK in 1962. In the UK the signing of an Anglo-Japanese trade agreement during 1962 enabled the sale of Japanese lightweight motorcycles and scooters in Britain. At that time, competition between the many motorcycle producers in Japan had reduced numbers significantly and by the end of the sixties, only the big-four which are familiar with today remained.

Yamaha Europe was founded in 1968 and based in Holland. Although originally set up to market marine products, the Dutch base is now the official European Headquarters and distribution centre. Yamaha motorcycles are built at factories in Holland, Denmark, Norway, Italy, France, Spain and Portugal. Yamahas are imported into the UK by Yamaha Motor UK Ltd, formerly Mitsui Machinery Sales (UK) Ltd. Mitsui and Co. were originally a trading house, handling the shipping, distribution and marketing of Japanese products into western countries. Ultimately Mitsui Machinery Sales was formed to handle Yamaha motorcycles and outboard motors.

Based on the technology derived from its motorcycle operation, Yamaha have produced many other products, such as automobile and lightweight aircraft engines, marine engines and boats, generators, pumps, ATVs, snowmobiles, golf cars, industrial robots, lawnmowers, swimming pools and archery equipment.

Two-strokes first

Part of Yamaha's success was a whole string of innovations in the two-stroke world. Autolube engine lubrication, torque induction, multi-ported engines, reed valves and power valves kept their two-strokes at the forefront of technology. Many advances were achieved with the use of racing as a development laboratory. They went to the USA in the late 1950s with an air-cooled 250cc twin but didn't hit the GPs until the early 1960s when Fumio Ito scored a hat-trick of sixth places in the Isle of Man TT, the Dutch TT and the Belgian GP. This experiment gave rise to the idea of the over-the-counter racer, an idea that became reality in the TD1, the first in an unmatched series of two-stroke racers that were the standard issue for privateers at national and international level for years and helped Yamaha develop their road engines. While privateers raced the twins, Yamaha built the outrageously complicated vee-four 250 for Phil Read and followed it with a vee-four 125 that Bill Ivy lapped the Isle of Man on at over 100mph! When the FIM regulations were changed to limit the smaller GP classes to two cylinders, these exotic bikes died but set the scene for an unparalleled dynasty of mass-produced racers based on the same technology as the road bikes.

In the 1960s and 70s the two-stroke engined YAS3 125, YDS1 to YDS7 250 and YR5 350 formed the core of Yamaha's range. By the mid-70s they had been superseded by the RD (Race-Developed) 125, 250, and 350 range of two-stroke twins, featuring improved 7-port engines with reed valve induction. Braking was improved by the use of an hydraulic brake on the front wheel of DX models, instead of the drum arrangement used previously, and cast alloy wheels were available as an option on later RD models. The RD350 was replaced by the RD400 in 1976.

Running parallel with the RD twins was a range of single-cylinder two-strokes. Used in a variety of chassis types, the engine was used in the popular 50 cc FS1-E moped, the V50 to 90 step-thrus, RS100 and 125, YB100 and the DT trail range.

The TD racers got water-cooling in 1973 to become the TZs, the most successful and numerous over-the-counter racers ever built. That same year, Jarno Saarinen became the first rider to win a 500cc GP on a four-cylinder two-stroke on the new in-line four which was effectively a pair of TZs side-by-side. TZs won everywhere – including the Daytona 200 and 500 races when overbored to 351cc. A 700cc TZ also appeared, one year later taken out to 750cc. Steve Baker won the first Formula 750 world title – one of the precursors of Superbike – on one in 1977. The following year Kenny Roberts won Yamaha's first world 500 title and would be succeeded by Wayne Rainey and Eddie Lawson before Mick Doohan and the NSR500 took over.

The air-cooled single and twin cylinder RD road bikes were eventually replaced by the LC series in 1980, featuring liquid-cooled engines, radical new styling, spiral pattern cast wheels and cantilever rear suspension (Yamaha's Monoshock). Of all the LC models, the RD350LC, or RD350R as it was later known, has made the most impact in the market. Later models had YPVS (Yamaha Power Valve System) engines, another first for Yamaha – this was essentially a valve located in the exhaust ports which was electronically operated to alter port timing to achieve maximum power output. The RD500LC was the largest two-stroke made by Yamaha and differed from the other LCs by the use of its vee-four cylinder engine.

With the exception of the RD350R, now manufactured in Brazil, the LC range has been discontinued. Two-stroke engined models have given way to environmental pressure, and thus with a few exceptions, such as the TZR125 and TZR250, are used only in scooters and small capacity bikes.

The distinctive paintwork and trim of the RD models

The Four-strokes

Yamaha concentrated solely on two-stroke models until 1970 when the XS1 was produced, their first four-stroke motorcycle. It was perhaps Yamaha's success with two-strokes that postponed an earlier move into the four-stroke motorcycle market, although their work with Toyota during the 1960s had given them a sound base in four-stroke technology.

The XS1 had a 650 cc twin-cylinder SOHC engine and was later to become known as the XS650, appearing also in the popular SE custom form. Yamaha introduced a three cylinder 750 cc engine in 1976, fitted in a sport-tourer frame and called the XS750, TX750 in the USA . The XS750 established itself well in the sport tourer class and remained in production with very few changes until uprated to 850 cc in 1980.

Other four-strokes followed in 1976, with the introduction of the XS250/360/400 series twins. The XS range was strengthened in 1978 by the four-cylinder XS1100.

The 1980s saw a new family of four-strokes, the XJ550, 650, 750 and 900 Fours. Improvements over the XS range amounted to a slimmer DOHC engine unit due to the relocation of the alternator behind the cylinders, electronic ignition and uprated braking and suspension systems. Models were available mainly in standard trim, although custom-styled Maxims were produced especially for the US market. The

The XS650 led the way for Yamaha's four-stroke range

XJ650T was the first model from Yamaha to have a turbo-charged engine. Although these early XJ models have now been discontinued, their roots live on in the XJ600S and XJ900S Diversion (Seca II) models.

The FZR prefix encompasses the pure sports Yamaha models. With the exception of the 16-valve FZR400 and FZR600 models, the FZ/FZR750 and FZR1000 used 20-valve engines, two exhaust valves and three inlet

Yamaha's XS750 was produced from 1976 to 1982 and then uprated to 850 cc

valves per cylinder. This concept was called Genesis and gave improved gas flow to the combustion chambers. Other features of the new engine were the use of down-draught carburetors and the engine's inclined angle in the frame, plus the change to liquid-cooling. Lightweight Deltabox design aluminium frames and uprated suspension improved the bikes's handling. The Genesis engine lives on in the YZF750 and 1000 models.

The Genesis concept was the basis of Yamaha's foray into four-stroke racing, first with a bike known simply as 'The Genesis', an FZ750 motor in a TT Formula 1 bike with which the factory attempted to steal the Honda RVF750's thunder at important events like the Suzuka 8 Hours and the Bol d'Or although they never fielded it for a whole World Championship season. That had to wait for the advent of the World Superbike Championship, although there was no full works team until 1995, instead it was left to individual importers to support teams. It was the Australian Dealer Team Yamaha which scored the factory's first World Superbike win in the series debut year of 1988. The rider? Mick Doohan. Slightly, embarrassingly, it was the steel framed FZ750 rather than the FZR homologation special that won races. The OW01 was a race winner, mainly in the hands of Fabrizio Pirovano, the factory's most successful Superbike racer with ten victories, but national success in the UK, Japan, and in the Daytona 200 has not been translated into World Championships for any of Yamaha's 750s.

The vee-twin engine has been the mainstay of the XV Virago range. Since 1981 XVs have been produced in 535, 700, 750, 920, 1000 and 1100 engine sizes, all using the same basic air-cooled sohc vee-twin engine. Other uses of vee engines have been in the XZ550 of the early 1980s, the XVZ12 Venture and the mighty VMX-12 V-Max.

A new family of four-strokes was released in 1980 with the introduction of the XJ range

Yamaha has always been a sporting-orientated company whose motto could be 'Racing Improves the Breed', so it's no surprise that the latest generation of lightweight sportsters are at the cutting edge of performance on and off the track. The R6 won more races than any other machine in the inaugural year of the World Supersports Championship, the R7 won a race in its debut year in World Superbike in the hands of the mercurial Noriyuki Haga, and the mighty 1000cc R1 ended Honda's domination of the Isle of Man F1 TT when David Jefferies won three races in a week in 1999.

In Grand Prix racing, the factory took several years to get over the shock of Wayne Rainey's crippling accident. and first 500cc win since the American's enforced retirement didn't come until 1998 when Simon Crafar won at Donington Park. For 1999, Yamaha refocussed their ambitions and signed Italian superstar Max Biaggi plus Spanish trier Carlos Checa for the works team, while dashing young Frenchman Regis Laconi and tough little Aussie Gary McCoy rode for the WCM satellite team. Both teams got a win in the '99 season and with a new TZ250 being developed for 2000 it looks as if Yamaha's spirit of competition will go on unabated into the new Millenium.

The XV535 Virago vee-twin

The Mild Ones

Many manufacturers just don't put their hearts into making factory customs. Yamaha, however, got it right from the start. Not many people remember the original Virago, a 750 cc shaft-drive V-twin from the early 1980s but it worked well enough. Unfortunately it was brought out alongside the gruesomely underdeveloped TR1, which was an attempt at a mainstream V-twin.

Yamaha realised that if you took an existing bike and 'customised' it you usually got a bad bike, after all they did it themselves a couple of times. The first Virago was designed as a custom from the start, it was a coherent design that achieved its objectives. Customers who bought the bike weren't disappointed.

Then in 1988 came the the XV535, the bike on which the XVS650 would eventually be based. Again it was a shaft-drive V-twin with no relation to other bikes. It was small, cute and even sports-bike obsessed magazine testers agreed it was a good bike. It sold by the boat load. Its size, weight and manageability made it a favourite with new riders, returning bikers and especially women. The mix of style and practicality was just about perfect and it gave rise to a few companies specialising in Viragos.

Success in the custom field may have come as a surprise to Yamaha but they've picked up the ball and run with it. They learned (unlike other factories) that the bikes must have style and be easy to ride and look after. The 535 definitely had the hallmarks of a custom – peanut tank, large rear tyre, skinny front tyre, low seat, etc – but it had its own distinctive look. When the time came to completely rework the old Virago, Yamaha moved closer to the Harley-Davidson approach as seen in the lines of the two exhausts running down the right-hand side of the bike and the orange and black, Harley's factory racing colours, colour option. The new name – Drag Star in Europe and V-Star in the US – tells you exactly where Yamaha looked for the styling. All the cues are there, with the emphasis being on long and low. The XVS650's engine is based on that used in the 535, bored and stroked to provide the extra capacity. In addition to the standard, or custom as it is called in the US, the slightly more expensive Classic model took the custom look a stage further with valanced mudguards, chrome fork shrouds and different headlight and instruments.

The XVS1100 arrived two years after the 650 to complete the family tree. Although it's chassis was completely new and mirrored the styling of the smaller model it used the engine from its predecessor, the XV1100 Virago. The XVS1100 was available in standard or classic trim, plus a Silverago version for US owners which had a windshield, saddlebags, studded seat and passenger backrest.

Yamaha's custom savvy includes the understanding that their customers will want to, er, customise their bikes, so there are plenty of accessories around to let owners do just that. The Yamaha customs also have the advantage of a better than average finish, which means they stay shinier longer. There is nothing worse than a factory custom with dull paint and rusty chromework. The fact you don't see models in that state is a tribute not just to the owners but to the Yamaha designers who understood what they were doing when they took on the challenge of making a factory custom that rider would want to buy – and keep buying.

Acknowledgements

Our thanks are due to Fowlers Motorcycles of Bristol and Taylors Motorcycles of Crewkerne who supplied the machines featured in the illustrations throughout this manual. We would also like to thank NGK Spark Plugs (UK) Ltd for supplying the colour spark plug condition photographs, the Avon Rubber Company for supplying information on tyre fitting and Draper Tools Ltd for some of the workshop tools shown.

Thanks are also due to Julian Ryder who wrote the introduction 'Musical Instruments to Motorcycles' and Yamaha Motor (UK) Ltd for providing model photographs.

About this manual

The aim of this manual is to help you get the best value from your motorcycle. It can do so in several ways. It can help you decide what work must be done, even if you choose to have it done by a dealer; it provides information and procedures for routine maintenance and servicing; and it offers diagnostic and repair procedures to follow when trouble occurs.

We hope you use the manual to tackle the work yourself. For many simpler jobs, doing it yourself may be quicker than arranging an appointment to get the motorcycle into a dealer and making the trips to leave it and pick it up. More importantly, a lot of money can be saved by avoiding the expense the shop must pass on to you to cover its labour and overhead costs. An added benefit is the sense of satisfaction and accomplishment that you feel after doing the job yourself.

References to the left or right side of the motorcycle assume you are sitting on the seat, facing forward.

We take great pride in the accuracy of information given in this manual, but motorcycle manufacturers make alterations and design changes during the production run of a particular motorcycle of which they do not inform us. No liability can be accepted by the authors or publishers for loss, damage or injury caused by any errors in, or omissions from, the information given.

Illegal Copying

The XVS1100A

Frame and engine numbers

The frame serial number is stamped into the right-hand side of the frame steering head and printed on a label affixed to the frame. The engine number is stamped into the right upper side of the crankcase. Both of these numbers should be recorded and kept in a safe place so they can be furnished to law enforcement officials in the event of a theft.

The frame serial number, engine serial number and carburettor identification number should also be kept in a handy place (such as with your driving licence) so they are always available when purchasing or ordering parts for your machine.

The frame number is stamped in the right-hand side of the steering head and is also displayed on a label

The engine number is stamped in the upper right-hand side of the crankcase

Model codes

The procedures in this manual identify models by their production year. For Europe models refer to the model code label on the frame rail under the seat and cross-refer this to the accompanying table. The first four digits relate to the model code; this is followed by a production code and a colour code letter below.

US market models have a suffix letter after the model name to denote the production year, e.g. XVS1100M denotes a year 2000 Custom model and XVS1100AM a year 2000 Classic model. The letter C after the suffix letter indicates that the machine is a California market model. US market suffix letters and corresponding production years are as follows:

1998	K	2005	T
1999	L	2006	V
2000	M	2007	W
2001	N	2008	X
2002	P	2009	Y
2003	R	2010	Z
2004	S	2011	B

Europe models

Prod yr	Model name	Model code
1997	XVS650	4VR1, 4VR2, 4XR1, 4XR2
1998	XVS650	4VR3, 4VR4, 4XR3, 4XR4
1998	XVS650A	5BN4, 5BN9
1999	XVS650	4VR7, 4VR8, 4XR7, 4XR8
1999	XVS650A	5BNC, 5BND
1999	XVS1100	5EL1
2000	XVS650	4VRB, 4XRB
2000	XVS650A	5BNN, 5BNP
2000	XVS1100	5EL8
2000	XVS1100A	5KS4
2001	XVS650	4VRD, 4XRD
2001	XVS650A	5BNV, 5BNW
2001	XVS1100	5PB2
2001	XVS1100A	5KSB
2002-05	XVS650	4VRE, 4XRE
2002/03	XVS650A	5SC5, 5SC6
2002	XVS1100A	5KSG
2004	XVS650A	5SCE, 5SCK
2002-06	XVS1100	5PBB
2003/04	XVS1100A	5KSN
2005	XVS650A	5SCW, 5SCX
2005	XVS1100A	5YSF
2006	XVS650A	4C57, 4C58
2006-08	XVS1100A	5YSR

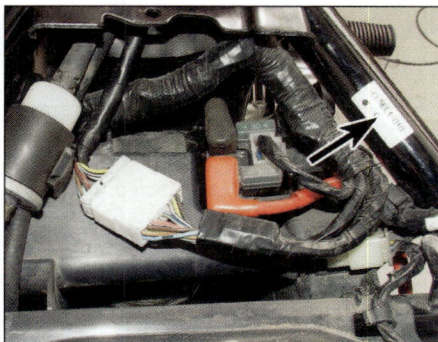

The model code label (arrowed) will be found on the left or right frame rail, under the rider's seat

Buying spare parts

Once you have found all the identification numbers, record them for reference when buying parts. Since the manufacturers change specifications, parts and vendors (companies that manufacture various components on the machine), providing the ID numbers is the only way to be reasonably sure that you are buying the correct parts.

Whenever possible, take the worn part to the dealer so direct comparison with the new component can be made. Along the trail from the manufacturer to the parts shelf, there are numerous places that the part can end up with the wrong number or be listed incorrectly.

The two places to purchase new parts for your motorcycle – the accessory store and the franchised dealer – differ in the type of parts they carry. While dealers can obtain virtually every part for your motorcycle, the accessory dealer is usually limited to normal high wear items such as filters, cables, spark plugs, brake pads/shoes, etc. Rarely will an accessory outlet have major suspension components, cylinders, transmission gears, or cases.

Used parts can be obtained for roughly half the price of new ones, but you can't always be sure of what you're getting. Once again, take your worn part to the breaker for direct comparison.

Whether buying new, used or rebuilt parts, the best course is to deal directly with someone who specialises in parts for your particular make.

650 models

1997

The 650 model was introduced in Europe as the XVS650 Drag Star.

The engine was an air-cooled, single overhead camshaft V-twin derived from the XV535 Virago and mounted in a newly designed steel twin cradle frame with single shock rear suspension. Drive was transmitted to the five-speed gearbox via a wet, multi-plate clutch, and to the rear wheel by shaft.

Front suspension was by conventional, non-adjustable telescopic forks and braking was by single disc at the front and a drum brake at the rear. The wheels were wire spoked.

The XVS650 was designed as a cruiser-style custom, with low seat height, forward mounted footrests and twin chromed exhaust pipes on the right-hand side. The handlebars were wide and raked back and the speedometer was mounted in a chromed cover on top of the fuel tank. The air intake to the twin carburettors was through a large chromed air filter housing on the right-hand side of the engine unit.

1998

The XVS650A Drag Star Classic model was introduced in Europe. Based on the original Drag Star, it was restyled with larger, valanced mudguards, front fork shrouds and redesigned head and tail lights. A 16 inch front wheel was fitted.

Both models were introduced in the US where they were called the XVS650 V-Star Custom and the XVS650A V-Star Classic respectively.

1999 to 2000

No change apart from colour schemes.

2001

The gearchange linkage and headlight beam adjustment mechanism were modified and a redesigned front brake caliper was introduced on all models. An alarm system was offered as an option.

Footboards were fitted to the Classic models in place of the rider footrests. The redesigned air induction system, formerly fitted to the Classic models, was fitted to the standard XVS650 Drag Star and XVS650 V-Star Custom.

2002

No change apart from colour schemes.

2003

The XVS650S V-Star Silverado model was introduced in the US. Based on the XVS650A V-Star Classic, it was equipped with a windshield, saddlebags, a studded seat and passenger backrest. XVS650A Europe models were equipped with an electronic immobiliser system.

2004-on

No change apart from colour schemes.

1100 models

1999

The 1100 model was introduced in Europe as the XVS1100 Drag Star and in the US as the XVS1100 V-Star Custom.

The engine was an air-cooled, single overhead camshaft V-twin derived from the XV1100 Virago and mounted in a steel twin cradle frame with detachable right-hand frame down-tube to facilitate engine removal. Twin carburettors were fitted. Drive was transmitted to the five-speed gearbox via a wet, multi-plate clutch, and to the rear wheel by shaft.

Front suspension was by conventional, non-adjustable telescopic forks, and rear suspension was by single shock with a rising rate linkage. Braking was by twin discs at the front and a single disc at the rear. The wheels were wire spoked. An alarm system was offered as an option.

Like the 650 models, the 1100 Drag Star and V-Star Custom were designed as a cruiser-style machines, with similar low seat, forward mounted footrests and twin chromed exhaust pipes.

2000

The XVS1100A Drag Star Classic model was introduced in Europe, and the XVS1100A V-Star Classic model was introduced in the US.

Based on the original 1100 Drag Star and V-Star, they were restyled with larger, valanced mudguards, rider footboards instead of footrests, front fork shrouds and redesigned head and tail lights. A redesigned front brake caliper and 16 inch front wheel were fitted.

2001

The redesigned front brake caliper was fitted to the standard XVS1100 Drag Star and V-Star Custom models.

2002

The XVS1100S V-Star Silverado model was introduced in the US. Based on the XVS1100A V-Star Classic, it was equipped with a windshield, saddlebags, a studded seat and passenger backrest.

2003

The XVS1100A and XVS1100S models were fitted with cast alloy wheels. XVS1100A Europe models were equipped with an electronic immobiliser system.

2004-on

No change apart from colour schemes.

Bike Spec

Engine – 650 models

Type	Air cooled, 75° V-twin
Capacity	649 cc
Bore and stroke	81 x 63 mm
Compression ratio	9.0:1
Camshafts	SOHC, chain driven
Valves	2 valves per cylinder
Fuel system	2 x 28 mm Mikuni carburettors
Clutch	Wet multi-plate, cable operated
Transmission	5-speed constant mesh
Final drive	Shaft

Engine – 1100 models

Type	Air cooled, 75° V-twin
Capacity	1063 cc
Bore and stroke	95 x 75 mm
Compression ratio	8.3:1
Camshafts	SOHC, chain driven
Valves	2 valves per cylinder
Fuel system	2 x 37 mm Mikuni carburettors
Clutch	Wet multi-plate, cable operated
Transmission	5-speed constant mesh
Final drive	Shaft

Chassis – 650 models

Type . . . . .Tubular double cradle
Rake and trail
  XVS650 . . . . .35°, 153 mm
  XVS650A and XVS650S . . . . .35°, 145 mm
Front suspension . . . . .Telescopic forks, non adjustable
Rear suspension . . . . .Monoshock with spring preload adjustment
Fuel tank capacity . . . . .16 litres
Tyre sizes . . . . **Front**   **Rear**
  XVS650 . . . . 100/90 19 57S   170/80 15M/C 77S
  XVS650A and XVS650S 130/90 16 67S   170/80 15M/C 77S
Front brake . . . . .Single disc with double-piston caliper
Rear brake . . . . .Drum

Chassis – 1100 models

Type . . . . .Tubular double cradle
Rake and trail
  XVS1100 . . . . .33°, 136 mm
  XVS1100A and XVS1100S . . . . .33°, 132 mm
Front suspension . . . . .Telescopic forks, non adjustable
Rear suspension . . . . .Monoshock with spring preload adjustment
Fuel tank capacity . . . . .17 litres
Tyre sizes . . . . **Front**   **Rear**
  XVS1100 . . . . 110/90 18 61S   170/80 15M/C 77S
  XVS1100A and XVS1100S . . 130/90 16 67S   170/80 15M/C 77S
Front brake . . . . .Twin discs with double-piston calipers
Rear brake . . . . .Single disc with opposed-piston caliper

Weights and dimensions – Europe models

XVS650

Wheelbase . . . . .1610 mm
Overall length . . . . .2340 mm
Overall width . . . . .880 mm
Overall height . . . . .1065 mm
Seat height . . . . .695 mm
Ground clearance (minimum) . . . . .140 mm
Weight (with oil and full fuel tank)
  1997 to 2000 models . . . . .227 kg
  2001-on models . . . . .233 kg

XVS650A

Wheelbase . . . . .1625 mm
Overall length . . . . .2450 mm
Overall width . . . . .930 mm
Overall height . . . . .1105 mm
Seat height . . . . .710 mm
Ground clearance (minimum)
  1998 to 2003 models . . . . .145 mm
  2004-on models . . . . .140 mm
Weight (with oil and full fuel tank)
  1998 to 2000 models . . . . .242 kg
  2001 to 2003 models . . . . .247 kg
  2004-on models . . . . .249 kg

XVS1100

Wheelbase . . . . .1640 mm
Overall length . . . . .2405 mm
Overall width . . . . .895 mm
Overall height . . . . .1095 mm
Seat height . . . . .690 mm
Ground clearance (minimum) . . . . .145 mm
Weight (with oil and full fuel tank)
  1999 to 2000 models . . . . .274 kg
  2001-on models . . . . .275 kg

XVS1100A

Wheelbase . . . . .1645 mm
Overall length . . . . .2465 mm
Overall width . . . . .945 mm
Overall height . . . . .1095 mm
Seat height . . . . .710 mm
Ground clearance (minimum) . . . . .145 mm
Weight (with oil and full fuel tank) . . . . .274 kg

Weights and dimensions – US models

XVS650

Wheelbase . . . . .1610 mm
Overall length . . . . .2295 mm
Overall width . . . . .880 mm
Overall height . . . . .1065 mm
Seat height . . . . .695 mm
Ground clearance (minimum) . . . . .140 mm
Weight (with oil and full fuel tank) . . . . .227 kg

XVS650A and XVS650S

Wheelbase . . . . .1625 mm
Overall length . . . . .2450 mm
Overall width . . . . .930 mm
Overall height
  XVS650A . . . . .1105 mm
  XVS650S . . . . .1135 mm
Seat height . . . . .710 mm
Ground clearance (minimum) . . . . .145 mm
Weight (with oil and full fuel tank)
  XVS650A . . . . .243 kg
  XVS650S . . . . .247 kg

XVS1100

Wheelbase . . . . .1640 mm
Overall length . . . . .2405 mm
Overall width . . . . .895 mm
Overall height . . . . .1095 mm
Seat height . . . . .690 mm
Ground clearance (minimum) . . . . .145 mm
Weight (with oil and full fuel tank) . . . . .275 kg

XVS1100A and XVS1100S

Wheelbase . . . . .1645 mm
Overall length . . . . .2465 mm
Overall width . . . . .945 mm
Overall height . . . . .1095 mm
Seat height . . . . .710 mm
Ground clearance (minimum)
  XVS1100A . . . . .145 mm
  XVS1100S . . . . .140 mm
Weight (with oil and full fuel tank) . . . . .288 kg

Professional mechanics are trained in safe working procedures. However enthusiastic you may be about getting on with the job at hand, take the time to ensure that your safety is not put at risk. A moment's lack of attention can result in an accident, as can failure to observe simple precautions.

There will always be new ways of having accidents, and the following is not a comprehensive list of all dangers; it is intended rather to make you aware of the risks and to encourage a safe approach to all work you carry out on your bike.

Asbestos

● Certain friction, insulating, sealing and other products - such as brake pads, clutch linings, gaskets, etc. - contain asbestos. Extreme care must be taken to avoid inhalation of dust from such products since it is hazardous to health. If in doubt, assume that they do contain asbestos.

Fire

● Remember at all times that petrol is highly flammable. Never smoke or have any kind of naked flame around, when working on the vehicle. But the risk does not end there - a spark caused by an electrical short-circuit, by two metal surfaces contacting each other, by careless use of tools, or even by static electricity built up in your body under certain conditions, can ignite petrol vapour, which in a confined space is highly explosive. Never use petrol as a cleaning solvent. Use an approved safety solvent.

● Always disconnect the battery earth terminal before working on any part of the fuel or electrical system, and never risk spilling fuel on to a hot engine or exhaust.

● It is recommended that a fire extinguisher of a type suitable for fuel and electrical fires is kept handy in the garage or workplace at all times. Never try to extinguish a fuel or electrical fire with water.

Fumes

● Certain fumes are highly toxic and can quickly cause unconsciousness and even death if inhaled to any extent. Petrol vapour comes into this category, as do the vapours from certain solvents such as trichloroethylene. Any draining or pouring of such volatile fluids should be done in a well ventilated area.

● When using cleaning fluids and solvents, read the instructions carefully. Never use materials from unmarked containers - they may give off poisonous vapours.

● Never run the engine of a motor vehicle in an enclosed space such as a garage. Exhaust fumes contain carbon monoxide which is extremely poisonous; if you need to run the engine, always do so in the open air or at least have the rear of the vehicle outside the workplace.

The battery

● Never cause a spark, or allow a naked light near the vehicle's battery. It will normally be giving off a certain amount of hydrogen gas, which is highly explosive.

● Always disconnect the battery ground (earth) terminal before working on the fuel or electrical systems (except where noted).

● If possible, loosen the filler plugs or cover when charging the battery from an external source. Do not charge at an excessive rate or the battery may burst.

● Take care when topping up, cleaning or carrying the battery. The acid electrolyte, evenwhen diluted, is very corrosive and should not be allowed to contact the eyes or skin. Always wear rubber gloves and goggles or a face shield. If you ever need to prepare electrolyte yourself, always add the acid slowly to the water; never add the water to the acid.

Electricity

● When using an electric power tool, inspection light etc., always ensure that the appliance is correctly connected to its plug and that, where necessary, it is properly grounded (earthed). Do not use such appliances in damp conditions and, again, beware of creating a spark or applying excessive heat in the vicinity of fuel or fuel vapour. Also ensure that the appliances meet national safety standards.

● A severe electric shock can result from touching certain parts of the electrical system, such as the spark plug wires (HT leads), when the engine is running or being cranked, particularly if components are damp or the insulation is defective. Where an electronic ignition system is used, the secondary (HT) voltage is much higher and could prove fatal.

Remember...

✗ **Don't** start the engine without first ascertaining that the transmission is in neutral.

✗ **Don't** suddenly remove the pressure cap from a hot cooling system - cover it with a cloth and release the pressure gradually first, or you may get scalded by escaping coolant.

✗ **Don't** attempt to drain oil until you are sure it has cooled sufficiently to avoid scalding you.

✗ **Don't** grasp any part of the engine or exhaust system without first ascertaining that it is cool enough not to burn you.

✗ **Don't** allow brake fluid or antifreeze to contact the machine's paintwork or plastic components.

✗ **Don't** siphon toxic liquids such as fuel, hydraulic fluid or antifreeze by mouth, or allow them to remain on your skin.

✗ **Don't** inhale dust - it may be injurious to health (see Asbestos heading).

✗ **Don't** allow any spilled oil or grease to remain on the floor - wipe it up right away, before someone slips on it.

✗ **Don't** use ill-fitting spanners or other tools which may slip and cause injury.

✗ **Don't** lift a heavy component which may be beyond your capability - get assistance.

✗ **Don't** rush to finish a job or take unverified short cuts.

✗ **Don't** allow children or animals in or around an unattended vehicle.

✗ **Don't** inflate a tyre above the recommended pressure. Apart from overstressing the carcass, in extreme cases the tyre may blow off forcibly.

✔ **Do** ensure that the machine is supported securely at all times. This is especially important when the machine is blocked up to aid wheel or fork removal.

✔ **Do** take care when attempting to loosen a stubborn nut or bolt. It is generally better to pull on a spanner, rather than push, so that if you slip, you fall away from the machine rather than onto it.

✔ **Do** wear eye protection when using power tools such as drill, sander, bench grinder etc.

✔ **Do** use a barrier cream on your hands prior to undertaking dirty jobs - it will protect your skin from infection as well as making the dirt easier to remove afterwards; but make sure your hands aren't left slippery. Note that long-term contact with used engine oil can be a health hazard.

✔ **Do** keep loose clothing (cuffs, ties etc. and long hair) well out of the way of moving mechanical parts.

✔ **Do** remove rings, wristwatch etc., before working on the vehicle - especially the electrical system.

✔ **Do** keep your work area tidy - it is only too easy to fall over articles left lying around.

✔ **Do** exercise caution when compressing springs for removal or installation. Ensure that the tension is applied and released in a controlled manner, using suitable tools which preclude the possibility of the spring escaping violently.

✔ **Do** ensure that any lifting tackle used has a safe working load rating adequate for the job.

✔ **Do** get someone to check periodically that all is well, when working alone on the vehicle.

✔ **Do** carry out work in a logical sequence and check that everything is correctly assembled and tightened afterwards.

✔ **Do** remember that your vehicle's safety affects that of yourself and others. If in doubt on any point, get professional advice.

● If in spite of following these precautions, you are unfortunate enough to injure yourself, seek medical attention as soon as possible.

Note: *The daily (pre-ride) checks outlined in the owner's manual covers those items which should be inspected on a daily basis.*

Engine/transmission oil level check

Before you start:
✔ Run the engine and allow it to reach normal operating temperature.
Caution: Do not run the engine in an enclosed space such as a garage or shop.
✔ Stop the engine and allow the machine to sit undisturbed for about five minutes.

Bike care:
● If you have to add oil frequently, you should check whether you have any oil leaks. If there is no sign of oil leakage from the joints and gaskets the engine could be burning oil (see *Fault Finding*).

The correct oil
● Modern, high-revving engines place great demands on their oil. It is very important that the correct oil for your bike is used.
● Always top up with a good quality oil of the specified type and viscosity and do not overfill the engine.
● Use an oil designed for motorcycle use. Oils for use in car engines (often labelled 'energy conserving II') contain anti-friction additives which can cause clutch slip and starter clutch slip.

Oil type	API grade SE, SF or SG (minimum)
Oil viscosity	Refer to the accompanying table

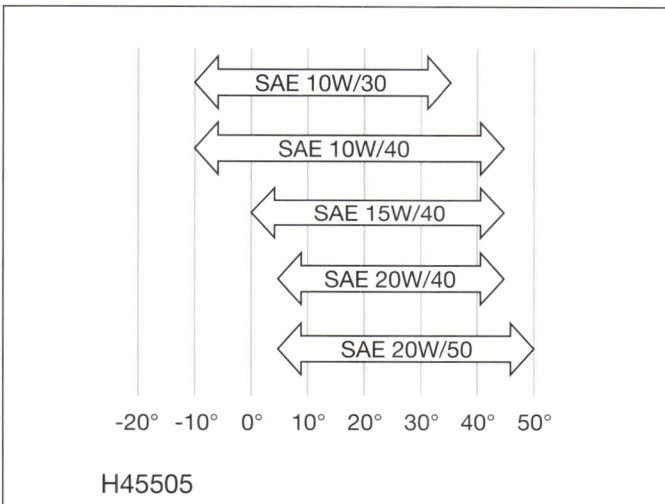

Oil viscosity chart; select the oil best suited to the conditions.

1 Hold the motorcycle upright. Check the oil level in the window in the lower part of the left crankcase – the level should be between the Maximum and Minimum marks next to the window.

2 If the level is below the Minimum mark, remove the oil filler cap from the left side engine cover

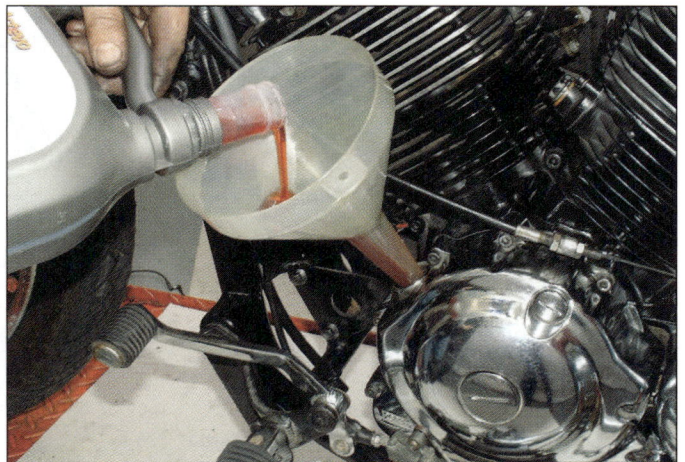

3 Add enough oil of the recommended grade and type to bring the level up to the Maximum mark. Do not overfill.

Brake fluid level checks

> ⚠️ **Warning: Brake hydraulic fluid can harm your eyes and damage painted surfaces, so use extreme caution when handling and pouring it and cover surrounding surfaces with rag. Do not use fluid that has been standing open for some time, as it absorbs moisture from the air which can cause a dangerous loss of braking effectiveness.**

Before you start:

✔ Hold the motorcycle upright. Turn the handlebars until the top of the front master cylinder reservoir is as level as possible. On 1100 models, the rear master cylinder reservoir is located at the front of the engine.
✔ Make sure you have the correct hydraulic fluid. DOT 4 is recommended.
✔ Wrap a rag around the reservoir being worked on to ensure that any spillage does not come into contact with painted surfaces.

Bike care:

● The fluid in the front and rear brake master cylinder reservoirs will drop slightly as the brake pads wear down, although the need for repeated topping-up is an indication of a leak somewhere in the system, which should be investigated immediately.
● Check for signs of fluid leaks from the hydraulic hoses and brake system components – if found, rectify immediately (see Chapter 6).
● Check the operation of both brakes before taking the machine on the road; if there is evidence of air in the system (spongy feel to lever or pedal), it must be bled (see Chapter 6).

FRONT BRAKE FLUID LEVEL

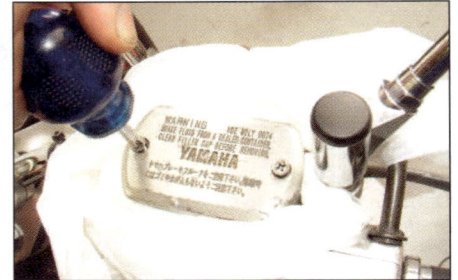

1 The front brake fluid level is visible through the inspection window in the master cylinder reservoir. Make sure that the fluid level is above the LOWER mark on the reservoir. If the level is low, the fluid must be topped-up.

2 Protect the surrounding area from brake fluid spills (which will damage the paint) with a clean cloth and remove all dust and dirt from around the reservoir cover, then remove the screws.

3 Lift off the cover, diaphragm plate and diaphragm. **Note:** *Do not operate the front brake with the cover removed.*

4 Top-up with new, clean DOT 4 hydraulic fluid, until the level is just above the inspection window – do not overfill. Reinstall the diaphragm, plate and the cover. Tighten the screws securely, but do not overtighten them.

REAR BRAKE FLUID LEVEL (1100 MODELS)

1 The rear brake fluid level is visible through the reservoir body – if required, remove the metal cover to check the level.

2 Support the reservoir upright – the fluid must be above the LOWER level line. If the level is below the level line, unscrew the cap and remove the diaphragm.

3 Top-up with new, clean DOT 4 hydraulic fluid, until the level is above the LOWER level line – do not overfill. Take care to avoid spills (see **Warning** above). Ensure that the diaphragm is correctly seated before installing the cap. Tighten the cap securely. Install the reservoir and metal cover, then tighten the mounting screw.

Clutch checks

Bike care:

● Correct clutch freeplay is necessary to ensure proper clutch operation and reasonable clutch service life. Freeplay normally changes because of cable stretch and clutch wear, so it should be checked and adjusted periodically.

● If the lever is stiff to operate and doesn't return quickly, lubricate the cable (see Chapter 1).

● Too little freeplay might result in the clutch not engaging completely. If there is too much freeplay, the clutch might not release fully.

● If a small amount of cable adjustment is required, use the adjuster on the handlebar lever. If a large amount of adjustment is required, use the adjuster at the lower end of the cable. If freeplay still can't be adjusted within the Specifications, the cable may be stretched or the clutch may be worn. Refer to Chapter 2 for cable renewal and clutch overhaul procedures.

Clutch cable freeplay
650 models – 10 to 15 mm
1100 models – 5 to 10 mm

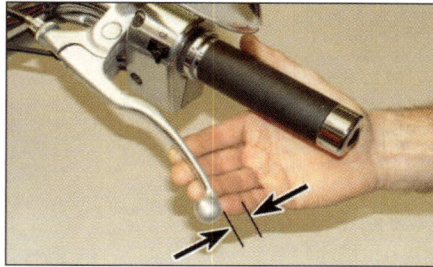

1 Clutch cable freeplay is measured at the handlebar lever ball end. Slowly pull in on the lever until resistance is felt, then note the amount of lever movement. Compare this distance with the specified value.

2 Normal freeplay adjustments are made at the clutch lever by loosening the lockwheel and turning the adjuster until the desired freeplay is obtained. Always retighten the lockwheel once the adjustment is complete.

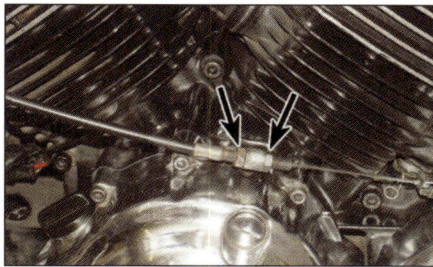

3 If freeplay can't be adjusted at the lever on 650 models, check the initial adjustment at the engine. Loosen the locknuts at the clutch cable bracket on the engine. Turn the nuts to achieve the correct freeplay, then tighten them. Make final adjustments at the lever adjuster (see Step 2).

4 If freeplay can't be adjusted at the lever on 1100 models, remove the cover from the clutch adjuster on the left side of the engine. Loosen the locknut and turn the adjuster screw clockwise until it seats lightly, then back it out 1/4 turn and tighten the locknut. Make final adjustments at the lever adjuster (see Step 2).

Suspension, steering and final drive checks

Suspension and Steering:

● Make sure the steering operates smoothly, without looseness and without binding.

● Check the front and rear suspension for smooth operation.

Final drive:

● Check that there is no oil leakage around the final drive housing. If any is evident, check the final drive oil level (Chapter 1).

Legal and safety checks

Lighting and signalling:

● Take a minute to check that the headlight, tail light, brake light and turn signals all work correctly.

● Check that the horn sounds when the switch is operated.

● A working speedometer is a statutory requirement in the UK.

Safety:

● Check that the throttle grip rotates smoothly and snaps shut when released, in all steering positions.

● Check that the engine shuts off when the kill switch is operated.

● Check that sidestand return spring holds the stand securely up when retracted.

● Following the procedure in your owner's manual, check the operation of the sidestand switch.

Fuel:

● This may seem obvious, but check that you have enough fuel to complete your journey. If you notice signs of fuel leakage – rectify the cause immediately.

● Ensure you use the correct grade fuel (see Chapter 3 Specifications).

Tyre checks

The correct pressures:

● Tyre pressures must be checked when **cold**, not immediately after riding. Note that very low tyre pressures may cause the tyre to slip on the rim or come off. High tyre pressures will cause abnormal tread wear and unsafe handling.
● Use an accurate pressure gauge.
● Proper air pressure will increase tyre life and provide maximum stability and ride comfort.

Tyre care:

● Check the tyres for cuts, tears, nails or other sharp objects and wear. Riding on worn tyres is extremely hazardous, as traction and handling are directly affected.
● Check the condition of the tyre valve and ensure the dust cap is in place.
● Pick out any stones or nails which may have become embedded in the tyre tread. If left, they will eventually penetrate through the tyre and cause a puncture.
● If tyre damage is apparent, or unexplained loss of pressure is experienced, seek the advice of a tyre fitting specialist without delay.

Tyre tread depth:

● At the time of writing UK law requires that tread depth must be at least 1 mm over 3/4 of the tread breadth all the way around the tyre, with no bald patches. Yamaha specify a minimum tread depth of 1.6 mm, although many riders prefer to renew tyres at 2 mm.
● Many tyres now incorporate wear indicators in the tread. Identify the triangular pointer or TWI mark on the tyre sidewall to locate the indicator bar and renew the tyre if the tread has worn down to the bar.

Loading*/speed	Front	Rear
XVS650 Europe models:		
Up to 90 kg load	29 psi (2.0 Bar)	32 psi (2.2 Bar)
90 kg to max load of 180 kg	29 psi (2.0 Bar)	36 psi (2.5 Bar)
High speed riding	29 psi (2.0 Bar)	36 psi (2.5 Bar)
XVS650A Europe models:		
Up to 90 kg load	33 psi (2.3 Bar)	33 psi (2.3 Bar)
90 kg to max load of 180 kg	33 psi (2.3 Bar)	36 psi (2.5 Bar)
XVS650 US models:		
Up to 90 kg load	29 psi (2.0 Bar)	33 psi (2.3 Bar)
90 kg to max load of 180 kg	29 psi (2.0 Bar)	36 psi (2.5 Bar)
XVS650A and XVS650S US models:		
Up to 90 kg load	33 psi (2.3 Bar)	33 psi (2.3 Bar)
90 kg to max load of 200 kg	33 psi (2.3 Bar)	36 psi (2.5 Bar)
High speed riding	33 psi (2.3 Bar)	36 psi (2.5 Bar)
XVS1100 Europe models:		
Up to 90 kg load	29 psi (2.0 Bar)	33 psi (2.3 Bar)
90 kg to max load of 200 kg	33 psi (2.3 Bar)	36 psi (2.5 Bar)
High speed riding	33 psi (2.3 Bar)	36 psi (2.5 Bar)
XVS1100A Europe models:		
Up to 90 kg load	33 psi (2.3 Bar)	33 psi (2.3 Bar)
90 kg to max load of 200 kg	33 psi (2.3 Bar)	36 psi (2.5 Bar)
XVS1100 US models:		
Up to 90 kg load	29 psi (2.0 Bar)	32 psi (2.2 Bar)
90 kg to max load of 200 kg	32 psi (2.2 Bar)	36 psi (2.5 Bar)
High speed riding	32 psi (2.3 Bar)	36 psi (2.5 Bar)
XVS1100A and XVS1100S US models:		
Up to 90 kg load	33 psi (2.3 Bar)	33 psi (2.3 Bar)
90 kg to max load of 200 kg	33 psi (2.3 Bar)	36 psi (2.5 Bar)
High speed riding	33 psi (2.3 Bar)	36 psi (2.5 Bar)

Note that load is the total weight of the rider, passenger, cargo and accessories

1 Check the tyre pressures when the tyres are **cold** and keep them properly inflated.

2 Measure the tread depth at the centre of the tyre using a tread depth gauge.

3 Tyre tread wear indicator bar and its location marking on the sidewall (arrowed).

Chapter 1
Routine maintenance and Servicing

Contents

Degrees of difficulty

Easy, suitable for novice with little experience | **Fairly easy,** suitable for beginner with some experience | **Fairly difficult,** suitable for competent DIY mechanic | **Difficult,** suitable for experienced DIY mechanic | **Very difficult,** suitable for expert DIY or professional

Engine

Spark plugs	
Type	NGK DPR7EA-9 or X22EPR-U9
Gap	0.8 to 0.9 mm
Valve clearances (COLD engine)	
Intake	0.07 to 0.12 mm
Exhaust	0.12 to 0.17 mm
Engine idle speed	1150 to 1250 rpm
Cylinder compression pressure (at sea level)	
Standard	11 Bar (160 psi)
Maximum	12 Bar (174 psi)
Minimum	10 Bar (145 psi)
Maximum difference between cylinders	1 Bar (15 psi)
Carburettor synchronisation	
Vacuum at idle speed	220 mm Hg
Maximum vacuum difference between cylinders	10 mm Hg
Cylinder numbering	No. 1 cylinder rear, no. 2 cylinder front

Cycle parts

Brake pedal position	
XVS650 (all models), XVS650A (1998 to 2000)	85 mm (top of footrest to top of pedal)
XVS650A and S (2001-on)	108 mm (top of footrest to top of footboard)
Gearchange rod length	
XVS650 (1997 to 2000), XVS650A (1998 to 2000)	188 mm
XVS650 (2001-on)	156 mm
XVS650A and S (2001-on)	168 mm
Freeplay adjustments	
Throttle twistgrip	4 to 6 mm
Clutch lever	10 to 15 mm
Front brake lever	10 to 15 mm
Rear brake pedal	20 to 30 mm
AIS reed valve clearance	0.4 mm

Torque settings

Oil drain plug	43 Nm
Oil filter cover bolts	10 Nm
Spark plugs	18 Nm
Steering head bearing adjuster nut	
Initial torque	52 Nm
Final torque	18 Nm
Steering stem nut	110 Nm
Front fork top yoke clamp bolts	
XVS650	20 Nm
XVS650A and S	23 Nm
Valve adjuster locknuts	14 Nm
Rocker cover bolts	10 Nm
Camshaft sprocket cover bolts	10 Nm
Front brake caliper mounting bolts	40 Nm
Front brake caliper pin bolt	
1997 to 2000 models	23 Nm
2001-on models	27 Nm
Final drive oil level and drain plugs	23 Nm

Recommended lubricants and fluids

Fuel grade	Unleaded, minimum 91 RON (Research Octane Number)
Engine/transmission oil	
Type	API grade SE, SF or SG (minimum)
Viscosity	Refer to the oil viscosity chart in Daily (pre-ride) checks
Capacity	
With filter change	2.8 litres
Oil change only	2.6 litres
Brake fluid	DOT 4
Final gear	
Type	SAE 80 API GL-4 hypoid gear oil
Capacity	0.19 litre
Wheel bearings	Medium weight, lithium-based multi-purpose grease
Swingarm pivot bearings	Medium weight, lithium-based multi-purpose grease
Cables and lever pivots	Chain or cable lubricant or 10W30 motor oil
Stand and footrest pivots	Chain or cable lubricant or 10W30 motor oil
Brake pedal and gearchange lever pivots	Chain and cable lubricant or 10W30 motor oil
Throttle twistgrip	Multi-purpose grease or dry film lubricant

Engine

Spark plugs	
Type	NGK BP7ES or ND W22EPR-U
Gap	0.7 to 0.8 mm
Valve clearances (COLD engine)	
Intake	0.07 to 0.12 mm
Exhaust	0.12 to 0.17 mm
Engine idle speed	950 to 1050 rpm
Cylinder compression pressure (at sea level)	
Standard	10 Bar (145 psi)
Maximum	11 Bar (160 psi)
Minimum	9 Bar (131 psi)
Maximum difference between cylinders	1 Bar (15 psi)
Carburettor pilot screw setting	3 turns out
Carburettor synchronisation	
Vacuum at idle speed	260 to 280 mm Hg
Maximum vacuum difference between cylinders	10 mm Hg
Cylinder numbering	No. 1 cylinder rear, no. 2 cylinder front

Cycle parts

Brake pedal position	
XVS1100	81.8 mm (top of footrest to top of pedal)
XVS1100A and S	98.5 mm (top of footrest to top of footboard)
Gearchange rod length	
XVS1100	114.7 mm
XVS1100A and S	114.9 mm
Freeplay adjustments	
Throttle twistgrip	4 to 6 mm
Clutch lever	5 to 10 mm
Front brake lever	5 to 8 mm

Torque settings

Oil drain plug	43 Nm
Oil filter cover bolts	10 Nm
Spark plugs	20 Nm
Steering head bearing adjuster nut	
Initial torque	52 Nm
Final torque	18 Nm
Steering stem nut	110 Nm
Front fork top yoke clamp bolts	20 Nm
Valve adjuster locknuts	27 Nm
Rocker cover bolts	10 Nm
Camshaft sprocket cover bolts	10 Nm
Front brake caliper pin bolt	23 Nm
Front brake caliper mounting bolts	40 Nm
Final drive oil level and drain plugs	23 Nm

Recommended lubricants and fluids

Fuel grade	Unleaded, minimum 91 RON (Research Octane Number)
Engine/transmission oil	
Type	API grade SE, SF or SG (minimum)
Viscosity	Refer to oil viscosity chart in Daily (pre-ride) checks
Capacity	
With filter change	3.1 litres
Oil change only	3.0 litres
Brake fluid	DOT 4
Final gear	
Type	SAE 80 API GL-4 hypoid gear oil
Capacity	0.20 litre
Wheel bearings	Medium weight, lithium-based multi-purpose grease
Swingarm pivot bearings	Medium weight, lithium-based multi-purpose grease
Cables and lever pivots	Chain and cable lubricant or 10W30 motor oil
Stand and footrest pivots	Chain and cable lubricant or 10W30 motor oil
Brake pedal and gearchange lever pivots	Chain and cable lubricant or 10W30 motor oil
Throttle twistgrip	Multi-purpose grease or dry film lubricant

650 models right side

1 Battery
2 Air filter
3 Front brake fluid reservoir
4 Throttle cable upper adjuster
5 Steering head bearing adjuster
6 Rear brake pedal height adjuster
7 Oil filter cover
8 Rear brake freeplay adjuster

650 models left side

1 In-line fuel filter
2 Clutch cable upper adjuster
3 Idle speed adjuster
4 Clutch cable lower adjuster
5 Rear shock preload adjuster
6 Final drive oil filler/level plug
7 Final drive oil drain plug
8 Timing inspection cap
9 Engine oil drain plug
10 Centre cap in alternator cover
11 Engine oil level window
12 Engine oil filler cap

1100 models right side

1 Battery
2 Air filter
3 Throttle cable upper adjuster
4 Front brake fluid reservoir
5 Steering head bearing adjuster
6 Rear brake fluid reservoir
7 Oil filter cover

1100 models left side

1 Clutch cable upper adjuster
2 Idle speed adjuster
3 Rear shock pre-load adjuster
4 In-line fuel filter
5 Final drive oil filler/level plug
6 Final drive oil drain plug
7 Clutch adjuster
8 Timing inspection cap
9 Centre cap in alternator cover
10 Engine oil level window
11 Engine oil drain plug
12 Engine oil filler cap

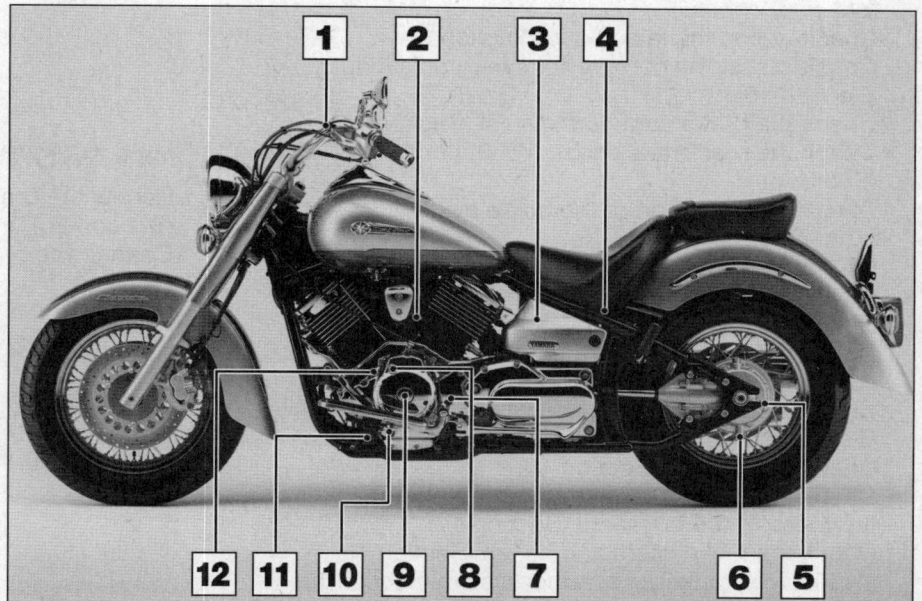

Note: *The intervals listed below are those recommended by the manufacturer for each particular operation during the model years covered in this manual. Your owner's manual may have slightly different intervals for some items in which case use the intervals in the owners manual.*

Daily or pre-ride
☐ See 'Daily (pre-ride) checks' at the beginning of this manual.

After the initial 600 miles (1000 km)
Note: *This check is usually performed by a Yamaha dealer after the first 600 miles (1000 km) from new. Thereafter, maintenance is carried out according to the following intervals of the schedule.*

Europe models – every 6000 miles (10,000 km)
US models – every 4000 miles (7000 km)
☐ Change the engine oil (Section 1)
☐ Clean the air filter element (Section 2)
☐ Adjust the valve clearances (Section 3)
☐ Clean and gap the spark plugs (Section 4)
☐ Check final drive oil level (Section 5)
☐ Lubricate the stand and lever pivots and cables (Section 6)
☐ Check the operation of the sidestand switch (Section 7)
☐ Check/adjust throttle cable freeplay (Section 8)
☐ Check/adjust clutch cable freeplay (see *Daily (pre-ride) checks*)
☐ Check/adjust the idle speed (Section 9)
☐ Check/adjust the carburettor synchronisation (Section 10)
☐ Check the brake pads and disc(s) (Section 11)
☐ Check the rear brake shoes – 650 models (Section 11)
☐ Check the operation of the brake system (Section 12)
☐ Lubricate the gearchange/brake pedal pivots (Section 6)
☐ Check the steering head bearings (Section 13)
☐ Check the suspension for proper operation and fluid leaks (Section 14)
☐ Check the tyres, wheels and wheel bearings (Section 15)
☐ Check the battery (Section 16)
☐ Check the exhaust system for leaks and check the tightness of the fasteners (Section 17)
☐ Check the fuel system and hoses (Section 18)
☐ Inspect the crankcase breather system (Section 19)
☐ Check the air induction system (AIS) (Section 20)
☐ Check the handlebar switches and headlight beam (Section 21)
☐ Check the security of all fasteners (Section 22)

Europe models – every 12,000 miles (20,000 km)
US models – every 8000 miles (13,000 km)
☐ Change the engine oil and oil filter (Section 1)
☐ Renew the air filter element (Section 2)
☐ Renew the fuel filter (Section 18)
☐ Check the EVAP system – California models (Section 24)
☐ Renew the spark plugs (Section 4)
☐ Change final drive oil (Section 25)
☐ Re-grease the steering head bearings (Chapter 5)

Europe models – every 30,000 miles (50,000 km)
US models – every 16,000 miles (25,000 km)
☐ Re-grease the swingarm bearings (Chapter 5)

Every two years
☐ Renew the brake master cylinder and caliper seals (Section 26)
☐ Change the brake fluid (Section 27)

Every four years
☐ Renew the brake hose(s) (Section 28)

Non-scheduled maintenance
☐ Check cylinder compression (Section 29)
☐ Change front fork oil (Section 30)

1 This Chapter is designed to help the home mechanic maintain his/her motorcycle for safety, economy, long life and peak performance.

2 Deciding where to start or plug into the routine maintenance schedule depends on several factors. If the warranty period on your motorcycle has just expired, and if it has been maintained according to the warranty standards, you may want to pick up routine maintenance as it coincides with the next mileage or calendar interval. If you have owned the machine for some time but have never

performed any maintenance on it, then you may want to start at the beginning and include all frequent procedures to ensure that nothing important is overlooked. If the engine has just had a major overhaul, then you should start the engine maintenance items from the beginning. If you have a used machine and have no knowledge of its history or maintenance record, you should combine all the checks into one large initial service and then settle into the maintenance schedule prescribed.

3 Before beginning any maintenance or repair, the machine should be cleaned

thoroughly, especially around the oil filter area, spark plugs, valve cover, carburettors, etc. Cleaning will help ensure that dirt does not contaminate the engine and will allow you to detect wear and damage that could otherwise easily go unnoticed.

4 Certain maintenance information is sometimes printed on decals attached to the motorcycle. If any information on the decals differs from that included here, use the information on the decal.

Read the *Safety first!* section of this manual carefully before starting work.

Maintenance procedures

1 Engine oil and oil filter change

1 Regular oil and filter changes are the single most important maintenance procedure you can perform on a motorcycle. The oil not only lubricates the internal parts of the engine, transmission and clutch, but it also acts as a coolant, a cleaner and corrosion inhibitor. Because of these demands, the oil takes a terrific amount of abuse and should always be changed at the recommended service interval. The oil filter should be changed with every second oil change.

HAYNES HiNT *Saving a little money on the difference in cost between a good oil and a cheap oil won't pay off if the engine is damaged.*

2 Before changing the oil, warm up the engine so the oil will drain easily. Be careful when draining the oil, as the exhaust pipes, the engine, and the oil itself can cause severe burns.

3 Support the motorcycle upright over a clean drain tray. Remove the oil filler cap to vent the crankcase and act as a reminder that there is no oil in the engine **(see illustration)**.

4 Refer to the appropriate procedure below according to your model.

All 650 models

5 Remove the oil drain plug, located in the left-hand side of the engine, and allow the old oil to drain fully into the tray **(see illustration)**. Discard the sealing washer as a new one must be used.

6 To remove the oil filter, first undo the bolts from the engine side cover and remove it, then undo the bolts from the filter cover and remove it **(see illustrations)**. Withdraw the filter from the engine **(see illustration)**.

7 Clean all traces of old oil from the filter

1.3 Remove the filler cap as a reminder that the engine oil has been drained

1.5 Location of the oil drain plug

1.6a Remove the engine side cover . . .

1.6b . . . then remove the filter cover bolts (arrowed) . . .

1.6c . . . and lift off the cover

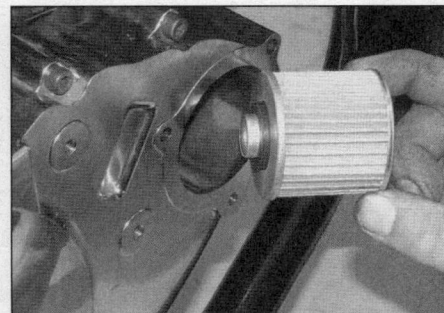
1.6d Pull the filter out of the engine, noting which way round it fits

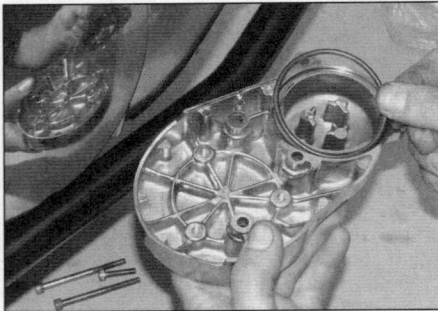
1.7 Fit a new cover O-ring on reassembly

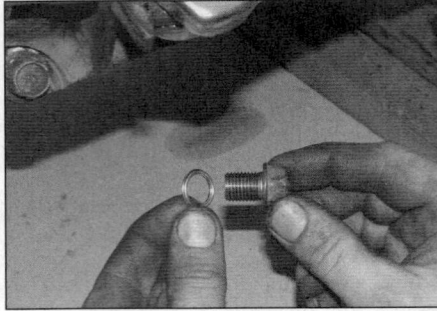
1.9 Fit a new sealing washer on the drain plug

1.11 Remove the oil drain plug

housing and cover. Discard the cover O-ring as a new one must be used **(see illustration)**.
8 Install the new filter in the casing with its shoulder facing **inwards (see illustration 1.6d)**. Install a new O-ring in the cover, then fit

the cover and tighten the bolts to the specified torque setting. Fit the engine side cover.
9 Clean the drain plug threads and install a new sealing washer on the plug **(see**

illustration). Install the plug and tighten it to the specified torque setting.
10 Fill the engine with the correct amount and type of oil (see Specifications at the beginning of this Chapter) and install the filler cap. Run the engine for a few minutes, then recheck the oil level and top-up if necessary (see *Daily (pre-ride) checks*). Check that there are no leaks from the filter cover or drain plug.

All 1100 models

11 Remove the oil drain plug, located in the left-hand side of the engine, and allow the old oil to drain fully into the tray **(see illustration)**. Discard the sealing washer as a new one must be used.
12 Remove the exhaust system (see Chapter 3).
13 To remove the oil filter, first undo the bolts securing the right-hand engine cover and lift it off **(see illustration)**. Note that the lower bolt is a larger diameter than the rest **(see illustration)**.
14 Pull out the filter cover **(see illustration)**. Note the location of the two O-rings on the cover and the small O-ring set in the engine case oil passage **(see illustrations)**. Discard the O-rings as new ones must be fitted.
15 Withdraw the filter from the engine **(see illustration)**. Clean all traces of old oil from the filter housing and cover.
16 Install the new filter in the casing with its shoulder facing **outwards (see illustration 1.15)**. Check that the two new cover O-rings are correctly positioned and the small O-ring is located in the oil passage, then refit the cover and tighten its bolts to the specified torque setting.

1.13a Undo the cover bolts . . .

1.13b . . . noting that the lower bolt has a larger diameter

1.14a Remove the filter cover . . .

1.14b . . . noting the location of the thick . . .

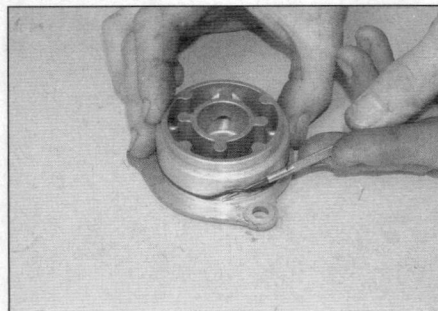
1.14c . . . and thin O-rings on the cover

1.14d Note the small O-ring in the oil passage

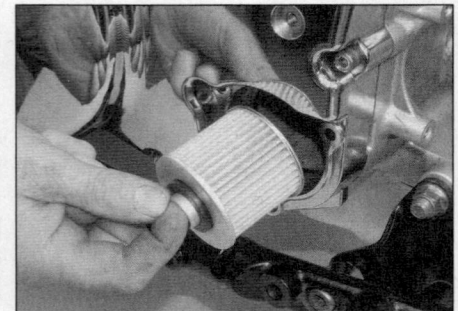
1.15 Pull the filter out of the engine, noting which way round it fits

17 Install the right-hand engine cover and tighten its bolts.

18 Clean the drain plug threads and install a new sealing washer on the plug. Install the plug and tighten it to the specified torque setting.

19 Fill the engine with the correct amount and type of oil (see *Specifications* at the beginning of this Chapter) and install the filler cap. Run the engine for a few minutes, then recheck the oil level and top-up if necessary (see *Daily (pre-ride) checks*). Check that there are no leaks from the filter cover or drain plug.

> **HAYNES HiNT** *Check the old oil carefully – if it is very metallic-coloured, then the engine is experiencing wear from running-in (new engine) or insufficient lubrication. If there are flakes or chips of metal in the oil, then something is drastically wrong internally and the engine will have to be disassembled for inspection and repair. If there are pieces of fibre-like material in the oil, the clutch plates are wearing excessively and should be checked.*

2.1a Remove the housing cover screws . . .

2.1b . . . and lift off the cover

2.2a Remove the clip (arrowed) . . .

2.2b . . . and lift off the filter element noting how it locates

2 Air filter element clean

650 models

1 Undo the screws and remove the air filter housing cover (see illustrations).

2 Remove the clip securing the filter element, then lift out the element noting how it fits (see illustrations).

3 Tap the element on a hard surface to shake out dirt. If compressed air is available, use it to clean the element by blowing from the inside out. If the element is extremely dirty or damaged, replace it with a new one.

4 Installation is the reverse of removal. Ensure the filter element is correctly seated in the air filter housing (see illustration 2.2b).

1100 models

5 Undo the screws and remove the air filter housing cover, then lift off the filter element noting how it fits (see illustrations).

6 Tap the element on a hard surface to shake out dirt. If compressed air is available, use it to clean the outside of the element. If the element is extremely dirty or damaged, replace it with a new one.

7 Installation is the reverse of removal. Ensure the filter element is correctly located and sealed against the air filter housing.

3 Valve clearance check

1 The engine must be completely cold for this maintenance procedure, so let the machine sit overnight before beginning.

2 Disconnect the cable from the negative terminal of the battery. Remove the spark plugs (see Section 4) so the crankshaft is easier to turn.

3 Remove the fuel tank (see Chapter 3).

650 models

4 Remove the carburettors and heat shield (see Chapter 3).

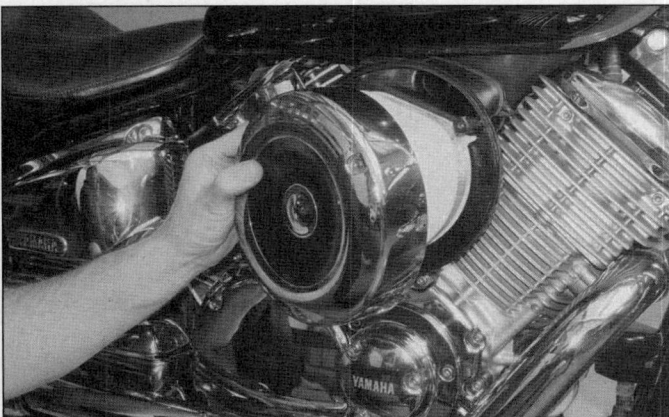
2.5a Remove the filter cover . . .

2.5b . . . and lift off the filter element, noting how it fits

3.5a Remove the upper . . .

3.5b . . . and lower cylinder head covers

3.5c Note how the peg (arrowed) locates on the rear cylinder lower cover

3.6a Undo the bolts (arrowed) . . .

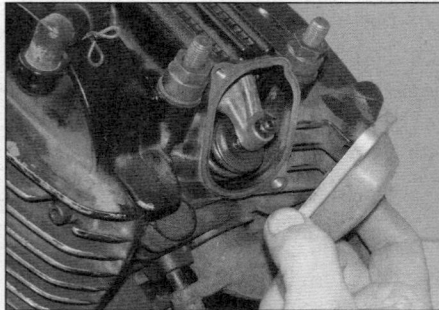

3.6b . . . and remove the rocker covers

3.7a Undo the bolts (arrowed) . . .

3.7b . . . and remove the camshaft sprocket covers. Note the front cover O-ring (arrowed) . . .

3.7c . . . and the rear cover O-ring

5 Undo the bolts and remove the upper and lower covers from the front and rear cylinder heads (see illustrations).

6 Undo the bolts and remove the rocker covers (see illustrations). Discard the cover O-rings as new ones must be fitted.

7 Undo the bolts and remove the camshaft sprocket covers, noting the O-rings (see illustrations). A baffle plate is fitted in the rear cover – if it does not come off with the cover, remove it from the cylinder head, noting the location of the O-ring (see illustrations).

8 Undo the timing inspection cap and the centre cap in the alternator cover on the left-hand side of the engine (see illustration).

9 Turn the crankshaft clockwise with a socket on the alternator centre bolt until the rear

3.7d A baffle plate is fitted in the rear cover

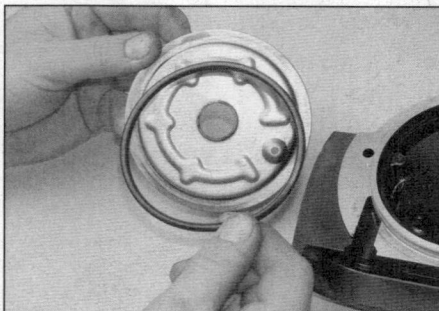

3.7e Note the baffle plate O-ring

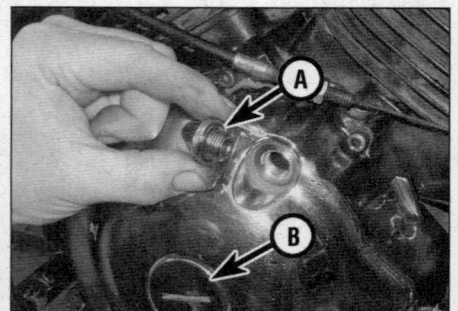

3.8 Remove the timing (A) and centre (B) caps from the alternator cover

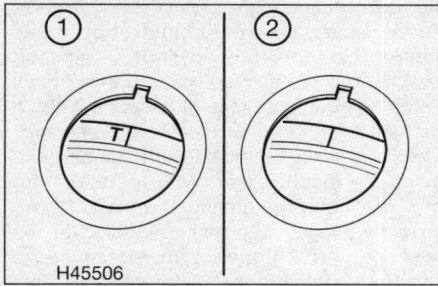

3.9a Cylinder timing marks

1 Rear cylinder timing mark aligned with notch
2 Front cylinder timing mark aligned with notch

3.9b Rear cylinder camshaft sprocket timing marks

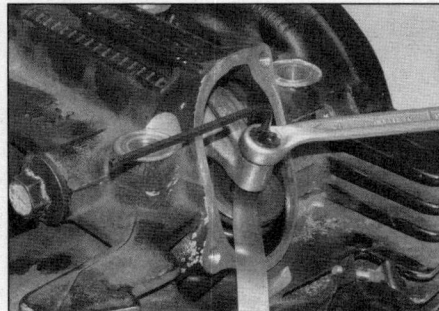

3.11 Checking the valve clearance with a feeler gauge

cylinder timing mark on the edge of the alternator rotor is aligned with the notch inside the inspection hole (see illustration). Check that the rear cylinder camshaft sprocket mark is aligned with the index mark on the cylinder head (see illustration). If the camshaft sprocket mark is not correctly aligned, turn the crankshaft one full turn and check the marks again. With the alternator rotor mark and the camshaft sprocket mark correctly aligned, the rear cylinder is at top dead centre (TDC) on its compression stroke with both valves closed (there should be a small amount of play between the rocker arms and the valve stems).
10 With the engine in this position, the clearances for both of the rear cylinder valves can be checked.
11 Start with the intake valve clearance. Insert a feeler gauge of the thickness listed in this Chapter's Specifications between the rocker arm and valve stem (see illustration). Pull the feeler gauge out slowly – you should feel a slight drag. If there's no drag, the clearance is too loose. If there's a heavy drag, or if the feeler gauge won't fit, the clearance is too tight.
12 To adjust the clearance, loosen the adjuster locknut, then turn the adjuster with an Allen key to obtain the correct clearance (see illustration). Turn the adjuster clockwise to decrease the clearance and anti-clockwise to increase the clearance.
13 Hold the adjuster to prevent it turning and tighten the locknut. Recheck the clearance with the feeler gauge to make sure it didn't

change when you tightened the locknut and readjust it if necessary.
14 Turn the crankshaft clockwise to align the front cylinder's timing mark on the edge of the alternator rotor with the notch inside the inspection hole (see illustration 3.9a). Check that the front cylinder camshaft sprocket mark is aligned with the index mark on the cylinder head (see illustration). With the alternator rotor mark and the camshaft sprocket mark correctly aligned, the front cylinder is at top dead centre (TDC) on its compression stroke with both valves closed (there should be a small amount of play between the rocker arms and the valve stems).
15 With the engine in this position, follow the procedure in Steps 11 to 13 to check and adjust both valves for the front cylinder.
16 Check the O-rings on the timing inspection cap and the cover centre cap and fit new ones if they're flattened, broken or have been leaking.

17 On the rear cylinder, check the condition of the baffle plate O-ring and fit a new one if necessary, then install the baffle plate in the cover. Install both camshaft sprocket covers and tighten their bolts to the torque listed in this Chapter's Specifications.
18 Ensure the new rocker cover O-rings are correctly installed, then fit the rocker covers and tighten their bolts to the specified torque (see illustration).
19 Install the remaining components in the reverse order of removal.

1100 models

20 Remove the air intake duct (see Chapter 3).
21 Undo the bolts and remove the front and rear cylinder head covers (see illustration).
22 Undo the bolts and remove the rocker covers (see illustration). Note the location of the cover O-rings.
23 Undo the bolts and remove the camshaft

3.12 Adjusting the valve clearance with an Allen key

3.14 Front cylinder camshaft sprocket timing marks

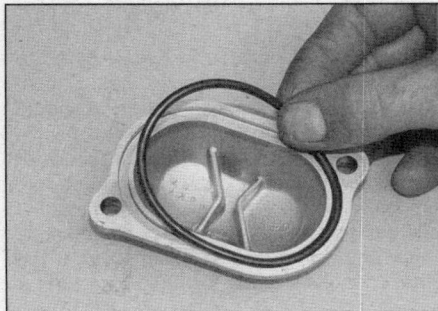

3.18 Fit new O-rings into the groove in the covers

3.21 Remove the cylinder head covers

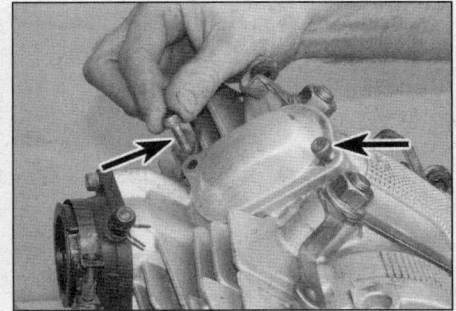

3.22 Undo the bolts (arrowed) and remove the rocker covers

3.23a Undo the bolts (arrowed) . . .

3.23b . . . and remove the camshaft sprocket covers, noting the O-rings

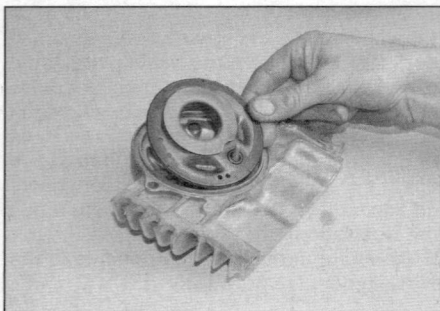

3.23c Baffle plate is a press fit in the front camshaft sprocket cover

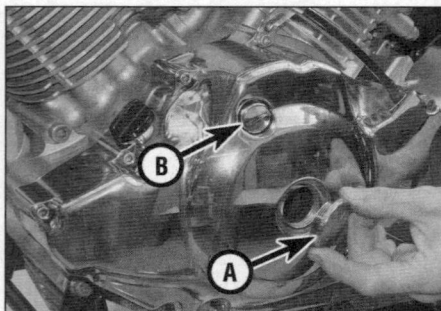

3.24 Remove the centre (A) and timing (B) caps from the alternator cover

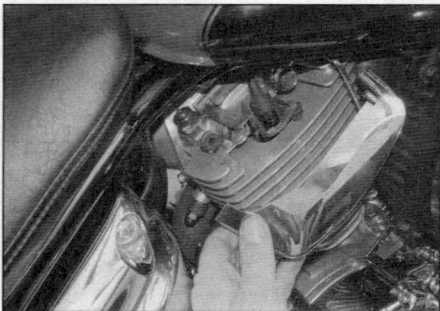

4.2 Pull off the spark plug covers on 1100 models

4.3 Pull the cap off each spark plug

4.4a Using the plug socket and spanner . . .

4.4b . . . to remove a spark plug

sprocket covers, noting the location of the cover O-rings **(see illustrations)**. A baffle plate is fitted in the front cover – if it does not come off with the cover, remove it from the cylinder head, noting the location of the O-ring **(see illustration)**.

24 Undo the centre cap and timing inspection cap in the alternator cover on the left-hand side of the engine **(see illustration)**.
25 Turn the crankshaft clockwise with a socket on the alternator centre bolt until the rear cylinder timing mark on the edge of the

alternator rotor is aligned with the notch inside the inspection hole **(see illustration 3.9a)**. Check that the rear cylinder camshaft sprocket mark is aligned with the index mark on the cylinder head **(see illustration 3.9b)**. If the camshaft sprocket mark is not correctly aligned, turn the crankshaft one full turn and check the marks again. With the alternator rotor mark and the camshaft sprocket mark correctly aligned, the rear cylinder is at top dead centre (TDC) on its compression stroke with both valves closed (there should be a small amount of play between the rocker arms and the valve stems).
26 With the engine in this position, follow the procedure in Steps 11 to 13 to check and adjust both valves for the rear cylinder.
27 Now turn the crankshaft clockwise until the front cylinder timing marks are correctly aligned (see Step 14). With the engine in this position, follow the procedure in Steps 11 to 13 to check and adjust both valves for the front cylinder.
28 Check the O-rings on the rocker and camshaft sprocket covers and on the timing inspection cap and the cover centre cap and fit new ones if they're flattened, broken or have been leaking.
29 Ensure the cover O-rings are correctly installed, then fit the covers and tighten their bolts to the torque listed in this Chapter's Specifications.
30 Install the remaining components in the reverse order of removal.

4 Spark plug check

1 Make sure your spark plug socket is the correct size before attempting to remove the plugs – a suitable one is supplied in the motorcycle's toolkit.
2 On 1100 models, pull off the front and rear spark plug covers **(see illustration)**.
3 Disconnect the spark plug caps from the spark plugs **(see illustration)**. If available, use compressed air to blow away any accumulated debris from around the base of the spark plugs.
4 Using either the plug socket supplied in the bike's tool kit or a deep socket wrench, unscrew the plugs from the cylinder head **(see illustrations)**.
5 Inspect the electrodes for wear. Both the centre and side electrodes should have square edges and the side electrode should be of uniform thickness. Look for excessive deposits and evidence of a cracked or chipped insulator around the centre electrode. Compare your spark plugs to the colour spark plug reading chart at the end of this manual. Check the threads, the washer and the ceramic insulator body for cracks and other damage.
6 If the electrodes are not excessively worn, and if the deposits can be easily removed with

8 Since the cylinder head is made of aluminium, which is soft and easily damaged, thread the plugs into the heads by hand.

HAYNES HINT *Since the plugs are recessed, slip a short length of hose over the end of the plug to use as a tool to thread it into place. The hose will grip the plug well enough to turn it, but will start to slip if the plug begins to cross-thread in the hole – this will prevent damaged threads. Refer to Tools and Workshop Tips in the Reference section for thread repair methods.*

9 Once the plugs are finger tight, the job can be finished with a socket. If a torque wrench is available, tighten the plugs to the torque listed in this Chapter's Specifications. If you do not have a torque wrench, tighten the plugs finger tight (until the washers bottom on the cylinder head) then use a socket to tighten them an additional 1/4 to 1/2 turn. Regardless of the method used, do not over-tighten the plugs.
10 Reconnect the spark plug caps. On 1100 models, install the front and rear spark plug covers.

5 Final drive oil level check

1 Support the motorcycle in an upright position.

⚠ *Warning: If the bike has just been ridden the final drive unit may be hot enough to cause burns. Wait until the final drive unit is cool to the touch before checking the level.*

2 Remove the oil level plug from the final drive housing **(see illustration)**.
3 The oil should be level with the lower edge of the hole **(see illustration)**. If it's low, add oil of the type listed in this Chapter's Specifications with a funnel or hose.
4 Check the level plug sealing washer – if it is damaged or has been leaking, fit a new one.
5 Install the level plug and tighten it to the torque listed in this Chapter's Specifications.

6 Stand and lever pivots and cable lubrication

Pivot points

1 Since the stand and lever pivots and various other components are exposed to the elements, they should be lubricated periodically to ensure safe and trouble-free operation.
2 The footrest pivots, clutch and brake lever pivots, brake pedal and gearchange lever pivots and linkage and stand pivot should be lubricated frequently **(see illustrations)**. On 650 models, remove the rear right-hand frame cover to access the rear brake rod pivot **(see illustration)**.

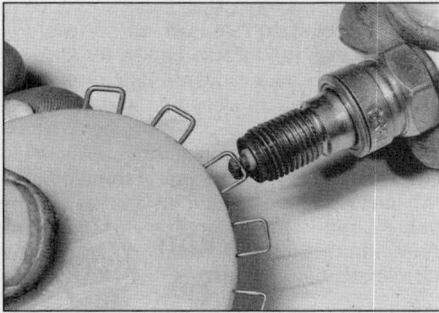
4.7a Using a wire type gauge to measure the spark plug electrode gap

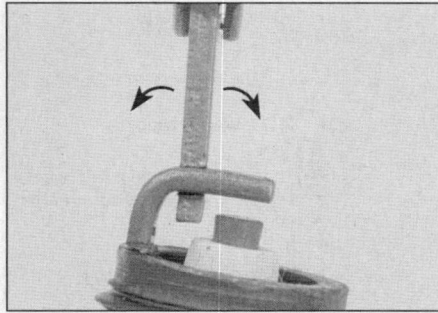
4.7b Adjust the electrode gap by bending the side electrode only

5.2 Location of the final drive oil level plug

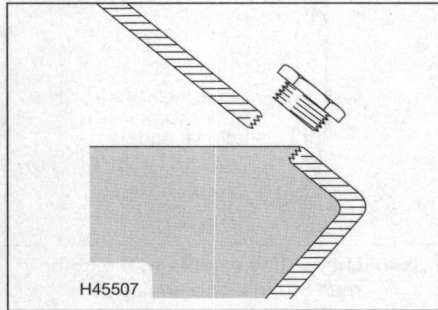
5.3 Final drive oil level

a wire brush, the plugs can be re-gapped and reused. If in doubt concerning the condition of the plugs, replace them with new ones, as the expense is minimal.
7 Before installing new spark plugs, make sure they are the correct type and heat range. Check the gap between the electrodes, as they are not preset. For best results, use a wire-type gauge rather than a flat gauge to check the gap **(see illustration)**. If the gap must be adjusted, bend the side electrode only and be very careful not to chip or crack the insulator nose **(see illustration)**. Make sure the washer is in place before installing each plug.

6.2a Lubricate the pivots on the levers ...

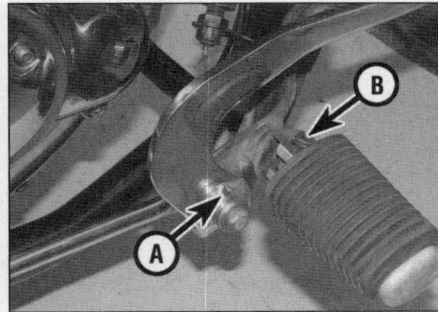
6.2b ... pedals (A) and footrests (B) ...

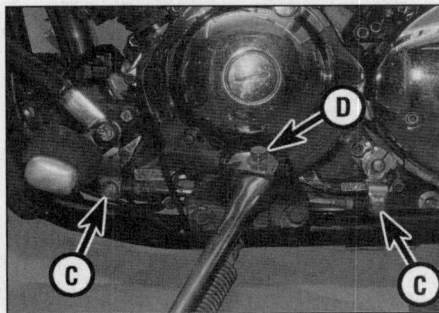
6.2c ... gearchange linkage (C) and sidestand (D)

6.2d Location of rear brake rod pivot on 650 models

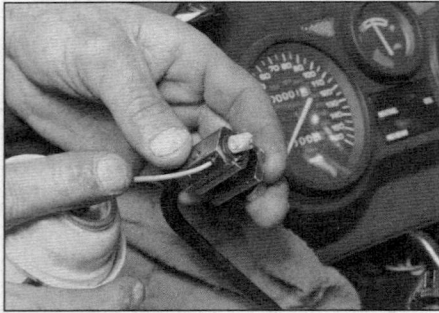

6.4a Lubricating a cable with a pressure adapter. Ensure the tool seals around the inner cable

3 In order for the lubricant to be applied where it will do the most good, the component should be disassembled. However, if chain or cable lubricant is being used, it can be applied to the pivot joint gaps and will usually work its way into the areas where friction occurs. If engine oil or light grease is being used, apply it sparingly as it may attract dirt (which could cause the controls to bind or wear at an accelerated rate). **Note:** *One of the best lubricants for the control lever pivots is a dry-film lubricant.*

Cables

4 To lubricate the throttle and choke cables, disconnect the cable(s) at the lower end (see Chapter 3). To lubricate the clutch cable, first disconnect it from the handlebar lever (see Chapter 5). Lubricate the cable with a pressure lube adapter **(see illustration)**. If you

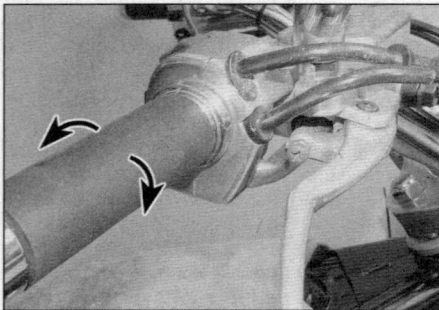

8.2 Throttle cable freeplay is measure in terms of twistgrip rotation

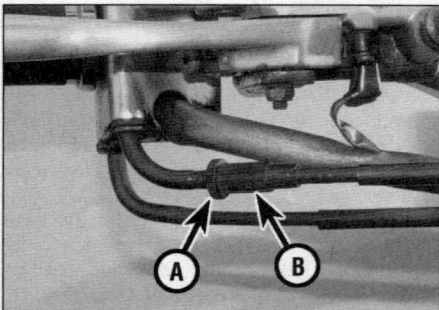

6.4b Lubricating a cable with a home-made funnel and engine oil

don't have one, disconnect both ends of the cable and remove it from the machine and use a funnel and engine oil **(see illustration)**.

7 Sidestand switch check

Inspect the sidestand switch for security, and check for correct operation (Chapter 8).

8 Throttle cable freeplay check

Check

1 Make sure the throttle twistgrip rotates easily from fully closed to fully open with the front wheel turned at various angles. The grip

should return automatically from fully open to fully closed when released. If the twistgrip sticks, check the throttle cables for kinks or cracks in the outer covers. Also, make sure the inner cables are clean and well-lubricated (see Section 6).

2 Check for a small amount of freeplay at the twistgrip before the carburettor throttle pulley is activated and compare the freeplay to the value listed in this Chapter's Specifications **(see illustration)**. If required, adjust the accelerator cable as follows.

Adjustment

3 Loosen the accelerator cable adjuster lockwheel at the handlebar end of the cable, then turn the adjuster in or out until the specified amount of freeplay is obtained at the twistgrip **(see illustration)**. Tighten the lockwheel.

4 If this adjuster has reached its limit of adjustment, reset it so that the freeplay is at a maximum, then adjust the cable at the carburettor end.

5 Remove the fuel tank; on 650 models remove the air filter housing and on 1100 models remove the cover on the left-hand side of the carburettor assembly (see Chapter 3).

6 Identify the accelerator (opening) cable **(see illustrations)**. Slacken the upper adjuster locknut, then, holding the lower locknut against the bracket, turn the adjuster out, making sure the lower nut remains on the adjuster threads. Turn the adjuster until the specified amount of freeplay is obtained, then tighten the upper locknut. Further adjustments can now be made at the twistgrip end. If the cable cannot be adjusted as specified, install a new one (see Chapter 3)

7 Make sure the throttle pulley on the carburettor contacts the idle adjusting screw when the twistgrip is in the closed position (see Chapter 3).

8 Install the components as applicable in the reverse order of removal.

⚠️ *Warning: Turn the handlebars all the way through their travel with the engine idling. Idle speed should not change. If it does, the cables may be routed incorrectly. Correct this condition before riding the bike.*

8.3 Accelerator cable adjuster lockwheel (A) and adjuster (B) – 650 model shown

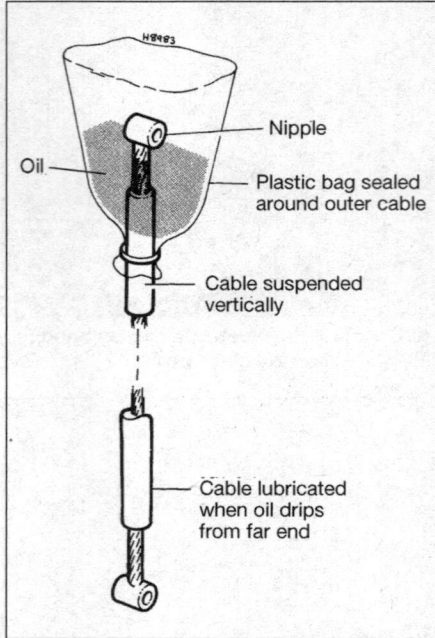

8.6a Accelerator cable – 650 models

8.6b Accelerator cable – 1100 models

9.3a Location of the idle speed adjuster – 650 models

9.3b Location of the idle speed adjuster – 1100 models

9 Idle speed check

1 The idle speed should be checked and adjusted before and after the carburettors are synchronized and when it is obviously too high or too low. Before adjusting the idle speed, make sure the valve clearances and spark plug gaps are correct. Also, turn the handlebars back-and-forth and see if the idle speed changes as this is done. If it does, the accelerator cable may not be adjusted correctly, or it may be trapped (see Section 8). This is a dangerous condition that can cause loss of control of the bike. Be sure to correct this problem before proceeding.

2 The engine should be at normal operating temperature, which is usually reached after 10 to 15 minutes of stop and go riding. Support the motorcycle securely in an upright position.

3 With the engine idling, turn the idle speed adjuster until the idle speed listed in this Chapter's Specifications is obtained. **Note:** *As the machine is not fitted with a tachometer in the instrument panel the only accurate means of measuring engine speed is using an auxiliary tachometer with an inductive pick-up which clamps around the rear cylinder HT lead.* The idle speed adjuster is located on the left-hand side of the carburettor assembly **(see illustrations)**. Turn the adjuster clockwise to increase idle speed and anti-clockwise to decrease it.

4 Snap the throttle open and shut a few times, then recheck the idle speed. If

necessary, repeat the adjustment procedure.

5 If a smooth, steady idle can't be achieved, the fuel/air mixture may be incorrect (see Chapter 3) or the carburettors may need synchronising (see Section 10). Also check the intake manifold rubbers for cracks which will cause an air leak, resulting in a weak mixture. Check the air induction system (see Section 20).

10 Carburettor synchronisation

⚠️ *Warning: Petrol (gasoline) is extremely flammable, so take extra precautions when you work on any part of the fuel system. Don't smoke or allow open flames or bare light bulbs near the work area, and don't work in a garage where a natural gas-type appliance (such as a water heater or clothes dryer) is present. If you spill any fuel on your skin, rinse it off immediately with soap and water. When you perform any kind of work on the fuel system, wear safety glasses and have a class B type fire extinguisher on hand.*

1 Carburettor synchronisation is simply the process of adjusting the carburettors so they pass the same amount of fuel/air mixture to each cylinder. This is done by measuring the vacuum produced in each cylinder. Carburettors that are out of synchronisation will result in decreased fuel mileage, increased engine temperature, less

than ideal throttle response and higher vibration levels.

2 To properly synchronize the carburettors, you will need a vacuum gauge set-up with a gauge for each cylinder, or a mercury manometer, which is a calibrated tube arrangement that utilizes columns of mercury to indicate engine vacuum. **Note:** *Because of the nature of the synchronisation procedure and the need for special instruments, most owners leave the task to a Yamaha dealer or a reputable motorcycle repair shop.*

3 Temporarily remove the fuel tank (see Chapter 3). Remove the air filter housing and, on 1100 models, remove the intake duct (see Chapter 3).

4 Remove the blanking caps from the intake joint fittings **(see illustration)**. Connect the vacuum gauges or manometer to the fittings.

5 Install the fuel tank and start the engine and let it run until it reaches normal operating temperature. Check the engine idle speed and adjust it if necessary (see Section 9).

6 With the engine idling, the vacuum readings for both cylinders should be the same, or at least within the tolerance listed in this Chapter's Specifications. If the vacuum readings vary, adjust carburettor No. 1 to match No. 2 by turning the synchronising screw (see Chapter 3).

7 After adjustment, snap the throttle open and shut 2 or 3 times, then recheck the vacuum readings and readjust as necessary.

8 When the adjustment is complete, turn the engine OFF. Remove the vacuum gauges or manometer and reinstall the blanking caps. Check the throttle cable freeplay and adjust it if necessary (see Section 8).

9 Install all the parts removed for access.

10 Start the engine and check the idle speed (see Section 9).

11 Brake pads and brake shoes check

⚠️ *Warning: The dust created by the brake system may contain asbestos, which is harmful to your health. Never blow it out with compressed air and don't inhale any of it. An approved filtering mask should be worn when working on the brakes.*

Brake pads

1 Always renew the disc brake pads in complete sets; on 1100 models with two front brake calipers, replace all four pads at the same time.

2 To check the front brake pads on all 650 models, follow the procedure in Chapter 6 and displace the caliper assembly, then remove the pads from the caliper bracket **(see illustration)**.

3 To check the front brake pads on all 1100 models, follow the procedure in Chapter 6 and displace the caliper, then remove the

10.4 Blanking caps on intake joint fittings – 650 model shown

11.2 Remove the pads from the caliper bracket – 650 models

11.3 Displace the caliper to access the pads (arrowed) – 1100 models

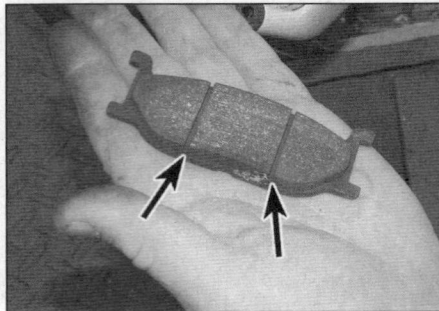

11.4 Front brake pad wear indicators (arrowed)

11.7 Inspecting the rear brake caliper pads (arrowed) – 1100 models

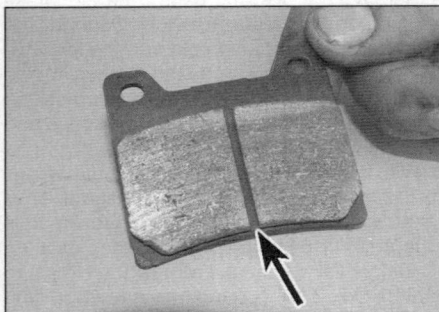

11.8 Rear brake pad wear indicator (arrowed) – 1100 models

11.11 Rear drum brake wear indicator – 650 models

pads from the caliper bracket **(see illustration)**.

4 If the pads are worn nearly to the bottom of the wear indicators, fit new ones **(see illustration). Note:** *Some after-market pads may use different indicators; always check with your supplier before fitting.* If required, measure the amount of friction material remaining – the minimum is 0.8 mm.

5 Yamaha recommend that new pad springs should be fitted whenever the pads are renewed – refer to Chapter 6 for full details of pad removal, inspection and installation.

6 On reassembly, don't forget to tighten the caliper mounting bolts and caliper pin to the specified torque setting.

7 To check the rear brake pads on 1100 models, follow the procedure in Chapter 6 and displace the caliper **(see illustration)**.

8 If the pads are worn nearly to the bottom of

the wear indicator, fit new ones **(see illustration). Note:** *Some after-market pads may use different indicators; always check with your supplier before fitting.* If required, measure the amount of friction material remaining – the minimum is 0.5 mm.

9 Yamaha recommend that a new pad spring should be fitted whenever the pads are renewed – refer to Chapter 6 for full details of pad removal, inspection and installation.

10 On reassembly, don't forget to tighten the caliper mounting bolts to the specified torque setting.

Brake shoes

11 650 models are fitted with a drum rear brake. To check the rear brake shoes for wear, have an assistant press the brake pedal firmly while you look at the wear indicator on the brake backplate **(see illustration)**. If the

indicator pointer is close to the end of its travel, the brake shoes must be renewed (see Chapter 6).

12 Brake system check

1 A routine general check of the brakes will ensure that any problems are discovered and remedied before the rider's safety is jeopardised.

2 Check the brake lever and pedal for loose fixings, rough action, excessive play, bends, and other damage. Replace any damaged parts with new ones (see Chapter 6).

3 Make sure all brake fasteners are tight. Check the brake pads and shoes for wear (see Section 11) and make sure the fluid level in the brake reservoir is correct (see *Daily (pre-ride) checks* at the beginning of this Manual).

4 Inspect the brake hose(s) for cracks and look for leaks at the brake hose connections **(see illustration)**. The brake hoses should be renewed if they have deteriorated, or every four years irrespective of their condition (see Section 28).

5 If the lever or pedal action of hydraulic brakes is spongy, bleed the brakes (see Chapter 6).

6 The seals in the brake master cylinder and caliper and the brake fluid should be changed every two years (see Sections 26 and 27).

7 Make sure the brake light operates when the front brake lever is pulled in. The front brake light switch is not adjustable. If it fails to operate properly, check it (see Chapter 8).

8 Make sure the brake light is activated just before the rear brake takes effect. If adjustment is necessary, hold the switch so it won't rotate and turn the adjusting nut on the switch body until the brake light is activated when required **(see illustration)**. If the switch doesn't operate the brake light, check it (see Chapter 8).

Front brake lever

9 The front brake lever must have the amount of free play listed in this Chapter's Specifications to prevent brake drag.

10 Operate the lever and check freeplay at the ball end of the lever. If it's not correct,

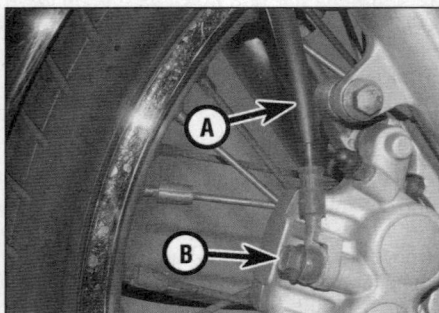

12.4 Inspect the brake hose (A) and hose connections (B)

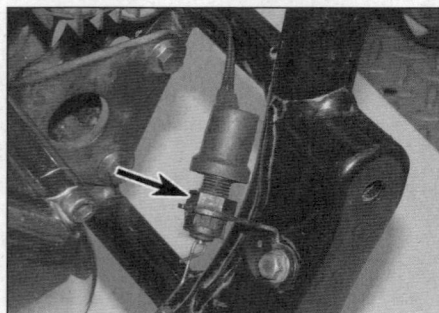

12.8 Rear brake light switch adjuster nut (arrowed)

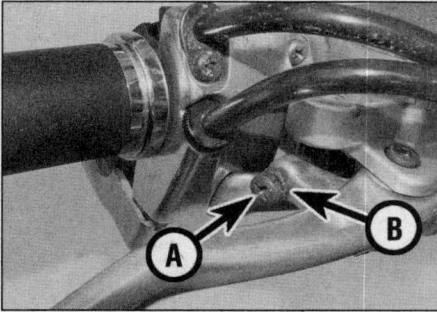

12.10 Front brake lever adjuster (A) and locknut (B)

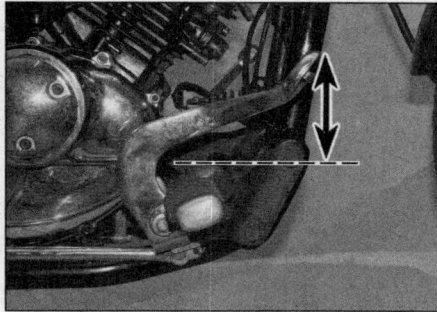

12.11 Distance (A) between the top edge of the brake pedal and the footrest should be as specified

12.12 Location of the brake pedal height adjuster – 650 models

loosen the adjuster locknut, turn the adjuster to bring freeplay within the Specifications and tighten the locknut **(see illustration)**.

Rear brake pedal

11 The top edge of the rear brake pedal should be positioned above the footrest or footboard the distance listed in this Chapter's Specifications **(see illustration)**.

650 models

12 To adjust the position of the pedal, first loosen the locknut on the adjuster, then turn the adjuster to set the pedal position **(see illustration)**. Tighten the locknut.
13 Now check the pedal freeplay and compare it to the value listed in this Chapter's Specifications. Adjust if necessary by turning the adjuster at the rear end of the brake rod **(see illustration)**.
14 Support the machine with the rear wheel off the ground. Apply the brake several times and ensure that the wheel turns freely without the brake binding when the pedal is released. If the brake binds, recheck the pedal freeplay and, if necessary, check the operation of the rear brake (see Chapter 6).
15 If necessary, adjust the brake light switch (see Step 8).

1100 models

16 To adjust the position of the pedal, first loosen the locknut on the brake rod, then turn the adjuster to set the pedal position **(see illustration)**. After adjustment, check that the end of the rod is visible through the hole in the clevis. Tighten the locknut.

12.13 Rear brake pedal freeplay adjuster – 650 models

17 Support the machine with the rear wheel off the ground. Apply the brake several times and ensure that the wheel turns freely without the brake binding when the pedal is released. If the brake binds, recheck the pedal position and, if necessary, check the operation of the rear brake master cylinder and caliper (see Chapter 6).
18 If necessary, adjust the brake light switch (see Step 8).

---

13 Steering head bearings check

1 The steering head bearings can become dented, rough or loose during normal use of the machine. In extreme cases, worn or loose steering head bearings can cause steering wobble which is potentially dangerous.

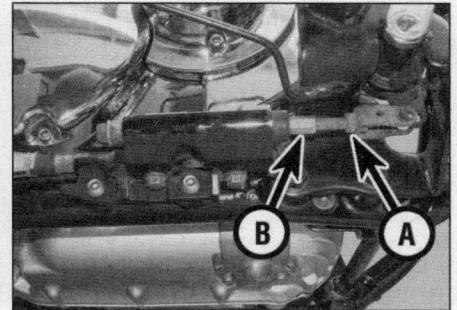

12.16 Loosen locknut (A) then turn adjuster (B) – 1100 models

Check

2 To check the bearings, support the motorcycle securely in an upright position using an auxiliary stand with the front wheel off the ground.
3 Point the wheel straight ahead and slowly turn the handlebars from lock-to-lock. Dents or roughness in the bearing races will be felt and if the bearings are too tight the bars will not move smoothly and freely. If the bearings are damaged they should be renewed (see Chapter 5).
4 Next, grasp the bottom of the forks and try to move them forwards and backwards **(see illustration)**. Any looseness in the steering head bearings will be felt as front-to-rear movement of the forks. If play is felt in the steering head bearings, adjust them as follows.

> **HAYNES HINT** *Freeplay in the fork due to worn fork bushes can be misinterpreted as steering head bearing play – do not confuse the two.*

Adjustment

5 Although not essential, it is wise to remove the fuel tank to avoid the possibility of damage during this procedure (see Chapter 3). Alternatively, place a suitable cover over the tank.
6 Loosen the two front fork top yoke clamp bolts **(see illustration)**.

13.4 Checking for play in the steering head bearings

13.6 Front fork top yoke clamp bolt (arrowed)

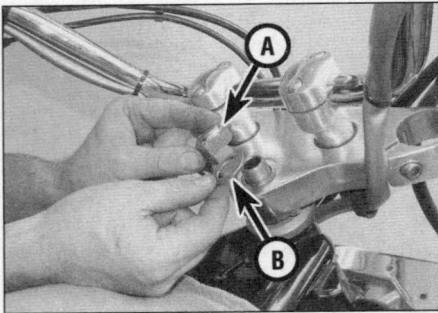

13.7 Steering stem nut (A) and washer (B)

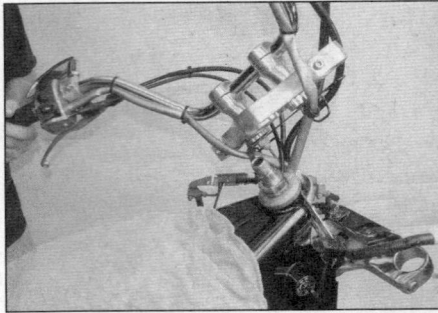

13.8 Lift off the top yoke and handlebar assembly

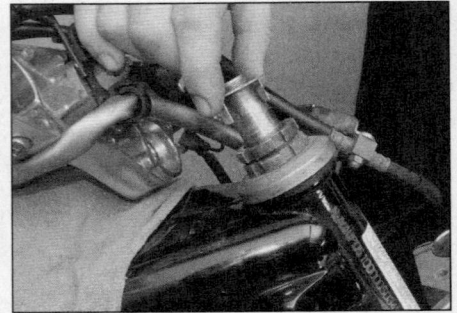

13.9 Remove the lock washer

7 Remove the steering stem nut and washer **(see illustration)**.

8 Lift off the fork top yoke and handlebar assembly and support them so that they are clear of the steering head **(see illustration)**. Ensure no strain is placed on the brake hose or wiring. Keep the brake reservoir upright to prevent fluid spills.

9 Remove the lock washer, noting how it fits **(see illustration)**.

10 Using either a C-spanner or suitable drift, undo the adjuster locknut and remove it, then remove the rubber washer **(see illustrations)**.

11 To adjust the bearings as specified by Yamaha, a service tool (Pt. No. 90890-01403 for Europe or YU-33975 for US) and a torque wrench are required. If the tool is available, first slacken the adjuster nut slightly to take pressure off the bearing, then tighten the nut to the initial torque setting specified at the beginning of this Chapter. Make sure the torque wrench handle is at right-angles (90°) to the centre line between the adjuster nut and the service tool wrench socket **(see illustration)**. Now slacken the nut, then tighten it to the final torque setting specified.

12 If the Yamaha tool is not available, using either a C-spanner, a peg spanner or a drift located in one of the notches, slacken the adjuster nut slightly to take pressure off the bearing then tighten the nut until all freeplay is removed **(see illustration)**. Now tighten the nut a little more to pre-load the bearings. Now slacken the nut and retighten it, setting it so that all freeplay is just removed from the bearings, yet the steering is able to move freely from lock-to-lock. Tighten the nut only a little at a time, and after each adjustment repeat the checks outlined in Steps 3 and 4.

Caution: Take great care not to apply excessive pressure because this will cause premature failure of the bearings.

13 Turn the steering from lock-to-lock several times to settle the bearings, then recheck the adjustment or the torque setting. The object is to set the adjuster nut so that the bearings are under a very light loading, just enough to remove any freeplay. If any roughness or binding is felt in the bearings, remove the steering stem and inspect them (see Chapter 5).

14 With the bearings correctly adjusted, install the rubber washer and the locknut **(see illustrations 13.10b and a)**. Tighten the locknut finger-tight, then tighten it further until its notches align with those in the adjuster nut, making sure the adjuster nut does not turn as well. Install the lock washer so that the tabs fit into the notches in both the locknut and adjuster nut **(see illustration 13.9)**.

15 Fit the top yoke and handlebar assembly onto the steering stem and the fork legs. Install the washer and steering stem nut and tighten it to the torque setting specified at the beginning of this Chapter. Tighten the top yoke clamp bolts to the specified torque.

16 Check the bearing adjustment as described above and re-adjust if necessary.

Note: *Periodic cleaning and re-greasing of the steering head bearings is recommended by the manufacturer. Refer to Chapter 5 for steering head bearing lubrication and renewal procedures.*

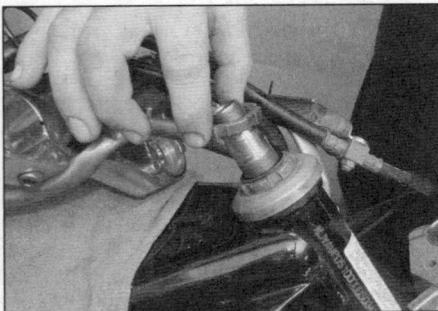

13.10a Remove the adjuster locknut . . .

13.10b . . . and the rubber washer

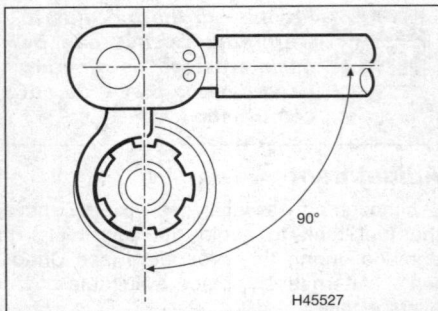

13.11 Ensure the torque wrench arm is at right-angles (90°) to the service tool

13.12 Adjusting the bearings with a C-spanner

14 Suspension checks

1 The suspension components must be maintained in top operating condition to ensure rider safety. Loose, worn or damaged suspension parts decrease the vehicle's stability and control.

Front suspension

2 While standing alongside the motorcycle, apply the front brake and push on the handlebars to compress the forks several times. Check that they move up-and-down smoothly without binding. If binding is felt, the

14.3 Inspect the fork tubes (A) and dust seals (B)

forks should be disassembled and inspected (see Chapter 5).

3 Inspect the fork tubes for signs of scratches, corrosion and pitting, and oil leaks **(see illustration)**. Carefully lever up the dust seals using a flat-bladed screwdriver and inspect the area around the fork seals. Any scratches, corrosion and pitting will cause premature seal failure. If oil leaks are evident, new seals must be fitted (see Chapter 5). If the damage is excessive, new fork tubes should be installed (see Chapter 5).

4 Check the tightness of all suspension nuts and bolts to be sure none have worked loose, referring to the torque settings specified at the beginning of Chapter 5.

Rear suspension

5 Inspect the shock for fluid leaks and tightness of the mountings (see Chapter 5). If leaks are found, the shock should be renewed.

6 With the aid of an assistant to support the bike, compress the rear suspension several times. It should move up and down freely without binding. If any binding is felt, the worn or faulty component must be identified and renewed. The problem could be due to either the shock absorber or the swingarm components.

7 Support the motorcycle using an auxiliary stand so that the rear wheel is off the ground. Grab the swingarm and rock it from side to side – there should be no discernible movement at the rear. If there is a little

14.11 Location of the rear suspension adjuster on 650 models

movement or a slight clicking can be heard, check the tightness of all the rear suspension mounting bolts and nuts, referring to the torque settings specified at the beginning of Chapter 5, then re-check for movement. Next, grasp the top of the rear wheel and pull it upwards – there should be no discernible freeplay before the shock absorber begins to compress **(see illustration)**. Any freeplay felt in either check indicates worn bearings in the swingarm, or, on 1100 models, the suspension linkage, or worn shock absorber mountings. The worn components must be renewed (see Chapter 5).

8 To make an accurate assessment of the swingarm bearings it is necessary to first remove the rear wheel (see Chapter 5). On 650 models, detach the rear shock from the swingarm; on 1100 models, remove the bolt securing the suspension linkage plates to the swingarm (see Chapter 5). Grasp the rear of the swingarm with one hand and place your other hand at the junction of the swingarm and the frame. Try to move the rear of the swingarm from side to side. Any wear (play) in the bearings should be felt as movement between the swingarm and the frame at the front. If there is any play, the swingarm will be felt to move forward and backward at the front (not from side-to-side). Next, move the swingarm up and down through its full travel. It should move freely, without any binding or rough spots. If any play in the swingarm is noted or if the swingarm does not move freely, the bearings must be removed for inspection or renewal (see Chapter 5).

14.13 Location of the rear suspension adjuster on 1100 models

Adjustment

9 Only the rear suspension setting can be adjusted. The rear shock absorber on all models is adjustable for spring preload. There are seven positions. Position 1 is the softest setting, position 3 is the standard, and position 7 is the hardest. A C-spanner and extension bar is provided in the bike's toolkit for adjusting the shock.
Caution: Never turn the adjuster beyond the maximum or minimum adjustment number.

650 models

10 Remove the seats (see Chapter 7).
11 Adjust the spring pre-load by turning the spring seat on the bottom of the shock **(see illustration)**. Align the setting required with the adjustment stopper. Turn the spring seat clockwise to increase pre-load and anti-clockwise to decrease it.

1100 models

12 Remove the seats and the rear mudguard (see Chapter 7).
13 Adjust the spring pre-load by turning the spring seat on the top of the shock **(see illustration)**. Align the setting required with the adjustment stopper. Turn the spring seat clockwise to decrease pre-load and anti-clockwise to increase it.

15 Tyre, wheel and bearing checks

Tyres

1 Check the tyre condition and tread depth thoroughly – see *Daily (pre-ride) checks*.

Wheels

2 Check wire spoke wheels for cracks, flat spots on the rim, bent spokes and other damage. Tap the spokes with a metal screwdriver blade or similar tool and listen to the sound. If the spoke makes a 'clunk' or low-pitched sound it is loose. Spoke tensioning or renewal is a task for a wheel building expert.

3 Cast wheels, where fitted, are virtually maintenance free, but they should be kept clean and checked periodically for cracks and other damage. Never attempt to repair damaged cast wheels; they must be replaced with new ones.

4 Check the valve rubber for signs of damage or deterioration and have it renewed if necessary. Also, make sure the valve cap is in place and tight. Check that the wheel balance weights are fixed firmly to the wheel rim – two types are fitted, those that clip around the spokes and those that adhere to the rim itself

15.4a Wheel balance weight clipped to spoke

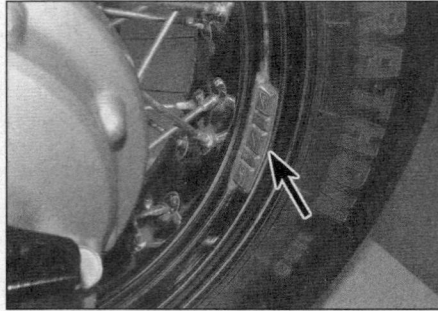
15.4b Wheel balance weights fixed to the wheel rim

15.7 Checking for play in the wheel bearings

(see illustrations). If there are signs that the weights have fallen off, have the wheel rebalanced by a motorcycle tyre specialist.

5 Check the wheel runout and alignment (see Chapter 6).

Wheel bearings

6 Wheel bearings will wear over a period of time and result in handling problems.

7 Support the motorcycle upright using an auxiliary stand. Check for any play in the bearings by pushing and pulling the wheel against the hub **(see illustration)**. Also raise the wheel off the ground and check that it rotates smoothly.

8 If any play is detected in the hub, or if the wheel does not rotate smoothly (and this is not due to brake or transmission drag), the wheel must be removed and the bearings inspected for wear or damage (see Chapter 6).

16 Battery check

1 All models are fitted with a sealed, maintenance-free battery. **Note:** *Do not attempt to open the battery as resulting damage will mean it will be unfit for further use.*

2 All that should be done is to check that the terminals are clean and tight and that the casing is not damaged or leaking. See Chapter 8 for further details.

3 If the machine is not in regular use, disconnect the battery and give it a refresher charge every month to six weeks (see Chapter 8).

17 Exhaust system check

1 Periodically check all the exhaust system joints and mountings for leaks and loose fasteners, referring to the torque settings specified at the beginning of Chapter 3. **Note:** *The exhaust pipe-to-cylinder head fixings are*

prone to corrosion. Lubricate the threads of the studs and bolts with copper-based grease to preserve them.

2 If tightening the exhaust pipe-to-cylinder head fixings or the silencer clamp bolts fails to stop any leaks, replace the joint gaskets with new ones (see Chapter 3). **Note:** *On the rear cylinder head, an exhaust manifold fixes directly to the head and the exhaust pipe bolts to the manifold. There is a gasket between the head and the manifold and a gasket between the manifold and the pipe.*

18 Fuel system and hoses check

⚠️ *Warning: Petrol (gasoline) is extremely flammable, so take extra precautions when you work on any part of the fuel system. Don't smoke or allow open flames or bare light bulbs near the work area, and don't work in a garage where a natural gas-type appliance is present. If you spill any fuel on your skin, rinse it off immediately with soap and water. When you perform any kind of work on the fuel system, wear safety glasses and have a class B type fire extinguisher on hand.*

1 Check the fuel tank, the fuel tap, the hoses and the carburettors for leaks and evidence of damage.

2 If carburettor gaskets are leaking, the carburettors should be disassembled and rebuilt using new gaskets and seals (see Chapter 3).

3 If the fuel tap to tank joint is leaking, or the tap body is leaking, tightening the screws may help **(see illustration)**. If leaks persist, follow the procedure in Chapter 3 and renew the tap seal and O-ring.

4 Whenever the fuel tank, air filter housing or airbox are removed, check the condition of the fuel hoses and their clips. Note that on 1100 models, the fuel pump is located behind the left-hand frame panel – periodically remove the panel and check the condition of the supply (from the tank) and delivery (to the carburettors) hoses. If the fuel hoses are cracked or otherwise deteriorated, replace them with new ones.

5 On 650 models, remove the instrument panel and check the condition of the fuel tank breather hose (see Chapter 3). Ensure the hose is not trapped or blocked. On California models, ensure the EVAP canister is not damaged and replace it with a new one if necessary (see Chapter 3).

In-line fuel filter

6 An in-line fuel filter is fitted between the fuel tap and the fuel pump. At the service interval, or if the filter is dirty or clogged, replace it with a new one – this type of filter cannot be cleaned.

7 On 650 models, remove the fuel tank (see Chapter 3). On 1100 models remove the seats and displace the ICU panel underneath the rider's seat.

8 Have a rag ready to soak up any residual fuel, then release the clips and disconnect the hoses from the filter. Pull the filter out of its holder, noting how it fits **(see illustrations)**.

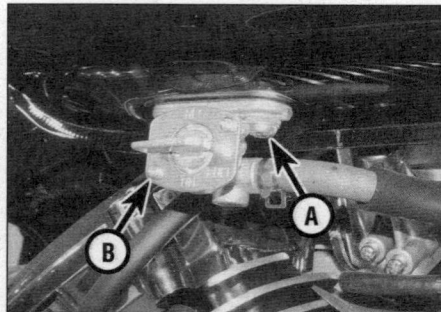
18.3 Fuel tap to tank screws (A) and tap body screws (B)

18.8a Location of the fuel filter – 650 models

18.8b Location of the fuel filter – 1100 models

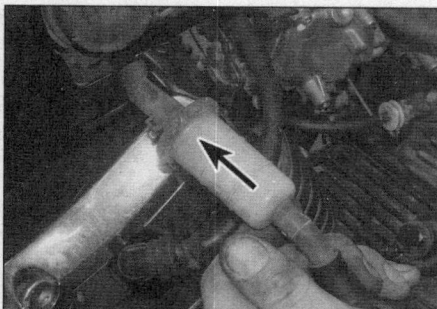
18.9 Arrow should point in direction of fuel flow

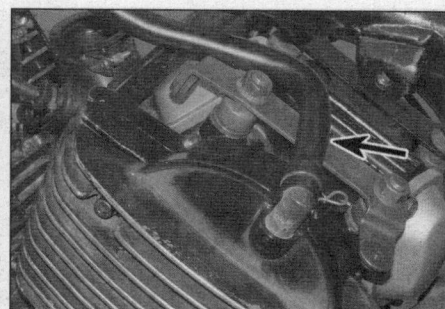
19.2 Location of the breather hose – 650 model shown

9 Install the new filter so that its arrow points in the direction of fuel flow, i.e. away from the tap **(see illustration)**. Fit the hoses onto the filter unions and secure them with the clips.
10 Install the remaining components, then start the engine and check that there are no leaks.

19 Crankcase breather system check

1 On 650 models, remove the rear cylinder head covers (see Chapter 2A). On 1100 models, remove the fuel tank (see Chapter 3).
2 Inspect the hose that runs from the breather union on the top of the engine to the air filter housing **(see illustration)**. Make sure the hose is attached at both ends and secured by the clips. If the hose is cracked or deteriorated replace it with a new one.

20 Air induction system (AIS) check

1 An air induction system (AIS) is fitted to certain market models. The system sucks fresh air into the exhaust ports, allowing combustion to continue longer, thus reducing the level of unburned hydrocarbons in the exhaust.
2 The components of the air induction system (AIS) should be checked at the specified service interval, or if a smooth, steady idle can't be achieved (see Section 9).
3 Full details and service information for the AIS can be found in Chapter 3.

21 Handlebar switches and headlight beam check

Handlebar switches

1 Switch operation should be checked at the service interval or as soon as a problem occurs.
2 The switch contacts may become dirty or corroded in use. Undo the screws securing the two halves of the switch unit together and separate them **(see illustration)**. If required, clean the contacts with a knife or polish with crocus cloth. Spray the contacts with electrical contact cleaner or corrosion inhibitor.
3 If necessary, follow the procedure in Chapter 8 and check the individual switches for continuity.

Headlight beam

4 An improperly adjusted headlight may cause problems for oncoming traffic or provide poor, unsafe illumination of the road ahead. Before adjusting the headlight, be sure to consult with local traffic laws and regulations. UK owners refer to MOT test checks in the Reference section.

5 The headlight beam can be adjusted both vertically and horizontally. Before performing the adjustment, make sure the fuel tank is at least half full and have an assistant sit on the seat.
XVS650 and 1999 to 2000 XVS1100 models
6 The horizontal adjusting screw is at the upper left of the headlight rim **(see illustration)**. Turn the screw clockwise to move the beam to the left and anti-clockwise to move it to the right.
7 The vertical adjusting screw is located at the lower right of the headlight rim **(see illustration 21.6)**. Turn the screw clockwise to raise the beam and anti-clockwise to lower it.
XVS650A/S and XVS1100A/S models
8 The horizontal adjusting screw is at the lower right of the headlight rim **(see illustration)**. Turn the screw clockwise to move the beam to the left and anti-clockwise to move it to the right.
9 The vertical adjusting screw is located at the lower left of the headlight rim **(see illustration 21.8)**. Turn the screw clockwise to raise the beam and anti-clockwise to lower it.
2001-on XVS1100 models
10 The horizontal adjusting screw is at the lower left of the headlight rim. Turn the screw clockwise to move the beam to the left and anti-clockwise to move it to the right.
11 The vertical adjusting screw is located at the lower right of the headlight rim. Turn the screw clockwise to raise the beam and anti-clockwise to lower it.

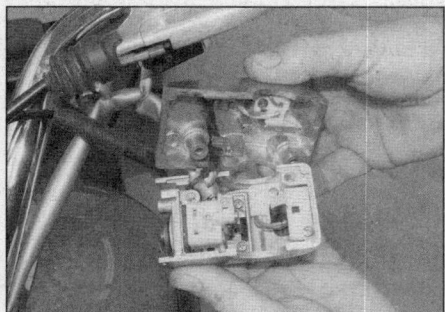
21.2 Separate the halves of the switch units to inspect the electrical contacts

21.6 Horizontal headlight beam adjusting screw (A) and vertical adjusting screw (B) – XVS650 models

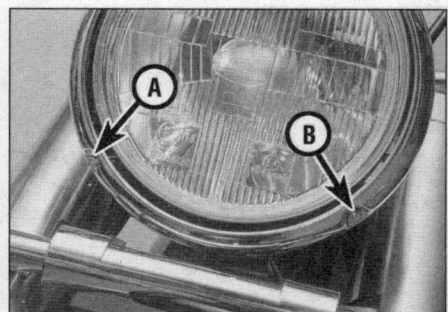
21.8 Horizontal headlight beam adjusting screw (A) and vertical adjusting screw (B) – XVS650A models

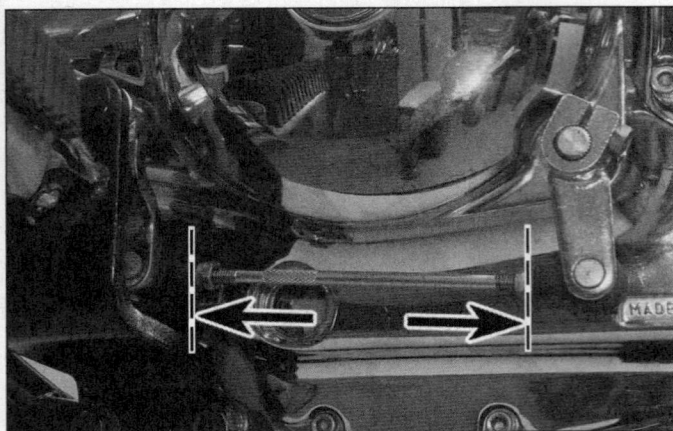

23.1 Gearchange rod length (A) should be as specified

23.2 Gearchange rod locknut (arrowed)

22 Fastener tightness check

1 Since vibration of the machine tends to loosen fasteners, all nuts, bolts, screws, etc. should be periodically checked for proper tightness.
2 Pay particular attention to the following:
  Spark plugs
  Engine oil drain plug
  Oil filter cover bolts and drain plug
  Gearchange lever and linkage
  Footrest and sidestand pivots
  Engine mounting bolts
  Rear shock absorber mounting bolts
  Front wheel axle and axle pinch bolt
  Rear wheel axle nut
3 If a torque wrench is available, use it along with the torque specifications at the beginning of this, or other, Chapters.

23 Gearchange linkage check and adjustment

1 Check the alignment of the gearchange lever and the arm at the other end of the linkage with the linkage rod. The lever and the arm should be at right angles to the rod and the rod should be the specified length **(see illustration)**. Measure the rod as shown and compare the result with the specifications at the beginning of this Chapter.
2 To adjust, loosen the locknuts at both ends of the linkage rod and turn the rod to change its length **(see illustration)**. The rod is reverse threaded on one end, so will screw into or out of the lever and arm simultaneously when turned. Don't forget to tighten the locknuts after adjustment.

24 Evaporative emission control (EVAP) system check

1 California models are fitted with an evaporative emission control (EVAP) system which prevents fuel vapour escaping from the tank into the atmosphere. When the engine isn't running, the vapour is stored in a canister, then drawn into the combustion chambers for burning when the engine starts.
2 The hoses should be checked periodically for loose connections, damage and deterioration. Tighten or renew the hoses as needed.
3 A rollover valve prevents the flow of fuel through the EVAP system if the bike falls over. To test the valve, disconnect its hoses and remove the mounting screw. It should be possible to blow air through the valve when it's upright, but not when it's turned upside down. If the valve doesn't perform as described, fit a new one.
4 XVS1100 models are fitted with an EVAP system solenoid valve located behind the left-hand side cover. Follow the procedure in Chapter 8, Section 27, to check the valve.

25 Final drive oil change

1 Ride the bike to warm the oil so it will drain completely.

> **Warning: Be careful not to touch hot components (including the oil); they may be hot enough to cause burns.**

2 Support the machine in an upright position and place a drain tray below the final drive housing.
3 Remove the filler plug to vent the housing, then remove the drain plug and let the oil drain for 10 to 15 minutes **(see illustration)**.

> **HAYNES HINT** *Check the old oil carefully – if it is very metallic coloured, then the final drive is experiencing wear from break-in (new engine) or from insufficient lubrication. If there are flakes or chips of metal in the oil, then something is drastically wrong internally and the final drive will have to be disassembled for inspection and repair.*

4 Check the condition of the sealing washer on the drain plug and discard it if it is damaged or worn – it is always advisable to use a new washer even if the old one looks good **(see illustration)**.
5 Clean the drain plug and fit the sealing washer, then reinstall the plug and tighten it to the torque listed in this Chapter's Specifications.

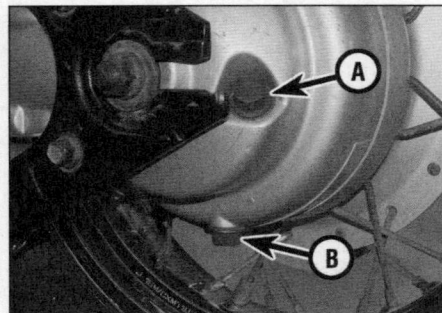

25.3 Final drive unit filler plug (A) and drain plug (B)

25.4 Always fit a new sealing washer to the drain plug

6 Fill the final drive unit to the correct level with oil of the type listed in this Chapter's Specifications (see Section 5).

7 Install the filler plug and tighten it to the torque listed in this Chapter's Specifications.

26 Brake master cylinder and caliper seals renewal

1 Yamaha specify that the brake master cylinder and caliper seals should be renewed every two years.

2 Refer to the procedures in Chapter 6.

27 Brake fluid renewal

1 Brake system hydraulic fluid will deteriorate with age and must be replaced with new fluid every two years.

2 Refer to the procedure in Chapter 6.

28 Brake hose renewal

1 Brake system hydraulic hoses will deteriorate with age and must be replaced with new ones every four years.

2 Refer to the procedure in Chapter 6.

29 Cylinder compression check

1 Among other things, poor engine performance may be caused by leaking valves, incorrect valve clearances, a leaking head gasket, or worn pistons, rings and/or cylinder walls. A cylinder compression check will help pinpoint these conditions and can also indicate the presence of excessive carbon deposits in the cylinder heads.

2 The only tools required are a compression gauge with a threaded adapter to suit the spark plug hole in the cylinder head, and a spark plug socket. Depending on the outcome of the initial test, a squirt-type oil can may also be needed.

3 Make sure the valve clearances are correctly set (see Section 3) and that the cylinder head bolts/nuts are tightened to the correct torque setting (see Chapter 2A or 2B as applicable).

4 Refer to *Fault Finding Equipment* in the Reference section at the end of this manual for details of the compression test, and to the Specifications at the beginning of this Chapter for the test data.

30 Front fork oil change

1 Fork oil will degrade over a period of time – there is no set interval for changing the oil.

2 Refer to Chapter 5, Section 6 and remove one of the fork legs from the machine. Note that it is advisable to loosen the fork top bolt whilst it is securely clamped in the top yoke.

3 Unscrew the top bolt from the fork leg **(see illustration)**. Discard the O-ring as a new one must be fitted on reassembly.

⚠️ *Warning: The fork spring is pressing on the fork top bolt with considerable pressure. Unscrew the bolt very carefully, keeping a downward pressure on it and release it slowly as it is likely to spring clear as the last threads are freed. It is advisable to wear some form of eye and face protection when carrying out this operation.*

4 Withdraw the spacer, washer and spring from the fork leg **(see illustrations)**.

5 Invert the fork leg over a suitable container and pump the fork vigorously to expel as much fork oil as possible.

6 Compress the fork tube fully into the slider, then slowly pour in the correct quantity of the specified grade of fork oil (refer to the Specifications section at the beginning of Chapter 5). Pump the fork tube in the slider slowly to distribute the oil, then leave the leg upright for ten minutes to allow any air bubbles to disperse.

7 With the fork tube fully compressed into the slider; measure the fork oil level from the top of the tube **(see illustration)**. Add or subtract fork oil until it is at the level specified (see Chapter 5 Specifications).

8 Pull the fork tube out of the slider to its full extension and install the spring with the closer-wound coils at the top, followed by the washer and spacer.

9 Lubricate a new O-ring with fork oil and fit it onto the top bolt. Screw the top bolt into the tube carefully, making sure it is not cross-threaded. **Note:** *The top bolt can be tightened to the specified torque setting at this stage if the tube is held between the padded jaws of a vice, but do not risk distorting the tube by doing so. A better method is to tighten the top bolt when the fork leg has been installed and is securely held in the bottom yoke.*

10 Install the fork leg in the yokes then change the oil in the other fork leg. Note that it is essential that the oil quantity and level are the same in each fork.

30.3 Unscrew the top bolt – discard the O-ring (arrowed)

30.4a Withdraw the spacer . . .

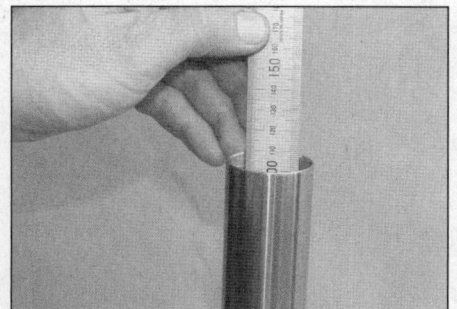

30.4b . . . the washer . . .

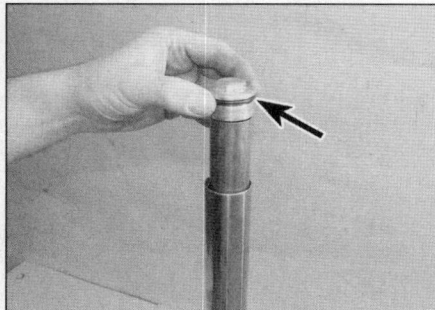

30.4c . . . and the fork spring

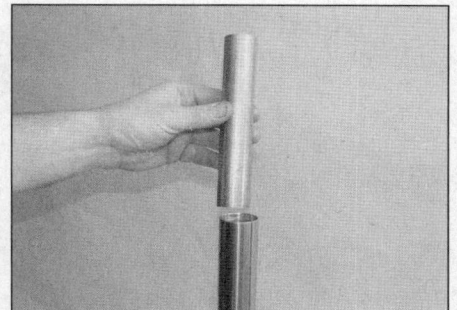

30.7 Measure the oil level with the fork held upright and fully compressed

Chapter 2 Part A
Engine, clutch and transmission – 650 models

Contents

Degrees of difficulty

Easy, suitable for novice with little experience	**Fairly easy,** suitable for beginner with some experience	**Fairly difficult,** suitable for competent DIY mechanic	**Difficult,** suitable for experienced DIY mechanic	**Very difficult,** suitable for expert DIY or professional

Specifications

General

Bore x stroke	81 x 63 mm
Displacement	649 cc
Compression ratio	9.0 to 1

Camshafts

Lobe height	
Intake (standard)	39.73 mm
Intake (service limit)	39.63 mm
Exhaust (standard)	39.77 mm
Exhaust (service limit)	39.67 mm
Bush oil clearance	0.020 to 0.061 mm
Journal diameter (standard)	27.96 to 27.98 mm
Bush inside diameter (standard)	28.00 to 28.02 mm

Rocker arms

Rocker inside diameter (standard)	14.00 to 14.02 mm
Shaft outside diameter (standard)	13.98 to 13.99 mm
Rocker-to-shaft clearance (service limit)	0.08 mm

Cylinders

Bore diameter	
Standard	80.97 to 81.02 mm
Service limit	81.10 mm
Bore measuring point	40 mm from top of cylinder

Cylinder head, valves and valve springs

Cylinder head warpage limit	0.03 mm
Valve stem runout limit	0.03 mm
Valve stem diameter	
Intake (standard)	6.975 to 6.990 mm
Intake (service limit)	6.955 mm
Exhaust (standard)	6.960 to 6.975 mm
Exhaust (service limit)	6.935 mm
Valve guide inside diameter (intake and exhaust)	
Standard	7.000 to 7.012 mm
Service limit	7.04 mm
Valve stem-to-guide clearance (service limit)	
Intake	0.08 mm
Exhaust	0.10 mm
Valve head diameter	
Intake	36.9 to 37.1 mm
Exhaust	31.9 to 32.1 mm
Valve face width (intake and exhaust)	2.3 mm
Valve head margin thickness (intake and exhaust)	
Standard	1.0 to 1.4 mm
Limit	0.8 mm
Valve seat width (intake and exhaust)	
Standard	1.0 to 1.2 mm
Limit	1.8 mm
Valve spring free length (intake and exhaust)	
Standard	43.2 mm
Service limit	42.0 mm
Valve spring bend limit	1.9 mm

Pistons

Piston diameter	
Standard	80.92 to 80.97 mm
First oversize	81.50 mm
Second oversize	82.00 mm
Diameter measuring point	6 mm from bottom of skirt
Piston-to-cylinder clearance	
Standard	0.035 to 0.055 mm
Service limit	0.15 mm
Piston pin diameter	19.99 to 20.00 mm
Piston pin to piston bore clearance	0.004 to 0.020 mm

Piston rings

Ring side clearance	
Top ring	
Standard	0.03 to 0.07 mm
Service limit	0.12 mm
Second ring	
Standard	0.02 to 0.06 mm
Service limit	0.12 mm
Ring end gap	
Top ring	
Standard	0.15 to 0.30 mm
Service limit	0.55 mm
Second ring	
Standard	0.30 to 0.45 mm
Service limit	0.80 mm
Oil ring side rails	
Standard	0.2 to 0.7 mm

Clutch

Friction plate thickness	
Standard	2.9 to 3.1 mm
Service limit	2.6 mm
Steel plate thickness	1.5 to 1.7 mm
Steel plate warpage limit	0.2 mm
Pushrod bend limit	0.5 mm
Spring free length	
Standard	39.5 mm
Service limit	38.5 mm

Oil pump

Inner to outer rotor clearance
    Standard . . . .   0.12 mm
    Service limit . . . .   0.20 mm
Outer rotor to body clearance
    Standard . . . .   0.03 to 0.08 mm
    Service limit . . . .   0.15 mm

Crankshaft, connecting rods and bearings

Connecting rod big-end side clearance . . . .   0.270 to 0.424 mm
Connecting rod big-end bearing oil clearance . . . .   0.026 to 0.050 mm
Crankshaft runout limit . . . .   0.02 mm
Main bearing journal service limit . . . .   44.95 mm
Main bearing oil clearance . . . .   0.020 to 0.052 mm
Main bearing seat service limit . . . .   49.02 mm

Transmission

Gear ratios
    1st gear 2.714:1 (38/14T)
    2nd gear 1.900:1 (38/20T)
    3rd gear 1.458:1 (35/24T)
    4th gear 1.167:1 (28/24T)
    5th gear 0.967:1 (29/30T)
Input shaft and output shaft runout limit . . . .   0.06 mm
Input shaft gearset length . . . .   103 to 103.2 mm

Torque settings

Alternator cover bolts . . . .   10 Nm
Alternator rotor bolt . . . .   80 Nm
Cam chain tensioner blade bolts . . . .   10 Nm
Cam chain tensioner bolts . . . .   12 Nm
Cam chain tensioner centre bolt . . . .   20 Nm
Camshaft retainer bolts . . . .   20 Nm
Camshaft sprocket bolt . . . .   55 Nm
Camshaft sprocket cover bolts . . . .   10 Nm
Clutch actuating lever screw . . . .   12 Nm
Clutch adjuster locknut . . . .   8 Nm
Clutch centre nut . . . .   70 Nm*
Clutch cover bolts . . . .   10 Nm
Clutch pressure plate screws . . . .   8 Nm
Connecting rod nuts . . . .   36 Nm**
Crankcase bolts (6 mm) . . . .   10 Nm
Crankcase bolts (8 mm) . . . .   24 Nm
Cylinder bolt . . . .   10 Nm
Cylinder head bolts (8 mm) . . . .   20 Nm
Cylinder head nuts (10 mm) . . . .   35 Nm
Cylinder head cover bolts . . . .   10 Nm
Engine mountings
    Front upper bracket bolts . . . .   40 Nm
    Front lower bracket bolts . . . .   30 Nm
    Front lower mounting bolt . . . .   40 Nm
    Rear upper mounting bolts . . . .   40 Nm
    Rear lower mounting bolt . . . .   74 Nm
Gearchange lever pinch bolt . . . .   10 Nm
Middle drive gear assembly bolts . . . .   25 Nm
Middle drive gear locknut . . . .   120 Nm***
Oil strainer cover bolts . . . .   10 Nm
Oil pump bolts . . . .   7 Nm
Output shaft bearing retainer screws . . . .   25 Nm***
Primary drive gear nut . . . .   70 Nm
Rocker cover bolts . . . .   10 Nm
Rocker shaft retaining bolts . . . .   38 Nm****
Starter clutch bolts . . . .   20 Nm

*   Use a new lock washer.
** Apply molybdenum disulfide grease to the threads and nut surfaces; follow special tightening procedures in the text.
*** Stake after installation.
**** Use new sealing washers.

1 General information

The engine unit is an air-cooled V-twin with the transmission housed within the crankcases. The valves are operated by overhead camshafts which are chain driven off the crankshaft. The engine/transmission assembly is constructed from aluminium alloy. The crankcase is divided vertically.

The crankcase incorporates a wet sump, pressure-fed lubrication system which uses a gear-driven oil pump and an oil filter mounted in the right-hand side of the crankcase.

Power from the crankshaft is routed to the transmission via the clutch, which is of the coil spring, wet multi-plate type and is gear-driven off the crankshaft. The transmission is a five-speed, constant-mesh unit.

2 Operations possible with the engine in the frame

The components and assemblies listed below can be removed without having to remove the engine from the frame. If, however, a number of areas require attention at the same time, removal of the engine is recommended.

Starter motor
Alternator rotor
Starter clutch
Cam chain tensioners
Clutch and primary drive gear
Oil pump
External gearchange mechanism

3 Operations requiring engine removal

1 It is necessary to remove the engine/transmission unit from the frame to gain access to the following components:

Cylinder heads, rocker arms and camshafts
Cylinders and pistons
Cam chains, tensioner blades and guides
Middle driven gear
Oil strainer

2 The crankcase halves must be separated to gain access to the following components:

Crankshaft, connecting rods and bearings
Transmission shafts
Selector drum and forks

4 Major engine repair – general note

1 It is not always easy to determine when or if an engine should be completely overhauled, as a number of factors must be considered.
2 High mileage is not necessarily an indication that an overhaul is needed, while low mileage, on the other hand, does not preclude the need for an overhaul. Frequency of servicing is probably the single most important consideration. An engine that has regular oil and filter changes, as well as other required maintenance, will most likely give many miles of reliable service. Conversely, a neglected engine, or one which has not been run-in properly, may require an overhaul very early in its life.
3 Exhaust smoke and excessive oil consumption are both indications that piston rings and/or valve guides are in need of attention. Make sure oil leaks are not responsible before deciding that the rings and guides are worn. Refer to Chapter 1 and perform a cylinder compression check to determine for certain the nature and extent of the work required.
4 If the engine is making obvious knocking or rumbling noises, the connecting rod and/or main bearings are probably at fault.
5 Loss of power, rough running, excessive valve train noise and high fuel consumption rates may also point to the need for an overhaul, especially if they are all present at the same time. If a complete tune-up does not remedy the situation, major mechanical work is the only solution.
6 An engine overhaul generally involves restoring the internal parts to the specifications of a new engine. During an overhaul the piston rings are renewed and the cylinders are bored. If a rebore is done, then new pistons are also required. The main and connecting rod bearings are generally replaced with new ones and, if necessary, the crankshaft is also renewed. Generally the valves are serviced as well, since they are usually in less than perfect condition at this point. While the engine is being overhauled, other components such as the carburettors and the starter motor can be rebuilt also. The end result should be a like-new engine that will give as many trouble free miles as the original.
7 Before beginning the engine overhaul, read through all of the related procedures to familiarise yourself with the scope and requirements of the job. Overhauling an engine is not all that difficult, but it is time consuming. Plan on the motorcycle being tied up for a minimum of two weeks. Check on the availability of parts and make sure that any necessary special tools, equipment and supplies are obtained in advance.
8 Most work can be done with typical workshop hand tools, although a number of precision measuring tools are required for inspecting parts to determine if they must be renewed. Often a dealer service department or motorcycle repair shop will handle the inspection of parts and offer advice concerning reconditioning and replacement.

HAYNES HINT *As a general rule, time is the primary cost of an overhaul so it doesn't pay to install worn or substandard parts.*

9 As a final note, to ensure maximum life and minimum trouble from a rebuilt engine, everything must be assembled with care in a spotlessly clean environment.

5 Engine – removal and installation

Caution: The engine is very heavy. Engine removal and installation should be done with the aid of an assistant to avoid damage or injury that could occur if the engine is dropped. An hydraulic floor jack should be used to support and lower the engine if possible.

Removal

1 If the engine is dirty, particularly around its mountings, wash it thoroughly before starting any major dismantling work. This will make work much easier and rule out the possibility of dirt falling inside.
2 Support the motorcycle securely in an upright position using an auxiliary stand. Work can be made easier by raising the machine to a suitable working height on a hydraulic ramp or a suitable platform. Make sure the motorcycle is secure and will not topple over (see Section 1 of *Tools and Workshop Tips* in the *Reference* section). When disconnecting any wiring, cables and hoses, it is advisable to mark or tag them as a reminder of where they connect.
3 Drain the engine oil (see Chapter 1).
4 Remove the battery cover (see Chapter 7). Disconnect the battery negative lead, then disconnect the positive lead (see Chapter 8).
5 Remove the fuel tank, carburettor assembly and, where fitted, the air induction system (see Chapter 3). Plug the intake manifolds with clean rag.
6 Remove the rear cylinder exhaust pipe and silencer assembly (see Chapter 3).
7 Remove the rear brake linkage, pedal and right-hand footrest assembly (see Chapter 6).
8 Remove the front cylinder exhaust pipe (see Chapter 3).
9 Undo the screws and remove the right-hand frame cover (see Chapter 7).
10 If required, to avoid damaging the chromed finish of the covers, remove the bolts from the engine side cover and remove it, then undo the bolts from the oil filter cover and remove the cover and the filter (see Chapter 1, Section 1). Discard the filter cover O-ring as a new one must be used. Remove the bolts from the clutch cover and remove the cover; discard the gasket as a new one must be used (see Section 18). Note the location of the clips for the starter motor lead on the lower cover bolts. Note the location of the two cover dowels and remove them for safekeeping if they are loose.
11 Remove the starter motor (see Chapter 8). If the clutch cover has not been removed, loosen the lower cover bolts and free the

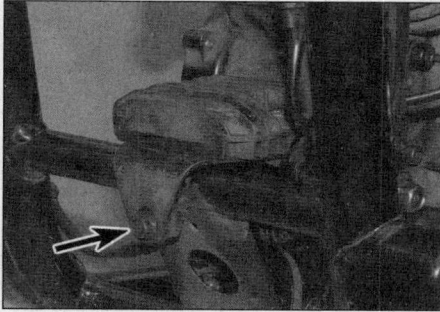
5.12 Regulator/rectifier mounting bolt (arrowed)

5.13 Displace the rear brake light switch

5.14 Note the register mark (arrowed) on the gearchange shaft

5.15 Remove the sidestand bolts

5.16 Remove the transmission cover

5.17a Middle gear covers are secured by two bolts

5.17b Discard the inner cover O-ring

5.19a Trace the wiring from the alternator cover . . .

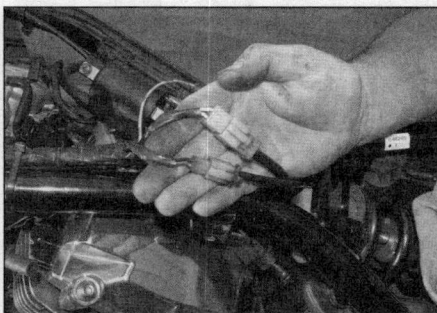
5.19b . . . and disconnect it at the connectors

5.19c Note the location of the clutch cable bracket

starter motor lead from the clips, then position the lead clear of the engine.

12 Undo the regulator/rectifier mounting bolt, then disconnect the wiring connector and remove the regulator/rectifier (see illustration).

13 Undo the bolt and displace the rear brake light switch (see illustration).

14 Check for the mark on the gearchange shaft that aligns with the slot in the lever (see illustration). If the mark isn't visible, make your own with a sharp punch then remove the pinch bolt and pull the lever off the shaft. Undo the bolts securing the left-hand footrest bracket and remove the gearchange pedal, gearchange linkage and footrest as an assembly (see Chapter 5).

15 Undo the screws securing the sidestand switch and displace the switch, then undo the nuts and bolts securing the sidestand assembly and remove it (see illustration).

16 Remove the toolbox cover (see Chapter 7). Remove the four bolts securing the transmission cover and remove the cover (see illustration).

17 Remove the bolts securing the middle gear covers and remove the outer cover (see illustration). If the inner cover comes away with the outer cover, note the O-ring fitted to the inner cover and discard it as a new one must be fitted (see illustration).

18 Disconnect the clutch cable from the release mechanism arm and the cable bracket (see Section 17).

19 Trace the wiring from the back of the alternator cover and disconnect it at the connectors, then free the wiring from any clips or ties and note its routing (see illustrations). Working evenly in a criss-cross pattern, loosen the cover bolts, then remove them noting the location of the clutch cable bracket (see illustration). Draw off the cover, noting how it fits over the gearchange shaft (see

5.19d Draw off the alternator cover

5.20 Disconnect the neutral switch wire from the terminal

5.21a Upper cylinder head covers are secured by two bolts on each side

5.21b Manoeuvre the lower covers out carefully

5.22 Pull off the spark plug caps

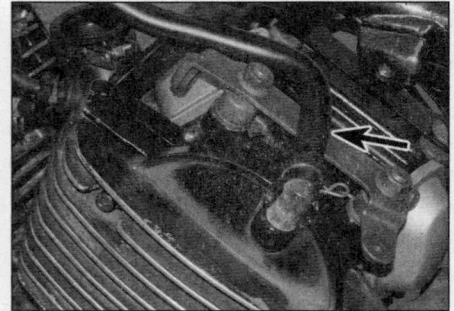
5.23 Disconnect the engine breather hose

illustration). Discard the cover gasket as a new one must be used. Note the location of the cover dowels and remove them for safekeeping if they are loose.

> **HAYNES HINT** *Make a cardboard template of the alternotor cover and punch a hole for each bolt location. As each bolt is removed, store it in its relative position in the template. This will ensure all bolts are installed correctly on reassembly – this is important, as many bolts differ slightly in length.*

20 Loosen the screw securing the neutral switch wire and disconnect the wire from the switch terminal **(see illustration)**.

21 Undo the bolts and remove the upper and lower covers from the front and rear cylinder heads **(see illustrations)**.
22 Pull the spark plug caps off the plugs **(see illustration)**.
23 Release the clip securing the breather hose to the rear cylinder head and disconnect the hose **(see illustration)**.
24 Disconnect the earth (ground) wire from the rear of the engine on the right-hand side **(see illustration)**.
25 Pull the rubber driveshaft boot away from the back of the engine unit **(see illustration)**.
26 Check around the engine and frame to make sure all the necessary wiring, cables and hoses have been disconnected, and that any which remain connected to the engine are

not retained by any clips, guides or brackets on the frame.
27 Position a jack under the engine with a block of wood between the jack head and the crankcase **(see illustration)**. Make sure the jack is centrally positioned so the engine will not topple in any direction when the last mounting bolt is removed and the engine is supported only by the jack.
28 Undo the nuts and bolts securing the left and right front upper mounting brackets to the frame and the bolts securing the brackets to the engine and remove the brackets **(see illustrations)**. Note the location of the clutch cable guide on the left-hand side.
29 Undo the front lower engine mounting nut and bolt and remove the bolt, then undo the bolts securing the left and right front lower

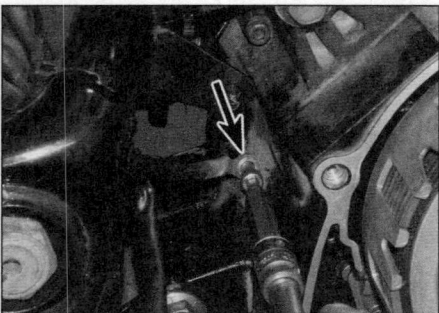
5.24 Remove the bolt and disconnect the engine earth wire

5.25 Pull the driveshaft boot away from the engine unit

5.27 Support the engine with a jack and a block of wood

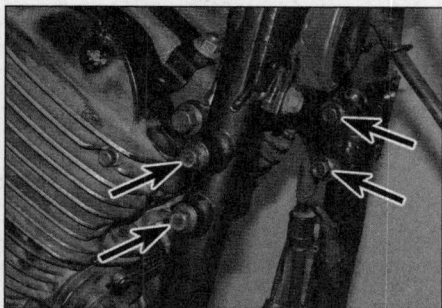

5.28a Undo the upper mounting bracket bolts on the frame . . .

5.28b . . . and on the engine . . .

5.28c . . . then remove the brackets. Note the clutch cable guide (arrowed)

mounting brackets to the frame and remove the brackets **(see illustrations)**.

30 Undo the left and right rear upper mounting bolts and remove them **(see illustrations)**. Note that the left-hand bolt is longer than the right-hand bolt.

31 Counter-hold the nut on the lower rear mounting bolt then undo the bolt and remove it **(see illustration)**. **Note:** *On the machine photographed, the bolt and hole through the crankcase were extremely corroded and required soaking in penetrating oil before the bolt could be removed.*

32 Slowly and carefully lift the engine assembly out of the frame on the right-hand side – note that the final drive coupling on the rear of the engine unit must be disengaged from the driveshaft as the engine is lifted out.

Installation

33 Installation is the reverse of removal, noting the following:

● With the aid of an assistant, lift the engine unit into the frame and support it on the jack and block of wood. Ensure the splines on the final drive coupling are engaged with the driveshaft. Manoeuvre the engine unit into position so that the mounting bolt holes align. Make sure no wires, cables or hoses become trapped between the engine and the frame.

● Remove any corrosion from the engine mounting bolts with a wire brush and apply a smear of copper-based grease to the shanks of the bolts before installation.

● Don't tighten any of the engine mounting bolts until they all have been installed. Make sure the correct bolt is installed in its correct location.

● Tighten all the bolts to the torque settings specified at the beginning of this Chapter.

● Always use new gaskets on the engine covers where removed, and fit new O-rings where recommended.

● Make sure all wires, cables and hoses are correctly routed and connected, and secured by any clips or ties.

● Refill the engine with oil (see Chapter 1).

● Check the throttle and clutch cable freeplay (see Chapter 1).

● Adjust the engine idle speed (see Chapter 1).

6 Engine disassembly and reassembly – general information

1 Before disassembling the engine, the external surfaces of the unit should be thoroughly cleaned and degreased. This will prevent contamination of the engine internals, and will also make working a lot easier and cleaner. A high flash-point solvent, such as paraffin (kerosene) can be used, or better still, a proprietary engine degreaser such as Gunk. Use old paintbrushes and toothbrushes to work the solvent into the various recesses of the engine casings. Take care to exclude solvent or water from the electrical components and from the intake and exhaust ports.

⚠ **Warning: The use of petrol (gasoline) as a cleaning agent should be avoided because of the risk of fire.**

2 When clean and dry, arrange the unit on the workbench, leaving a suitable clear area for working. Gather a selection of small containers and plastic bags so that parts can be grouped together in an easily identifiable manner. Some paper and a pen should be on

5.29a Remove the front lower engine mounting bolt (arrowed) . . .

5.29b . . . then the bracket-to-frame bolts and brackets

5.30a Remove the left-hand rear upper mounting bolt . . .

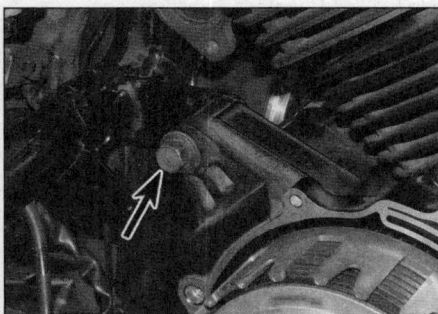

5.30b . . . and the right-hand rear upper mounting bolt

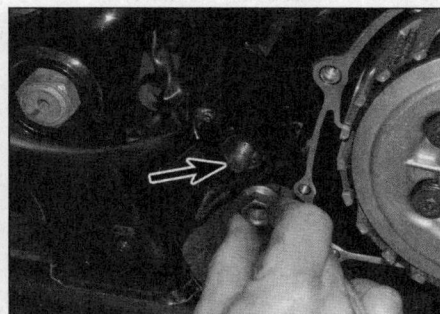

5.31 Location of the lower rear mounting bolt

hand so that notes can be made and labels attached where necessary. In addition, a digital camera is often useful for recording images of component positions or alignment markings before they are disturbed. A supply of clean rag is also required.

> **HAYNES HiNT** *A useful engine support stand can be made from short lengths of 2 x 4 inch wood screwed together into a rectangle. The stand should be just big enough to accommodate the sump within it, so that the engine rests on its crankcase.*

3 Before commencing work, read through the appropriate section so that some idea of the necessary procedure can be gained. When removing components it should be noted that great force is seldom required, unless specified. In many cases, a component's reluctance to be removed is indicative of an incorrect approach or removal method – if in any doubt, re-check with the text.

4 When disassembling the engine, keep "mated" parts together (eg. valve assemblies, cylinders, pistons and connecting rods, that have been in contact with each other during engine operation). These "mated" parts must be reused or replaced as assemblies.

5 Engine/transmission disassembly should be done in the following general order with reference to the appropriate Sections.

Remove the cylinder heads
Remove the camshafts
Remove the rocker arms
Remove the cylinders
Remove the pistons
Remove the alternator rotor
Remove the clutch
Remove the oil pump
Remove the external gearchange mechanism
Remove the middle driven gear
Separate the crankcase halves
Remove the crankshaft and connecting rods
Remove the selector drum and forks
Remove the transmission shafts/gears

6 Reassembly is accomplished by reversing the general disassembly sequence.

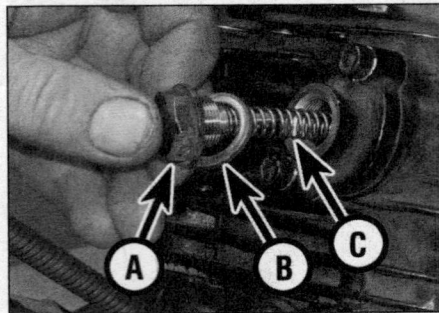
7.1 Remove the tensioner centre bolt (A), sealing washer (B) and spring (C)

7 Cam chain tensioners

Note: *This procedure can be carried out with the engine in the frame.*

Removal

1 Remove the tensioner centre bolt and sealing washer, then pull out the spring (see illustration).

2 Remove the tensioner mounting bolts and draw it out of the cylinder noting which way round it fits (see illustration). Discard the sealing washer as a new one must be fitted.

Inspection

3 Release the catch on the tensioner plunger and check that the plunger moves smoothly in an out of the tensioner body (see illustration). Inspect the teeth on the plunger and the spring for wear and damage. If any part of the tensioner assembly is worn or damaged replace it with a new one – individual parts are not available.

4 Check the sealing washer on the centre bolt for cracks or hardening. It's a good idea to renew this washer whenever the bolt is removed.

Installation

5 Release the catch on the tensioner plunger and compress it into the tensioner body.

6 Turn the tensioner so the catch is facing upwards and install the tensioner into the cylinder, using a new gasket.

7 Tighten the mounting bolts to the torque listed in this Chapter's Specifications.

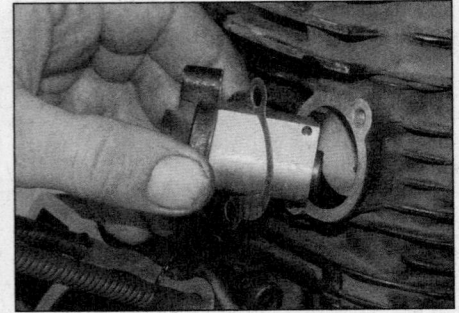
7.2 Draw out the tensioner noting how it fits

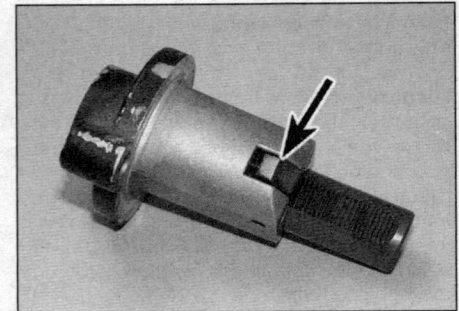
7.3 Release the catch (arrowed) and check the operation of the plunger

8 Install the spring, sealing washer and centre bolt. Tighten the bolt to the torque listed in this Chapter's Specifications.

9 Install the remaining components in the reverse order of removal.

8 Cylinder head removal and refitting

Removal

Note: *If only one cylinder head is being removed, ignore the Steps which do not apply.*

1 Remove the engine from the frame (see Section 5). Lift the heat shield off the cylinder head intake manifolds.

2 Undo the nuts and remove the front and rear cylinder head cover brackets (see illustrations).

8.2a Undo the nuts (arrowed) . . .

8.2b . . . and lift off the cover brackets . . .

8.2c . . . noting how they fit

8.2d Lift off the engine mounting bracket

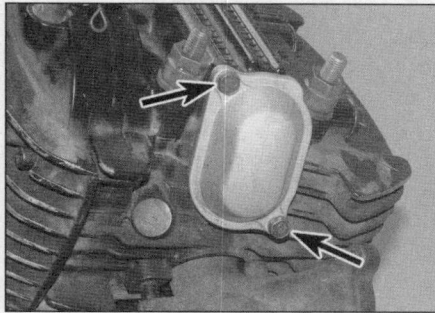

8.3 Undo the bolts and remove the rocker covers

8.4 Undo the bolts and remove the camshaft sprocket covers

Lift the engine mounting bracket off the front cylinder head (see illustration).

3 Undo the bolts and remove the rocker covers (see illustration). Discard the cover O-rings as new ones must be fitted.

4 Undo the bolts and remove the camshaft sprocket covers (see illustration). Note the location of the cover O-rings (see Chapter 1, Section 3). **Note:** *A baffle plate is fitted in the rear cover – if it does not come off with the cover, remove it from the cylinder head (see Step 5).*

Rear cylinder head

5 If not already done, remove the baffle plate, noting how it locates on the pin in the camshaft sprocket cover (see illustration). Note the location of the O-ring.

6 Temporarily install the alternator cover.

Remove the timing inspection cap and the centre cap from the cover (see illustration).

7 Follow the procedure in Chapter 1, Section 3, and turn the crankshaft clockwise with a socket on the alternator centre bolt until the rear cylinder is at top dead centre (TDC) on its compression stroke with both valves closed.

8 Counter-hold the alternator centre bolt to prevent the engine turning and loosen the camshaft sprocket bolt (see illustration).

9 Remove the cam chain tensioner for the rear cylinder (see Section 7).

Caution: Stuff clean rag into the opening below the camshaft sprocket so nothing is accidentally dropped into it.

10 Remove the camshaft sprocket bolt and the sprocket plate (see illustration).

11 Label the sprocket "R" (for rear cylinder)

and slide it off the camshaft with the cam chain (see illustration). Lift the cam chain off the sprocket and secure the chain with a length of wire. Make sure the camshaft dowel doesn't fall out of the camshaft and remove it for safekeeping if it is loose (see illustration).

12 Loosen the cylinder head bolts and nuts evenly in the **reverse** of the tightening order (see illustration 8.28e). Remove the nuts, washers and bolts.

13 Lift the cylinder head off the studs. If it's stuck, tap around the joint face between the head and the cylinder with a soft-faced mallet or block of wood to free it. Don't attempt to lever the head off the cylinder – you will damage the sealing surface. Feed the cam chain down the tunnel and secure it with a cable tie or piece of wire to prevent it falling

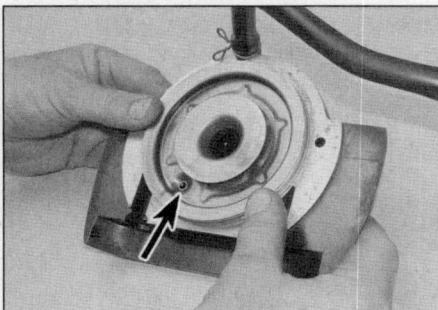

8.5 Baffle plate locates on pin (arrowed) in rear camshaft sprocket cover

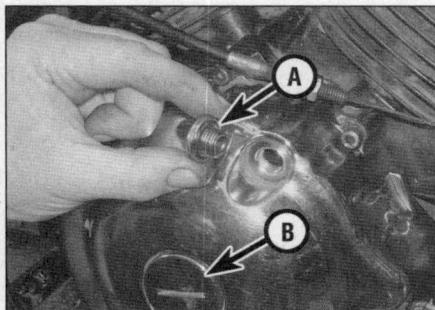

8.6 Remove the timing (A) and centre (B) caps from the alternator cover

8.8 Loosen the camshaft sprocket bolt

8.10 Remove the sprocket bolt and plate

8.11a Pull the sprocket off the end of the camshaft

8.11b Remove the dowel (arrowed) for safekeeping if it is loose

8.13 Hold the cam chain and lift off the cylinder head

8.14 Discard the old cylinder head gasket

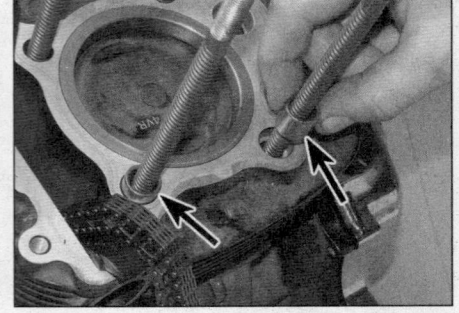

8.15 If required, remove the dowels for safekeeping

into the crankcase and jamming on the crankshaft sprocket **(see illustration)**.

14 Remove the gasket and discard it as a new one must be used **(see illustration)**.

15 Note the two dowels either on the cylinder studs or in the underside of the head and remove them for safekeeping if they are loose **(see illustration)**.

16 Check the old cylinder head gasket and the mating surfaces on the cylinder head and cylinder for evidence of leaks, which could indicate that the head is warped. Refer to Section 11 and check the flatness of the cylinder head.

17 Clean all traces of old gasket material from the cylinder head and cylinder. Be careful not to let any of the gasket material fall into the crankcase, the cylinder bore or the oil passage.

18 If required, undo the bolts securing the intake manifold to the cylinder head and remove the manifold. Discard the O-ring as a new one must be fitted.

19 If required, undo the nuts securing the exhaust manifold to the cylinder head and remove the manifold. Discard the gasket as a new one must be fitted.

Front cylinder head

20 Follow the procedure in Chapter 1, Section 3, and turn the crankshaft clockwise with a socket on the alternator centre bolt until the **front** cylinder is at top dead centre (TDC) on its compression stroke with both valves closed.

21 Follow Steps 8 to 18 to remove the front cylinder head. Note that there is no plate fitted to the front camshaft sprocket. If required, label the camshaft sprocket "F" (for front cylinder).

Installation

Rear cylinder head

22 If both cylinder heads have been removed, install the rear head first.

23 If removed, fit a new gasket to the exhaust manifold and install the manifold.

24 If removed, fit a new O-ring to the intake manifold and install the manifold.

25 If removed, install the dowels on the cylinder studs **(see illustration 8.15)**.

26 Install the new head gasket on top of the cylinder **(see illustration 8.14)**.

27 Lower the cylinder head onto the studs and feed the cam chain and guide through the tunnel in the head. Ensure the upper end of the guide fits into the notch in the upper end of the tunnel **(see illustration)**. Secure the chain.

28 Install the cylinder head bolts, washers and nuts and tighten them finger-tight **(see illustrations)**. If required, use a screwdriver to slide the washer and nut into place on the stud next to the spark plug **(see illustration)**. Tighten the nuts and bolts in the order shown in two stages to the torques specified at the beginning of this Chapter **(see illustration)**.

8.27 Ensure the cam chain guide is correctly located in the notch (arrowed)

8.28a Install the cylinder head bolts . . .

8.28b . . . washers . . .

8.28c . . . and nuts

8.28d Slide the washer (arrowed) down a screwdriver onto the recessed stud

8.28e Cylinder head fixings TIGHTENING sequence

8.32 Tension the cam chain and check the camshaft sprocket (A) and alternator rotor (B) timing marks as described

29 If removed, install the camshaft dowel. Ensure the camshaft dowel is aligned with the index mark on the cylinder head.

30 Check that the alternator rotor timing mark for the rear cylinder is aligned with the notch in the inspection hole (see Step 7). If it's necessary to turn the crankshaft, hold the cam chain up to prevent it falling off the crankshaft sprocket and becoming jammed.

31 Engage the camshaft sprocket with the cam chain so its dowel hole aligns with the camshaft dowel and fit the sprocket onto the camshaft (**see illustration 8.11a**). Ensure the sprocket timing mark is facing out.

32 Turn the camshaft sprocket just far enough to remove all slack in the cam chain on the exhaust side. Tension the chain by pressing on the tensioner blade through the tensioner hole in the cylinder and check that the timing marks on the camshaft sprocket and alternator rotor are aligned correctly (**see illustration**).

33 Install the sprocket plate with its concave side out, and fit the bolt finger-tight (**see illustration 8.10**).

34 Install the cam chain tensioner (see Section 7).

35 Counter-hold the alternator centre bolt and tighten the camshaft sprocket bolt to the specified torque.

36 Check the valve clearances (see Chapter 1).

37 Check the condition of the baffle plate O-ring and fit a new one if necessary, then install the baffle plate in the camshaft sprocket cover (**see illustration 8.5**). Check the condition of the sprocket cover O-ring and fit a new one if necessary, then install the cover and tighten the bolts to the specified torque.

9.4b Remove the bolts and lockwasher – note the bolts are different lengths

9.2 Remove the rocker shaft retaining bolts and washers

38 Install the rocker covers with new O-rings and tighten the bolts to the specified torque.

Front cylinder head

39 Follow Steps 24 to 36 to install the front cylinder head, noting that the **front** cylinder's timing mark on the edge of the alternator rotor must be aligned with the notch in the inspection hole before the camshaft sprocket is installed. There is no plate fitted to the front camshaft sprocket

40 Check the condition of the camshaft sprocket cover O-ring and fit a new one if necessary, then install the cover and tighten the bolts to the specified torque.

41 Install the rocker covers with new O-rings and tighten the bolts to the specified torque.

42 Install the remaining components in the reverse order of removal.

---

9 Camshafts and rockers

Removal

Note: *Before proceeding, arrange to label and store the camshafts and rockers along with their related components so they can be returned to their original locations without getting mixed up*

1 Remove the cylinder heads (see Section 8). If not already done, remove the dowel from the end of each camshaft if it is loose.

2 Working on one cylinder head at a time, remove the rocker shaft retaining bolts and sealing washers (**see illustration**). Discard the washers as new ones must be fitted.

9.4c Remove the camshaft retainer

9.3 Draw out the shafts as described and remove the rockers

9.4a Flatten the lockwasher tabs

3 Thread an 8 mm bolt into the end of the rocker shafts, then draw the shafts out from the cylinder head and remove the rockers (**see illustration**). Assemble each rocker on its shaft and label them (e.g. RI – rear intake/RE – rear exhaust) so that they can be installed in their original positions. **Note:** *If the intake valve rockers are a tight fit through the rocker cover opening, lift them out through the hole for the camshaft after it has been removed.*

4 Flatten the tabs on the camshaft bolt lockwasher (**see illustration**). Remove the bolts, lockwasher and camshaft retainer (**see illustrations**). Note that the bolts are different lengths and mark them to aid reassembly.

5 Pull the camshaft and bush out of the cylinder head. If it doesn't come easily, use the camshaft sprocket bolt to draw it out. Remove the bush from the camshaft.

6 Note that the camshafts are numbered – the No. 1 camshaft fits in the rear cylinder head and the No. 2 camshaft fits in the front cylinder head (**see illustration**).

9.6 Note the numbers cast into the camshafts

9.9 Inspect the camshaft bearing surface (arrowed)

7 Repeat the procedure for the other head. Remember to keep the parts for each head together and labelled so they can be reinstalled in their original locations.

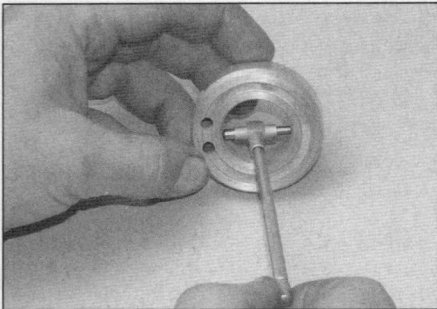

9.10b ... and the inside diameter of the camshaft bush

9.11 Measuring the camshaft lobe height

9.14a Measuring the rocker shaft ...

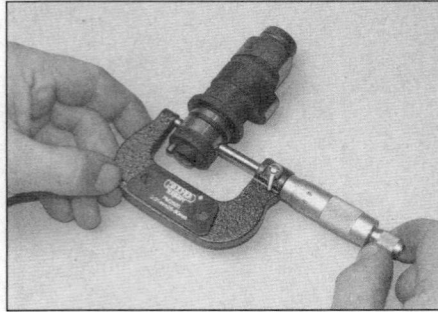

9.10a Measuring the camshaft journal ...

Inspection

8 Clean all of the components with solvent and dry them thoroughly. Blow through the oil passages with compressed air, if available.

9 Inspect the cam bearing surface inside the head (see illustration). Look for score marks, deep scratches and evidence of spalling (a pitted appearance). If the head is worn or damaged a new one will have to be fitted.

10 Next, check the camshaft bush oil clearance. Measure the outer diameter of the camshaft journal and the inner diameter of the bush (see illustrations). Subtract the journal diameter from the bush diameter to obtain the clearance. If it's greater than that listed in this Chapter's Specifications, compare the measurements with the standard specifications and renew whichever part is worn.

11 Check the camshaft lobes for heat

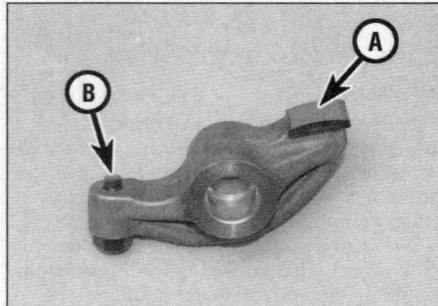

9.13 Inspect the contact surfaces of the rocker faces (A) and adjusting screws (B)

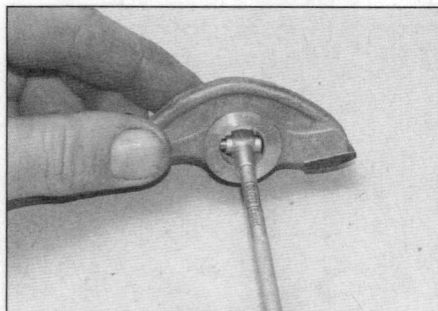

9.14b ... and the inside diameter of the rocker arm

discoloration (blue appearance), score marks, chipped areas, flat spots and spalling. Measure the height of each lobe with a micrometer (see illustration) and compare the results to the Specifications. If the camshaft is damage or worn beyond the service limit a new one must be fitted.

> **HAYNES HiNT** *Before renewing the camshaft or cylinder head because of damage, check with local machine shops specialising in motorcycle engine work. In the case of the camshafts, it may be possible for cam lobes to be welded, reground and hardened, at a cost far lower than that of a new camshaft. If the bearing surface in the head is damaged, it may be possible for it to be bored out to accept a bearing insert. Due to the cost of new components it is recommended that all options are explored!*

12 Check the camshaft sprocket for wear, cracks and other damage, renewing it if necessary. If the sprocket is worn, it is likely the chain will be worn and should be checked (see Section 12).

13 Inspect the rocker faces for pits, spalling, score marks and rough spots (see illustration). Also check the contact areas between the adjusting screws and the valve stem. Look for cracks in each rocker arm. If the faces of the rockers are damaged, the rocker arms and the camshaft should be renewed as an assembly.

14 Measure the outside diameter of each rocker shaft and the inside diameter of the corresponding rocker arm (see illustrations). Calculate the difference and compare the result with this Chapter's Specifications. If the clearance is beyond the service limit, renew the rocker and shaft as an assembly.

Installation

15 Lubricate the camshaft with molybdenum disulphide oil (a 50/50 mixture of molybdenum disulphide grease and engine oil) and install it in the cylinder head with the dowel hole facing the index mark at the top of the head (see illustration).

9.15 Install the camshaft with the dowel hole facing up

9.16 Install the camshaft bush with the cut-out (arrowed) at the top

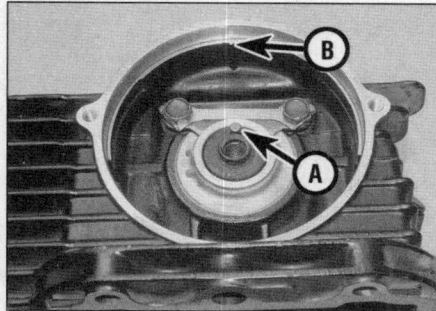

9.17 Secure the bolts with the lockwasher. Note the alignment of the camshaft dowel (A) with the index mark (B)

9.20 Slots in the rocker shafts should be vertical

16 Position the camshaft bush on the camshaft with the cutout for the retainer at the top, then press it carefully into place until the cutout is flush with the cylinder head **(see illustration)**.

17 Install the retainer, a new lockwasher and the retainer bolts. Ensure the bolts are fitted in the correct locations **(see illustration 9.4b)**. Tighten the bolts to the torque listed in this Chapter's Specifications, then bend the lockwasher tabs against the bolt heads **(see illustration)**. If removed, install the dowel in the end of the camshaft.

18 If required, thread a bolt into the end of the rocker shafts to aid assembly – if this method is not used, ensure the threaded end of the shaft with the small slot faces out. Lubricate the rocker shafts and the rocker arm bores with clean engine oil. Install the rocker shaft partway into its location in the cylinder head, then hold the corresponding rocker in position and press the shaft all the way in **(see illustration 9.3)**. Note that the adjuster end of the rocker must be accessible through the rocker cover hole. If applicable, remove the assembly bolt.

19 Repeat the procedure and install the other rocker.

20 Check the position of the slots in the ends of the rocker shafts – they should be vertical **(see illustration)**. If necessary, turn the shafts with a screwdriver to align them correctly and ensure that the shafts are pressed all the way in.

21 Install new sealing washers on the rocker shaft retaining bolts, then install the bolts and tighten them to the torque listed in this Chapter's Specifications **(see illustration 9.2)**.

10 Valves/valve seats/valve guides – servicing

1 Because of the complex nature of this job and the special tools and equipment required, most owners leave servicing of the valves, valve seats and valve guides to a professional. However, you can make an initial assessment of whether the valves are seating, and therefore sealing, correctly by pouring a small amount of solvent into each of the valve ports. If the solvent leaks past any valve into the combustion chamber the valve is not seating and sealing correctly.

2 Once the camshaft and rockers have been removed, you can also remove the valves from the cylinder head, clean the components, check them for wear to assess the extent of the work needed and, unless a valve service is required, grind in the valves (see Section 11). The head can then be reassembled.

3 The dealer service department will remove the valves and springs, renew the valves and guides, recut the valve seats, check and renew the valve springs, spring retainers and collets (as necessary), replace the valve seals with new ones and reassemble the valve components.

11.6 Compress the valve spring carefully to avoid damage

4 After the valve service has been performed, the head will be in like-new condition. When the head is returned, be sure to clean it again very thoroughly before installation on the engine, to remove any metal particles or abrasive grit that may still be present from the valve service operations. Use compressed air, if available, to blow out all the holes and passages.

11 Cylinder head and valve overhaul

1 As mentioned in the previous Section, valve overhaul should be left to a Yamaha dealer. However, disassembly, cleaning and inspection of the valves and related components can be done by the home mechanic if the necessary tools are available. This way no expense is incurred if the inspection reveals that overhaul is not required at this time.

2 To disassemble the valve components without the risk of damaging them, a valve spring compressor is absolutely essential. Make sure it is suitable for motorcycle work.

Disassembly

3 Before proceeding, arrange to label and store the valves along with their related components so they can be returned to their original locations without getting mixed up **(see illustration)**. If possible, obtain a container divided into compartments and label each with the identity of the valve which will be stored in it. Alternatively, labelled plastic bags will do just as well.

4 Clean all traces of old gasket material from the cylinder heads with a suitable solvent. If you need to use a scraper, take care not nick or gouge the soft aluminium.

5 Remove the camshafts and rocker arms if not already done (see Section 9).

6 Working on one cylinder head at a time, compress the spring on the first valve with a spring compressor, making sure it is correctly located on each end of the valve assembly **(see illustration)**. Do not compress the spring any more than is absolutely necessary

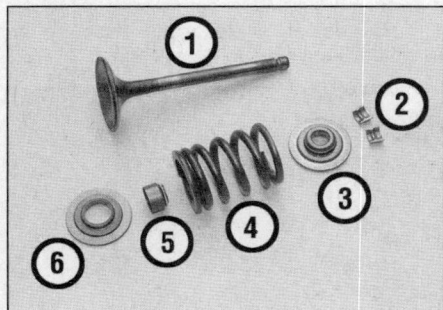

11.3 Valve components

1 Valve
2 Collets
3 Spring retainer
4 Spring
5 Valve stem oil seal
6 Spring seat

11.7a Remove the collets as described

11.7b Remove the spring retainer . . .

11.7c . . . the valve spring . . .

11.7d . . . and the valve

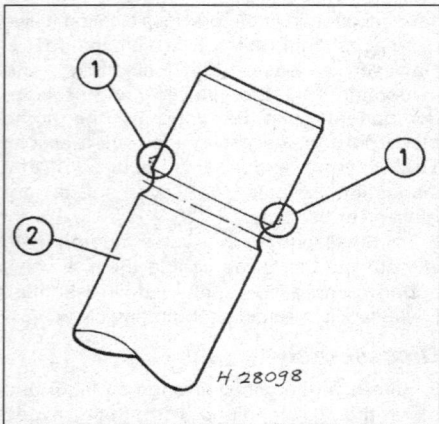

11.7e If the valve stem (2) won't pull through the guide, deburr the area above the collet groove (1)

7 Remove the collets using either needle-nose pliers, tweezers, a magnet or a screwdriver with a dab of grease on it **(see illustration)**. Carefully release the valve spring compressor and remove the spring retainer, noting which way up it fits, the spring and the valve **(see illustrations)**. If the valve binds in the guide (won't pull through), push it back into the head and deburr the area around the collet groove with a very fine file **(see illustration)**.

8 Pull the valve stem seal off the top of the valve guide with pliers and discard it (the old seals should never be reused), then remove the spring seat **(see illustrations)**.

9 Repeat the procedure for the remaining valve. Remember to keep the parts for each valve together and labelled so they can be reinstalled in the correct location. Repeat the procedure for the other cylinder head.

10 Carefully scrape all carbon deposits out of the combustion chamber area. A hand held wire brush or a piece of fine emery cloth can be used once the majority of deposits have been scraped away. Do not use a wire brush mounted in a drill motor as the head material is soft and may be eroded away. Next, clean the cylinder head with solvent and dry it thoroughly. Compressed air will speed the drying process and ensure that all holes, recessed areas and oil passages are clean.

11 Scrape off any deposits that may have formed on the valves, then use a motorized wire brush to remove deposits from the valve heads and stems. Again, make sure the valves do not get mixed up. Clean the valve springs, collets, retainers and spring seats with solvent and dry them thoroughly. Clean the parts from one valve at a time so as not to mix them up.

Inspection

12 Inspect each cylinder head very carefully for cracks and other damage. If cracks are found, a new head will be required. Check the cam bearing surfaces for wear and evidence of seizure. Check the camshaft and rockers for wear as well (see Section 9).

13 Using a precision straightedge and a feeler gauge, check the head gasket mating surface for warpage. Lay the straightedge lengthwise, across the head and diagonally (corner-to-corner), intersecting the head stud holes, and try to slip the feeler gauge under it around the side of the combustion chamber (see Section 3 of *Tools and Workshop Tips* in the Reference section at the end of this manual). The gauge should be the same thickness as the cylinder head warp limit listed in this Chapter's Specifications. If the feeler gauge can be inserted between the head and the straightedge, the head is warped and must either be machined or, if warpage is excessive, replaced with a new one. Consult a Yamaha dealer or take the head to an automotive engineer for rectification.

14 Examine the valve seats in the combustion chamber. If they are pitted, cracked or burned, the head will require work beyond the scope of the home mechanic. Measure the valve seat width and compare it to this Chapter's Specifications **(see illustration)**. If it exceeds the service limit, or if it varies around its circumference, consult a Yamaha dealer or take the head to an automotive engineer for rectification.

11.8a Pull off the valve stem seal (arrowed) . . .

11.8b . . . and lift out the spring seat

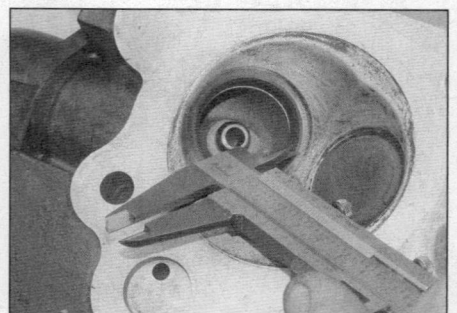

11.14 Measuring the valve seat width

15 Examine each valve face for cracks, pits and burned spots **(see illustration)**. **Note:** *Slight imperfections between the valve face and seat may be over come by grinding the valves (see Steps 23 to 27).*

16 Rotate the valve and check for any obvious indication that it is bent. Using V-blocks and a dial gauge if available, measure the valve stem runout and compare the result to the Specifications at the beginning of this Chapter **(see illustration)**. If the runout exceeds the service limit, the valve must be replaced with a new one. Note that a slightly bent valve stem will prevent the valve from seating properly in the head.

17 Measure the various aspects of the valve head and compare them with the listed specifications **(see illustration)**.

18 Measure the valve stem diameter **(see illustration)**. Clean the valve guides to remove any carbon build-up, then measure the inside diameters of the guides (at both ends and the centre of the guide) with a small hole gauge and micrometer (see *Tools and Workshop Tips* in the *Reference* section). The guides are measured at the ends and at the centre to determine if they are worn in a bell-mouth pattern (more wear at the ends). Subtract the valve stem diameter from the guide diameter to obtain the valve stem-to-guide clearance. If the clearance is greater than the service limit listed in the Specifications, renew whichever components are worn beyond their specified limit. Note that if the valve guide is worn unevenly, it should be renewed.

19 Inspect the valve stem and the collet groove area for scuffing and cracks **(see illustration 11.15)**. Check the end of the stem for pitting and wear. The presence of any of the above conditions indicates the need for fitting new valves.

20 Check the end of each valve spring for wear. Measure the spring free length and compare it to this Chapter's Specifications **(see illustration)**. Any spring that is shorter than specified must be replaced with a new one. Stand the spring on a flat surface and check it for squareness **(see illustration)**. If the bend in any spring exceeds the specified limit it must be renewed.

21 Check the spring retainers and collets for obvious wear and cracks. Any questionable parts should not be reused, as extensive damage will occur in the event of failure during engine operation.

22 If the inspection indicates that no overhaul work is required, the valve components can be reinstalled in the head.

Reassembly

23 Unless a valve service has been performed, before installing the valves in the head, they should be ground-in (lapped) to ensure a positive seal between the valves and seats. This procedure requires coarse and fine valve grinding compound and a valve grinding tool. If a grinding tool is not available, a piece of rubber or plastic hose can be slipped over the

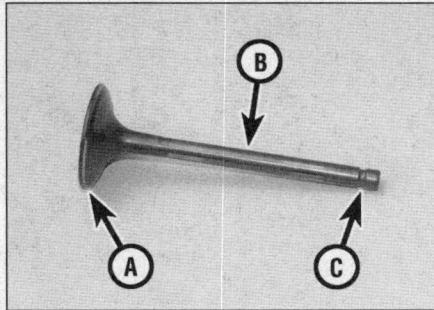

11.15 Check the valve face (A), stem (B) and collet groove (C) for signs of wear and damage

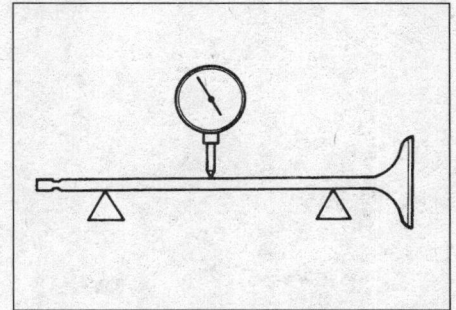

11.16 Measure valve stem runout with V-block and a dial gauge

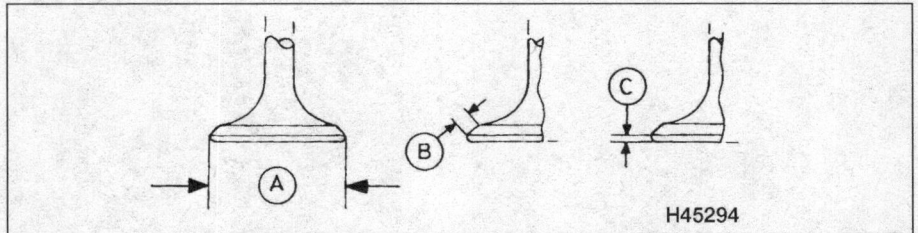

H45294

11.17 Valve head measurement points

A Head diameter   *B Face width*   *C Margin thickness*

valve stem (after the valve has been installed in the guide) and used to turn the valve.

24 Apply a small amount of coarse grinding compound to the valve face **(see illustration)**. Lubricate the valve stem with some molybdenum disulphide oil (a 50/50 mixture of molybdenum disulphide grease and engine

11.18 Measuring the valve stem diameter with a micrometer

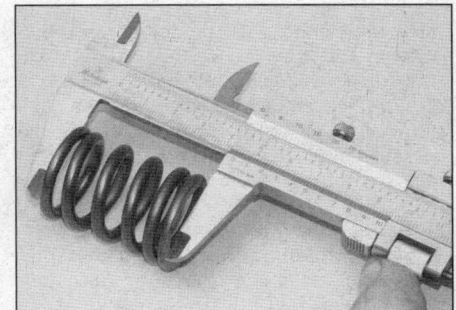

11.20b Check the valve springs for squareness

oil), then slip the valve into the guide. **Note:** *Make sure the valve is installed in the correct guide and be careful not to get any grinding compound on the valve stem.*

25 Attach the grinding tool (or hose) to the valve and rotate the tool between the palms of your hands. Use a back-and-forth motion (as

11.20a Measuring the free length of a valve spring

11.24 Apply small dabs of grinding compound to the valve face only

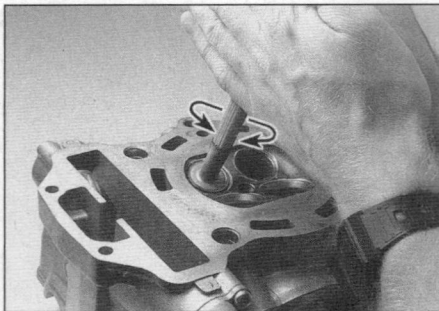

11.25 Rotate the valve grinding tool back and forth between the palms of your hands

11.28 Press the new stem seal into place with a suitable deep socket

11.30 A small dab of grease will hold the collets in place on the valve while the spring is released

11.32 Tap the valve stem gently to seat the collets in the groove

though rubbing your hands together) rather than a circular motion to that the valve rotates alternately clockwise and anti-clockwise on its seat **(see illustration)**. Lift the valve off the seat and turn it at regular intervals to distribute the grinding compound evenly. Continue the grinding procedure until the valve face and seat contact areas are of uniform and correct width and unbroken around their entire circumference.

26 Carefully remove the valve from the guide and wipe off all traces of grinding compound. Use solvent to clean the valve and wipe the seat area thoroughly with a solvent soaked cloth.

27 Repeat the procedure with fine valve grinding compound, then repeat the entire procedure for the remaining valve and cylinder head.

28 Working on one valve at a time, lay the spring seat in place in the cylinder head so

that its shouldered side faces up **(see illustration 11.8b)**. Fit a new stem seal onto the valve guide and use an appropriate size deep socket to press the seal over the end of the guide until it is felt to clip into place **(see illustration)**. Don't twist or cock the seal, or it will not seal properly against the valve stem. Also, don't remove it again or it will be damaged.

29 Coat the valve stem with molybdenum disulphide oil, then install it into its guide, rotating it slowly to avoid damaging the seal. Check that the valve moves up and down freely in the guide. Next, install the spring with its closer-wound coils facing down against the head, and the retainer, with its shouldered side facing down so that it fits into the top of the spring **(see illustrations 11. 7c and 7b)**.

30 Apply a small amount of grease to the inside of the collets – this will help hold them in place when fitting them on the valve stem

(see illustration). Compress the spring with the valve spring compressor and install the collets **(see illustration 11.7a)**. When compressing the spring, do so only as far as is necessary to slip the collets into place. Make certain that the collets are securely located in the collet groove and release the spring compressor.

31 Repeat the procedure for the remaining valve and cylinder head.

32 Support each cylinder head on blocks so the valves can't contact the workbench top, then very gently tap each of the valve stems to seat the collets in their grooves **(see illustration)**.

33 Install the camshafts and rocker arms (see Section 9).

12 Cam chains, tensioner blades and guides

Removal

1 Remove the cylinder heads (see Section 8).
2 Check the visible portion of each cam chain for obvious wear or damage. Except in cases of oil starvation, Hy-Vo type chains wear very little.
3 Check the camshaft sprocket for wear, cracks and other damage. If the sprocket is worn, it is likely the chain and the sprocket on the crankshaft will also be worn. If wear this severe is apparent, the entire engine should be disassembled for inspection.
4 Lift out the cam chain guide, noting how it fits **(see illustration)**. Check the sliding surface of the guide for excessive wear, deep grooves, cracking and other obvious damage, and renew it if necessary.
5 Follow the appropriate procedure to remove the cam chain and tensioner blade. Work on one cylinder at a time and keep the parts for each cylinder together so that they can be reinstalled in the correct location.

Rear cylinder

6 Remove the alternator rotor, starter clutch and idler gear (see Section 16).
7 Undo the bolts securing the lower end of the tensioner blade and lift it out **(see illustrations)**.

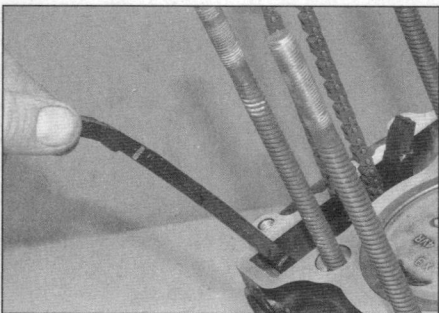

12.4 Lift out the cam chain guide

12.7a Undo the bolts (arrowed) . . .

12.7b . . . and lift out the rear cylinder tensioner blade

12.8 Lift out the cam chain

12.10a Undo the bolts (arrowed) . . .

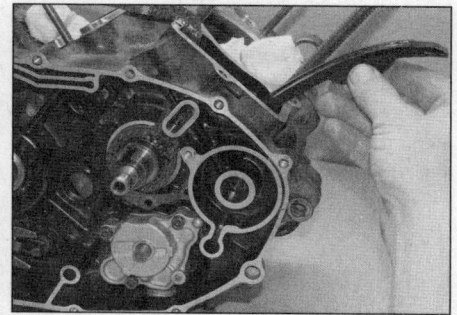

12.10b . . . and lift out the front cylinder tensioner blade . . .

8 The cam chain is marked with paint on the outside to identify which way round it is fitted – if no mark is visible, apply your own. Slip the cam chain off the crankshaft sprocket and remove it **(see illustration)**.

Front cylinder

9 Remove the clutch and primary gears (see Section 18).

10 Follow the procedure in Steps 7 and 8 and remove the tensioner blade and cam chain **(see illustrations)**.

Inspection

11 If the chain is stiff or the links are binding, or if the links are loose, discard the chain. A chain in poor condition will wear the sprocket teeth and ideally a chain and sprockets should be replaced as a set. The camshaft sprockets are easily renewed, but if the crankshaft sprocket is unfit for further use a new crankshaft will have to be fitted.

12 Follow the procedure in Step 4 and check the tensioner blade.

Installation

13 Installation is the reverse of removal, noting the following:

● If the original chain is being used, ensure it is refitted the correct way round (see Step 8).

● Tighten the tensioner blade bolts to the torque setting specified at the beginning of this Chapter.

● Install the guide blade with the end marked

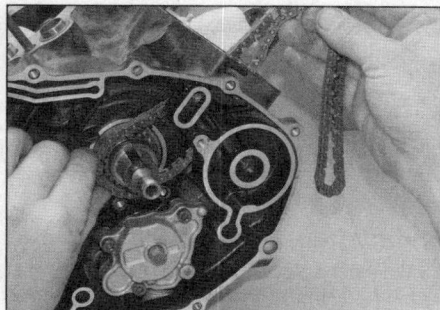

12.10c . . . then lift out the cam chain

UP at the top and ensure the lower end of the blade locates in the slot in the crankcase.

● When the cylinder head is installed, ensure the upper end of the guide blade locates correctly in the notch inside the head (see Section 8).

13 Cylinders

Note: *The procedure is the same for both cylinders.*

Removal

1 Remove the cylinder heads (see Section 8).

13.3 Remove the Allen bolt that secures the cylinder to the crankcase

2 Lift out the cam chain guide **(see illustration 12.4)**.

3 Remove the cylinder bolt **(see illustration)**.

4 Lift the cylinder off the studs **(see illustration)**. If it's stuck, tap around the joint face between the cylinder and the crankcase with a soft-faced mallet or block of wood to free it. Don't attempt to lever the cylinder off the crankcase – you will damage the sealing surface. Feed the cam chain down the tunnel and secure it with a cable tie or piece of wire to prevent it falling into the crankcase and jamming on the crankshaft sprocket. Support the piston to prevent it hitting the crankcase as the cylinder is lifted off.

5 Remove the gasket and discard it as a new one must be used **(see illustration)**.

6 Note the location of the dowels on the crankcase or in the underside of the cylinder and remove them for safekeeping if they are loose **(see illustration)**. Note the O-ring on

13.4 Lift the cylinder straight up off the studs

13.5 Discard the old cylinder base gasket

13.6a Note the locations of the dowels (arrowed)

13.6b Note the O-ring fitted on the large dowel

13.8 Remove the O-ring from the base of the cylinder

13.11 Measuring the cylinder bore with a telescoping gauge

the large dowel and discard it as a new one must be fitted **(see illustration)**.

7 Stuff clean rag into the crankcase opening around the piston and remove all traces of old gasket material from the surface of the crankcase with a suitable solvent.

8 Remove the O-ring from the base of the cylinder and discard it as a new one must be fitted **(see illustration)**. Clean all traces of old gasket material from the joint face of the cylinder with a suitable solvent.

9 Repeat the procedure to remove the remaining cylinder.

Inspection

10 Inspect the cylinder wall carefully for scratches and score marks.

11 Using telescoping gauges and a micrometer (see *Tools and Workshop Tips*), check the diameter of the cylinder bore at a point 40 mm down from the top of the cylinder. Measure both parallel to and across the crankshaft axis and calculate the average cylinder dimension **(see illustration)**. Compare the results to the specifications at the beginning of this Chapter.

12 To calculate the piston-to-cylinder clearance, first measure the piston diameter (see Section 14). Subtract the piston diameter from the cylinder diameter obtained in Step 11 to obtain the clearance and compare the result with the service limit specified at the beginning of this Chapter.

13 If the cylinders are badly scratched, scuffed or scored, tapered or worn beyond the service limit, have them rebored by a Yamaha dealer or specialist engineer. If a rebore is done, oversize pistons and rings will be required as well.

14 If the precision measuring tools are not available, take the cylinder and piston to a Yamaha dealer or specialist engineer for assessment and advice.

Installation

15 Install the dowels on the crankcase and fit a new O-ring on the large dowel **(see illustration 13.6b)**. Place a new cylinder base gasket on the crankcase **(see illustration 13.5)**. Install a new O-ring around the base of the cylinder **(see illustration 13.8)**.

16 Lubricate the cylinder bore and piston with plenty of clean engine oil. Check that the piston ring end gaps are correctly positioned (see Section 15).

17 Install the cylinder on the studs and carefully lower it down until the piston crown fits into the bottom of the cylinder bore **(see illustration)**. At the same time, pull the cam chain up through the tunnel, using a hooked piece of wire or cable tie.

18 Push down on the cylinder, making sure the piston doesn't get cocked sideways, and slide the piston up into the bore. Compress each ring by hand and feed it into the bottom of the bore.

19 Once the piston is fitted inside the cylinder press the cylinder down onto the crankcase. If necessary, use a wood or plastic hammer handle to gently tap the cylinder

down, but don't use too much force or the piston will be damaged.

20 Install the cylinder bolt and tighten it to the specified torque **(see illustration 13.3)**.

21 Repeat the procedure to install the remaining cylinder.

22 Install the remaining components in the reverse order of removal.

14 Pistons

Removal

1 Remove the cylinders (see Section 13).

2 Stuff a clean rag into the crankcase opening around the connecting rod. This will prevent the circlips from falling into the crankcase if they are inadvertently dropped.

3 Using a sharp scribe or paint, mark the location of each piston (front or rear cylinder) into its crown or on the inside of the piston skirt **(see illustration)**. Each piston should have an EX mark on its crown – this mark faces the exhaust side of the cylinder when the piston is installed. If not, scribe an arrow into the piston crown before removal.

4 Carefully prise out the circlips on each side of the piston pin using a small flat-bladed screwdriver inserted into the notch **(see illustration)**. Check for burring around the circlip grooves and remove any with a very fine file or penknife blade, then push the

13.17 Fit the piston crown into the bottom of the cylinder bore

14.3 Identify the piston location and note the EX mark (arrowed)

14.4a Prise out the circlips . . .

14.4b . . . then push out the piston pin

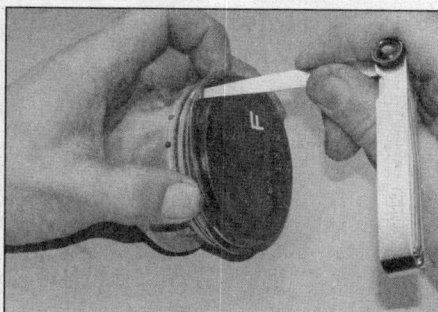
14.5a Removing the piston rings with a feeler gauge blade

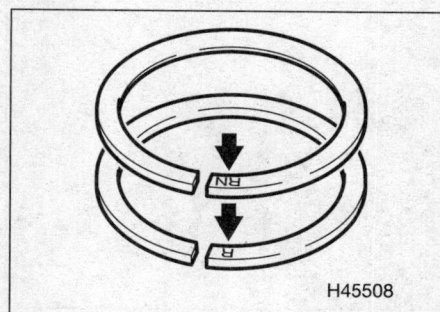
H45508
14.5b Note the marks on the ends of the two top rings (arrowed)

piston pin out to free the piston from the connecting rod (see illustration). Discard the circlips as new ones must be used on reassembly. When the piston has been removed from the rod, keep the piston and its pin together so that related parts do not get mixed up.

> **HAYNES HINT**
> If a piston pin is a tight fit in the piston, heat the piston gently with a hot air gun – this will expand the alloy piston sufficiently to release its grip on the pin. If the piston pin is particularly stubborn, extract it using a drawbolt tool, but be careful to protect the piston's working surfaces.

5 Using a feeler gauge blade or a piston ring removal and installation tool, carefully remove the rings from the pistons, working on one piston at a time (see illustration). Do not nick or gouge the piston in the process. Note which way up each ring fits and in which groove, as they must be installed in their original positions if being re-used. The upper surface of the top two rings should have a manufacturer's mark or letter at one end – if the mark on each ring is different, note which mark is for the top ring and which is for the second (see illustration). Note: Do not use a piston ring tool on the oil ring side rails as they may be damaged.
6 Scrape all traces of carbon from the top of

the piston. A hand-held wire brush or a piece of fine emery cloth can be used once most of the deposits have been scraped away. Do not, under any circumstances, use a wire brush mounted in a drill motor; the piston material is soft and is easily damaged.
7 Use a piston ring groove cleaning tool to remove any carbon deposits from the ring grooves. If a tool is not available, a piece broken off an old ring will do the job. Be very careful to remove only the carbon deposits. Do not remove any metal and do not nick or gouge the sides of the ring grooves.
8 Once the carbon has been removed, clean the piston with a suitable solvent and dry it thoroughly. Make sure the oil return holes at the back of the oil ring groove are clear. If the identification previously marked on the piston is cleaned off, be sure to re-mark it correctly.

Inspection

9 Inspect each piston for cracks around the skirt, at the pin bosses and at the ring lands. Normal piston wear appears as even, vertical wear on the thrust surfaces of the piston and slight looseness of the top ring in its groove. If the skirt is scored or scuffed, the engine may have been suffering from overheating and/or abnormal combustion, resulting in excessively high operating temperatures.
10 A hole in the top of the piston (only likely in extreme circumstances), or burned areas around the edge of the piston crown, indicate that pre-ignition or knocking under load have

occurred. If you find evidence of any problems the cause must be corrected or the damage will occur again (see Fault Finding in the Reference section).
11 Calculate the piston-to-bore clearance by measuring the cylinder bore (see Section 13) and the piston diameter. Make sure each piston is matched to its correct cylinder. Measure the piston 6 mm up from the bottom of the skirt and at 90° to the piston pin axis (see illustration). Subtract the piston diameter from the cylinder diameter to obtain the clearance and compare the result with the service limit specified at the beginning of this Chapter. If it is greater than specified, the cylinders will have to be rebored and new oversized pistons and rings installed.
12 Measure the piston ring-to-groove clearance by laying each of the top two rings in its groove and slipping a feeler gauge in beside it (see illustration). Make sure you have the correct ring for the groove (see Step 5). Check the clearance at three or four locations around the groove. If the clearance is greater than specified, renew both the piston and rings as a set. If new rings are being used, measure the clearance using the new rings. If the clearance is greater than that specified, the piston is worn and must be renewed.
13 Apply clean engine oil to the piston pin, insert it part way into the piston and check for any freeplay between the two (see illustration). Measure the pin external diameter, and the pin bore in the piston (see

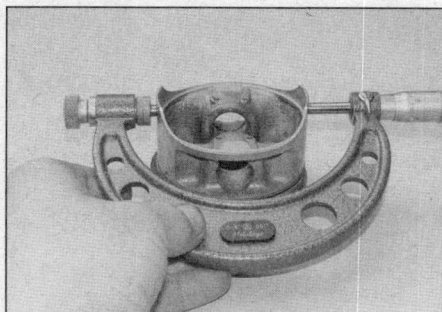
14.11 Measuring the piston diameter

14.12 Measuring the piston ring-to-groove clearance

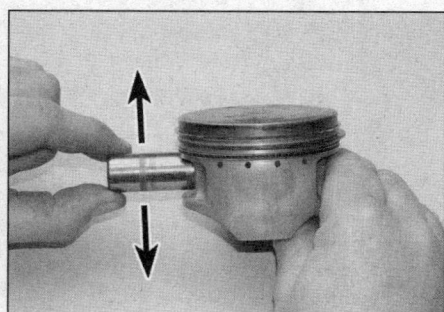
14.13a Check for freeplay between the piston and pin

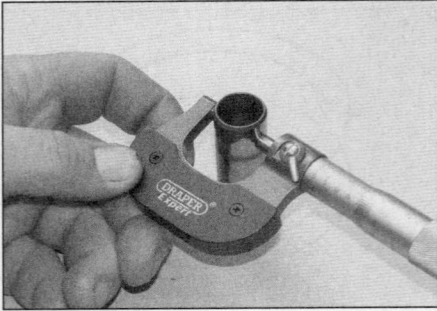

14.13b Measuring the piston pin diameter . . .

14.13c . . . and the pin bore in the piston

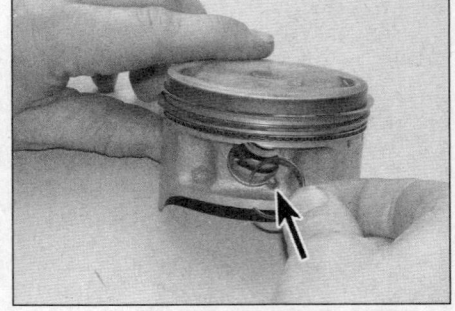

14.15 Install the circlips with the ends away from the removal notch (arrowed)

illustrations). Subtract the pin diameter from the piston bore diameter to obtain the clearance. If it is greater than the specified figure, check whether it is the piston or pin that is worn beyond its service limit and renew them as required. Repeat the checks between the pin and the connecting rod small-end (see Section 25).

Installation

14 Inspect and install the piston rings (see Section 15).

15 Install a **new** circlip into one side of the piston (never re-use old circlips), then lubricate the piston pin, the piston pin bore and the connecting rod small-end bore with clean engine oil. When installing the circlips, compress them only just enough to fit them in the piston, and make sure they are properly

15.3 Measuring piston ring end gap

seated in their grooves with the open end away from the removal notch **(see illustration)**.

16 Line up the piston on its connecting rod with the EX mark towards the exhaust side of the cylinder (see Step 3). Insert the piston pin from the side without the circlip and secure it with the other **new** circlip.

17 Install the remaining components in the reverse order of removal.

15 Piston rings

1 It is good practice to renew the piston rings when an engine is being overhauled. Before installing the rings on the pistons, the ring end gaps must be checked with the rings installed in the cylinder.

Inspection

2 Lay out the pistons and the new ring sets so the rings will be matched with the same piston and cylinder during the end gap measurement procedure and engine assembly. The upper surface of the top two rings should have a manufacturer's mark or letter at one end – if the mark on each ring is different, note which mark is for the top ring and which is for the second **(see illustration 14.5b)**.

3 To measure the ring end gap, insert the ring

into the top of the cylinder and square it up with the cylinder walls by pushing it in with the top of the piston. The ring should be about 40 mm below the top edge of the cylinder. Slip a feeler gauge between the ends of the ring and compare the measurement to the specifications at the beginning of this Chapter **(see illustration)**.

4 If the gap is larger or smaller than specified, double check to make sure that you have the correct rings before proceeding. Excess end gap is not critical unless it is greater than the service limit.

5 Repeat the procedure for each ring that will be installed in the first cylinder and for each ring in the remaining cylinder. Note that the end gaps differ between the top, second and oil rings. Remember to keep the matched rings, pistons and cylinders together. Note that Yamaha specify no service limit for the oil control ring side rails.

Installation

6 Once the ring end gaps have been checked the rings can be installed on the pistons.

7 The oil control ring (lowest on the piston) is installed first. It is composed of three separate components. Slip the expander into the groove, then install the lower side rail **(see illustrations)**. **Note:** *Do not use a piston ring installation tool on the oil ring side rails as they may be damaged. Instead, place one end of the side rail into the groove between the*

15.7a Fit the oil ring expander in its groove . . .

15.7b . . . then fit the lower side rail

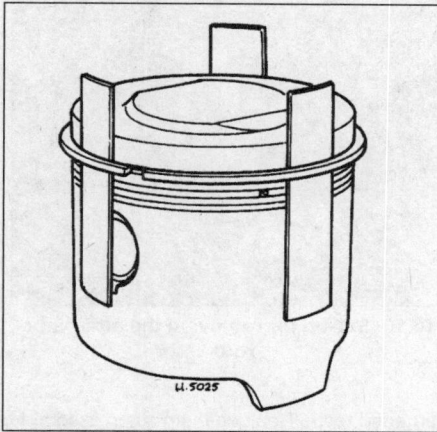

15.9 Old pieces of feeler gauge blade can be used to guide the ring over the piston

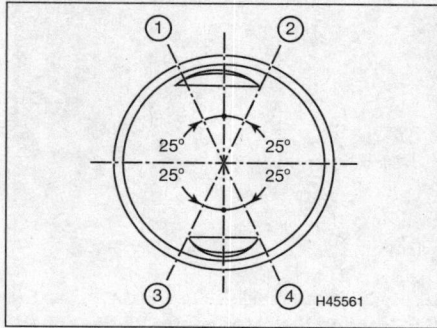

15.12 Stagger the ring end gaps as shown

1 Top ring
2 Oil ring lower side rail
3 Oil ring upper side rail
4 Second ring

16.5a Pull off the alternator cover . . .

expander and the ring land. Hold it firmly in place and slide a finger around the piston while pushing the rail into the groove. Next, install the upper side rail in the same manner. Make sure the ends of the expander touch but do not overlap.

8 After the three oil ring components have been installed, check to make sure that both the upper and lower side rails can be turned smoothly in the ring groove.

9 The upper surface of each compression ring should have a mark or letter at one end which must face up when the ring is installed on the piston (see Step 2). Fit the second ring into the middle groove in the piston. Do not expand the ring any more than is necessary to slide it into place. To avoid breaking the ring, use a piston ring installation tool or a feeler gauge blade (see illustration).

10 Finally, install the top ring in the same manner into the top groove in the piston.

11 Repeat the procedure for the remaining piston.

12 Once the rings have been properly installed, stagger the end gaps, including

those of the oil ring side rails (see illustration).

16 Alternator rotor, starter clutch and gears

Note: This procedure can be carried out with the engine in the frame.

Removal

1 Drain the engine oil (see Chapter 1).

2 Disconnect the clutch cable from the release mechanism arm and the cable bracket (see Section 17).

3 Follow the procedure in Section 21 and pull the gearchange lever off the gearchange shaft.

4 If the alternator cover is being removed from the bike, first remove the fuel tank (see Chapter 3). Follow the procedure in Section 5, Step 19, and trace the wiring from the back of the alternator cover and disconnect it at the connectors. Free the wiring from any clips or ties and note its routing. Working evenly in a criss-cross

HAYNES HiNT Make a cardboard template of the alternator cover and punch a hole for each bolt location. As each bolt is removed, store it in its relative position in the template. This will ensure all bolts are installed correctly on reassembly – this is important, as many bolts differ slightly in length.

pattern, loosen the alternator cover bolts, then remove them noting the location of the clutch cable bracket.

5 Draw off the cover, noting how it fits over the gearchange shaft, then discard the cover gasket as a new one must be used (see illustrations). Note the location of the cover dowels and remove them for safekeeping if they are loose.

6 If the cover is just being displaced, secure it to the machine with a cable tie to avoid straining the alternator wiring.

7 Pull out the intermediate gear shaft and remove the gear, noting which way round it fits (see illustration).

8 If required, the operation of the starter clutch can be checked while it is in place. Check that the idler gear is able to rotate freely anti-clockwise, but locks when rotated

16.5b . . . and discard the gasket. Note the cover dowels (arrowed)

16.7 Pull out the shaft (A) and remove the gear (B)

16.8 Idler gear should rotate freely anti-clockwise

16.9 Holding the rotor centre as described to undo the bolt

16.10 Set-up for removing the alternator rotor

clockwise **(see illustration)**. If not, the starter clutch is faulty and should be removed for inspection.

9 To remove the alternator rotor bolt it is necessary to stop the rotor from turning. If a rotor holding strap or tool is not available, use a spanner on the flats on the outside of the rotor centre **(see illustration)**. Alternatively, if the engine is still in the frame, place the transmission in gear and have an assistant apply the rear brake, then unscrew the bolt. **Caution: If a rotor holding strap is used, make sure it does not contact the raised sections on the outside of the rotor.**

10 To remove the rotor from the shaft it is necessary to use a rotor puller. Yamaha

provide a service tool (Europe Part Nos. 90890–01362 and 90890–04089 or US Part Nos. YU-33270 and YU-04089), or alternatively a similar tool can be obtained commercially **(see illustration)**. **Note:** *Remove three starter clutch bolts then thread the puller legs into the bolt holes.*

11 Pull the rotor off the shaft and remove the Woodruff key from its slot **(see illustrations)**.

12 Draw the idler gear off the crankshaft and remove its thrust washer **(see illustrations)**. Note that the washer may stick to the back of the gear – remove it for safekeeping.

Inspection

13 Check the gears for cracks, chips, or

damaged teeth. Replace them as an assembly if they are worn or damaged. Check the intermediate gear shaft and bearing surface for signs of wear and replace it if necessary **(see illustration)**.

14 Place the alternator rotor face down on the workbench and fit the idler gear hub into the starter clutch on the back of the rotor. Rotate the gear clockwise as you do to spread the clutch sprags and allow it to enter. With the gear in place, hold the rotor and check that the gear rotates freely in a clockwise direction and locks against the rotor in an anti-clockwise direction **(see illustration)**. If it doesn't, the starter clutch should be dismantled.

16.11a Pull the rotor off the shaft . . .

16.11b . . . and remove the Woodruff key

16.12a Remove the idler gear . . .

16.12b . . . and the thrust washer

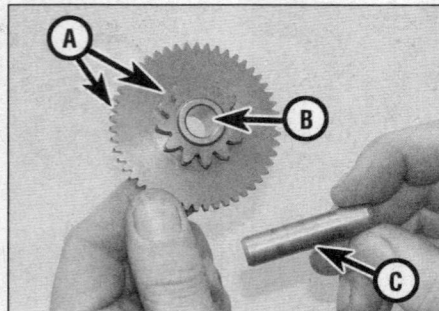

16.13 Check both sets of teeth (A) on the intermediate gear, the bearing surface (B) and the shaft (C)

16.14 Idler gear should rotate freely clockwise

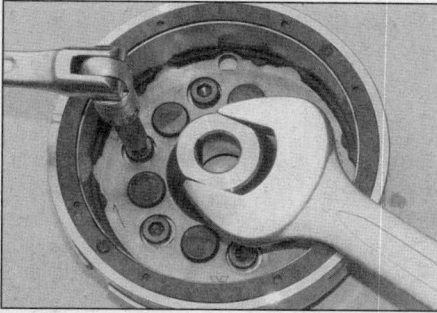
16.15a Remove the starter clutch bolts . . .

16.15b . . . then lift off the starter clutch assembly

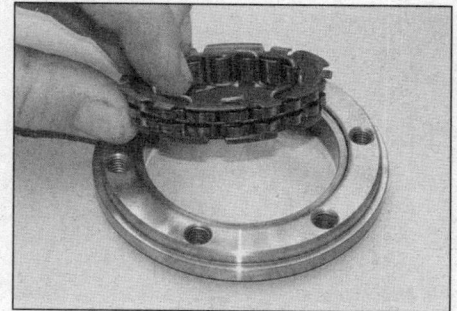
16.16 Check the condition of the sprags

15 Lift out the idler gear. Hold the alternator rotor and undo the bolts securing the starter clutch, then lift it off **(see illustrations)**.
16 Inspect the condition of the sprags inside the clutch assembly **(see illustration)**. If they are damaged or worn at any point, the clutch assembly should be renewed – individual components are not available.
17 Inspect the idler gear hub for signs of wear and scoring where it fits inside the starter clutch. If the hub surface shows signs of excessive wear, renew the idler gear and the starter clutch assembly.

Installation

18 Clean the starter clutch bolts and apply a suitable non-permanent locking compound to their threads **(see illustration)**. Position the housing on the back of the alternator rotor, then install the bolts and tighten them to the torque setting specified at the beginning of this Chapter.
19 Fit the thrust washer onto the crankshaft then lubricate the idler gear hub with engine oil and slide the gear onto the shaft.
20 Fit the Woodruff key into its slot in the crankshaft. Clean the tapered end of the shaft and the corresponding mating surface on the inside of the alternator rotor with a suitable solvent **(see illustration)**.
21 Make sure no metal objects have attached themselves to the magnets on the inside of the

16.18 Thread-lock the starter clutch bolts

16.20 Clean the end of the crankshaft (arrowed) with solvent

rotor. Lubricate the starter clutch with a few drops of engine oil, then align the rotor with the Woodruff key and slide it onto the shaft. Ensure the starter clutch engages all the way onto the idler gear hub and check the operation of the starter clutch as described in Step 8.
22 Fit the washer onto the rotor bolt and tighten the bolt to the torque setting specified at the beginning of this Chapter **(see illustration)**. Use the method employed on removal to prevent the rotor from turning (see Step 9).
23 Lubricate the intermediate gear shaft with engine oil. Hold the gear in position, making sure the smaller pinion faces inwards, and insert the shaft **(see illustration 16.7)**.

24 Check the condition of the gearchange shaft seal in the alternator cover and renew it if necessary (see *Tools and Workshop Tips* in the *Reference* section) **(see illustration)**.
25 Remove all traces of old gasket from the crankcase and cover surfaces. Ensure the cover dowels are in position, then install a new cover gasket **(see illustration 16.5b)**.
26 Install the cover, then install the bolts and clutch cable bracket. Tighten the bolts evenly in a criss-cross pattern, to the specified torque setting.
27 Install the remaining components in the reverse order of removal. Don't forget to fill the engine with the recommended type and amount of oil (see Chapter 1).

16.22 Fit the washer (arrowed) before installing the rotor bolt

16.24 Check the gearchange shaft seal (arrowed) in the cover

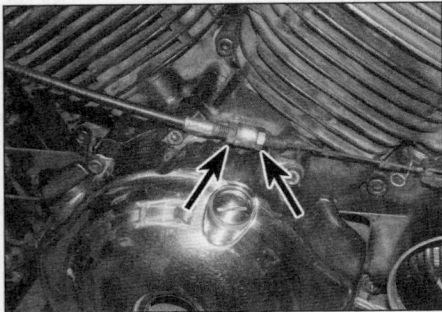

17.1a Loosen the locknuts (arrowed) . . .

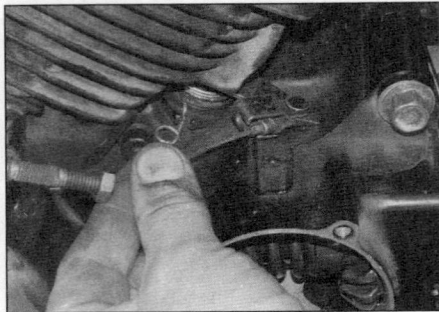

17.1b . . . then disconnect the cable from the release mechanism arm

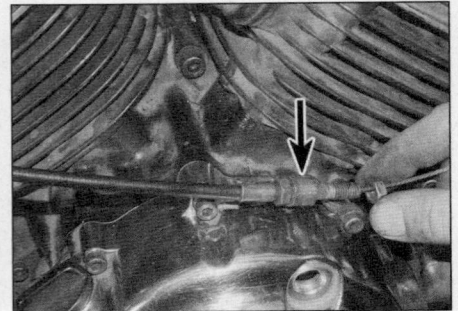

17.1c Pull the cable out of the bracket (arrowed)

17 Clutch cable

1 Loosen the locknuts on the adjuster on the lower (engine) end of the cable until there is sufficient freeplay to disconnect the inner cable end from the clutch release mechanism arm **(see illustrations)**. Remove the lower locknut and pull the cable out of the bracket on the alternator cover **(see illustration)**.

2 Displace the rubber boot from the adjuster on the handlebar lever **(see illustration)**. Loosen the lockwheel on the adjuster, then screw the adjuster into the lever bracket and align the slot in the adjuster with the slot in the bracket **(see illustration)**.

3 Pull the outer cable end from the socket in the adjuster and release the inner cable end from the lever **(see illustration)**.

4 Remove the cable from the bike, noting its routing through the guides on the underside of the fork top yoke and the left-hand side of the frame.

5 Before installing the new cable, push the release mechanism arm forwards and check that the pointer on the end of the arm aligns with the index mark on the engine casing **(see illustration)**. If necessary, follow the procedure in Section 18 and adjust the release mechanism freeplay.

6 Installation is the reverse of removal. Lubricate the cable ends with multi-purpose

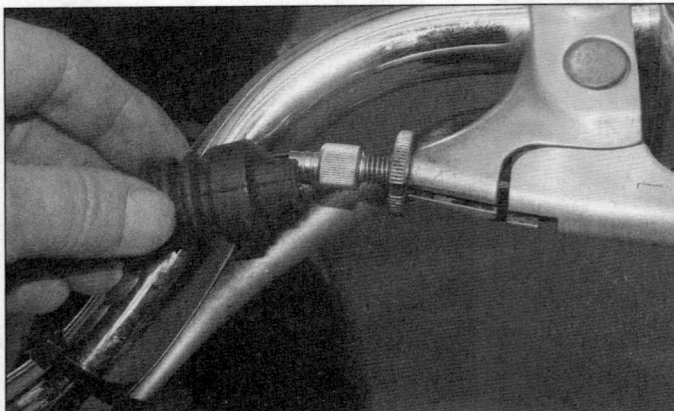

17.2a Pull the rubber boot off the adjuster

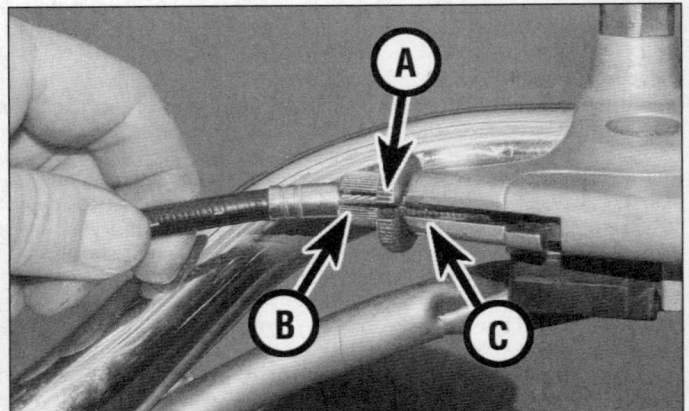

17.2b Loosen the lockwheel (A) and align the slots in the adjuster (B) and the bracket (C)

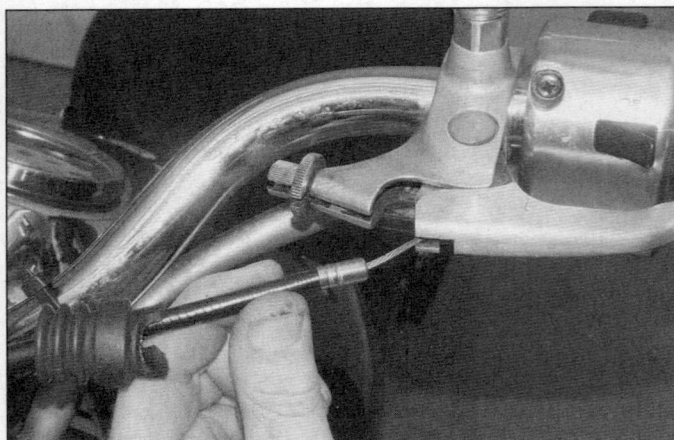

17.3 Release the cable from the lever

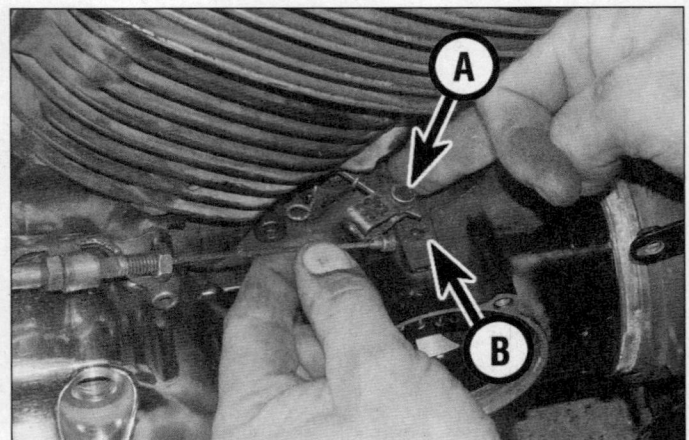

17.5 Check that the arm (A) aligns with the index mark (B)

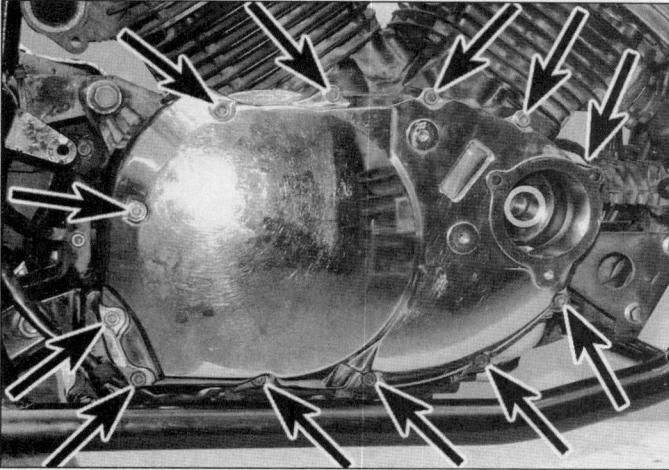

18.3a Remove the bolts (arrowed) . . .

18.3b . . . and lift off the cover

grease and make sure the cable is correctly routed. Adjust the cable freeplay (see *'Daily (pre-ride) checks'* at the beginning of this Manual).

18 Clutch and primary gears

Note: *This procedure can be carried out with the engine in the frame.*

Removal

1 Drain the engine oil and remove the oil filter (see Chapter 1).
2 Remove the exhaust system (see Chapter 3).
3 Working evenly in a criss-cross pattern, loosen the clutch cover bolts, then remove the bolts and take off the cover **(see illustrations)**. Note the wiring clips secured by the lower cover bolts.
4 Remove the cover gasket as a new one

must be used. Note the position of the locating dowels and remove them for safekeeping if they are loose **(see illustration)**.
5 Remove the circlip and take off the oil pump driven gear noting which way round it fits **(see illustrations)**.
6 Loosen the clutch spring bolts evenly in a criss-cross pattern, then remove the bolts and springs **(see illustrations)**.
7 Remove the pressure plate together with the short pushrod located on the back of the plate **(see illustration)**.

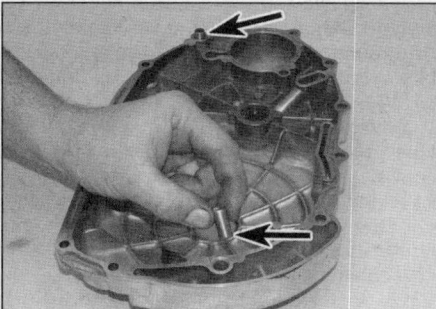

18.4 Remove the dowels (arrowed) for safekeeping

18.5a Remove the circlip . . .

18.5b . . . and take off the oil pump driven gear

18.6a Loosen the clutch spring bolts evenly . . .

18.6b . . . then remove the bolts and springs

18.7 Lift off the clutch pressure plate

18.8a Remove the steel ball . . .

18.8b . . . and long pushrod

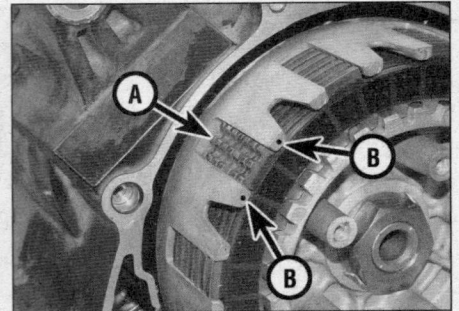
18.9 Note the alignment of the plate tabs (A) with the marks on the housing (B)

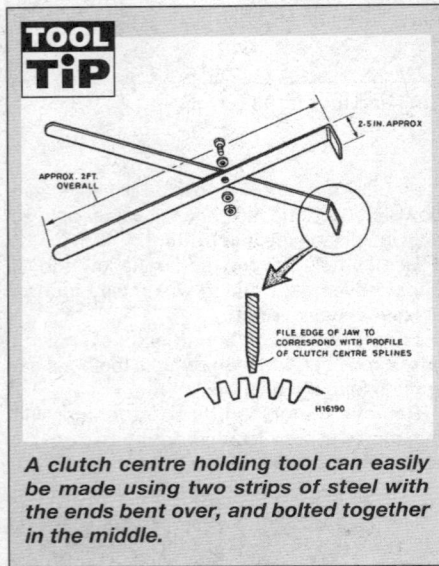

TOOL TiP

A clutch centre holding tool can easily be made using two strips of steel with the ends bent over, and bolted together in the middle.

18.10a Bend back the lockwasher tabs

18.10b Hold the clutch centre as described and loosen the centre nut

8 Use a magnet to draw out the steel ball and the long pushrod from the input shaft **(see illustrations)**.
9 Note the alignment of the notched clutch friction plate tabs with the match marks on the clutch housing **(see illustration)**. Grasp the complete set of clutch plates and remove them as a pack – unless the plates are being replaced

with new ones, keep them in their original order.
10 Bend back the tabs on the clutch centre nut lockwasher **(see illustration)**. To loosen the centre nut, the transmission input shaft must be locked. This can be done in several ways. If the engine is in the frame, engage 1st gear and have an assistant hold the rear brake on hard with the rear tyre in firm contact with the ground. Alternatively, the Yamaha service tool – Part No. 90890-04086 (Europe models) or YM-91042 (US models) – a similar commercially available or a home-made tool **(see Tool Tip)**, can be used to stop the clutch centre from turning **(see illustration)**.
11 Undo the nut and remove the lockwasher from the input shaft, noting how they fit **(see illustrations)**. Discard the lockwasher, as a new one must be fitted on reassembly.
12 Slide the clutch centre and the thrust washer off the input shaft **(see illustrations)**. If required, the clutch housing can be removed at this stage **(see illustration)**.
13 Bend back the lockwasher on the nut that

18.11a Remove the centre nut . . .

18.11b . . . and lockwasher

18.12a Slide off the clutch centre . . .

18.12b . . . and the thrust washer

18.12c Slide off the clutch housing

18.13a Bend back the lockwasher on the oil pump and primary drive gear nut

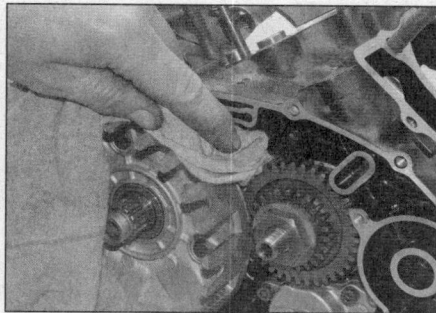

18.13b Wedge a rag between the gears to lock the crankshaft

18.14a Remove the nut . . .

18.14b . . . lockwasher. . .

18.14c . . . and retaining plate

18.15 Remove the oil pump drive gear

18.16a Remove the primary drive gear . . .

18.16b . . . and square key

secures the oil pump and primary drive gears **(see illustration)**. To loosen the nut, the crankshaft must be locked. Either remove the alternator cover centre cap and counter-hold the shaft on the alternator centre bolt, or wedge a rag between the teeth of the primary drive gear and the driven gear on the back of the clutch housing to prevent them turning, then loosen the nut **(see illustration)**. Once the nut is loose, pull the clutch housing off.

14 Remove the nut, lockwasher and retaining plate, noting how the plate fits **(see illustrations)**. Discard the lockwasher, as a new one must be fitted.

15 Remove the oil pump drive gear **(see illustration)**.

16 Remove the primary drive gear and square key **(see illustrations)**.

Inspection

17 After an extended period of service the clutch friction plates will wear and promote clutch slip. Measure the thickness of each

friction plate using a vernier caliper **(see illustration)**. If any plate has worn to or beyond the service limit given in the Specifications at the beginning of this Chapter, the friction plates must be renewed as a set. Also, if any of the plates smell burnt or are glazed, they must be renewed as a set.

18 The plain plates should not show any

signs of excess heating (bluing). Check for warpage using a flat surface and feeler gauges **(see illustration)**. If any plate exceeds the maximum permissible amount of warpage, or shows signs of bluing, all the plain plates must be renewed as a set.

19 Measure the free length of each clutch spring **(see illustration)**. If any spring is below

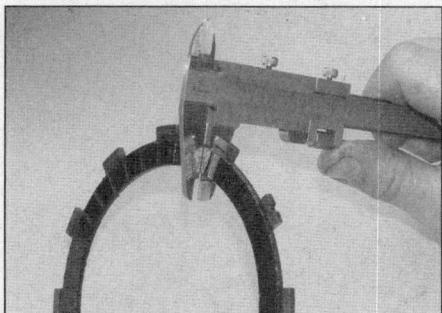

18.17 Measuring the thickness of a clutch friction plate

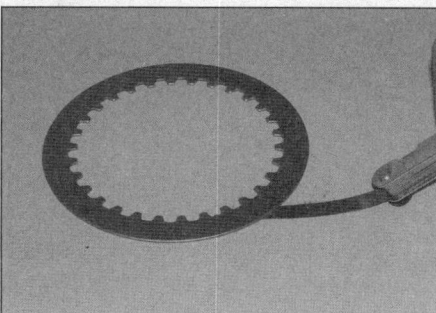

18.18 Checking a plain clutch plate for warpage

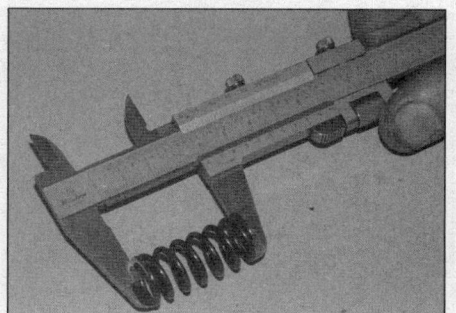

18.19 Measuring clutch spring free length

18.21 Primary driven gear is integral with the clutch housing – check the condition of the springs

18.22 Inspect the bearing surface (arrowed)

18.24a Discard the short pushrod O-ring

the service limit specified, renew all the springs as a set.

20 Inspect the clutch assembly for burrs and indentations on the edges of the protruding tangs of the friction plates and/or slots in the edge of the housing with which they engage; similarly check for wear between the inner teeth of the plain plates and the slots in the clutch centre. Wear will cause clutch drag and slow disengagement during gear changes, as the plates will snag when the pressure plate is lifted. With care, a small amount of wear can be corrected by dressing with a fine file, but if it is excessive the worn components should be renewed.

21 Check the teeth on the primary drive gear and driven gear for wear or damage and

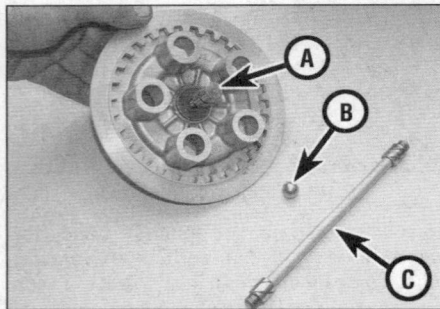

18.24b Examine the contact surfaces of the short pushrod (A), ball (B) and long pushrod (C)

replace them if defects are found. Note that the driven gear is integral with the clutch housing (see illustration). Check the condition of the springs in the back of the housing.

22 Check the bearing surface in the centre of the clutch housing and replace the clutch housing if it's worn or damaged (see illustration). If the bearing surface is damaged, inspect the corresponding surface of the transmission input shaft and renew the shaft if necessary (see Section 28).

23 Check the pressure plate for wear and damage.

24 The short pushrod is a loose fit in the pressure plate and is retained by the freeplay adjuster and locknut. It is not necessary to remove the short pushrod unless any of the components are damaged. Discard the pushrod O-ring as a new one must be fitted (see illustration). Examine the contact surfaces of the short pushrod, ball and long pushrod for wear and pitting and renew any worn or damaged parts (see illustration).

25 The clutch release mechanism shaft is located in the left-hand side of the engine case and cannot be removed with the transmission output shaft in place. If the shaft seal or bearing is worn, refer to the procedure in Section 28 to renew them.

Installation

26 Install the primary drive gear key, then install the primary drive gear, oil pump drive

gear and retaining plate (see illustrations 18.16b and a, 18.15 and 18.14c).

27 Install a new lockwasher on the retaining plate, ensuring the lockwasher tab fits into the notch in the retaining plate (see illustration 18.14b). Install the nut finger-tight.

28 Lubricate the clutch housing bearing surface with clean engine oil, then install the clutch housing on the transmission input shaft (see illustration 18.12c). Ensure the primary driven gear teeth on the back of the housing engage with the primary drive gear correctly.

29 Using the method employed on removal to lock the crankshaft, tighten the nut to the torque listed in this Chapter's Specifications, then bend the lockwasher against the nut to secure it (see illustrations).

30 Install the thrust washer and the clutch centre on the transmission input shaft (see illustrations 18.12b and a). Install a new lockwasher then fit the nut recessed side inwards and tighten it finger-tight (see illustrations 18.11b and a).

31 Using the method employed on removal to lock the input shaft, tighten the nut to the torque listed in this Chapter's Specifications, then bend the lockwasher against the nut to secure it (see illustration).

32 Coat the clutch friction plates with clean engine oil. Build up the plates as follows: first fit the thick plain plate, then a friction plate with the double notch on the plate tab aligned with the match marks on the clutch housing

18.29a Tighten the primary drive gear nut to the specified torque . . .

18.29b . . . then bend the new lockwasher to secure it

18.31 Secure the clutch centre nut with the lockwasher

18.32a Install the thick plain plate first . . .

18.32b . . . then align the notched tab on a friction plate with the housing and fit the plate

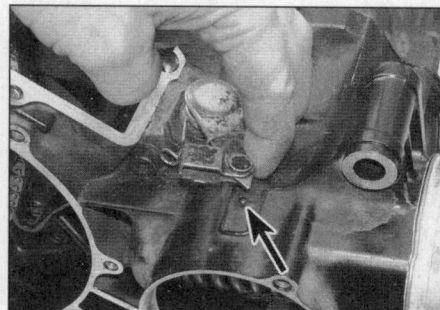

18.36a Ensure the pointer on the clutch release mechanism arm aligns with the index mark (arrowed)

(see illustrations). Now fit a standard plain plate, then alternate friction and plain plates. Ensure all the notched tabs on the friction plates are aligned with the marks on the clutch housing **(see illustration 18.9)**. The last plate to be fitted should be a friction plate.

33 Lubricate the long pushrod with engine oil and install it in the input shaft, then install the steel ball.

34 Fit a new O-ring onto the short pushrod on the back of the pressure plate and lubricate it with lithium soap grease, then install the pressure plate **(see illustration 18.7)**.

35 Install the clutch springs and spring bolts, then tighten the bolts finger-tight **(see illustration 18.6b)**. Now tighten the bolts evenly in a criss-cross pattern to the torque listed in this Chapter's Specifications.

36 Push the clutch release mechanism arm forwards and check that the pointer on the end of the arm aligns with the index mark on the engine casing **(see illustration)**. If they aren't aligned, loosen the locknut on the freeplay adjuster in the centre of the pressure plate and turn the adjuster in or out until they are **(see illustration)**. Hold the adjuster and tighten the locknut.

37 Install the oil pump driven gear and secure it with a new circlip **(see illustrations 18.5b and a)**.

38 Remove the circlip and lever the seal out of the clutch cover; lubricate a new seal with engine oil, then press it into place with a suitably sized socket and secure it with a new circlip **(see illustrations)**.

39 Remove all traces of old gasket from the crankcase and clutch cover surfaces. Ensure the clutch cover dowels are in position, then install a new cover gasket **(see illustration)**.

40 Install the clutch cover ensuring it is correctly aligned, then install the bolts finger-tight **(see illustrations 18.3b and a)**. Don't forget to fit the wiring clips on the lower bolts.

41 Tighten the bolts evenly in a criss-cross pattern, to the specified torque setting.

42 Install the remaining components in the reverse order of removal. Don't forget to fill the engine with the recommended type and amount of oil (see Chapter 1).

18.36b Adjusting the clutch release mechanism freeplay

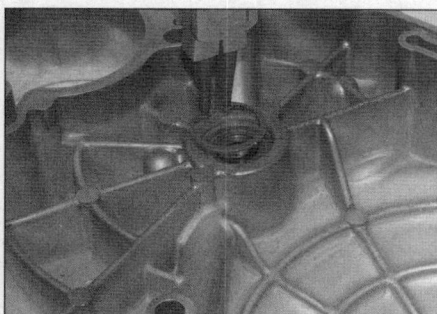

18.38a Remove the circlip . . .

18.38b . . . and lever out the seal

18.38c Install a new seal . . .

18.38d . . . and press it in with a suitable sized socket

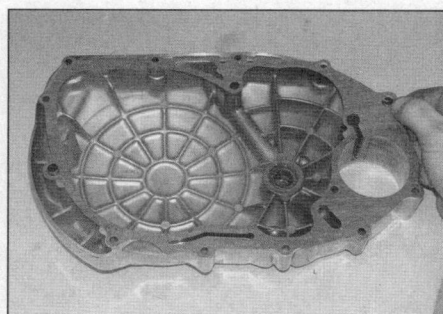

18.39 Install a new gasket on the cover

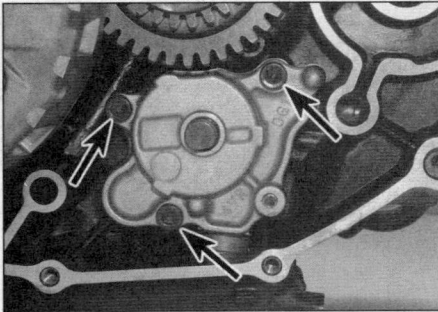
19.3a Remove the oil pump mounting bolts . . .

19.3b . . . and lift out the pump

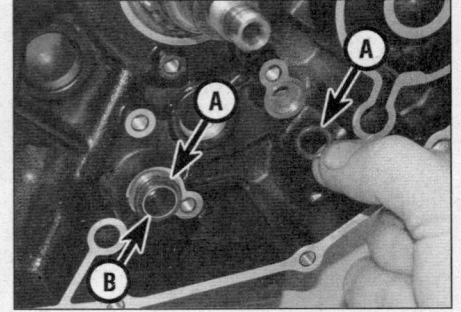
19.4 Remove the two O-rings (A) and dowel (B)

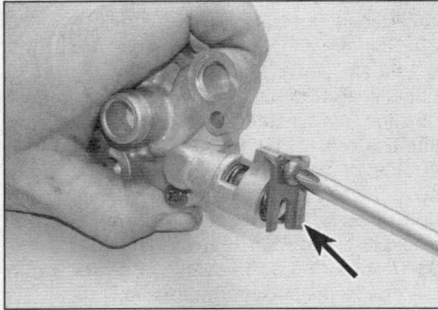
19.5a Remove the retaining plate (arrowed) . . .

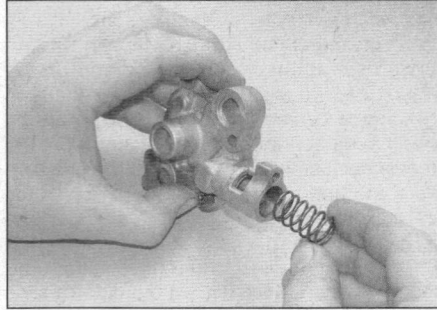
19.5b . . . then pull out the spring . . .

19 Oil pump

Note: *This procedure can be carried out with the engine in the frame.*

Removal

1 Follow the procedure in Section 18, Steps 1 to 4, and remove the clutch cover.
2 Remove the circlip and take off the oil pump driven gear noting which way round it fits **(see illustrations 18.5a and 5b)**.
3 Remove the oil pump mounting bolts and lift out the pump, noting how it fits **(see illustrations)**.
4 Remove the oil pump O-rings and dowel **(see illustration)**.

Inspection

5 Undo the screw on the bottom of the pump and remove the retaining plate, then take out the spring and relief valve, noting which way round it fits **(see illustrations)**.
6 Undo the cover screw on the back of the pump body and lift off the cover **(see illustrations)**.
7 Note the location of the inner rotor drive pin in the shaft, then lift the shaft out of the pump body **(see illustration)**.
8 Lift the inner and outer rotors out of the pump body, noting how they fit **(see illustration)**. Note that the rotors are not

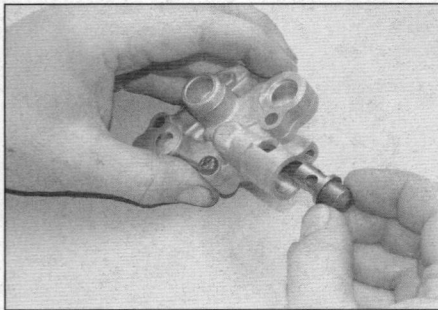
19.5c . . . and relief valve

19.6a Undo the cover screw . . .

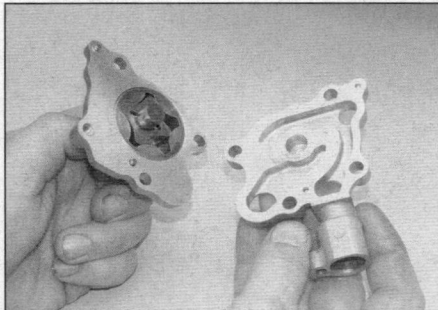
19.6b . . . and lift off the cover

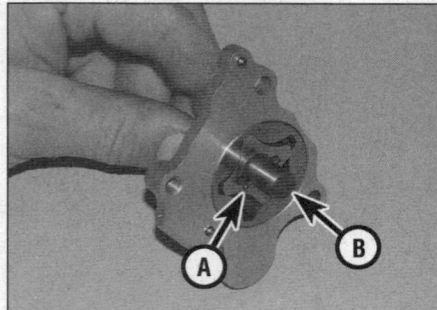
19.7 Note the location of the pin (A) then lift out the shaft (B)

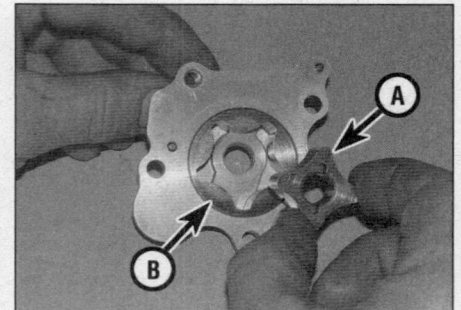
19.8 Lift out the inner (A) and outer (B) pump rotors

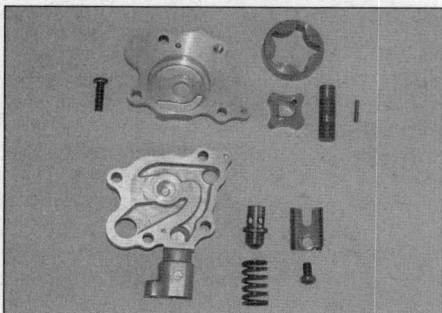

19.9 Clean the pump components and inspect them for wear

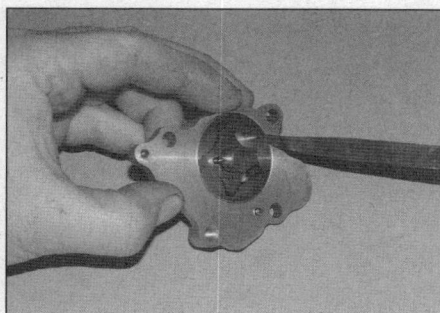

19.11 Measure the outer rotor to body clearance as shown

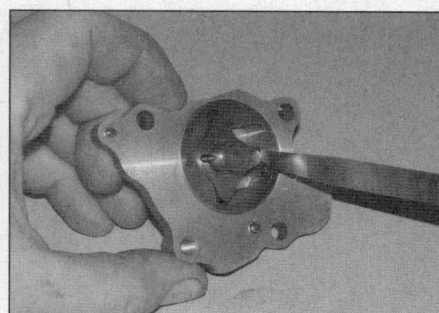

19.12 Measure the inner rotor tip to outer rotor clearance as shown

marked, but they should be installed in the pump the same way round on reassembly.

9 Clean all the components with a suitable solvent **(see illustration)**. Check that the oilways in the body are clear by blowing them through with compressed air, if available.

10 Inspect the components for scoring and wear. If any damage, scoring or uneven or excessive wear is evident, renew the pump – individual components are not available.

11 Install the rotors and shaft in the body and measure the clearance between the outer rotor and the body with a feeler gauge and compare it to the service listed in the specifications at the beginning of this Chapter **(see illustration)**. If the clearance is greater than the service limit, renew the pump.

12 Measure the clearance between the inner rotor tip and the outer rotor with a feeler gauge and compare it to the service limit listed in the specifications **(see illustration)**. If the clearance is greater than the service limit, renew the pump.

13 Check the pump driven gear for wear or damage, and replace it with a new one if necessary. If the driven gear is worn, inspect the drive gear on the crankshaft and renew it if necessary (see Section 18).

14 If the pump is good, make sure all the components are clean, then lubricate them with fresh engine oil.

15 Install the outer and inner rotors in the pump body, then fit the drive pin into the shaft and install the shaft **(see illustration 19.7)**

16 Fit the cover and secure it with the screw **(see illustrations 19.6b and a)**.

17 Rotate the pump shaft by hand and check

that the rotors turn freely – if not, strip and reassemble the pump.

18 Install the relief valve, spring and retaining plate, and secure them with the screw **(see illustrations 19.5c, b and a)**.

Installation

19 Before installing the pump, prime it by pouring oil into it while turning the shaft by hand – this will ensure that it begins to pump oil quickly.

Caution: Also pour oil into the crankcase oil passages to prevent engine damage on start-up.

20 Installation is the reverse of removal, noting the following:

● Ensure the dowel is in place and fit new O-rings in the crankcase **(see illustration 19.4)**.
● Lubricate the O-rings with clean engine oil.
● Tighten the pump mounting bolts to the torque listed in this Chapter's Specifications.
● Note how the pump driven gear locates on the pump shaft and secure it with a new circlip.
● Follow the procedure in Section 18, Steps 38 to 42, and install the clutch cover.

20 Oil strainer

1 Remove the engine from the frame (see Section 5).

2 Be prepared to catch any residual oil when the strainer is removed.

3 Undo the bolts securing the oil strainer cover and lift it off – note that the strainer will come out with the cover **(see illustrations)**.

4 Pull the strainer out of the cover. Note the position of the O-ring on the strainer and the O-ring and gasket on the cover – discard them as new ones must be fitted **(see illustration)**.

5 Clean the strainer with a suitable solvent. If the strainer is so clogged it can't be cleaned, fit a new one.

6 Fit a new O-ring onto the strainer then install it in the crankcase – ensure the strainer is installed with the gauze side down and is pushed all the way in.

7 Fit a new O-ring and gasket to the strainer cover. Lubricate the O-rings with a smear of lithium soap grease. Install the cover, pressing it over the end of the strainer, and tighten the bolts to the torque listed in this Chapter's Specifications.

8 Install the remaining components in the reverse order of removal.

21 Gearchange mechanism

Note: *This procedure can be carried out with the engine in the frame.*

Gearchange lever and pedal

1 Check for the register mark on the gearchange shaft that aligns with the slot in the lever **(see illustration 5.14)**. If the mark isn't visible, make your own with a sharp

20.3a Undo the cover bolts (arrowed) . . .

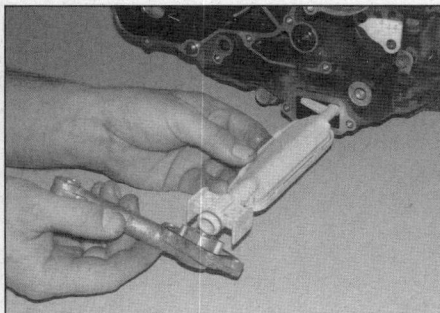

20.3b . . . and remove the cover and strainer

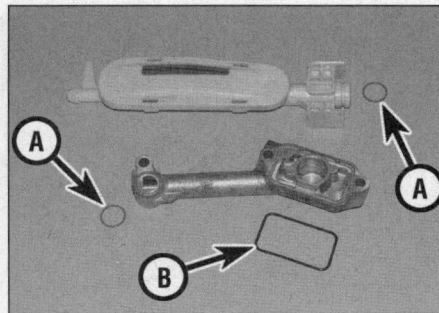

20.4 Note the location of the O-rings (A) and gasket (B)

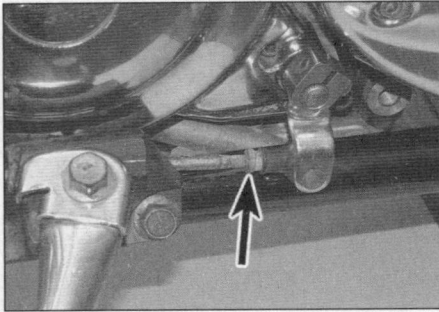

21.2 Gearchange rod locknut (arrowed)

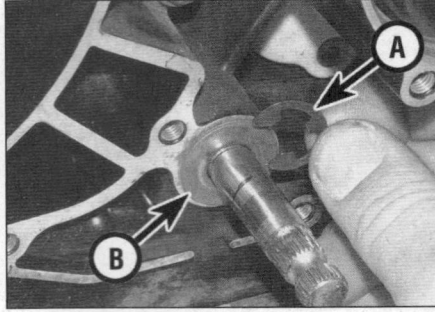

21.7 Remove the circlip (A) and washer (B)

Gearchange mechanism

Removal

5 Make sure the transmission is in neutral. Disconnect the gearchange lever from the shaft (see Step 1).
6 Remove the alternator cover (see Section 16).
7 Remove the circlip and washer from the gearchange shaft **(see illustration)**.
8 Remove the clutch (see Section 18).
9 Note how the gearchange shaft centralising spring locates on the pin and how the stopper arm spring locates against the post in the case **(see illustration)**. Pull the selector arm back to disengage it from the selector drum **(see illustration)**. Pull the shaft assembly out.
10 Note the order of the components on the shaft to aid reassembly **(see illustration)**.

Inspection

11 Inspect the splines on the gearchange

punch then remove the pinch bolt and pull the lever off the shaft.
2 If required, remove the gearchange pedal, gearchange linkage and left-hand footrest as an assembly (see Chapter 5). Alternatively, note the position of the lever locknut on the rod to aid reassembly, then loosen the locknut

and unscrew the lever from the shaft **(see illustration)**.
3 If required, refer to the procedure in Chapter 5 to separate the gearchange pedal from the footrest assembly.
4 Installation is the reverse of removal. Adjust the gearchange linkage as described in Chapter 1.

21.9a Centralising spring locates on pin (A) and stopper arm spring locates on post (B)

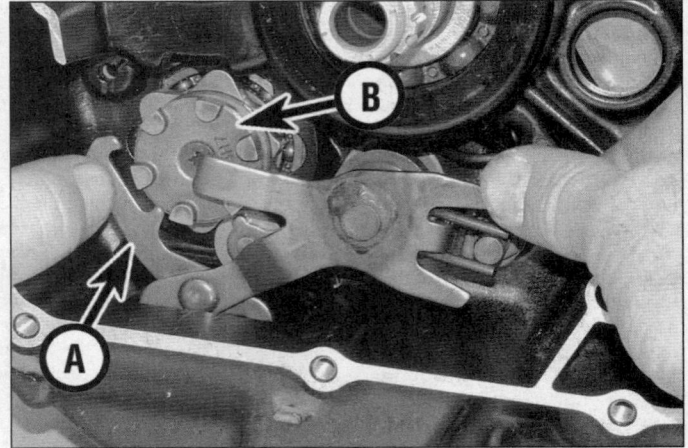

21.9b Disengage the arm (A) from the drum (B)

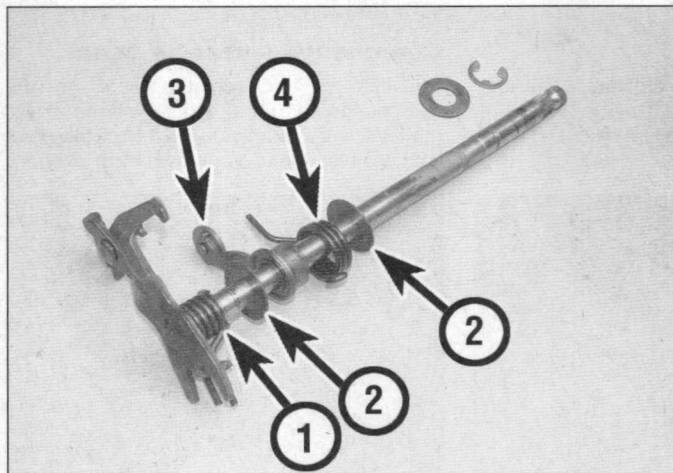

21.10 Gearchange shaft assembly

1 Centralising spring and circlip   3 Stopper arm
2 Washer   4 Stopper arm spring

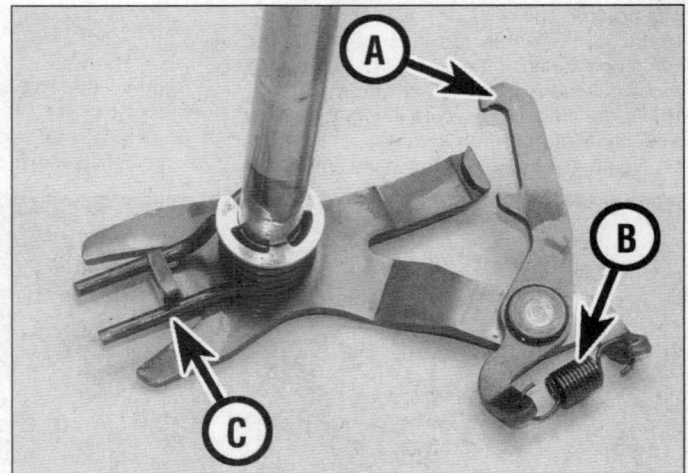

21.12a Check the selector arm (A) and spring (B); note the centralising spring (C)

21.12b Check the pins and cam lobes on the selector drum

21.13 Location of the centralising spring pin

21.14 Note the needle bearing (arrowed) in the stopper arm

shaft; if they are worn or damaged, or if the shaft is bent, renew the shaft.

12 Check the selector arm for distortion and wear of its pawls, check for any corresponding wear on the selector pins on the selector drum, and check the selector arm spring **(see illustrations)**. Renew any components that are worn or damaged.

13 Inspect the shaft centralising spring **(see illustration 21.12a)**. To renew the spring, first slide the washer, stopper arm spring, stopper arm and second washer off the shaft **(see illustration 21.10)**. Remove the circlip and slide off the old spring, noting which way round it fits. Install the new spring and secure it with a new circlip. After inspection, install the remaining components in the reverse order of removal. If the centralising spring pin in the casing is worn or loose, bend back its lockwasher and unscrew it **(see illustration)**. Install the pin with a new lockwasher and tighten it securely, then bend the new lockwasher against the nut to secure it.

14 Check the stopper arm roller, needle bearing and the detents in the selector cam for any wear or damage, and make sure the roller turns freely **(see illustration)**. Replace any components that are worn or damaged with new ones. Renew the stopper arm spring if it's worn or distorted.

15 Inspect the pins on the end of the selector

cam. If they're worn or damaged, remove the centre screw and lift off the selector cam, then withdraw the pins **(see illustration 21.12b)**. See Section 27 for details of the selector drum.

16 Inspect the gearchange shaft seal in the left-hand engine case and replace it if it's worn or damaged (see *Tools and Workshop Tips* in the *Reference* section) **(see illustration)**. It's a good idea to renew the seal whenever the shaft is removed.

Installation

17 Lubricate the gearchange shaft with clean engine oil. Make sure the centralising spring ends are correctly positioned over each side of the selector arm tab **(see illustration 21.12a)**.

18 Check that the stopper arm components are assembled on the shaft in the correct order **(see illustration 21.10)**. Slide the shaft assembly into the crankcase and engage the stopper arm with the selector cam and position its spring against the post **(see illustrations 21.9b and a)**. Pull the selector arm back and engage it on the selector drum and locate the ends of the centralising spring over the pin. Ensure the gearchange shaft is pressed all the way in.

19 Install the plain washer and a new circlip on the left-hand end of the shaft **(see illustrations 21.7)**.

20 Install the remaining components in the reverse order of removal.

21 Don't forget to fill the engine with the recommended type and amount of oil (see Chapter 1).

22 Middle driven gear

Note: *Because of the complex nature of this job and the special tools and equipment required, most owners leave servicing and repair of the middle driven gear assembly to a professional. However, you can make an initial assessment of whether any work is required as follows.*

Removal

1 Remove the engine from the frame (see Section 5).

2 If not already done, remove the middle gear inner cover; discard the cover O-ring as a new one must be fitted (see Section 5, Step 17).

3 Loosen four bolts that secure the bearing housing to the engine case, then pull the housing out a short way and remove the shims between the housing and the case **(see illustrations)**. Note the number and location of the shims to aid installation.

21.16 Location of the gearchange shaft seal

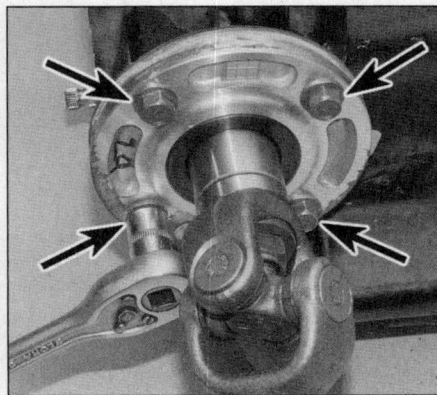

22.3a Loosen the four bolts . . .

22.3b . . . and remove the shims, noting how they fit

22.4a Pull the bearing housing out of the casing . . .

22.4b . . . and discard the O-ring

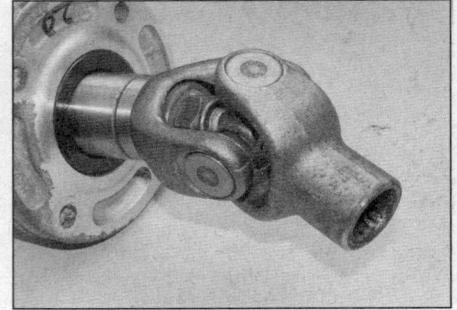

22.5 Check the bearings in the universal joint for wear or damage

4 Remove the bolts and pull the bearing housing out of the case, then remove the O-ring from the housing and discard it as a new one must be used **(see illustrations)**.

Inspection

5 Check the final drive coupling universal joint for looseness or stiff movement **(see illustration)**. If the coupling is worn or damaged, follow the procedure in Chapter 2B, Section 21, to renew the coupling.
6 Check for play between the middle gear shaft and the bearing in the housing **(see illustration)**.
7 Inspect the shaft splines and the teeth of the middle driven gear for wear or damage. If the gear is worn, check the teeth of the middle drive gear also (see Section 28).
8 Check the damper spring for looseness or obvious damage such as breakage.
9 If any of the above conditions exist, have the middle driven gear assembly stripped and repaired by a Yamaha dealer or other qualified motorcycle repair shop **(see illustration)**. It is important that they should also install the assembly in the case and adjust the gear backlash.
10 Check the condition of the middle driven gear bearing in the crankcase **(see illustration)** and renew it if necessary (see *Tools and Workshop Tips* in the *Reference* section).

Installation

11 If the middle driven gear assembly is

good, installation is the reverse of removal, noting the following:
● Install new O-rings on the bearing housing and inner cover and lubricate them with lithium soap grease.
● Lubricate the middle driven gear with clean engine oil.
● Install the bearing housing shims in their original positions and the right way round.
● Tighten the bearing housing bolts to the torque specified at the beginning of this Chapter.
Note: *If the middle driven gear assembly is repaired it must be installed by a Yamaha dealer who will re-shim the bearing housing to engine case clearance.*

23 Crankcase

1 To examine and repair or renew the crankshaft, connecting rods, bearings, or transmission components, the crankcase must be split into two parts.

Separation

2 Remove the engine from the frame (see Section 5).
3 Before the crankcases can be separated the following components must be removed:
Cylinder heads (see Section 8)
Cam chains (see Section 12)
Cylinders (see Section 13)

Pistons (see Section 14)
Alternator rotor and gears (see Section 16)
Clutch and primary gears (see Section 18)
Oil pump (see Section 19)
Oil strainer (see Section 20)
Gearchange mechanism (see Section 21)
Middle driven gear (see Section 22)
4 If not already done, wrap clean rag around the connecting rods to prevent them striking the crankcase.
5 Loosen the crankcase bolts a ¼ turn at a time in the **reverse** of the tightening sequence (start with the highest-numbered bolt and work to the lowest) and remove them **(see illustration 23.20a and b)**.

> **HAYNES HiNT** *Make a cardboard template of the crankcase and punch a hole for each bolt location. Number the holes to match the numbers cast in the crankcase. As each bolt is removed, store it in its relative position in the template. This will ensure all bolts are installed correctly on reassembly – this is important, as many bolts differ slightly in length.*

6 Position the selector cam so that the cam lobes align with the cut-outs in the crankcase, then carefully lift the right-hand crankcase half

22.6 Check for play between the shaft and the bearing housing (arrowed)

22.9 Check the components of the middle driven gear as described

22.10 Check the condition of the bearing (arrowed) in the crankcase

23.6a Position the selector cam as described . . .

23.6b . . . then carefully lift off the right-hand crankcase half

off the left-hand half **(see illustrations)**. As you lift, pry gently and evenly at the pry points around the crankcase seam. Using a soft-faced mallet, tap alternately on the transmission and crankshafts and the upper rear crankcase mounting lugs. If the halves won't separate easily, make sure all fasteners have been removed. Don't attempt to lever the crankcase halves apart – you will damage the sealing surface.

7 Note the location of the crankcase dowels and remove them for safekeeping if they are loose **(see illustration)**. Discard the O-ring on the dowel inside the cases as a new one must be fitted **(see illustration)**.

8 Refer to Sections 25 to 28 for the removal and installation of the components housed within the crankcase.

Inspection

9 After the crankshaft and transmission components have been removed, the crankcases should be cleaned thoroughly with suitable solvent and dried with compressed air. All oil passages should be blown out with compressed air.

10 Check the cases for any damage. Small cracks or holes in aluminium castings can be repaired with an epoxy resin adhesive as a temporary measure. Permanent repairs can only be effected by argon-arc welding, and only a specialist in this process is in a position

to advise on the economy or practical aspect of such a repair. If any damage is found that can't be repaired, renew the crankcase halves as a set.

11 Damaged threads can be economically reclaimed by using a diamond section wire thread insert. These are easily fitted after drilling and re-tapping the affected thread.

12 Sheared studs or bolts can usually be removed with stud extractors; if you are in any doubt consult your Yamaha dealer or specialist motorcycle engineer.

> **HAYNES HINT** Refer to Tools and Workshop Tips in the Reference section for details of installing a thread insert and using stud extractors.

Reassembly

13 Remove all traces of sealant from the crankcase mating surfaces with a suitable solvent. If a scraper must be used, take care not to gouge the soft aluminium.

14 Install the crankcase dowels and fit a new O-ring to the dowel inside the cases **(see illustration 23.7b)**. **Note:** *On the machine photographed the rear crankcase dowel was extremely corroded – if required, clean the dowels with wire wool and lubricate them with a smear of copper-based grease.*

15 Make sure the crankshaft and transmission shafts are correctly positioned in the left-hand crankcase half (see Sections 26, 27 and 28).

16 Generously lubricate the transmission gears, the selector drum and the crankshaft main bearings with fresh engine oil. Don't get any oil on the crankcase mating surfaces.

17 Apply a thin, even bead of suitable sealant (such as Yamaha Bond 1215) to the mating surface of one crankcase half **(see illustration)**. *Caution: Don't apply an excessive amount of sealant as it will ooze when the case halves are assembled and may obstruct oil passages.*

18 Align the right-hand crankcase half with the crankshaft and transmission shafts and position the selector cam so that it will pass through the cut-outs in the crankcase **(see illustration 23.6a)**. Lower the right-hand half down onto the left-hand half, ensuring the dowels align correctly. *Caution: The crankcase halves should fit together completely without being forced. If they're not correctly seated, separate them and investigate the problem. DO NOT attempt to pull them together by tightening the crankcase bolts.*

19 Clean the threads of the crankcase bolts and lubricate them with fresh engine oil, then install the bolts in their holes.

23.7a Note the location of the dowels (arrowed)

23.7b Discard the O-ring

23.17 Apply a thin bead of sealant to one half of the crankcase

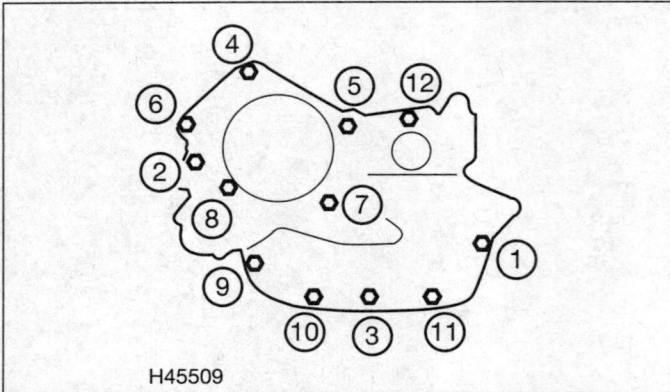

H45509

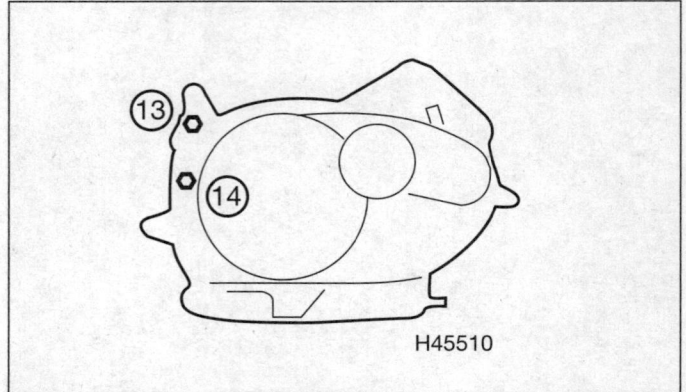

H45510

23.20a Crankcase bolt TIGHTENING sequence – left-hand side

23.20b Crankcase bolt TIGHTENING sequence – right-hand side

20 Tighten the bolts evenly and a little at a time in numerical order shown, starting with the lowest-numbered bolt and working to the highest (see illustrations). Tighten all bolts to the torque listed in this Chapter's Specifications. Note: *There are different torque settings for the 8 mm bolts and the 6 mm bolts.*

21 With all the crankcase bolts tightened, check that the crankshaft and transmission shafts turn smoothly and freely. Support the connecting rods to prevent them striking the crankcase. Rotate the selector cam to ensure the gear selection is operating correctly. If there are any signs of undue stiffness or rough spots, or any other problems, the fault must be rectified before proceeding further.

22 Install the remaining assemblies in the reverse order of removal.

23 Don't forget to fill the engine with the recommended type and amount of oil (see Chapter 1).

24 Main and connecting rod bearings – general information

1 Even though main and connecting rod bearings are generally replaced with new ones during the engine overhaul, the old bearings should be retained for close examination as they may reveal valuable information about the condition of the engine.

2 Bearing failure occurs mainly because of lack of lubrication, the presence of dirt or other foreign particles, overloading the engine and/or corrosion. Regardless of the cause of bearing failure, it must be corrected before the engine is reassembled to prevent it from happening again.

3 When examining the bearings, match them with their corresponding journal on the crankshaft to help identify the cause of any problem. Note that the main bearings are pressed into the crankcase halves and should only be disturbed if new ones are to be fitted.

4 Dirt and other foreign particles get into the engine in a variety of ways. They may be left in the engine during assembly or they may pass

through filters or breathers, then get into the oil and from there into the bearings. Metal chips from machining operations and normal engine wear are often present. Abrasives are sometimes left in engine components after reconditioning operations, especially when parts are not thoroughly cleaned using the proper cleaning methods. Whatever the source, foreign objects often end up imbedded in the soft bearing material and are easily recognized. Large particles will not imbed in the bearing and will score or gouge the bearing and journal. The best prevention for this type of bearing failure is to clean all parts thoroughly and keep everything spotlessly clean during engine assembly. Regular oil and filter changes are also essential.

5 Lack of lubrication or lubrication breakdown has a number of interrelated causes. Excessive heat (which thins the oil), overloading (which squeezes the oil from the bearing face) and oil leakage or throw off (from excessive bearing clearances, worn oil pump or high engine speeds) all contribute to a breakdown of the protective lubricating film. Blocked oil passages will starve a bearing of lubrication and destroy it. When lack of lubrication is the cause of bearing failure, the bearing material is wiped or extruded from the steel backing of the bearing. Temperatures may increase to the point where the steel backing and the journal turn blue from overheating.

HAYNES HINT *Refer to Tools and Workshop Tips (Section 5) in the Reference section for bearing fault finding.*

6 Riding habits can have a definite effect on bearing life. Full throttle, low speed operation, or lugging the engine, puts very high loads on bearings, which tend to squeeze out the oil film. These loads cause the bearings to flex, which produces fine cracks in the bearing face (fatigue failure). Eventually the bearing material will loosen in pieces and tear away from the steel backing. Short trip riding leads to corrosion of bearings, as

insufficient engine heat is produced to drive off the condensed water and corrosive gases produced. These products collect in the engine oil, forming acid and sludge. As the oil is carried to the engine bearings, the acid attacks and corrodes the bearing material.

7 Incorrect bearing installation during engine assembly will lead to bearing failure as well. Tight fitting bearings which leave insufficient bearing oil clearances result in oil starvation. Dirt or foreign particles trapped behind a bearing insert result in high spots on the bearing which lead to failure.

8 To avoid bearing problems, clean all parts thoroughly before reassembly, double check all bearing clearance measurements and lubricate the new bearings with clean engine oil during installation.

25 Connecting rods and bearings

Removal

1 Separate the crankcase halves (see Section 23).

2 Lift out the crankshaft together with the connecting rods (see illustration).

3 Before removing the connecting rods, push them to one side on the crankshaft and measure the clearance between the crankshaft and the connecting rod big-end

25.2 Lift out the crankshaft assembly

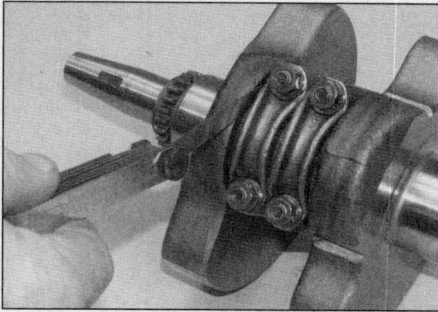

25.3 Measuring the connecting rod side clearance

25.4a Mark the position of the connecting rods and caps

25.4b Big-ends are marked for alignment and bearing size code

with a feeler gauge **(see illustration)**. Compare the result with the specification at the beginning of this Chapter; if the clearance is greater than the service limit, examine the sides of the rod big-ends when they have been removed from the crankshaft and renew any component that shows signs of wear or abrasion.

4 Using paint or a marker pen, mark the position of each connecting rod and cap relative to its position on the crankshaft **(see illustration)**. Note that the letter already written on the rod and cap is for alignment on reassembly and the number is the big-end bearing size code **(see illustration)**. Note the position of the 'Y' mark on the connecting rods to aid reassembly – on the machine photographed, the 'Y' mark on each rod faced towards the outside of the crankcase **(see illustration)**.

5 Unscrew the connecting rod cap nuts and remove the bolts if they are loose, then separate the caps, complete with the lower bearing shells, from the crankshaft **(see illustrations)**. If the cap appears stuck, tap it on one end with a soft-faced hammer while pulling it.

6 Detach the connecting rods, complete with the upper bearing shells, from the crankshaft.

7 Press the bearing shells sideways to separate them from the rods and caps and keep the rods, caps and shells in order so they can be reinstalled in their original locations **(see illustration)**. It is not necessary to remove the bolts from the rods unless they are damaged and new ones need to be fitted – note the alignment of each bolt head with the recess in the rod.

8 Wash the parts in suitable solvent and dry them with compressed air, if available.

Inspection

9 Check the connecting rods for cracks and other obvious damage.

10 To check the rod small-end, lubricate the appropriate piston pin with clean engine oil, then insert it in the rod and check for freeplay **(see illustration)**. If freeplay is excessive, measure the pin external diameter and compare the result with the specifications at the beginning of this Chapter **(see illustration)**. If the pin is worn beyond its service limit, renew it, otherwise a new connecting rod will have to be fitted.

11 Refer to Section 24 and examine the connecting rod bearing shells. If they are scored, badly scuffed or appear to have been seized, new shells must be installed. Always renew the shells in the connecting rods as a set. If they are badly damaged, check the

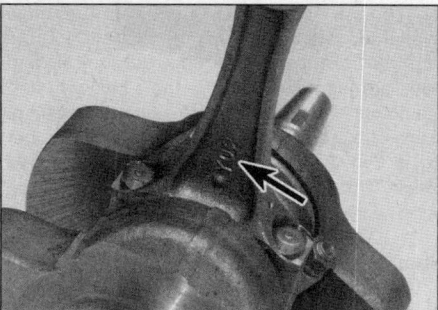

25.4c Note the 'Y' mark to ensure correct reassembly

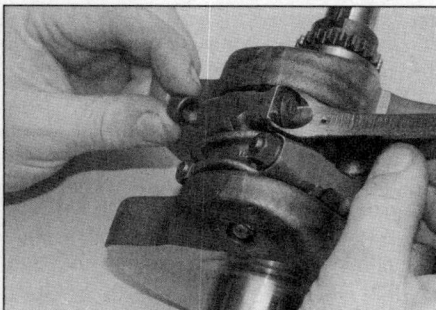

25.5a Remove the cap nuts . . .

25.5b . . . and pull off the caps

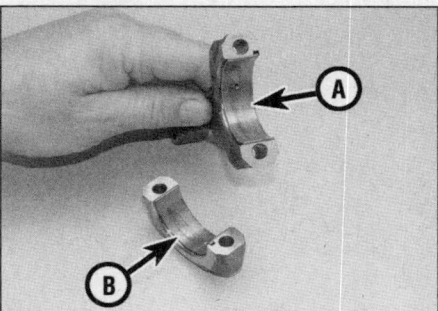

25.7 Press the shells sideways to remove them from the rod (A) and cap (B)

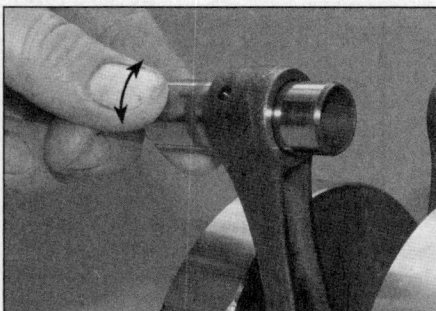

25.10a Check for freeplay between the piston pin and the connecting rod small-end

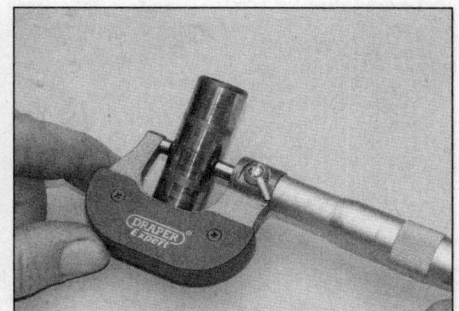

25.10b Measure the piston pin diameter where it fits in the rod

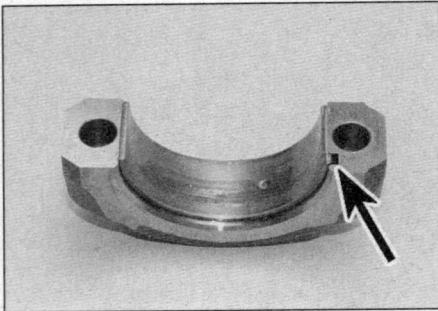

25.15 **Tab on the shell should locate in the notch (arrowed)**

25.16 **Place a strip of Plastigauge on the bearing journal**

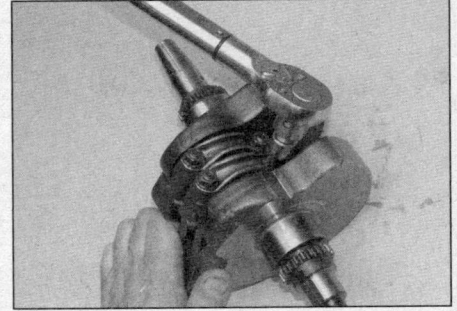

25.18 **Tighten the cap nuts as described to the specified torque setting**

corresponding crankshaft journal. Evidence of extreme heat, such as bluing, indicates that lubrication failure has occurred. Refer to Section 19 and thoroughly check the oil pump and pressure relief valve, as well as all oil holes and passages, before reassembling the engine.

12 If you are in doubt about their straightness, have the rods checked for twist and bending by a Yamaha dealer or specialist engineer.

Oil clearance check

13 Whether new bearing shells are being fitted or the original ones are being re-used, the connecting rod big-end bearing oil clearance should be checked prior to reassembly. Bearing oil clearance is measured with a product known as Plastigauge.

14 If not already done, remove the bearing shells from the rods and caps, keeping them in order (see Step 7). Clean the backs of the shells, the bearing locations in both the connecting rods and caps, and the crankshaft journal with a suitable solvent.

15 Press the shells into their locations, ensuring that the tab on each shell engages the notch in the connecting rod or cap (**see illustration**). Make sure the shells are fitted in the correct locations and take care not to touch the bearing surfaces with your fingers.

16 Cut an appropriate size length of Plastigauge (it should be slightly shorter than the width of the crankshaft journal) and place it on the journal (**see illustration**). Do not

place Plastigauge over the oil holes in the journal.

17 Apply molybdenum disulphide grease to the bolt shanks and threads and to the seats of the nuts. Fit the connecting rods and caps onto the crankshaft (**see illustration 25.5b**). Make sure the caps are fitted the correct way around so the previously made markings align (see Step 4), and that the 'Y' marks on the rods are facing the correct way round. Fit the nuts and tighten them finger-tight. **Note:** *It is essential that, throughout this procedure, the connecting rods do not rotate on the crankshaft.*

18 Tighten the cap nuts to the torque setting specified at the beginning of this Chapter (**see illustration**). Yamaha emphasise that each nut should be tightened in one continuous movement to the final torque setting, and that if tightening is paused between 30 and 36 Nm the nut should be loosened to below 30 Nm and the procedure repeated.

19 Unscrew the nuts and remove the connecting rods and caps from the crankshaft, being very careful not to disturb the Plastigauge.

20 Compare the width of the crushed Plastigauge on the crankshaft journal to the scale printed on the Plastigauge envelope to obtain the bearing oil clearance (**see illustration**). Compare the result to the specifications at the beginning of this Chapter. If the clearance is within the range specified and the bearings are in perfect condition, they can be reused.

21 Carefully clean away all traces of the

Plastigauge from the crankshaft and bearing shells using a fingernail or other object which will not score the bearing surfaces.

22 If the clearance is beyond the service limit, replace the bearing shells with new ones (see Steps 24 and 25) and check the oil clearance once again. Always renew all of the shells at the same time.

23 If the clearance is still greater than the service limit, the crankshaft journal is worn and the crankshaft should be replaced with a new one.

Bearing shell selection

24 Replacement shells for the big-end bearings are supplied on a selected fit basis. The code number for the crankshaft journal is stamped on the outside of the crankshaft web (**see illustration**). Each connecting rod size code number is marked in ink on the flat face of the rod and cap (**see illustration 25.4b**).

25 To select the correct shells from the range available, subtract the crankshaft journal number from the connecting rod number and compare the result with the table below to find the colour coding of the replacement shells e.g. connecting rod number 4 minus journal number 2 = 2; No. 2 bearing shells are colour coded black. The colour codes are painted on the edge of the bearing shells (**see illustration**).

Number	Colour
1	blue
2	black
3	brown
4	green

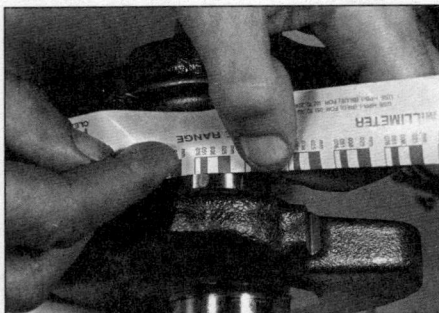

25.20 **Measure the crushed Plastigauge using the printed scale**

25.24 **Location of crankshaft journal code number**

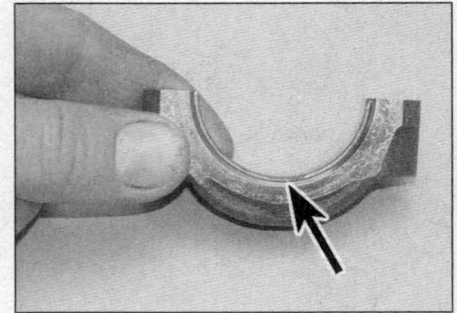

25.25 **Location of the bearing shell colour code**

Installation

26 Ensure that the crankshaft journal, the backs of the bearing shells and the bearing seats in the caps and rods are clean. If new shells are being fitted, ensure that all traces of protective grease are removed using paraffin (kerosene). Dry the shells, caps, rods and journal with a clean, lint-free cloth. Install the shells, making sure the tab on each shell engages the notch in the cap or rod **(see illustration 25.15)**.

27 Ensure the bearings are fitted in their correct locations and take care not to touch any bearing surface with your fingers. Lubricate the shells with clean engine oil.

28 Follow the procedure in Step 17 and assemble the connecting rods on the crankshaft, then follow the procedure in Step 18 and tighten the cap nuts to the specified torque setting.

29 Check that the rods rotate smoothly and freely on the crankshaft. If either of them feels tight, tap on the bottom of the cap with a soft-faced hammer – this should free it up. If not, detach the rods and recheck the assembly.

30 Follow the procedure in Section 26 and install the crankshaft assembly in the crankcase.

26 Crankshaft and main bearings

Removal

1 Separate the crankcase halves (see Section 23).

2 Lift out the crankshaft together with the connecting rods, then follow the procedure in Section 25 and remove the connecting rods from the crankshaft.

3 Clean the crankshaft with a suitable solvent, paying particular attention to flush out the oil passages. If available, blow the crank dry with compressed air and also blow through the oil passages.

Inspection

4 Check the cam chain sprockets on the

26.4 Inspect the cam chain sprockets for wear and damage

26.5 Use V-blocks or a holding fixture together with a dial gauge to check the crankshaft runout

26.6 Examine the surface of the main bearing journals . . .

crankshaft for chipped teeth and excessive wear **(see illustration)**. If any damage is found, replace the crankshaft with a new one and check the condition of the chains and camshaft sprockets (see Section 12).

5 Place the crankshaft on V-blocks and check the runout with a dial gauge **(see illustration)**. Compare the result with this Chapter's Specifications. If the runout exceeds the limit, renew the crankshaft.

6 Refer to Section 24 and examine the main bearing journals **(see illustration)**. Evidence of extreme heat, such as bluing, indicates that lubrication failure has occurred. Refer to Section 19 and thoroughly check the oil pump and pressure relief valve, as well as all oil holes and passages, before reassembling the engine. If the journals are scored, badly scuffed or pitted, renew the crankshaft.

7 Measure the outside diameter of the main bearing journals and compare the results with the specifications at the beginning of this Chapter **(see illustration)**. Measure each journal in two places to ensure the crank has not worn unevenly. If either journal has worn beyond the service limit, or is worn unevenly, a new crankshaft will have to be fitted.

8 Examine the main bearings in the crankcases for uneven wear, scoring and pits **(see illustration)**. If the bearings are damaged, new ones will have to be fitted. If the bearings appear to be in good condition, calculate the journal-to-bearing oil clearance as follows. First measure the inside diameter of each bearing and note the results. Measure

the bearings in two places to ensure they have not worn unevenly – if they have, renew them. Next, subtract the outside diameter of the appropriate crankshaft journal (see Step 7) from the inside diameter of the matching bearing and compare the result with the specification at the beginning of this Chapter. If either clearance is greater than the service limit, both bearings will have to be renewed. You will need telescoping gauges and a micrometer to measure the bearing **(see illustration)**.

Note: *Because removal and installation of the main bearings requires special tools and equipment the task should be left to a Yamaha dealer or automotive engineer. However, the following points are included for your information.*

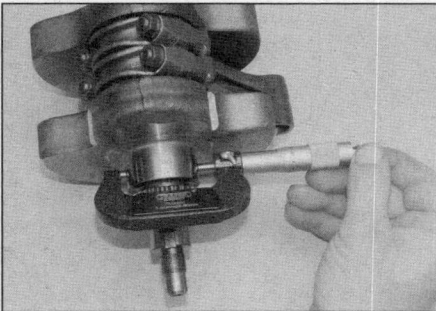

26.7 . . . then measure the journals with a micrometer

26.8a Examine the surface of the main bearings . . .

26.8b . . . then measure the bearings as described

26.9 Bearing tab (arrowed)

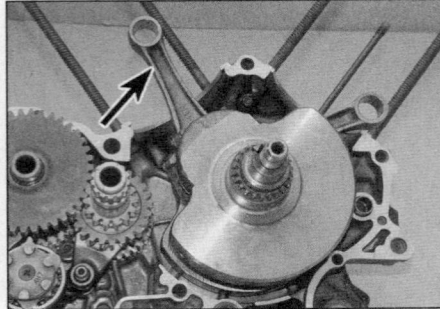

26.14 Left-hand connecting rod aligns with mouth of rear cylinder

27 Selector drum and forks

Main bearing selection

9 Note the tab on the side of the bearing (see illustration) and press the bearing out from the opposite side of the crankcase.
10 Measure the inside diameter of the bearing seats in the crankcase halves and compare the result with the specification at the beginning of this Chapter. If either measurement is greater than the service limit, replace the crankcases as a set. New crankcases are supplied with bearings fitted. If the bearing seats are within the specification, refer to the table below and select the appropriate colour coded main bearing.

Diameter of the bearing seat	Colour
49.000 to 49.010 mm	blue
49.011 to 49.020 mm	green

11 When the new bearings are installed, ensure the tab on the side of the bearing is aligned with the slot on the edge of the bearing seat.

Installation

12 Follow the procedure in Section 25 and install the connecting rods on the crankshaft.
13 Lubricate the main bearings with clean engine oil.
14 Carefully lower the crankshaft assembly into the left-hand crankcase half. Ensure the left-hand connecting rod is aligned with the mouth of the rear cylinder in the crankcase (see illustration).
15 Follow the procedure in Section 23 and assemble the crankcase halves.

Removal

1 Separate the crankcase halves (see Section 23).
2 Note how the input shaft selector fork locates in the groove on the 3rd gear pinion and how the guide pin on the fork locates in the selector drum (see illustration). The input shaft fork is lettered 'C' for identification – if the letter is not visible, mark the fork before removing it. Support the fork and pull out the fork shaft, then remove the fork and slide it back onto the shaft (see illustrations).
3 Note how the output shaft selector forks locate in the grooves on the 4th and 5th gear pinions and how the guide pins on the forks locate in the grooves in the selector drum (see illustration). The forks are lettered for identification – the right-hand fork has an 'R' and the left-hand fork has an 'L'. If the letters are not visible, mark the forks before removing them.
4 Support the output shaft selector forks and pull the fork shaft from the crankcase (see illustration). Lift out the right-hand fork and slide it back onto the shaft the right way round (see illustration). Note that the output fork shaft is longer than the input fork shaft.

27.2a Note the location of the input shaft selector fork (arrowed)

27.2b Pull out the fork shaft . . .

27.2c . . . and lift out the fork – note the letter 'C' (arrowed)

27.3 Note the location of the output shaft selector forks (arrowed)

27.4a Pull out the fork shaft . . .

27.4b . . . and lift out the right-hand fork – note the letter 'R' (arrowed)

27.5 Lift out the selector drum

27.6 Lift out the left-hand fork – note the letter 'L' (arrowed)

27.7 Check the selector forks for wear and damage

5 Note the position of the selector drum, then lift it out of the case **(see illustration)**.

6 Lift out the left-hand fork and slide it back onto the shaft the right way round **(see illustration)**.

Inspection

7 Inspect the selector forks for any signs of wear or damage, especially around the fork ends where they engage with the grooves in the pinions **(see illustration)**. Check that each fork fits correctly in its pinion groove. Check closely to see if the forks are bent. If the forks are in any way damaged they must be replaced with new ones.

8 Check that the forks fit correctly on their shaft. They should move freely with a light fit but no appreciable freeplay. Check that the fork shaft holes in the casing are not worn or damaged.

9 Check the selector fork shaft is straight using V-blocks and a dial gauge or by rolling it along a flat surface. A bent shaft will cause difficulty in selecting gears and make the gearchange action heavy and should be replaced with a new one.

10 Inspect the selector drum grooves and selector fork guide pins for signs of wear or damage **(see illustrations)**. If either show signs of wear or damage they must be replaced with new ones.

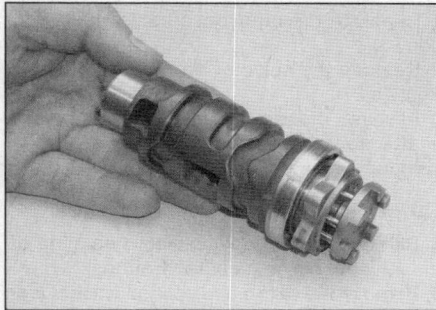

27.10a Check the grooves in the selector drum . . .

11 Check the selector drum bearing referring to *Tools and Workshop Tips* (Section 5) in the *Reference* section. If the bearing is worn, remove the screw securing the selector cam and lift off the cam, noting the location of the dowel, then draw the bearing off **(see illustration)**. Install the new bearing, then align the dowel and install the cam and tighten the screw securely.

12 Check the operation of the spring-loaded neutral switch plunger **(see illustration)**. If the plunger is damaged, remove the screw securing the retaining plate and lift out the plunger and spring. Renew the damaged components as necessary.

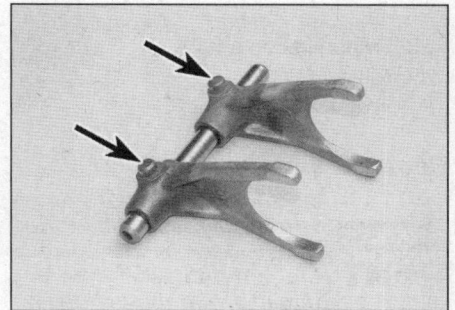

27.10b . . . and the guide pins (arrowed) on the forks

Installation

13 Installation is the reverse of removal, noting the following:

● Lubricate all components with clean engine oil before installing them.
● Use the letters on the selector forks to position them correctly (see Steps 2 and 3). The letters face the right-hand side of the engine when installed.
● Ensure the selector fork guide pins are located in their grooves in the selector drum before installing the fork shafts.
● Ensure the selector drum is in the neutral position.

27.11 Remove the cam (B) then pull off the bearing (A)

27.12 Check the operation of the neutral switch plunger (arrowed)

28.4a Remove the 1st gear pinion . . .

28.4b . . . and the 4th gear pinion

28.5a Remove the circlip . . .

28 Transmission shafts

Removal and disassembly

HAYNES HiNT *When disassembling the transmission shafts, place the parts on a long rod or thread a wire through them to keep them in order and facing the proper direction.*

1 Separate the crankcase halves (see Section 23).
2 Remove the selector drum and forks (see Section 27).
3 Always disassemble the transmission shafts separately to avoid mixing up the components.

Output shaft and middle drive gear

4 Remove the 1st gear pinion then slide off the 4th gear pinion **(see illustrations)**.
5 Remove the circlip and splined washer **(see illustrations)**. Discard the circlip as a new one must be fitted.
6 Slide the 3rd gear pinion up off the output

shaft and lift out the input shaft assembly with it **(see illustration)**.
7 Remove the 5th gear pinion **(see illustration)**.
8 Remove the circlip and splined washer **(see illustrations)**. Discard the circlip as a new one must be fitted.
9 Remove the 2nd gear pinion **(see illustration)**.
10 The output shaft and middle drive gear pinion can be left in the crankcase unless they or their bearing need to be renewed. If any of these parts are worn or damaged, first bend back the staked portion of the middle drive gear locknut, then secure the output shaft in a

28.5b . . . and splined washer

28.6 Remove the 3rd gear pinion (A) and input shaft assembly (B)

28.7 Remove the 5th gear pinion

28.8a Remove the circlip . . .

28.8b . . . and splined washer

28.9 Remove the 2nd gear pinion

28.10a Hold the output shaft (arrowed) in a soft-jawed vice . . .

28.10b . . . and undo the locknut (arrowed)

28.11 Bearing retainers are secured by four Torx screws – screw (A) is shorter than the others

soft-jawed vice and undo the locknut (see illustrations). Remove the drive gear pinion and pull the output shaft out of the bearing. Discard the locknut as a new one must be used.

11 To remove the bearing, undo its four retainer screws with a No. 30 Torx bit and remove the two retainers (see illustration). Discard the screws as new ones must be used.

Caution: The screws are staked or thread-locked in place. Don't use anything other than the correct bit to loosen them or they'll be rounded out. Note that one of the screws is shorter than the other three (see illustration 28.11). Be sure to reinstall the short screw in the correct location or the clutch release mechanism will be obstructed.

12 Press the bearing out of its seat, then remove the shims. Store the shims carefully so the correct number can be reinstalled.

13 If required, undo the set screw that secures the clutch release mechanism shaft and remove the screw and sealing washer (see illustration). Pull the shaft out of the casing, noting how the return spring locates, and remove the washer (see illustration). Examine the shaft for wear and renew it if necessary.

14 If the shaft seal has been leaking, lever it out carefully with a flat-bladed screwdriver and discard it. Examine the shaft bearing for wear and pitting on the rollers and renew it if necessary (see *Tools and Workshop Tips* in

28.13a Screw (arrowed) secures the clutch release mechanism shaft

the *Reference* section). Lubricate the new seal with grease and press it into place with a suitably sized socket.

Input shaft

Note: *Disassembly and reassembly of the input shaft requires an hydraulic press.*

15 Before disassembly, measure the length of the gearset on the input shaft (see illustration). The length is determined by how far the gears are pressed onto the shaft. Compare it to the manufacturer's specification of 103.0 to 103.2 mm.

16 Place the input shaft in a press with a bearing splitter behind the 2nd gear pinion (see illustration). Press the shaft out of the gear pinion. Once the pinion is loose, take it off the shaft.

17 Slide the 5th gear pinion off the shaft, then

28.13b Note the location of the shaft return spring (arrowed)

slide off the 3rd gear pinion (see illustration).
18 Remove the circlip and splined washer, then slide off the 4th gear pinion.

Inspection

19 Wash all the components in suitable solvent and dry them off.
20 Check the gear teeth for cracking, chipping, pitting and other obvious wear or damage. Any pinion that is damaged must be renewed.
21 Inspect the dogs and the dog holes in the gears for cracks, chips, and excessive wear especially in the form of rounded edges. Make sure mating gears engage properly. Renew mating gears as a set if necessary.
22 Check for signs of scoring or blueing on the pinions and shafts. This could be caused by overheating due to inadequate lubrication.

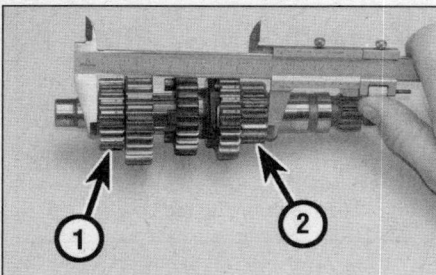
28.15 Measure the length of the input shaft gearset
1 *2nd gear pinion*
2 *Integral 1st gear pinion*

28.16 Press the input shaft out of the 2nd gear pinion

28.17 Slide off the 5th gear pinion (A) and the 3rd gear pinion (B); note the 4th gear pinion (C)

Check that all the oil holes and passages are clear. Replace any worn or damaged parts with new ones.

23 Check that each pinion moves freely on the shaft without undue freeplay.

24 The shafts are unlikely to sustain damage unless the engine has seized, placing an unusually high loading on the transmission, or after the machine has covered a very high mileage. Check the surface of each shaft, especially where a pinion turns on it, and replace the shaft with a new one if it has scored or picked up, or if there are any cracks. Check the shaft runout using V-blocks and a dial gauge and replace the shaft with a new one if the runout exceeds the limit specified at the beginning of this Chapter.

25 Check the splined washers and renew any that are bent or worn.

26 Check the bearings referring to *Tools and Workshop Tips* (Section 5) in the *Reference* section.

Assembly and installation

Note: *During assembly and installation, lubricate the bearings with clean engine oil and the transmission shafts and pinions with molybdenum disulphide oil (a 50/50 mix of engine oil and molybdenum grease).*

27 If removed, slide the return spring and washer onto the clutch release mechanism shaft. Lubricate the shaft seal with clean engine oil, then install the shaft ensuring it is the correct way round. Locate the spring over the clutch arm **(see illustration 28.13b).** Fit a new sealing washer onto the set screw and install the screw tightening it securely **(see illustration 28.13a).**

28 If the middle gear pinion, output shaft or shaft bearing were removed, reverse the removal steps to install them. Ensure the shims are installed in the seat before the bearing. Apply a suitable non-permanent thread-locking compound to the bearing retainer Torx screws and tighten them to the torque setting specified at the beginning of this Chapter. Ensure the short Torx screw goes in the correct hole **(see illustration 28.11).** Install a new middle drive gear locknut, tighten it to the specified torque and stake it **(see illustration).**

29 Reverse Steps 17 and 18 to assemble the input shaft, then carefully press the 2nd gear pinion onto the shaft until the gearset is the specified length **(see illustration 28.15).**

30 Install the 2nd gear pinion and splined washer on the output shaft and secure them with a new circlip **(see illustrations 28.9, 28.8b and a).**

31 Slide the 5th gear pinion onto the output shaft **(see illustration 28.7).**

32 Hold the 3rd gear pinion and input shaft assembly together, then slide the pinion onto

28.28 Don't forget to stake the middle drive gear locknut

the output shaft while lowering the input shaft into position in the case **(see illustration 28.6).**

33 Reverse Steps 4 and 5 using a new circlip to secure the 3rd gear pinion and splined washer. Check that the assembled gears turn smoothly without binding **(see illustration).**

34 Install the selector drum and forks (see Section 27).

29 Initial start-up after overhaul

1 Make sure the engine oil level is correct (see *Daily (pre-ride) checks*).

2 Make sure there is fuel in the tank, then turn the fuel tap to the ON position and operate the choke.

3 Start the engine and allow it to run at a moderately fast idle until it reaches operating temperature.

4 Ensure that the engine warning light is not illuminated.

5 Check carefully that there are no oil leaks and make sure the transmission and controls, especially the brakes, function properly before road testing the machine. Refer to Section 30 for the recommended running-in procedure.

6 Upon completion of the road test, and after the engine has cooled down completely, recheck the valve clearances (see Chapter 1).

28.33 Check that the gears turn smoothly

30 Recommended running-in procedure

1 Treat the machine gently for the first few miles to allow the oil to circulate throughout the engine and any new parts installed to seat.

2 Great care is necessary if the engine has been extensively overhauled – the bike will have to be run in as when new. This means more use of the transmission and a restraining hand on the throttle until at least 600 miles (1000 km) have been covered. There is no point in keeping to any set road speed – the main idea is to keep from labouring the engine and to gradually increase performance up to the 1000 mile (1600 km) mark. These recommendations apply less when only a partial overhaul has been done, though it does depend to an extent on the nature of the work carried out and which components have been renewed. Experience is the best guide, since it is easy to tell when an engine is running freely. If in any doubt, consult a Yamaha dealer. The following maximum engine speed limitations, which Yamaha provide for new motorcycles, can be used as a guide.

3 If a lubrication failure is suspected, stop the engine immediately and try to find the cause. If an engine is run without oil, even for a short period of time, severe damage will occur.

Up to 600 miles (1000 km)	No more than 1/3 throttle – vary throttle position and speed.
600 to 1000 miles (1000 to 1600 km)	No more than 1/2 throttle – vary throttle position and speed
Over 1000 miles (1600 km)	Normal riding – do not exceed tachometer red line

Chapter 2 Part B
Engine, clutch and transmission – 1100 models

Contents

Degrees of difficulty

Easy, suitable for novice with little experience	Fairly easy, suitable for beginner with some experience	Fairly difficult, suitable for competent DIY mechanic	Difficult, suitable for experienced DIY mechanic	Very difficult, suitable for expert DIY or professional

Specifications

General
Bore x stroke .... 95 x 75 mm
Displacement .... 1063 cc
Compression ratio .... 8.3 to 1

Camshafts
Lobe height
  Intake (standard) .... 39.112 to 39.212 mm
  Intake (service limit) .... 39.012 mm
  Exhaust (1999 to 2000)
    Standard .... 39.145 to 39.245 mm
    Service limit .... 39.045 mm
  Exhaust (2001-on)
    Standard .... 39.112 to 39.212 mm
    Service limit .... 39.012 mm
Bush oil clearance .... 0.020 to 0.061 mm
Journal diameter .... 24.96 to 24.98 mm
Bush bore .... 25.00 to 25.021 mm

Rocker arms

Rocker inside diameter (standard)	14.000 to 14.018 mm
Shaft outside diameter (standard)	13.985 to 13.991 mm
Rocker-to-shaft clearance (service limit)	0.086 mm

Cylinder head, valves and valve springs

Cylinder head warpage limit	0.03 mm
Valve stem bend limit	0.03 mm
Valve stem diameter	
Intake (standard)	7.975 to 7.990 mm
Exhaust (standard)	7.960 to 7.975 mm
Valve guide inside diameter (intake and exhaust)	
Standard	8.000 to 8.012 mm
Valve stem-to-guide clearance (service limit)	
Intake	0.08 mm
Exhaust	0.10 mm
Valve head diameter	
Intake	47.0 to 47.2 mm
Exhaust	39.0 to 39.2 mm
Valve face width (intake and exhaust)	2.1 mm
Valve head margin thickness (intake and exhaust)	
Standard	1.1 to 1.5 mm
Service limit	0.8 mm
Valve seat width (intake and exhaust)	
Standard	1.2 to 1.4 mm
Service limit	1.8 mm
Valve spring free length (intake and exhaust)	
Standard	44.6 mm
Service limit	43.5 mm
Valve spring bend limit	1.9 mm

Cylinders

Bore diameter	
Standard	95.00 to 95.01 mm
Service limit	95.10 mm
Bore measuring point	40 mm from top of cylinder

Pistons

Piston diameter (standard)	94.960 to 94.975 mm
Diameter measuring point	5 mm from bottom of piston skirt
Piston-to-cylinder clearance	
Standard	0.025 to 0.050 mm
Service limit	0.15 mm
Piston pin diameter	21.99 to 22.0 mm
Piston pin bore in piston	22.004 to 22.015 mm
Piston pin to piston bore clearance	0.004 to 0.024 mm

Piston rings

Ring side clearance	
Top ring	
Standard	0.04 to 0.08 mm
Service limit	0.1 mm
Second ring	
Standard	0.03 to 0.07 mm
Service limit	0.1 mm
Ring end gap	
Top ring	
Standard	0.3 to 0.5 mm
Service limit	0.8 mm
Second ring	
Standard	0.3 to 0.45 mm
Service limit	0.8 mm
Oil ring	
Standard	0.2 to 0.7 mm
Service limit	Not applicable

Clutch

Friction plate thickness	
Standard	2.9 to 3.1 mm
Service limit	2.8 mm
Steel plate thickness	1.9 to 2.1 mm
Steel plate warpage limit	0.1 mm
Pushrod bend limit	0.5 mm
Diaphragm spring height	
Standard	7.2 mm
Minimum	6.5 mm

Oil pump

	Standard	Service limit
Inner to outer rotor clearance	0.03 to 0.09 mm	0.15 mm
Outer rotor to housing clearance	0.03 to 0.08 mm	0.15 mm
Rotor to straightedge clearance	0.03 to 0.08 mm	0.15 mm

Crankshaft, connecting rods and bearings

Connecting rod big-end side clearance	0.320 to 0.474 mm
Connecting rod big-end bearing oil clearance	0.044 to 0.073 mm
Crankshaft runout limit	0.02 mm

Transmission

Gear ratios	
1st gear	2.353:1 (40/17T)
2nd gear	1.667:1 (40/24T)
3rd gear	1.286:1 (36/28T)
4th gear	1.032:1 (32/31T)
5th gear	0.853:1 (29/34T)
Gearshaft runout limit	0.08 mm

Torque settings

Alternator cover bolts	10 Nm
Alternator rotor nut	175 Nm
Cam chain gear shaft retainer bolt	10 Nm
Cam chain tensioner blade bolts	10 Nm
Cam chain tensioner bolts	10 Nm
Cam chain tensioner centre bolt	8 Nm
Camshaft retainer bolts	20 Nm
Camshaft sprocket bolt	55 Nm
Camshaft sprocket cover bolts	10 Nm
Clutch adjuster locknut	12 Nm
Clutch centre nut	70 Nm *
Clutch cover bolts	10 Nm
Clutch diaphragm spring bolts	8 Nm
Connecting rod nuts	48 Nm **
Crankcase bolts (6 mm)	10 Nm
Crankcase bolts (10 mm)	39 Nm
Cylinder bolts	10 Nm
Cylinder head bolts	20 Nm
Cylinder head nuts (12 mm)	50 Nm
Cylinder head nuts (10 mm)	35 Nm
Engine front mounting bracket bolts	48 Nm
Engine mounting bolts	48 Nm
Front cylinder head mounting bracket nuts	74 Nm
Gearchange lever pinch bolt	10 Nm
Oil pipe union bolts (internal)	10 Nm ***
Oil pipe union bolts (external)	20 Nm ***
Oil pump bolts	7 Nm
Oil pump chain cover bolts	10 Nm
Oil pump sprocket bolt	12 Nm
Primary drive gear nut	110 Nm *
Rocker cover bolts	10 Nm
Rocker shaft retaining bolts	38 Nm ***
Selector fork shaft stopper plate screws	7 Nm ****
Starter clutch bolts	12 Nm

* Use a new lockwasher.
** Apply molybdenum disulfide grease to the threads and nut surfaces; follow special tightening procedure in the text.
***Use new sealing washers.
**** Apply suitable thread locking compound.

1 General information

The engine unit is an air-cooled V-twin with the transmission housed within the crankcases. The valves are operated by overhead camshafts which are chain driven via intermediate gears off the crankshaft. The engine/transmission assembly is constructed from aluminium alloy. The crankcase is divided vertically.

The crankcase incorporates a wet sump, pressure-fed lubrication system which uses a chain-driven oil pump mounted in the left-hand side of the crankcase and an oil filter mounted in the right-hand side.

Power from the crankshaft is routed to the transmission via the clutch, which is of the diaphragm spring, wet multi-plate type and is gear-driven off the crankshaft. The transmission is a five-speed, constant-mesh unit.

2 Operations possible with the engine in the frame

The components and assemblies listed below can be removed without having to remove the engine from the frame. If, however, a number of areas require attention at the same time, removal of the engine is recommended.

Starter motor
Alternator rotor
Starter clutch
Cam chain tensioners, blades and gears
Oil pump
Clutch and primary drive gear
Gearchange mechanism

3 Operations requiring engine removal

1 It is necessary to remove the engine/transmission assembly from the frame to gain access to the following components:
Cylinder heads, rocker arms and camshafts
Cylinders and pistons
Cam chains and intermediate gears
2 The crankcase halves must be separated to gain access to the following components:
Crankshaft, connecting rods and bearings
Transmission shafts
Selector drum and forks
Oil pressure relief valve
Middle driven pinion and final drive coupling

4 Major engine repair – general information

Refer to Section 4 of Chapter 2A.

5 Engine removal and installation

Caution: The engine is very heavy. Engine removal and installation should be done with the aid of an assistant to avoid damage or injury that could occur if the engine is dropped. An hydraulic floor jack should be used to support and lower the engine if possible.

Removal

1 If the engine is dirty, particularly around its mountings, wash it thoroughly before starting any major dismantling work. This will make work much easier and rule out the possibility of dirt falling inside.
2 Support the motorcycle securely in an upright position using an auxiliary stand. Work can be made easier by raising the machine to a suitable working height on an hydraulic ramp or a suitable platform. Make sure the motorcycle is secure and will not topple over (see Section 1 of *Tools and Workshop Tips* in the *Reference* section). When disconnecting any wiring, cables and hoses, it is advisable to mark or tag them as a reminder of where they connect.
3 If the engine is going to be disassembled, drain the engine oil (see Chapter 1).
4 Remove the seat, the tool box and battery covers (see Chapter 7). Disconnect the battery negative lead, then disconnect the positive lead and remove the battery (see Chapter 8).

5 Remove the carburettor assembly and, where fitted, the air induction system (see Chapter 3). Plug the intake manifolds with clean rag.
6 Remove the exhaust system (see Chapter 3).
7 Place a rag underneath the oil filter cover to catch any residual oil, then remove the cover and filter (see Chapter 1).
8 Remove the rear brake pedal and right-hand footrest assembly, then displace the rear brake master cylinder and fluid reservoir (see Chapter 6). Unclip the rear brake light switch wiring from the frame and position it clear of the engine.
9 Remove the screws securing the left and right-hand frame covers and remove the covers (see Chapter 7).
10 If required, to avoid damaging the chrome finish, remove the bolts from the clutch cover and remove the cover (see Section 19).
11 Remove the starter motor (see Chapter 8).
12 Trace the wire from the oil level sensor and disconnect it at the connector, then undo the bolts securing the cover and sensor unit in the underside of the crankcase and pull out the sensor **(see illustrations)**.
13 Remove the screws securing the cylinder head covers and remove the covers **(see illustration)**.
14 Pull off the spark plug covers, then pull the spark plug caps off the plugs **(see illustration)**.
15 On the left-hand side of the bike, unclip the wiring loom from the backing panel and

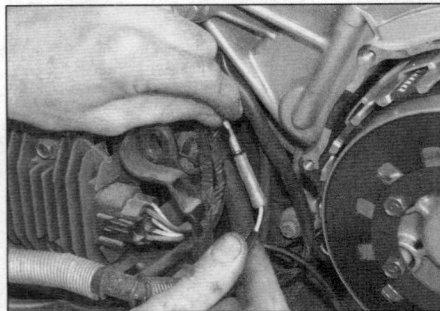
5.12a Disconnect the oil level sensor wire

5.12b Remove the sensor from the crankcase

5.13 Remove the cylinder head covers . . .

5.14 . . . and pull off the spark plug covers

5.15a Pull the wiring connectors out of the cover (arrowed)

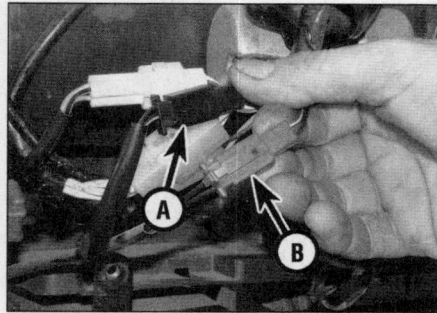

5.15b Disconnect the fuel pump (A) and sidestand switch (B) connectors . . .

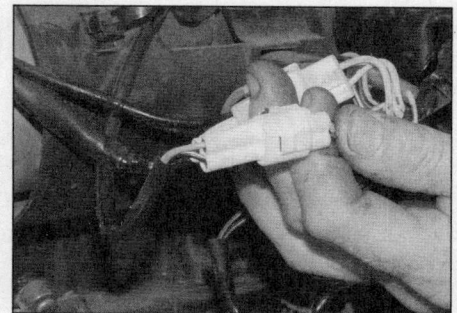

5.15c . . . the speed sensor connector . . .

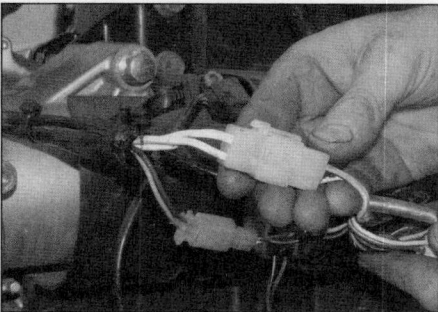

5.15d . . . the alternator connector . . .

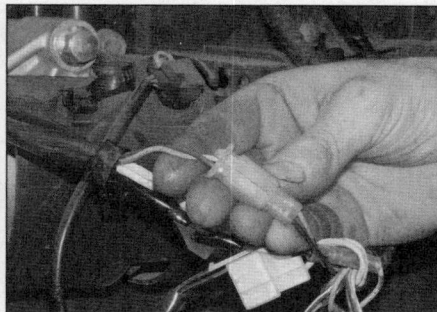

5.15e . . . the pick-up coil connector . . .

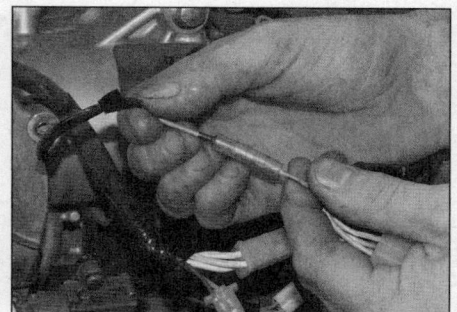

5.15f . . . and the neutral switch connector

pull the wiring connectors out of the cover **(see illustration)**. Identify and then disconnect the connectors for the fuel pump, sidestand switch, speed sensor, alternator, pick-up coil and neutral switch **(see illustrations)**. Position the wiring clear of the engine unit.

16 Disconnect the clutch cable (see Section 18).

17 Undo the bolts securing the sidestand assembly and remove it **(see illustration)**.

18 Check for a mark on the gearchange shaft that aligns with the slot in the lever. If necessary, make your own with a sharp punch, then remove the pinch bolt and pull the lever off the shaft (see Section 20).

19 Remove the left-hand footrest, gearchange pedal and linkage as an assembly (see Chapter 5).

20 Undo the screws securing the fuel hose

guide plate and remove the plate **(see illustration)**. Pull the fuel pump off the left-hand backing panel and secure it clear of the engine unit **(see illustration)**.

21 Unclip the immobiliser wiring from the backing panel **(see illustration)**.

22 Unclip the fusebox from the backing panel **(see illustration)**.

5.17 Sidestand assembly is secured by two bolts (arrowed)

5.20a Remove the fuel hose guide plate . . .

5.20b . . . and displace the fuel pump

5.21 Displace the immobiliser wiring . . .

5.22 . . . and the fusebox

5.23 Displace the fuel filter

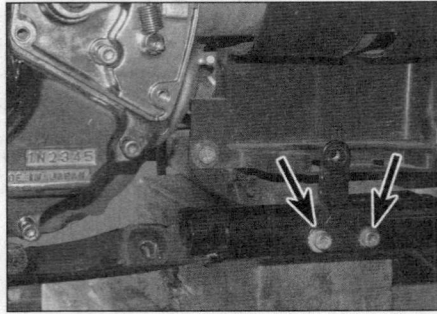

5.24a Frame cover bracket is secured by two bolts

5.24b Note the bolt (arrowed) behind the battery position

5.24c Lift off the backing panel

5.25 Remove the speed sensor (arrowed)

5.26 Pull back the driveshaft boot

5.27 Disconnect the earth (ground) wire from the back of the engine unit

5.29 Disconnect the wire from the neutral switch

23 Unclip the fuel filter from the top of the backing panel (see illustration).
24 Undo the bolts securing the bracket for the left-hand frame cover and remove the

bracket (see illustration). Undo the bolts securing the left-hand tool box and backing panel, noting that one bolt is located on the right-hand side behind the battery position

(see illustration). Lift off the backing panel (see illustration).
25 Undo the bolt securing the speed sensor and remove the sensor (see illustration).
26 Pull the rubber driveshaft boot away from the engine (see illustration).
27 Disconnect the earth (ground) wire from the back of the engine on the right-hand side (crankcase bolt No. 18) (see illustration).
28 If required, to avoid damaging the chrome finish, remove the bolts from the alternator cover and remove the cover (see Section 16). If the engine is going to be disassembled, loosen the alternator centre nut (see Section 16).
29 Loosen the neutral switch terminal screw and disconnect the wire (see illustration).
30 Remove the two bolts securing the steering head panels then pull off the fuel tank rubbers (see illustrations). The covers lock

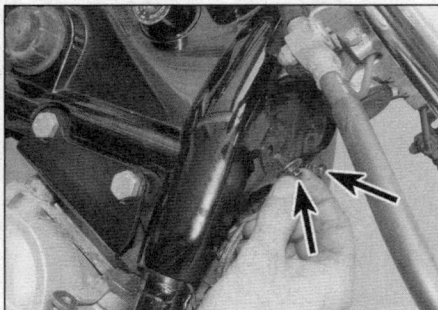

5.30a Remove the bolts (arrowed) . . .

5.30b . . . and the tank rubbers

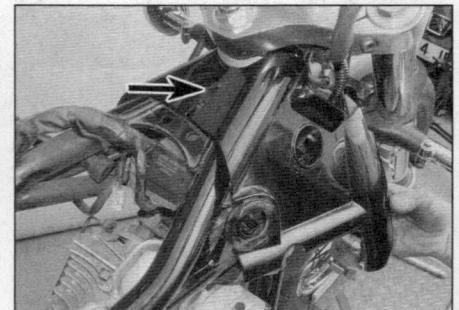

5.30c Note how the panels lock together on the top edge

5.34a Undo the long front bolt . . .

5.34b . . . and pull it out

5.34c Undo the left-hand bolt
(arrowed) . . .

together on the top edge – fold them upwards to remove them **(see illustration)**.

31 Remove the horn (see Chapter 8).

32 Check around the engine and frame to make sure all the necessary wiring, cables and hoses have been disconnected, and that any that remain connected to the engine are not retained by any clips, guides or brackets on the frame.

33 Position a jack under the engine with a block of wood between the jack head and the crankcase. Make sure the jack is centrally positioned so the engine will not topple in any direction when the last mounting bolt is removed and the engine is supported only by the jack.

34 The engine front mounting bracket is secured to the frame by three bolts. Undo the long front bolt and pull it out **(see illustrations)**. Next undo the two short bolts and remove them **(see illustrations)**. Note that the short bolts are different lengths – the longer fits on the right-hand side.

35 Undo the nuts and bolts securing the right-hand frame tube to the steering head and the bolts securing the rear of the frame tube and lift-off the tube **(see illustrations)**.

36 Undo the long bolt securing the engine front mounting bracket to the engine and lift it off **(see illustration)**.

37 Undo the bolts securing the front cylinder head mounting bracket to the frame – note that the left-hand bolts are longer **(see illustrations)**.

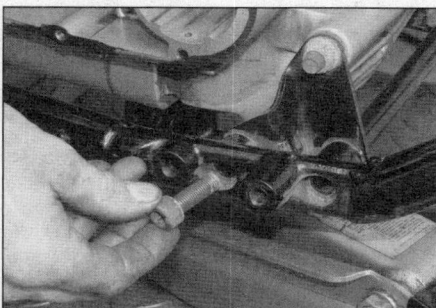

5.34d . . . and the longer right-hand bolt

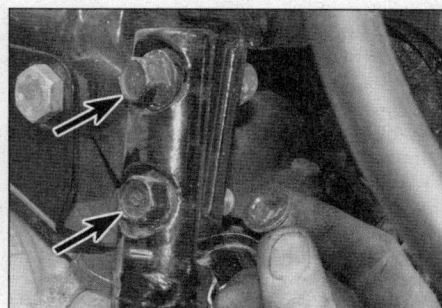

5.35a Undo the nuts and bolts at the steering head . . .

5.35b . . . and the bolts (arrowed) at the rear of the frame tube . . .

5.35c . . . and remove the frame tube

5.36 Remove the engine front mounting bracket

5.37a Remove the left-hand . . .

5.37b . . . and right-hand mounting bracket to frame bolts

5.38a Remove the left . . .

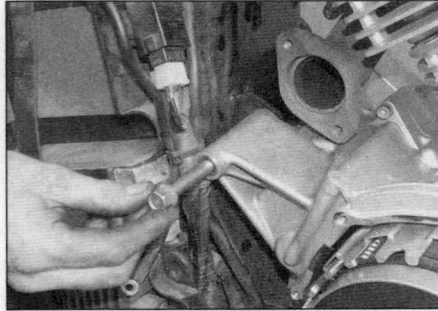

5.38b . . . and right rear upper mounting bolts

5.39a Counter-hold the nut (arrowed) . . .

38 Undo the left and right rear upper mounting bolts and remove them **(see illustrations)**.

39 Counter-hold the nut on the lower rear mounting bolt then undo the bolt and remove it **(see illustrations)**.

40 Undo the bolts securing the rear upper and lower mounting brackets to the frame and remove them **(see illustrations)**.

41 Slowly and carefully manoeuvre the engine assembly out of the frame on the right-hand side – note that the final drive coupling on the rear of the engine unit must be disengaged from the driveshaft as the engine is lifted out **(see illustrations)**.

Installation

42 Installation is the reverse of removal, noting the following:

● With the aid of an assistant, lift the engine

unit into the frame and support it on the jack and block of wood. Ensure the splines on the final drive coupling are engaged with the driveshaft. Manoeuvre the engine unit into position so that the mounting bolt holes align. Make sure no wires, cables or hoses become trapped between the engine and the frame.

● Don't tighten any of the engine mounting bolts until they have all been installed. Make sure the correct bolt is installed in its correct location.

● Tighten all the bolts in the order shown to the torque settings specified at the beginning of this Chapter.

　1 Rear lower mounting bolt (see illustration 5.39b).
　2 Rear upper mounting bolts (see illustrations 5.38a and b).
　3 Front cylinder mounting bracket-to-frame bolts (see illustrations 5.37a and b).

　4 Right-hand frame tube bolts (see illustrations 5.35a and b).
　5 Front mounting bracket bolts (see illustrations 5.34a, c and d).

● Make sure all wires, cables and hoses are correctly routed and connected, and secured by any clips or ties.

● Refill the engine with oil (see Chapter 1).

● Check the throttle and clutch cable freeplay (see Chapter 1).

● Adjust the engine idle speed (see Chapter 1).

6 Engine disassembly and reassembly –
general information

1 Before disassembling the engine, the external surfaces of the unit should be thoroughly cleaned and degreased. This will prevent contamination of the engine internals, and will also make working a lot easier and cleaner. A high flash-point solvent, such as paraffin (kerosene) can be used, or better still, a proprietary engine degreaser such as Gunk. Use old paintbrushes and toothbrushes to work the solvent into the various recesses of the engine casings. Take care to exclude solvent or water from the electrical components and from the intake and exhaust ports.

⚠ *Warning: The use of petrol (gasoline) as a cleaning agent should be avoided because of the risk of fire.*

5.39b . . . and remove the bolt on the left-hand side

5.40a Remove the rear upper (arrowed) . . .

5.40b . . . and rear lower mounting brackets

5.41a Disengage the coupling from the driveshaft . . .

5.41b . . . and manoeuvre the engine out

2 When clean and dry, arrange the unit on the workbench, leaving a suitable clear area for working. Gather a selection of small containers and plastic bags so that parts can be grouped together in an easily identifiable manner. Some paper and a pen should be on hand so that notes can be made and labels attached where necessary. A supply of clean rag is also required.

> **HAYNES HINT** *A useful engine support stand can be made from short lengths of 2 x 4 inch wood screwed together into a rectangle. The stand should be just big enough to accommodate the sump within it, so that the engine rests on its crankcase.*

3 Before commencing work, read through the appropriate section so that some idea of the necessary procedure can be gained. When removing components it should be noted that great force is seldom required, unless specified. In many cases, a component's reluctance to be removed is indicative of an incorrect approach or removal method – if in any doubt, re-check with the text.
4 When disassembling the engine, keep "mated" parts together (e.g. valve assemblies, cylinders, pistons and connecting rods, that have been in contact with each other during engine operation). These "mated" parts must be reused or renewed as assemblies.
5 Engine/transmission disassembly should be done in the following general order with reference to the appropriate Sections.

Remove the cylinder heads
Remove the camshafts
Remove the rocker arms
Remove the cylinders
Remove the pistons
Remove the alternator rotor
Remove the clutch
Remove the cam chains
Remove the oil pump
Remove the gearchange mechanism
Separate the crankcase halves

7.2a Undo the centre bolt (arrowed) . . .

Remove the crankshaft and connecting rods
Remove the selector drum and forks
Remove the transmission shafts/gears
Remove the oil pressure relief valve
6 Reassembly is accomplished by reversing the general disassembly sequence.

7 Cam chain tensioners

Note: *This procedure can be carried out with the engine in the frame.*

Removal

1 For improved access to the front cylinder tensioner, remove the air filter housing (see Chapter 3).
2 Unscrew the tensioner centre bolt and remove the bolt and sealing washer **(see illustrations)**. Discard the washer as a new one must be fitted.
3 Insert a small flat-bladed screwdriver into the tensioner and turn it clockwise to retract and lock the tensioner plunger **(see illustration)**. Remove the tensioner mounting bolts and draw it out of the cylinder, noting which way round it fits **(see illustration)**. Discard the sealing washer as a new one must be fitted. Note the position of the air filter housing bracket on the front cylinder tensioner body.

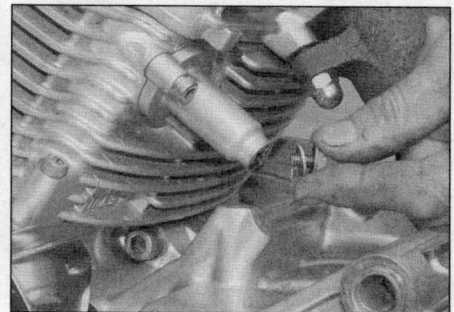

7.2b . . . and remove the bolt and washer

Inspection

4 With the tensioner plunger fully retracted, turn the screwdriver anti-clockwise – the plunger should extend under spring pressure **(see illustration)**. If it doesn't, renew the tensioner.

Installation

5 Install a new gasket on the tensioner body, then follow the procedure in Step 3 to retract and lock the plunger.
6 Install the tensioner on the engine, ensuring the UP mark is facing up, then tighten the mounting bolts to the torque listed in this Chapter's Specifications. Turn the screwdriver anti-clockwise to release the plunger. Don't forget to fit the air filter housing bracket on the front cylinder tensioner.
7 Fit a new washer to the centre bolt and tighten the bolt securely.
8 Install the remaining components in the reverse order of removal.

8 Cylinder head removal and installation

Removal

Note: *If only one cylinder head is being removed, ignore the Steps which do not apply.*
1 Remove the engine from the frame (see Section 5).

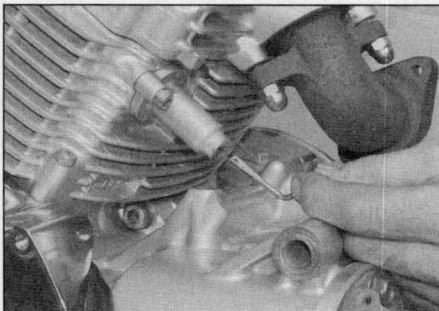

7.3a Turn the tensioner clockwise to lock the plunger

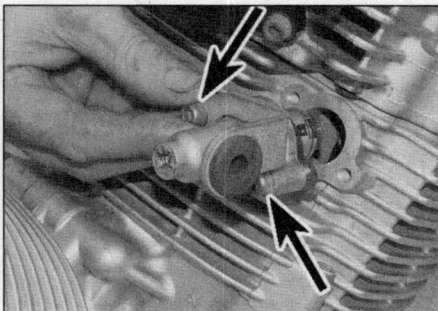

7.3b Undo the bolts (arrowed) and draw out the tensioner

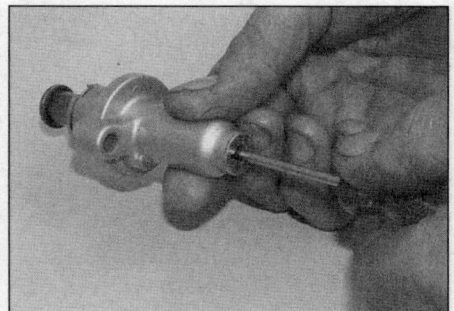

7.4 Check the operation of the plunger as described

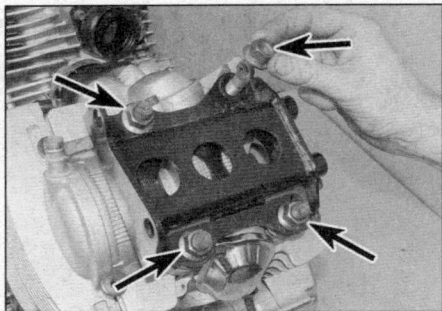
8.2a Remove the nuts . . .

8.2b . . . and lift off the mounting bracket

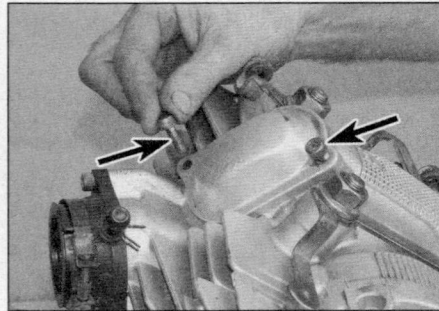
8.3 Each rocker cover is secured by two bolts

2 Undo the nuts securing the front cylinder head mounting bracket and remove the bracket (see illustrations).
3 Undo the bolts and remove the rocker covers (see illustration). Discard the cover O-rings as new ones must be fitted.
4 Undo the bolts and remove the camshaft sprocket covers (see illustrations). Note the location of the cover O-ring.
5 Undo the external oil feed union bolts and remove the pipes, noting how they fit (see illustrations). Discard the sealing washers as new ones must be fitted – note that the washers on the central bottom union bolt have internal tabs (see illustration).
6 Remove the timing inspection cap and the centre cap in the alternator cover on the left-hand side of the engine (see illustration).

Rear cylinder head
7 Follow the procedure in Chapter 1, Sec-

8.4a Undo the bolts (arrowed) . . .

8.4b . . . and remove the camshaft sprocket covers – note the cover O-ring (arrowed)

tion 3, and turn the crankshaft clockwise with a socket on the alternator centre bolt until the rear cylinder is at top dead centre (TDC) on its compression stroke with both valves closed.

8 Counter-hold the alternator centre bolt to prevent the engine turning and loosen the camshaft sprocket bolt (see illustration).
9 Remove the cam chain tensioner for the rear cylinder (see Section 7).

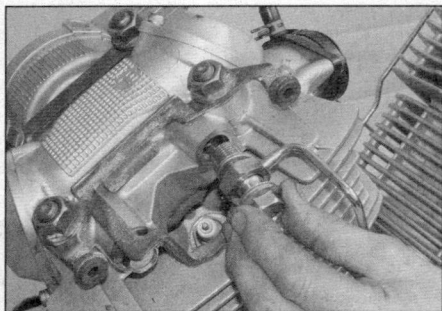
8.5a Undo the oil feed union bolts on the cylinder heads . . .

8.5b . . . and on the crankcase . . .

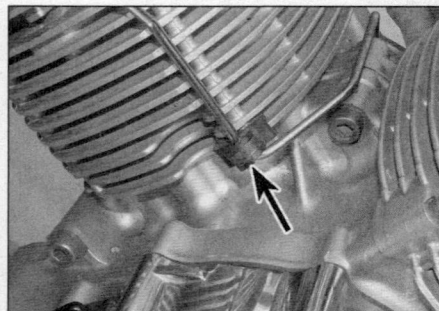
8.5c . . . noting the location of the buffer (arrowed) on the front cylinder pipe

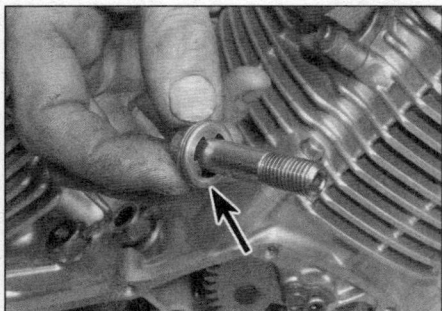
8.5d Note the special washers (arrowed) on the bottom union bolt

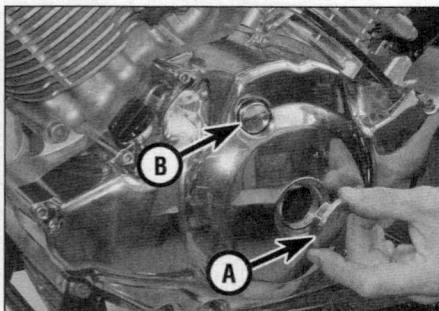
8.6 Remove the timing (B) and centre caps (A) from the alternator cover

8.8 Loosen the camshaft sprocket bolt as described

8.10 Remove the sprocket bolt and washer

8.11a Remove the sprocket and lift off the chain

8.11b Remove the dowel (arrowed) if it is loose

Caution: Stuff clean rag into the opening below the cam sprocket so nothing is accidentally dropped into it.

10 Remove the camshaft sprocket bolt and washer **(see illustration)**.

11 Label the sprocket 'R' (for rear cylinder). Slide the sprocket off the camshaft and lift the cam chain off the sprocket **(see illustration)**. Make sure the camshaft dowel doesn't fall out of the camshaft and remove it for safekeeping if it is loose **(see illustration)**. Secure the chain with a length of wire or temporarily install the sprocket bolt and loop the chain over it to prevent it falling into the engine.

12 Loosen the cylinder head bolts and nuts evenly in the **reverse** of the tightening order **(see illustration 8.31b)**. Remove the nuts, bolts and washers.

13 Lift off the cylinder head cover brackets, noting how they fit **(see illustration)**.

14 Lift the cylinder head off the studs **(see illustration)**. If it's stuck, tap around the joint face between the head and the cylinder with a soft-faced mallet or block of wood to free it. Don't attempt to lever the head off the cylinder – you will damage the sealing surface. Feed the cam chain down the tunnel and secure it with a cable tie or piece of wire to prevent it falling into the crankcase and jamming on the drive sprocket.

15 Remove the gasket and discard it as a new one must be used **(see illustration)**.

16 Note the two dowels either on the cylinder studs or in the underside of the head and remove them for safekeeping if they are loose **(see illustration)**.

17 Check the old cylinder head gasket and the mating surfaces on the cylinder head and cylinder for evidence of leaks, which could indicate that the head is warped. Refer to

Section 11 and check the flatness of the cylinder head.

18 Clean all traces of old gasket material from the cylinder head and cylinder. Be careful not to let any of the gasket material fall into the crankcase, the cylinder bore or the oil passage.

19 If required, undo the bolts securing the intake manifold to the cylinder head and remove the manifold **(see illustration)**. Discard the O-ring as a new one must be fitted.

20 If required, undo the nuts securing the exhaust manifold to the cylinder head and remove the manifold **(see illustration)**. Discard the gasket as a new one must be fitted.

Front cylinder head

21 If required, remove the baffle plate from

8.13 Lift off the head cover brackets (arrowed)

8.14 Lift off the cylinder head

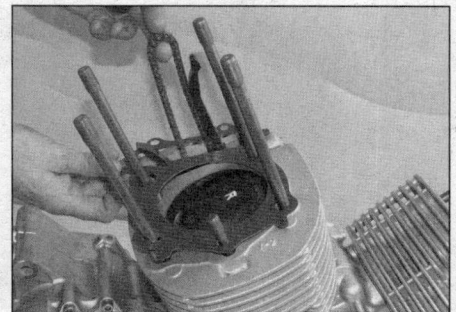

8.15 Discard the old cylinder head gasket

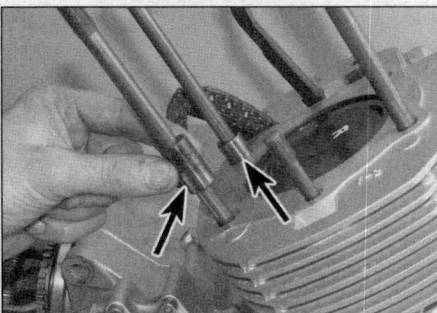

8.16 If required, remove the dowels for safekeeping

8.19 Intake manifold is secured by two bolts

8.20 Exhaust manifold is secured by two nuts

8.21 Baffle plate is located inside the front camshaft sprocket cover

8.23 Note the plate (arrowed) fitted to the front camshaft sprocket

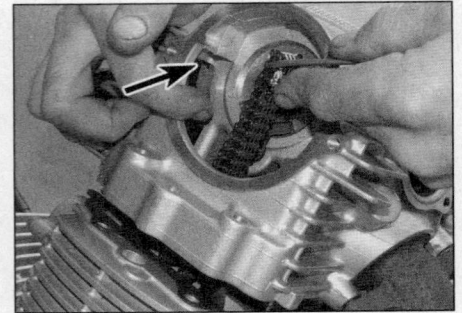

8.29 Upper end of cam chain guide fits in notch (arrowed)

inside the camshaft sprocket cover (see illustration).

22 Follow the procedure in Chapter 1, Section 3, and turn the crankshaft clockwise with a socket on the alternator centre bolt until the **front** cylinder is at top dead centre (TDC) on its compression stroke with both valves closed.

23 Follow Steps 8 to 19 of this section to remove the front cylinder head. Note that a plate is fitted to the front camshaft sprocket (see illustration). If required, label the camshaft sprocket 'F' (for front cylinder). **Note:** *The nuts on the front cylinder head*

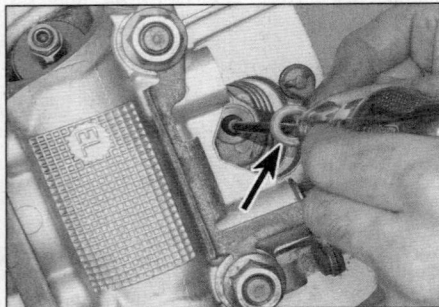

8.31a Slide the washer (arrowed) down a screwdriver onto the recessed stud

12 mm studs are longer than those on the rear head – don't mix them up.

Installation

Rear cylinder head

24 If both cylinder heads have been removed, install the rear cylinder head first.

25 If removed, fit a new gasket to the exhaust manifold and install the manifold. Tighten the manifold nuts securely.

26 If removed, fit a new O-ring to the intake manifold and install the manifold. Tighten the manifold bolts securely.

27 If removed, install the dowels on the cylinder studs (see illustration 8.16).

28 Install the new head gasket on top of the cylinder with the '5EL' mark facing up (see illustration 8.15).

29 Lower the cylinder head onto the studs and feed the cam chain and guide through the tunnel in the head. Ensure the upper end of the guide fits into the notch in the upper end of the tunnel (see illustration). Secure the chain.

30 Install the cylinder head cover brackets (see illustration 8.13).

31 Install the cylinder head bolts and nuts and tighten them finger-tight. **Note:** *The nuts on the rear cylinder head 12 mm studs are*

shorter than those on the front head. Don't forget the washer on the 10 mm stud next to the spark plug hole – if required, slide the washer and nut down the shaft of a screwdriver to locate them on the stud (see illustration). Tighten the nuts and bolts in the order shown in two stages to the torque settings specified at the beginning of this Chapter (see illustration).

32 If removed, install the camshaft dowel. Ensure the camshaft dowel is aligned with the index mark on the cylinder head (see illustration).

33 Check that the alternator rotor timing mark for the rear cylinder is aligned with the notch in the inspection hole (see Step 7). If it's necessary to turn the crankshaft, hold the cam chain up to prevent it falling off the drive sprocket and becoming jammed.

34 Engage the camshaft sprocket with the cam chain so its dowel hole aligns with the camshaft dowel and fit the sprocket onto the camshaft (see illustration 8.11a). Ensure the sprocket timing mark is facing out.

35 Install the sprocket bolt and washer and tighten them finger-tight.

36 Turn the camshaft sprocket just far enough to remove all slack in the cam chain on the intake side, then tension the chain by

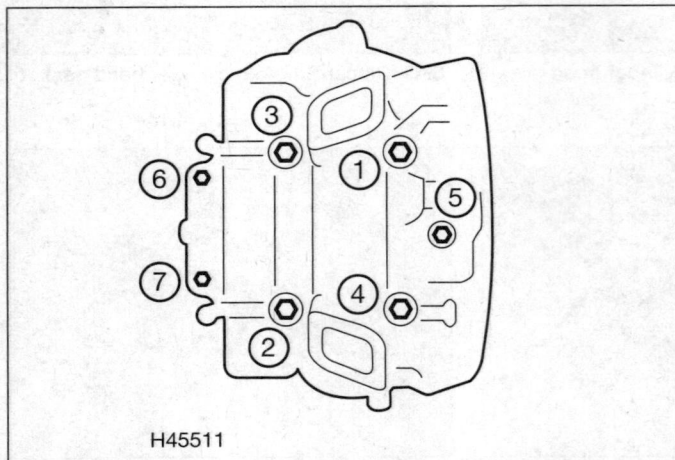

8.31b Cylinder head nut and bolt TIGHTENING sequence

H45511

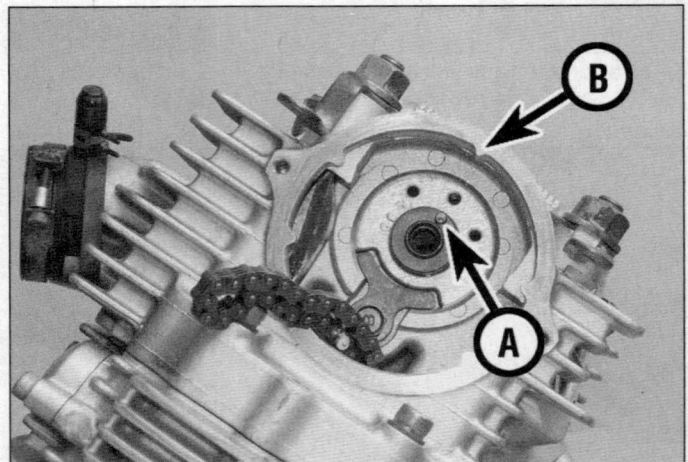

8.32 Ensue the dowel (A) is aligned with the index mark (B)

8.36 Tension the cam chain and check that the timing marks are aligned

pressing on the tensioner blade through the tensioner hole in the cylinder **(see illustration)**. Check that the timing marks on the camshaft sprocket and alternator rotor are aligned correctly.

37 Install the cam chain tensioner (see Section 7).

38 Counter-hold the alternator centre bolt and tighten the camshaft sprocket bolt to the specified torque.

39 Check the valve clearances (see Chapter 1).

40 Check the condition of the camshaft sprocket cover O-ring and fit a new one if necessary. Install the cover and tighten the bolts to the specified torque.

41 Install the rocker covers with new O-rings and tighten the bolts to the specified torque.

Front cylinder head

42 Follow Steps 26 through 39 to install the front cylinder head, noting that the long nuts on the 12 mm studs secure the head **(see**

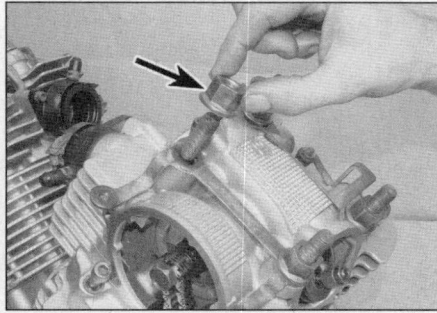

8.42 Use the long nuts to secure the front cylinder head

illustration). Ensure that the **front** cylinder's timing mark on the edge of the alternator rotor is aligned with the notch in the inspection hole before the camshaft sprocket is installed. Fit the plate on the camshaft sprocket before installing the sprocket bolt and washer **(see illustration 8.23)**.

43 If removed, fit the baffle plate into the camshaft sprocket cover **(see illustration 8.21)**.

44 Check the condition of the camshaft sprocket cover O-ring and fit a new one if necessary. Install the cover and tighten the bolts to the specified torque.

45 Install the rocker covers with new O-rings and tighten the bolts to the specified torque.

46 Install the front cylinder head mounting bracket and tighten the nuts to the specified torque **(see illustrations 8.2b and a)**.

47 Fit new sealing washers on the external oil feed pipe union bolts and install the pipes, noting the location of the buffer on the front cylinder pipe (see Step 5). Hold the unions to

prevent them twisting and tighten the bolts to the specified torque setting.

48 Install the remaining components in the reverse order of removal.

9   Camshafts and rockers

Removal

1 Remove the appropriate cylinder head (see Section 8). If not already done, remove the dowel from the end of the camshaft if it is loose.

2 Remove the bolt and camshaft retainer, noting how it fits **(see illustration)**.

3 Pull the camshaft and bush out from the cylinder head **(see illustration)**. If it doesn't come easily, thread a 10 mm bolt into the sprocket bolt hole and pull the camshaft out with the bolt.

4 Note that the camshafts are numbered – the No. 1 camshaft fits in the rear cylinder head and the No. 2 camshaft fits in the front cylinder head **(see illustration)**.

5 Remove the rocker shaft retaining bolt and sealing washer – note that one shaft is retained by the oil feed union bolt. Discard the washer as new ones must be fitted.

6 Using a slide-hammer or similar tool, draw the rocker shafts out from the cylinder head and remove the rockers **(see illustrations)**. Assemble each rocker on its shaft and label them (e.g. RI – rear intake/RE – rear exhaust) so that they can be installed in their original positions.

9.2 Remove the bolt and camshaft retainer (arrowed)

9.3 Pull out the camshaft and bush (arrowed)

9.4 Note the numbers cast into the camshafts

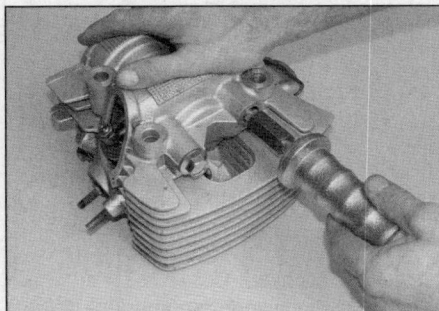

9.6a Use a slide-hammer . . .

9.6b . . . to draw out the rocker shafts . . .

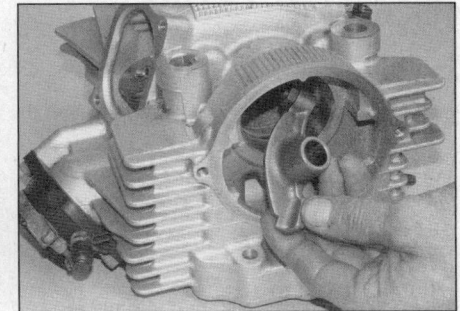

9.6c . . . then remove the rockers

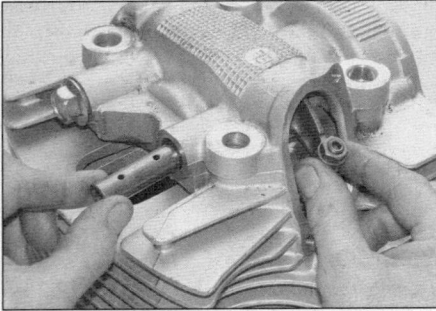
9.10a Note the position of the oil holes when installing the rocker shafts

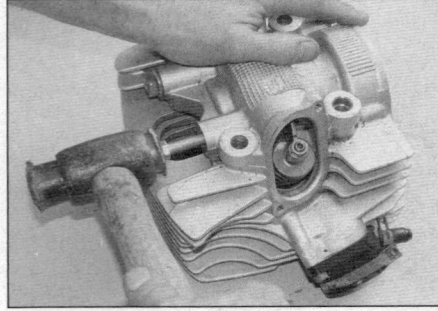
9.10b Drive the shafts in carefully with a soft-faced mallet

9.10c Position the camshaft bush with the cut-out (arrowed) as shown

HAYNES HiNT *If you don't have a slide-hammer, a similar tool can be made using a long bolt, a large flat washer and a short piece of pipe. Tap the pipe against the washer to pull the rocker shaft out of the rocker arm.*

7 Repeat the procedure for the other head. Remember to keep the parts for each head together and labelled so they can be reinstalled in their original locations.

Inspection

8 The procedure for cleaning and inspecting the camshaft and rocker components is the same as for XVS650 models (see Chapter 2A).
9 Refer to the Specifications at the beginning of this Chapter for the XVS1100 engine.

Installation

10 The procedure for installing the camshaft and rocker components is the same as for XVS650 models (see Chapter 2A) noting the following:
● Install the rockers and shafts first.
● There are no slots in the ends of the rocker shafts. Position the shafts with the oil holes along the top and bottom edges with the threaded end facing out. If necessary, thread a bolt into the shaft and drive it into place carefully with a soft-faced mallet **(see illustrations)**.
● Install the left-hand rocker shaft retaining bolts only – the right-hand bolts secure the external oil feed pipe unions.

● Position the camshaft bush with the cut-out for the retainer at the bottom **(see illustration)**.
● No lockwasher is fitted to the retainer bolt.
● Refer to the Specifications at the beginning of this Chapter for torque settings.

10 Valves/valve seats/valve guides – servicing

1 Because of the complex nature of this job and the special tools and equipment required, most owners leave servicing of the valves, valve seats and valve guides to a professional. However, you can make an initial assessment of whether the valves are seating, and therefore sealing, correctly by pouring a small amount of solvent into each of the valve ports. If the solvent leaks past any valve into the combustion chamber the valve is not seating and sealing correctly.
2 You can also remove the valves from the cylinder head, clean the components, check them for wear to assess the extent of the work needed and, unless a valve service is required, grind in the valves (see Section 11). The head can then be reassembled.
3 The dealer service department will remove the valves and springs, renew the valves and guides, recut the valve seats, check and renew the valve springs, spring retainers and collets (as necessary), replace the valve seals with new ones and reassemble the valve components.

4 After the valve service has been performed, the head will be in like-new condition. When the head is returned, be sure to clean it again very thoroughly before installation on the engine, to remove any metal particles or abrasive grit that may still be present from the valve service operations. Use compressed air, if available, to blow out all the holes and passages.

11 Cylinder head and valve overhaul

1 The procedure is the same as for XVS650 models (see Chapter 2A).
2 Refer to the Specifications at the beginning of this Chapter for the XVS1100 engine.

12 Cylinders

Note: *The procedure is the same for both cylinders.*

Removal

1 Remove the appropriate cylinder head (see Section 8).
2 Lift out the cam chain guide, noting which way round it fits **(see illustration)**.
3 Remove the cylinder bolts **(see illustration)**.
4 Lift the cylinder off the studs **(see illustration)**. If it's stuck, tap around the joint

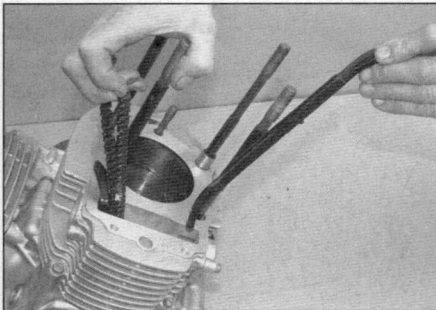
12.2 Lift out the cam chain guide

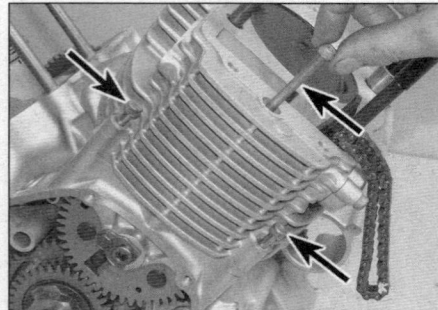
12.3 Remove the cylinder bolts (arrowed)

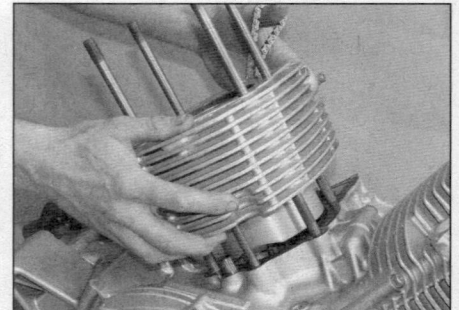
12.4 Lift the cylinder straight up off the studs

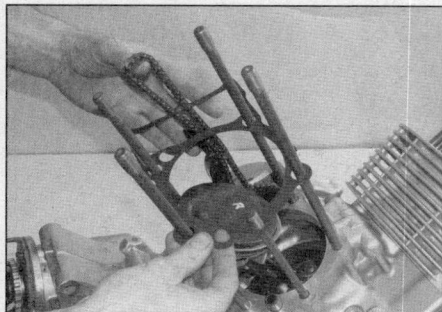

12.5 Discard the old cylinder base gasket

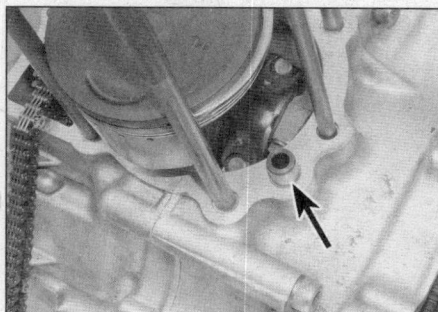

12.6a Note the location of the dowels (arrowed) . . .

12.6b . . . and remove them if they are loose

face between the cylinder and the crankcase with a soft-faced mallet or block of wood to free it. Don't attempt to lever the cylinder off the crankcase – you will damage the sealing surface. Feed the cam chain down the tunnel to prevent it jamming in the crankcase. Support the piston to prevent it hitting the crankcase as the cylinder is lifted off.

5 Remove the gasket and discard it as a new one must be used (see illustration).

6 Note the location of the dowels on the crankcase or in the underside of the cylinder and remove them for safekeeping if they are loose (see illustrations).

7 Stuff clean rag into the crankcase opening around the piston and remove all traces of old gasket material from the surface of the crankcase with a suitable solvent.

8 Clean all traces of old gasket material from the joint face of the cylinder with a suitable solvent.

9 Repeat the procedure to remove the other cylinder.

Inspection

10 The procedure for inspecting the cylinder is the same as for XVS650 models (see Chapter 2A).

11 Refer to the Specifications at the beginning of this Chapter for the XVS1100 engine. **Note:** *The bores on the XVS1100 engine are electro-plated with a highly wear resistant coating which should last the life of the engine. If a cylinder bore is badly scratched, scuffed or scored, it must be*

renewed – reboring is not possible. The bore surface should not be honed.

Installation

12 If removed, install the dowels on the crankcase, then fit a new cylinder base gasket (see illustration 12.5).

13 Lubricate the cylinder bore and piston with plenty of clean engine oil. Check that the piston ring end gaps are correctly positioned (see Chapter 2A, Section 15).

14 Install the cylinder on the studs and carefully lower it down until the piston crown fits into the bottom of the cylinder bore (see illustration). At the same time, pull the cam chain up through the tunnel, using a hooked piece of wire or cable tie.

15 Push down on the cylinder, making sure the piston doesn't get cocked sideways, and slide the piston up into the bore. Compress each ring by hand and feed it into the bottom of the bore (see illustration).

16 Once the piston is fitted inside the cylinder press the cylinder down onto the crankcase (see illustration). If necessary, use a wood or plastic hammer handle to gently tap the cylinder down, but don't use too much force or the piston will be damaged.

17 Install the cylinder bolts and tighten them to the specified torque (see illustration 12.3).

18 Repeat the procedure to install the remaining cylinder.

19 Install the remaining components in the reverse order of removal.

13 Pistons

1 The procedure is the same as for XVS650 models (see Chapter 2A).

2 Refer to the Specifications at the beginning of this Chapter for the XVS1100 engine.

14 Piston rings

1 The procedure is the same as for XVS650 models (see Chapter 2A).

2 Refer to the Specifications at the beginning of this Chapter for the XVS1100 engine.

15 Cam chains, timing drive gears, tensioner blades and guides

Removal

1 Remove the cylinder heads (see Section 8).

2 Check the visible portion of each cam chain for obvious wear or damage. Except in cases of oil starvation, Hy-Vo type chains wear very little.

3 Check the camshaft sprocket for wear,

12.14 Install the cylinder on the studs

12.15 Compress the rings and feed them into the cylinder bore

12.16 Press the cylinder down onto the crankcase

15.9 Remove the bolt and the shaft
retainer (arrowed)

15.10a Draw out the shaft . . .

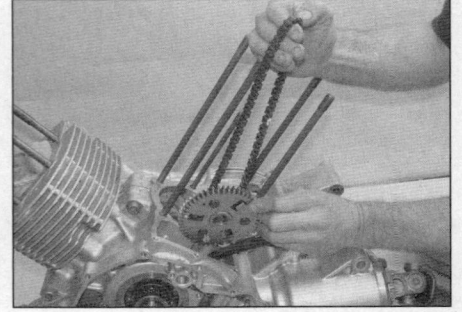

15.10b . . . then lift out the gear and chain

cracks and other damage. If the sprocket is worn, it is likely the chain and the sprocket on the back of the cam chain gear will also be worn. If wear this severe is apparent, the entire engine should be disassembled for inspection.

4 Lift out the cam chain guide, noting how it fits **(see illustration 12.2)**. Check the sliding surface of the guide for excessive wear, deep grooves, cracking and other obvious damage, and renew it if necessary.

5 Follow the appropriate procedure to remove the cam chain and tensioner blade. Work on one cylinder at a time and keep the parts for each cylinder together so that they can be reinstalled in the correct location.

Rear cylinder

6 Remove the cylinder (see Section 12).

7 Insert a suitable 6 mm dowel, drill bit or short bolt through the hole in the cam chain gear to keep both halves of the gear aligned **(see illustration 15.10c)**. Follow the procedure in Section 16 and remove the alternator rotor, starter clutch assembly and timing drive gear.

8 Mark the cam chain with paint on the outside to identify which way round it is fitted.

9 Remove the bolt and the cam chain gear shaft retainer **(see illustration)**. Note how the retainer locates in the end of the shaft.

10 Draw out the shaft, then lift out the cam chain gear and chain **(see illustrations)**. If not already done, remove the tool used to align the halves of the gear **(see illustration)**. Note that the rear cylinder cam chain gear is stamped '2'.

11 Undo the bolts securing the lower end of the tensioner blade and lift it out **(see illustration)**.

Front cylinder

12 Remove the cylinder (see Section 12).

13 Mark the cam chain with paint on the outside to identify which way round it is fitted.

14 Insert a suitable 6 mm dowel, drill bit or short bolt through the hole in the cam chain gear to keep both halves of the gear aligned **(see illustration)**. Remove the bolt and the cam chain gear shaft retainer **(see illustration)**. Note how the retainer locates in the end of the shaft.

15 Draw out the shaft, then lift out the cam chain gear and chain **(see illustrations)**. Note that the front cylinder cam chain gear is stamped '3'.

15.10c Remove the tool used to align the
halves of the gear

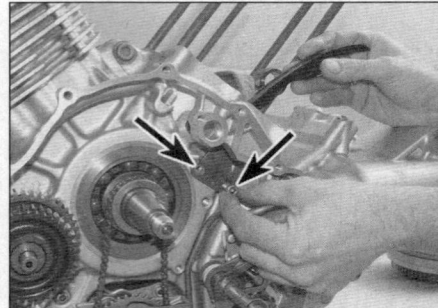

15.11 Remove the bolts (arrowed) and lift
out the rear cylinder tensioner blade

15.14a Align the halves of the cam chain
gear with a suitable tool

15.14b Remove the bolt and the shaft
retainer (arrowed)

15.15a Draw out the shaft . . .

15.15b . . . then lift out the gear and chain

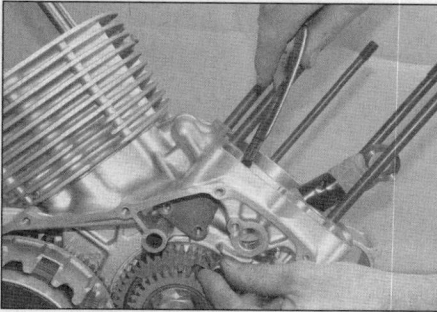

15.16 Remove the bolts and lift out the front cylinder tensioner blade

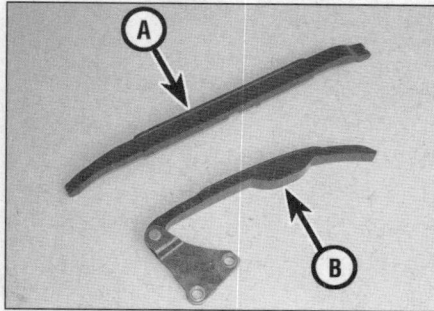

15.18 Inspect the cam chain guide (A) and tensioner (B) blades for wear and damage

15.19 Inspect the gear teeth for wear and damage

16 Undo the bolts securing the lower end of the tensioner blade and lift it out **(see illustration)**.

Inspection

17 If the chain is stiff or the links are binding, or if the links are loose, discard the chain. A chain in poor condition will wear the sprocket teeth and ideally a chain and sprockets should be renewed as a set.
18 Follow the procedure in Step 4 and check the tensioner blade **(see illustration)**.
19 Inspect the teeth on the cam chain gears and the corresponding teeth on the timing drive gears for wear and renew any components as necessary **(see illustration)**.
20 Check that the two halves that make up each cam chain gear move separately from each other against the pressure of the three springs built into the gear, then return to their original relationship by spring pressure **(see illustration)**. If the halves don't move separately or don't return, renew the gear. Also renew the gear if the springs are loose or damaged.

Installation

Rear cylinder

21 Install the tensioner blade and tighten the bolts to the torque setting specified at the beginning of this Chapter **(see illustration 15.11)**.
22 Use the method employed on removal to

align the halves of the cam chain gear (stamped '2'). Slip the gear into the chain, ensuring the chain is the correct way round, then position the gear in the crankcase and install the gear shaft **(see illustration 15.10a)**. Install the shaft retainer and secure it with the bolt – tighten the bolt to the specified torque.
23 Align the punch mark on the cam chain gear with the slot in the crankshaft **(see illustration)**. Secure the chain with wire or a cable tie to prevent it falling off the sprocket. Follow the procedure in Section 16 and install the alternator rotor, starter clutch assembly and timing drive gear.
24 Don't forget to remove the tool used to align the halves of the gear.
25 Install the remaining components in the reverse order of removal.

Front cylinder

26 Install the tensioner blade and tighten the bolts to the torque setting specified at the beginning of this Chapter **(see illustration 15.16)**.
27 Use the method employed on the rear cylinder to align the halves of the cam chain gear (stamped '3').
28 Slip the gear into the chain, ensuring the chain is the correct way round, then position the gear in the crankcase ensuring that the punch mark on the gear aligns with the mark on the timing drive gear **(see illustration)**. Install the gear shaft and shaft retainer, then fit the bolt and

15.20 Check the operation of the cam chain gear halves

tighten it to the specified torque **(see illustrations 15.15a and 15.14b)**.
29 Don't forget to remove the tool used to align the halves of the gear **(see illustration 15.14a)**.
30 Install the remaining components in the reverse order of removal.

16 Alternator rotor, starter clutch and gears

Note: *This procedure can be carried out with the engine in the frame.*

Removal

1 Drain the engine oil (see Chapter 1).

15.23 Align the punch mark (A) with the slot (B)

15.28 Align the punch mark (A) with the timing mark (B)

16.6a Remove the alternator cover bolts . . .

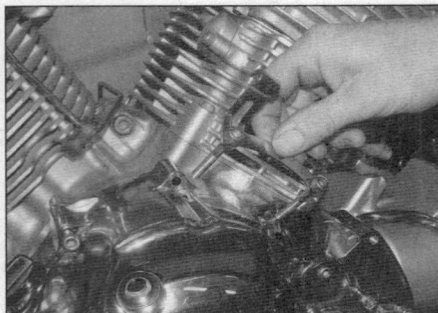

16.6b . . . noting the location of the clutch cable bracket . . .

16.7a . . . and draw off the cover

2 Disconnect the clutch cable from the release mechanism arm and the cable bracket (see Section 18).
3 Follow the procedure in Section 20 and remove the gearchange lever from the gearchange shaft.
4 Remove the left-hand footrest, gearchange pedal and linkage as an assembly (see Chapter 5).
5 Remove the left-hand frame cover (see Chapter 7) and disconnect the alternator and pick-up coil wiring connectors (see Section 5).
6 Working evenly in a criss-cross pattern, loosen the alternator cover bolts, then remove them noting the location of the clutch cable bracket **(see illustrations)**. Note the sealant on the three bolts immediately below the rear cylinder.

> **HAYNES HiNT**
> *Make a cardboard template of the alternator cover and punch a hole for each bolt location. As each bolt is removed, store it in its relative position in the template. This will ensure all bolts are installed correctly on reassembly – this is important, as many bolts differ slightly in length.*

7 Draw off the cover, noting how it fits over the gearchange shaft **(see illustration)**. Note the plain washer on the outer end of the gearchange shaft – it may be stuck inside the cover **(see illustration)**. Discard the cover

16.7b Note the washer on the gearchange shaft

gasket as a new one must be used. Note the location of the cover dowels and remove them for safekeeping if they are loose **(see illustration)**.
8 If required, the operation of the starter clutch can be checked while the alternator rotor is in place. Check that the idler gear on the back of the rotor is able to rotate freely anti-clockwise, but locks when rotated clockwise **(see illustration)**. If not, the starter clutch is faulty and should be removed for inspection.
9 To loosen the alternator rotor nut it is necessary to stop the rotor from turning. If the engine is in the fame, engage 1st gear and have an assistant apply the rear brake, then unscrew the nut. Alternatively, if a rotor holding strap or tool is not available, remove the clutch cover and lock the primary drive gear and the driven gear on the back of the

16.7c Note the location of the cover dowels (arrowed)

clutch (see Section 19). Remove the rotor nut and washer **(see illustration)**.
Caution: If a rotor holding strap is used, make sure it does not contact the raised sections on the outside of the rotor.
10 To remove the rotor from the shaft it is necessary to use a rotor puller. Yamaha provide a service tool (Part Nos. 90890–01362 and 90890–04131 Europe models, and YU-33270 and YM-38145 US models), or alternatively a similar tool can be obtained commercially **(see illustration)**. **Note:** *Three threaded holes are provided in the rotor for the puller legs.*
11 Pull the rotor off the shaft by using the puller.
Caution: When the rotor is pulled off, the rear cylinder timing drive gear may remain in place on the shaft and if so the springs and dowels normally retained in the back

16.8 Turn the intermediate gear (A) to rotate the idler gear on the back of the rotor (B) as described

16.9 Remove the rotor nut and washer

16.10 An aftermarket puller suitable for removing the rotor

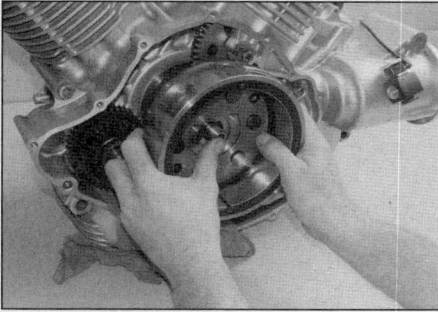

16.12a Grip the rotor, starter clutch and timing drive gear . . .

16.12b . . . and draw them off as an assembly

16.13 If required, remove the Woodruff key

of the starter clutch idler gear will fall out. To prevent this happening, first follow the procedure in Section 15 and insert a suitable tool through the hole in the rear cylinder cam chain gear to prevent the gear gripping the timing drive gear. Temporarily install the rotor nut on the crankshaft with just enough clearance between the nut and the rotor to allow the rotor to be pulled away from the tapered section of the shaft but no further. As a final precaution, stuff clean rag into the crankcase behind the rotor to prevent any loose parts falling into the engine.

12 Once the joint between the rotor and crankshaft has been broken, remove the rotor nut, then grip the rotor, starter clutch and timing drive gear and draw them off as an assembly **(see illustrations)**.

13 Remove the Woodruff key from its slot for safekeeping if it is loose **(see illustration)**.

14 Pull out the intermediate gear and shaft, noting which way round the gear fits **(see illustration)**.

Inspection

15 Note that the punch mark on the back of the timing drive gear aligns with the slot in the centre of the rotor, then pull the gear off the back of the rotor assembly **(see illustrations)**.
16 Note the position of the springs and dowel pins – there should be two springs and two pins in each of the three slots **(see illustration)**. The dogs on the timing drive gear should be a press fit between the springs. If the gear is loose, if the dogs or springs are worn, renew the appropriate parts.
17 Place the alternator rotor face down on the workbench, then hold the rotor and check that the idler gear rotates freely in a clockwise direction and locks against the rotor in an anti-clockwise direction **(see illustration)**. If it

16.14 Remove the intermediate gear and shaft

doesn't, the starter clutch should be dismantled.
18 To remove the idler gear, first remove the retaining circlip then lift off the spacer **(see illustrations)**.

16.15a Note that punch mark (A) aligns with slot (B) . . .

16.15b . . . then pull off the gear

16.16 Note the position of the springs and dowel pins

16.17 Idler gear should rotate freely clockwise

16.18a Remove the circlip . . .

16.18b . . . and the spacer

16.19a Lift off the idler gear . . .

16.19b . . . then lift out the bearing

16.20a Undo the bolts . . .

19 Lift off the idler gear, then lift out the bearing **(see illustrations)**.

20 Hold the alternator rotor and undo the bolts securing the starter clutch, then lift it off, noting the alignment of the hole in the clutch housing and the rotor **(see illustrations)**.

21 Press the sprag ring out of the housing and inspect the condition of the sprags **(see illustration)**. If they are damaged or worn, the starter clutch should be renewed – individual components are not available.

22 Check the condition of the idler gear bearing; if the rollers are worn or pitted, renew the bearing **(see illustration 16.19b)**.

23 Inspect the idler gear hub on the back of the rotor and the bearing surface inside the idler gear for signs of wear and scoring. Check the teeth of the idler gear and intermediate gear for cracks, chips, or damaged teeth. Check the intermediate gear shaft and bearing surface for signs of wear. If any parts are damaged or worn, renew them.

Installation

24 Press the starter clutch sprag ring into the housing **(see illustration 16.21)**. Position the housing on the back of the alternator rotor so that the holes align **(see illustration 16.20b)**. Clean the starter clutch bolts and apply a suitable non-permanent locking compound to their threads **(see illustration)**. Install the bolts and tighten them to the torque setting specified at the beginning of this Chapter **(see illustration 16.20a)**.

25 Lubricate the idler gear bearing and the starter clutch with engine oil, then fit the bearing, the gear and the spacer and secure them with the circlip **(see illustrations 16.19b and a, 16.18b and a)**.

26 Ensure the springs and dowel pins are correctly installed in the back of the rotor, then align the punch mark on the timing drive gear with the slot in the alternator rotor and install the drive gear **(see illustrations 16.15b and a)**.

27 Lubricate the intermediate gear shaft with engine oil. Hold the gear in position, making sure the smaller pinion faces outwards, and insert the shaft **(see illustration 16.14)**.

28 If removed, install the Woodruff key in its slot in the crankshaft and align the punch mark on the cam chain gear with the key **(see illustration)**. Ensure that the two halves of the gear are still aligned with a suitable tool **(see illustration)**. Stuff a clean rag around the oil pump to prevent any parts falling into the engine.

29 Clean the tapered end of the crankshaft and the corresponding mating surface on the inside of the alternator rotor with a suitable solvent. Make sure no metal objects have attached themselves to the magnets on the inside of the rotor.

30 To aid installation, highlight the two teeth of the timing drive gear immediately adjacent to the punch mark on the gear with white paint **(see illustration)**.

31 Grip the rotor, starter clutch and timing

16.20b . . . and remove the starter clutch –
note the alignment of the holes (arrowed)

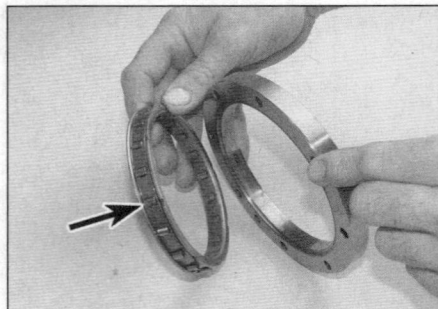

16.21 Check the condition of the sprags in
the sprag ring (arrowed)

16.24 Thread lock the starter clutch bolts

16.28a Align the punch mark (A) with the
Woodruff key (B)

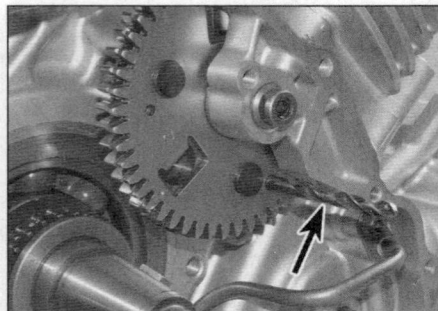

16.28b Using a drill bit to align the halves
of the cam chain gear

16.30 Highlight the gear teeth adjacent to
the punch mark (arrowed)

16.35 Check the condition of the gearchange shaft seal (arrowed)

16.36 Install a new cover gasket

17.2a Undo the bolts (arrowed) . . .

drive gear as an assembly, then align the slot in the rotor with the Woodruff key and carefully install the assembly on the crankshaft, using the highlighted teeth on the timing drive gear to ensure the cam chain gear remains correctly aligned **(see illustration 16.12b)**.

32 Press the rotor all the way on, ensuring the teeth of the timing drive gear and cam chain gear and the starter idler gear and intermediate gear mesh correctly, then secure the rotor with the washer and nut **(see illustration 16.9)**. Remove the tool used to align the halves of the cam chain gear and remove the rag from around the oil pump.

33 Check the operation of the starter clutch as described in Step 8.

34 Use the method employed on removal to prevent the rotor from turning and tighten the rotor nut to the specified torque.

35 Check the condition of the gearchange shaft seal in the alternator cover and renew it

if necessary (see *Tools and Workshop Tips* in the *Reference* section) **(see illustration)**.

36 Remove all traces of old gasket from the crankcase and cover surfaces. Ensure the cover dowels are in position, then install a new cover gasket **(see illustration)**.

37 Check that the plain washer is in place on the end of the gearchange shaft, then install the cover. Install the bolts and clutch cable bracket. Note that the old sealant should be cleaned off the appropriate bolts and fresh sealant applied. Tighten the bolts evenly in a criss-cross pattern, to the specified torque setting.

38 Install the remaining components in the reverse order of removal. Don't forget to connect the alternator and pick-up coil wiring connectors and to fill the engine with the recommended type and amount of oil (see Chapter 1). Adjust the clutch cable freeplay (see *Daily (pre-ride) checks*).

17 Oil pump

Note: *This procedure can be carried out with the engine in the frame.*

Removal

1 Remove the alternator rotor and timing drive gear assembly (see Section 16).

2 Undo the chain cover bolts and take off the cover **(see illustrations)**.

3 Undo the driven sprocket bolt and lift off the sprocket **(see illustrations)**. Mark the chain with paint on the outside to identify which way round it is fitted, then lift it off the crankshaft sprocket **(see illustration)**.

4 Remove the oil pump mounting bolts and lift out the pump, noting the location of the pump dowel **(see illustrations)**. Remove the

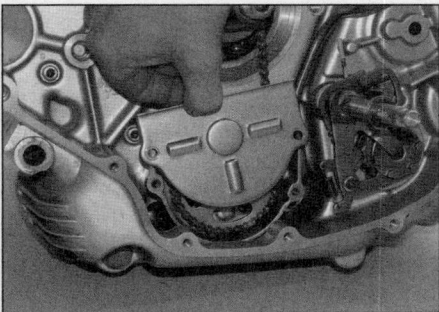

17.2b . . . and remove the chain cover

17.3a Undo the bolt (arrowed) . . .

17.3b . . . and lift off the sprocket

17.3c Mark the chain then lift it off

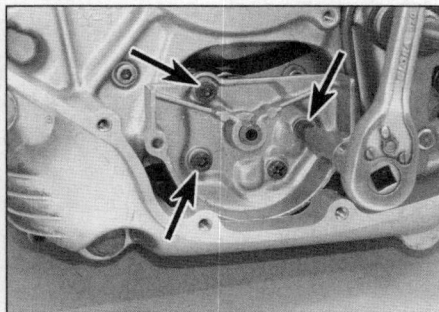

17.4a Remove the mounting bolts (arrowed) . . .

17.4b . . . and lift out the pump – note the location of the dowel

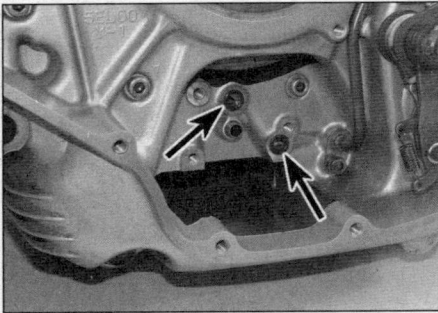
17.4c Discard the O-rings (arrowed)

17.5 Remove the internal oil pipe

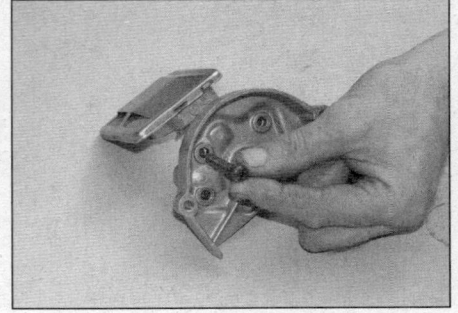
17.6a Undo the cover screw . . .

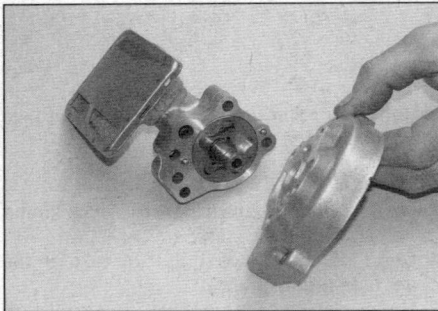
17.6b . . . and lift off the cover

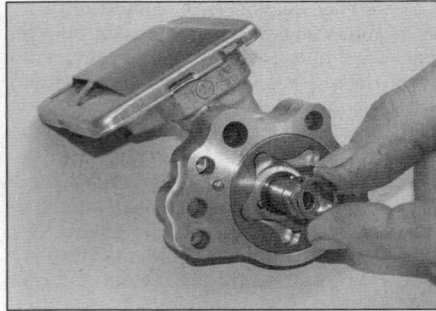
17.7a Remove the plain washer . . .

17.7b . . . then remove the circlip from the shaft

17.8a Lift out the outer rotor . . .

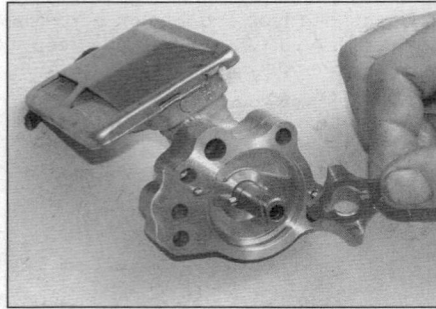
17.8b . . . and the inner rotor . . .

Inspection

Note: *The pump is fitted with two sets of rotors – take care to note their positions to aid reassembly.*

6 Undo the cover screw that holds the pump assembly together and lift off the outer cover **(see illustrations)**.

7 Remove the plain washer and circlip from the pump shaft **(see illustrations)**.

8 Lift out the outer (thinner) set of rotors and the drive pin **(see illustrations)**. Note that the rotors are marked and should be installed in the pump the same way round on reassembly.

9 Lift off the inner cover **(see illustration)**.

10 Lift out the shaft and drive pin and the inner (thicker) set of rotors **(see illustrations)**.

11 Remove the dowels from the pump

two O-rings and discard them as new ones must be fitted **(see illustration)**.

5 Undo the bolts securing the internal oil pipe

and pull the pipe away from the crankcase, noting the location of the two O-rings **(see illustration)**. Discard the O-rings as new ones must be fitted.

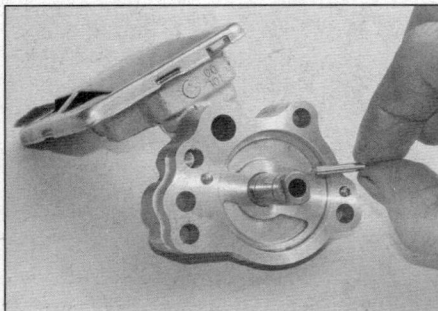
17.8c . . . and the drive pin

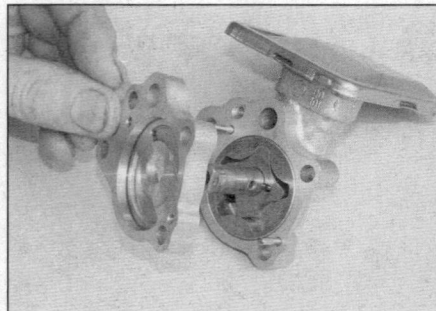
17.9 Remove the inner cover

17.10a Lift out the shaft and drive pin . . .

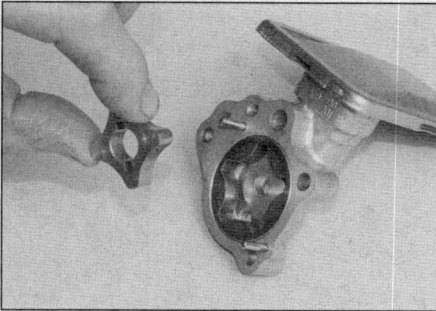

17.10b . . . then lift out the inner rotor . . .

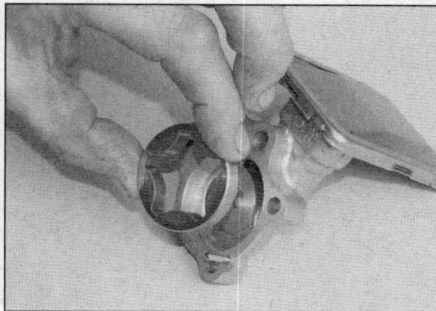

17.10c . . . and the outer rotor

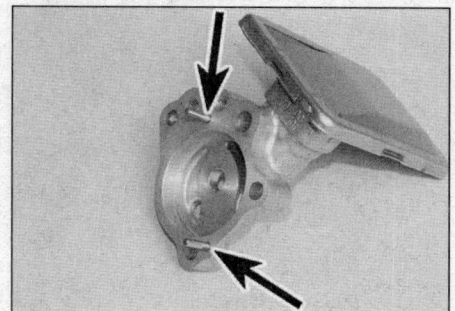

17.11 Remove the dowels (arrowed) for safekeeping

housing for safekeeping if they are loose (see illustration).

12 Unclip the strainer screen from the pump housing and lift out the plastic insert (see illustrations).

13 Clean all the components with a suitable solvent.

14 Inspect the components for scoring and wear. If any damage, scoring or uneven or excessive wear is evident, renew the pump – individual components are not available.

15 Install the inner rotors and shaft in the housing and measure the clearance between the outer rotor and the housing with a feeler gauge and compare it to the service listed in the specifications at the beginning of this Chapter (see illustration). If the clearance is greater than the service limit, renew the pump.

16 Measure the clearance between the inner rotor tip and the outer rotor with a feeler gauge and compare it to the service limit listed in the specifications (see illustration). If the clearance is greater than the service limit, renew the pump.

17 If removed, install the dowels in the pump housing and fit the inner cover, then install the outer rotors; follow the procedure in Steps 15 and 16 and measure the outer rotor clearances.

18 Check the pump driven sprocket for wear or damage, and replace it with a new one if necessary. If the driven sprocket is worn, inspect the drive sprocket and the chain and renew them as a set if necessary.

19 If required, remove the drive sprocket from the crankshaft with a puller. **Note:** *Removal will damage the sprocket. It must be*

replaced with a new one if it's removed from the crankshaft. Position the new sprocket on the crankshaft with the teeth toward the crankcase, then drive it all the way on with a hammer and suitable spacer.

20 If the pump is good, make sure all the components are clean, then lubricate them with clean engine oil.

21 If removed, install the dowels in the pump housing.

22 Install the inner rotors in the housing, then fit the drive pin through the lower hole in the shaft and install the shaft (see illustration 17.10a).

23 Install the inner cover, the drive pin and the outer rotors (see illustrations 17.9, 8c, 8b and 8a).

24 Fit the circlip and then the plain washer on the shaft, then install the outer cover and secure it with the screw (see illustrations 17.7b, 7a, 6b and 6a).

25 Rotate the pump shaft by hand and check that the rotors turn freely – if not, strip and reassemble the pump.

26 Install the plastic insert and clip the strainer screen onto the pump housing.

27 Blow through the internal oil pipe with compressed air to ensure that it is clear.

Installation

28 Before installing the pump, prime it by pouring oil into it while turning the shaft by hand – this will ensure that it begins to pump oil quickly.

Caution: Also pour oil into the crankcase oil passages to prevent engine damage on start-up.

29 Fit new O-rings onto the ends of the internal oil pipe and install the pipe. Tighten the pipe bolts to the torque setting specified at the beginning of this Chapter.

30 Fit the pump dowel and new O-rings into the crankcase (see illustration 17.4c). Position the pump on the engine and tighten its mounting bolts to the specified torque setting.

31 Slip the chain over the drive sprocket, ensuring it is the correct way round (see Step 3). Engage the driven sprocket with the chain, then install the sprocket on the pump

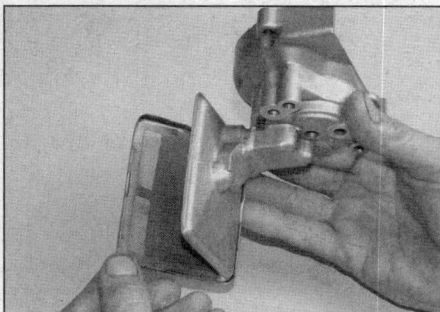

17.12a Unclip the strainer screen . . .

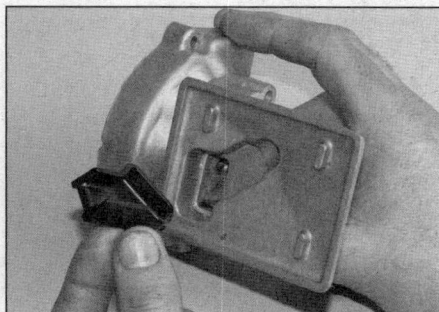

17.12b . . . and lift out the plastic insert

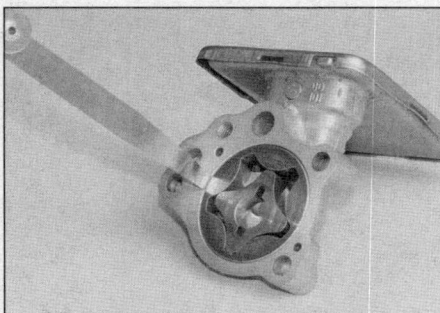

17.15 Measure the outer rotor to body clearance as shown

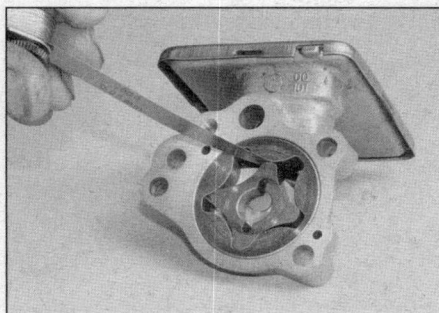

17.16 Measure the inner rotor tip to outer rotor clearance as shown

17.31 Fit the sprocket onto the pump shaft

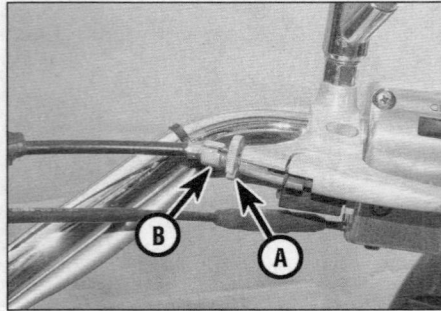

18.1a Loosen the lockwheel (A) and screw the adjuster (B) into the bracket

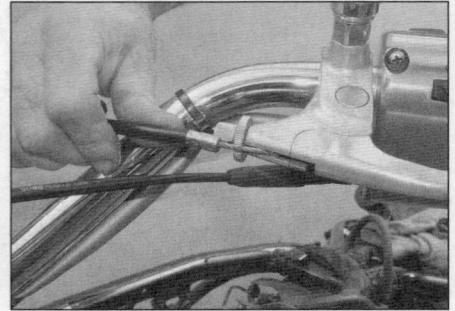

18.1b Pull the cable out of the adjuster . . .

shaft (see illustration). Install the sprocket bolt and tighten it to the specified torque setting.

32 Install the chain cover and tighten the bolts to the specified torque setting (see illustration 17.2b).

33 Install the remaining components in the reverse order of removal.

18 Clutch cable and release mechanism

Note: *This procedure can be carried out with the engine in the frame.*

Clutch cable

1 Displace the rubber boot from the adjuster on the handlebar lever, then loosen the adjuster lockwheel and screw the adjuster into the lever bracket (see illustration). Align the slot in the adjuster with the slot in the bracket, then pull the outer cable end from the socket in the adjuster and release the inner cable end from the lever (see illustrations).

2 Remove the frame cover from the left-hand side of the bike (see Chapter 7). Undo the bolts and lift off the clutch release mechanism cover (see illustrations).

3 Bend back the metal tang and disconnect the lower end of the inner cable from the release lever (see illustrations).

4 Remove the cable from the bike, noting its routing through the guides and support bracket on the alternator cover.

5 Installation is the reverse of removal. Lubricate the cable ends with multi-purpose grease and make sure the cable is correctly routed. Adjust the cable freeplay (see *Daily (pre-ride) checks*).

Release mechanism

6 Disconnect the lower end of the clutch cable from the release lever (see above).

7 Remove the alternator cover (see Section 16).

8 Disconnect the lever return spring (see illustration).

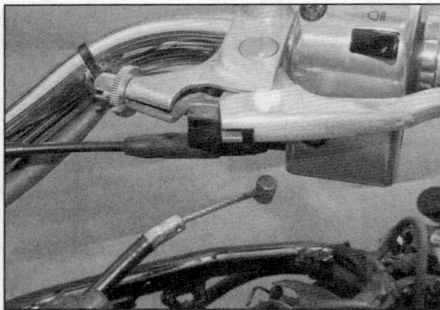

18.1c . . . and release the cable end from the lever

18.2a Undo the bolts (arrowed) . . .

18.2b . . . and lift off the clutch release mechanism cover

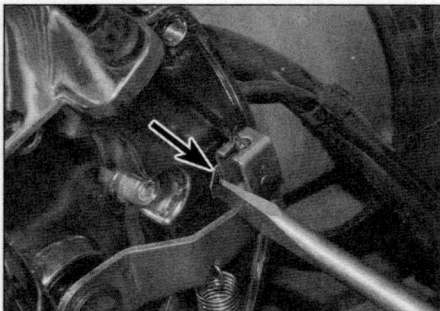

18.3a Bend back the tang (arrowed) . . .

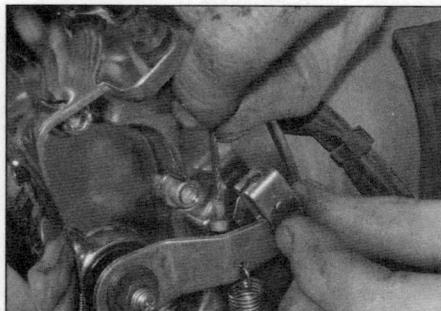

18.3b . . . and disconnect the cable from the lever

18.8 Disconnect the return spring (arrowed)

18.9a Remove the nut and washer . . .

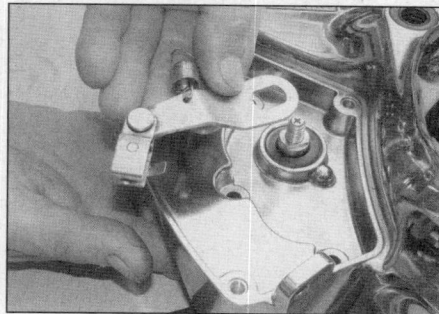

18.9b . . . and lift off the lever

18.10a Pull out the push screw and cover . . .

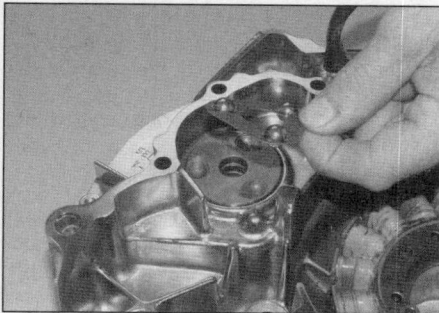

18.10b . . . and lift out the ball retainer

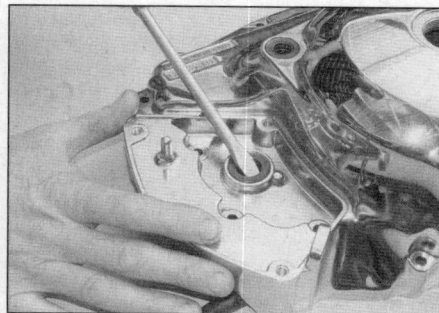

18.12 Lever out the old oil seal

damage, especially the contact surfaces of the push screw cover and balls, and renew any as necessary

12 Lever the release mechanism oil seal out of the alternator cover with a flat-bladed screwdriver, noting which way round it fits **(see illustration)**. Lubricate the new seal with lithium soap grease and press it into place with a suitably sized socket.

13 Installation is the reverse of the removal. Lubricate the push screw and ball retainer with clean engine oil.

14 Adjust clutch freeplay (see *Daily (pre-ride) checks*).

9 Remove the nut and washer and detach the clutch operating lever from the push screw, noting which way round it fits **(see illustrations)**.

10 Turn the cover over and pull out the push screw and cover, then lift off the ball retainer **(see illustrations)**.

11 Inspect the components for wear and

19 Clutch and primary gears

Note: *This procedure can be carried out with the engine in the frame.*

Removal

1 Drain the engine oil and remove the oil filter (see Chapter 1).

2 Remove the air filter housing and exhaust system (see Chapter 3)

3 Displace the right-hand footrest and brake pedal assembly (see Chapter 6).

4 Working evenly in a criss-cross pattern, loosen the clutch cover bolts, then remove them noting the location of the air filter housing bracket and the wiring clips secured by the lower cover bolts **(see illustrations)**. Note the sealant on the two bolts immediately below the front cylinder.

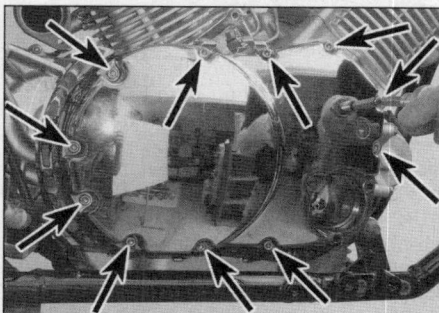

19.4a Remove the clutch cover bolts

19.4b Note the location of the air filter housing bracket . . .

HAYNES HiNT *Make a cardboard template of the clutch cover and punch a hole for each bolt location. As each bolt is removed, store it in its relative position in the template. This will ensure all bolts are installed correctly on reassembly – this is important, as many bolts differ slightly in length.*

19.4c . . . and the wiring clips

19.5 Note the location of the cover dowels (arrowed)

5 Remove the cover and discard the gasket as a new one must be used. Note the position of the locating dowels and remove them for safekeeping if they are loose **(see illustration)**.

19.6a Loosen the spring bolts evenly . . .

19.6b . . . then remove the bolts and the spring plate (arrowed)

19.6c Lift off the diaphragm spring . . .

19.6d . . . and spring seat

19.7 Lift off the pressure plate

6 Loosen the clutch spring bolts evenly, then remove the bolts and lift off the spring plate **(see illustrations)**. Remove the clutch diaphragm spring and spring seat **(see illustrations)**.

7 Lift off the pressure plate **(see illustration)**.

8 Draw out the short pushrod together with the thrust washer and thrust bearing **(see illustration)**. Use a magnet to draw out the long pushrod from the input shaft **(see illustration)**. Note which way round the pushrod fits.

9 Note the alignment of the notched clutch friction plate tabs with the match marks on the clutch housing, then grasp the complete set of clutch plates and remove them as a pack **(see illustration)**. Unless the plates are being replaced with new ones, keep them in their original order.

10 Bend back the tabs on the clutch centre nut lockwasher **(see illustration)**. To loosen the centre nut it is necessary to stop the transmission input shaft from turning. If the engine is in the frame, engage 1st gear and have an assistant apply the rear brake. Alternatively, the Yamaha service tool – Part No. 90890-04086 (European models) or YM-91042 (US models) – a similar commercially available or a home-made tool (see Tool Tip, Chapter 2A, Section 18) can be used **(see illustration)**.

11 Remove the nut and lockwasher, noting

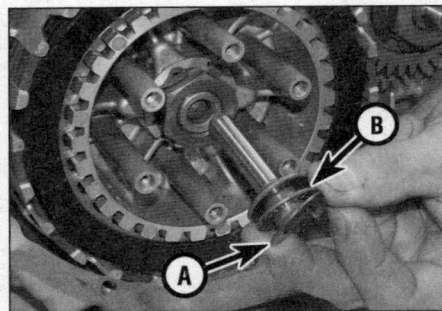

19.8a Draw out the short pushrod, thrust washer (A) and bearing (B)

19.8b Draw out the long pushrod

19.9 Note the alignment of the plate tabs (A) with the marks on the housing (B)

19.10a Bend back the lockwasher tabs

19.10b Hold the clutch centre as described and loosen the centre nut

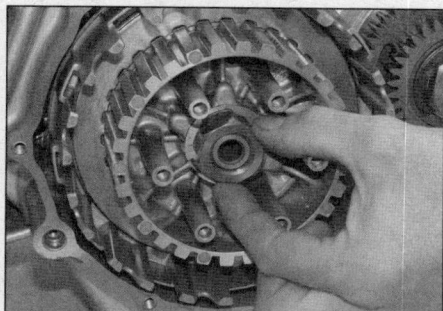
19.11a Remove the centre nut . . .

19.11b . . . and the lockwasher

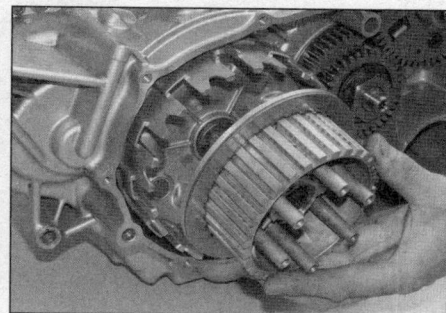
19.12a Slide off the clutch centre . . .

how the washer fits **(see illustrations)**. Discard the lockwasher, as a new one must be used on reassembly.

12 Slide the clutch centre and the thrust washer off the input shaft **(see illustrations)**. If required, the clutch housing can be removed at this stage **(see illustration)**.

13 Bend back the lockwasher on the nut that secures the timing and primary drive gears **(see illustration)**. To loosen the nut it is necessary to stop the crankshaft from turning. Either remove the alternator cover centre cap and counter-hold the shaft on the alternator centre bolt, or wedge a rag or short length of soft metal such as aluminium or brass between the teeth of the primary drive gear and the driven gear on the back of the clutch housing then loosen the nut **(see illustrations)**. Once the nut is loose, pull the clutch housing off. Do not remove the nut at this stage.

14 Align the punch mark on the timing drive gear with the mark on the front cylinder cam chain gear, then follow the procedure in Section 15 to align the halves of the cam chain gear and draw out the cam chain gear shaft. Lift the cam chain gear up to disengage it from the timing drive gear.

15 Remove the nut, lockwasher and retaining plate, noting how they fit **(see illustrations)**.

19.12b . . . and the thrust washer

19.12c Slide off the clutch housing

19.13a Bend back the lockwasher tabs

19.13b Lock the primary drive gear and driven gear with a soft metal wedge . . .

19.13c . . . or rag and loosen the timing and primary drive gear nut

19.15a Remove the nut . . .

19.15b . . . the lockwasher . . .

19.15c . . . and the retaining plate

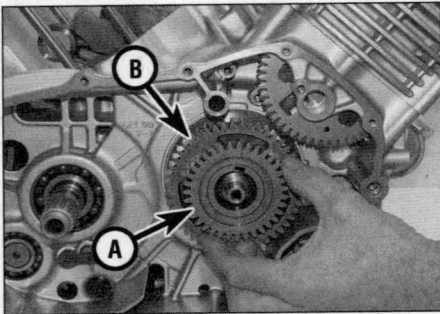

19.16 Pull the timing (A) and primary (B) drive gears off together

19.18a Note that punch mark (A) aligns with slot (B)

19.18b Separate the gears carefully

Discard the lockwasher, as a new one must be used.

16 Lift the cam chain gear up to provide sufficient clearance to pull the timing drive gear and primary drive gear off the shaft as an assembly **(see illustration)**. **Note:** *If the two gears become separated, the springs and dowels normally retained in the primary drive gear will fall out – as a precaution, stuff clean rag into the crankcase below the gears to prevent any loose parts falling into the engine.*

17 Remove the square key from the slot in the crankshaft.

Inspection

18 Note the punch mark on the timing drive gear aligns with the slot in the centre of the primary drive gear, then carefully separate the two gears **(see illustrations)**.

19 Note the position of the springs and dowel pins – there should be two springs and two pins in each of the three slots **(see illustration)**. The dogs on the timing drive gear should be a press fit between the springs. If the gear is loose, if the dogs or springs are worn, renew the appropriate parts.

20 After an extended period of service the clutch friction plates will wear and promote clutch slip. Measure the thickness of each friction plate using a vernier caliper **(see illustration)**. If any plate has worn to or beyond the service limit given in the Specifications at the beginning of this Chapter, the friction plates must be renewed as a set. Also, if any of the plates smell burnt or are glazed, they must be renewed as a set.

21 The plain plates should not show any signs of excess heating (bluing). Check for warpage using a flat surface and feeler gauges **(see illustration)**. If any plate exceeds the maximum permissible amount of warpage, or shows signs of bluing, all the plain plates must be renewed as a set.

22 Check the diaphragm spring and spring seat for warpage and measure the free height of the spring **(see illustration)**. Renew any components as necessary.

23 Inspect the clutch assembly for burrs and indentations on the edges of the protruding tangs of the friction plates and/or slots in the edge of the housing with which they engage. Similarly check for wear between the inner teeth of the plain plates and the slots in the clutch centre. Wear will cause clutch drag and slow disengagement during gear changes, as the plates will snag when the pressure plate is lifted. With care, a small amount of wear can be corrected by dressing with a fine file, but if it is excessive the worn components should be renewed.

24 Check the teeth on the primary drive gear and driven gear for wear or damage and renew them if defects are found. Note that the driven gear is integral with the clutch housing **(see illustration)**. Check the condition of the springs in the back of the housing.

25 Check the bearing surface in the centre of the clutch housing and renew the clutch housing if it's worn or damaged **(see**

19.19 Note the position of the springs and dowel pins

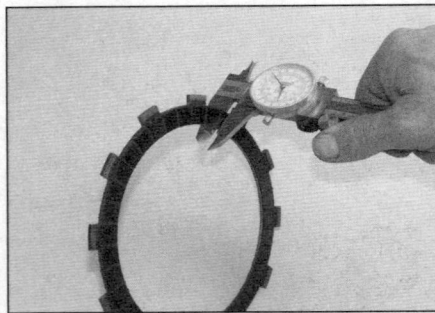

19.20 Measuring the thickness of a clutch friction plate

19.21 Checking a plain clutch plate for warpage

19.22 Measuring the free height of the diaphragm spring

19.24 Primary driven gear is integral with the clutch housing – check the condition of the springs

19.25 Inspect the bearing surface (arrowed)

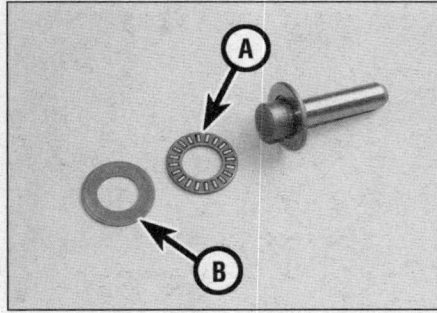

19.27 Inspect the thrust bearing (A) and washer (B) for wear or damage

19.28a Locate the ends of the wire retainer (arrowed)

illustration). If the bearing surface is damaged, inspect the corresponding surface of the transmission input shaft and renew the shaft if necessary (see Section 28).

26 Check the pressure plate for wear and damage.

27 Check the thrust bearing and washer for wear or damage **(see illustration)**. Examine the contact surfaces of the clutch pushrods for wear and pitting. Renew any worn or damaged parts.

28 The clutch centre is fitted with an anti-judder assembly. Note that these parts need not be removed unless the clutch has been juddering, in which case all the components

should be renewed as a set. To remove the assembly, locate the ends of the wire retainer and press them out of the clutch housing, then press down on the steel plate and pull the wire out of its groove **(see illustrations)**. Lift off the thick steel plate, spring and spring seat **(see illustrations)**. Renew the components, including the wire retainer, as a set. Install the spring seat with the inner lip uppermost, then the spring with the inner lip down. Install the thick steel plate. Insert one end of the wire retainer in the hole in the clutch centre and ensure it locks in place **(see illustration)**. Press down firmly on the steel plate and pull the wire into its groove **(see**

illustration 19.28b). Press the other end of the wire into the hole in the clutch centre and ensure it locks in place.

29 Refer to Section 18 for details of the clutch release mechanism.

Installation

30 Ensure the springs and dowel pins are correctly installed in the primary drive gear, then align the punch mark on the timing drive gear with the slot in the primary and install the drive gear **(see illustrations 19.18b and a)**.

31 Slide the gear assembly onto the crankshaft and install the square key **(see illustration)**.

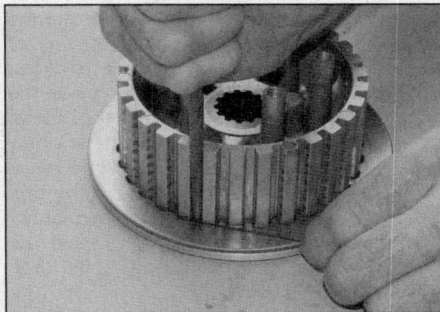

19.28b Press down on the steel plate and pull out the wire

19.28c Lift off the thick steel plate . . .

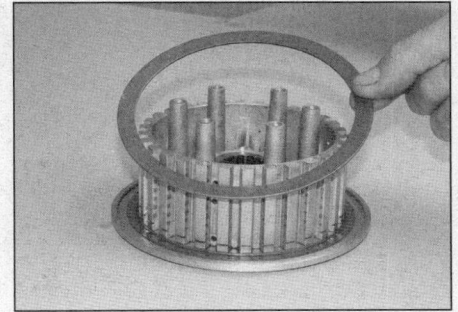

19.28d . . . the spring . . .

19.28e . . . and spring seat

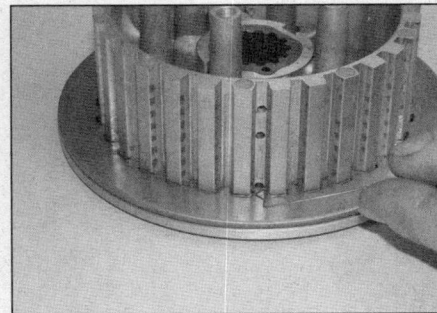

19.28f Ensure the wire retainer locks in place

19.31 Install the gear assembly and the square key

19.32a Engage the cam chain gear with the timing drive gear as described

19.32b Ensure the punch marks align

19.35 Secure the nut with the new lockwasher

32 Insert a suitable tool through the hole in the cam chain gear to align both halves of the gear, then engage the cam chain gear with the timing drive gear, ensuring the punch marks align **(see illustrations)**. Follow the procedure in Section 15 and install the cam chain gear shaft.

33 Install the retaining plate and a new lockwasher on the timing drive gear, ensuring the lockwasher tab fits into the notch in the retaining plate, then install the nut finger-tight **(see illustrations 19.15c, b and a)**.

34 Lubricate the clutch housing bearing surface with clean engine oil, then install the clutch housing on the transmission input shaft **(see illustration 19.12c)**. Ensure the primary driven gear teeth on the back of the housing engage with the primary drive gear correctly.

35 Use the method employed on removal to prevent the crankshaft turning and tighten the nut to the torque listed in this Chapter's Specifications, then bend the lockwasher against the nut to hold it **(see illustration)**.

36 Install the thrust washer and the clutch centre on the transmission input shaft **(see illustrations 19.12b and a)**. Install a new lockwasher then fit the nut recessed side inwards and tighten it finger-tight **(see illustrations 19.11b and a)**.

37 Use the method employed on removal to prevent the input shaft turning and tighten the nut to the specified torque setting, then bend the lockwasher against the nut to secure it **(see illustration)**.

38 Coat the clutch friction plates with clean engine oil. Build up the plates as follows: first

fit a friction plate with the notch on the plate tab aligned with the match marks on the clutch housing **(see illustration)**. Now fit a plain plate, then alternate friction and plain plates. Ensure all the notched tabs on the friction plates are aligned with the marks on the clutch housing **(see illustration 19.9)**. The last plate to be fitted should be a friction plate.

39 Lubricate the long pushrod with clean engine oil and install it in the input shaft, then lubricate the inner end of the short pushrod with lithium soap grease and install it **(see illustrations 19.8b and a)**.

40 Lubricate the thrust bearing with engine oil and fit the bearing and thrust washer onto the short pushrod.

41 Install the pressure plate, spring seat, diaphragm spring and spring plate and secure them with the spring bolts **(see illustrations 19.7, 19.6d, c and b)**. Now tighten the bolts evenly in a criss-cross pattern to the torque listed in this Chapter's Specifications.

42 Undo the bolts securing the seal retaining plate inside the clutch cover and remove the plate **(see illustration)**. Lever the seal out of the cover **(see illustration)**. Lubricate a new seal with engine oil, then press it into place with a suitably sized socket. Clean the bolt threads and apply a suitable non-permanent thread-locking compound, then install the plate and secure it with the bolts **(see illustration)**.

43 Remove all traces of old gasket from the crankcase and clutch cover surfaces. Ensure the clutch cover dowels are in

19.37 Secure the clutch centre nut with the lockwasher

19.38 Align the notched tab (arrowed) on a friction plate with the housing and fit the plate

19.42a Remove the seal retaining plate inside the clutch cover . . .

19.42b . . . and lever out the old seal

19.42c Apply thread locking compound to the plate retaining bolts

19.43 Install a new cover gasket

20.1a Note the register mark (arrowed) on the gearchange shaft

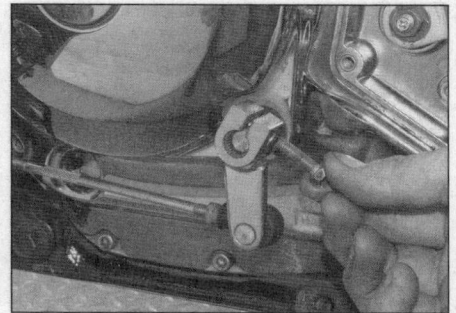

20.1b Remove the pinch bolt and pull the lever off the shaft

position, then install a new cover gasket **(see illustration)**.

44 Install the clutch cover ensuring it is correctly aligned, then install the bolts finger-tight. Don't forget to fit the bracket for the air filter housing and the wiring clips on the lower bolts **(see illustrations 19.4b and c)**.

45 Tighten the bolts evenly in a criss-cross pattern, to the specified torque setting.

46 Install the remaining components in the reverse order of removal. Don't forget to fill the engine with the recommended type and amount of oil (see Chapter 1).

20 Gearchange mechanism

Note: *This procedure can be carried out with the engine in the frame.*

Gearchange lever and pedal

1 Check for a register mark on the gearchange shaft that aligns with the slot in the lever **(see illustration)**. If necessary, make your own with a sharp punch then remove the pinch bolt and pull the lever off the shaft **(see illustration)**.

2 If required, remove the gearchange pedal, gearchange linkage and left-hand footrest as an assembly (see Chapter 5). Alternatively, note the position of the lever locknut on the shaft to aid reassembly, then loosen the locknut and unscrew the lever from the shaft.

3 If required, refer to the procedure in Chapter 5 to separate the gearchange pedal from the footrest assembly.

4 Installation is the reverse of removal. Adjust the gearchange linkage as described in Chapter 1.

Gearchange mechanism

Removal

5 Make sure the transmission is in neutral. Disconnect the gearchange lever from the shaft (see Step 1).

6 Remove the alternator cover (see Section 16).

7 Note how the gearchange shaft centralising spring locates on the pin and how the stopper arm spring locates against the case **(see**

illustration). Pull the selector arm back to disengage it from the selector drum and pull the gearchange shaft assembly out **(see illustrations)**. Note the washers on both ends of the shaft and remove them for safekeeping if required.

8 Note the order of the components on the shaft to aid reassembly **(see illustration)**. **Note:** *If any of the shaft assembly components are disturbed, fit new circlips on reassembly.*

Inspection

9 Inspect the splines on the gearchange shaft; if they are worn or damaged, or if the shaft is bent, renew the shaft.

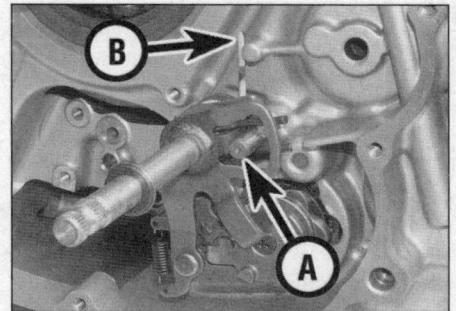

20.7a Location of centralising spring pin (A) and stopper arm spring (B)

20.7b Disengage the selector arm (A) from the selector drum (B) . . .

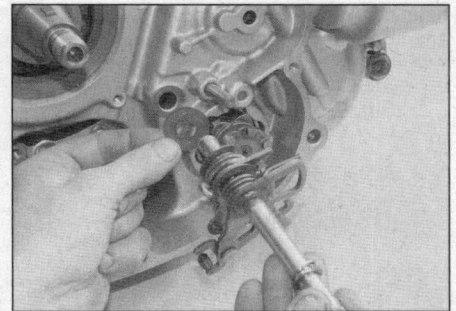

20.7c . . . and pull the gearchange shaft out

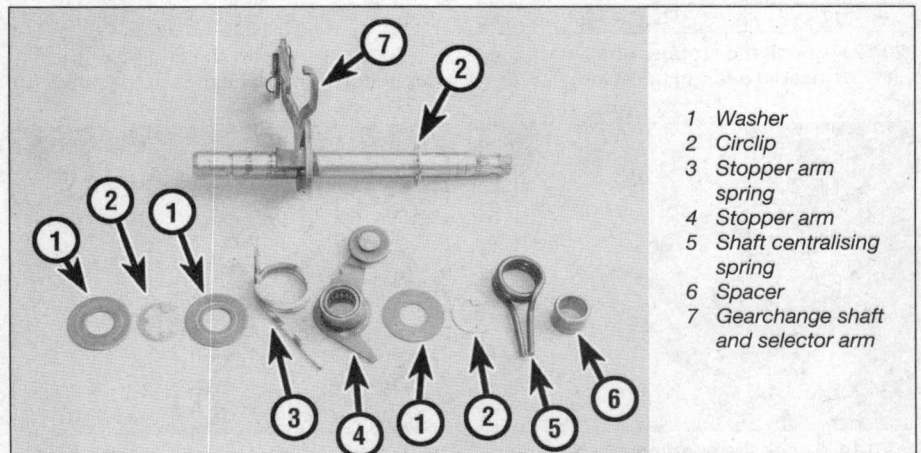

20.8 Gearchange shaft components

1 Washer
2 Circlip
3 Stopper arm spring
4 Stopper arm
5 Shaft centralising spring
6 Spacer
7 Gearchange shaft and selector arm

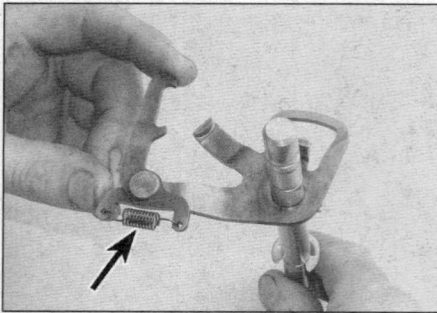

20.10 Check the selector arm for wear – note the spring (arrowed)

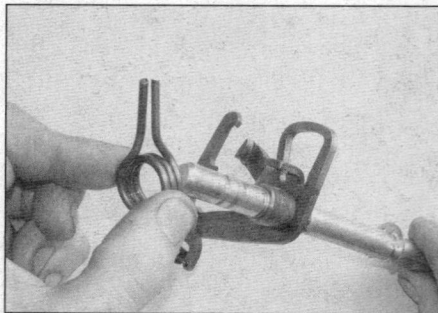

20.11a Install the centralising spring . . .

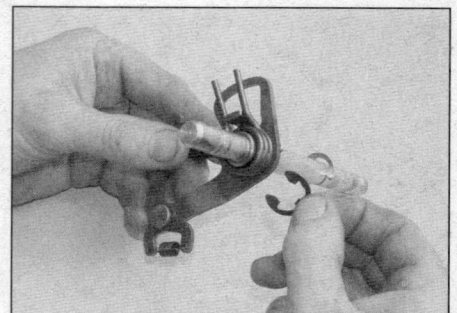

20.11b . . . and secure it with a new circlip

10 Check the selector arm for distortion and wear of its pawls and check the selector arm spring **(see illustration)**. Check for any corresponding wear on the selector pins on the selector drum and renew any components that are worn or damaged.

11 Inspect the shaft centralising spring. To renew the spring, first slide the circlip, washer, stopper arm spring, stopper arm and washer off the shaft **(see illustration 20.8)**. Remove the circlip and slide off the old spring, noting which way round it fits. Install the new spring and secure it with a new circlip **(see illustrations)**.

12 Check the stopper arm roller, needle bearing and the detents in the selector cam for any wear or damage, and make sure the roller turns freely **(see illustration)**. Replace any components that are worn or damaged with new ones. Renew the stopper arm spring if it's worn or distorted **(see illustration)**. After inspection, install the remaining components in the reverse order of removal and secure them with a new circlip.

13 Inspect the pins on the end of the selector cam. If they're worn or damaged, remove the centre screw and lift off the selector cam, then withdraw the pins (see Section 27 for details of the selector drum).

14 Inspect the gearchange shaft seal and needle bearing in the alternator cover and renew them if they are worn or damaged (see *Tools and Workshop Tips* in the *Reference* section) **(see illustration)**. It's a good idea to renew the seal whenever the cover is removed.

Installation

15 Lubricate the gearchange shaft with clean engine oil. Make sure the centralising spring ends are correctly positioned either side of the selector arm tab.

16 Check that the stopper arm components are assembled on the shaft in the correct order **(see illustration 20.8)**. Fit the washer onto the right-hand end of the shaft, then slide the shaft assembly into the crankcase **(see illustration 20.7c)**. Engage the stopper arm with the selector cam and position its spring against the post **(see illustration)**. Pull the selector arm back and engage it on the selector drum and locate the ends of the centralising spring on the pin. **(see illustrations 20.7b and a)**. Ensure the shaft is pressed all the way in.

17 Install the plain washer on the left-hand end of the shaft **(see illustration)**.

18 Install the remaining components in the reverse order of removal.

19 Don't forget to fill the engine with the recommended type and amount of oil (see Chapter 1).

21 Middle driven pinion and final drive coupling

Note: *The middle driven pinion is located in the left-hand side of the crankcase. Access to the pinion and its shaft can only be gained after splitting the crankcases and removing the middle drive pinion and shaft. Because of the complex nature of this job and the special tools and equipment required to dismantle and reassemble the shafts, most owners leave servicing and repair of the middle driven pinion assembly to a Yamaha dealer. However, you can make an initial assessment of whether any work is required as follows.*

20.12a Check the stopper arm – note the needle bearing (arrowed)

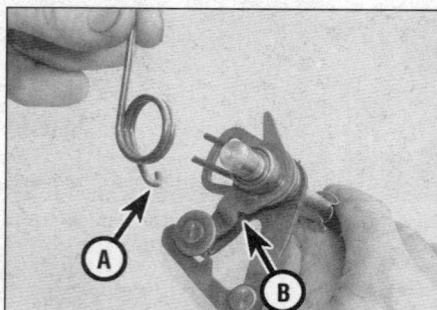

20.12b Note how the end (A) of the stopper arm spring locates in the notch (B)

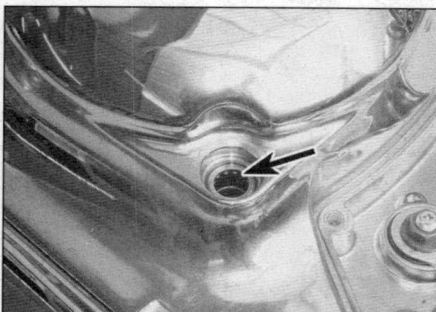

20.14 Check the shaft needle bearing (arrowed) in the alternator cover

20.16 Stopper arm locates against selector cam (A) and spring (B) against post

20.17 Don't forget to fit the washer on the end of the shaft

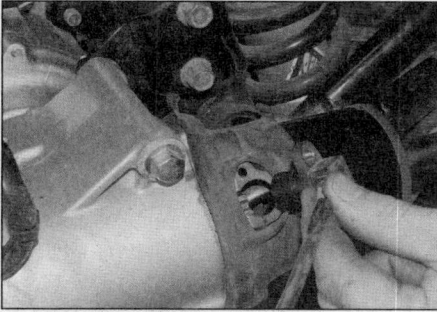

21.3a Displace the speed sensor . . .

21.3b . . . and pull back the driveshaft boot

21.3c Pull off the shaft cover

Middle driven pinion

1 Remove the rear wheel (see Chapter 6).
2 Follow the procedure in Chapter 7 and remove the toolbox and backing panel
3 Undo the bolt securing the speed sensor and displace the sensor, then pull the rubber driveshaft boot away from the engine and pull off the rubber shaft cover **(see illustrations)**.
4 Grasp the inner half of the final drive coupling and check for play in the shaft bearing.
5 If play exists, the engine will have to be removed from the frame and the crankcases split (see Sections 5 and 22). However, first check with your Yamaha dealer or specialist engineer as to how much disassembly to do.

Final drive coupling

6 Inspect the splines on the end of the driveshaft (see Chapter 5). If they are worn it is likely the internal splines on the back half of the drive coupling will be worn also **(see illustration)**.
7 Check the final drive coupling universal joint for looseness or stiff movement.
8 If the drive coupling is worn or damaged, first follow the procedure in Section 5 and remove the engine from the frame.
9 To remove the back half of the coupling, first remove the circlips securing the bearing caps in the front half of the coupling **(see illustrations)**.

10 Support the assembly on a suitably sized tube or socket and drive the lower bearing cap partially out **(see illustrations)**. Now turn the coupling through 180° and drive down on the back half of the coupling to knock out the opposite bearing cap **(see illustrations)**.
11 Remove the back half of the coupling together with the central joint assembly and

21.6 Check the splines (arrowed) in the drive coupling

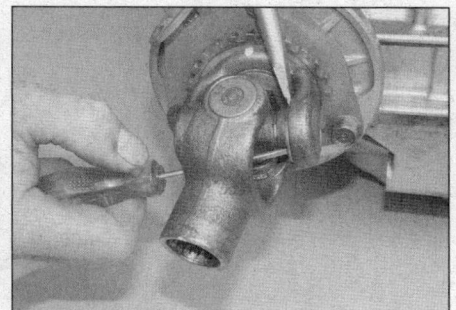

21.9a Lever out the circlips . . .

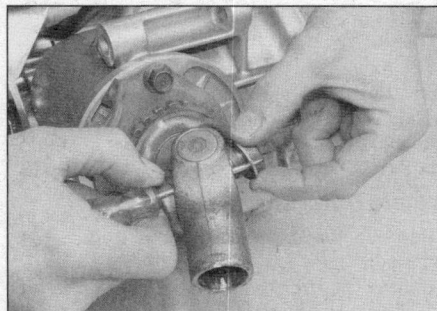

21.9b . . . on the front half of the coupling

21.10a Drive the lower bearing cap partially out . . .

21.10b . . . then turn the coupling . . .

21.10c . . . and drive out the opposite bearing cap as described . . .

21.10d . . . until the central joint (arrowed) is free

21.11 Remove the back half of the coupling

21.12 Drive out the remaining bearing cap

21.13a Partially install one new bearing cap (arrowed) . . .

21.13b . . . then install the new back coupling . . .

21.13c . . . drive the bearing cap all the way in . . .

21.13d . . . and secure it with the circlip

discard it as individual components are not available **(see illustration)**.
12 Drive the remaining bearing cap out of the front bearing coupling **(see illustration)**.
13 Drive one new bearing cap partially into the front bearing coupling, install the new back coupling, then support the assembly and drive the bearing cap all the way in and secure it with a new circlip **(see illustrations)**.
14 Turn the coupling through 180° and drive in the second new bearing cap and secure it with a new circlip.
15 Ensure that all the circlips are pressed fully home **(see illustration)**.
16 Check that the coupling moves freely in all directions without binding **(see illustration)**.

22 Crankcase

1 To examine and repair or renew the crankshaft, connecting rods, bearings, transmission components or middle drive and driven shafts, the crankcase must be split into two parts.

Separation

2 Remove the engine from the frame (see Section 5).
3 Before the crankcases can be separated the following components must be removed:

Cylinder heads (see Section 8)
Cylinders (see Section 12)
Pistons (see Section 13)
Alternator rotor and gears (see Section 16)
Clutch and primary gears (see Section 19)
Cam chains (see Section 15)
Oil pump (see Section 17)
Oil level switch (see Chapter 8)
Gearchange mechanism (see Section 20)

4 If not already done, wrap clean rag around the connecting rods to prevent them striking the crankcase.
5 Loosen the crankcase bolts a 1/4 turn at a time in the **reverse** of the tightening sequence (start with the highest-numbered bolt and work to the lowest) and remove them **(see illustration 22.20a and b)**. Note the sealing washer on the No. 15 bolt and discard it as a new one must be used.

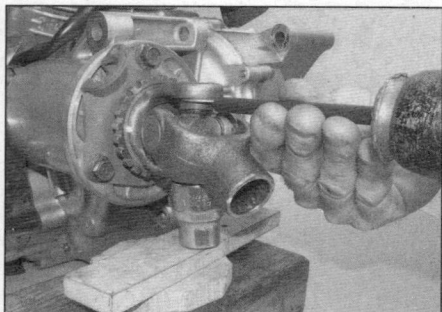
21.15 Ensure all the circlips are pressed fully home

21.16 Check that the new coupling moves freely in all directions

HAYNES HINT *Make a cardboard template of the crankcase and punch a hole for each bolt location. Number the holes. As each bolt is removed, store it in its relative position in the template. This will ensure all bolts are installed correctly on reassembly – this is important, as many bolts differ slightly in length.*

22.6 Carefully lift off the right-hand crankcase half

22.7a Note the location of the dowels (arrowed)

22.7b Note the location of the O-rings . . .

6 Carefully lift the right-hand crankcase half off the left-hand half **(see illustration)**. As you lift, pry gently and evenly at the pry points around the crankcase seam. Using a soft-faced mallet, tap alternately on the transmission and crankshafts and the upper rear crankcase mounting lugs. If the halves won't separate easily, make sure all fasteners have been removed. Don't attempt to lever the crankcase halves apart – you will damage the sealing surface.

7 Note the location of the 3 crankcase dowels and remove them for safekeeping if they are loose **(see illustration)**. Note the location of the two O-rings and the spacer on the central O-ring **(see illustrations)**. Discard the O-rings as new ones must be fitted.

8 Refer to Sections 23 to 28 for the removal and installation of the components housed within the crankcase.

Inspection

9 After the crankshaft and transmission components have been removed, the crankcases should be cleaned thoroughly with suitable solvent and dried with compressed air. All oil passages should be blown out with compressed air.

10 Check the cases for any damage. Small cracks or holes in aluminium castings can be repaired with an epoxy resin adhesive as a temporary measure. Permanent repairs can only be effected by argon-arc welding, and

only a specialist in this process is in a position to advise on the economy or practical aspect of such a repair. If any damage is found that can't be repaired, renew the crankcase halves as a set.

11 Damaged threads can be economically reclaimed by using a diamond section wire thread insert. These are easily fitted after drilling and re-tapping the affected thread.

12 Sheared studs or bolts can usually be removed with stud extractors; if you are in any doubt consult your Yamaha dealer or specialist motorcycle engineer.

> **HAYNES HINT** *Refer to Tools and Workshop Tips in the Reference section for details of installing a thread insert and using stud extractors.*

Reassembly

13 Remove all traces of sealant from the crankcase mating surfaces with a suitable solvent. If a scraper must be used, take care not to gouge the soft aluminium.

14 Install the crankcase dowels and fit the new O-rings **(see illustrations 22.7a, b and c)**.

15 Make sure the crankshaft and transmission shafts are correctly positioned in the left-hand crankcase half (see Sections 26 to 28). If removed, don't forget to install the oil

pressure relief valve in the right-hand crankcase half (see Section 23). Make sure the selector drum is correctly aligned with the neutral switch (see Section 27).

16 Generously lubricate the transmission gears, the selector drum and the crankshaft main bearings with fresh engine oil. Don't get any oil on the crankcase mating surfaces.

17 Apply a thin, even bead of suitable sealant (such as Yamaha Bond 1215) to the mating surface of the left-hand crankcase half **(see illustration)**.

Caution: Don't apply an excessive amount of sealant as it will ooze when the case halves are assembled and may obstruct oil passages.

18 Align the right-hand crankcase half with the crankshaft and transmission shafts. Lower the right-hand half down onto the left-hand half, ensuring the dowels align correctly.

Caution: The crankcase halves should fit together completely without being forced. If they're not correctly seated, separate them and investigate the problem. DO NOT attempt to pull them together by tightening the crankcase bolts.

19 Clean the threads of the crankcase bolts and lubricate them with clean engine oil, then install the bolts in their holes. Don't forget to fit a new sealing washer on the No. 15 bolt **(see illustration)**.

20 Tighten the bolts evenly and a little at a time in numerical order shown, starting with the lowest-numbered bolt and working to the

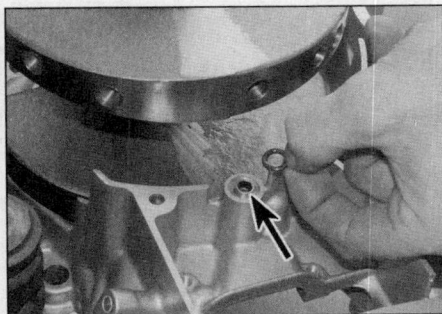

22.7c . . . and the spacer on the central O-ring

22.17 Apply a thin bead of sealant to one half of the crankcase

22.19 Don't forget the sealing washer on bolt No. 15

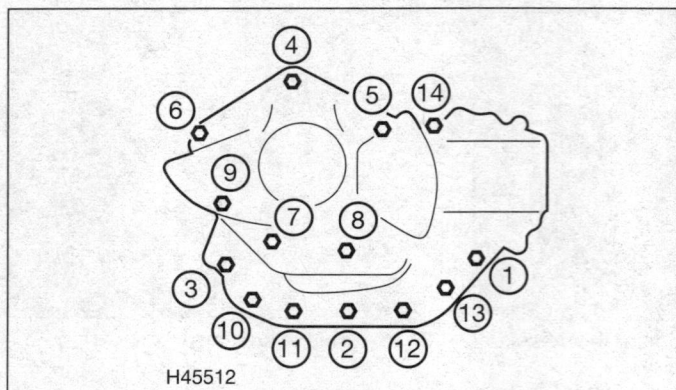

22.20a Crankcase bolt TIGHTENING sequence – left-hand side

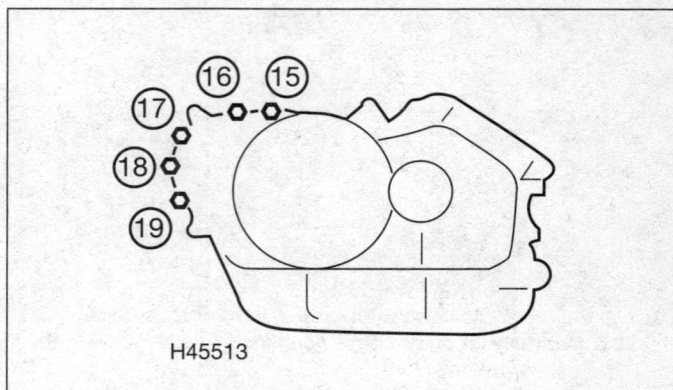

22.20b Crankcase bolt TIGHTENING sequence – right-hand side

highest (see illustrations). Tighten all bolts to the torque listed in this Chapter's Specifications. Note: *There are different torque settings for the 10 mm bolts and the 6 mm bolts.*

21 With all the crankcase bolts tightened, check that the crankshaft and transmission shafts turn smoothly and freely. Support the connecting rods to prevent them striking the crankcase. Rotate the selector cam to ensure the gear selection is operating correctly. If there are any signs of undue stiffness or rough spots, or any other problems, the fault must be rectified before proceeding further.

22 Install the remaining assemblies in the reverse order of removal.

23 Don't forget to fill the engine with the

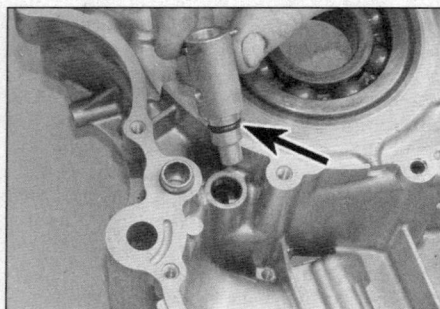

23.2 Draw out the oil pressure relief valve – note the O-ring

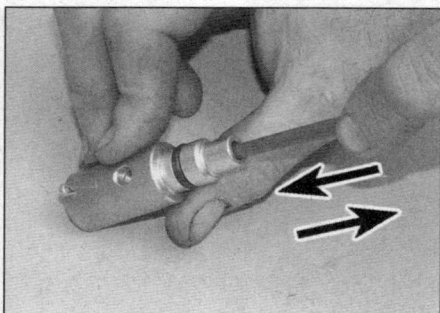

23.3 Checking the operation of the valve plunger

recommended type and amount of oil (see Chapter 1).

23 Oil pressure relief valve

1 Separate the crankcase halves (see Section 22).

2 Draw the pressure relief valve out of the right-hand crankcase half and discard the O-ring as a new one must be fitted (see illustration).

3 Check that the plunger moves smoothly in and out of the valve body (see illustration). If the plunger sticks, disassemble the valve as follows.

4 Straighten the split pin and pull it out, then remove the spring retainer, spring and plunger (see illustration).

5 Clean the parts thoroughly and check them for wear and damage. If the components are good, lubricate them with clean engine oil and reassemble the valve using a new split pin. Recheck the plunger movement. If it still sticks, or if any components are worn, fit a new valve.

6 Fit a new O-ring on the valve body and lubricate it with engine oil. Carefully press the valve back into its bore in the crankcase.

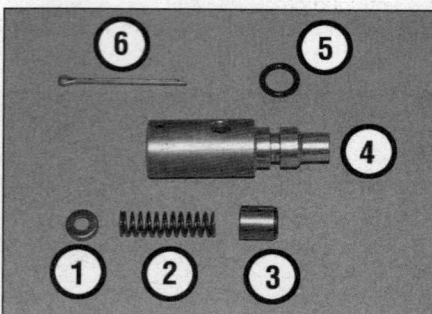

23.4 Components of the oil pressure relief valve

1	Spring retainer	4	Valve body
2	Spring	5	O-ring
3	Plunger	6	Split pin

24 Main and connecting rod bearings – general information

Refer to Chapter 2A, Section 24.

25 Connecting rods and bearings

Removal

1 Separate the crankcase halves (see Section 22).

2 Follow the procedure in Section 26 and remove the crankshaft, together with the connecting rods, from the left-hand crankcase half.

3 Before removing the connecting rods, push them to one side on the crankshaft and measure the clearance between the crankshaft and the connecting rod big-end with a feeler gauge (see illustration). Compare the result with the specification at the beginning of this Chapter; if the clearance is greater than the service limit, examine the sides of the rod big-ends when they have been removed from the crankshaft and renew any component that shows signs of wear or abrasion.

4 Using paint or a marker pen, mark the

25.3 Measuring the connecting rod side clearance

25.4a Mark the position of the connecting rods and caps

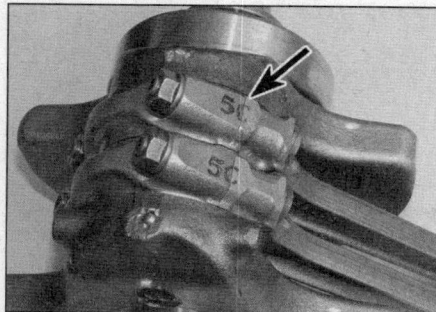

25.4b Big-ends are marked for alignment and bearing size code

25.4c Note the 'Y' marks to ensure correct reassembly

position of each connecting rod and cap relative to its position on the crankshaft **(see illustration)**. Note that the letter already written on the rod and cap is for alignment on reassembly and the number is the big-end bearing size code **(see illustration)**. Note the position of the 'Y' mark on the connecting rods to aid reassembly – the 'Y' marks should face the left-hand side of the crankshaft **(see illustration)**.

5 Unscrew the connecting rod cap nuts and separate the caps, complete with the lower bearing shells, from the crankshaft **(see illustrations)**. If the cap appears stuck, tap it on one end with a soft-faced hammer while pulling it.

6 Detach the connecting rods, complete with the upper bearing shells, from the crankshaft.

7 Press the bearing shells sideways to separate them from the rods and caps and keep the rods, caps and shells in order so they can be reinstalled in their original locations **(see illustrations)**. It is not necessary to remove the bolts from the rods unless they are damaged and new ones need to be fitted – note the alignment of each bolt head with the recess in the rod.

8 Wash the parts in suitable solvent and dry them with compressed air, if available.

Inspection

9 Check the connecting rods for cracks and other obvious damage.

10 To check the rod small-end, lubricate the appropriate piston pin with clean engine oil, then insert it in the rod and check for freeplay **(see illustration)**. If freeplay is excessive, measure the pin external diameter and compare the result with the specifications at the beginning of this Chapter **(see**

illustration). If the pin is worn beyond its service limit, renew it, otherwise a new connecting rod will have to be fitted.

11 Refer to Section 24 and examine the connecting rod bearing shells. If they are scored, badly scuffed or appear to have been seized, new shells must be installed. Always renew the shells in the connecting rods as a set. If they are badly damaged, check the corresponding crankshaft journal. Evidence of extreme heat, such as bluing, indicates that lubrication failure has occurred. Refer to Section 17 and thoroughly check the oil pump and pressure relief valve, as well as all oil holes and passages, before reassembling the engine.

12 If you are in doubt about their straightness, have the rods checked for twist and bending by a Yamaha dealer or specialist engineer.

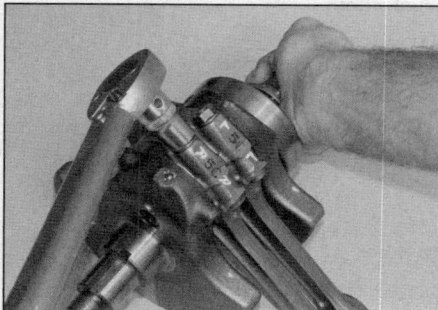

25.5a Remove the cap nuts . . .

25.5b . . . and separate the caps from the crankshaft

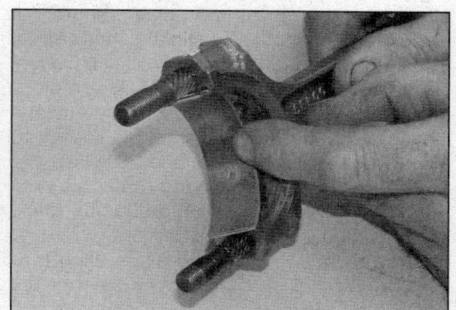

25.7a Press the bearing shells sideways to remove them

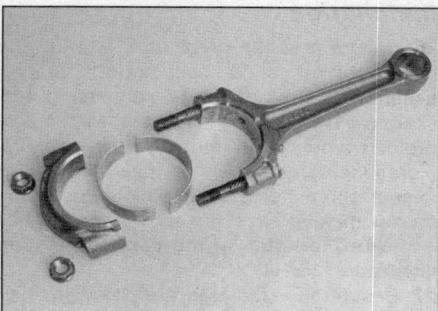

25.7b Keep the rods, caps and shells in order

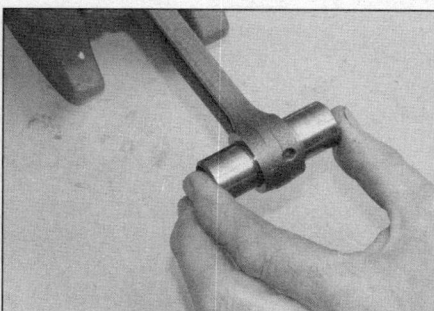

25.10a Check for freeplay between the piston pin and the connecting rod small-end

25.10b Measure the piston pin diameter where it fits in the rod

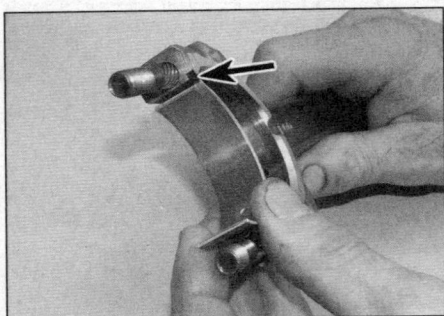
25.15 Tab on the shell should locate in the notch (arrowed)

25.16 Place a strip of Plastigauge on the bearing journal

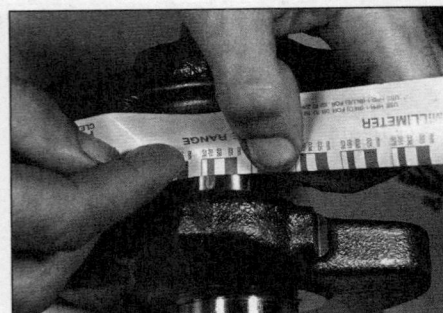
25.20 Measure the crushed Plastigauge using the printed scale

Oil clearance check

13 Whether new bearing shells are being fitted or the original ones are being re-used, the connecting rod big-end bearing oil clearance should be checked prior to reassembly. Bearing oil clearance is measured with a product known as Plastigauge.

14 If not already done, remove the bearing shells from the rods and caps, keeping them in order (see Step 7). Clean the backs of the shells, the bearing locations in both the connecting rods and caps, and the crankshaft journal with a suitable solvent.

15 Press the shells into their locations, ensuring that the tab on each shell engages the notch in the connecting rod or cap (see illustration). Make sure the shells are fitted in the correct locations and take care not to touch the bearing surfaces with your fingers.

16 Cut an appropriate size length of Plastigauge (it should be slightly shorter than the width of the crankshaft journal) and place it on the journal (see illustration). Do not place Plastigauge over the oil holes in the journal.

17 Apply molybdenum disulphide grease to the bolt shanks and threads and to the seats of the nuts. Fit the connecting rods and caps onto the crankshaft (see illustration 25.5b). Make sure the caps are fitted the correct way around so the previously made markings align (see Step 4), and that the 'Y' marks on the rods are facing the correct way round. Fit the nuts and tighten them finger-tight. **Note:** *It is essential that, throughout this procedure, the connecting rods do not rotate on the crankshaft.*

18 Tighten the cap nuts to the torque setting specified at the beginning of this Chapter. Yamaha emphasise that each nut should be tightened in one continuous movement to the final torque setting, and that if tightening is paused between 43 and 48 Nm the nut should be loosened to below 43 Nm and the procedure repeated.

19 Unscrew the nuts and remove the connecting rods and caps from the crankshaft, being very careful not to disturb the Plastigauge.

20 Compare the width of the crushed Plastigauge on the crankshaft journal to the scale printed on the Plastigauge envelope to obtain the bearing oil clearance (see illustration). Compare the result to the specifications at the beginning of this Chapter. If the clearance is within the range specified and the bearings are in perfect condition, they can be reused.

21 Carefully clean away all traces of the Plastigauge from the crankshaft and bearing shells using a fingernail or other object which will not score the bearing surfaces.

22 If the clearance is beyond the service limit, replace the bearing shells with new ones (see Steps 24 and 25) and check the oil clearance once again. Always renew all of the shells at the same time.

23 If the clearance is still greater than the service limit, the crankshaft journal is worn and the crankshaft should be replaced with a new one.

Bearing shell selection

24 Replacement shells for the big-end bearings are supplied on a selected fit basis.

The code number for the crankshaft journal is stamped on the outside of the crankshaft web (see illustration). Each connecting rod size code number is marked in ink on the flat face of the connecting rod cap (see illustration 25.4b). Note that there are two ranges of bearing shells – the first range (Table 1) is for the front cylinder, upper and lower bearing shells, and rear cylinder lower bearing shell; the second range (Table 2) is for the rear cylinder upper bearing shell only.

25 To select the correct shells, subtract the crankshaft journal number from the connecting rod number and compare the result with the appropriate table below to find the colour coding of the replacement shells e.g. connecting rod number 4 minus journal number 2 = 2; No. 2 bearing shells are colour-coded black. The colour codes are painted on the edge of the bearing shells (see illustration).

Table 1

Number	Colour
1	blue
2	black
3	brown
4	green
5	yellow

Table 2

Number	Colour
1) 2)	black
3	brown
4) 5)	green

Installation

26 Ensure that the crankshaft journal, the backs of the bearing shells and the bearing seats in the caps and rods are clean. If new shells are being fitted, ensure that all traces of protective grease are removed using paraffin (kerosene). Dry the shells, caps, rods and journal with a clean, lint-free cloth. Install the shells, making sure the tab on each shell engages the notch in the cap or rod (see illustration 25.15).

27 Ensure the bearings are fitted in their correct locations and take care not to touch any bearing surface with your fingers. Lubricate the shells with clean engine oil.

25.24 Location of the crankshaft journal code number

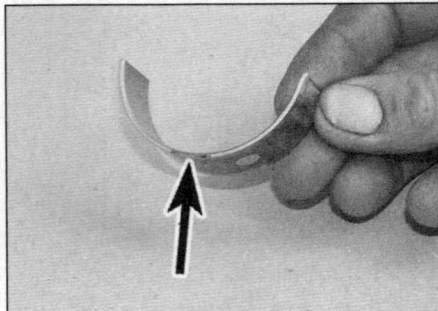
25.25 Location of the bearing shell colour code

26.2a Set-up for pressing the crankshaft out of the crankcase

26.2b Support the crankshaft assembly as it is removed

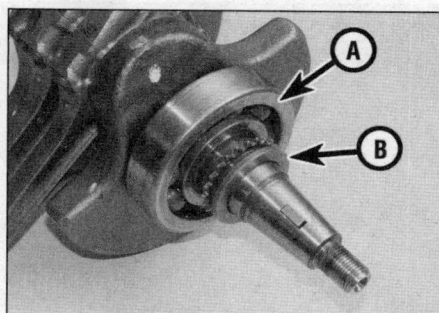

26.3 Left-hand main bearing (A) and oil pump drive sprocket (B)

28 Follow the procedure in Step 17 and assemble the connecting rods on the crankshaft, then follow the procedure in Step 18 and tighten the cap nuts to the specified torque setting.

29 Check that the rods rotate smoothly and freely on the crankshaft. If either of them feels tight, tap on the bottom of the cap with a soft-faced hammer – this should free it up. If not, detach the rods and recheck the assembly.

30 Follow the procedure in Section 26 and install the crankshaft assembly in the crankcase.

26 Crankshaft and main bearings

Removal

1 Separate the crankcase halves (see Section 22).

2 Support the left-hand crankcase half and press out the crankshaft. The crankshaft is a very tight fit in the bearing in the left-hand crankcase half. Yamaha produce a service tool (Part No. 90890-01135 Europe models or YU-01135-A US models) to press the crankshaft out. Alternatively, use the set-up shown **(see illustrations)**. **Note:** *If the crankshaft does not come out easily, apply steady pressure with the tools described and heat the bearing housing with a hot air gun.* **DO NOT** *try to drive the crankshaft out – if necessary, take the crankcase to a Yamaha dealer or specialist engineer for crankshaft removal and installation.*

3 The left-hand main bearing and the oil pump drive sprocket will come out with the crankshaft – unless the bearing or sprocket need to be renewed, they can be left in place **(see illustration)**.

4 Follow the procedure in Section 25 and remove the connecting rods from the crankshaft.

5 Clean the crankshaft with a suitable solvent, paying particular attention to flush out the oil passages. If available, blow the crank dry with compressed air and also blow through the oil passages.

Inspection

6 Check the oil pump drive sprocket for chipped teeth and excessive wear. If any damage is found, use an external bearing puller to remove the sprocket **(see illustration)**. Check the condition of the chain and oil pump sprocket (see Section 17).

26.6 Using a bearing puller to remove the oil pump drive sprocket

7 Place the crankshaft on V-blocks and check the runout with a dial gauge **(see illustration)**. Compare the result with this Chapter's Specifications. If the runout exceeds the limit, renew the crankshaft.

8 Check the main bearings referring to *Tools and Workshop Tips* (Section 5) in the *Reference* section **(see illustrations)**. If the right-hand bearing needs to be renewed, heat the bearing housing with a hot air gun and tap it out using a bearing driver or suitably sized socket. Note which way round the bearing is fitted. If the left-hand bearing needs to be removed, use an external bearing puller to draw it off the crankshaft. **Note:** *If not already done, the oil pump drive sprocket must be removed before the bearing (see Step 6).*

9 Refer to Section 24 and examine the crankshaft where it passes through the main bearings **(see illustration)**. Evidence of extreme heat, such as bluing, indicates that

26.7 Checking the crankshaft runout

26.8a Check the left-hand main bearing on the crankshaft . . .

26.8b . . . and the right-hand main bearing (arrowed) in the crankcase

26.9 Examine the surface of the crankshaft

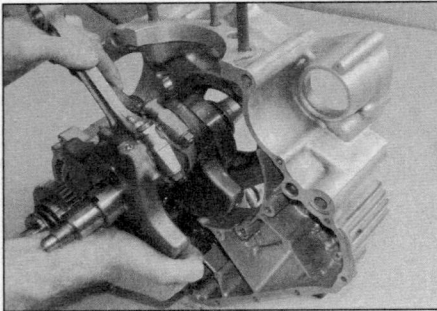

26.14a Position the crankshaft in the left-hand case . . .

26.14b . . . then draw it in using the set-up shown

26.14c Left-hand connecting rod aligns with mouth of rear cylinder

lubrication failure and bearing seizure has occurred. Refer to Sections 17 and 23 and thoroughly check the oil pump and pressure relief valve, as well as all oil holes and passages, before reassembling the engine. If the journals are scored, badly scuffed or pitted, renew the crankshaft.

Installation

10 If applicable, fit the new right-hand bearing into the crankcase. Heat the bearing housing and carefully tap the bearing in using a bearing driver or suitable socket which bears on the bearing outer race.
11 If applicable, fit the new left-hand bearing onto the crankshaft. Support the crankshaft and drive the bearing on using a suitable length of tube which bears on the bearing

inner race. Use the same method to install the new oil pump drive sprocket, ensuring the sprocket teeth are facing in (see illustration 26.3).
12 Follow the procedure in Section 25 and install the connecting rods on the crankshaft.
13 Lubricate the main bearings with clean engine oil.
14 Position the crankshaft in the left-hand crankcase half (see illustration). Ensure the main bearing is aligned with the bearing housing, then heat the housing with a hot air gun and draw the crankshaft assembly in using the set-up shown (see illustration). Note that the bearing is a very tight fit in its housing and considerable heat will have to be applied throughout the procedure. Ensure the left-hand connecting rod is aligned with the mouth of the rear cylinder in the crankcase

(see illustration). Ensure the main bearing is drawn all the way into its housing.
15 Follow the procedure in Section 22 and assemble the crankcase halves.

27 Selector drum and forks

Removal

1 Separate the crankcase halves (see Section 22).
2 Note how the flat on the selector fork shaft aligns with the middle drive gear pinion (see illustration).
3 Note how the selector forks locate in the grooves in the gear pinions and how the guide pins on the forks locate in the grooves in the selector drum.
4 The forks are lettered for identification. Note: *The letters are not visible when the forks are in place in the transmission – if required, make your own marks before removing them.* The right-hand fork (R) locates in the groove on the output shaft 4th gear pinion, the middle fork (C) locates in the groove on the input shaft 2nd/3rd gear pinion and the left-hand fork (L) locates in the groove on the output shaft 5th gear pinion.
5 Pull out the fork shaft then lift out the R fork (see illustrations). Note the position of the middle fork (C), then turn it and draw it out (see illustrations). Slide the forks back onto the shaft the right way round for safekeeping.

27.2 Flat (arrowed) on the shaft aligns with the middle driven gear pinion

27.5a Pull out the fork shaft . . .

27.5b . . . and the 'R' fork

27.5c Note the location of the middle 'C' fork (arrowed) . . .

27.5d . . . then turn it and draw it out

27.6a Support the left-hand 'L' fork (arrowed) . . .

27.6b . . . and lift out the selector drum . . .

27.6c . . . then lift out the left-hand fork

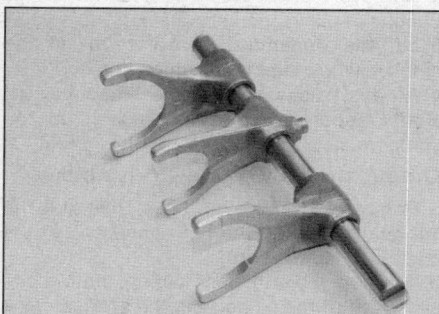

27.7 Check the selector forks for wear and damage

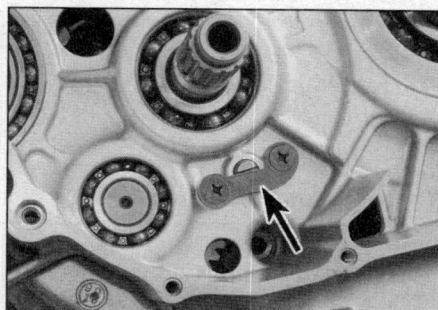

27.10 Ensure that the shaft stopper plate (arrowed) is secure

27.11a Check the selector drum grooves (arrowed) . . .

6 Note how the selector drum aligns with the neutral switch, then carefully lever up the remaining fork (L) and pull the drum out of the case (see illustrations). Lift out the left-hand fork (see illustration).

Inspection

7 Inspect the selector forks for any signs of wear or damage, especially around the fork ends where they engage with the grooves in the pinions (see illustration). Check that each fork fits correctly in its pinion groove. Check closely to see if the forks are bent. If the forks are in any way damaged they must be replaced with new ones.
8 Check that the forks fit correctly on the shaft. They should move freely with a light fit

but no appreciable freeplay. Check that the fork shaft holes in the casing are not worn or damaged.
9 Check the selector fork shaft is straight using V-blocks and a dial gauge or by rolling it along a flat surface. A bent shaft will cause difficulty in selecting gears and make the gearchange action heavy and should be replaced with a new one.
10 Check the shaft stopper plate in the right-hand crankcase half for looseness (see illustration). If the plate is loose, remove its screws and apply a suitable thread locking compound to the threads. Reinstall the screws and tighten them to the torque listed in this Chapter's Specifications.
11 Inspect the selector drum grooves and

selector fork guide pins for signs of wear or damage (see illustrations). If either show signs of wear or damage they must be replaced with new ones.
12 Check the selector drum bearing referring to *Tools and Workshop Tips* (Section 5) in the *Reference* section. If the bearing is worn, remove the screw securing the selector cam and lift off the cam, noting the location of the dowel, then draw the bearing off (see illustration). Install the new bearing, then align the dowel and install the cam and tighten the screw securely.
13 Check the operation of the spring-loaded neutral switch plunger in the left-hand crankcase half (see illustration). If the plunger is damaged, unscrew the switch from

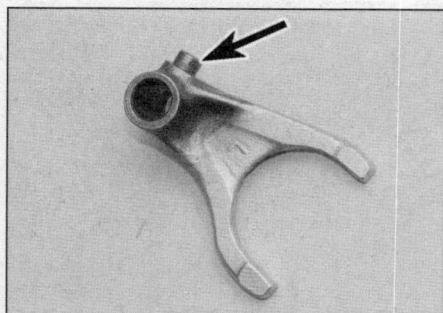

27.11b . . . and the fork guide pins for wear and damage

27.12 Selector drum bearing (A), cam (B) and screw (C)

27.13a Check the operation of the neutral switch plunger (arrowed)

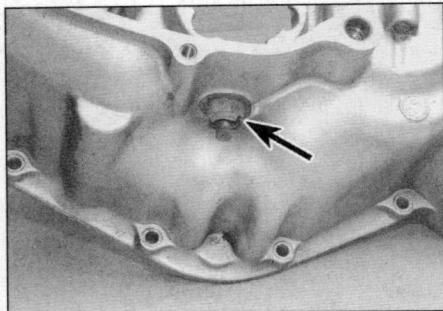

27.13b Unscrew the switch (arrowed) from the outside of the case

27.14a Support the left-hand fork before installing the selector drum

27.14b Fork guide pins must be located in the selector drum grooves

the crankcase and fit a new one with a new sealing washer **(see illustration)**.

Installation

14 Installation is the reverse of removal, noting the following:

● Lubricate all components with clean engine oil before installing them.
● Use the letters on the selector forks to position them correctly (see Step 4). The letters face the right-hand side of the engine when installed.
● Hold the left-hand fork in position before installing the selector drum **(see illustration)**.
● Ensure the selector fork guide pins are located in their grooves in the selector drum before installing the fork shaft **(see illustration)**.
● Ensure the selector drum is in the neutral position.

● Align the flat on the forks shaft with the middle drive gear pinion.

28 Transmission shafts

Removal and disassembly

> **HAYNES HiNT** *When disassembling the transmission shafts, place the parts on a long rod or thread a wire through them to keep them in order and facing the proper direction.*

1 Separate the crankcase halves (see Section 22).

2 Remove the selector drum and forks (see Section 27).
3 Lift the transmission shafts out of the crankcase together **(see illustration)**.
4 Always disassemble the transmission shafts separately to avoid mixing up the components.

Output shaft and middle drive pinion

5 Remove the middle drive gear then slide the 1st gear pinion off the right-hand end of the shaft **(see illustration)**.
6 Remove the 4th gear pinion, noting the alignment of the oil holes in the shaft and the pinion **(see illustration)**.
7 Remove the circlip and splined washer **(see illustrations)**. Discard the circlip as a new one must be fitted.
8 Remove the 3rd gear pinion **(see illustration)**.
9 Remove the 5th gear pinion from the left-

28.3 Lift the shafts out together

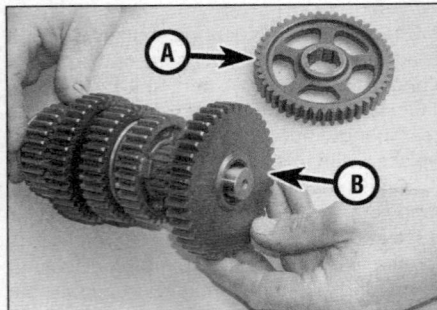

28.5 Remove the middle drive gear (A) then slide off the 1st gear pinion (B)

28.6 Remove the 4th gear pinion – note the alignment of the oil holes (arrowed)

28.7a Remove the circlip ...

28.7b ... and splined washer

28.8 Remove the 3rd gear pinion

28.9 Remove the 5th gear pinion – note the alignment of the oil holes (arrowed)

28.10a Remove the circlip . . .

28.10b . . . and splined washer

28.11 Remove the 2nd gear pinion

28.12 Lift off the middle driven gear pinion

28.13 Location of the middle drive shaft assembly

hand end of the shaft, noting the alignment of the oil holes in the shaft and the pinion (see illustration).
10 Remove the circlip and splined washer (see illustrations). Discard the circlip as a new one must be fitted.
11 Remove the 2nd gear pinion (see illustration).

12 Lift the middle driven gear pinion off the middle drive shaft (see illustration).
13 The middle drive shaft assembly should be left in the crankcase (see illustration). Special tools and equipment are required to dismantle and reassemble the assembly. If any of the components appear worn or damaged, consult a Yamaha dealer or specialist engineer.

Input shaft

14 Remove the circlip and thrust washer (see illustrations). Discard the circlip as a new one must be fitted.
15 Remove the 5th gear pinion then slide off the 2nd/3rd gear pinion (see illustrations).
16 Remove the circlip and splined washer (see illustrations). Discard the circlip as a new one must be fitted.

28.14a Remove the circlip . . .

28.14b . . . and thrust washer

28.15a Remove the 5th gear pinion . . .

28.15b . . . and the 2nd/3rd gear pinion

28.16a Remove the circlip . . .

28.16b . . . and splined washer

28.17 Remove the 4th gear pinion

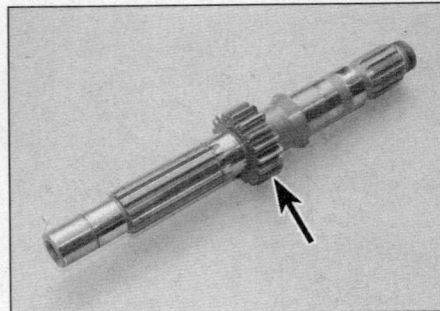

28.18 The 1st gear pinion (arrowed) is integral with the shaft

17 Remove the 4th gear pinion (see illustration).
18 The 1st gear pinion is integral with the input shaft (see illustration).

Inspection

19 Wash all the components in suitable solvent and dry them off.
20 Check the gear teeth for cracking, chipping, pitting and other obvious wear or damage. Any pinion that is damaged must be renewed.
21 Inspect the dogs and the dog holes in the gears for cracks, chips, and excessive wear especially in the form of rounded edges (see illustration). Make sure mating gears engage properly. Renew mating gears as a set if necessary.
22 Check for signs of scoring or blueing on

the pinions and shafts. This could be caused by overheating due to inadequate lubrication. Check that all the oil holes and passages are clear. Replace any worn or damaged parts with new ones.
23 Check that each pinion moves freely on the shaft without undue freeplay.
24 The shafts are unlikely to sustain damage unless the engine has seized, placing an unusually high loading on the transmission, or after the machine has covered a very high mileage. Check the surface of each shaft, especially where a pinion turns on it, and replace the shaft with a new one if it has scored or picked up, or if there are any cracks (see illustration). Check the shaft runout using V-blocks and a dial gauge and replace the shaft with a new one if the runout exceeds the limit specified at the beginning of this Chapter.

25 Check the splined washers and renew any that are bent or worn.
26 Check the transmission bearings in the crankcase halves referring to Tools and Workshop Tips (Section 5) in the Reference section (see illustration). Note that an oil seal is fitted behind the input shaft bearing in the left-hand side of the crankcase (see illustration). If the bearing is removed, remove the seal and check that the oil passage in the bearing seat is clear. Fit a new oil seal. Don't forget to check the bearing on the middle driven gear (see illustration).

Assembly and installation

Note: During assembly and installation, lubricate the bearings with clean engine oil and the transmission shafts and pinions with molybdenum disulphide oil (a 50/50 mix of engine oil and molybdenum grease).

Output shaft

27 Slide the 2nd gear pinion and splined washer onto the left-hand end of the shaft and secure them with a new circlip (see illustrations 28.11, 28.10b and a). Align the ends of the circlip with the splines on the shaft.
28 Install the 5th gear pinion (see illustration 28.9).
29 Slide the 3rd gear pinion and splined washer onto the right-hand end of the shaft and secure them with a new circlip (see illustrations 28.8, 28.7b and a).
30 Slide on the 4th and 1st gear pinions, then install the middle drive gear (see illustrations 28.6 and 28.5).

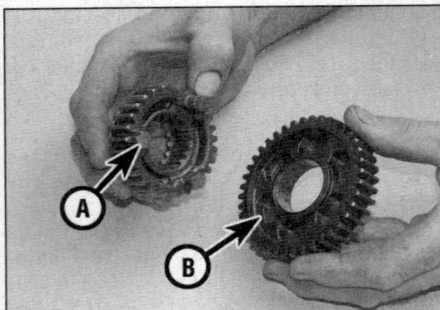

28.21 Check the condition of the dogs (A) and dog holes (B)

28.24 Check the shafts for wear and damage

28.26a Check the transmission bearings as described

28.26b Note the location of the input shaft oil seal

28.26c Check the bearing on the middle driven gear

Input shaft

31 Slide the 4th gear pinion and splined washer onto the left-hand end of the shaft and secure them with a new circlip **(see illustrations 28.17, 28.16b and a)**.

32 Slide on the 2nd/3rd gear pinion and the 5th gear pinion **(see illustrations 28.15b and a)**.

33 Install the thrust washer and secure it with a new circlip **(see illustration 28.14b and a)**.

34 Mesh the gears on both transmission shafts **(see illustration)**. Install the transmission assembly in the crankcase **(see illustration 28.3)**.

35 Install the middle driven gear pinion on the middle drive shaft **(see illustration 28.12)**.

36 Install the selector drum and forks (see Section 27).

29 Initial start-up after overhaul

1 Make sure the engine oil level is correct (see *Daily (pre-ride) checks*).

2 Make sure there is fuel in the tank, then turn the fuel tap to the ON position and operate the choke.

3 Start the engine and allow it to run at a moderately fast idle until it reaches operating temperature.

4 Ensure that the engine warning light is not illuminated.

5 Check carefully that there are no oil leaks

28.34 Mesh the gears on both transmission shafts

and make sure the transmission and controls, especially the brakes, function properly before road testing the machine. Refer to Section 30 for the recommended running-in procedure.

6 Upon completion of the road test, and after the engine has cooled down completely, recheck the valve clearances (see Chapter 1).

30 Recommended running-in procedure

1 Treat the machine gently for the first few miles to allow the oil to circulate throughout the engine and any new parts installed to seat.

2 Great care is necessary if the engine has been extensively overhauled – the bike will have to be run in as when new. This means

more use of the transmission and a restraining hand on the throttle until at least 600 miles (1000 km) have been covered. There is no point in keeping to any set road speed – the main idea is to keep from labouring the engine and to gradually increase performance up to the 1000 mile (1600 km) mark. These recommendations apply less when only a partial overhaul has been done, though it does depend to an extent on the nature of the work carried out and which components have been renewed. Experience is the best guide, since it is easy to tell when an engine is running freely. If in any doubt, consult a Yamaha dealer. The following maximum engine speed limitations, which Yamaha provide for new motorcycles, can be used as a guide.

3 If a lubrication failure is suspected, stop the engine immediately and try to find the cause. If an engine is run without oil, even for a short period of time, severe damage will occur.

Up to 600 miles (1000 km)	No more than 1/3 throttle – vary throttle position and speed.
600 to 1000 miles (1000 to 1600 km)	No more than 1/2 throttle – vary throttle position and speed
Over 1000 miles (1600 km)	Normal riding – do not exceed tachometer red line

Chapter 3
Fuel and exhaust systems

Contents

Degrees of difficulty

Easy, suitable for novice with little experience	**Fairly easy,** suitable for beginner with some experience	**Fairly difficult,** suitable for competent DIY mechanic	**Difficult,** suitable for experienced DIY mechanic	**Very difficult,** suitable for expert DIY or professional

Specifications

Fuel
Grade .... Unleaded, minimum 91 RON (Research Octane Number)
Fuel tank capacity (including reserve)
  650 models .... 16 litres
    Reserve .... 3 litres
  1100 models .... 17 litres
    Reserve .... 4.5 litres

Carburettors – 650 models
Type .... 2 x Mikuni BDS28
Fuel level .... 7.5 to 8.5 mm below line on float chamber
Idle speed .... see Chapter 1
Pilot screw setting
  UK models
    1997 to 2000 .... 2 turns out
    2001-on .... 2 1/2 turns out
  US models .... 2 1/2 turns out
Main jet 90
Main air jet 50
Jet needle/clip position from top
  UK models
    1997 to 2000 .... 4CP10 / 3
    2001-on .... 4CT2 / 2
  US models .... 4CT3 / 1
Needle jet
  UK models
    1997 to 2000 .... O–6
    2001-on O–4
  US models O–4
Pilot jet 20
Pilot air jet 100
Valve seat size 1.0

Carburettors – 1100 models

Type	2 x Mikuni BSR37
Fuel level	4 to 5 mm below top edge of float chamber
Idle speed	see Chapter 1
Pilot screw setting	
UK models	3 turns out
US models	Pre-set
Main jet	
Front cylinder	112.5
Rear cylinder	110
Main air jet	55
Jet needle/clip position from top	
UK models	
XVS1100 (all models), XVS1100A (1999)	
Front cylinder	5DL40-53-3 / 5
Rear cylinder	5DL39-53-3 / 5
XVS1100A and S (2000-on)	5DL44-53-3
US models	5DL43-53-1
Needle jet	P – 0M
Pilot jet	17.5
Pilot air jet	
Front cylinder	145
Rear cylinder	63.8
Valve seat size	1.2

Throttle position sensor

Resistance	4 to 6 K-ohms @ 20°C

Fuel pump

Output pressure	0.12 Bar (1.74 psi)
Resistance	1.6 to 2.2 ohms @ 20°C

AIS

Reed valve clearance	0.4 mm

Torque settings

Carburettor assembly bolts	12 Nm
Exhaust pipe-to-cylinder head nuts	20 Nm
Silencer clamp bolts	20 Nm
Exhaust system mounting bolts	25 Nm

1 General information and precautions

General information

The fuel system consists of the fuel tank, the fuel tap, filter and pump, the carburettors and the connecting hoses and control cables.

The carburettors used on these motorcycles are CV type Mikunis with butterfly throttle valves. For cold starting, a cable-operated choke mechanism is fitted. In certain markets the carburettors are fitted with electronically operated heaters to prevent carburettor icing.

Air is drawn into the carburettors first through a filter, which is located on the side of the machine below the fuel tank. It then passes into an airbox mounted immediately above the carburettors.

The exhaust system routes exhaust gases from the engine into twin silencers mounted on the right-hand side of the bike. Certain models have an air induction system (AIS) to reduce harmful emissions.

Many of the fuel system service procedures are considered routine maintenance items and for that reason are included in Chapter 1.

Precautions

⚠️ **Warning: Petrol (gasoline) is extremely flammable, so take extra precautions when you work on any part of the fuel system. Don't smoke or allow open flames or bare light bulbs near the work area, and don't work in a garage where a natural gas-type appliance is present. If you spill any fuel on your skin, wash it off immediately with soap and water. When you perform any kind of work on the fuel system, wear safety glasses and have a fire extinguisher suitable for a class B type fire (flammable liquids) on hand.**

Always perform service procedures in a well-ventilated area to prevent a build-up of fumes.

Never work in a building containing a gas appliance with a pilot light, or any other form of naked flame. Ensure that there are no naked light bulbs or any sources of flame or sparks nearby.

Do not smoke (or allow anyone else to smoke) while in the vicinity of petrol (gasoline), or of components containing petrol. Remember the possible presence of vapour from these sources and move well clear before smoking.

Check all electrical equipment belonging to the house, garage or workshop where work is being undertaken (see the *Safety First!* section of this manual). Remember that certain electrical appliances such as drills, cutters etc. create sparks in the normal course of operation and must not be used near petrol (gasoline) or any component containing it. Again, remember the possible presence of fumes before using electrical equipment.

Always mop up any spilt fuel and safely dispose of the rag used.

Any stored fuel that is drained off during servicing work must be kept in sealed containers that are suitable for holding petrol (gasoline), and clearly marked as such; the containers themselves should be kept in a safe place. Note that this last point applies equally to the fuel tank if it is removed from the machine; also remember to keep its filler cap closed at all times.

Read the *Safety first!* section of this manual carefully before starting work.

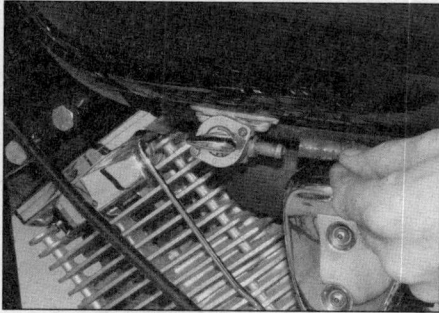

2.2 Detach the fuel hose from the tap

2.4 Detach the fuel tank breather hose (arrowed)

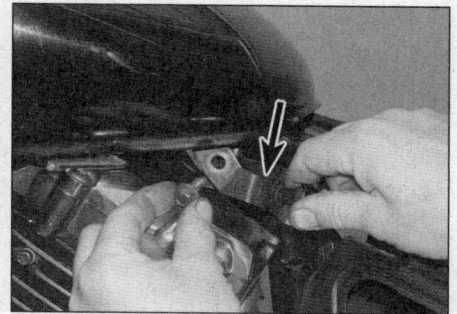

2.6 Remove the tank mounting bolts – note the location of the choke bracket (arrowed)

2 Fuel tank, tap and filter

Warning: Refer to the precautions given in Section 1 before starting work.

Fuel tank

1 Make sure the fuel filler cap is secure.

2 Turn the fuel tap OFF. Have a rag ready to catch any residual fuel from the hose, then release the clip securing the hose to the tap and detach the hose **(see illustration)**.

650 models

3 Remove the instrument panel and disconnect the speedometer cable and instrument wiring (see Chapter 8).

4 Release the clip securing the tank breather hose and detach the hose, noting how it fits **(see illustration)**.

5 Remove the seats (see Chapter 7).

6 Remove the two bolts securing the rear of the tank to the frame, noting the location of the choke bracket **(see illustration)**.

7 Lift the tank off, pulling it to the rear of the bike to release it from the front mounting rubbers.

8 Inspect the tank mounting rubbers for signs of damage or deterioration and replace them with new ones, if necessary **(see illustration)**.

9 Installation is the reverse of removal, noting the following:

● Push the tank all the way forward onto the mounting rubbers.

● Make sure the hoses are properly attached and secured by their clips. Make sure the breather hose is correctly routed through its guide **(see illustration 2.4)**.

● Make sure the instrument wiring is securely connected.

● Tighten the mounting bolts securely.

● Start the engine and check that there are no sign of fuel leaks.

1100 models

10 Remove the seats (see Chapter 7).

11 Release the trim clips securing the ICU panel underneath the seat, then lift the panel and disconnect the instrument panel wiring connector **(see illustration)**.

12 Remove the two bolts securing the tank rear bracket, then lift the tank off, pulling it to the rear of the bike to release it from the front mounting rubbers **(see illustrations)**.

13 Inspect the tank mounting rubbers for signs of damage or deterioration and replace them with new ones, if necessary **(see illustration 2.8)**.

14 Installation is the reverse of removal, noting the points in Step 9. Note there is no breather hose fitted on this model.

Fuel tap

15 The tap should not be removed unnecessarily from the tank, otherwise there is a possibility of damaging the seal. If the fuel tap-to-tank joint is leaking, first ensure that the retaining screws are tightened to the specified torque setting **(see illustration)**. If the leak persists, remove the tap (see Steps 17 to 19) and renew the seal.

16 If the tap body is leaking, first ensure that the body screws are tight. If the leak

2.8 Check the condition of the tank mounting rubbers

2.11 Disconnect the instrument panel wiring connector

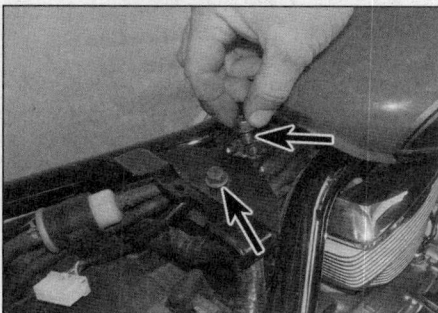

2.12a Remove the tank mounting bolts (arrowed) . . .

2.12b . . . and lift the tank off

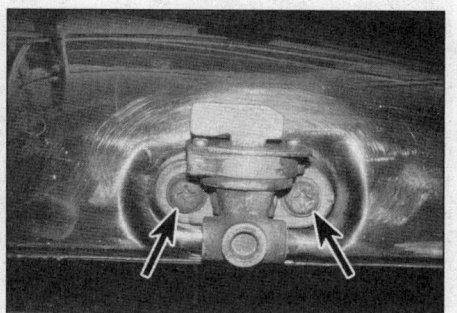

2.15 Fuel tap retaining screws (arrowed)

2.19 Fuel tap assembly and seal (arrowed)

2.20a Remove the body screws (arrowed) . . .

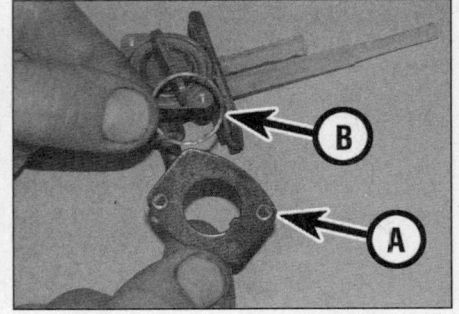
2.20b . . . then lift off the front plate (A) and washer (B) . . .

2.20c . . . and remove the lever and O-ring (arrowed)

persists, remove the tap as follows and renew the seal.

17 Remove the fuel tank (see Steps above as appropriate).

18 Connect a drain hose to the tap and insert its end in a container suitable and large enough for storing the fuel in the tank. Turn the fuel tap to RES and allow the tank to drain fully. When the tank has drained, turn the tap OFF.

19 Remove the screws securing the tap to the tank and withdraw the tap assembly (see illustration). Discard the seal, as a new one must be used.

20 Remove the body screws, front plate, washer, lever and O-ring (see illustrations).

21 Clean any sediment out of the tap body and ensure the body and lever are not worn, then reassemble the tap fitting a new O-ring. Tighten the body screws securely.

22 Fit a new tap seal, then install the tap in the tank and tighten the screws securely.

23 Install the fuel tank (see Steps above as appropriate).

Fuel filter

24 An in-line fuel filter is fitted between the fuel tap and the fuel pump. The filter should be renewed at the specified service interval, or if it becomes dirty or clogged (see Chapter 1, Section 18).

3 Fuel tank cleaning and repair

1 All repairs to the fuel tank should be carried out by a professional who has experience in this critical and potentially dangerous work. Even after cleaning and flushing of the fuel

system, explosive fumes can remain and ignite during repair of the tank.

2 If the fuel tank is removed from the bike, it should not be placed in an area where sparks or open flames could ignite the fumes coming out of the tank. Be especially careful inside garages where a natural gas-type appliance is located, because the pilot light could cause an explosion.

4 Air filter housing and airbox

Removal

1 Remove the fuel tank (see Section 2).

2 Release the clip securing the air filter housing to the airbox duct (see illustration).

3 Remove the bolts securing the air filter housing, then carefully pull the housing away from the bike to release the peg on the back of the housing from the grommet on the support bracket (see illustration).

4 On 1100 models, release the clip securing the air duct to the airbox and pull off the duct

4.2 Release the clip (A) between the duct (B) and the filter housing (C)

4.3 Note the mounting peg (arrowed)

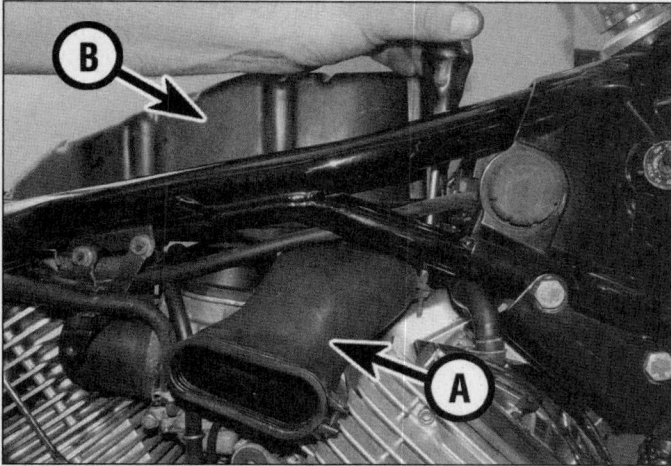
4.4a On 1100 models, separate the air duct (A) from the airbox (B) . . .

4.4b . . . then release the clips on the underside of the airbox . . .

(see illustration). Release the clips securing the front and rear carburettor intake ducts to the underside of the airbox (see illustration). Remove the airbox rear mounting bolt (see illustration).

5 On 650 models, release the clips securing the underside of the airbox front and rear carburettor intakes (see illustration).

6 Lift the airbox and release the clip securing the engine breather hose and detach the hose, then remove the airbox (see illustrations).

7 On 1100 models, note how the carburettor breather locates in the underside of the airbox (see illustration).

Installation

8 Installation is the reverse of removal, noting the following:

● Check the condition of the various ducts and hoses and their clips and replace them with new ones, if necessary.

● Don't forget to connect the engine breather hose and secure it with the clip.

● Ensure the airbox is pressed firmly down onto the carburettor intake ducts before tightening the clips.

4.4c . . . and remove the rear mounting bolt

5 Air/fuel mixture adjustment

Note: *Due to the increased emphasis on controlling exhaust emissions in certain world markets, regulations have been formulated which prevent adjustment of the air/fuel mixture. On such models the pilot screw positions are pre-set at the factory and in some cases have a limiter cap fitted to prevent tampering. Where adjustment is possible, it*

4.5 On 650 models release the clips on the carburettor intakes (arrowed) . . .

can only be made in conjunction with an exhaust gas analyser to ensure that the machine does not exceed emissions regulations.

1 If the engine runs extremely rough at idle or continually stalls, and if carburettor overhaul does not cure the problem (and it definitely is a carburation problem – see Section 6), the pilot screws may require adjustment. It is worth noting at this point that unless you have the experience to carry this out it is best to entrust the task to a motorcycle dealer, tuner or fuel systems specialist. The pilot screw is

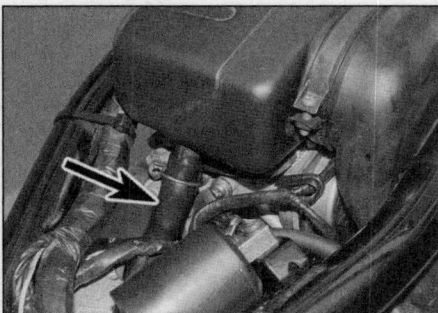
4.6a . . . then detach the breather hose (arrowed) . . .

4.6b . . . and remove the airbox

4.7 On 1100 models note the location of the breather (arrowed)

located on the top of each carburettor on 650 models (see illustration 8.13) and underneath each carburettor on 1100 models (see illustration 8.47). Make sure the valve clearances are correct and the carburettors are synchronised before adjusting the pilot screws (see Chapter 1).

2 Before adjusting the pilot screws, warm the engine up to normal working temperature, then stop it. Screw both pilot screws in until they seat lightly, counting the number of turns as an analysis check, then back them out to the number of turns specified (see this Chapter's Specifications). This is the base position for adjustment.

3 Start the engine and reset the idle speed to the correct level (see Chapter 1) – note that you'll need access to an auxiliary tachometer with inductive pick-up to set the idle speed accurately. Working on one carburettor at a time, turn the pilot screw by a small amount either side of this position to find the point at which the highest consistent idle speed is obtained. When you've reached this position, reset the idle speed to the specified amount (see Chapter 1). Repeat on the other carburettor.

6 Carburettor overhaul – general information

1 Poor engine performance, hesitation, hard starting, stalling, flooding and backfiring are all signs that major carburettor maintenance may be required.

2 Keep in mind that many so-called carburettor problems are really not carburettor problems at all, but mechanical problems within the engine or an ignition system fault. Try to establish for certain that the carburettors are in need of maintenance before beginning a major overhaul.

3 Check the fuel tap, fuel filter, the fuel lines, the fuel tank breather hose (where fitted), the EVAP system rollover valve (California models), the intake manifold hose clamps, the vacuum hose (AIS where fitted), the air filter element, the spark plugs, cylinder compression, carburettor synchronisation and the fuel pump before assuming that a carburettor overhaul is required.

4 Most carburettor problems are caused by dirt particles, varnish and other deposits which build up in and block the internal fuel and air passages. Also, in time, gaskets and O-rings shrink or deteriorate and cause fuel and air leaks which lead to poor performance.

5 When overhauling the carburettors, disassemble them completely and clean the parts thoroughly with a carburettor cleaning solvent, then dry them with filtered, unlubricated compressed air. Blow through the fuel and air passages with compressed air to force out any dirt that may have been loosened but not removed by the solvent. Once the cleaning process is complete, reassemble the carburettors using new gaskets and O-rings.

6 Before disassembling the carburettors, make sure you have a carburettor rebuild kit, some carburettor cleaner, a supply of rags, some means of blowing out the carburettor

passages and a clean place to work. It is recommended that only one carburettor be overhauled at a time to avoid mixing up parts.

7 Carburettor removal and installation

Warning: Refer to the precautions given in Section 1 before starting work.

Removal

1 Remove the fuel tank (see Section 2).

2 Remove the air filter housing and airbox (see Section 4).

3 Place a suitable container below the float chambers, then slacken the drain screw on each chamber and drain all the fuel from the carburettors (see illustration). Tighten the drain screws securely once all the fuel has been drained.

4 On 1100 models, remove the chrome cover on the left-hand side of the carburettor assembly (see illustration). Release the clips securing the front and rear carburettor intake ducts to the carburettors and pull off the ducts (see illustration). Note that the ducts are different shapes and are numbered – No. 1 duct fits the rear cylinder carburettor and No. 2 duct fits the front cylinder carburettor (see illustration). If the numbers are not clear, make your own marks to aid reassembly.

5 Release the clip securing the fuel hose and disconnect the hose (see illustrations).

6 Disconnect the wiring connectors for the

7.3 Carburettor drain screws (arrowed) – 650 model shown

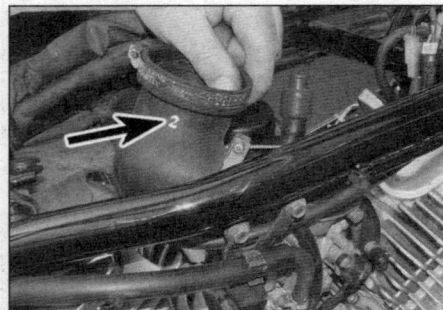

7.4a On 1100 models, remove the chrome cover . . .

7.4b . . . then remove the intake ducts . . .

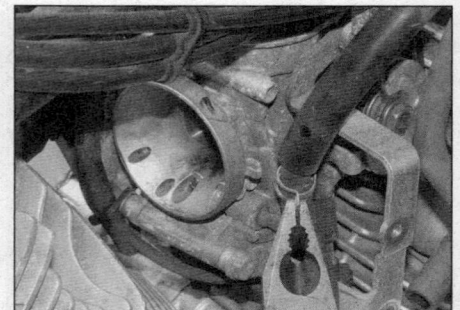

7.4c . . . noting the identification number (arrowed)

7.5a Release the clip securing the fuel hose – 650 model shown

7.5b Release the clip securing the fuel hose – 1100 model shown

7.6a Carburettor heater wiring connector

7.6b Throttle position sensor wiring connector – 650 model shown

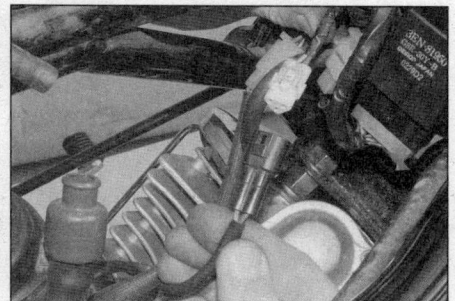

7.6c Throttle position sensor wiring connector – 1100 model shown

carburettor heaters and the throttle position sensor **(see illustrations)**.

7 On 650 models, disconnect the carburettor breather hose from the bracket on the front cylinder **(see illustration)**.

8 If the carburettors are being displaced but not removed completely from the bike, the throttle and choke cables can be left attached to the carburettor assembly. If the carburettors are being removed, first loosen the locknuts on the outer cable ends and disconnect outer cables from the bracket, then disconnect the inner cable ends from the throttle pulley **(see illustration)**. **Note:** *On 650 models, it is easier to disconnect the cables once the carburettors have been displaced.*

9 Disconnect the choke cable from the carburettor assembly **(see illustrations)**.

10 Release the clips securing the carburettors to the cylinder head intake manifolds, then carefully ease the carburettor assembly off **(see illustrations)**.

11 Note how the clips align with the intake manifolds **(see illustration)**. Stuff clean rag into the manifolds to prevent anything falling inside.

Installation

12 Installation is the reverse of removal, noting the following.

● Check for cracks or splits in the cylinder head intake manifolds and replace them with new ones, if necessary.

● Make sure the carburettors are fully engaged with the intake manifolds – they can be difficult to engage, so a squirt of WD40 or a smear of grease inside the manifolds will ease fitting.

● Make sure the clips are correctly positioned

7.7 Disconnect the breather hose from the bracket

7.8 Disconnect the throttle cables from the bracket (A) and the pulley (B)

7.9a Disconnect the choke cable – 650 model shown

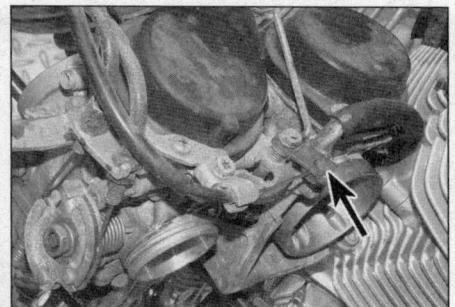

7.9b Disconnect the choke cable – 1100 model shown

on the manifolds **(see illustration 7.11)**. Tighten the clips securely.

● Make sure all hoses are correctly routed and secured and not trapped or kinked.

● Don't forget to connect the throttle position sensor and carburettor heater wiring connectors.

● Refer to Section 10 for installation of the throttle and choke cables. Check the operation of the cables and adjust them as necessary (see Chapter 1).

● Check idle speed and carburettor synchronisation and adjust as necessary (see Chapter 1).

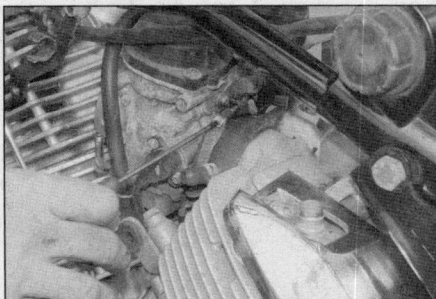

7.10a Release the clips on the intake manifolds . . .

7.10b . . . and ease the carburettor assembly off

7.11 Note how the clips align with the intake manifolds

8 Carburettor stripdown and rebuild

⚠️ **Warning: Refer to the precautions given in Section 1 before starting work.**

Note: *Before disassembly, ensure a rebuild kit is available so that all O-rings and seals can be renewed.*

650 models
Disassembly

1 Remove the carburettor assembly from the bike (see Section 7). Disconnect the carburettor heater wiring loom from the heaters and earth terminal and remove the loom **(see illustration)**. Work on one carburettor at a time to avoid getting parts mixed up **(see illustration)**.

2 Remove the top cover screws, noting the location of the wiring clips **(see illustration)**. Note the location of the throttle cable bracket on the front cylinder carburettor **(see illustration)**. Lift off the cover and remove the spring **(see illustration)**.

3 Note how the tab on the piston diaphragm locates around the air passage in the

8.1a Remove the heater wiring loom

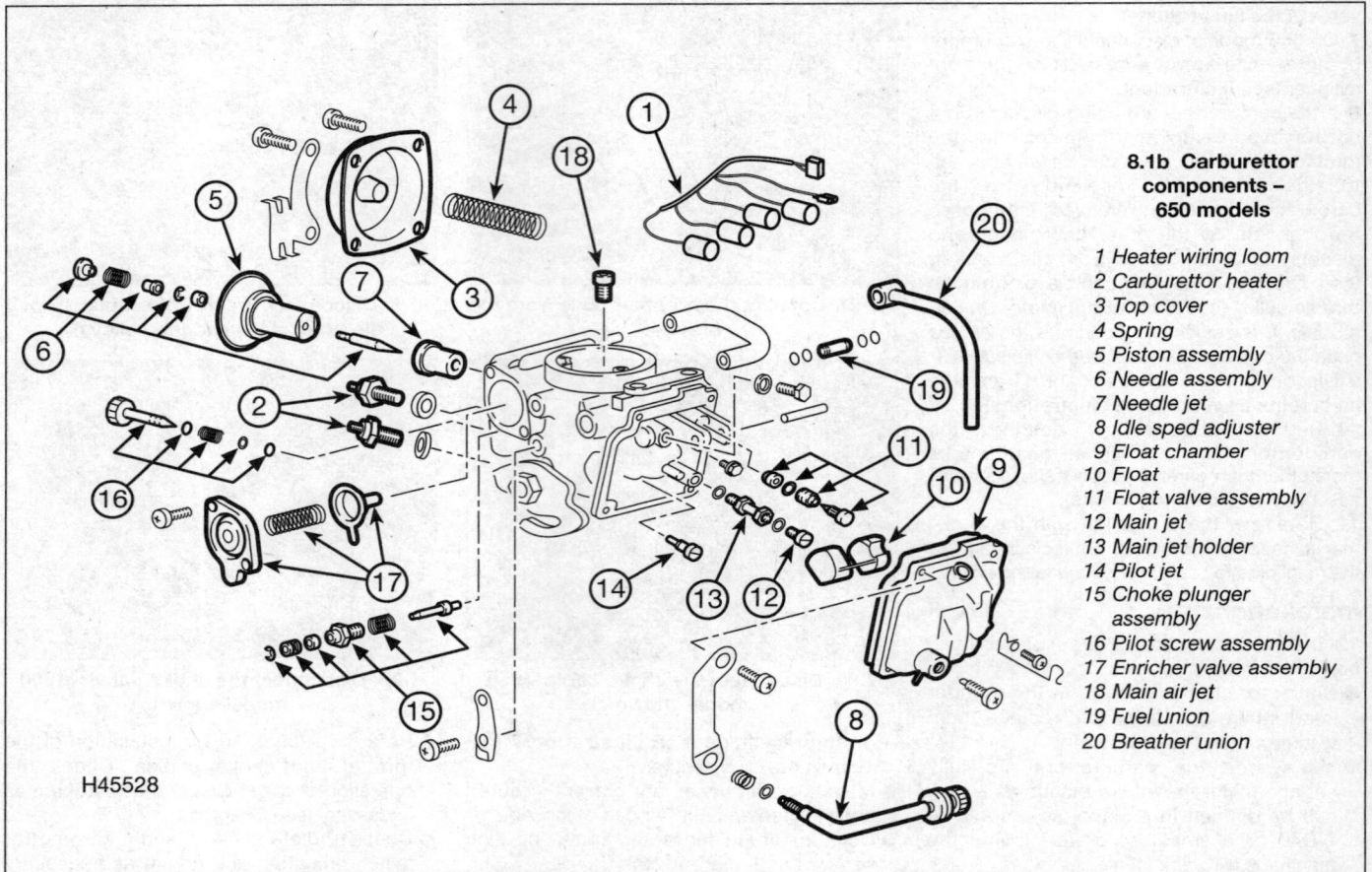

8.1b Carburettor components – 650 models

1 Heater wiring loom
2 Carburettor heater
3 Top cover
4 Spring
5 Piston assembly
6 Needle assembly
7 Needle jet
8 Idle sped adjuster
9 Float chamber
10 Float
11 Float valve assembly
12 Main jet
13 Main jet holder
14 Pilot jet
15 Choke plunger assembly
16 Pilot screw assembly
17 Enricher valve assembly
18 Main air jet
19 Fuel union
20 Breather union

H45528

8.2a Remove the top cover screws

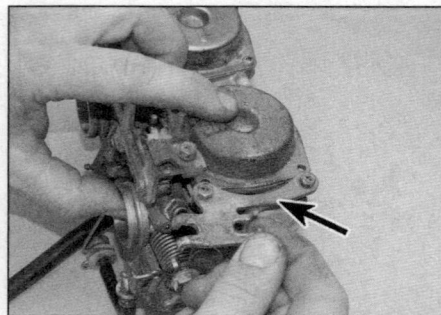

8.2b Note the location of the throttle cable bracket (arrowed)

8.2c Lift off the cover and remove the spring

8.3a Note the location of the piston diaphragm tab (arrowed) . . .

8.3b . . . then lift out the piston assembly

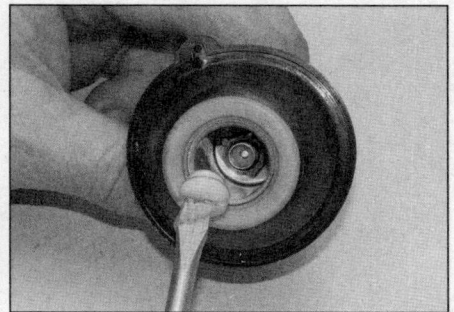
8.4a Unscrew the needle retainer . . .

carburettor body **(see illustration)**. Carefully peel the rim of the diaphragm out of its sealing groove and withdraw the piston assembly **(see illustration)**.

Caution: Do not use a sharp instrument to displace the diaphragm from its groove, as it is easily damaged.

4 Unscrew the needle retainer from inside the piston and lift it out, then lift out the spring and spring seat **(see illustrations)**.

5 Push the needle up from the bottom of the piston and withdraw it from the top, noting how the pin on the needle collar locates in the hole in the bottom of the piston **(see illustration)**.

6 Remove the enricher valve cover screws carefully – the cover is under spring pressure – and remove the cover and spring **(see illustrations)**. Lift out the valve diaphragm, noting how it fits **(see illustration)**. **Note:** *The enricher valve for the rear cylinder carburettor*

cannot be accessed until the carburettors have been separated (see Steps 16 to 20).

7 Note the location of the idle speed adjuster and its support bracket on the front cylinder carburettor **(see illustration)**. Undo the float

chamber screws and remove them, the lift off the float chamber; note how the gasket fits then discard it as a new one must be used **(see illustrations)**.

8 Pull out the float pivot pin and lift the float

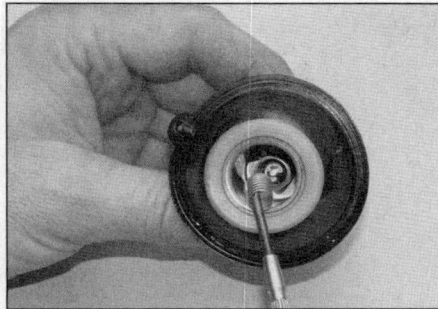
8.4b . . . then lift out the spring and spring seat

8.5 Push the needle up from the bottom of the piston

8.6a Undo the enricher valve cover screws . . .

8.6b . . . and remove the cover and spring

8.6c Lift out the valve diaphragm

8.7a Note the location of the idle speed adjuster and its support bracket

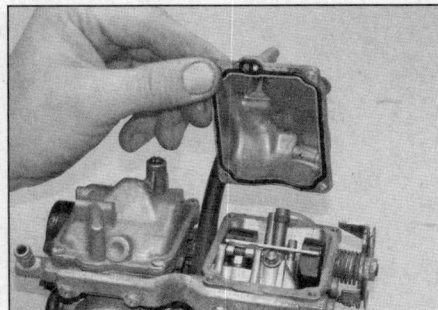
8.7b Lift off the float chamber . . .

8.7c . . . and discard the old gasket

8.8a Pull out the float pin . . .

8.8b . . . and lift off the float assembly

8.9a Unscrew the main jet . . .

assembly out of the carburettor **(see illustrations)**. Unhook the needle from the tab on the float, noting how it fits

9 Unscrew and remove the main jet and the main jet holder **(see illustrations)**.

10 Unscrew and remove the needle jet holder and washer, then carefully press the needle

jet out through the body of the carburettor **(see illustrations)**.

11 Unscrew and remove the pilot jet **(see illustration)**.

12 If required, undo the screw securing the float valve and pull the valve out **(see illustration)**. **Note:** *An O-ring is fitted to the*

valve; if the O-ring is damaged a new float needle valve assembly will have to be fitted, individual components are not available.

13 The pilot screw assembly can be removed from the carburettor if necessary, but note that its setting will be disturbed **(see Haynes Hint)**. Unscrew and remove the pilot screw along with its spring and O-ring **(see illustration)**. **Note:** *If any components are damaged the pilot screw assembly must be renewed as a set, individual components are not available.*

8.9b . . . and main jet holder

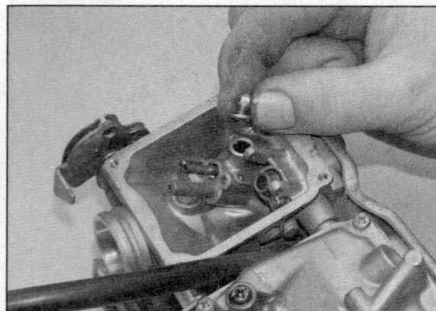
8.10a Unscrew the needle jet holder and washer . . .

> **HAYNES HiNT** *To record the pilot screw's current setting, turn the screw in until it seats lightly, counting the number of turns necessary to achieve this, then fully unscrew it. On installation, the screw is simply backed out the number of turns you've recorded.*

14 Unscrew and remove the main air jet **(see illustration)**.

8.10b . . . then push the needle jet (arrowed) . . .

8.10c . . . out through the carburettor body

8.11 Remove the pilot jet

8.12 Float valve assembly is secured by screw (arrowed)

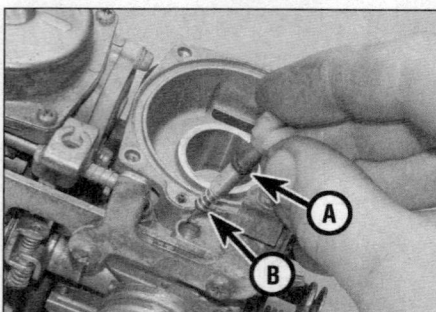
8.13 Pilot screw assembly – note the O-ring (A) and spring (B)

8.14 Remove the main air jet

8.15 Location of the throttle position sensor

8.16 Note the arrangement of the linkage and synchronising springs

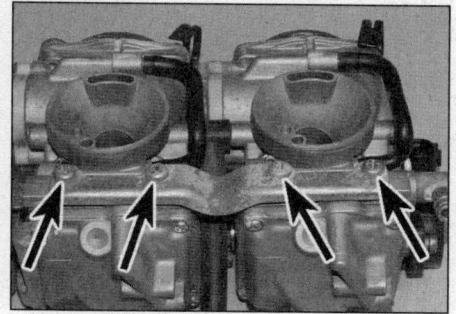

8.17 Remove the screws securing the upper stay

15 A throttle position sensor is mounted on the outside of the rear cylinder carburettor **(see illustration)**. Do not remove the sensor from the carburettor unless it is known to be faulty and is being replaced with a new one. Refer to Chapter 4 for checking and adjustment of the sensor.

16 Before separating the carburettors make a note of how the throttle linkage and synchronising springs are arranged **(see illustration)**.

17 Remove the screws from the carburettor upper stay and lift off the stay **(see illustration)**.

18 Remove the screws from the carburettor lower stay and lift off the stay and the choke cable bracket **(see illustrations)**.

19 Remove the circlips and disconnect the choke linkage bar from the choke plungers, noting the location of the plastic washers **(see illustration)**.

20 Separate the carburettors carefully, noting the location of the breather union and the fuel union. Discard the O-rings on the fuel union as new ones must be fitted.

21 If required, unscrew the choke plunger nut, using a pair of thin-nosed pliers if access is too restricted for a spanner, and withdraw the plunger assembly from the carburettor body.

22 The carburettor heaters are threaded into each carburettor body **(see illustration)**. Do not remove the heaters unless they are known to be faulty and are being replaced with new ones. Refer to Chapter 8 for carburettor heater checks.

Cleaning

Caution: Use only a dedicated carburettor cleaner or petroleum-based solvent for carburettor cleaning. Do not use caustic cleaners.

23 Soak the carburettor body and individual components in the cleaner to loosen and dissolve the varnish and other deposits (always check the directions for use of solvent products, especially when applying them to non-metallic items). Then use a nylon-bristle brush to remove the stubborn deposits, rinse, and dry the components with compressed air.

24 Use compressed air to blow out all the fuel and air passages in the carburettor body and the jets and emulsion tube.

Caution: Never clean the jets or passages with a piece of wire or a drill bit, as they will be enlarged, causing the fuel and air metering rates to be upset.

Inspection

25 Check the operation of the choke plunger assembly. If it doesn't move smoothly, inspect the needle on the end of the plunger, the spring and the plunger linkage bar. Replace the plunger assembly with a new one if any component is worn, damaged or bent – individual parts are not available.

26 If removed, check the tapered portion of the pilot screw and the spring and O-ring for wear or damage **(see illustration 8.13)**. Replace the assembly with a new one if necessary – individual parts are not available.

27 Check the carburettor body, float chamber and top cover for cracks, distorted sealing surfaces and other damage. If any

8.18a Remove the screws securing the lower stay . . .

8.18b . . . then remove the stay and choke cable bracket

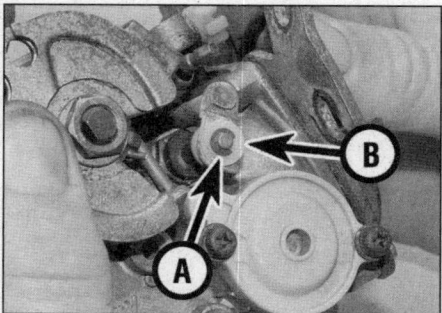

8.19 Remove circlip (A) to disconnect choke plunger – note the washer (B)

8.22 Location of the carburettor heaters

defects are found, renew the faulty component, although replacement of the entire carburettor will probably be necessary (check with a Yamaha dealer on the availability of separate components).

28 Inspect the piston diaphragm for splits, holes and general deterioration. Holding it up to a light will help to reveal problems of this nature.

29 Insert the piston into the carburettor body and check that it moves up-and-down smoothly. Check the surface of the piston for wear. If it's worn excessively or doesn't move smoothly in the body, replace it with a new one.

30 Check the jet needle for straightness by rolling it on a flat surface (such as a piece of glass). Replace it with a new one if it is bent, or if the tip is worn.

31 Operate the throttle shaft to make sure the throttle butterfly valve opens and

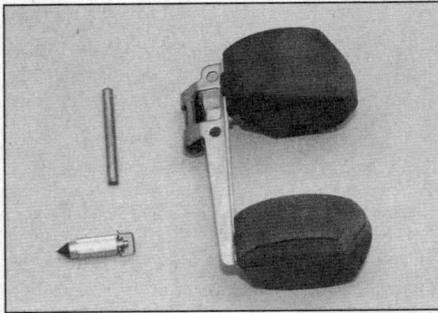

8.34 Check the floats and float needle as described

8.35 Pin on the needle collar locates in hole (arrowed)

8.36a Remove the carburettor heater wiring loom

closes smoothly. If it doesn't, renew the carburettor.

32 Inspect the enricher valve diaphragm for splits or brittleness and renew the diaphragm if necessary **(see illustration 8.6c)**.

33 Check the floats for damage. This will usually be apparent by the presence of fuel inside one of the floats. If the floats are damaged, they must be renewed.

34 Inspect the float needle – if a pronounced groove has formed on the taper, renew the needle. Gently push down on the plunger on the top of the needle then release it – it should spring back immediately. If any defects are found, replace the needle with a new one **(see illustration)**. Also, check the needle valve for wear and renew it if necessary.

Reassembly

Note: *When reassembling the carburettors, be sure to use the new O-rings, seals and other parts supplied in the rebuild kit. Do not overtighten the carburettor jets and screws, as they are easily damaged.*

35 Reassembly is the reverse of disassembly, noting the following:

● Before joining the carburettors, ensure the choke plunger assembly and enricher valve are installed in the rear cylinder carburettor. Lubricate the O-rings on the fuel union with a light film of oil and position the breather union correctly.

● When joining the carburettors together, lay them on a surface plate while tightening the stay screws to ensure proper alignment.

● Check the operation of the choke linkage bar.

● If removed, install the pilot screw along with its spring and O-ring, turning it in until it seats lightly. Now, turn the screw out the number of turns previously recorded, or as specified at the beginning of this Chapter.

● Don't forget to fit the washer on the needle jet holder **(see illustration 8.10a)**.

● Ensure the float needle locates in its seat in the valve before installing the float pivot pin.

● Don't forget to fit the idle speed adjuster and its support bracket on the front cylinder carburettor before installing the float chamber screws **(see illustration 8.7a)**.

● Ensure the pin on the needle collar is correctly located in the hole in the bottom of the piston **(see illustration)**.

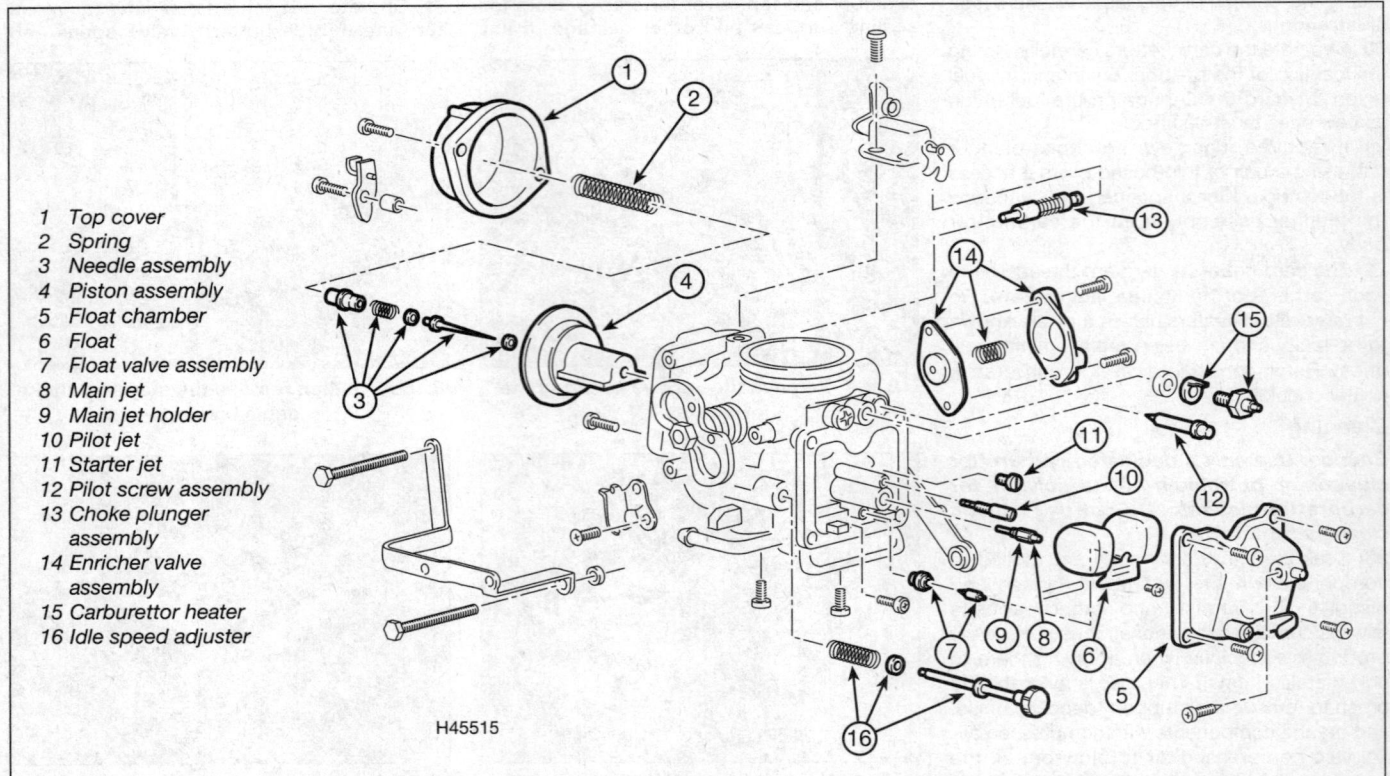

1 Top cover
2 Spring
3 Needle assembly
4 Piston assembly
5 Float chamber
6 Float
7 Float valve assembly
8 Main jet
9 Main jet holder
10 Pilot jet
11 Starter jet
12 Pilot screw assembly
13 Choke plunger assembly
14 Enricher valve assembly
15 Carburettor heater
16 Idle speed adjuster

H45515

8.36b Carburettor components – 1100 models

8.37a Note the location of the choke cable bracket (arrowed)

8.37b Remove the top cover screws . . .

8.37c . . . then lift off the cover and remove the spring

● Don't forget to fit the throttle cable bracket and the wiring clips on the carburettors before installing the top cover screws (see illustration 8.2b).

1100 models

Disassembly

36 Remove the carburettor assembly from the bike (see Section 7). Release the carburettor heater wiring loom from the cable ties and clips and remove it (see

illustration). Work on one carburettor at a time to avoid getting parts mixed up (see illustration).
37 Note the location of the choke cable bracket on the rear cylinder carburettor (see illustration). Remove the top cover screws, then lift off the cover and remove the spring (see illustrations).
38 Carefully peel the rim of the diaphragm out of its sealing groove and withdraw the piston assembly, noting how the piston and slide locate in the carburettor body (see illustration).

Caution: Do not use a sharp instrument to displace the diaphragm from its groove, as it is easily damaged.
39 Note the location of the O-ring on the top edge of the carburettor body, then discard it as a new one must be fitted (see illustration).
40 Pull the needle retainer out from inside the piston and lift out the spring and spring seat, then push the needle up from the bottom of the piston and withdraw it from the top, noting the location of the washers underneath the needle clip (see illustrations).

8.38 Lift out the piston assembly

8.39 Note the location of the O-ring

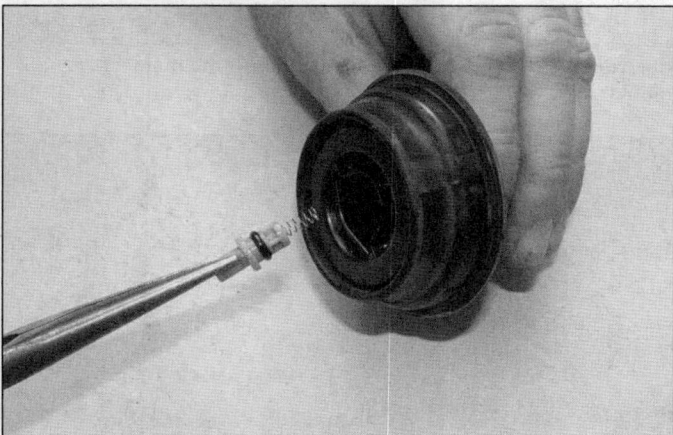
8.40a Pull out the needle retainer . . .

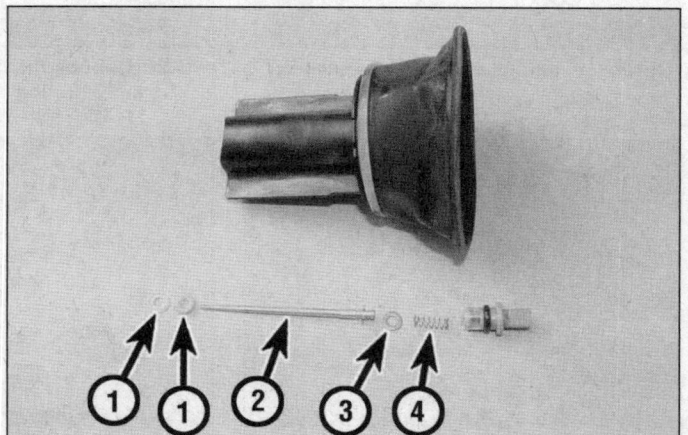
8.40b . . . and note the order of the components
1 Washers   2 Needle   3 Spring seat   4 Spring

8.41a Undo the float chamber screws . . .

8.41b . . . noting the location of the vent hose bracket (arrowed)

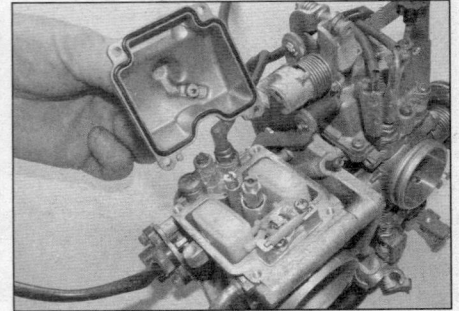

8.41c Lift off the float chamber . . .

41 Undo the float chamber screws and remove them **(see illustration)**. Note the location of the vent hose bracket on the front cylinder carburettor **(see illustration)**. Lift off the float chamber; note how the gasket fits then discard it as a new one must be used **(see illustrations)**.

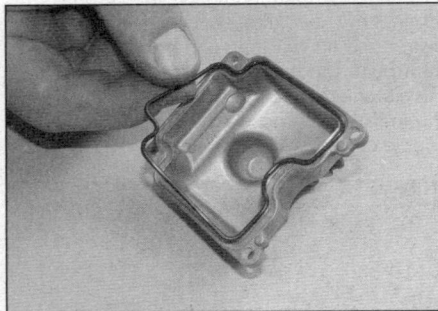

8.41d . . . and discard the old gasket

8.42a Remove the screw securing the float pivot pin . . .

42 Remove the screw securing the float pivot pin and lift the float assembly out of the carburettor **(see illustrations)**. Unhook the needle from the tab on the float, noting how it fits **(see illustration)**.

43 Hold the main jet holder with a suitable spanner and unscrew and remove the main jet, then unscrew the main jet holder **(see illustrations)**.

44 Unscrew and remove the starter jet **(see illustration)**.

45 Unscrew and remove the pilot jet and washer **(see illustration)**.

46 If required, undo the screw securing the float valve and pull the valve out **(see illustration)**. **Note:** *An O-ring is fitted to the valve; if the O-ring is damaged a new float needle valve assembly will have to be fitted, individual components are not available.*

8.42b . . . and lift off the float assembly

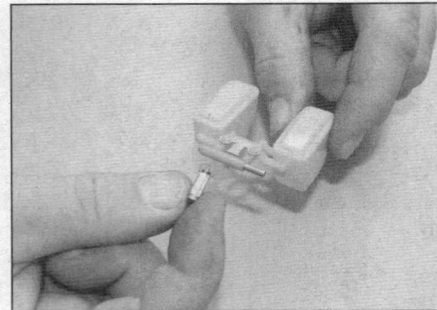

8.42c Unhook the needle from the float, noting how it fits

8.43a Unscrew the main jet . . .

8.43b . . . and the main jet holder

8.44 Remove the starter jet

8.45 Remove the pilot jet and washer

8.46 Float valve assembly is secured by screw (arrowed)

8.47 Remove the pilot screw (arrowed) as described

8.48 Unscrew the idle speed adjuster (arrowed)

8.49 Location of the throttle position sensor

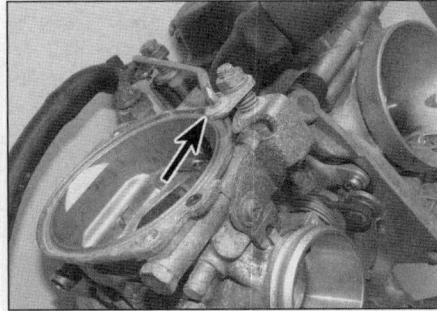

8.50a Note the arrangement of the choke linkage (arrowed) . . .

8.50b . . . throttle linkage (A) and synchronising springs (B)

47 The pilot screw assembly can be removed from the carburettor if necessary, but note that its setting will be disturbed **(see Haynes Hint on page 3•10)**. Unscrew and remove the pilot screw along with its spring and O-ring **(see illustration)**. **Note:** *If any components are damaged the pilot screw assembly must be renewed as a set, individual components are not available.*

48 Unscrew and remove the idle speed adjuster and spring from the outside of the rear cylinder carburettor **(see illustration)**.

49 A throttle position sensor is mounted on the outside of the front cylinder carburettor **(see illustration)**. Do not remove the sensor from the carburettor unless it is known to be faulty and is being replaced with a new one.

Refer to Chapter 4 for checking and adjustment of the sensor.

50 Before separating the carburettors make a note of how the choke linkage, throttle linkage and synchronising springs are arranged **(see illustrations)**. If not already done, cut the cable ties securing the wiring to the central support bracket.

51 Remove the screws securing the choke linkage bracket and lift it off, noting how the choke lever locates on the choke plunger **(see illustrations)**.

52 Remove one carburettor from the central support bracket at a time. Remove the split pin and washer from the throttle linkage of the first carburettor, then remove the two carburettor mounting bolts **(see illustrations)**.

8.51a Remove the choke linkage bracket . . .

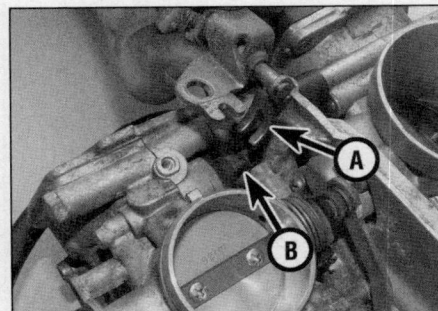

8.51b . . . noting how the lever (A) locates on the plunger (B)

8.52a Remove split pin (A) and washer (B) from linkage (C) . . .

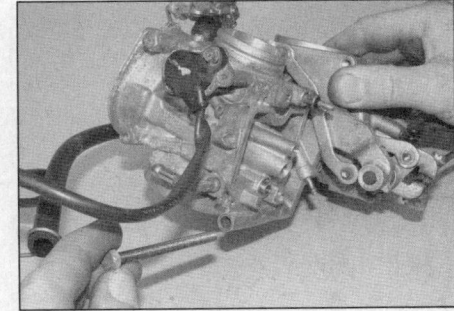

8.52b . . . then remove the mounting bolts

8.53a Separate the carburettors carefully . . .

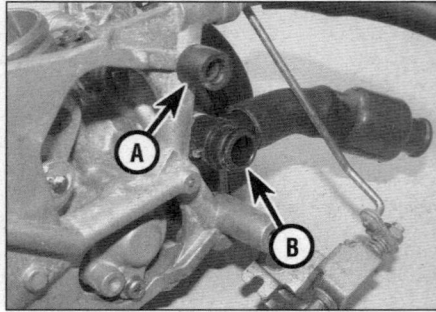

8.53b . . . noting the location of the balance hose (A) and breather union (B)

8.54a Undo the enricher valve cover screws . . .

53 Separate the carburettors carefully, noting the location of the balance hose and the breather union **(see illustrations)**. Discard the O-rings on the breather union as new ones must be fitted.

54 Remove the enricher valve cover screws carefully – the cover is under spring pressure – and remove the cover and spring **(see illustrations)**. Lift out the valve diaphragm, noting how it fits **(see illustration)**.

55 If required, unscrew the choke plunger nut, using a pair of thin-nosed pliers if access is too restricted for a spanner, and withdraw the plunger assembly from the carburettor body.

56 A carburettor heater is mounted on each carburettor body. Do not remove the heaters unless they are known to be faulty and are

being replaced with new ones. Refer to Chapter 8 for carburettor heater checks.

Cleaning

57 Follow the procedures in Steps 23 and 24 to clean the carburettor components.

Inspection

58 Follow the procedures in Steps 25 to 34 to inspect the carburettor components.

Reassembly

Note: *When reassembling the carburettors, be sure to use the new O-rings, seals and other parts supplied in the rebuild kit. Do not overtighten the carburettor jets and screws, as they are easily damaged.*

59 Reassembly is the reverse of disassembly, noting the following:

● Before joining the carburettors, ensure the choke plunger assemblies and enricher valves are installed. Lubricate the O-rings on the breather union with a light film of oil and position the breather union correctly.

● When joining the carburettors together, ensure the throttle linkage is correctly aligned before installing the mounting bolts **(see illustrations)**. Secure the throttle linkage with new split pins **(see illustration)**.

● Check the operation of the choke linkage **(see illustration 8.37a)**.

● If removed, install the pilot screw along with its spring and O-ring, turning it in until it seats lightly. Now, turn the screw out the number of turns previously recorded, or as specified at the beginning of this Chapter.

● Don't forget to fit the washer on the pilot jet.

● Ensure the float needle locates in its seat in the valve before securing the float pivot pin.

● Don't forget to fit the vent hose bracket on the front cylinder carburettor before installing the float chamber screws.

● Don't forget to fit the O-ring on the top edge of the carburettor body.

● Ensure the washers are in place on the jet needle before it is installed in the piston.

● Secure the throttle position sensor and carburettor heater wiring to the central support bracket with new cable ties **(see illustration 8.36a)**.

8.54b . . . and remove the cover and spring

8.54c Lift out the valve diaphragm

8.59a Check the throttle linkage alignment . . .

8.59b . . . before installing the mounting bolts

8.59c Use new split pins on the throttle linkage

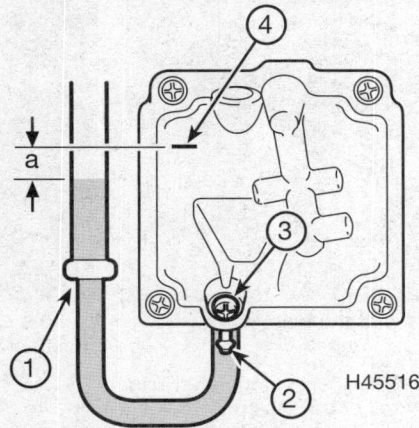

9.2 Fuel level check set-up

1 Gauge assembly
2 Union
3 Drain screw
4 Fuel level line
a) Fuel level measurement

H45516

9 Carburettor fuel level check

⚠️ **Warning: Refer to the precautions given in Section 1 before starting work.**

1 To check the fuel level, position the motorcycle upright on level ground; support it using an auxiliary stand if necessary. Remove the fuel tank (see Section 2) and the air filter housing (see Section 4), then arrange a temporary fuel supply to the carburettors.

2 Yamaha produce a fuel level gauge (Part No. 90890-01312 for Europe or YM-01312-A

for US), or alternatively a suitable length of clear plastic tubing can be used. Attach the gauge or tubing to the drain hose union on the bottom of one of the carburettor float chambers, then secure it vertically alongside the carburettor using tape to hold it in place **(see illustration)**. Identify the datum mark on the carburettor and mark a line on the tube level with this mark, or if using the Yamaha tool align the zero on the gauge scale with the datum mark. On 650 models the datum mark is a cast line on the float chamber, whereas on 1100 models the datum mark is the gasket joint of the carburettor.

3 Turn the fuel supply ON and loosen the drain screw to allow the fuel to flow into the tube – do not move the tube from its original

position otherwise a false reading will be obtained. The level at which the fuel stabilises in the tube indicates the fuel level in the float chamber. Refer to the relevant Specifications at the beginning of this Chapter for to your machine and measure the level relative to the original line with corresponds with the datum mark.

4 Repeat the procedure for the other carburettor. The fuel level must the same in each carburettor.

5 If the level in either carburettor is incorrect, turn the fuel tap OFF and drain the carburettors, then remove the float chamber (see Section 8). **Note:** *It isn't necessary to remove the carburettors from the motorcycle since the float chamber screws are accessible.*

6 The fuel level is adjusted by altering the float height. Adjust the float height by carefully bending the float tab a little at a time until the correct height is obtained. This will involve repeated checking of the fuel level as described above.

10 Throttle and choke cables

Throttle cables

Removal

1 Remove the fuel tank (see Section 2) and the air filter housing (see Section 4). On 1100 models, remove the airbox and the chrome cover on the left-hand side of the carburettor assembly.

2 Mark each cable according to its location at both ends. If new cables are being fitted, match them to the old cables to ensure they are correctly installed.

3 Loosen the lower throttle cable elbow locknuts and slide the cables out of the bracket on the carburettor assembly **(see illustrations)**.

4 Detach the inner throttle cable ends from the throttle pulley on the carburettors **(see illustration)**.

5 Remove the screw securing the accelerator (opening) cable to the twistgrip/switch unit and unscrew the decelerator (closing) cable lockring **(see illustration)**. Remove the unit

10.3a Location of the throttle cable bracket – 650 models

10.3b Location of the throttle cable bracket – 1100 models

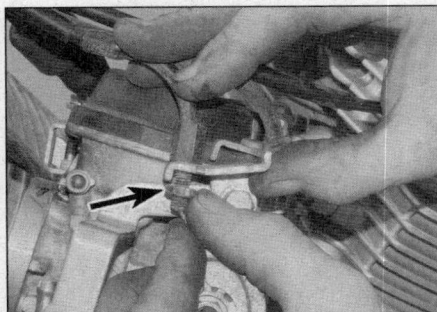
10.3c Loosen the lower locknut (arrowed) and slide the cable off the bracket

10.4 Detach the cables from the throttle pulley (arrowed) – 650 model shown

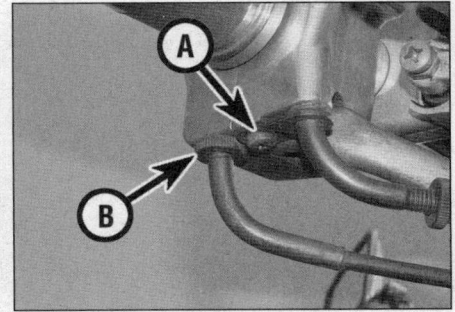
10.5a Remove the screw (A) and cable lockring (B)

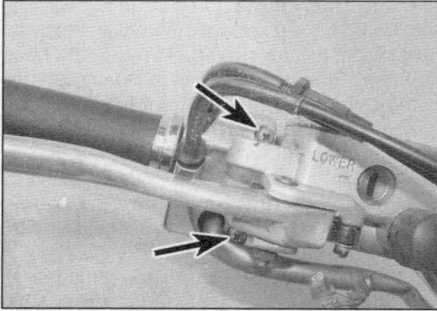

10.5b Remove the screws (arrowed) . . .

10.5c . . . and split the twistgrip/switch unit

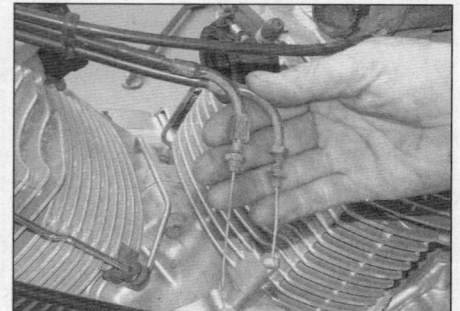

10.8 Ensure the cables are correctly positioned before connecting them to the carburettors

screws and separate the halves of the unit (see illustrations). Detach both inner cable ends from the twistgrip and withdraw the cables from the unit.

6 Remove the throttle cables from the bike, noting how they are routed.

Installation

7 Lubricate the cable ends with multi-purpose grease, then install the upper ends through the lower half of the twistgrip/switch unit and secure them in the twistgrip. Fit the outer cable ends into the unit, making sure they locate correctly. Tighten the decelerator cable lockring finger-tight and install the accelerator cable retaining screw. Join the unit halves, making sure the pin in the upper half locates in the hole in the handlebar, and tighten the screws.

8 Feed the cables through to the carburettors, making sure they are correctly routed (see illustration). The cables must not interfere with any other component and should not be kinked or bent sharply.

9 Fit the accelerator inner cable into the lower socket on the carburettor pulley and the decelerator inner cable into the upper socket, then slide the outer cables into the bracket and tighten the locknuts (see illustration).

10 Follow the procedure in Chapter 1 and adjust the throttle cable freeplay.

Choke cable

Removal

11 Loosen the bolt securing the cable clamp on the carburettor assembly and slip the cable out of the clamp (see illustration).

12 Detach the inner cable end from the choke lever (see illustrations 7.9a or b).

13 On 650 models, the choke knob is held in a bracket secured by the fuel tank left-hand mounting bolt. Unscrew the knob from the bracket and remove the cable.

14 On 1100 models, the choke cable is retained in a pulley on the underside of the left-hand handlebar switch unit. Remove the unit screws and separate the halves of the unit from the handlebar, then remove the plate from the bottom of the unit to access the choke pulley (see illustrations). Pull the outer cable end out of the socket in the unit and detach the inner cable end from the pulley.

Installation

15 Installation is the reverse of removal. Note that on 1100 models, freeplay can be removed from the cable by use of the adjuster at the handlebar end.

11 Fuel pump

⚠️ **Warning: Refer to the precautions given in Section 1 before starting work.**

Check

1 The fuel pump is powered by the ignition control unit via the fuel pump relay. It will run whenever the ignition is switched ON and the ignition is operative i.e. only when the engine is turning over. As soon as the ignition is killed, power to the relay is cut so that there is no risk of fuel being sprayed out under pressure in the event of an accident.

2 On 650 models, the fuel pump is mounted on a bracket behind the steering head (see illustration). To access the pump, remove the

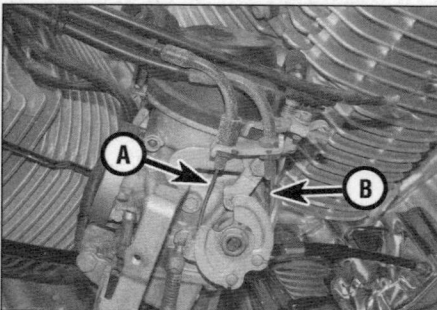

10.9 Accelerator cable (A) and decelerator cable (B)

10.11 Location of the choke cable clamp – 650 model shown

10.14a Undo the screw and remove the plate . . .

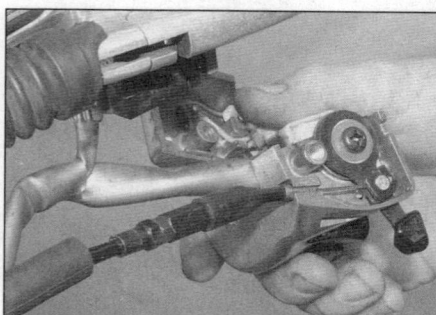

10.14b . . . to access the choke pulley

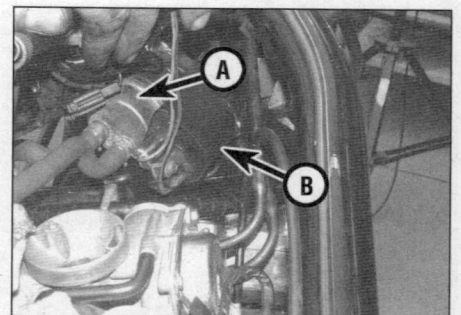

11.2 Location of the fuel pump (A) – 650 models. Note the ignition coil (B)

11.3 Location of the fuel pump – 1100 models

fuel tank, air filter housing and airbox (see Sections 2 and 4), then remove the steering head panels (see Chapter 7).

3 On 1100 models, the fuel pump is located behind the left-hand frame cover **(see illustration)**. Remove the cover to access the pump (see Chapter 7).

4 If fuel is not being delivered to the carburettors, first check that it is flowing from the tank to the pump. Refer to Chapter 1, Section 18 and check the in-line fuel filter.

5 To check pump operation, release the clip securing the fuel hose to the carburettors and detach the hose. Place the open end of the hose in a container suitable for storing petrol (gasoline) **(see illustration)**.

6 Trace the wiring from the fuel pump and disconnect it at the connector. Ensure that the fuel tap is ON. Using a fully charged battery (the motorcycle's battery will do) and jumper wires, connect the battery positive (+ve) terminal to the blue/black wire terminal on the pump side of the connector and the battery negative (-ve) terminal to the black wire terminal. The pump should operate and fuel should flow into the container. If not, the pump is faulty and a new one must be fitted.

7 If the pump is good, refer to the procedures in Chapter 8, Section 23, and check the fuel pump electrical system. **Note:** *On 1100 models from 2003, fuel supply to the carburettors is cut by the solenoids in the ignition fault self-diagnosis system if an ignition coil fails. Refer to Chapter 4, Section 6, for details.*

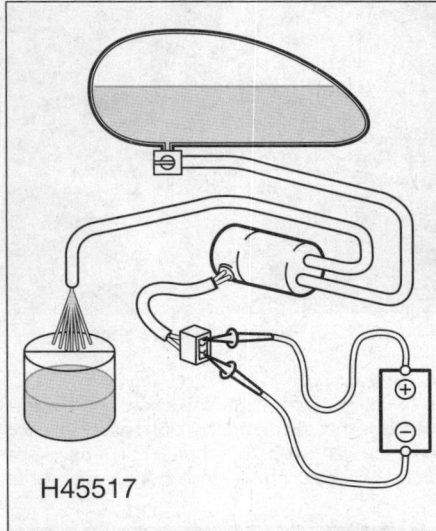

H45517

11.5 Set-up for checking the operation of the fuel pump – connect the battery as described

Removal

650 models

8 Make sure the ignition is switched OFF. Remove the fuel tank, air filter housing and airbox (see Sections 2 and 4), then remove the steering head panels (see Chapter 7). Trace the wiring from the fuel pump and the front cylinder ignition coil and disconnect it at the connectors **(see illustration 11.2)**. Pull the cap off the front cylinder spark plug.

9 Make a note of which fuel hose fits which union on the pump (supply from the tank and delivery to the carburettors) as an aid to installation. Either release the clips securing the hoses to the pump and disconnect the hoses, or disconnect the delivery hose from the carburettor assembly and unclip the fuel filter from the frame. Use a rag to mop up any residual fuel.

10 Remove the bolts securing the mounting bracket to the frame and lift out the pump and front cylinder coil assembly, noting how it fits **(see illustrations)**. Unclip the pump from the bracket.

11.10a Pump bracket is secure by bolt (arrowed) on each side

1100 models

11 Make sure the ignition is switched OFF. Remove the left-hand frame cover (see Chapter 7).

12 Pull the wiring out of the rubber cover and disconnect the fuel pump wiring connector.

13 Make a note of which fuel hose fits which union on the pump (supply from the tank and delivery to the carburettors) as an aid to installation. Release the clips securing the hoses to the pump and disconnect the hoses. Use a rag to mop up any residual fuel.

14 Unclip the pump from the bracket **(see illustration 11.3)**.

Installation

15 Installation is a reverse of removal, noting the following:
● Ensure the fuel hoses are fitted correctly and secured with the clips.
● On 650 models, don't forget to reconnect the ignition coil wiring connector.
● Start the engine and check carefully that there are no leaks at the hose connections.

12 Exhaust system

650 models

1 Loosen the clamp bolt securing the (upper) rear cylinder silencer to the rear cylinder exhaust pipe **(see illustration)**.

11.10b Lift out the pump/coil assembly

11.10c Note how the bracket locates on the pin (arrowed)

12.1 Loosen the rear cylinder silencer clamp (arrowed)

12.2a Remove the mounting bolt . . .

12.2b . . . and pull off the silencer

12.3a Loosen the front cylinder silencer clamp (arrowed) . . .

2 Loosen the bolt securing the rear cylinder silencer to the silencer bracket, then support the silencer and remove the bolt and pull the silencer off the pipe **(see illustrations)**.

3 The (lower) front cylinder silencer and the rear cylinder exhaust pipe are a welded assembly and must be removed together. First loosen the clamp bolt securing the front cylinder silencer to the front cylinder exhaust pipe, then remove the bolts securing the rear exhaust pipe to the exhaust manifold **(see illustrations)**.

4 Loosen the bolt securing the front cylinder silencer to the silencer bracket, then support the silencer/exhaust pipe assembly and remove the bolt and pull the silencer off the front exhaust pipe **(see illustrations)**.

5 Remove the manifold nuts that secure the front exhaust pipe to the cylinder head **(see illustration)**. Support the pipe and ease it forward off the manifold studs and manoeuvre it off the bike.

6 Prise the gaskets out of the exhaust ports and discard them as new ones must be fitted.

7 Before installation, check the condition of the silencer sealing rings and fit new ones if necessary **(see illustration)**.

8 Scrape any excess carbon out of the exhaust ports, especially where the gaskets seat. Clean any corrosion off the manifold bolts and studs and lubricate them with copper based grease. During installation, tighten the nuts and bolts finger-tight until all the components are in place.

9 Fit a new gasket into the front cylinder exhaust port **(see illustration)**. If necessary, apply a smear of grease to the gasket to keep it in place.

10 Manoeuvre the front exhaust pipe into position and secure it with the manifold nuts **(see illustration 12.5)**.

11 Fit a new gasket into the rear cylinder exhaust manifold **(see illustration)**.

12.3b . . . then remove the rear exhaust pipe manifold bolts (arrowed)

12.4a Remove the mounting bolt . . .

12.4b . . . and pull off the silencer/exhaust pipe assembly

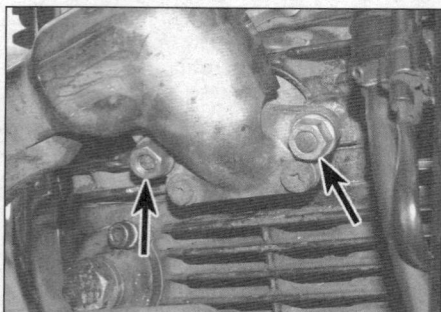
12.5 Front exhaust pipe is secured by manifold nuts (arrowed)

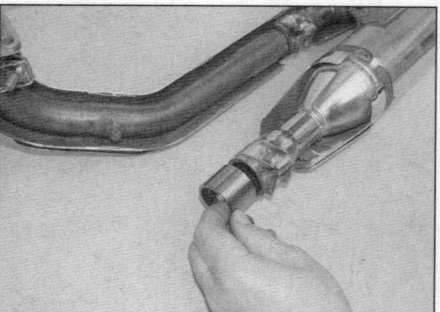
12.7 Check the silencer sealing rings

12.9 Fit a new front cylinder exhaust port gasket

12.11 Fit a new rear cylinder exhaust manifold gasket

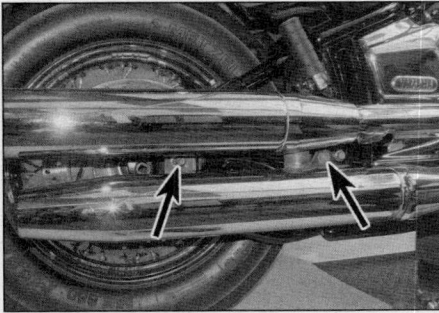

12.15a Loosen the silencer assembly to bracket bolts (arrowed)

12.15b Pull the silencer assembly off

12.16 Silencer bracket is secured by two bolts

12 Manoeuvre the front cylinder silencer/rear cylinder exhaust pipe assembly into position so that the pipe aligns with the manifold and the silencer mounting point aligns with the bracket **(see illustration 12.4b)**. Install the mounting bolt and the manifold bolts.

13 Install the rear cylinder silencer and secure it with the mounting bolt.

14 Tighten the manifold nuts and bolts, the silencer clamp bolts and mounting bolts to the torque settings specified at the beginning of this Chapter.

1100 models

15 The front and rear cylinder silencers are a welded assembly and must be removed together. First loosen the clamp bolts securing the silencers to the exhaust pipes, then loosen the bolts securing the silencer assembly to the silencer bracket **(see illustration)**. Support the silencer assembly, remove the bolts and pull the assembly off the pipes **(see illustration)**.

16 If required, undo the bolts securing the silencer bracket to the frame and remove the bracket **(see illustration)**.

17 Remove the bolts securing the rear exhaust pipe to the exhaust manifold and lift off the pipe **(see illustration)**.

18 Remove the bolt securing the rear brake fluid reservoir to the frame and displace the reservoir **(see illustration)**.

19 Remove the manifold nuts that secure the front exhaust pipe to the cylinder head **(see illustration)**. Support the pipe and ease it

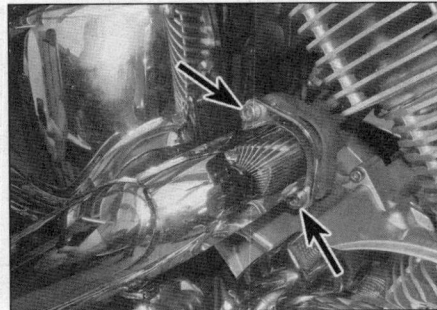

12.17 Remove the rear exhaust pipe manifold bolts (arrowed)

forward off the manifold studs and manoeuvre it off the bike **(see illustration)**.

20 Before installation, follow Steps 6 to 9 above. During installation, tighten the exhaust system nuts and bolts finger-tight until all the components are in place.

21 Manoeuvre the front exhaust pipe into position and secure it with the manifold nuts, then install the rear brake fluid reservoir and its cover and tighten the reservoir mounting bolt securely.

22 Fit a new gasket into the rear cylinder exhaust manifold, then install the rear exhaust pipe and secure it with the bolts.

23 Manoeuvre the silencer assembly into position so that the silencer mounting points align with the bracket. Install the mounting bolts.

24 Tighten the manifold nuts and bolts, the

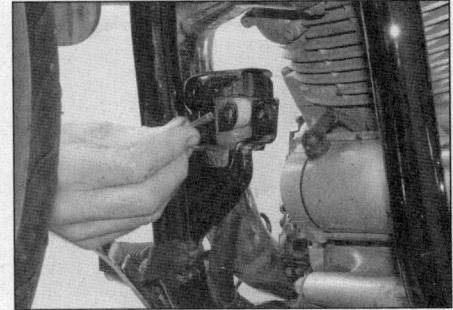

12.18 Displace the rear brake fluid reservoir

silencer clamp bolts and mounting bolts to the torque settings specified at the beginning of this Chapter.

13 Air induction system (AIS)

1 The air induction system, where fitted, uses exhaust gas pulses to suck fresh air into the exhaust ports, where it mixes with hot combustion gases. The additional oxygen provided by the fresh air allows combustion to continue for a longer time, reducing unburned hydrocarbons in the exhaust gas content.

2 Reed valves control the flow of air into the ports and prevent exhaust gas from flowing back into the system. An air cut-off valve is operated by intake manifold pressure and shuts off the flow of air into the system during deceleration to prevent backfiring. Air drawn into the system passes through a filter element.

3 Periodically, or at the specified service interval for your machine, check the system components for loose connections, damaged or deteriorated hoses.

650 models

4 On 1997 to 2000 models, the AIS components are located underneath the fuel tank on the left-hand side **(see illustration)**. On later models, the components are mounted on the left-hand side of the engine.

12.19a Remove the front exhaust pipe manifold nuts (arrowed) . . .

12.19b . . . and lift off the pipe

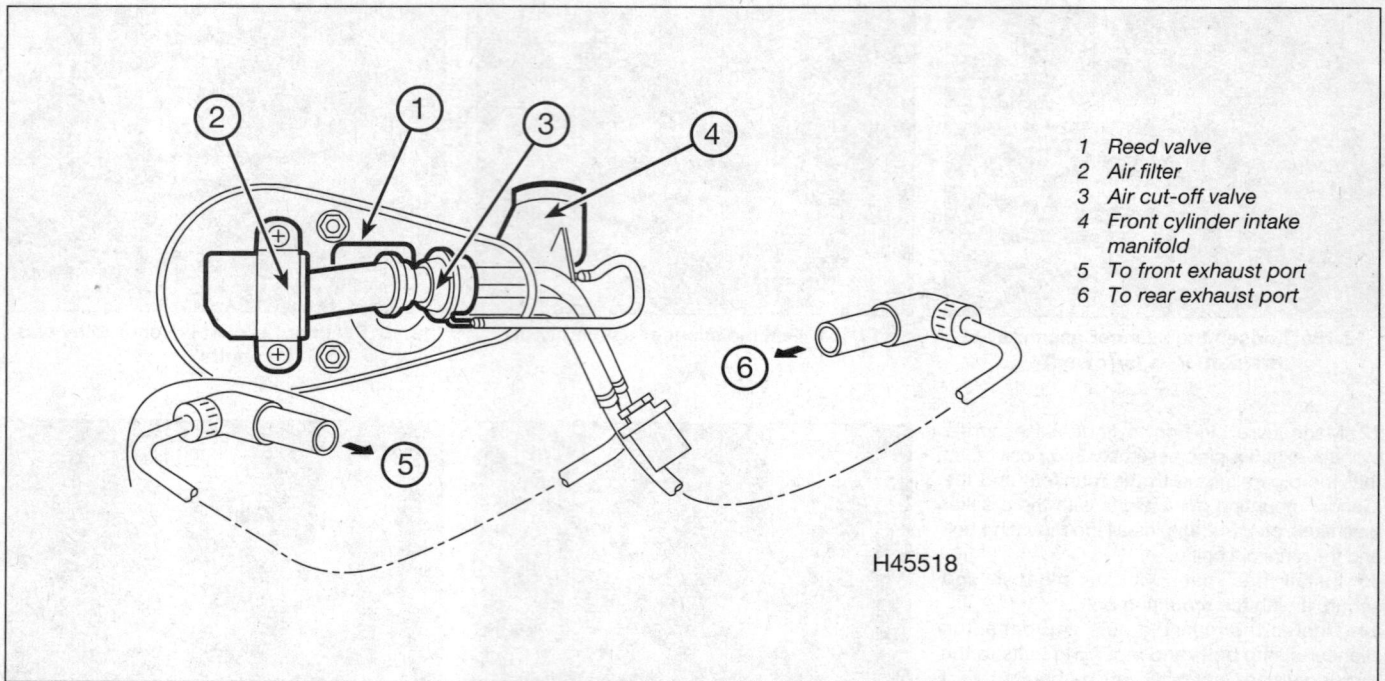

1 Reed valve
2 Air filter
3 Air cut-off valve
4 Front cylinder intake manifold
5 To front exhaust port
6 To rear exhaust port

H45518

13.4 AIS components – 1997 to 2000 650 models

5 Undo the housing cover screws and lift off the cover (see illustration). Undo the screws securing the filter in the housing and lift it out (see illustration). Remove the filter element from the filter case and clean it with compressed air. If the element is extremely dirty or damaged, replace it with a new one.

6 Installation is the reverse of removal. Ensure the filter element seals correctly against the case.

7 The reed valves are located inside the reed valve housing; release the clips securing the housing to the AIS assembly hoses and remove it, noting how it fits (see illustrations).

8 Undo the screws securing the two halves of the reed valve housing and lift out the reed valve assembly.

9 If required, clean the reeds carefully with a suitable solvent. Measure the clearance between the reeds and the reed holders and compare the result with the specification at the beginning of this Chapter (see illustration). If the clearance is greater than the specification, or if the reeds are cracked or damaged, fit a new housing assembly – individual components are not available.

10 Installation is the reverse of removal. Ensure the reed valve assembly is fitted correctly in the housing and secure the AIS hoses with the clips.

13.5a Remove the housing cover

13.5b Remove the filter (arrowed) from the housing

13.7a Detach the hoses (arrowed) from the reed valve

13.7b Location of the reed valve – 2001-on 650 models

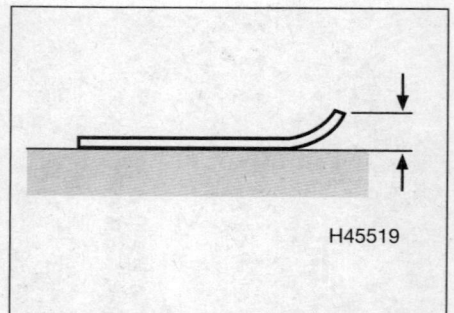

H45519

13.9 Measure the reed valve clearance

1 *Pipe to front exhaust port*
2 *Pipe to rear exhaust port*
3 *Gasket*
4 *Vacuum hose*
5 *Reed valve*
6 *Air cut-off valve*
7 *Air filter*
8 *Air filter case*

H45520

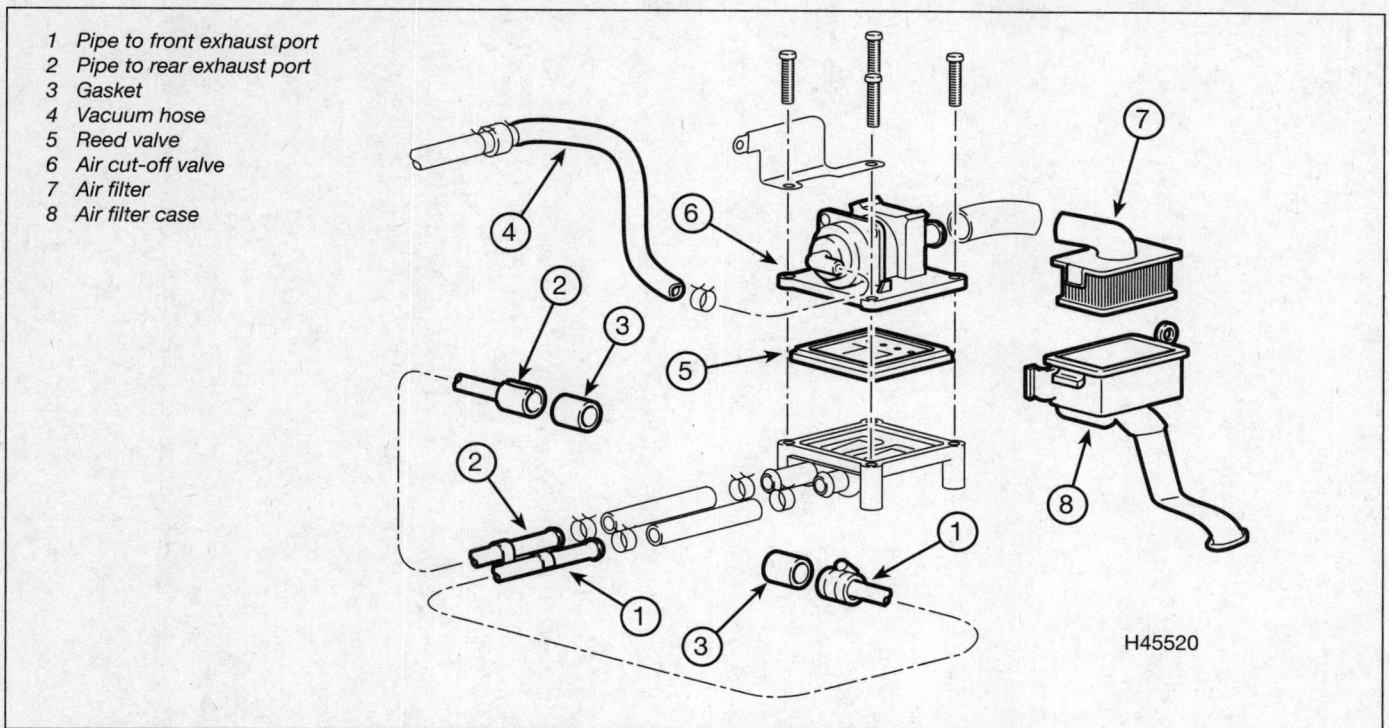

13.12 AIS components – 1100 models

1100 models

11 Remove the left-hand frame cover.
12 Detach the hoses from the air filter housing, then remove the mounting screw and lift off the housing **(see illustration)**.
13 Unclip the filter element and lift it out of the housing. Clean the filter with compressed air. If the element is extremely dirty or damaged, replace it with a new one.
14 Installation is the reverse of removal. Ensure the filter element seals correctly against the case.
15 The reed valves are located inside the reed valve housing. Release the clips securing the housing to the AIS assembly hoses and detach the hoses, noting how they fit. Undo the screws securing the housing bracket and remove the housing.
16 Undo the screws securing the reed valve housing to the air cut-off valve and lift out the reed valve assembly.
17 Follow the procedure in Step 9 and clean the reeds, then measure the reed clearance. If the clearance is greater than the specification, or if the reeds are cracked or damaged, fit a new cut-off valve assembly – individual components are not available.
18 Installation is the reverse of removal. Ensure the reed valve assembly is fitted correctly to the cut-off valve and secure the AIS hoses with the clips.

14 Evaporative emission control (EVAP) system

1 California models are fitted with an evaporation control (EVAP) system which prevents fuel vapour escaping from the tank into the atmosphere. For details of the system and service information refer to Chapter 1, Section 24.

Chapter 4
Ignition system

Contents

Degrees of difficulty

Easy, suitable for novice with little experience	Fairly easy, suitable for beginner with some experience	Fairly difficult, suitable for competent DIY mechanic	Difficult, suitable for experienced DIY mechanic	Very difficult, suitable for expert DIY or professional

Specifications

General
Ignition timing .... Not adjustable
Spark plug .... see Chapter 1

Ignition HT coil
Primary resistance .... 3.8 to 4.6 ohms at 20°C
Secondary resistance .... 10.1 to 15.1 K-ohms at 20°C
Spark plug cap resistance .... 10 K-ohms at 20°C

Pick-up coil
Resistance .... 182 to 222 ohms at 20°C

Throttle position sensor
Maximum resistance .... 4.0 to 6.0 K-ohms at 20°C
Resistance range .... Zero to 5.0 ± 1.0 K-ohms at 20°C

Torque settings
Pick-up coil bolts .... 7 Nm
Alternator cover bolts .... 10 Nm

1 General information

All models are fitted with a fully transistorised electronic ignition system which, due to its lack of mechanical parts, is totally maintenance-free. The system comprises a trigger, pick-up coil, ignition control unit (ICU) and ignition HT coils (refer to *Wiring Diagrams* at the end of Chapter 8 for details). A throttle position sensor on the carburettor assembly provides information for the ignition control unit.

The ignition trigger, which is on the alternator rotor on the left-hand end of the crankshaft, operates the pick-up coil magnetically as the crankshaft rotates. The pick-up coil sends a signal to the ICU which then supplies the HT coils with the power necessary to produce a spark at the plugs.

The ICU incorporates an electronic advance system controlled by signals from the ignition trigger and pick-up coil, and from the throttle position sensor.

The system also incorporates a safety interlock circuit which will cut the ignition if the sidestand is extended whilst the engine is running and in gear, or if a gear is selected whilst the engine is running and the sidestand is extended. It also prevents the engine from being started if the engine is in gear unless the clutch lever is pulled in (see Chapter 8).

Note: *Individual ignition system components can be checked but not repaired. If ignition system troubles occur, and the faulty component can be isolated, the only cure for the problem is to replace the part with a new one. Keep in mind that most electrical parts, once purchased, cannot be returned. To avoid unnecessary expense, make very sure the faulty component has been positively identified before buying a replacement part.*

2 Ignition system fault finding

Warning: The energy levels in electronic systems can be very high. On no account should the ignition be switched on whilst the plugs or plug caps are being held. Shocks from the HT circuit can be most unpleasant. Secondly, it is vital that the engine is not turned over or run with either of the plug caps removed, and that the plugs are soundly earthed (grounded) when the system is checked for sparking. The ignition system components can be seriously damaged if the HT circuit becomes isolated.

Note: *Refer to Section 6 for details of the engine warning light function.*

1 As no means of adjustment is available, any failure of the system can be traced to failure of

TOOL TIP

A simple spark gap testing fixture can be made from a block of wood, a large alligator clip, and two nails, one of which is fashioned so that a spark plug cap or bare HT lead can be connected to its end. Make sure the gap between the ends of the two nails is the same as specified.

a system component or a simple wiring fault. Of the two possibilities, the latter is by far the most likely. In the event of failure, check the system in a logical fashion, as described below.

2 Pull one of the spark plug caps off the plug and reconnect it to a spare spark plug (preferably use a new plug, properly gapped – see Chapter 1). Lay the plug on the engine with the threads contacting the engine. If necessary, hold the spark plug with an insulated tool.

Warning: Don't remove one of the spark plugs from the engine to perform this check – atomised fuel being pumped out of the open spark plug hole could ignite, causing severe injury!

3 Check that the kill switch is in the RUN position and the transmission is in neutral, then turn the ignition (main) switch ON and turn the engine over on the starter motor. If the system is in good condition a regular, fat blue spark should be evident at the plug electrodes. If the spark appears thin or yellowish, or is non-existent, further investigation will be necessary. Turn the ignition OFF and repeat the test for the other spark plug.

4 The ignition system must be able to produce a spark which is capable of jumping

2.4 An adjustable spark gap tester

a particular size gap. Yamaha specify that a healthy system should produce a spark capable of jumping at least 6 mm. A simple testing tool can be made to test the minimum gap across which the spark will jump (**see Tool Tip**) or, alternatively, it is possible to buy an ignition spark gap tester tool, some of which are adjustable to alter the spark gap (**see illustration**).

5 Pull one of the spark plug caps off the plug and reconnect it to the protruding contact on the test tool, then clip the tool to a good earth (ground) on the engine or frame. Check that the kill switch is in the RUN position, turn the ignition switch ON and turn the engine over on the starter motor. If the system is in good condition a regular, fat blue spark will be seen to jump the gap between the electrodes. Repeat the test for the other cylinder. If the test results are good the entire ignition system can be considered good. If the spark appears thin or yellowish, or is non-existent, further investigation will be necessary.

6 Ignition faults can be divided into two categories, namely those where the ignition system has failed completely, and those which are due to a partial failure. The likely faults are listed below, starting with the most probable source of failure. Work through the list systematically, referring to the appropriate Sections of this Chapter (or other Chapters, as indicated) for full details of the necessary checks and tests. **Note:** *Before checking the following items ensure that the battery is fully charged and that all fuses are in good condition.*

Loose, corroded or damaged wiring connections; broken or shorted wiring between any of the component parts of the ignition system (see Chapter 8).

● Faulty spark plug, dirty, worn or corroded plug electrodes, or incorrect gap between electrodes (Chapter 1).
● Faulty spark plug cap.
● Faulty ignition (main) switch or engine kill switch (see Chapter 8).
● Faulty neutral, clutch or sidestand switch, or starting circuit cut-off relay (see Chapter 8).
● Faulty pick-up coil or damaged trigger.
● Faulty ignition HT coil(s).
● Faulty ignition control unit.

7 If the above checks don't reveal the cause of the problem, have the ignition system tested by a Yamaha dealer.

3 Ignition HT coils and spark plug caps

Check

1 Remove the fuel tank (see Chapter 3) and the steering head panels (see Chapter 7). On 650 models the HT coils are located behind the steering head and behind the airbox. On 1100 models, both HT coils are located behind the steering head.

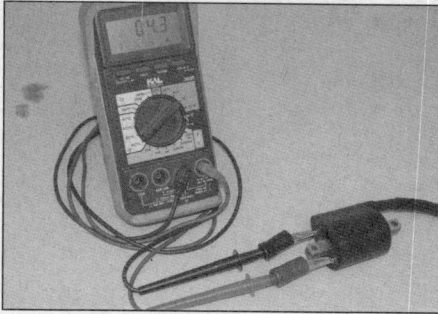

3.3 Measuring primary resistance between the terminals on the coil

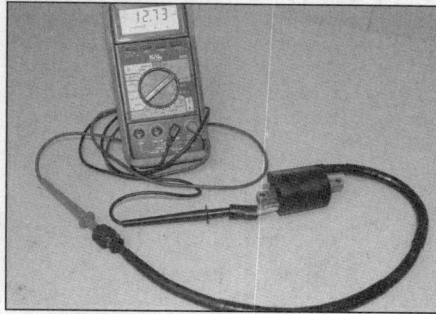

3.4 Measuring secondary resistance between the HT lead and the primary terminal as described

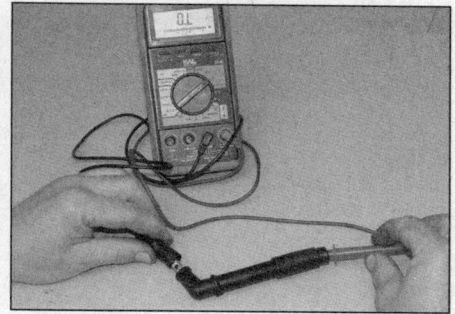

3.6 Measuring spark plug cap resistance

3.8 Disconnect the coil primary circuit connectors (arrowed)

3.9a Remove the coil/fuel pump assembly bracket on 650 models as described . . .

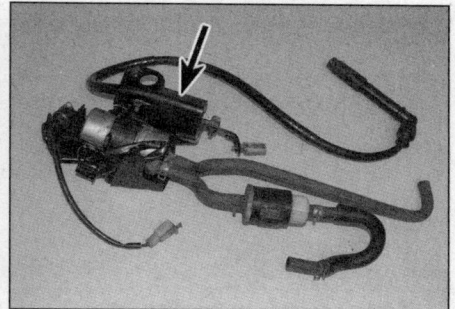

3.9b . . . then remove the coil (arrowed) from the bracket

2 Check each coil visually for cracks and other damage. Inspect the wiring terminals and the spark plug lead.

3 Using a multimeter, test each coil in turn as follows. First disconnect the primary circuit wiring connectors from the coil terminals, noting where they fit. Set the meter to the ohms x 1 scale and connect the positive (+ve) lead to the red/black wire terminal on the coil and the negative (-ve) lead to the orange (or grey) wire terminal to measure the coil primary resistance (see illustration). If the reading obtained is not within the range shown in the Specifications, it is likely that the coil is defective.

4 Next measure the secondary coil resistance as follows. Unscrew the spark plug cap from the end of the HT lead and set the meter to the K-ohms scale. Connect the positive (+ve) meter lead to the end of the HT lead and the negative (-ve) lead to the red/black wire

terminal on the coil (see illustration). If the reading obtained is not within the range shown in the Specifications, it is likely that the coil is defective.

5 If a coil is confirmed to be faulty, it must be replaced with a new one: the coils are sealed units and cannot therefore be repaired.

6 Check the spark plug cap resistance with the meter set to the K-ohms scale. Connect the meter leads to the terminals in both ends of the cap (see illustration). If the reading obtained is not within the range shown in the Specifications, it is likely that the cap is defective.

Removal and installation

7 To remove the coils, first remove the fuel tank, air filter housing and air box (see Chapter 4). Remove the steering head panels (see Chapter 7).

8 Disconnect the spark plug leads from the plugs. Label the coil primary circuit wiring connectors to aid in reconnection, then disconnect them (see illustration).

9 On 650 models, remove the bolts securing the rear cylinder coil to the frame and lift it off. The front cylinder coil is secured to the same bracket behind the steering head as the fuel pump; follow the procedure in Chapter 3, Section 11, and remove the bolts securing the bracket to the frame, then lift the coil and fuel pump assembly off (see illustration). Remove the bolts securing the front cylinder coil to the bracket and lift it off (see illustration).

10 On 1100 models, remove the bolts securing the coils to the frame and lift them off (see illustration).

11 Installation is the reverse of removal. Make sure the primary circuit electrical connectors are firmly attached to the coil terminals.

3.10 On 1100 models the coils are secured by two bolts (arrowed)

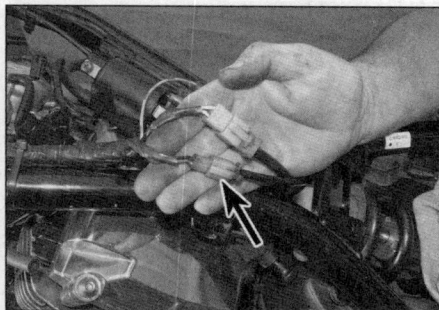

4.2 Location of the pick-up coil wiring connector (arrowed) – 650 models

4 Pick-up coil

Check

1 Disconnect the battery negative (–ve) lead (see Chapter 8).

2 On 650 models, remove the fuel tank (see Chapter 3). Trace the wiring from the back of the alternator cover and disconnect it at the white two-pin connector (see illustration).

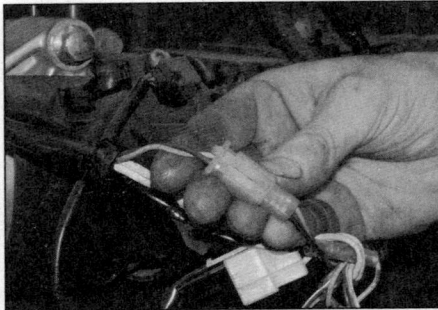

4.3 Location of the pick-up coil wiring connector (arrowed) – 1100 models

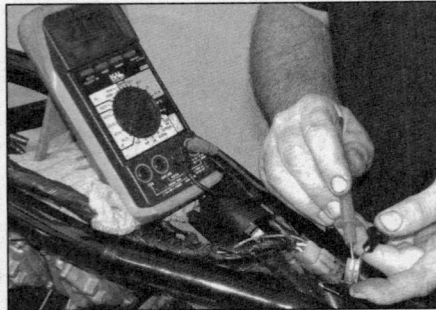

4.4 Measuring the pick-up coil resistance

4.8 On 650 models, release the wiring (arrowed) from the clip

4.12a Location of the pick-up coil – 650 models

4.12b Location of the pick-up coil – 1100 models

3 On 1100 models, remove the left-hand frame cover (see Chapter 7). Trace the wiring from the back of the alternator cover and disconnect it at the white two-pin connector **(see illustration)**.

4 Using a multimeter set to the ohms x 100 scale, measure the resistance between the terminals on the pick-up coil side of the connector **(see illustration)**.

5 Compare the reading obtained with that given in the Specifications at the beginning of this Chapter. The pick-up coil must be replaced with a new one if the reading obtained differs greatly from that given, particularly if the meter indicates a short circuit (no measurable resistance) or an open circuit (infinite, or very high resistance).

6 If the pick-up coil is thought to be faulty, first check that the wiring from the connector to the pick-up coil is not damaged. Pinched or broken wires can usually be repaired. If the

wiring is good, replace the pick-up coil with a new one. **Note:** *On 1100 models, the pick-up coil and alternator stator are listed as an integral assembly.*

Removal and installation

7 Disconnect the battery negative (–ve) lead.

8 On 650 models, refer to Step 2 and disconnect the wiring connector. Remove the transmission cover and the middle gear cover (see Chapter 2A). Release the wiring from the clip on the back of the crankcase **(see illustration)**.

9 On 1100 models, refer to Step 3 and disconnect the wiring connector.

10 Feed the wiring back to the alternator cover, noting its routing and releasing it from any clips.

11 Disconnect the clutch cable from the bracket on the alternator cover, then remove the alternator cover (see Chapter 2A or 2B applicable).

12 Unscrew the bolts securing the pick-up coil and the wiring clamp to the inside of the cover, then free the wiring grommets from the cut-out in the cover and remove the coil **(see illustrations)**. On 1100 models, unscrew the bolts securing the alternator stator and remove the pick-up coil and stator assembly.

13 Fit the pick-up coil and the wiring grommets into their locations in the cover. On 1100 models, install the pick-up coil and stator assembly. Apply a suitable non-permanent thread locking compound to the fixing bolts and tighten them to the torque setting specified at the beginning of this Chapter. Install the wiring clamp and tighten the clamp bolt securely.

14 Follow the procedure in Chapter 2A or 2B as applicable and install the alternator cover and clutch cable.

15 Feed the pick-up coil wiring up to the connector, securing it with any clips. Check that the contacts inside the wiring connector are clean and free from corrosion, then reconnect it securely **(see illustration 4.2 or 4.3)**.

16 Reconnect the battery negative (-ve) terminal and install the remaining components in the reverse order of removal.

5 Throttle position sensor

1 The throttle position sensor is mounted on the outside of the front cylinder carburettor and is keyed to the throttle shaft. The sensor provides the ignition control unit with information on throttle position and rate of opening or closing.

Check

2 Remove the fuel tank, the air filter housing and the air box (see Chapter 3). Make sure the ignition is switched OFF.

3 On 650 models, disconnect the throttle position sensor wiring directly from the sensor **(see illustration)**.

4 On 1100 models, trace the wiring from the sensor and disconnect it at the connector **(see illustration)**.

5.3 Throttle position sensor wiring connector – 650 models

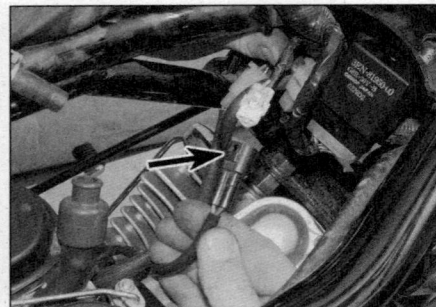

5.4 Throttle position sensor wiring connector – 1100 models

5.10 Throttle position sensor mounting screws – 1100 model shown

5 Using a multimeter set to the K-ohms range, measure the sensor's maximum resistance (throttle fully open). Connect the meter probes between the black wire terminal and the blue wire terminal on the sensor side of the connector. Compare the reading obtained with that given in the Specifications at the beginning of this Chapter; if it differs greatly, replace the sensor with a new one.

6 Now check the sensor's resistance range by connecting the positive meter probe to the yellow terminal and the negative probe to the black terminal, and slowly opening the throttle from fully closed to fully open. If the readings obtained differ greatly from those specified at the beginning of this Chapter, replace the sensor with a new one. **Note:** *When checking the resistance range, it is more important that there is a smooth and constant change in the resistance as the throttle is opened, than that the figures themselves are exactly as specified.*

7 If the checks made in Steps 5 and 6 produce different readings from those specified, remove the sensor as described below and inspect it for signs of damage or wear to the slot where the throttle shaft connects. Repeat the checks described, turning the sensor by hand as required in Step 6. If the results are still outside those specified, renew the sensor.

8 If the test results are as specified, use a multimeter to check for continuity between the terminals on the wiring loom side of the sensor wiring connector and the corresponding terminals on the ignition control unit connector, referring to *Wiring Diagrams* at the end of Chapter 8. There should be continuity between each terminal. If not, this is probably due to a damaged or broken wire between the connectors: pinched or broken wires can usually be repaired. Also check the connectors for loose or corroded terminals, and check the sensor itself for cracks and other damage. If the wiring and connectors are good, check the adjustment of the sensor as described below.

Adjustment

Note: *On 650 models, it may be necessary to displace the carburettor assembly to access*

the throttle position sensor mounting screws – see Chapter 3.
9 Before adjusting the sensor, check the engine idle speed and carburettor synchronisation (see Chapter 1).
10 Loosen the sensor mounting screws, then connect the multimeter as described in Step 6 **(see illustration)**. With the throttle fully closed, turn the sensor clockwise or anti-clockwise until the closed throttle resistance is indicated. If the sensor cannot be adjusted to obtain the correct reading, replace it with a new one.
11 Tighten the sensor mounting screws securely.

Renewal

12 Remove the fuel tank, the air filter housing and the air box (see Chapter 3). Make sure the ignition is switched OFF.
13 Follow the procedure in Steps 3 or 4 as applicable and disconnect the wiring connector. Unscrew the sensor mounting screws and remove the sensor, noting how it fits.
14 Install the sensor, ensuring it is keyed correctly onto the throttle shaft, and tighten the screws lightly. Connect the wiring connector and adjust the sensor as described in Steps 9 to 11.
15 Install the remaining components in the reverse order of removal.

---

6   Fault self-diagnosis

1 When the ignition (main) switch is turned ON, the engine warning light in the speedometer will come on for 1.4 seconds and then go out. If, however, there is a fault in the ignition system, the warning light will then begin to flash. If a fault develops while the engine is running, the warning light will come on and stay on.
2 On all models, a fault with the throttle position sensor, or the sensor wiring, is indicated by a flashing warning light. Follow the procedure in Section 5 and check the sensor.

7.4 Unscrew the timing inspection cap (arrowed)

3 On 1100 models, a fault with the speed sensor will also cause the warning light to flash. Follow the procedure in Chapter 8 to check the sensor back-up fuse and output. Additionally on models from 2003, a fault with either of the ignition HT coils will cause the warning light to flash and the safety solenoids in the ignition system will cut the fuel supply to the carburettors. Follow the procedure in Section 3 to check the HT coils.

---

7   Ignition timing

General information

1 Since no provision exists for adjusting the ignition timing, and since no ignition component is subject to mechanical wear, there is no need for regular checks. However, the ignition timing should be checked if investigating a fault such as a loss of power or a misfire, but only after a thorough examination of all the other ignition system components and wiring.
2 The ignition timing is checked dynamically (engine running) using a stroboscopic lamp. The inexpensive neon lamps should be adequate in theory, but in practice may produce a pulse of such low intensity that the timing mark remains indistinct. If possible, one of the more precise xenon tube lamps should be used, powered by an external source of the appropriate voltage. **Note:** *Do not use the machine's own battery, as an incorrect reading may result from stray impulses within the machine's electrical system.*

Check

3 Warm the engine up to normal operating temperature, then turn it OFF.
4 Unscrew the timing inspection cap in the alternator cover on the right-hand side of the engine **(see illustration)**.
5 The mark on the edge of the alternator rotor which indicates the firing point at idle speed for the rear cylinder is an 'H' mark **(see illustration)**. The static timing mark with

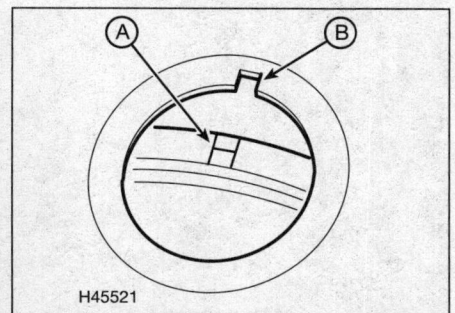

7.5 'H' mark on alternator rotor (A) and static timing mark (B)

which this should align is the cut-out in the inspection hole.

> **HAYNES HiNT**
>
> *The timing mark can be highlighted with white paint to make them more visible under the stroboscope light*

6 Connect the timing lamp to the rear cylinder ignition coil as described in the manufacturer's instructions.

7 Start the engine and aim the light at the inspection hole.

8 With the machine idling at the specified speed, the 'H' mark should appear precisely in the middle of the cut-out in the inspection hole (see illustration 7.5). Note: *It is essential that the reading is taken at the specified idling speed.*

9 If the ignition timing is incorrect, or suspected of being incorrect, one of the ignition system components is at fault, and the system must be tested as described in the preceding Sections of this Chapter.

10 When the check is complete, install the timing inspection cap, using a new sealing washer if the old one is damaged or deformed, and tighten it securely.

8.2a Lift out the panel behind the battery . . .

8 Ignition control unit (ICU)

1 If the tests shown in the preceding Sections have failed to isolate the cause of an ignition fault, it is possible that the ICU itself is faulty. No details are available with which the unit can be tested. The best way to determine whether it is faulty is to substitute it with a known good one. Otherwise, take the unit to a Yamaha dealer for assessment.

Removal

2 On 650 models, remove the battery (see Chapter 8). Lift out the panel at the back of the battery housing to access the ICU (see illustrations).

3 On 1100 models, remove the rider's seat (see Chapter 7). The ICU is located on the panel underneath the seat (see illustration). Disconnect the battery negative (–ve) lead.

4 Disconnect the wiring connectors from the ICU.

5 Remove the screws securing the ICU and remove the unit.

Installation

6 Installation is the reverse of removal. Make sure the wiring connectors are correctly and securely connected.

9 Immobiliser system (late 650/1100A Europe models)

General information

1 The system comprises a security coded ignition key with integral transponder, the immobiliser unit and the ICU. When the key is inserted into the ignition (main) switch the security code is transmitted from the key to the immobiliser. The code deactivates the immobiliser and the warning LED stops flashing. When the key is removed, the immobiliser is activated and the warning LED starts flashing. Note: *To minimise battery discharging, the warning LED goes out after 24 hours although the immobiliser system remains active. Disconnecting the battery does not deactivate the immobiliser system.*

2 One red master key and two black ignition keys are supplied with each machine from new. The keys and the immobiliser are encoded by the factory. The master key should be kept in a safe place and not used on a day-to-day basis – if the master key is lost you will need a new immobiliser system!

3 If a black ignition key is lost, obtain a replacement from a Yamaha dealer and encode the new key and the second black ignition key as described below. You will require the red master key for this purpose. Once the system is recoded the lost key will not deactivate the immobiliser.

Key encoding

4 Check that the warning LED is flashing normally. Insert the red master key in the ignition switch and turn it ON, then turn it OFF and insert the new black ignition key in the switch and turn it ON. The LED will flash rapidly, indicating the key registration mode. Within five seconds, turn the new key OFF and insert the second black ignition key. Turn the switch ON, then turn it OFF again. Both ignition keys and the immobiliser system have now been recoded. Note: *Keys can only be recoded while the system is in key registration mode indicated by the rapidly flashing LED. Both keys must be recoded before the mode is finished.*

5 Check that the engine can be started with the two black keys – if not, repeat the procedure.

System check

6 If the immobiliser system is thought to be faulty, first check the main, ignition and back-

8.2b . . . to gain access to the ICU (arrowed) – 650 models

8.3 Location of the ICU (arrowed) – 1100 models

9.8 Disconnect the speedometer wiring connector

up fuses, then check the battery and the ignition (main) switch (see Chapter 8).

7 If the warning LED fails to illuminate, remove the seats, then displace the ICU panel to access the speedometer wiring connector (see Chapter 7).

8 Disconnect the speedometer wiring connector **(see illustration)**. Using a multimeter set to the DC20V scale, connect the meter positive (+ve) probe to the green/blue wire terminal in the loom side of the connector and the negative (-ve) probe to black wire terminal, then turn the ignition (main) switch ON and check for battery voltage. If voltage is present, it is likely the LED within the speedometer unit has failed – have it checked by a Yamaha dealer. If no voltage is present, check the immobiliser wiring as follows. Turn the ignition (main) switch OFF.

9 To check the immobiliser wiring, first remove the left-hand frame cover (see Chapter 7). The immobiliser is clipped to the backing panel below the fuel pump. Using a multimeter set to the DC20V scale, connect the meter positive (+ve) probe to the red/green wire terminal in the loom side of connector and the negative (-ve) probe to the black wire terminal, then turn the ignition (main) switch ON and check for battery voltage. If no voltage is present, refer to the *Wiring Diagrams* at the end of this Chapter and check the wiring between the battery and the immobiliser. Turn the ignition (main) switch OFF.

10 Now connect the meter positive (+ve) probe to the yellow/blue wire terminal in the loom side of the connector and the negative (-ve) probe to the black wire terminal, then turn the ignition (main) switch ON and check for battery voltage. If no voltage is present, refer to the *Wiring Diagrams* at the end of this Chapter and check the wiring between the ignition switch and the immobiliser. Turn the ignition (main) switch OFF.

11 Now connect the meter positive (+ve) probe to the green/blue wire terminal in the loom side of the connector and the negative (-ve) probe to the black wire terminal, then turn the ignition (main) switch ON and check for battery voltage. If voltage is present, refer to the *Wiring Diagrams* at the end of this Chapter and check the wiring between the speedometer and the immobiliser. If no voltage is present, it is likely the immobiliser is faulty – have it checked by a Yamaha dealer. Turn the ignition (main) switch OFF. **Note:** *If a new immobiliser is fitted, a new ignition (main) switch and keys will also be required – refer to your Yamaha dealer for details.*

Chapter 5
Frame, suspension and final drive

Contents

Degrees of difficulty

Easy, suitable for novice with little experience	Fairly easy, suitable for beginner with some experience	Fairly difficult, suitable for competent DIY mechanic	Difficult, suitable for experienced DIY mechanic	Very difficult, suitable for expert DIY or professional

Specifications

Front forks – Europe 650 models

Fork oil type (all models) .... SAE 10W fork oil

XVS650 (1997 to 2000)
Fork oil capacity .... 454 cc
Fork oil level .... 114 mm below top of inner fork tube*
Fork spring free length
    Standard .... 295 mm
    Service limit .... 289 mm

XVS650 (2001-on)
Fork oil capacity .... 462 cc
Fork oil level .... 110 mm below top of inner fork tube*
Fork spring free length
    Standard .... 303 mm
    Service limit .... 292 mm

XVS650A
Fork oil capacity .... 507 cc
Fork oil level .... 95 mm below top of inner fork tube*
Fork spring free length
    Standard .... 332.5 mm
    Service limit .... 325.9 mm

Front forks – US 650 models

Fork oil type (all models) .... SAE 10W fork oil
Fork oil capacity .... 507 cc
Fork oil level .... 95 mm below top of inner fork tube*
Fork spring free length
    Standard .... 332.5 mm
    Service limit .... 325.9 mm

*With spring removed and fork fully compressed.

Front forks – 1100 models

Fork oil type . . . . SAE 10W fork oil
Fork oil capacity . . . . 464 cc
Fork oil level . . . . 108 mm below top of inner fork tube*
Fork spring free length
  Standard
    XVS1100 . . . . 356.9 mm
    XVS1100A and S . . . . 361.9 mm
  Service limit . . . . 350.0 mm
*With spring removed and fork fully compressed.

Rear suspension – 650 models

Rear spring installed length
  XVS650 . . . . 160.5 mm
  XVS650A and S . . . . 165.5 mm
Swingarm endplay and side play limits . . . . 1.0 mm

Rear suspension – 1100 models

Rear spring installed length . . . . 163.0 mm
Swingarm endplay and side play limits . . . . 0 mm

Torque specifications

Footrest bracket bolts
  Rider's footrests . . . . 64 Nm
  Passenger's footrests . . . . 26 Nm
Fork clamp bolts
  Bottom yoke . . . . 30 Nm
  Top yoke (all 1100 models and XVS650) . . . . 20 Nm
  Top yoke (XVS650A and S models) . . . . 23 Nm
Fork damper bolt . . . . 30 Nm**
Fork top bolt . . . . 23 Nm
Front brake master cylinder clamp bolts . . . . 10 Nm
Front wheel axle pinch bolt . . . . 20 Nm
Front turn signal pinch bolts . . . . 7 Nm
Handlebar clamp bolts
  650 models . . . . 23 Nm
  1100 models . . . . 28 Nm
Handlebar mounting bracket nuts
  650 models . . . . 20 Nm
  1100 models . . . . 32 Nm
Rear shock absorber upper bolt
  650 models . . . . 62 Nm
  1100 models . . . . 40 Nm
Rear shock absorber lower bolt
  650 models . . . . 62 Nm
  1100 models . . . . 48 Nm
Rear suspension linkage bolts (1100 models only) . . . . 48 Nm
Rear wheel hub pinion nuts . . . . 62 Nm
Sidestand bracket to frame . . . . 64 Nm
Sidestand to bracket . . . . 56 Nm
Steering stem nut . . . . 110 Nm
Steering head bearing adjuster nut
  Initial setting . . . . 52 Nm
  Final setting . . . . 18 Nm
Swingarm pivot shaft
  650 models
    Left-hand shaft . . . . 100 Nm**
    Right-hand shaft . . . . 7 Nm
    Right-hand shaft locknut . . . . 100 Nm
  1100 models . . . . 90 Nm
**Apply non-permanent thread locking compound to the bolt threads.

1 General information

All models use a full cradle, twin spar steel frame. On 1100 models, the right-hand frame down-tube is detachable to facilitate engine removal.

Front suspension is by a pair of oil-damped, telescopic forks with internal coil springs. The forks are not adjustable.

The rear suspension consists of a swingarm acting on a single shock absorber. The shock is adjustable for spring preload only. On 1100 models, swingarm movement is transferred to the shock via a rising-rate linkage.

Final drive is by shaft.

2 Frame

1 The frame should not require attention unless accident damage has occurred. In most cases, frame renewal is the only satisfactory remedy for such damage. A few frame specialists have the jigs and other equipment necessary for straightening the frame to the required standard of accuracy, but even then there is no simple way of assessing to what extent the frame may have been over-stressed.
2 Loose engine mounting bolts can cause ovaling or fracturing of the mounts themselves. On 1100 models, ensure that the bolts retaining the detachable right-hand frame down-tube are tight (see Chapter 2B). On a high mileage bike, the frame should be examined closely for signs of cracking or splitting at the welded joints. Minor damage can often be repaired by welding, depending on the extent and nature of the damage, but this is a task for an expert.
3 Remember that a frame which is out of alignment will cause handling problems. If misalignment is suspected as the result of an accident, first check the wheel alignment (see Chapter 6). To check the frame thoroughly it will be necessary to strip the machine completely.

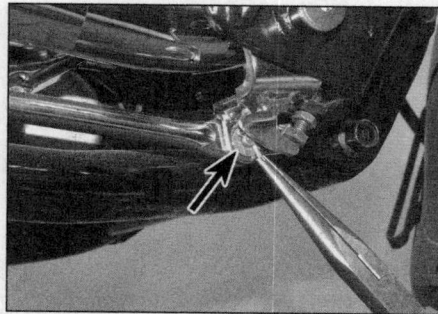
3.1a Remove the split pin and washer (arrowed) . . .

3.1b . . . then pull out the clevis pin

3 Brake pedal, gearchange lever and footrests

Brake pedal

650 models

1 Remove the split pin and washer from the clevis pin connecting the brake rod to the brake pedal, then pull out the clevis pin and separate the rod from the pedal (see illustrations). Discard the split pin, as a new one must be used on reassembly.
2 Loosen the bolts securing the footrest bracket to the frame, then support the footrest assembly and remove the bolts (see illustration).
3 Disconnect the rear brake light switch

spring from the brake pedal and lift off the footrest assembly (see illustration).
4 If required, disconnect the pedal return spring from the bracket, then undo the pivot bolt securing the pedal to the bracket and remove the pedal (see illustrations).
5 If required, to remove the brake rod and rear brake arm, first check for a register mark on the rear brake arm that aligns with a punch mark on the brake intermediate shaft (see illustration). Remove the pinch bolt and pull the lever off the shaft.
6 Installation is the reverse of removal. Apply grease to the brake pedal pivot. Tighten the footrest bracket bolts to the torque setting specified at the beginning of this Chapter. **Note:** *See Chapter 1, Section 12, for details of adjusting the pedal height and the operation of the rear brake light switch.*

3.2 Remove the footrest bracket bolts (arrowed)

3.3 Disconnect the brake light switch spring from the pedal

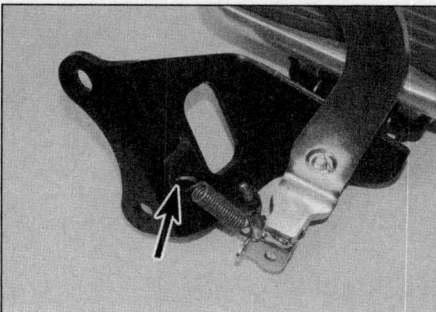
3.4a Disconnect the brake pedal return spring (arrowed) . . .

3.4b . . . and remove the pivot bolt (arrowed)

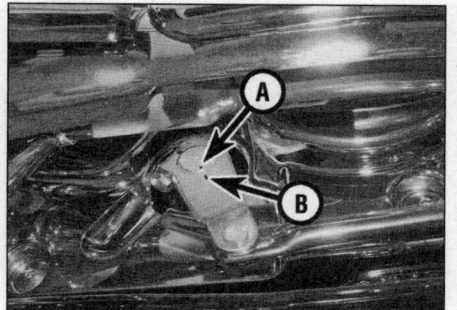
3.5 Note the alignment between the punch mark (A) and the register mark (B)

3.7 Disconnect the rear brake light switch connector

3.8 Remove the footrest bracket bolts (arrowed)

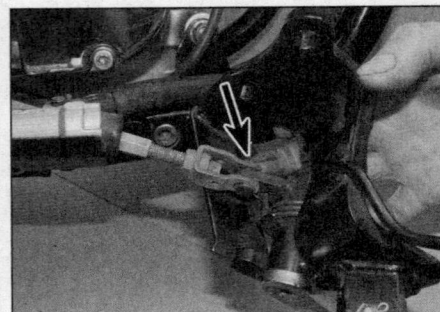

3.9a Remove the split pin and washer (arrowed) . . .

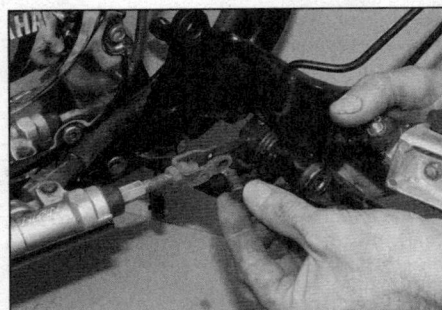

3.9b . . . then pull out the clevis pin

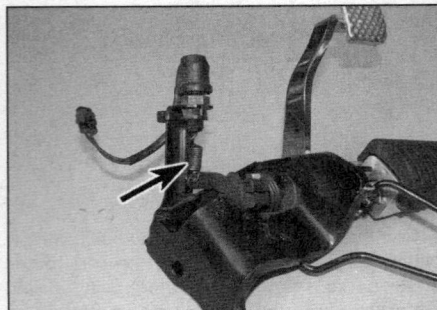

3.10 Disconnect the brake light switch spring (arrowed) from the lever

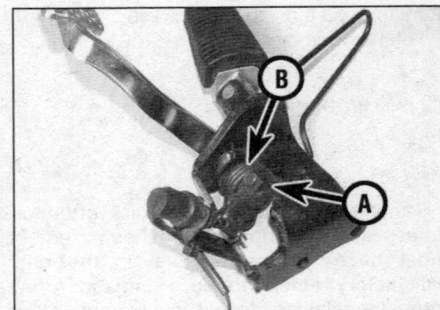

3.11 Pull off the lever (A) noting the location of the return spring (B)

1100 models

7 Disconnect the rear brake light switch wiring connector (see illustration).

8 Loosen the bolts securing the footrest bracket to the frame, then support the footrest assembly and remove the bolts (see illustration).

9 Remove the split pin and washer from the clevis pin connecting the brake pedal to the master cylinder pushrod, then remove the clevis pin and separate the pushrod from the pedal (see illustrations). Discard the split pin, as a new one must be used on reassembly.

10 To remove the brake pedal from the bracket, first disconnect the brake light switch spring from the actuating lever, then mark the pedal shaft where it aligns with the slot in the lever (see illustration).

11 Remove the pinch bolt and pull the lever

off the shaft, noting the location of the return spring (see illustration). Remove the pedal from the bracket.

12 Installation is the reverse of removal. Apply grease to the brake pedal pivot. Use a new split pin on the clevis pin securing the brake pedal to the master cylinder pushrod. Tighten the footrest bracket bolts to the torque setting specified at the beginning of this Chapter. Note: *See Chapter 1, Section 12, for details of adjusting the pedal height and the operation of the rear brake light switch.*

Gearchange lever

650 models

13 Check for the mark on the gearchange shaft that aligns with the slot in the lever (see illustration). If the mark isn't visible, make

your own with a sharp punch then remove the pinch bolt and pull the lever off the shaft. Undo the bolts securing the left-hand footrest bracket and remove the gearchange pedal, gearchange linkage and footrest as an assembly (see illustration).

14 If required, loosen the gearchange linkage rod locknuts, then unscrew the rod and separate it from the pedal and the lever – the rod is reverse-threaded on the lever end, so will unscrew from both lever and pedal simultaneously when turned in the one direction.

15 To remove the gearchange pedal from the bracket, remove the circlip and washer retaining the pedal and lift it off (see illustration).

16 Installation is the reverse of removal. Apply grease to the gearchange lever pivot and secure the lever with a new circlip. Tighten the

3.13a Note the punch mark (arrowed) on the gearchange shaft

3.13b Bolts (arrowed) secure the footrest/gearchange lever assembly

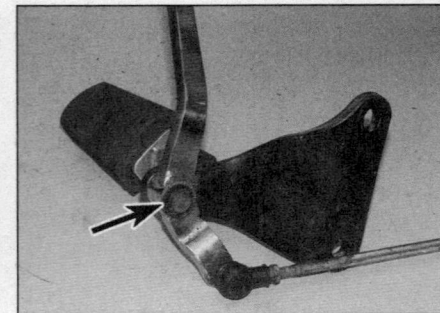

3.15 Gearchange pedal is secured by circlip and washer

3.17a Note the punch mark (arrowed) on the gearchange shaft . . .

3.17b . . . then remove the pinch bolt and pull off the lever

3.17c Undo the bolts (arrowed) . . .

3.17d . . . and remove the footrest/gearchange pedal assembly

footrest bracket bolts to the torque setting specified at the beginning of this Chapter. If required, adjust the length of the gearchange rod (see Chapter 1, Section 23).

1100 models

17 Check for the punch mark on the gearchange shaft that aligns with the slot in the lever – if the mark isn't visible, make your own with a sharp punch, then remove the pinch bolt and pull the lever off the shaft (see illustrations). Undo the bolts securing the left-hand footrest bracket and remove the gearchange pedal, gearchange linkage and footrest as an assembly (see illustrations).
18 If required, loosen the gearchange linkage rod locknuts, then unscrew the rod and separate it from the pedal and the lever – the rod is reverse-threaded on the lever end, so will unscrew from both lever and pedal simultaneously when turned in the one direction.

19 To remove the gearchange pedal from the bracket, remove the circlip and washer retaining the pedal and lift it off (see illustration).
20 Installation is the reverse of removal. Apply grease to the gearchange lever pivot and secure the lever with a new circlip. Tighten the footrest bracket bolts to the torque setting specified at the beginning of this Chapter. If required, adjust the length of the gearchange rod (see Chapter 1, Section 23).

Rider footrests

21 To remove the footrest, first note the location of the return spring, then remove the split pin and washer and pull out the clevis pin (see illustrations).
22 To remove the footboard, remove the circlip from the pivot pin, then remove the pin, noting the location of the return spring, and lift the footboard off (see illustrations).

Passenger footrests

23 To remove the footrest assembly, remove the bolts securing the bracket to the frame and lift it off (see illustration).

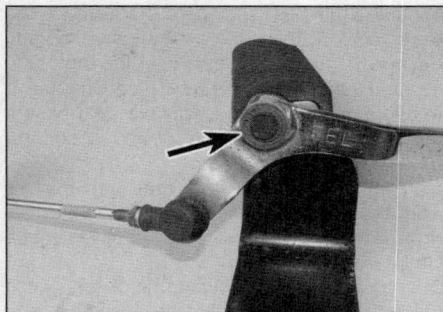

3.19 Gearchange pedal is secured by circlip and washer

3.21a Note the location of the return spring (arrowed) . . .

3.21b . . . then remove the split pin and washer (arrowed)

3.22a Remove the circlip (arrowed)

3.22b Note the location of the springs, them withdraw the pin

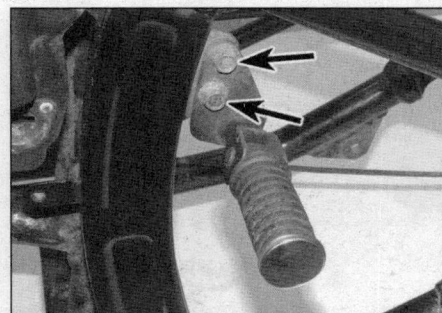

3.23 Footrest bracket is secured by two bolts (arrowed)

3.24 Footrest is held in position by rubber tension

24 To remove the footrest, remove the split pin and washer from the clevis pin, then remove the pin and lift the footrest off. Note that the footrest is held in either the up or down position by the tension of the footrest rubber **(see illustration)**.

25 Installation is the reverse of removal. Tighten the footrest bracket bolts to the torque setting specified at the beginning of this Chapter.

4 Sidestand

1 Support the motorcycle securely in an upright position using an auxiliary stand.

2 Undo the screws securing the sidestand switch and displace the switch **(see illustration)**. Alternatively, trace the wiring

4.2a Undo the screws (arrowed) and displace the switch

from the sidestand switch and disconnect it at the connector **(see illustration)**. On 650 models, the connector is located behind the left-hand steering head panel – remove the panel for access (see Chapter 7). On 1100 models, the connector is located behind the left-hand frame cover – remove the cover for access (see Chapter 7). Release the wiring from any clips or ties.

3 Undo the sidestand bracket bolts and lift off the stand assembly **(see illustration)**.

4 Note how the spring is attached to the lugs on the back of the stand **(see illustration)**. Note how the contact plate on the stand locates against the switch plunger **(see illustration)**.

5 If required, unhook the spring, then remove the locknut, pivot bolt and contact plate and separate the stand from the bracket **(see illustration)**.

6 Installation is the reverse of removal, noting the following:

4.2b Sidestand switch wiring connector – 650 model shown

● Apply grease to the stand pivot bolt and tighten the locknut securely.
● Tighten the stand bracket bolts to the specified torque setting.
● Check the spring tension – it must hold the stand up when it is not in use. If the spring has sagged, fit a new one.
● Ensure the contact plate actuates the stand switch when the stand is lowered – check the operation of the switch (see Chapter 8).

5 Handlebar and levers

Handlebars

1 The handlebar assembly can be displaced without removing the levers or switches, if for example, access is required only to the steering stem components. Either remove the handlebar clamps (see Step 9) or remove the bars and fork top yoke as an assembly (see Section 8), and lay the bars over the top of the frame. Remove the fuel tank (see Chapter 3) to avoid damaging the paintwork, and ensure the brake fluid reservoir cover is secure, before displacing the bars.

2 If required, unscrew the rear view mirrors from the handlebar brackets, noting that the right-hand mirror unscrews clockwise (see Chapter 7).

3 Undo the screws securing the clutch switch to the underside of the clutch lever and displace the switch, then disconnect the front brake light switch wiring connectors **(see illustrations)**.

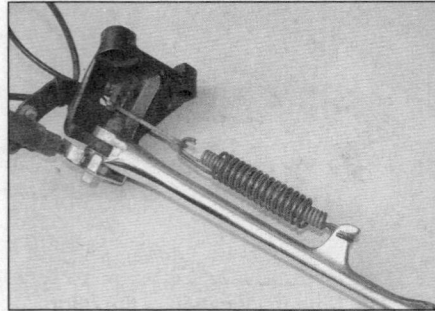

4.3 Sidestand is secured by two bolts

4.4a Note how the stand spring locates

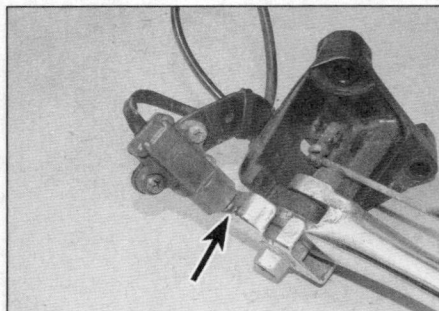

4.4b Note how the contact plate actuates the switch plunger

4.5 Location of the pivot bolt locknut

5.3a Clutch switch is secured by two screws (arrowed)

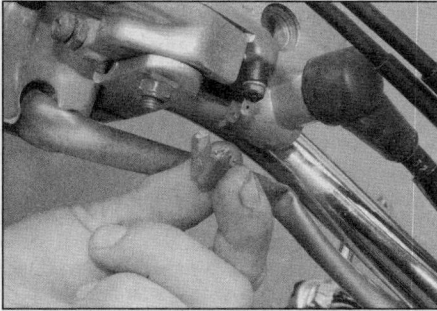
5.3b Disconnect the front brake light switch connectors

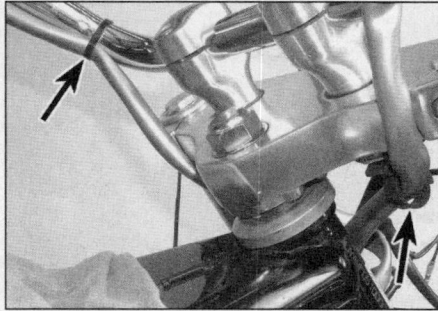
5.4 Free the wiring from the cable ties and clips (arrowed)

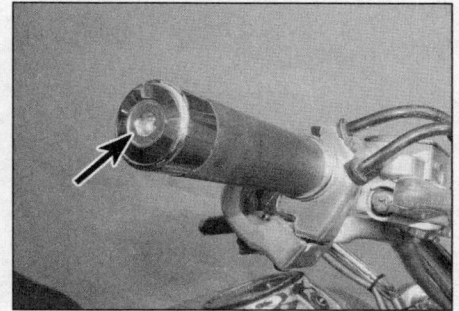
5.6 Unscrew the bar ends if fitted

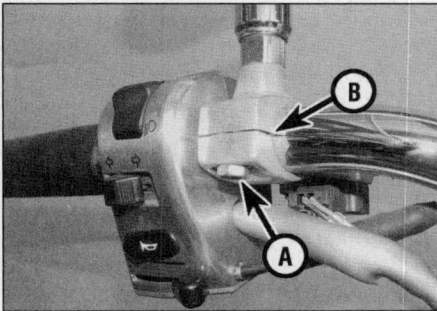
5.7 Clutch lever bracket pinch bolt (A) – note the punch mark (B)

5.8 Brake master cylinder clamp bolts (arrowed)

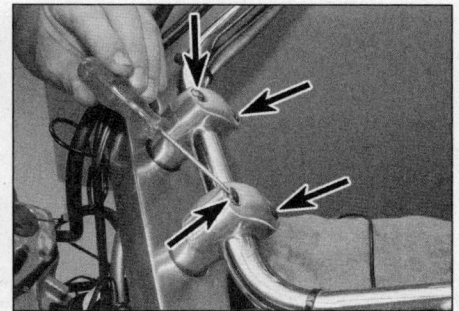
5.9a Remove the plugs from the tops of the bolts

4 Note the position of the cable ties securing the switch wiring to the handlebars, then remove the ties. Free the wiring from the clips on the underside of the top yoke (see illustration).
5 Remove the screws securing the two halves of the left and right-hand switch units and remove the backs of the units (see Chapter 8). The right-hand unit is a combined switch/throttle twistgrip – disconnect the throttle cables from the twistgrip (see Chapter 3).
6 Where fitted, unscrew the bar ends, then slide the grips off the bars (see illustration). Note: If the left-hand grip has been bonded in place you may need to cut it free.
7 Loosen the clutch lever bracket pinch bolt and slide the lever assembly off the bar (see illustration).
8 Unscrew the brake master cylinder clamp bolts and remove the clamp, noting how it fits,

then lift the master cylinder away from the handlebar (see illustration). Keep the reservoir upright to prevent fluid spills and make sure no strain is placed on the hose.
9 Remove the plugs from the tops of the handlebar clamp bolts (see illustration). Unscrew the bolts and remove the clamps and the handlebars. Note the location of the punch mark on the clamps to aid reassembly (see illustration).
10 The handlebar mounting brackets are secured by nuts on the underside of the top yoke. If required, remove the nuts and lift off the brackets, noting the location of the cable guide (see illustration).
11 Installation is the reverse of removal, noting the following:
● If removed, install the handlebar mounting brackets and tighten the nuts to the torque setting specified at the beginning of this Chapter.

● Install the handlebar clamps with the punch marks facing forward (see illustration 5.9b). Tighten the front clamp bolt first so that the gap is positioned at the rear joint of the clamp – tighten both bolts to the specified torque setting.
● Align the slot in the clutch lever bracket with the punch mark on the handlebar (see illustration 5.7).
● Lubricate the right-hand bar with a smear of grease before sliding on the throttle twistgrip.
● Install the brake master cylinder clamp with the UP mark facing up (see illustration). Tighten the bolts to the specified torque setting.
● Don't forget to reconnect the front brake light switch and clutch switch wiring connectors.
● Secure the switch wiring with new cable ties.

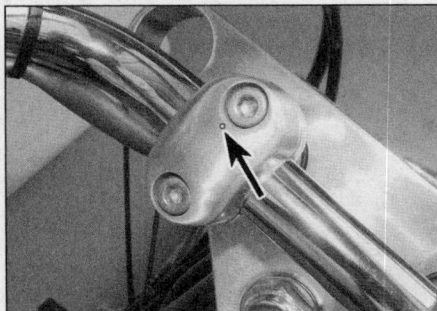
5.9b Note the location of the punch mark (arrowed)

5.10 Handlebar mounting brackets are secured by nuts (arrowed)

5.11 Ensure the clamp is fitted the correct way round, then tighten the two bolts (arrowed)

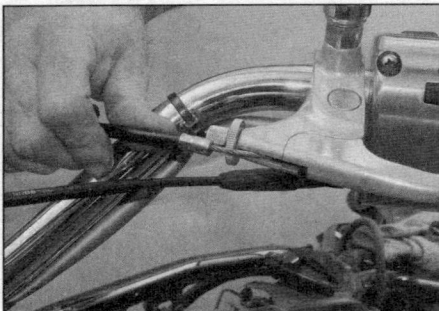

5.12 Detach the clutch cable from the lever

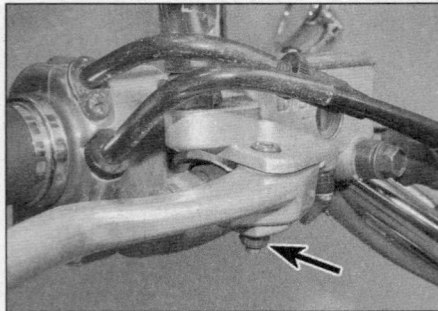

5.14a Front brake lever pivot bolt locknut

Front brake lever

14 Unscrew the lever pivot bolt locknut, then push the pivot bolt out of the bracket and remove the lever, noting the location of the return spring **(see illustrations)**. Note the bush inside the lever and remove it if it is loose. If either the bush or pivot bolt are worn replace them with new ones.

15 Installation is the reverse of removal. Apply grease to the pivot bolt shaft, the bush and the contact areas between the lever and its bracket. Don't forget to install the spring in the bracket before fitting the lever.

16 Check the brake lever freeplay as described in Chapter 1, Section 12 and adjust if necessary.

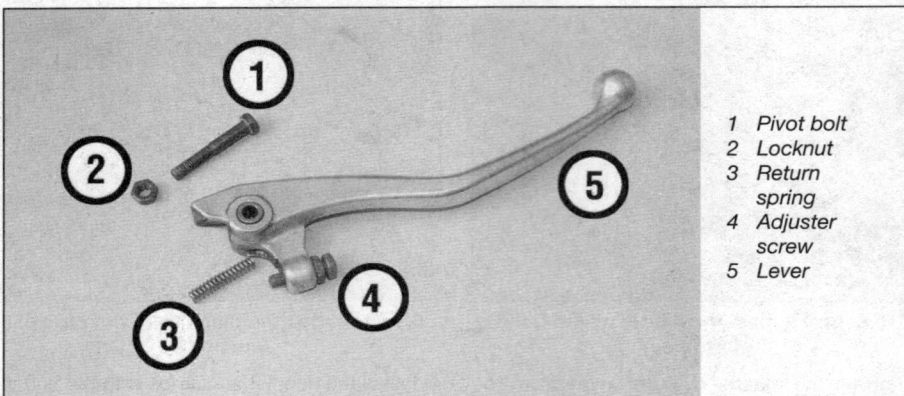

1 Pivot bolt
2 Locknut
3 Return spring
4 Adjuster screw
5 Lever

5.14b Components of the front brake lever

| 6 | Front fork removal and installation |

Removal

1 Support the motorcycle with an auxiliary stand so that the front wheel is off the ground.
2 Displace the front brake calipers (see Chapter 6). There is no need to disconnect the hydraulic hoses but support the calipers with cable ties to prevent straining the hoses.
3 Remove the front wheel (see Chapter 6).
4 Remove the front mudguard (see Chapter 7).
5 Work on each fork leg individually. Note the routing of the various cables and hoses around the forks.
6 Note the alignment between the top of the fork leg and the top yoke, then loosen the fork clamp bolt in the top yoke **(see illustration)**. If the fork legs are to be disassembled, or if the fork oil is being changed, loosen the fork top bolt now.
7 On XVS650A/S and XVS1100A/S models, the top fork covers must be removed to access the fork clamp bolts in the bottom yoke **(see illustration)**. First displace the

● Adjust throttle cable (see Chapter 1) and clutch cable (see *Daily (pre-ride) checks*).
● Check the operation of all switches and the front brake and clutch before taking the machine on the road.

Clutch lever

12 Thread the clutch cable adjuster fully into the bracket and detach the cable from the lever **(see illustration)**. Unscrew the lever pivot bolt locknut on the underside of the lever, then push the pivot bolt out of the bracket and remove the lever. Note the bush inside the lever and remove it if it is loose. If either the bush or pivot bolt are worn replace them with new ones.

13 Installation is the reverse of removal. Apply grease to the pivot bolt shaft, the bush and the contact areas between the lever and its bracket, and to the inner clutch cable. Adjust the clutch cable freeplay (see *Daily (pre-ride) checks*).

6.6 Top yoke fork clamp bolt (arrowed)

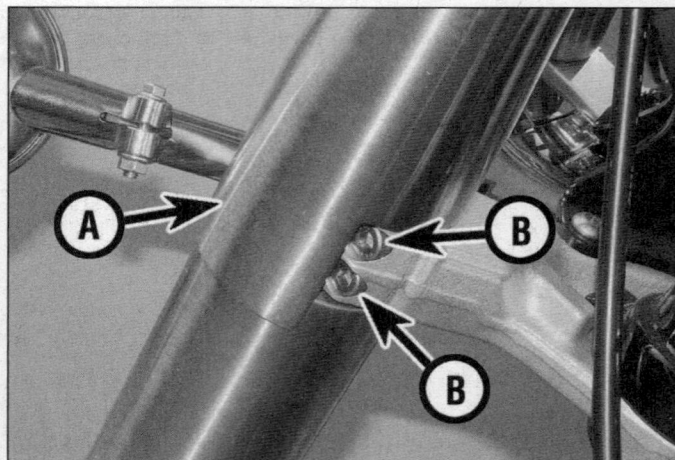

6.7 Where fitted, the cover (A) must be removed to access the bolts (B)

6.8 Loosen the front turn signal assembly pinch bolt

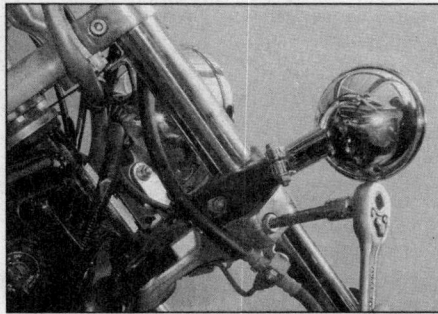

6.9a Loosen the clamp bolt in the bottom yoke . . .

6.9b . . . then remove the leg as described

handlebar assembly and fork top yoke (see Section 8). Lift off the fork top cover and the cover gasket and spacer, noting how they fit.

8 If applicable, loosen the front turn signal assembly pinch bolt so that the assembly no longer grips the fork leg **(see illustration)**.

9 Support the fork leg, then loosen but do not remove the fork clamp bolt(s) in the bottom yoke **(see illustration)**. Remove the fork leg by twisting it and pulling it downwards **(see illustration)**. Note which fork leg fits on which side.

> **HAYNES HiNT** *If the fork legs are seized in the yokes, spray the area with penetrating oil and allow time for it to soak in before trying again.*

Installation

10 Remove all traces of corrosion from the fork tubes and the yokes.

11 On XVS650A/S and XVS1100A/S models, temporarily install the fork top yoke and tighten the steering stem nut finger-tight (see Section 8).

12 Slide the fork leg up through the bottom yoke and into the top yoke, making sure the wiring, cables and hoses are the correct side of the leg as noted on removal. Make sure that the leg with the threaded section for the axle is on the left-hand side, and the leg with the axle pinch bolt is on the right.

13 Check that the amount of protrusion of the fork tube above the top yoke is as noted on removal and equal on both sides (see Step 6). Yamaha specify that the top of the fork inner tube (not the top bolt) should be flush with the upper surface of the top yoke.

14 Tighten the fork clamp bolt(s) in the bottom yoke to the torque setting specified at the beginning of this Chapter **(see illustration 6.9a)**. If the fork leg has been dismantled or if the oil has been changed, tighten the top bolt to the specified torque setting.

15 On XVS650A/S and XVS1100A/S models, remove the fork top yoke and install the spacer, gasket and fork top cover, then install the yoke and tighten the steering stem nut to the specified torque setting.

16 Tighten the clamp bolt(s) in the top yoke to the specified torque setting **(see illustration 6.6)**.

17 If applicable, tighten the front turn signal assembly pinch bolt to the specified torque setting.

18 Install the remaining components in the reverse order of removal.

19 Check the operation of the front forks and brakes before taking the machine out on the road.

7 Front fork overhaul

Disassembly

1 Always dismantle the fork legs separately to avoid interchanging any parts. Store all components in separate, clearly marked containers **(see illustration)**.

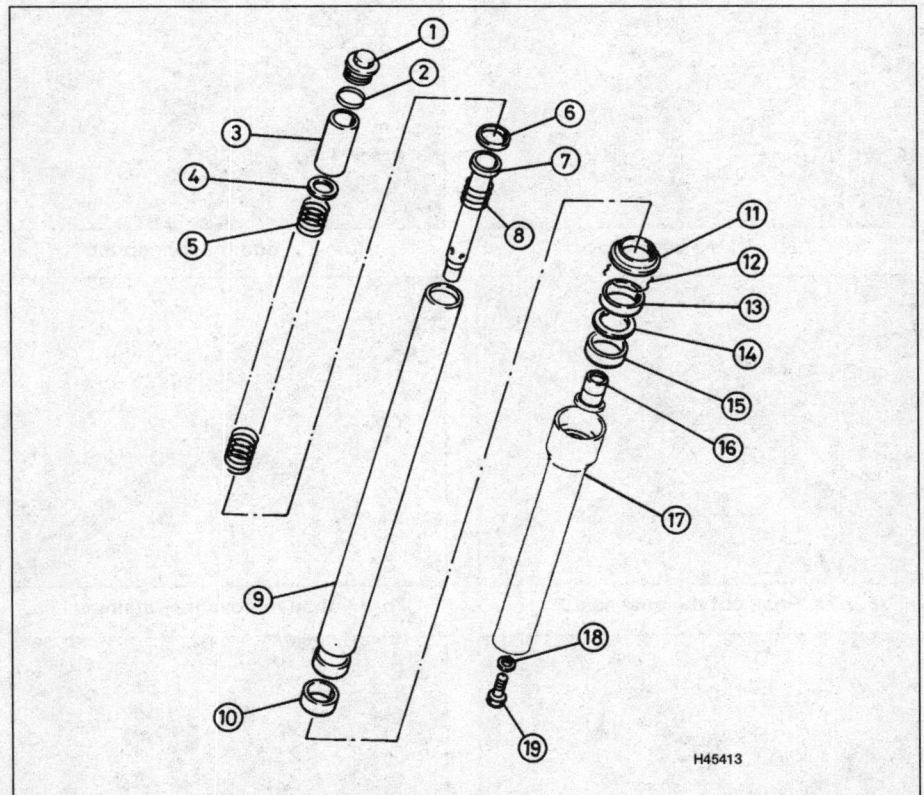

7.1 Front fork components

1 Top bolt	8 Rebound spring	14 Seal washer
2 O-ring	9 Fork tube	15 Top bush
3 Spacer	10 Bottom bush	16 Damper rod seat
4 Spring seat	11 Dust seal	17 Slider
5 Spring	12 Retaining clip	18 Sealing washer
6 Damper rod ring	13 Oil seal	19 Damper rod bolt
7 Damper rod		

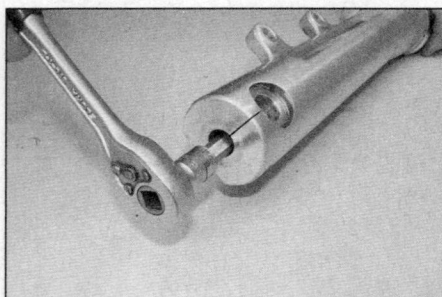

7.2 Loosen the damper rod bolt

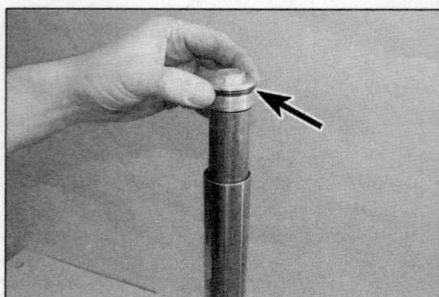

7.4 Unscrew the top bolt – discard the O-ring (arrowed)

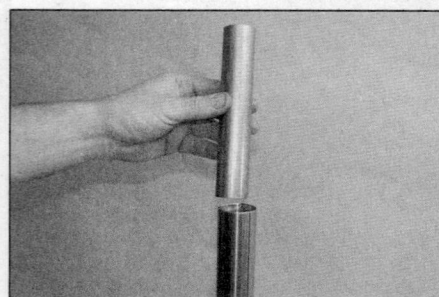

7.5a Withdraw the spacer . . .

2 Before dismantling the fork leg, it is advisable to loosen the damper rod bolt at this stage. Invert the leg and compress the fork tube in the slider so that the spring exerts the maximum pressure on the head of the damper rod, then loosen the bolt in the base of the fork slider **(see illustration)**.

3 If the fork top bolt was not loosened with the fork on the motorcycle, carefully clamp the fork tube in a vice equipped with soft jaws, taking care not to overtighten or score the tube's surface, and loosen the top bolt.

4 Unscrew the top bolt from the fork leg **(see illustration)**. Discard the O-ring as a new one must be fitted on reassembly.

⚠️ **Warning: The fork spring is pressing on the fork top bolt with considerable pressure. Unscrew the bolt very carefully, keeping a downward pressure on it and release it slowly as it is likely to spring clear as the last threads are freed. It is advisable to wear some form of eye and face protection when carrying out this operation.**

5 Withdraw the spacer, washer and spring from the fork leg **(see illustrations)**.

6 Invert the fork leg over a suitable container and pump the fork vigorously to expel as much fork oil as possible.

7 Prise out the dust seal from the top of the slider to gain access to the oil seal retaining clip, and remove the clip **(see illustrations)**. Take care not to scratch the fork leg. Discard the dust seal as a new one must be used. **Note:** *Where fitted, do not remove the fork leg protector from the top of the slider unless it is damaged and a new one is to be fitted.*

8 Remove the previously loosened damper rod bolt and its sealing washer from the bottom of the slider **(see illustration)**. Discard the sealing washer as a new one must be used on reassembly. If the damper rod bolt was not loosened before dismantling the fork, Yamaha provide a service tool (Part No. 90890-01460 for Europe or YM-1300-1 for US) and handle (Part No. 90890-01326 for Europe or YM-01326 for US) to hold the damper rod while the bolt is unscrewed. Alternatively, re-install the spring and spacer assembly (see Step 5) and top bolt, or pass a metal bar down through the fork tube and press hard onto the head of the damper rod to prevent it from turning.

9 To separate the tube from the slider it is necessary to displace the oil seal and top bush in the slider. The bottom bush on the tube will not pass through the top bush, and this can be used to good effect. Push the tube part-way into the slider, then pull it sharply outwards so that the bottom bush strikes the top bush and drives it out from the slider. Repeat this operation until the seal, seal washer and top bush are tapped out of the slider and the tube and bottom bush can be fully withdrawn **(see illustrations)**.

10 Slide the oil seal, its washer and the top bush off the fork tube, noting which way up they fit **(see illustration)**. Discard the oil seal as a new one must be fitted on reassembly.

7.5b . . . the washer . . .

7.5c . . . and the fork spring

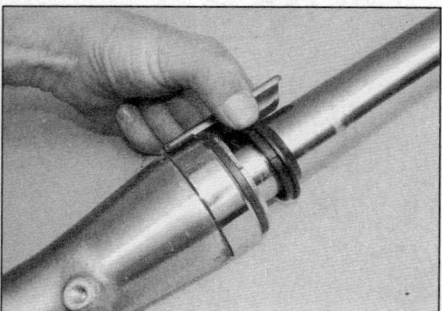

7.7a Prise out the dust seal . . .

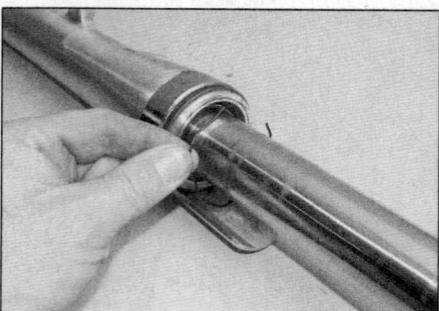

7.7b . . . then remove the retaining clip

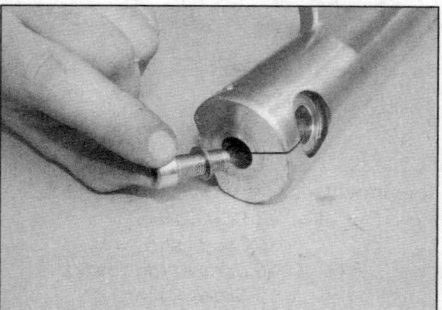

7.8 Remove the damper rod bolt and sealing washer

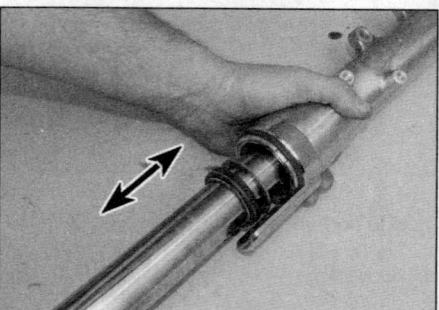

7.9a Pull the tube and slider apart firmly several times . . .

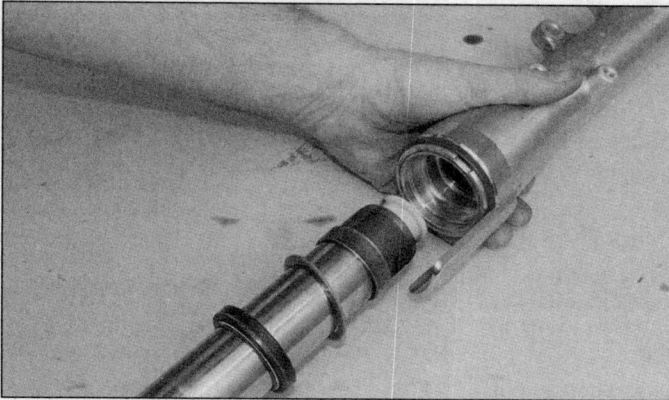

7.9b ... until they can be separated

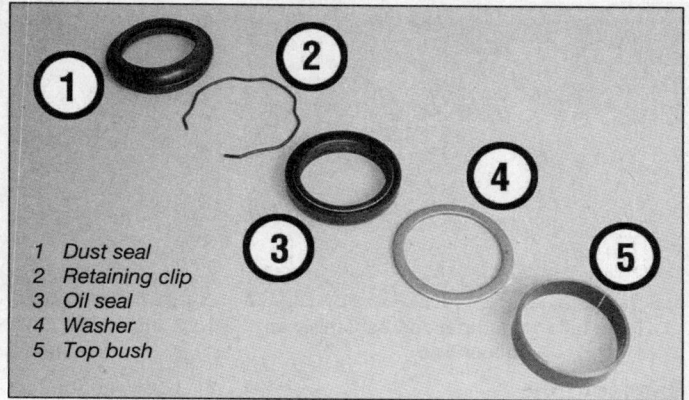

1 Dust seal
2 Retaining clip
3 Oil seal
4 Washer
5 Top bush

7.10 Fork slider components

11 Remove the damper rod seat, noting the small spring inside the seat, then tip the damper rod assembly out of the top of the fork tube **(see illustrations)**. **Note:** *Don't remove the Teflon ring from the damper rod unless it requires renewal.*

Inspection

12 Clean all parts in solvent and blow them dry with compressed air, if available. Check the fork tube for score marks, scratches, flaking or pitting of the chrome and excessive or abnormal wear. Look for dents in the tube. Renew the tube if excessive wear or damage are found.

13 Check the fork tube for runout (bending) using V-blocks and a dial gauge, or have it done by a Yamaha dealer or suspension specialist **(see illustration)**. Yamaha do not specify a runout limit, but if the tube is bent beyond the generally accepted limit of 0.2 mm, renew it.

⚠ **Warning: If the tube is bent, it should not be straightened – replace it with a new one.**

14 Inspect the internal surface of the fork slider for score marks, scratches and excessive or abnormal wear. Renew the slider if excessive wear or damage are found.

15 Check the spring for cracks and other damage. Measure the spring free length and compare the measurement to the specifications at the beginning of this Chapter. If a spring is defective or has sagged below the service limit, replace the springs in **both** fork legs with new ones. Never renew only one spring.

16 Examine the working surfaces of the two bushes; if worn or scuffed they must be renewed. **Note:** *Yamaha recommend that both the top and bottom bushes are renewed when the forks are disassembled.* The bottom bush (on the fork tube) can be removed by carefully easing apart the open ends with a large, flat bladed screwdriver and sliding it off the tube **(see illustration)**. Take care not to scratch the surface of the tube.

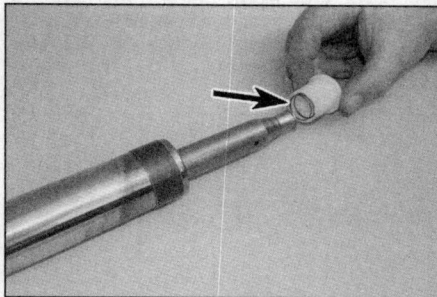

7.11a Remove the seat, noting the location of the small spring (arrowed)

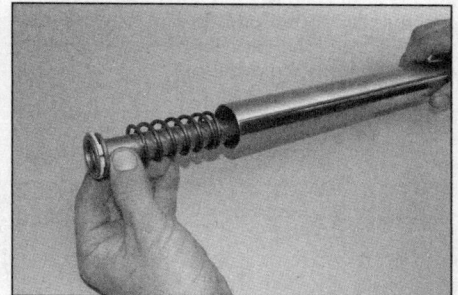

7.11b Tip the damper rod out of the top of the fork tube

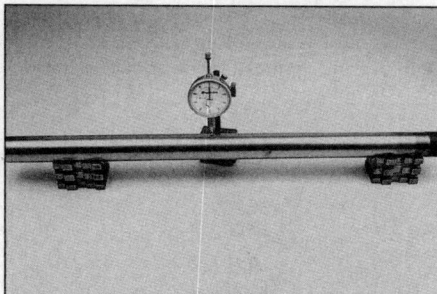

7.13 Check the fork tube runout using V-blocks and a dial gauge

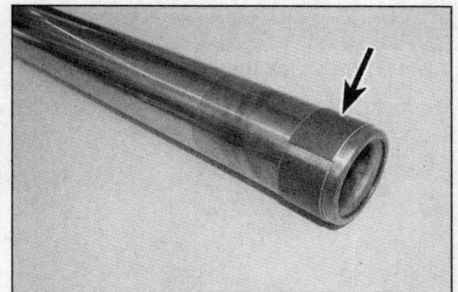

7.16 Check the condition of the bottom bush (arrowed)

17 Check the damper rod and rebound spring assembly for damage and wear, and renew it if necessary **(see illustration)**.

18 Examine the seat on the bottom of the damper rod and renew it if it is worn or distorted.

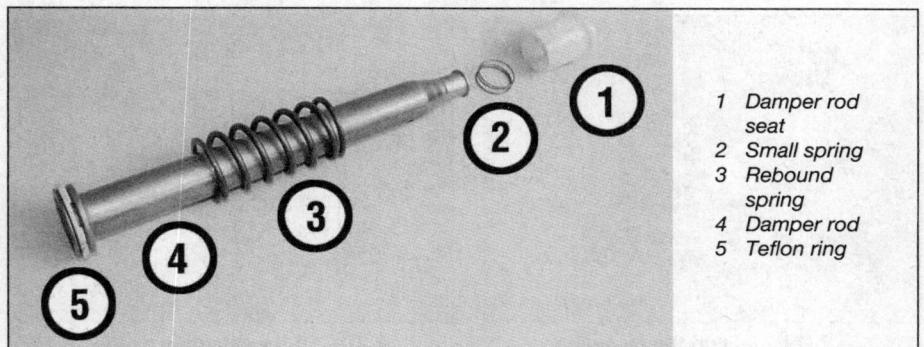

1 Damper rod seat
2 Small spring
3 Rebound spring
4 Damper rod
5 Teflon ring

7.17 Damper rod components

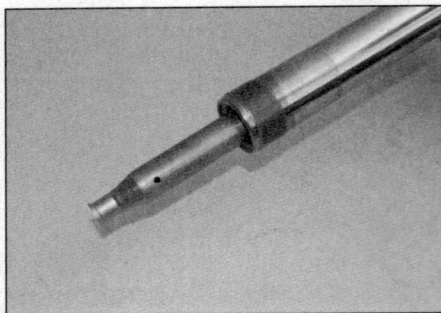
7.20 Install the damper rod assembly as described

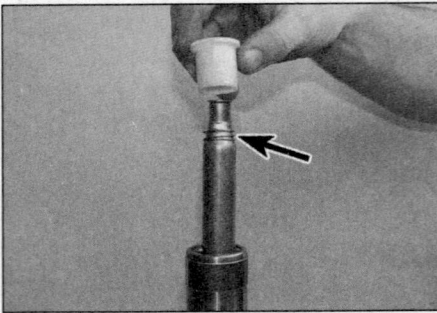
7.22 Install the damper rod seat – note the small spring

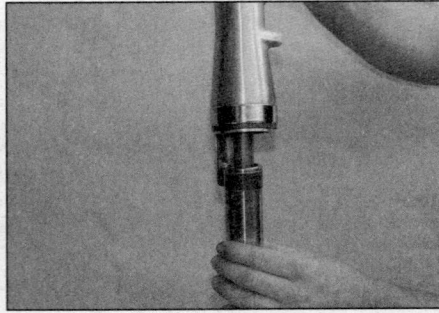
7.23 Fit the fork slider onto the tube

Reassembly

19 If applicable, install a new bottom bush onto the bottom of the fork tube.

20 Insert the damper rod and rebound spring into the top of the fork tube and slide it into place so that it projects fully from the bottom of the tube **(see illustration)**.

21 Lubricate the fork tube and bottom bush with the specified fork oil.

22 Install the seat on the bottom of the damper rod **(see illustration)**. Don't forget to fit the small spring inside the seat.

23 Install the slider onto the fork tube **(see illustration)**.

24 Fit a new sealing washer onto the damper rod bolt and apply a few drops of a suitable non-permanent thread-locking compound, then install the bolt into the bottom of the slider and tighten it to the specified torque setting **(see illustrations)**. If the damper rod rotates inside the tube, use the method employed on disassembly to hold the rod (see Step 8). Remove the tool or fork spring when the bolt has been tightened.

25 Push the fork tube fully into the slider, then oil the top bush and slide it down over the tube **(see illustration)**. Press the bush squarely into its recess in the slider. Use a hammer and a suitable piece of tubing to tap the bush lightly into place; note that excessive force should not be necessary. **Note:** *Take care not to scratch the fork tube during reassembly; if the tube is pushed fully into the slider any accidental scratching is confined to the area above the oil seal.*

26 Install the oil seal washer on top of the bush, then lubricate the new oil seal with lithium grease and slide it down over the tube with its markings facing upwards **(see illustrations)**. Press the seal squarely into the slider and tap it lightly into place as described in Step 25 until the retaining clip groove is visible above the seal.

27 Fit the retaining clip, making sure it is correctly located in its groove **(see illustrations)**.

28 Lubricate the inside of the new dust seal then slide it down the fork tube and press it into position **(see illustration)**.

29 Ensure the fork tube is still fully compressed into the slider, then slowly pour in the correct quantity of the specified grade of fork oil. Pump the fork tube in the slider

7.24a Thread lock the damper rod bolt . . .

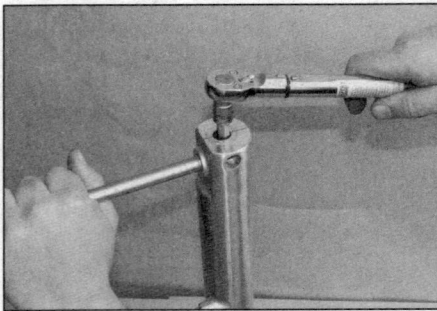
7.24b . . . and tighten it to the specified torque

7.25 Install the top bush . . .

7.26a . . . followed by the washer . . .

7.26b . . . and the oil seal

7.27a Fit the retaining clip . . .

7.27b . . . ensuring it is correctly located in its groove

7.28 Press the dust seal into place

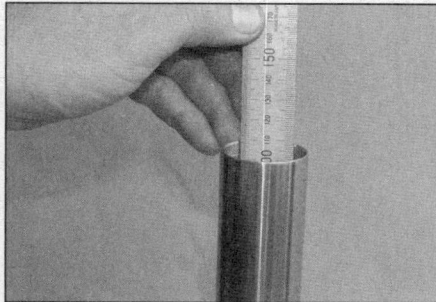

7.30 Measure the oil level with the fork held upright and fully compressed

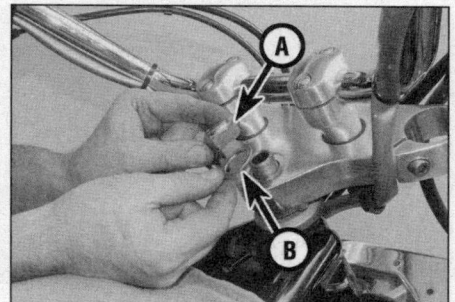

8.3 Remove the steering stem nut (A) and washer (B)

slowly to distribute the oil, then leave the leg upright for ten minutes to allow any air bubbles to disperse.

30 With the fork tube fully compressed into the slider; measure the fork oil level from the top of the tube **(see illustration)**. Add or subtract fork oil until it is at the level specified at the beginning of this Chapter.

31 Pull the fork tube out of the slider to its full extension and install the spring with the closer-wound coils at the top, followed by the washer and spacer.

32 Lubricate a new O-ring with fork oil and fit it onto the top bolt. Screw the top bolt into the tube carefully, making sure it is not cross-threaded. **Note:** *The top bolt can be tightened to the specified torque setting at this stage if the tube is held between the padded jaws of a vice, but do not risk distorting the tube by doing so. A better method is to tighten the top bolt when the fork leg has been installed and is securely held in the bottom yoke.*

33 Install the forks as described in Section 6.

TOOL TiP *Use a ratchet-type tool when installing the fork top bolt. This makes it unnecessary to remove the tool from the bolt whilst threading it in*

8 Steering stem

Removal

1 Remove the fuel tank to avoid damaging its paintwork (see Chapter 3). If the fork top yoke is going to be fully removed from the machine, remove the handlebar assembly and the handlebar bracket nuts, then separate the cable guide from the top yoke and free the wiring from the clips on its underside **(see illustrations 5.4 and 5.10)**. Note that, if

required, the fork top yoke can be displaced with the handlebars in place.

2 Note the alignment between the top of the fork leg and the top yoke, then loosen the fork clamp bolts in the top yoke **(see illustration 6.6)**.

3 Remove the steering stem nut and washer, then lift off the top yoke **(see illustration)**.

4 Remove the front forks (see Section 6). Remove the headlight unit and front turn signal assemblies (see Chapter 8).

5 Remove the lock washer, noting how it fits, then unscrew and remove the locknut using, if necessary, either a C-spanner or a drift located in one of the notches (though it shouldn't be tight and can probably be undone with your fingers) **(see illustrations)**. Remove the rubber washer **(see illustration)**.

6 Supporting the bottom yoke, unscrew the adjuster nut using either a C-spanner or a drift located in one of the notches, then remove the adjuster nut and the bearing cover from the steering stem **(see illustrations)**.

8.5a Remove the lock washer . . .

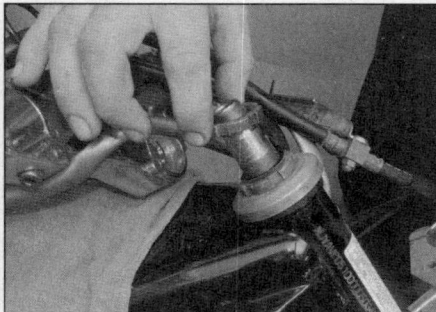

8.5b . . . the locknut . . .

8.5c . . . and the rubber washer

8.6a Unscrew the adjuster nut . . .

8.6b . . . then support the bottom yoke and remove the nut . . .

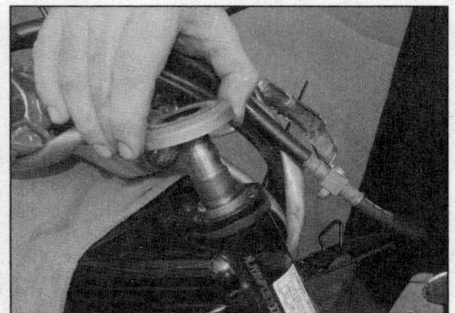

8.6c . . . and the bearing cover

8.7 Lower the steering stem out of the frame

8.8a Remove the inner race . . .

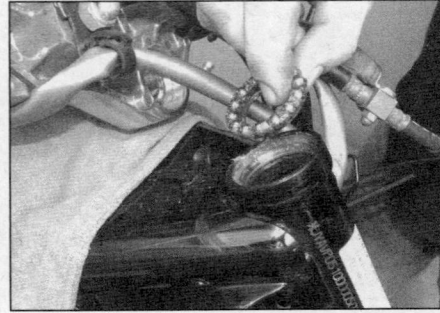

8.8b . . . and bearing from the top of the steering head

7 Gently lower the bottom yoke and steering stem out of the frame **(see illustration)**.

8 Remove the inner race and bearing from the top of the steering head **(see illustrations)**.

9 Remove the washer from the steering stem, then remove the bearing and dust seal from the base of the steering stem **(see illustrations)**. Discard the dust seal as a new one must be fitted on reassembly. Use a suitable solvent to remove all traces of old grease from the bearings and races and check them for wear or damage as described in Section 9. **Note:** *Do not remove the races from the steering head or the steering stem unless they are to be replaced with new ones – do not re-use the races if they have been removed.*

10 On XVS650A/S and XVS1100A/S models, if required, undo the bolts securing the lower

fork covers to the bottom yoke and remove the covers.

Installation

11 Smear a liberal quantity of lithium-based grease onto the bearing races and work some grease well into both the upper and lower bearings. Fit the new dust seal over the lower bearing inner race on the steering stem, then fit the bearing **(see illustrations 8.9c and b)**. Fit the washer on the stem **(see illustration 8.9a)**

12 Carefully lift the bottom yoke and steering stem up through the steering head, then install the upper bearing and the inner race into the top of the steering head, **(see illustrations 8.8b and a)**. Fit the bearing cover, then thread the adjuster nut onto the steering stem and adjust the bearings as described in Chapter 1, Section 13, noting

that you may need to carry out the procedure several times if new bearings have been fitted to allow them to settle **(see illustration)**.

13 Install the rubber washer and the locknut **(see illustrations 8.5c and b)**. Tighten the locknut finger-tight, then tighten it further until its notches align with those in the adjuster nut. If necessary, counter-hold the adjuster nut to prevent it turning. Install the lock washer so that the tabs fit into the notches in both the locknut and adjuster nut **(see illustration 8.5a)**.

14 Install the front forks (see Section 6).

15 Install the remaining components in the reverse order of removal.

9 Steering head bearing renewal

Inspection

1 Remove the steering stem (see Section 8) then use a suitable solvent to remove all traces of old grease from the bearings and races.

2 Check for wear or damage; the races should be polished and free from indentations **(see illustration)**. Inspect the bearing balls for signs of wear, pitting or discoloration, and examine the retainer cages for cracks or splits **(see illustration 8.8b)**.

3 Spin the bearing balls by hand. They should spin freely and smoothly. If there are signs of wear on any of the above components, both

8.9a Remove the washer . . .

8.9b . . . the bearing . . .

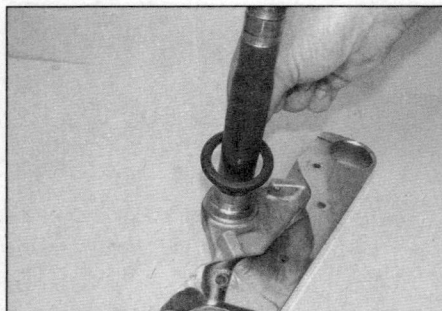

8.9c . . . and the dust seal

8.12 Check and adjust the steering head bearings

9.2 Inspect the races for wear and dents

9.4 Drive out the races with a suitable drift

upper and lower bearing assemblies must be renewed as a set. **Note:** *Do not remove the races from the steering head or the steering stem unless they are to be replaced with new ones – do not re-use the races if they have been removed.*

Renewal

4 The outer races are an interference fit in the steering head and can be tapped out with a suitable drift located in the cut-outs in the head **(see illustration)**. Alternate between the left and right-hand cut-outs so that the race is driven out squarely.

5 Alternatively, the races can be removed using a slide-hammer type bearing extractor – these can often be hired from tool shops.

6 The new outer races can be installed in the head using a drawbolt arrangement **(see illustration)**, or by using a large diameter tubular drift. Ensure that the drawbolt washer

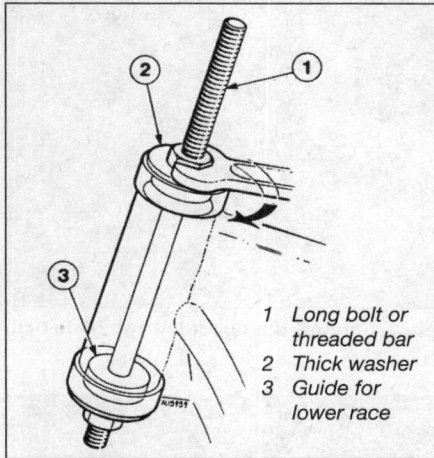
9.7a Loosen the bearing race with a hammer and chisel . . .

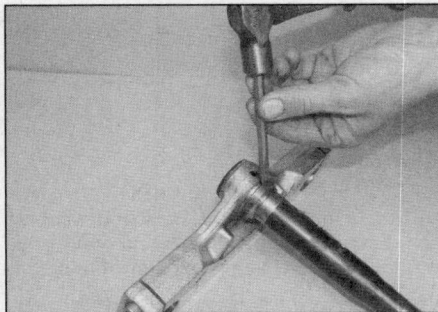
9.7c . . . or use a bearing puller

1 Long bolt or threaded bar
2 Thick washer
3 Guide for lower race

9.6 Drawbolt arrangement for fitting the steering head races

or drift (as applicable) bears only on the outer edge of the race and does not contact the bearing surface.

HAYNES HINT *Installation of new bearing outer races is made much easier if the races are left overnight in the freezer. This causes them to contract slightly making them a looser fit. Alternatively, use a freeze spray.*

7 To remove the lower bearing race from the steering stem, first drive a chisel between the base of the race and the bottom yoke (see

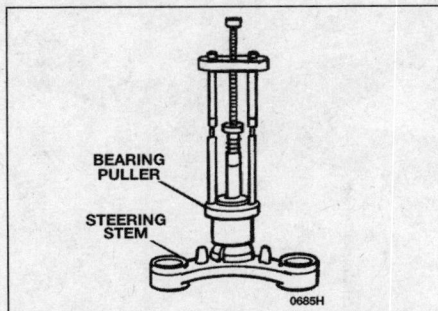
9.7b . . . then lever it off . . .

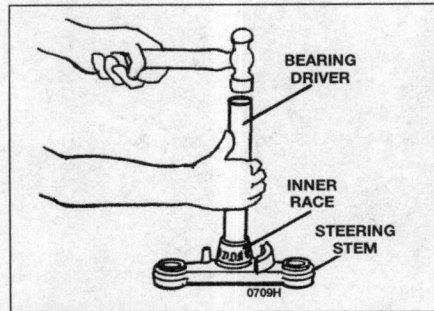
9.8 Install the lower race using a suitable driver or length of tubing

illustration). Work the chisel around the race to ensure it lifts squarely. Once there is clearance beneath the race, use two levers placed on opposite sides of the race to work it free, using blocks of wood to improve leverage and protect the yoke – if the race is firmly in place it will be necessary to use a bearing puller **(see illustrations)**. Alternatively, take the steering stem to a Yamaha dealer. **Note:** *On XVS650A/S and XVS1100A/S models, remove the lower fork covers from the bottom yoke to avoid damaging them before removing the lower bearing race.*

8 Fit the new lower race onto the steering stem. A length of tubing with an internal diameter slightly larger than the steering stem will be needed to tap the new race into position **(see illustration)**.

9 Install the steering stem (see Section 8).

10 Rear shock absorber

> **Warning: Do not attempt to disassemble the shock absorber. It is nitrogen-charged under high pressure. Improper disassembly could result in serious injury. Take the shock to a Yamaha dealer or suspension specialist for disposal.**

650 models

Adjustment

1 The rear shock absorber is adjustable for spring pre-load by turning the spring seat on the bottom of the shock – follow the procedure in Chapter 1, Section 14.

Removal

2 Support the motorcycle securely in an upright position using an auxiliary stand.

3 Remove the seats and the rear mudguard (see Chapter 7).

4 Remove the rear wheel (see Chapter 6).

5 Support the swingarm so that it does not drop when the shock absorber bolts are removed.

6 Undo the nuts securing the shock mounting bolts, then support the shock and withdraw the bolts **(see illustration)**. Note the collars on the lower mounting bolt.

10.6 Shock absorber mounting bolts (arrowed)

7 Lower the swingarm and manoeuvre the shock out.

Inspection

8 Inspect the body of the shock absorber for obvious physical damage and the coil spring for looseness, cracks or signs of fatigue.
9 Inspect the damper rod for signs of pitting and oil leakage.
10 Inspect the collars on the lower mounting for wear and replace as necessary.
11 Ensure that the spring pre-load adjusting ring is clean and free to rotate; inspect the indents on the ring for wear.
12 The shock cannot be dismantled for the renewal of individual components. If it is worn or damaged, it must be replaced with a new one.

Installation

13 Installation is the reverse of removal. Ensure the pre-load adjuster is at the rear end. Clean and apply a smear of grease to the mounting bolts and tighten them to the torque setting specified at the beginning of this Chapter.

1100 models

Adjustment

14 The rear shock absorber is adjustable for spring pre-load by turning the spring seat on the top of the shock – follow the procedure in Chapter 1, Section 14.

Removal

15 Support the motorcycle securely in an upright position using an auxiliary stand.
16 Remove the seats and the rear mudguard (see Chapter 7).
17 Remove the silencer assembly and rear exhaust pipe (see Chapter 3).
18 Remove the rear wheel (see Chapter 6).
19 Remove the tool box and backing panel (see Chapter 7).
20 Remove the battery tray and backing panel (see Chapter 7).
21 Support the swingarm so that it does not drop when the shock absorber bolts are removed.

10.22 Remove the upper linkage plate bolt

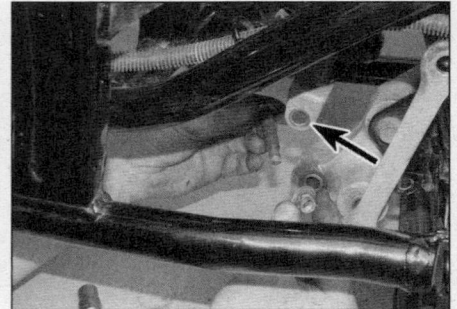
10.23 Remove the bolt on the lower end of the shock (arrowed)

10.24 Remove the bolt on the upper end of the shock

22 Undo the nut and washer from the upper linkage plate bolt, then remove the bolt **(see illustration)**.
23 Undo the nut and bolt securing the lower end of the shock to the link arm, then support the arm and withdraw the bolt **(see illustration)**.
24 Undo the nut and bolt securing the upper end of the shock, then support the shock and withdraw the bolt **(see illustration)**.
25 Manoeuvre the shock out **(see illustration)**.

Inspection

26 Follow the procedure in Steps 8 to 12, noting there are no collars fitted in the lower mounting on 1100 models.

10.25 Remove the shock absorber from the bike

Installation

27 Installation is the reverse of removal. Clean and apply a smear of grease to the mounting bolts and tighten them to the torque settings specified at the beginning of this Chapter.

11 Rear suspension linkage (1100 models)

Removal

1 Follow the procedure in Section 10, Steps 15 to 21, then undo the nuts and washers from both linkage plate bolts and remove the left-hand linkage plate **(see illustrations)**.

11.1a Undo the nuts and washers . . .

11.1b . . . and remove the left-hand linkage plate

11.5a Undo the nut and bolt (arrowed) . . .

11.5b . . . and remove the link arm

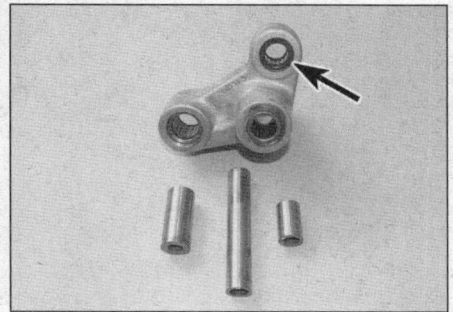

11.6 Prise out the bearing seals (arrowed)

11.7a Withdraw the collar . . .

11.7b . . . and check the upper linkage plate bearing

Installation

9 Installation is the reverse of removal, noting the following:

● Lubricate the new bearing seals with grease and press the seals squarely into place (see illustration).

● Lubricate the needle roller bearings and the collars with lithium-based grease (see illustration).

● Don't forget to install the right-hand linkage plate and lower bolt in the link arm before connecting the shock to the link arm.

● Install the nuts, bolts and washers finger-tight only until all components are in position, then tighten the nuts to the torque settings specified at the beginning of the Chapter (see illustration).

2 Remove the upper linkage plate bolt (see illustration 10.22).
3 Undo the nut securing the lower end of the shock to the link arm, then support the arm and withdraw the bolt (see illustration 10.23).
4 Lower the link arm and withdraw the lower linkage plate bolt and remove the right-hand linkage plate.
5 Remove the nut and bolt securing the link arm to the frame and remove the link arm, noting how it fits (see illustrations).

Inspection

6 Remove the collars from the link arm, then prise out the bearing seals and discard them as new ones must be fitted (see illustration). Clean all the components with a suitable solvent, removing all traces of dirt, corrosion and grease.

7 Inspect all components closely, looking for obvious signs of wear such as heavy scoring or pitting, or for damage such as cracks or distortion. Inspect the bolt holes in the linkage plates for elongation. Slip each collar back into its bearing and check that there is not an excessive amount of freeplay between the two components (see *Tools and Workshop Tips* in the *Reference* section). Don't forget to remove the collar from the upper linkage plate bolt location in the frame and check the condition of the bearings (see illustrations).
8 The bearings can be drifted out of their bores, but only remove them if new bearings are to be fitted. Take care when fitting new bearings; do not drift the bearings into place – a suitable drawbolt tool can be made up as described in *Tools and Workshop Tips* (Section 5) in the *Reference* section.

12 Swingarm removal and installation

650 models

Removal

1 Follow the procedure in Section 3 and remove the right-hand footrest assembly.
2 Follow the procedure in Section 10 and remove the rear shock absorber.
3 Before removing the swingarm it is advisable to check for play in the bearings (see Chapter 1, Section 14). Any problems which were not evident with the other

11.9a Seals can be installed with a suitably sized socket

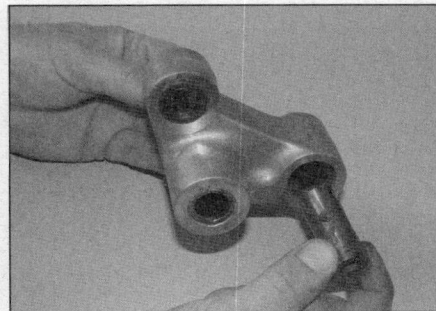

11.9b Lubricate the bearings and collars before installation

11.9c Ensure the components are correctly positioned before tightening the fixings

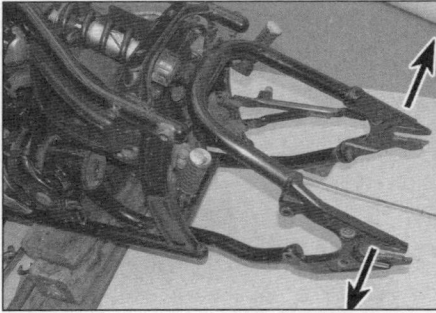

12.3 Check for play in the swingarm bearings

12.7a Undo the nut (A) and right-hand pivot shaft (B) . . .

12.7b . . . and the left-hand pivot shaft (arrowed)

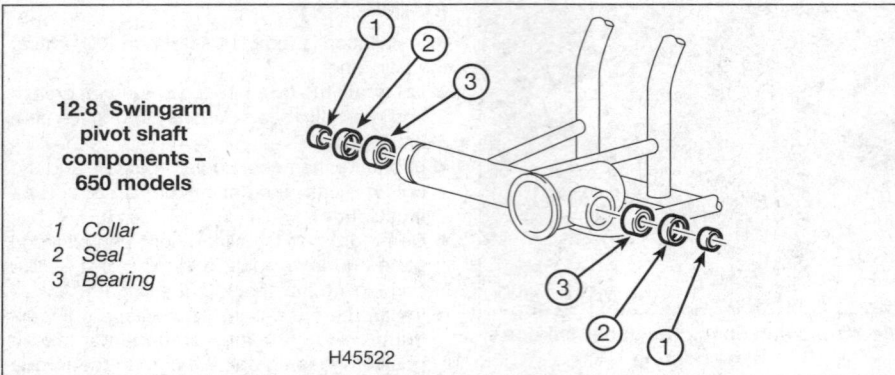

12.8 Swingarm pivot shaft components – 650 models

1 Collar
2 Seal
3 Bearing

H45522

suspension components attached may now show up (see illustration).

4 Remove the battery (see Chapter 8).

5 Remove the right-hand frame cover, the toolbox cover and the transmission cover (see Chapter 7).

6 Pull the rubber driveshaft boot away from the engine.

7 Undo the nut on the right-hand pivot shaft, then support the swingarm and remove the right-hand and left-hand pivot shafts (see illustrations).

8 Lift off the swingarm. Note the location of the pivot shaft collars inside the seals on both sides of the swingarm and remove them for safekeeping (see illustration).

9 Inspect all components for wear or damage as described in Section 13.

Installation

10 Ensure the driveshaft boot is in place and the pivot shaft collars are installed in the swingarm. Apply a suitable non-permanent thread locking compound to the threads of the left-hand pivot shaft. Hold the swingarm in position and install the shaft, then tighten it to the torque setting specified at the beginning of this Chapter.

11 Install the right-hand pivot shaft and tighten it to the specified torque setting, then install the right-hand pivot shaft nut and tighten it to the specified torque setting.

12 Ensure that the swingarm moves freely without binding, then install the remaining components in the reverse order of removal.

1100 models

Removal

13 Follow the procedure in Section 10 and remove the rear shock absorber. Undo the bolts securing the silencer bracket to the frame and remove the bracket.

14 Follow the procedure in Section 11 and remove both linkage plates.

15 Before removing the swingarm it is advisable to check for play in the bearings (see Chapter 1, Section 14). Any problems which were not evident with the other suspension components attached may now show up (see illustration 12.3).

16 Follow the procedure in Chapter 6 and remove the rear brake caliper.

17 Remove the clips securing the brake hose to the swingarm and the frame and position the hose clear of the swingarm (see illustrations).

18 Undo the bolt securing the speed sensor and displace the sensor, then pull the rubber driveshaft boot away from the engine and pull off the rubber shaft cover (see illustration).

19 Loosen the pivot shaft, then support the swingarm and pull the shaft out (see illustration).

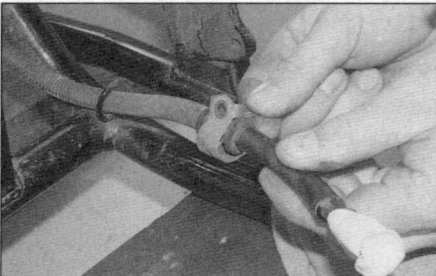

12.17a Release the rear brake hose form the clips . . .

12.17b . . . and pull the hose clear of the swingarm

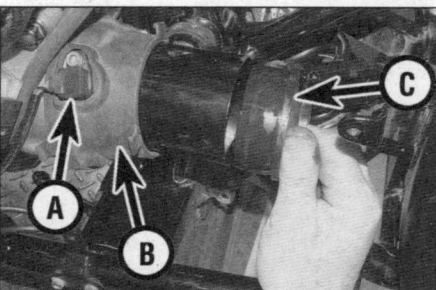

12.18 Displace the speed sensor (A), pull back the driveshaft boot (B) and remove the shaft cover (C)

12.19 Pull out the pivot shaft . . .

12.20 . . . and lift off the swingarm

12.21a Lift of the right-hand . . .

12.21b . . . and left-hand bearing covers

20 Lift off the swingarm **(see illustration)**.
21 Lift the covers off both sides of the swingarm bearing location on the frame **(see illustrations)**.
22 Inspect all components for wear or damage as described in Section 13.

Installation

23 Ensure the driveshaft boot is in place and the covers are installed on both sides of the swingarm bearing location.
24 Clean the pivot shaft threads in the left-hand side of the swingarm **(see illustration)**. Apply a suitable non-permanent thread locking compound to the threads **(see illustration)**.
25 Hold the swingarm in position and install the shaft, then tighten it to the torque setting specified at the beginning of this Chapter.
26 Ensure that the swingarm moves freely without binding, then install the remaining components in the reverse order of removal.

13 Swingarm bearing renewal

650 models

1 Remove the swingarm (see Section 12).
2 If not already done, remove the collars from inside the swingarm bearing seals, then prise out the seals and discard them as new ones must be fitted **(see illustration 12.8)**.
3 Clean the bearings carefully with a suitable solvent to remove all traces of dirt, corrosion and grease, then follow the procedure in *Tools and Workshop Tips* (Section 5) in the

12.24a Clean the pivot shaft threads . . .

12.24b . . . and apply a suitable thread locking compound

Reference section and check the bearings for roughness, looseness and any other damage.
4 The bearings can be driven out of their bores, but only remove them if new bearings are to be fitted. When fitting new bearings, drive them in carefully using a bearing driver or suitably sized socket, or use a suitable drawbolt tool as described in *Tools and Workshop Tips* in the *Reference* section.
5 Lubricate the bearing seals with lithium-based grease and press them into the swingarm, using a bearing driver or suitably sized socket.
6 Inspect the pivot shafts for signs of wear and renew them if necessary.

1100 models

7 Remove the swingarm (see Section 12).
8 If not already done, remove the covers from both sides of the swingarm bearing location on the frame. Pull the collar out of the bearings **(see illustration)**. Clean all the components with a suitable solvent, removing

all traces of dirt, corrosion and grease.
9 Inspect the bearings signs of wear such as heavy scoring or pitting. Slip the collar back into the bearings and check that there is not an excessive amount of freeplay between the two components (see *Tools and Workshop Tips* in the *Reference* section).
10 Remove any corrosion from the pivot shaft with steel wool. Check the shaft for straightness by rolling it on a flat surface such as a piece of plate glass. If available, check the run-out with V-blocks and fit a new one if it is bent.
11 The bearings can be drifted out of their bores, but only remove them if new bearings are to be fitted **(see illustration)**. Take care when fitting new bearings; *do not* drift the bearings into place – a suitable drawbolt tool can be made up as described in *Tools and Workshop Tips* (Section 5) in the *Reference* section.
12 Lubricate the needle roller bearings and the collar with lithium-based grease **(see illustration)**.

13.8 Withdraw the swingarm bearing collar

13.11 Drift out the old bearings if new ones are to be fitted

13.12 Lubricate the bearings and collar before installation

14.2a Lift off the final drive unit . . .

14.2b . . . and discard the old hub O-ring

14.3a Inspect the teeth on the hub pinion –
1100 model shown

14 Driveshaft and final drive unit

Note: *The final drive unit requires special tools to measure and adjust gear backlash. The procedure is complicated and should be done by a Yamaha dealer. However, you can make an initial assessment of whether any work is required as follows.*

Removal

1 Remove the rear wheel (see Chapter 6).
Caution: Don't lay the wheel down and allow it to rest on the disc – the disc could become warped. Set the wheel on wood blocks so the wheel rim supports the weight of the wheel.
2 Lift off the final drive unit **(see illustration)**. Note the O-ring fitted to the hub and discard it as a new one must be fitted **(see illustration)**.

Note: *Don't turn the final drive unit upside down – oil will leak out of the breather on the top of the unit.*
3 Clean the end of the driveshaft and the mating teeth on the hub pinion and the final drive unit gear with suitable solvent, then inspect the shaft splines and the drive teeth for wear or damage **(see illustrations)**. If the driveshaft splines are worn it is likely the internal splines on the back half of the drive coupling will be worn also. On 1100 models refer to the procedure in Chapter 2B, Section 21, and check the final drive coupling.
4 Rotate the driveshaft by hand. The final drive gear should rotate smoothly. If rotation feels rough or jerky or if it's noisy, have the final drive unit disassembled and inspected by a Yamaha dealer.
5 If the teeth on the hub pinion are worn, bend back the tabs on the lock washers and remove the nuts securing the pinion **(see illustration)**. Discard the lock washers as new

ones must be fitted. Pull the pinion off the hub; discard the two O-rings on the hub as new ones must be fitted.
6 The pinion studs are bonded into damper rubbers that are a press fit into the hub **(see illustration)**. If the rubbers have deteriorated or are loose, have new ones fitted by a Yamaha dealer or specialist engineer.

Installation

7 Installation is the reverse of the removal, noting the following:
● Lubricate the new hub O-rings with a smear of lithium soap grease before installation.
● Use new lock washers and tighten the hub pinion nuts to the torque setting specified at the beginning this Chapter.
● Lubricate the hub pinion, final drive gear and driveshaft splines with lithium-based grease.
● Check the oil level in the final drive unit and top up as needed (see Chapter 1).

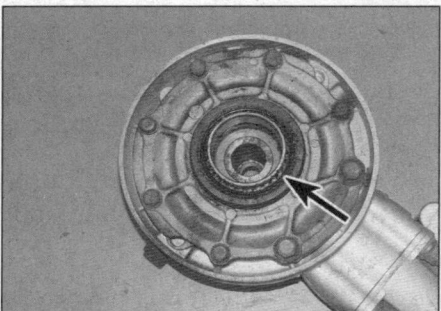
14.3b Inspect the teeth on the final drive
unit gear – 650 model shown

14.5 Hub pinion nuts are secured by lock
washer tabs (arrowed)

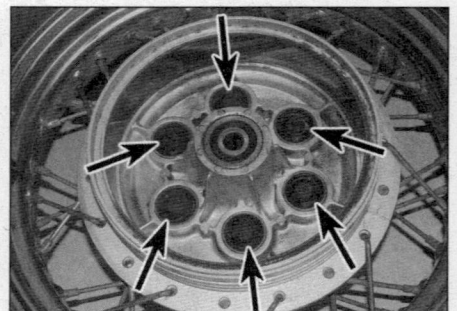
14.6 Pinion studs are bonded into rubber
dampers (arrowed)

Chapter 6
Brakes, wheels and tyres

Contents

Degrees of difficulty

Easy, suitable for novice with little experience	**Fairly easy,** suitable for beginner with some experience	**Fairly difficult,** suitable for competent DIY mechanic	**Difficult,** suitable for experienced DIY mechanic	**Very difficult,** suitable for expert DIY or professional

Specifications

Brakes

Brake fluid type	DOT 4
Brake pad friction material wear limit	see Chapter 1, Section 11
Front disc brake	
Disc thickness	
Standard	5.0 mm
Service limit*	4.5 mm
Disc runout limit	0.15 mm
Rear disc brake (1100 models)	
Disc thickness	
Standard	6.0 mm
Service limit*	5.5 mm
Disc runout limit	0.15 mm
Rear brake drum inside diameter (650 models)	
Standard	200 mm
Maximum	201 mm
Rear brake shoe lining thickness (650 models)	
Standard	4 mm
Minimum	2 mm

Refer to marks stamped into the disc (they supersede information printed here)

Wheels and tyres

Wheel runout
  650 models
    Radial (out of round) .... 2.0 mm
    Axial (side-to-side) .... 2.0 mm
  1100 models
    Radial (out of round) .... 1.0 mm
    Axial (side-to-side) .... 0.5 mm
Tyre pressures .... see *Daily (pre-ride) checks*
Tyre sizes
  XVS650
    Front 100/90-19 57S
    Rear 170/80-15 77S
  XVS650A and XVS650S
    Front 130/90-16 67S
    Rear 170/80-15 77S
  XVS1100
    Front 110/90-18 61S
    Rear 170/80-15 77S
  XVS1100A and XVS1100S
    Front 130/90-16 67S
    Rear 170/80-15 77S

Torque settings

Front brake caliper bolt
  650 models (1997 to 2000) .... 23 Nm
  650 models (2001-on) .... 27 Nm
  1100 models .... 23 Nm
Front brake caliper bracket bolts .... 40 Nm
Brake disc mounting bolts .... 23 Nm*
Brake hose banjo bolts .... 30 Nm
Final drive unit mounting bolts
  650 models .... 70 Nm
  1100 models .... 90 Nm
Front wheel axle .... 59 Nm
Front wheel axle pinch bolt .... 20 Nm
Front master cylinder mounting bolts .... 10 Nm
Rear brake arm pinch bolt (650 models) .... 10 Nm
Rear brake caliper bracket-to-frame bolt (1100 models) .... 40 Nm
Rear brake caliper mounting bolts (1100 models) .... 40 Nm
Rear brake master cylinder mounting bolts (1100 models) ... 23 Nm
Rear brake torque arm nuts (650 models) .... 20 Nm
Rear wheel axle clamp nuts (1100 models) .... 23 Nm
Rear wheel axle nut
  650 models .... 92 Nm
  1100 models .... 107 Nm
Apply non-permanent thread locking compound to the bolt threads.

1 General information

All 650 models are equipped with a single hydraulic disc front brake and a rod operated drum rear brake. All 1100 models have twin hydraulic disc front brakes and an hydraulic disc rear brake. Front disc brakes on all models have two-piston, sliding calipers; the rear brake on 1100 models has an opposed piston caliper.

2003-on XVS1100A and XVS1100S models are fitted with cast alloy wheels designed for tubeless tyres; all other models covered in this manual have wire spoked wheels fitted with tubed tyres.

Caution: Disc brake components rarely require disassembly. Do not disassemble components unless absolutely necessary. If any hydraulic brake hose connection is loosened, the system should be topped-up and bled upon reassembly. Do not use petroleum-based solvents to clean brake parts. Solvents will cause seals to swell and distort. Use clean brake fluid, brake cleaner or denatured alcohol only. Use care when working with brake fluid as it can injure your eyes and it will damage painted surfaces and plastic parts.

2 Front brake pads

Warning: The dust created by the brake system may contain asbestos, which is harmful to your health. Never blow it out with compressed air and don't inhale any of it. An approved filtering mask should be worn when working on the brakes.

650 models

Note: *Do not operate the brake lever while the caliper is off the disc.*

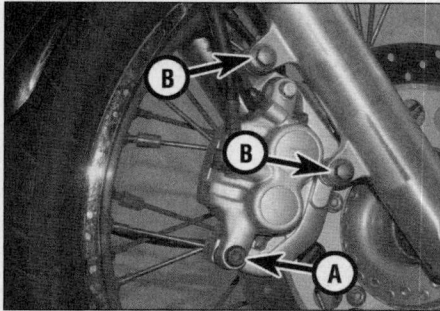

2.1a Loosen the caliper bolt (A), then undo the bracket bolts (B) . . .

2.1b . . . and slide the caliper assembly off the disc – 1997 to 2000 models

2.1c Remove the caliper bolt . . .

2.1d . . . and pivot the caliper up to expose the pads

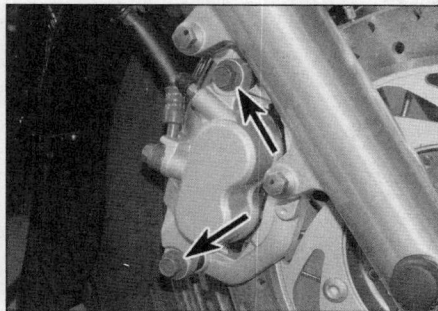

2.2 Caliper mounting bolts (arrowed) – 2001-on models

2.3a Remove the pads from the caliper bracket . . .

1 On 1997 to 2000 models, loosen the brake caliper bolt, then undo the brake caliper bracket bolts and slide the caliper assembly off the disc and fork **(see illustrations)**. Remove the caliper bolt and pivot the caliper up to expose the pads **(see illustrations)**. Secure the caliper to the motorcycle with a cable tie to avoid straining the hydraulic hose.
2 On 2001-on models, remove the two caliper bolts, then slide the caliper off the disc and caliper bracket **(see illustration)**. Secure the caliper to avoid straining the hydraulic hose.
3 Remove the pads from the caliper bracket, noting the location of the pad guide plates **(see illustrations)**.
4 Inspect the surface of each pad for contamination and check that the friction material has not worn beyond its service limit

(see Chapter 1, Section 11). If either pad is worn down to or beyond the service limit wear indicator, is fouled with oil or grease, or is heavily scored or damaged by dirt and debris, both pads must be renewed. Note that it is not possible to degrease the friction material; if the pads are contaminated in any way, new ones must be fitted.
5 Check that each pad has worn evenly at each end, and that each has the same amount of wear as the other. If uneven wear is noticed, one of the pistons is probably sticking in the caliper, in which case the caliper must be overhauled (see Section 3).
6 If the pads are in good condition clean them carefully, using a fine wire brush which is completely free of oil and grease, to remove all traces of road dirt and corrosion. Using a

pointed instrument, clean out the grooves in the friction material and dig out any embedded particles of foreign matter.
7 On 1997 to 2000 models, pull the caliper off the bracket **(see illustration)**. On all models, spray the inside of the caliper with a dedicated brake cleaner to remove any dust, noting the location of the pad spring inside the caliper **(see illustration)**. Remove any traces of corrosion from the caliper bolt(s) and the caliper pin, as applicable, which might cause sticking of the caliper/pad operation. Check the two dust seals on the caliper bracket and renew them if they are split or perished.
8 Check the condition of the brake disc (see Section 4).
9 If new pads are being installed, push the

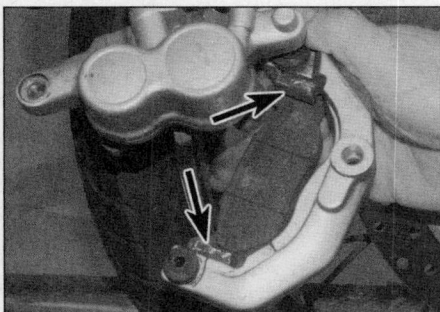

2.3b . . . noting the location of the pad guides (arrowed)

2.7a Pull the caliper off the bracket

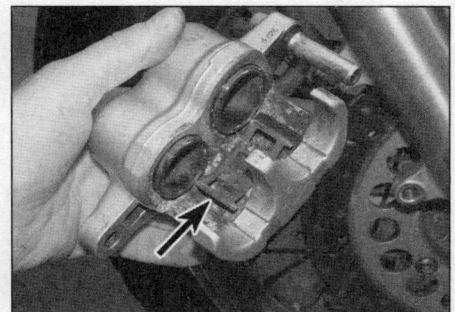

2.7b Note the location of the spring (arrowed) inside the caliper

2.9 Pushing the pistons back into the caliper as described

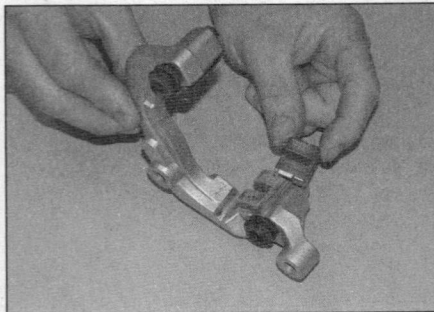

2.10 Ensure the guide plates are correctly installed on the bracket

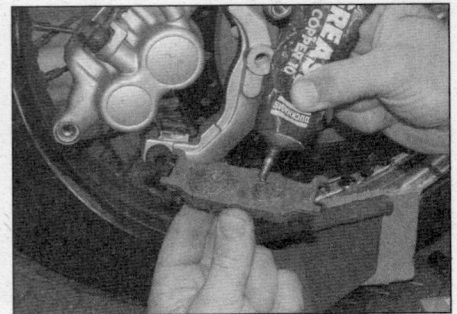

2.12 Smear the backs of the pads with copper-based grease

2.13 Check that the pads fit each side of the brake disc

2.17 Remove the brake hose guide bolt

pistons as far back into the caliper as possible, using hand pressure or grips and a piece of wood as leverage **(see illustration)**. This will displace brake fluid back into the brake fluid reservoir, so it may be necessary to remove the reservoir cap, plate and diaphragm and siphon out some fluid (depending on how much fluid was in there in the first place and how far the pistons have to be pushed in). If the pistons are difficult to push back, attach a length of clear hose to the bleed valve and place the open end in a suitable container, then open the valve and try again. Take great care not to draw any air into the system. If in doubt, bleed the brakes afterwards (see Section 11).

10 Ensure the pad guide plates are in place on the caliper bracket **(see illustration)**. Ensure the pad spring is in place inside the

caliper **(see illustration 2.7b)**; if it has been removed, it must be refitted so that its longer outer tangs point in the direction of forward disc/wheel rotation. **Note:** *Yamaha recommend that a new pad spring and new guide plates should be fitted whenever the pads are renewed.*

11 As applicable, lubricate the shank of the caliper bolt(s) and the caliper pin with copper-based grease. On 1997 to 2000 models, fit the caliper onto the caliper bracket **(see illustration 2.7a)**.

12 Smear the backs of the pads with copper-based grease, making sure that none gets on the front or sides of the pads **(see illustration)**. Install the pads in the bracket so that the friction material faces the disc.

13 On 1997 to 2000 models, rotate the caliper to cover the pads and install the

caliper bolt. Check that the pads are correctly positioned in the caliper so that they will fit each side of the disc **(see illustration)**. Slide the caliper assembly onto the disc and secure it with the bracket bolts. Tighten the bracket bolts to the torque setting specified at the beginning of this Chapter, then tighten the caliper bolt to the specified torque.

14 On 2001-on models, slide the caliper onto the disc, then secure it to the caliper bracket with the caliper bolts. Tighten the caliper bolts to the specified torque.

15 Operate the brake lever several times to bring the pads into contact with the disc. Top-up the fluid reservoir if necessary (see *Daily (pre-ride) checks*).

16 Check the operation of the brake carefully before riding the motorcycle.

1100 models

Note: *Do not operate the brake lever while the caliper is off the disc.*

17 Remove the brake hose guide bolt **(see illustration)**.

18 On 1999 to 2000 XVS1100 models, remove the caliper bolt, then pivot the caliper up to expose the pads and pull the caliper outwards so that its slider pin is withdrawn from the bracket **(see illustrations)**. Secure the caliper to the motorcycle with a cable tie to avoid straining the hydraulic hose.

19 On 2001-on models, remove the two caliper bolts, then slide the caliper off the disc and bracket **(see illustration 2.2)**. Secure the caliper to avoid straining the hydraulic hose.

2.18a Undo the caliper bolt . . .

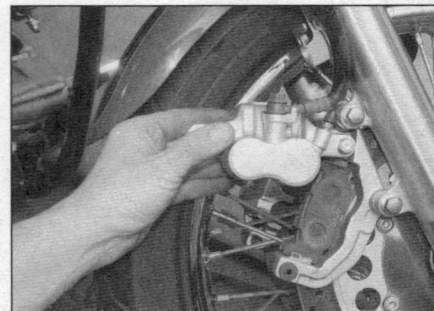

2.18b . . . then pivot the caliper up . . .

2.18c . . . and pull it off the bracket

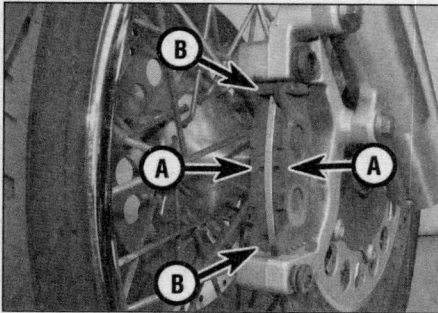

2.20 Remove the pads (A) – note the location of the guide plates (B)

20 Remove the pads from the caliper bracket, noting the location of the guide plates **(see illustration)**.

21 Follow the procedure in Steps 4 to 6 to check the condition of the pads. Note that both pads in both brake calipers must be renewed at the same time.

22 Spray the inside of the caliper with a dedicated brake cleaner to remove any dust, noting the location of the pad spring inside the caliper **(see illustration 2.7b)**. Remove any traces of corrosion from the caliper bolt(s) and the slider pin, as applicable, which might cause sticking of the caliper/pad operation. Check the two dust seals on the caliper bracket and renew them if they are split or perished.

23 Check the condition of the brake disc (see Section 4).

24 If required, follow the procedure in Step 9 and push the pistons back into the caliper.

25 Ensure the guide plates are in place on the caliper bracket. Smear the backs of the pads with copper-based grease, making sure that none gets on the front or sides of the pads, and install them on the bracket so that the friction material faces the disc **(see illustration 2.20)**. Ensure the pad spring is in place inside the caliper. If it has been removed, it must be refitted so that its outer longer tangs point in the direction of forward disc/wheel rotation. **Note:** *Yamaha recommend that a new pad spring and new guide plates should be fitted whenever the pads are renewed.*

26 On 1999 to 2000 XVS1100 models, fit the caliper onto the caliper bracket so that its

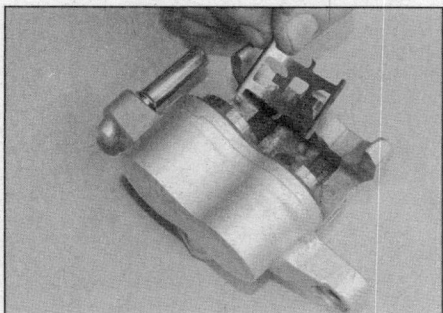

3.5 Remove the pad spring for safekeeping

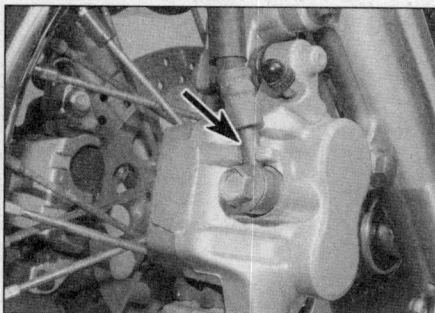

3.3 Note the alignment of the banjo fitting (arrowed) with the caliper

slider pin engages, then rotate the caliper to cover the pads and install the caliper bolt **(see illustrations 2.18c, 18b and 18a)**.

27 On all other models, slide the caliper onto the disc, then secure it with the caliper bolts.

28 Tighten the caliper bolt(s) to the torque setting specified at the beginning of this Chapter.

29 Install the brake hose guide bolt **(see illustration 2.17)**.

3 Front brake caliper

⚠ **Warning: If a caliper indicates the need for an overhaul (usually due to leaking fluid or sticky operation), all old brake fluid should be flushed from the system. To prevent damage from spilled brake fluid, always cover painted areas when disconnecting the caliper. Also, the dust created by the brake system may contain asbestos, which is harmful to your health. Never blow it out with compressed air and don't inhale any of it. An approved filtering mask should be worn when working on the brakes. Do not use petroleum-based solvents to clean brake parts. Use clean brake fluid, brake cleaner or denatured alcohol only.**

Removal

Note: *Do not operate the brake lever while the caliper is off the disc.*

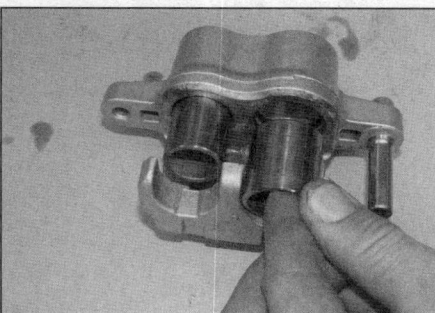

3.7 Displace the pistons from the caliper

1 Remove the brake hose guide bolt **(see illustration 2.17)**.

2 If the brake caliper is just being displaced, do not disconnect the brake hose. Remove the caliper bracket bolts and slide the caliper assembly off the disc and fork. Secure the caliper to the motorcycle with a cable tie to avoid straining the brake hose.

3 If the caliper is being completely removed or overhauled, first unscrew the brake hose banjo bolt and detach the banjo fitting, noting its alignment with the caliper **(see illustration)**. Discard the sealing washers, as new ones must be fitted. Wrap a clean plastic bag tightly around the end of the hose to prevent dirt entering the system, and secure it in an upright position to minimise fluid loss. **Note:** *If you are planning to overhaul the caliper and do not have a source of compressed air to blow out the pistons, just loosen the banjo bolt at this stage and retighten it lightly. The hydraulic system can then be used to force the pistons out of the caliper once the pads have been removed. Disconnect the hose once the pistons have been sufficiently displaced.* Now detach the caliper bracket from the fork and disc.

4 Remove the caliper-to-bracket lower bolt (1997 to 2000 models) or bolts (2001-on models) and separate the caliper body from the bracket/pads.

5 Note the location of the pad spring inside the caliper and remove it for safekeeping **(see illustration)**. If the spring is damaged or corroded, fit a new one on reassembly

Overhaul

6 Clean the exterior of the caliper with denatured alcohol or brake system cleaner. **Note:** *The pistons are different sizes. On the caliper we stripped, the pistons were clearly marked for identification. However, if required, mark each piston head and the caliper body with a suitable marker to ensure that the pistons can be matched to their original bores on reassembly.*

7 Displace the pistons from their bores using either compressed air or by carefully operating the front brake lever to pump them out **(see illustration)**. Ensure that both pistons are moving freely and evenly. If the pistons are being displaced hydraulically, it may be necessary to top-up the fluid reservoir during the procedure. Also, have some clean rag ready to catch the spilled fluid when the pistons reach the end of their bores. **Note:** *If the compressed air method is used, direct the air into the fluid inlet on the caliper. Use only low pressure to ease the pistons out – if the air pressure is too high and the pistons are forced out, the caliper and/or pistons may be damaged.*

⚠ **Warning: Never place your fingers in front of the pistons in an attempt to catch or protect them when applying compressed air, as serious injury could result.**

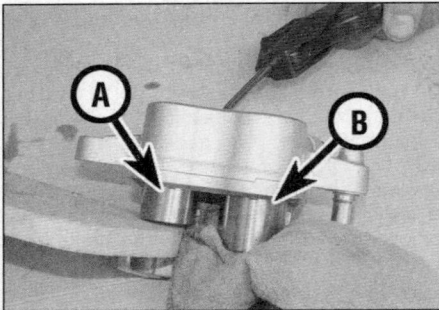

3.8 Hold piston (A) while displacing piston (B) with compressed air

3.9 Remove the seals from the grooves in the caliper

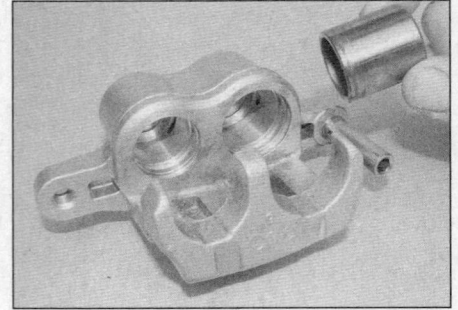

3.11 Inspect the pistons and bores for wear and damage

8 If a piston sticks in its bore, first remove the other piston and pack its bore tightly with clean rag or hold the free piston in place at the end of its bore with a small piece of wood **(see illustration)**. If not already done, disconnect the brake hose (see Step 3) then try and displace the stuck piston with compressed air (see Step 8). If the piston cannot be displaced, the caliper will have to be replaced with a new one.
Caution: Do not try to remove the pistons by levering them out, or by using pliers or any other grips.
9 Remove the dust seals and the piston seals from the piston bores using a soft wooden or plastic tool to avoid scratching the bores **(see illustration)**. Discard the seals as new ones must be fitted on reassembly.
10 Clean the pistons and bores with clean brake fluid of the specified type. If compressed air is available, blow it through the fluid galleries in the caliper to ensure they

are clear and use it to dry the parts thoroughly (make sure it is filtered and unlubricated).
Caution: Do not, under any circumstances, use a petroleum-based solvent to clean brake parts.
11 Inspect the bores and pistons for signs of corrosion, nicks and burrs and loss of plating **(see illustration)**. If surface defects are present, the caliper assembly must be renewed. If the caliper is in bad shape the master cylinder should also be checked.
12 Lubricate the new piston seals with clean brake fluid and install them in their grooves in the bores. Compare the seals and measure them if necessary to ensure that the correct seals are fitted in the correct bores. The same applies when fitting the new dust seals and pistons **(see illustration)**.
13 Lubricate the new dust seals with clean brake fluid and install them in their grooves in the bores.
14 If a special seal lubricant has been

supplied with the seal kit, use it to lubricate the outer lip of the bores and the dust seals, otherwise lubricate the pistons with clean brake fluid. Install the pistons, closed-end first, into the caliper bores, then, using your thumbs, push the pistons all the way in, making sure they enter the bores squarely **(see illustrations)**.

Installation

15 Ensure the pad spring is correctly installed inside the caliper so that its outer longer tangs point in the direction of forward disc/wheel rotation **(see illustration)**.
17 Fit the caliper onto the bracket and install the caliper over the disc and secure it to the fork. Tighten the caliper bolts and caliper bracket bolts to the specified torque settings.
18 If removed, connect the brake hose to the caliper, using **new** sealing washers on each side of the banjo union **(see illustration)**. Align the union as noted on removal. Tighten

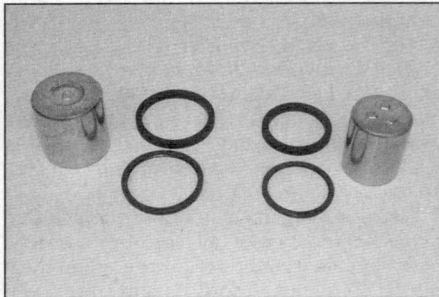

3.12 Pistons are different sizes – ensure the seals are matched before installation

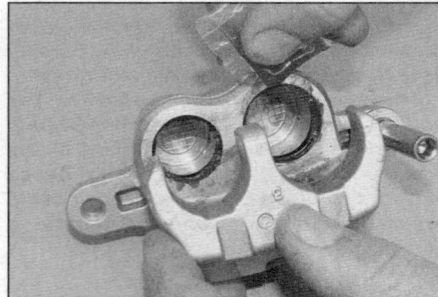

3.14a Lubricate the outer lip of the bores and dust seals . . .

3.14b . . . then install the pistons closed end first . . .

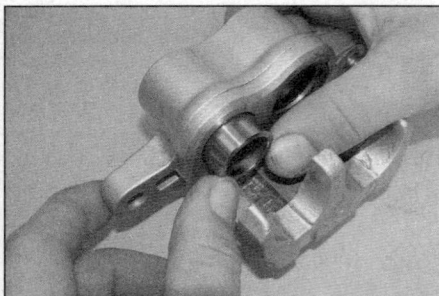

3.14c . . . and push them all the way into the caliper

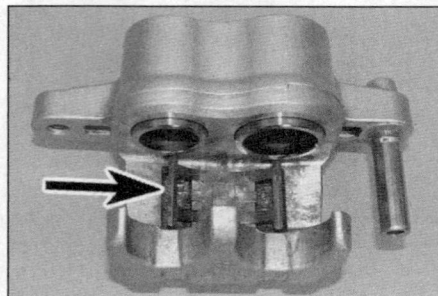

3.15 Ensure the pad spring (arrowed) is correctly installed

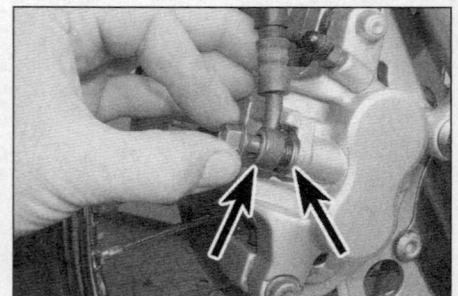

3.18 Fit new sealing washers (arrowed) on the banjo union

the banjo bolt to the torque setting specified at the beginning of this Chapter.

20 Install the brake hose guide bolt.

21 Top-up the fluid reservoir with DOT 4 brake fluid (see *Daily (pre-ride) checks*) and bleed the system (see Section 11).

22 Check that there are no fluid leaks and test the operation of the brake thoroughly before riding the motorcycle.

4 Front brake disc

Inspection

1 Inspect the surface of the disc for score marks and other damage **(see illustration)**. Light scratches are normal after use and won't affect brake operation, but deep grooves and heavy score marks will reduce braking efficiency and accelerate pad wear. If the disc is badly grooved, have it machined by a brake specialist, or fit a new one. Where twin discs are fitted (1100 models) renew both discs at the same time. Always fit new pads when you renew the disc(s).

2 The disc must not be machined or allowed to wear to a thickness below the service limit listed in this Chapter's Specifications. The thickness of the disc can be checked with a micrometer **(see illustration)**. If the thickness of the disc is less than the service limit, a new one must be fitted.

3 To check disc runout, support the bike on an auxiliary stand with the front wheel off the ground. Mount a dial gauge to the fork with the gauge plunger touching the surface of the disc about 10 mm from the outer edge **(see illustration)**. Rotate the wheel and watch the gauge needle, comparing the reading with the service limit listed in this Chapter's Specifications. If the runout is greater than the service limit, check the wheel bearings for play (see Chapter 1). If the bearings are worn, renew them (see Section 17), then repeat this check. If the disc runout is still excessive, a new one must be fitted.

Removal

4 Remove the wheel (see Section 15).

Caution: Don't lay the wheel down and allow it to rest on the disc – the disc could become warped. Set the wheel on wood blocks so the wheel rim supports the weight of the wheel.

5 If you are not replacing the disc with a new one, mark the relationship of the disc to the wheel so it can be installed in the same position. Unscrew the disc retaining bolts, loosening them evenly and a little at a time in a criss-cross pattern to avoid distorting the disc **(see illustration)**. Lift off the disc; note the location of the hub trim on 1100 models.

Installation

6 Before installing the disc, make sure there

4.1 Inspect the front brake disc for wear and damage

4.2 Measuring the disc thickness with a micrometer

4.3 Set-up for checking brake disc runout

4.5 Undo the bolts (arrowed) and remove the disc

is no dirt or corrosion where the disc seats on the hub, particularly right in the angle of the seat. If the disc does not sit flat when it is bolted down, it will appear to be warped when checked or when the front brake is used.

7 Install the disc on the wheel; align the previously applied register marks if you are reinstalling the original disc. On 1100 models, fit the hub trim.

8 Clean the threads of the disc mounting bolts, then apply a suitable non-permanent thread locking compound. Install the bolts and tighten them evenly and a little at a time in a criss-cross pattern to the torque setting specified at the beginning of this Chapter. Clean the brake disc using acetone or brake system cleaner. If a new disc has been installed, remove any protective coating from its working surfaces.

9 Install the front wheel (see Section 15).

10 Operate the brake lever several times to bring the pads into contact with the disc. Check the operation of the brake carefully before riding the motorcycle.

5 Front brake master cylinder

1 If the brake lever does not feel firm when the brake is applied, and the hydraulic hose and brake caliper are in good condition and bleeding the brake does not help (see Section 11), or if the master cylinder is leaking fluid, then master cylinder overhaul is recommended.

2 Before disassembling the master cylinder, read through the entire procedure and make sure that you have obtained all the new parts required including some new DOT 4 brake fluid, some clean rags and internal circlip pliers.

Caution: Disassembly, overhaul and reassembly of the brake master cylinder must be done in a spotlessly clean work area to avoid contamination and possible failure of the brake hydraulic system components. To prevent damage from spilled brake fluid, always cover painted areas when disconnecting the master cylinder. Do not use petroleum-based solvents to clean brake parts. Use clean brake fluid, brake cleaner or denatured alcohol only.

Removal

Note: *If the master cylinder is just being displaced and not completely removed from the motorcycle, follow the appropriate Steps in Chapter 5, Section 5. If required, secure the master cylinder to the motorcycle with a cable tie to avoid straining the brake hose and keep the reservoir upright to prevent fluid spills and air entering the system.*

3 Unscrew the rear view mirror, noting that the right-hand mirror unscrews clockwise.

4 Remove the front brake lever (see Chapter 5, Section 5). Disconnect the wiring connectors from the brake light switch. If required, remove the screw securing the switch to the master cylinder and remove the switch.

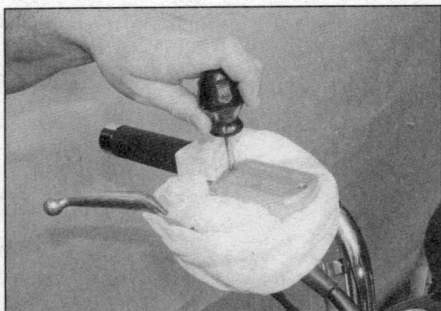

5.5 Loosen the reservoir cover screws

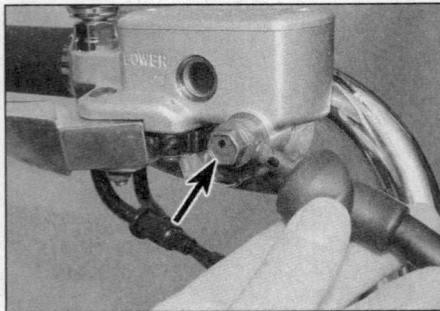

5.6 Unscrew the brake hose banjo bolt (arrowed)

5.7 Unscrew the master cylinder clamp bolts (arrowed)

5 Loosen the reservoir cover retaining screws **(see illustration)**.

6 If fitted, pull back the rubber boot, then unscrew the brake hose banjo bolt and separate the hose from the master cylinder, noting its alignment **(see illustration)**. Discard the sealing washers as they must be renewed. Wrap a plastic bag tightly around the end of the hose to stop dirt entering the system and secure the hose in an upright position to prevent fluid spills.

7 Support the master cylinder, then unscrew the master cylinder clamp bolts and remove the back of the clamp, noting how it fits **(see illustration)**. Lift the master cylinder away from the handlebar.

8 Undo the reservoir cover retaining screws and lift off the cover, the diaphragm plate and the diaphragm **(see illustration)**. Drain the brake fluid from the reservoir into a suitable container. Wipe any remaining fluid out of the reservoir with a clean rag. Inspect the reservoir diaphragm and renew it if it is damaged or deteriorated.

Overhaul

9 Carefully remove the dust boot from the end of the piston **(see illustration)**.

10 Using circlip pliers, remove the circlip, then withdraw the piston assembly and spring, noting how they fit **(see illustration 5.9)**. If the piston assembly is difficult to remove, apply low pressure compressed air to the fluid outlet. Lay the parts out in the proper order to prevent confusion during reassembly.

11 Clean all parts with clean brake fluid or denatured alcohol. If compressed air is available, blow it through the fluid galleries to ensure they are clear and use it to dry the parts thoroughly (make sure the air is filtered and unlubricated).

Caution: Do not, under any circumstances, use a petroleum-based solvent to clean brake parts.

12 Check the master cylinder bore for corrosion, scratches, nicks and score marks. If damage or wear is evident, the master cylinder must be renewed. If the master cylinder is in poor condition, then the caliper(s) should be checked as well.

13 The dust boot, circlip, piston assembly and spring are all included in the master cylinder overhaul kit. Use all of the new parts, regardless of the apparent condition of the old ones. If the seal and cup are not already on the piston, fit them according to the layout of the old piston assembly.

14 Install the new spring in the master cylinder, wide end first.

15 Lubricate the new piston assembly with clean brake fluid. Install the assembly into the master cylinder, making sure it is the correct way round **(see illustration 5.9)**. Make sure the lips on the cup do not turn inside out when they are slipped into the bore. Depress the piston and install the new circlip, making sure the circlip locates in its groove.

16 Install the new dust boot, making sure the lip is seated correctly.

Installation

17 Attach the master cylinder to the handlebar and fit the clamp with its UP mark facing up, then tighten the bolts to the torque setting specified at the beginning this Chapter **(see illustration 5.7)**.

18 Connect the brake hose to the master cylinder, using **new** sealing washers on each side of the banjo union. Align the union as noted on removal **(see illustration 5.6)**. Tighten the banjo bolt to the specified torque setting.

19 If removed, install the brake light switch, then connect the brake light wiring. Install the brake lever (see Chapter 5, Section 5).

20 Fill the fluid reservoir with new DOT 4 brake fluid, then bleed the hydraulic system (see Section 11).

21 Fit the diaphragm, making sure it is correctly seated, the diaphragm plate and the cover onto the reservoir **(see illustration 5.8)**. Install the cover screws and tighten them securely.

22 Install the rear view mirror.

23 Check that there are no fluid leaks and test the operation of the brakes thoroughly before riding the motorcycle.

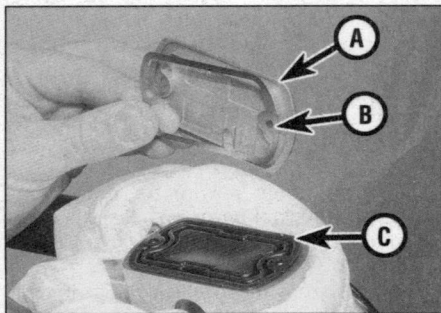

5.8 Lift off the cover (A), diaphragm plate (B) and diaphragm (C)

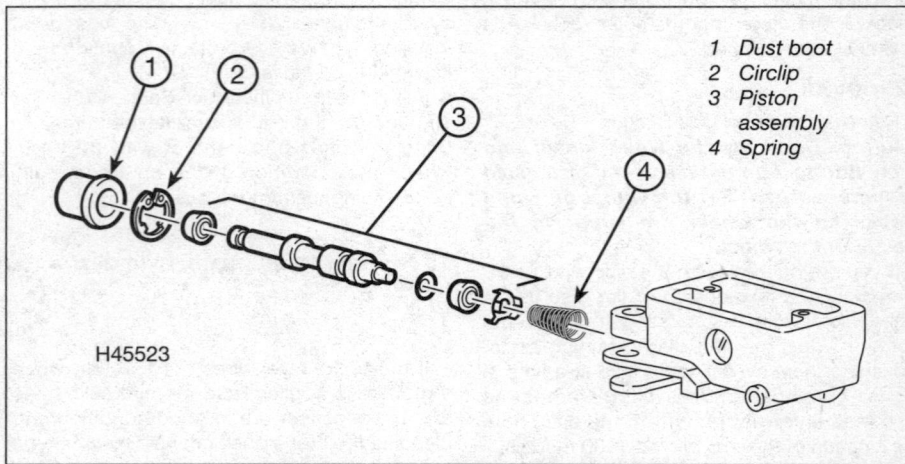

1 Dust boot
2 Circlip
3 Piston assembly
4 Spring

H45523

5.9 Front brake master cylinder components

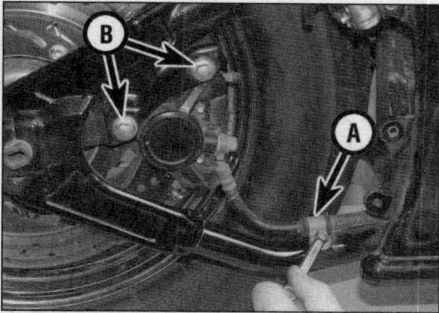

6.2a Release the brake hose from the clip (A), then undo the mounting bolts (B) . . .

6.2b . . . and slide the caliper off the disc

6.3 Prise off the caliper cover

6 Rear brake pads (1100 models)

Warning: The dust created by the brake system may contain asbestos, which is harmful to your health. Never blow it out with compressed air and do not inhale any of it. An approved filtering mask should be worn when working on the brakes.

Note: *Do not operate the brake pedal while the caliper is off the disc.*

1 Remove the silencer assembly and the silencer bracket (see Chapter 3).

2 Remove the clip securing the brake hose to the swingarm, then undo the brake caliper mounting bolts and slide the caliper off the disc **(see illustrations)**. **Note:** *Do not operate the brake pedal while the caliper is off the disc.*

3 Prise off the caliper cover **(see illustration)**.

4 Remove the R-clip from one pad pin, then pull out the pin and remove the pad spring, noting which way round it fits **(see illustrations)**.

5 Remove the R-clip from the second pad pin, then support the pads and pull out the pin **(see illustration)**. Lift out the pads.

6 Inspect the surface of each pad for contamination and check that the friction material has not worn beyond its service limit (see Chapter 1, Section 11). If either pad is worn down to or beyond the service limit wear indicator, is fouled with oil or grease, or is heavily scored or damaged by dirt and debris, both pads must be renewed as a set. Note that it is not possible to degrease the friction material; if the pads are contaminated in any way, new ones must be fitted.

7 Check that each pad has the same amount of wear as the other. If uneven wear is noticed, one of the pistons is probably sticking in the caliper, in which case the caliper must be overhauled (see Section 7).

8 If the pads are in good condition, clean them carefully using a fine wire brush which is completely free of oil and grease, to remove all traces of road dirt and corrosion. Using a pointed instrument, dig out any embedded particles of foreign matter.

9 Spray the inside of the caliper with a dedicated brake cleaner to remove any dust. Remove any traces of corrosion from the pad pins which might cause sticking of the caliper/pad operation.

10 Check the condition of the brake disc (see Section 8).

11 If new pads are being installed, push the pistons as far back into the caliper as possible using hand pressure or a piece of wood as leverage. This will displace brake fluid back into the brake fluid reservoir, so it may be necessary to remove the reservoir cap, plate and diaphragm, and siphon out some fluid (depending on how much fluid was in there in the first place and how far the pistons have to be pushed in). If the pistons are difficult to push back, attach a length of clear hose to the bleed valve and place the open end in a suitable container, then open the valve and try again. Take great care not to draw any air into

the system. If in doubt, bleed the brakes afterwards (see Section 11). **Note:** *Yamaha recommend that a new pad spring should be fitted whenever the pads are renewed.*

12 Smear the backs of the pads with copper-based grease, making sure that none gets on the front or sides of the pads, then install the pads in the caliper and secure them with one pad pin **(see illustration 6.5)**. Ensure the pads are installed so that the friction material faces the disc.

13 Install the pad spring so that its longer outside tangs face the direction of disc rotation and secure it with the second pad pin **(see illustration 6.4c)**.

14 Secure both pad pins with the R-clips – note that the R-clips fit between the inside edge of the caliper body and the back of the outer brake pad **(see illustration 6.4a)**.

15 Fit the caliper cover.

16 Check that the pads are correctly

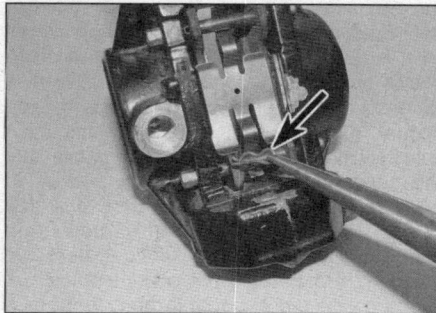

6.4a Remove the R-clip (arrowed) . . .

6.4b . . . then pull out the pad pin . . .

6.4c . . . and remove the pad spring

6.5 Remove the second pad pin

6.16a Check that the pads (arrowed) are correctly positioned

6.16b Install the caliper mounting bolts

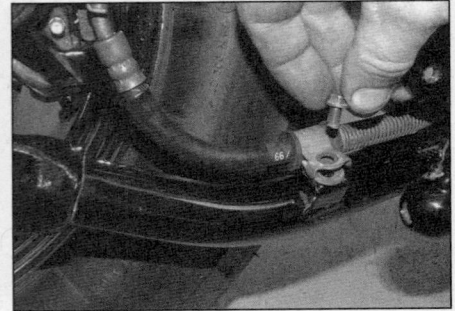

6.17 Secure the brake hose to the swingarm

positioned in the caliper so that they will fit each side of the disc, then slide the caliper onto the disc and secure it with the mounting bolts (see illustrations). Tighten the mounting bolts to the torque setting specified at the beginning of this Chapter.

17 Secure the brake hose to the swingarm (see illustration).

18 Operate the brake pedal several times to bring the pads into contact with the disc. Top-up the fluid reservoir if necessary (see *Daily (pre-ride) checks*).

19 Install the remaining components in the reverse order of removal.

20 Check the operation of the rear brake carefully before riding the motorcycle.

7 Rear brake caliper (1100 models)

⚠️ **Warning: If a caliper indicates the need for an overhaul (usually due to leaking fluid or sticky operation), all old brake fluid should be flushed from the system. To prevent damage from spilled brake fluid, always cover painted areas when disconnecting the caliper. Also, the dust created by the brake system may contain asbestos, which is harmful to your health. Never blow it out with compressed air and do not inhale any of it. An approved filtering mask should be worn when**

working on the brakes. Do not use petroleum-based solvents to clean brake parts. Use clean brake fluid, brake cleaner or denatured alcohol only.

Removal

Note: *Do not operate the brake pedal while the caliper is off the disc.*

1 Remove the silencer assembly and the silencer bracket (see Chapter 3).

2 If the caliper is just being displaced, do not disconnect the brake hose. Follow the procedure in Section 6, Step 2, then secure the caliper to the motorcycle with a cable tie to avoid straining the brake hose.

3 If the caliper is being completely removed or overhauled, unscrew the brake hose banjo bolt and detach the banjo fitting (see illustration). Note how the inner sealing washer locks against the caliper to prevent the banjo fitting rotating when the bolt is tightened, then discard the sealing washers as new ones must be used. Wrap a clean plastic bag tightly around the end of the hose to prevent dirt entering the system, and secure it in an upright position to minimise fluid loss. **Note:** *If you are planning to overhaul the caliper and do not have a source of compressed air to blow out the pistons, just loosen the banjo bolt at this stage and retighten it lightly. The hydraulic system can then be used to force the pistons out of the caliper once the pads have been removed. Disconnect the hose once the pistons have been sufficiently displaced.*

4 Unscrew the caliper mounting bolts and slide the caliper off the disc (see illustrations 6.2a and 2b). Follow the procedure in Section 6 and remove the pads from the caliper.

Overhaul

5 Clean the exterior of the caliper with denatured alcohol or brake system cleaner. Mark each piston head and the caliper body with a suitable marker to ensure that the pistons can be matched to their original bores on reassembly. **Note:** *On the caliper we overhauled, new pistons were supplied with the caliper seal kit.*

6 Displace the pistons from their bores using either compressed air or by carefully operating the rear brake pedal to pump them out. Ensure that both pistons are moving freely and evenly. If the pistons are being displaced hydraulically, it may be necessary to top-up the fluid reservoir during the procedure. Also, have some clean rag ready to catch any spilled fluid when the pistons reach the end of their bores. **Note:** *If the compressed air method is used, direct the air into the fluid inlet on the caliper. Use only low pressure to ease the pistons out – if the air pressure is too high and the pistons are forced out, the caliper and/or pistons may be damaged.*

⚠️ **Warning: Never place your fingers in front of the piston in an attempt to catch or protect it when applying compressed air, as serious injury could result.**

7 If a piston sticks in its bore, first remove the other piston and pack its bore with clean rag or hold the free piston in place at the end of its bore with a small piece of wood (see illustration). If not already done, disconnect the brake hose (see Step 2) then try and displace the stuck piston with compressed air (see Step 6). If the piston cannot be displaced, the caliper will have to be replaced with a new one.

Caution: Do not try to remove the pistons by levering them out, or by using pliers or any other grips.

8 Remove the dust seals and the piston seals from the piston bores using a wooden or plastic tool to avoid scratching the bores (see

7.3 Detach the rear caliper banjo fitting – note the inner sealing washer (arrowed)

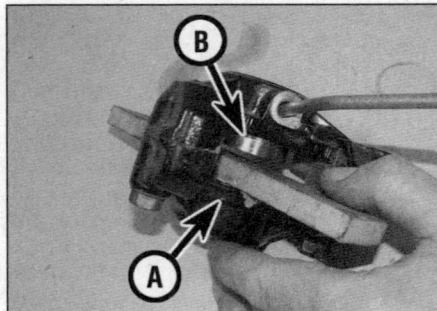

7.7 Hold piston (A) while displacing piston (B) with compressed air

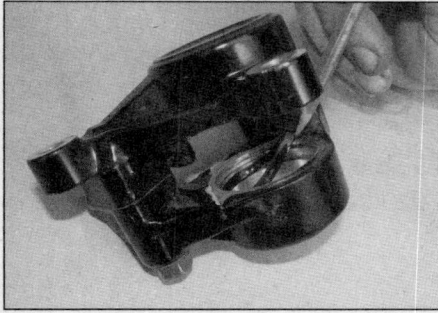

7.8 Remove the seals from the grooves in the caliper

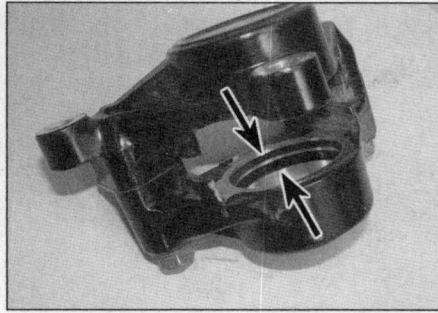

7.11 Lubricate the new seals (arrowed) and install them in the caliper

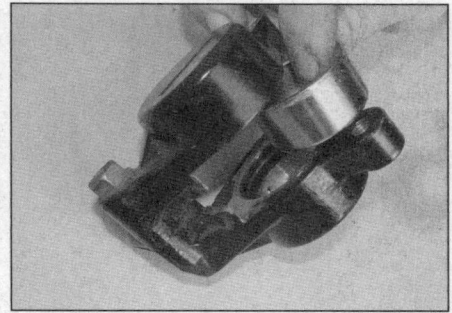

7.13 Install the pistons closed end first

illustration). Discard the seals as new ones must be fitted on reassembly.

9 Clean the pistons and bores with clean brake fluid of the specified type. If compressed air is available, blow it through the fluid galleries in the caliper to ensure they are clear and use it to dry the parts thoroughly (make sure it is filtered and unlubricated).

Caution: Do not, under any circumstances, use a petroleum-based solvent to clean brake parts.

10 Inspect the caliper bores and pistons for signs of corrosion, nicks and burrs and loss of plating. If surface defects are present, the caliper assembly must be renewed. If the caliper is in bad shape the master cylinder should also be checked.

11 Lubricate the new piston seals with clean brake fluid and install them in their grooves in the caliper bores **(see illustration)**.

12 Lubricate the new dust seals with clean brake fluid and install them in their grooves in the caliper bores.

13 If a special seal lubricant has been supplied with the seal kit, use it to lubricate the outer lip of the bores and the dust seals, otherwise lubricate the pistons with clean brake fluid. Install the pistons, closed-end first, into the caliper bores **(see illustration)**. Using your thumbs, push the pistons all the way in, making sure they enter the bores squarely.

Installation

14 Follow the procedure in Section 6 and install the pads in the caliper, then slide the caliper onto the disc and tighten the mounting bolts to the torque setting specified at the beginning of this Chapter.

15 If removed, connect the brake hose to the caliper, using **new** sealing washers on each side of the banjo union. Align the inner sealing washer with the caliper and the union as noted on removal **(see illustration 7.3)**. Tighten the banjo bolt to the torque setting specified at the beginning of this Chapter.

16 If removed, install the brake hose clip **(see illustration 6.17)**.

17 Top-up the fluid reservoir with DOT 4 brake fluid (see *Daily (pre-ride) checks*) and bleed the system (see Section 11).

18 Install the remaining components in the reverse order of removal.

19 Check that there are no fluid leaks and test the operation of the rear brake thoroughly before riding the motorcycle.

8 Rear brake disc (1100 models)

Inspection

1 Refer to the procedure in Section 4 of this Chapter, noting that when checking the disc runout the dial gauge should be attached to the swingarm.

Removal

2 Remove the rear wheel (see Section 16).
Caution: Don't lay the wheel down and allow it to rest on the disc – the disc could become warped. Set the wheel on wood blocks so the wheel rim supports the weight of the wheel.

3 If you are not replacing the disc with a new one, mark the relationship of the disc to the wheel so that it can be installed in the same position. Unscrew the disc retaining bolts, loosening them evenly and a little at a time in a criss-cross pattern to avoid distorting the disc, then remove the disc from the wheel **(see illustration)**.

Installation

4 Before installing the disc, make sure there is no dirt or corrosion where the disc seats on

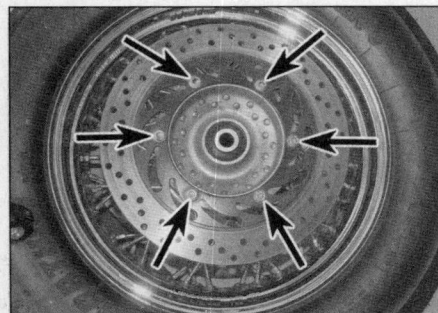

8.3 Undo the bolts (arrowed) and remove the disc

the hub, particularly right in the angle of the seat. If the disc does not sit flat when it is bolted down, it will appear to be warped when checked or when the rear brake is used.

5 Install the disc on the wheel; align the previously applied register marks if you are reinstalling the original disc.

6 Clean the threads of the disc mounting bolts, then apply a suitable non-permanent thread locking compound. Install the bolts and tighten them evenly and a little at a time in a criss-cross pattern to the torque setting specified at the beginning of this Chapter. Clean the brake disc using acetone or brake system cleaner. If a new disc has been installed, remove any protective coating from its working surfaces.

7 Install the rear wheel (see Section 16).

8 Operate the brake pedal several times to bring the pads into contact with the disc. Check the operation of the rear brake carefully before riding the motorcycle.

9 Rear brake master cylinder (1100 models)

1 If the brake pedal does not firm feel when the brake is applied, and the hydraulic hose and brake caliper are in good condition and bleeding the brakes does not help (see Section 11), or if the master cylinder is leaking fluid, then master cylinder overhaul is recommended.

2 Before disassembling the master cylinder, read through the entire procedure and make sure that you have obtained all the new parts required including some new DOT 4 brake fluid, some clean rags and internal circlip pliers.

Caution: Disassembly, overhaul and reassembly of the brake master cylinder must be done in a spotlessly clean work area to avoid contamination and possible failure of the brake hydraulic system components. To prevent damage from spilled brake fluid, always cover painted areas when disconnecting the master cylinder. Do not use petroleum-based solvents to clean brake parts. Use clean brake fluid, brake cleaner or denatured alcohol only.

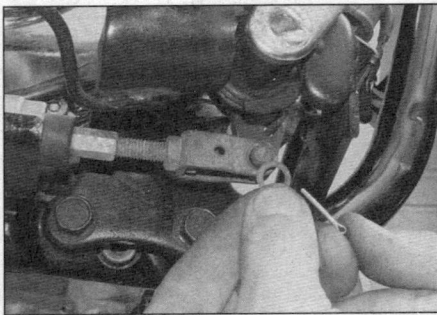
9.3 Remove the split pin and washer

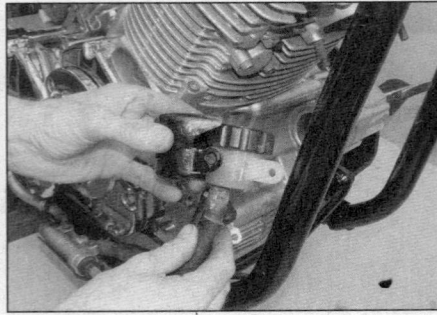
9.4a Displace the reservoir and metal cover . . .

9.4b . . . then remove the cap . . .

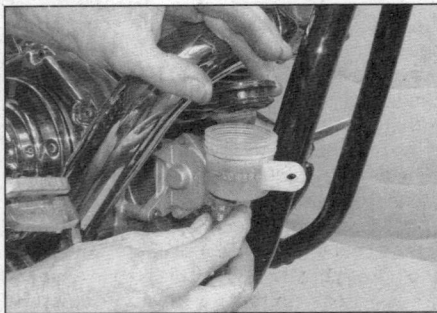
9.4c . . . and reservoir diaphragm

9.5 Remove the bolts and guard plate

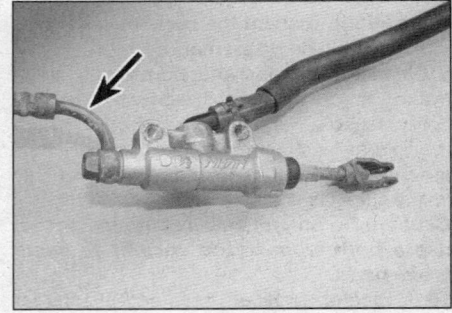
9.6 Undo the bolt and remove the banjo fitting (arrowed)

Removal

3 Remove the split pin and washer from the clevis pin connecting the brake pedal to the master cylinder pushrod (see illustration). Remove the clevis pin and separate the pushrod from the pedal. Discard the split pin, as a new one must be fitted.
4 Remove the bolt securing the fluid reservoir to the frame and remove the metal reservoir cover, then remove the reservoir cap and diaphragm (see illustrations). Drain the brake fluid into a suitable container. Release the clip securing the hose to the union on the reservoir and remove the reservoir. Wipe any remaining fluid out of the reservoir with a clean rag and replace the diaphragm and cap temporarily. Release the hose from any ties securing it to the frame.
5 Loosen the rear brake hose banjo bolt on the master cylinder and retighten it lightly.

Unscrew the two bolts securing the master cylinder to the frame and remove the guard plate (see illustration).
6 Lift off the master cylinder and withdraw the reservoir hose from the machine, noting its route. Unscrew the brake hose banjo bolt and separate the banjo fitting from the master cylinder, noting its alignment (see illustration). Discard the sealing washers, as new ones must be fitted. Wrap a clean plastic bag tightly around the end of the hose to prevent dirt entering the system and secure it in an upright position to prevent fluid spills.

Overhaul

7 If required, release the clip securing the reservoir hose to the union on the master cylinder and remove the hose.

8 Measure the position of the clevis on the pushrod, then loosen the locknut and thread the clevis and nut off the pushrod (see illustration).
9 Carefully remove the dust boot from the end of the master cylinder to reveal the pushrod retaining circlip (see illustration).
10 Depress the pushrod and use circlip pliers to remove the circlip, then slide out the pushrod, piston assembly and spring, noting how they fit (see illustration 9.9). If the piston assembly is difficult to remove, apply low pressure compressed air to the fluid outlet. Lay the parts out in the proper order to prevent confusion during reassembly.
11 Clean all of the parts with clean brake fluid or denatured alcohol. If compressed air is available, blow it through the fluid galleries to ensure they are clear and use it to dry the

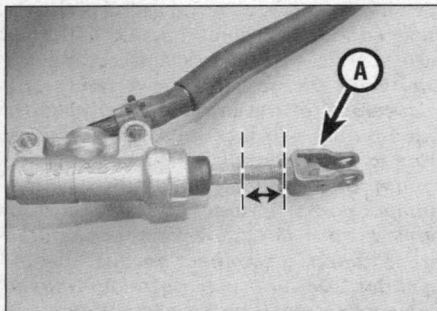
9.8 Measure the position of the clevis (A) on the pushrod as shown

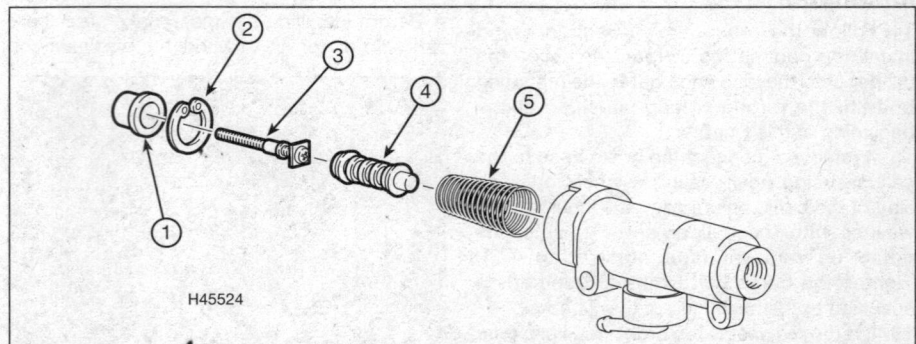
9.9 Rear brake master cylinder components

1 Dust boot   3 Pushrod   5 Spring
2 Circlip   4 Piston assembly

parts thoroughly (make sure the air is filtered and unlubricated).

Caution: Do not, under any circumstances, use a petroleum-based solvent to clean brake parts.

12 Check the master cylinder bore for corrosion, scratches, nicks and score marks. If damage or wear is evident, the master cylinder must be renewed. If the master cylinder is in poor condition, then the caliper should be checked as well.

13 The dust boot, circlip, pushrod, piston assembly and spring are included in the master cylinder rebuild kit. Use all of the new parts, regardless of the apparent condition of the old ones. Fit them according to the layout of the old piston assembly.

14 Fit the spring into the master cylinder, wide end first.

15 Lubricate the new piston assembly with clean brake fluid. Install the assembly into the master cylinder, making sure it is the correct way round **(see illustration 9.9)**. Make sure the lips on the cup do not turn inside out when they are slipped into the bore.

16 Install the pushrod, then press it in and fit the new circlip, making sure it is properly located in its groove.

17 Install the dust boot, making sure the lip is seated properly in the groove.

18 Thread the clevis locknut and the clevis onto the pushrod. Position the clevis as noted on removal (see Step 8), then tighten the locknut securely.

19 If removed, fit the reservoir hose onto its union and secure it with the clip.

20 Inspect the fluid reservoir cap and diaphragm and renew any parts if they are damaged or deteriorated.

Installation

21 Connect the brake hose to the master cylinder, using **new** sealing washers on each side of the banjo union. Align the union as noted on removal and tighten the banjo bolt finger-tight **(see illustration 9.6)**.

22 Fit the master cylinder onto its bracket and install the guard plate and mounting bolts. Feed the reservoir hose through to the reservoir location, then fit the reservoir onto the hose and secure it with the clip. Install the reservoir in position temporarily

23 Tighten the master cylinder mounting bolts to the torque setting specified at the beginning

of this Chapter. Tighten the brake hose banjo bolt to the specified torque setting.

24 Connect the master cylinder pushrod to the brake pedal with the clevis pin. Install the washer and secure the clevis pin with a new split pin **(see illustration 9.3)**.

25 Fill the fluid reservoir with new DOT 4 brake fluid, then bleed the hydraulic system (see Section 11).

26 Ensure the reservoir diaphragm is correctly seated, and that the cap is tightened securely, then fit the metal reservoir cover and secure the assembly with the mounting bolt.

27 Check that there are no fluid leaks and test the operation of the brake thoroughly before riding the motorcycle.

10 Brake hoses and unions

Inspection

1 Brake hose condition should be checked regularly and the hoses renewed at the specified interval (see Chapter 1).

2 Twist and flex the hoses while looking for cracks, bulges and seeping hydraulic fluid **(see illustration)**. Check extra carefully around the areas where the hoses connect with the banjo fittings, as these are common areas for hose failure.

3 Check the banjo fittings connected to the brake hoses. If the fittings are rusted, scratched or cracked, fit new hoses.

Renewal

4 The brake hoses have banjo fittings on each end. Cover the surrounding area with plenty of rags and unscrew the banjo bolt at each end of the hose, noting the alignment of the fitting with the master cylinder or brake caliper. Free the hose from any clips or guides and remove it, noting its routing. Discard the sealing washers as new ones must be used.

5 Position the new hose, making sure it is not twisted or otherwise strained, and ensure that it is correctly routed through any clips or guides and is clear of all moving components.

6 Check that the fittings align correctly, then install the banjo bolts, using **new** sealing washers on both sides of the fittings. Tighten the banjo bolts to the torque setting specified at the beginning of this Chapter. Note that on 1100

models, a special inner sealing washer is fitted on the rear brake caliper which locks against the caliper to prevent the banjo fitting rotating when the bolt is tightened **(see illustration 7.3)**.

7 Flush the old brake fluid from the system, refill with new DOT 4 brake fluid (see *Daily (pre-ride) checks*) and bleed the air from the system (see Section 11).

8 Check that there are no fluid leaks and test the operation of the brake thoroughly before riding the motorcycle.

11 Brake system bleeding and fluid change

Bleeding

1 Bleeding the brakes is simply the process of removing air from the brake fluid reservoir, the hose and the brake caliper. Bleeding is necessary whenever a brake system hydraulic connection is loosened, after a component or hose is renewed, or when the master cylinder or caliper is overhauled. Leaks in the system may also allow air to enter, but leaking brake fluid will reveal their presence and warn you of the need for repair.

2 To bleed the brakes, you will need some new DOT 4 brake fluid, a length of clear vinyl or plastic hose, a small container partially filled with clean brake fluid, some rags and a spanner to fit the brake caliper bleed valve.

3 Cover the fuel tank and other painted components to prevent damage in the event that brake fluid is spilled.

4 When bleeding the rear brake, remove the metal cover from the fluid reservoir then temporarily secure the reservoir to the frame with its mounting bolt.

5 Remove the reservoir cover or cap, diaphragm plate (if fitted) and diaphragm and slowly pump the brake lever (front brake) or pedal (rear brake) a few times, until no air bubbles can be seen floating up from the holes in the bottom of the reservoir. This bleeds the air from the master cylinder end of the line. Temporarily refit the reservoir cover or cap.

6 Pull the dust cap off the bleed valve. Attach one end of the clear vinyl or plastic hose to the bleed valve and submerge the other end in the clean brake fluid in the container **(see illustrations)**. Note: *To avoid*

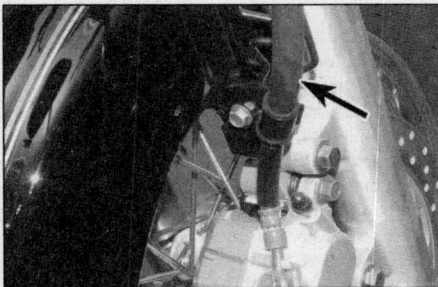

10.2 Flex the brake hose and check for cracks, bulges and seeping fluid

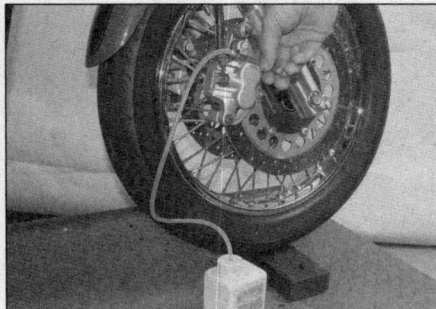

11.6a Set-up for bleeding the front brake

11.6b Set-up for bleeding the rear brake

damaging the bleed valve during the procedure, loosen it and then tighten it temporarily with a ring spanner before attaching the hose. With the hose attached, the valve can then be opened and closed with an open-ended spanner.

7 Remove the reservoir cover or cap and check the fluid level. Do not allow the fluid level to drop below the LOWER mark during the procedure.

8 Carefully pump the brake lever or pedal three or four times and hold it in (front) or down (rear) while opening the caliper bleed valve. When the valve is opened, brake fluid will flow out of the caliper into the clear tubing, and the lever will move toward the handlebar, or the pedal will move down. If there is air in the system there should be air bubbles in the brake fluid coming out of the caliper.

9 Retighten the bleed valve, then release the brake lever or pedal gradually. Top-up the reservoir and repeat the process until no air bubbles are visible in the brake fluid leaving the caliper, and the lever or pedal is firm when applied. On completion, disconnect the hose, then tighten the bleed valve and install the dust cap. If bleeding the front brake on an 1100 model, go on to bleed air from the other caliper.

> **HAYNES HINT** *If it is not possible to produce a firm feel to the lever or pedal, the fluid may be aerated. Let the brake fluid in the system stabilise for a few hours and then repeat the procedure when the tiny bubbles in the system have settled out.*

10 Top-up the reservoir, install the diaphragm, diaphragm plate (if fitted) and cover or cap. Wipe up any spilled brake fluid. Fit the metal cover to the rear brake fluid reservoir and secure the assembly with the mounting bolt.

11 Check that there are no fluid leaks and test the operation of the brakes thoroughly before riding the motorcycle.

Fluid change

12 Changing the brake fluid is a similar process to bleeding the brakes and requires

12.5 Fold the shoes as described to remove them

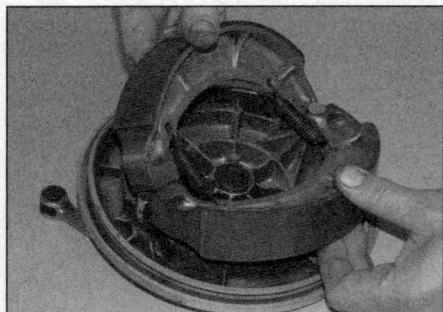
12.3 Remove the rear brake backplate

the same materials plus a suitable tool for siphoning the fluid out of the fluid reservoir. Also ensure that the container is large enough to take all the old fluid when it is flushed out of the system.

13 Follow Steps 3, 4 and 6, then remove the reservoir cover or cap, diaphragm plate (if fitted) and diaphragm and siphon the old fluid out of the reservoir. Fill the reservoir with new brake fluid, then follow Step 8.

14 Retighten the bleed valve, then release the brake lever or pedal gradually. Keep the reservoir topped-up with new fluid to above the LOWER level at all times or air may enter the system and greatly increase the length of the task. Repeat the process until new fluid can be seen emerging from the bleed valve.

> **HAYNES HINT** *Old brake fluid is invariably much darker in colour than new fluid, making it easy to see when all old fluid has been expelled from the system.*

15 Disconnect the hose, then tighten the bleed valve and install the dust cap.

16 Top-up the reservoir, install the diaphragm, diaphragm plate (if fitted) and cap. Wipe up any spilled brake fluid. Fit the metal cover to the rear brake fluid reservoir and secure the assembly with the mounting bolt.

17 Check that there are no fluid leaks and test the operation of the brakes thoroughly before riding the motorcycle.

12.7 Measure the thickness of the brake shoe linings

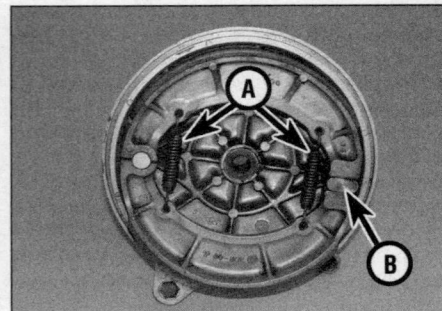
12.4 Note the position of the springs (A) and brake cam (B)

12 Rear drum brake (650 models)

Removal

1 Before you start, inspect the rear brake wear indicator (see Chapter 1, Section 11).

2 Remove the rear wheel and lift off the final drive unit (see Section 16).

3 Lift out the brake backplate **(see illustration)**.

4 Mark the brake shoes to aid reassembly; if they are not going to be renewed they must be installed in their original positions. Note the position of the brake springs and mark the end of the brake cam to aid reassembly **(see illustration)**.

5 Fold the shoes toward each other to release the spring tension and lift the shoes and springs off the backplate **(see illustration)**.

Inspection

6 Check the linings for wear, damage and signs of contamination. Note that it is not possible to degrease the friction material; if the linings are contaminated in any way, new ones must be fitted.

7 Measure the thickness of the lining material – just the lining material, not the metal backing **(see illustration)**. Check that the friction material has not worn beyond the service limit (see Specifications) and renew the shoes as a pair if necessary.

8 If the linings are in good condition, clean them carefully using a fine wire brush which is completely free of oil and grease, to remove all traces of dirt and corrosion. Using a pointed instrument, dig out any embedded particles of foreign matter.

9 Check the ends of the shoes where they contact the brake cam and pivot post. Renew the shoes if there's visible wear.

10 Clean all old grease from the brake cam and pivot post and check them for wear and damage **(see illustration)**. If the pivot post is worn or loose, a new backplate will have to be fitted. To renew the brake cam, first note the match marks on the brake arm and the outer end of the cam, then remove the brake arm pinch bolt and pull the arm off the cam. Note

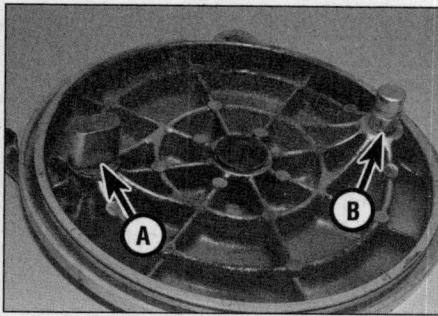

12.10 Check the brake cam (A) and pivot post (B) for wear

how the wear indicator locates on the shaft of the cam, them pull the cam out of the backplate. Lubricate the shaft of the new cam with lithium soap-based grease and install it in the backplate, then fit the wear indicator and brake arm. Check the alignment of the components, then tighten the pinch bolt to the specified torque setting.

11 Check the inside of the brake drum for wear or damage. Measure the inside diameter of the drum at several points with a vernier caliper. If the measurements are uneven (indicating that the drum is out-of-round) or if there are scratches deep enough to snag a fingernail, have the drum skimmed by a brake specialist to correct the surface. If the wear or damage cannot be corrected within the service limit specified at the beginning of this Chapter, the hub must be renewed.

Installation

12 Apply a smear of copper-based grease to the pivot post and the faces of the brake cam. *Caution: Do not apply too much grease otherwise there is a risk of it contaminating the brake drum and shoe linings.*

13 Hook the springs onto the shoes and position the shoes in a V on the brake backplate. Align the ends of the shoes with the pivot post and the brake cam, then fold the shoes down into position (see illustration 12.5). Make sure the ends of the shoes fit correctly on the cam and pivot post (see

illustration 12.4). Check the operation of the brake arm.

14 Install the brake backplate.

15 Install the rear wheel (see Section 16).

16 Check and adjust the rear brake freeplay (see Chapter 1, Section 12). Test the operation of the brake thoroughly before riding the motorcycle.

13 Wheel inspection and repair

1 In order to carry out a proper inspection of the wheels, it is necessary to support the motorcycle upright on an auxiliary stand so that the wheel being inspected is raised off the ground. Clean the wheels thoroughly to remove mud and dirt that may interfere with the inspection procedure or mask defects. Make a general check of the wheels (see Chapter 1) and tyres (see *Daily (pre-ride) checks*).

2 Attach a dial gauge to the fork or the swingarm and position its pointer against the side of the wheel rim. Spin the wheel slowly and check the axial (side-to-side) runout of the rim. In order to accurately check radial (out of round) runout with the dial gauge, the wheel would have to be removed from the machine, and the tyre from the wheel. With the axle clamped in a vice and the dial gauge positioned on the top of the rim, the wheel can be rotated to check the runout (see illustration).

3 An easier, though slightly less accurate, method is to attach a stiff wire pointer to the fork or the swingarm and position the end a fraction of an inch from the wheel (where the wheel and tyre join). If the wheel is true, the distance from the pointer to the rim will be constant as the wheel is rotated. **Note:** *If wheel runout is excessive, check the wheel bearings very carefully before renewing the wheel (see Section 17). It may be possible to correct the runout on a wire spoked wheel – consult a wheel specialist before buying a new item.*

4 The wheels should also be visually inspected for cracks, flat spots on the rim and other damage. Look very closely for dents in

the area where the tyre bead contacts the rim. On machines with cast alloy wheels, dents in this area may prevent complete sealing of the tyre against the rim, which leads to deflation of the tyre over a period of time. If damage is evident, or if runout in either direction is excessive, the wheel will have to be renewed. Wire spoked wheels can be rebuilt with new rims by a wheel specialist, but you should never attempt to repair a damaged cast alloy wheel.

14 Wheel alignment check

1 Misalignment of the wheels due to a bent frame or forks can cause strange and possibly serious handling problems. If the frame or forks are at fault, repair by a specialist or renewal are the only options.

2 To check wheel alignment you will need an assistant, a length of string or a perfectly straight piece of wood and a ruler. A plumb bob or other suitable weight will also be required.

3 In order to make a proper check of the wheels, support the motorcycle upright on an auxiliary stand. Measure the width of both tyres at their widest points. Subtract the smaller measurement from the larger measurement, then divide the difference by two. The result is the amount of offset that should exist between the front and rear tyres on both sides.

4 If a string is used, have your assistant hold one end of it about halfway between the floor and the rear axle, touching the rear sidewall of the tyre.

5 Run the other end of the string forward and pull it tight so that it is roughly parallel to the floor (see illustration). Slowly bring the string into contact with the front sidewall of the rear tyre, then turn the front wheel until it is parallel with the string. Measure the distance from the front tyre sidewall to the string.

6 Repeat the procedure on the other side of the motorcycle. The distance from the front tyre sidewall to the string should be equal on both sides.

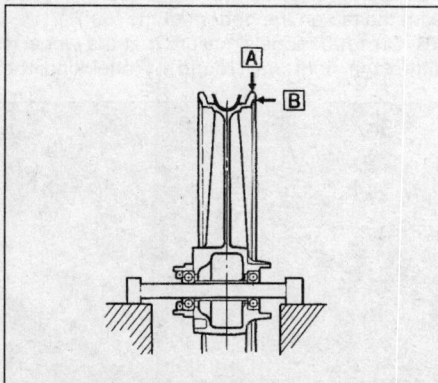

13.2 Check the wheel for radial (out-of-round) runout (A) and axial (side-to-side) runout (B)

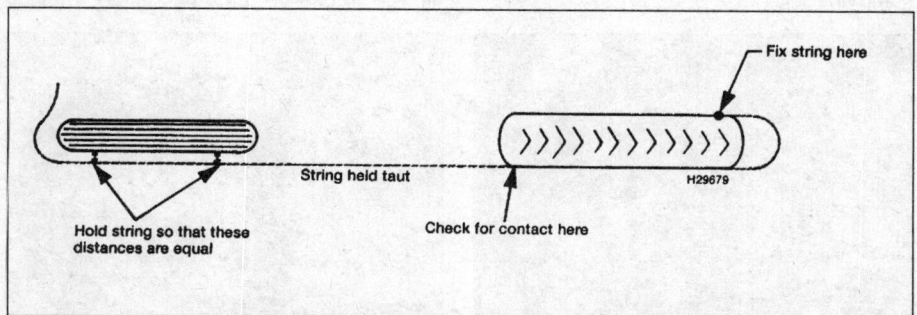

14.5 Wheel alignment check using string

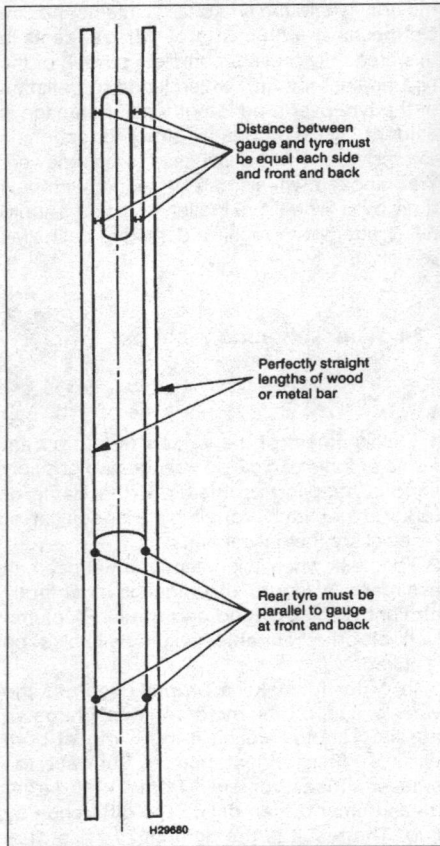

14.7 Wheel alignment check using a straight-edge

Distance between gauge and tyre must be equal each side and front and back

Perfectly straight lengths of wood or metal bar

Rear tyre must be parallel to gauge at front and back

7 If necessary, a perfectly straight length of wood or metal bar may be substituted for the string **(see illustration)**. The procedure is the same.

8 If the front-to-back alignment is correct, the wheels still may be out of alignment vertically.

9 Using the plumb bob, or other suitable weight and a length of string, check the rear wheel to make sure it is vertical. To do this, hold the string against the tyre upper sidewall and allow the weight to settle just off the floor. When the string touches both the upper and lower tyre sidewalls and is perfectly straight, the wheel is vertical. If it is not, adjust the stand until it is.

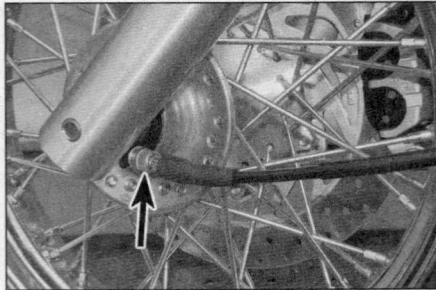

15.2 On 650 models, disconnect the speedometer cable (arrowed) from the drive unit

10 Once the rear wheel is vertical, check the front wheel in the same manner. If both wheels are not perfectly vertical, the frame and/or major suspension components are bent.

15 Front wheel

Removal

1 Using an auxiliary stand, support the motorcycle securely in an upright position so the front wheel is off the ground.

2 On 650 models, unscrew the speedometer cable from the drive unit and secure the cable clear of the wheel **(see illustration)**.

3 Displace the front brake caliper(s) (see Section 3).

4 Loosen the axle pinch bolt on the bottom of the right-hand fork, then loosen the axle **(see illustration)**.

5 Support the wheel, then withdraw the axle from the right-hand side and remove the wheel from between the forks **(see illustrations)**.

6 On 650 models, remove the speedometer drive unit from the left-hand side of the wheel and the axle spacer from the right-hand side, noting how they fit.

7 On 1100 models, remove the axle spacers from both sides of the wheel, noting how they fit **(see illustration)**.

Caution: Don't lay the wheel down and allow it to rest on the brake disc – the disc

15.4 Loosen the pinch bolt (A) then loosen the axle (B)

could become warped. Set the wheel on wood blocks so the wheel rim supports the weight of the wheel, or keep the wheel upright. Don't operate the front brake lever with the wheel removed.

8 Clean the axle and remove any corrosion using steel wool. Check the axle for straightness by rolling it on a flat surface such as a piece of plate glass. If available, place the axle in V-blocks and check for runout using a dial gauge. If the axle is bent, replace it with a new one.

9 Wipe any old grease off the bearing seals and check the condition of the seals and the wheel bearings (see Section 17).

10 Clean the axle spacer(s) and remove any corrosion with steel wool. The spacers should be perfectly smooth where they locate in the seals.

Installation

11 Apply lithium soap grease to the inside of the bearing seals.

12 On 650 models, install the speedometer drive unit in the left-hand side of the wheel and the axle spacer in the right-hand side.

13 On 1100 models, install the axle spacers in both sides of the wheel.

14 Apply a thin coat of lithium soap-based grease to the axle, then lift the wheel into position between the forks.

15 On 650 models, ensure that the speedometer drive unit is correctly aligned with the tab on the bottom of the fork.

16 On 1100 models, ensure that the wheel is fitted the right way round by checking the

15.5a Withdraw the axle . . .

15.5b . . . and lift out the wheel

15.7 Location of the axle spacer (arrowed)

15.21 Route the speedometer cable through the guide, where fitted

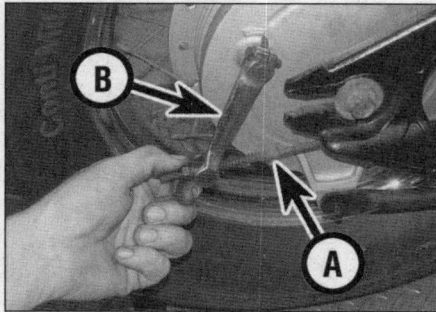

16.4 Unscrew the adjuster and disconnect the rod (A) from the arm (B)

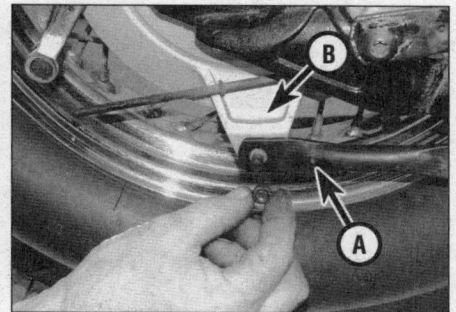

16.5a Disconnect the torque arm (A) from the brake backplate (B)

direction of rotation arrows on the tyre sidewalls **(see illustration 18.3)**.

17 Slide the axle in from the right-hand side, making sure that the spacers and speedometer drive unit (650 models) remain in place **(see illustration 15.5a)**.

18 Ensure that the axle aligns correctly with the threaded hole in the left-hand fork and tighten the axle to half the torque setting specified at the beginning of this Chapter, then take the bike off its auxiliary stand and compress the forks by pressing down on the handlebars to align the wheel and the suspension.

19 Tighten the axle to the full specified torque setting, then tighten the pinch bolt on the bottom of the right-hand fork slider to the specified torque setting **(see illustration 15.4)**.

20 Install the brake caliper(s), making sure

the pads sit squarely on each side of the discs (see Section 3).

21 On 650 models, reconnect the speedometer cable to the drive unit. Where fitted, ensure the cable is correctly routed through the guide on the mudguard **(see illustration)**.

22 Check the operation of the front brake before riding the motorcycle.

16 Rear wheel

650 models

Removal

1 Using an auxiliary stand, support the

motorcycle securely in an upright position with the rear wheel off the ground.

2 Remove the rear cylinder exhaust silencer (see Chapter 3).

3 Remove the rear mudguard (see Chapter 7).

4 Unscrew the rear brake adjuster nut and disconnect the brake rod from the brake arm **(see illustration)**. Note the position of the spring. Remove the brake rod pin from the brake arm if it is loose, thread it onto the brake rod and screw the adjuster nut onto the rod for safekeeping.

5 Remove the split pin from the bolt securing the brake torque arm to the brake backplate, then remove the nut and washer and disconnect the torque arm from the backplate **(see illustration)**. If necessary, remove the split pin from the bolt securing the brake torque arm to the bracket on the swingarm, then remove the nut and washer and lift off the torque arm **(see illustration)**. Note that the torque arm fits *behind* the bracket on the swingarm. Discard the split pins as new ones must be used.

6 Remove the bolts and washers securing the final drive unit, then undo the rear axle nut and remove the nut and washer **(see illustrations)**.

7 Draw the wheel back evenly until the axle rests in the cut-outs in the ends of the axle plates – in this position the driveshaft will have become disengaged from the final drive coupling on the back of the engine unit, and will be supported on a pin on the inside of the frame **(see illustrations)**.

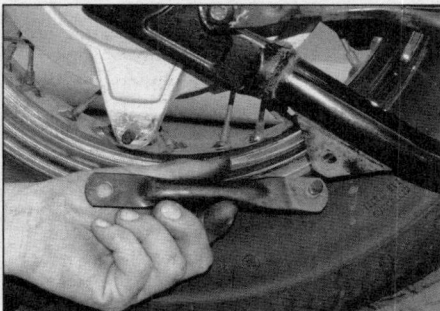

16.5b Remove the torque arm if necessary

16.6a Remove the bolts (arrowed) securing the final drive unit

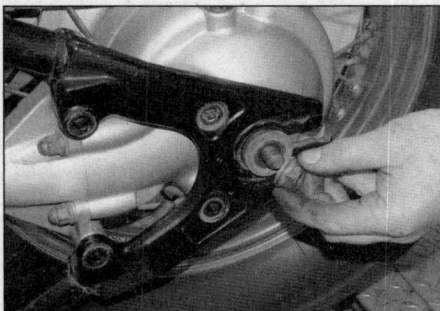

16.6b Remove the rear axle nut and washer

16.7a Draw the wheel back to the cut-outs (arrowed) in the axle plates

16.7b Driveshaft is supported by pin (arrowed) on the inside of the frame

16.8 Support the driveshaft and pull out the wheel

16.9a Lift off the final drive unit . . .

16.9b . . . and slide the long spacer off the axle

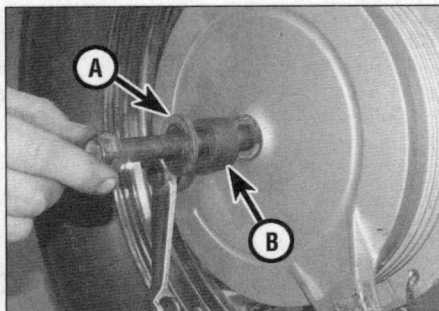

16.10 Note the location of the washer (A) and short spacer (B) on the axle

8 Support the driveshaft and lift the wheel out **(see illustration)**.

9 Lift off the final drive unit and slide the long spacer off the axle **(see illustrations)**. **Note:** *Stand the final drive unit the right way up – if it is turned upside down oil will leak out of the breather on the top of the unit.*

10 Pull out the axle and remove the washer and short spacer **(see illustration)**. Lift off the rear brake backplate **(see illustration 12.3)**.

11 Clean the axle and remove any corrosion using steel wool. Check the axle for straightness by rolling it on a flat surface such as a piece of plate glass. If available, place the axle in V-blocks and check for runout using a dial gauge. If the axle is bent, replace it with a new one.

12 Wipe any old grease off the wheel bearings and check the bearings (see Section 17).

16.18 Align the driveshaft with the final drive coupling

13 Clean the axle spacers and remove any corrosion with steel wool.

14 Lift out the final drive unit O-ring fitted to the hub and discard it as a new one must be used – if required, check the condition of the final drive unit (see Chapter 5, Section 14).

Installation

15 Apply lithium soap-based grease to the new final drive unit O-ring and fit it into the hub.

16 Apply a thin coat of lithium soap-based grease to the axle, then fit the washer and short spacer. Install the brake backplate, then insert the axle into the hub **(see illustration 16.10)**.

17 Slide the long spacer onto the axle, then fit the final drive unit **(see illustrations 16.9b and a)**.

18 Lift the wheel into position, ensuring the

driveshaft is aligned with the final drive coupling **(see illustration)**. Check that the short axle spacer is on the inside of the right-hand axle plate and the washer is on the outside of the plate. Rest the axle in the cut-outs in the ends of the axle plates and check that the driveshaft is supported on the pin on the inside of the frame **(see illustrations 16.7a and b)**. If accessible, pull the rubber shaft cover back over the driveshaft to make alignment with the final drive coupling easier.

19 Slide the wheel forwards carefully, ensuring the driveshaft engages with the final drive coupling – if necessary, turn the driveshaft to engage the splines. Push the wheel all the way in and check that the holes for the final drive unit bolts are aligned with the unit.

20 Install the final drive unit bolts and washers and tighten them to the torque setting specified at the beginning of this Chapter **(see illustration)**. If displaced, press the rubber shaft cover back into position.

21 Align the brake torque arm and backplate as noted on removal (see Step 5). Install the nuts finger-tight.

22 Install the axle washer and nut and tighten the nut to the specified torque setting.

23 Tighten the torque arm nuts to the specified torque setting and secure them with new split pins **(see illustrations)**.

24 If removed, install the brake rod pin in the brake arm. Fit the brake rod through the pin with the spring forward of the brake arm, then screw the adjuster nut onto the rod **(see**

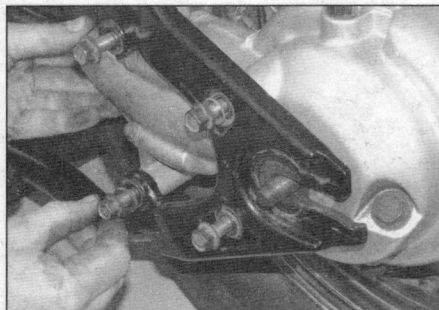

16.20 Install the final drive unit bolts and washers

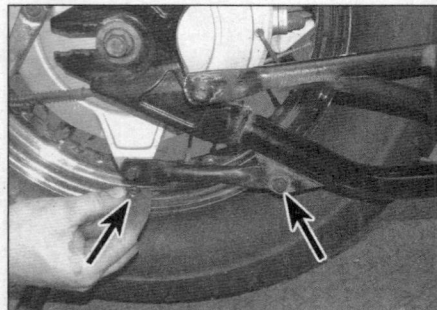

16.23a Tighten the torque arm nuts (arrowed) . . .

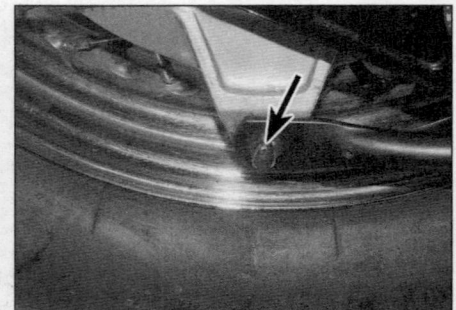

16.23b . . . and secure them with new split pins

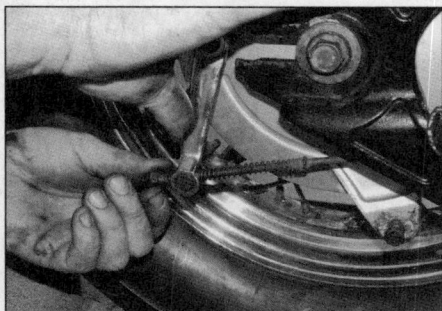
16.24 Screw the adjuster nut onto the brake rod

16.30 Undo the caliper bracket bolt

illustration). Adjust the rear brake (see Chapter 1, Section 12).
25 Install the remaining components in the reverse order of removal.

1100 models

Removal

26 Using an auxiliary stand, support the motorcycle securely in an upright position with the rear wheel off the ground.
27 Remove the exhaust silencer assembly

and the silencer bracket (see Chapter 3).
28 Displace the rear brake caliper (see Section 7).
29 Remove the rear mudguard (see Chapter 7).
30 Remove the bolt and washer securing the rear brake caliper bracket to the frame **(see illustration)**.
31 Remove the bolts and washers securing the final drive unit, then undo the rear axle nut and remove the nut and washer **(see illustrations)**.

32 Undo the nuts securing the axle clamp on the right-hand axle plate and remove the clamp, noting the punch mark on the clamp to aid installation **(see illustrations)**.
33 Draw the wheel back evenly until the axle rests in the cut-outs in the ends of the axle plates – in this position the driveshaft will have become disengaged from the final drive coupling on the back of the engine unit, and will be supported on a pin on the inside of the frame **(see illustrations 16.7a and b)**.
34 Support the driveshaft and lift the wheel out **(see illustration 16.8)**.
35 Lift off the final drive unit and slide the spacer off the axle **(see illustrations 16.9a and b)**. **Note:** *Stand the final drive unit the right way up – if it is turned upside down oil will leak out of the breather on the top of the unit.*
36 Pull out the axle and remove the brake caliper bracket and washer.
Caution: Don't lay the wheel down and allow it to rest on the brake disc – the disc could become warped. Set the wheel on wood blocks so the wheel rim supports the weight of the wheel, or keep the wheel upright. Don't operate the brake pedal with the wheel removed.

16.31a Remove the bolts (arrowed) securing the final drive unit

16.31b Remove the rear axle nut and washer

16.32a Undo the nuts (arrowed) . . .

16.32b . . . and remove the axle clamp – note the punch mark (arrowed)

16.37 Note the location of the spacer in the right-hand bearing seal

16.40 Fit spacer on the axle before installing the final drive unit

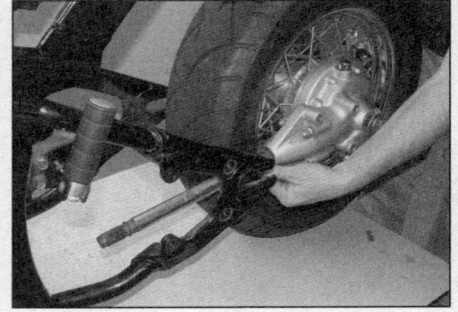

16.41a Support the driveshaft . . .

37 Follow the procedure in Steps 11 to 14, noting the spacer fitted in the bearing seal on the right-hand (brake disc) side of the hub (see illustration).

Installation

38 Apply lithium soap-based grease to the new final drive unit O-ring and fit it into the hub.
39 Apply a thin coat of lithium soap-based grease to the axle, then fit the washer and brake caliper bracket.
40 Insert the axle into the hub, then slide on the spacer and install the final drive unit (see illustration).
41 Lift the wheel into position, ensuring the driveshaft is aligned with the final drive coupling (see illustration). Check that the

washer on the right-hand end of the axle is on the inside of the right-hand axle plate next to the brake caliper bracket (see illustration). Rest the axle in the cut-outs in the ends of the axle plates and check that the driveshaft is supported on the pin on the inside of the frame. If accessible, pull the rubber shaft cover back over the driveshaft to make alignment with the final drive coupling easier.
42 Slide the wheel forwards carefully, ensuring the driveshaft engages with the final drive coupling – if necessary, turn the driveshaft to engage the splines. Support the caliper bracket so that it does not get trapped below the swingarm (see illustrations). Push the wheel all the way in and check that the holes for the final drive unit bolts are aligned with the unit. Install the caliper bracket bolt finger-tight.
43 Install the axle washer and nut finger-tight

– note that the outside edge of the washer is marked for identification (see illustration).
44 Install the axle clamp with the punch mark facing up, and tighten the clamp nuts finger-tight (see illustrations 16.32b and a).
45 Install the final drive unit bolts and washers and tighten them to the torque setting specified at the beginning of this Chapter (see illustration). If displaced, press the rubber shaft cover back into position.
46 Tighten the axle nut to the specified torque setting (see illustration 16.45).
47 Tighten the axle clamp nuts to the specified torque setting (see illustration).
48 Tighten the caliper bracket bolt to the specified torque setting (see illustration 16.30).
49 Install the remaining components in the reverse order of removal.

16.41b . . . and lift the wheel into position – ensure the washer (arrowed) is on the inside of the axle plate

16.42a Slide the wheel forwards carefully . . .

16.42b . . . supporting the caliper bracket

16.43 Note the mark on the axle washer

16.45 Tighten the final drive unit bolts (A), then tighten the axle nut (B)

16.47 Tighten the axle clamp nuts

17.3 Lever out the bearing seals as described

17.6a Drive out the bearings with a metal rod . . .

17 Wheel bearings

Caution: Once a wheel has been removed, don't lay it down and allow it to rest on the brake disc – the disc could become warped. Set the wheel on wood blocks so the wheel rim supports the weight of the wheel, or keep the wheel upright. Don't operate the front brake lever with the front wheel removed or the rear brake pedal (1100 models) with the rear wheel removed.

1 Follow the procedure in Chapter 1 to check the wheel bearings. If required, follow the appropriate procedure below to inspect and renew the bearings.

Front wheel bearings

2 Remove the front wheel and remove the axle spacer(s); on 650 models, remove the speedometer drive unit (see Section 15).

3 Lever out the bearing seals from both sides of the hub using a large, flat-bladed screwdriver and a piece of wood, taking care not to damage the hub **(see illustration)**. Discard the seals as new ones must be fitted on reassembly.

4 On 650 models, lift out the retainer and the tabbed speedometer drive plate from the left-hand side of the hub.

5 Check the condition of the bearings – see *Tools and Workshop Tips (Section 5)* in the *Reference* section.

6 Using a metal rod (preferably a brass punch) inserted through the centre of the bearing on one side of the hub, tap evenly around the inner race of the bearing on the other side to drive it from the hub **(see illustrations)**. The bearing spacer will fall free once the bearing is out of the hub. **Note:** *If it proves difficult to move the spacer aside sufficiently to gain purchase on the bearing's inner race, an alternative means of removal is to use a knife-edged puller inserted through the centre of the*

bearing to draw it outwards from the hub. Refer to 'Tools and Workshop Tips' (Section 5) in the Reference section for details.

7 Turn the wheel over and drive out the remaining bearing using the same procedure.

8 Thoroughly clean the hub area of the wheel with a suitable solvent and inspect the bearing seats for scoring and wear. If the seats are damaged, consult a Yamaha dealer before reassembling the wheel.

9 Install the new bearing into its seat in one side of the hub, with the marked or sealed side facing outwards. Using a bearing driver or a socket large enough to contact the outer

race of the bearing, drive it in until it's completely seated **(see illustration)**.

10 Turn the wheel over, install the bearing spacer and drive the other new bearing into place.

11 Lubricate the bearing seals with lithium soap-based grease and press them into the hub, using a bearing driver or a suitable socket – level the seals with the rim of the hub with a small block of wood **(see illustrations)**. **Note:** *On 650 models, don't forget to install the speedometer drive plate and retainer in the left-hand side of the hub before fitting the bearing seal.*

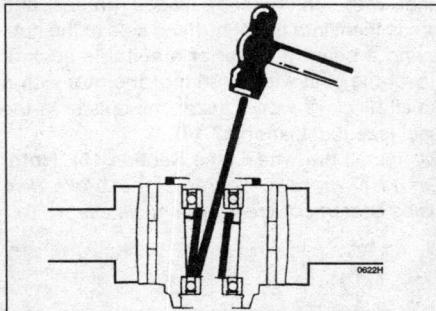
17.6b . . . locating it as shown

17.9 Install the new bearing with a suitable driver

17.11a Press in a new bearing seal . . .

17.11b . . . and level it with a block of wood

17.14 Remove the spacer then lever out the seal (arrowed)

17.16 Drive out the right-hand bearing as described

12 Degrease the brake disc(s) using acetone or brake system cleaner, then install the wheel (see Section 15).

Rear wheel bearings

13 Remove the rear wheel; lift off the final drive unit and pull out the axle (see Section 16).

14 On 1100 models, pull out the spacer fitted in the bearing seal on the right-hand (brake disc) side of the hub, then lever out the seal and discard it as a new one must be fitted (see illustration).

15 Check the condition of the bearings – see *Tools and Workshop Tips (Section 5)* in the *Reference* section.

16 Using a metal rod (preferably a brass punch) inserted through the left-hand side of the hub, tap evenly around the outer race of the right-hand bearing to drive it from the hub (see illustration). **Note:** *If it proves difficult to move the spacer aside sufficiently to gain purchase on the bearing's inner race, an alternative means of removal is to use a knife-edged puller inserted through the centre of the bearing to draw it outwards from the hub. Refer to 'Tools and Workshop Tips' (Section 5) in the Reference section for details.*

17 The bearing spacer (and bearing collar on 650 models) should fall free.

18 On 650 models, a single left-hand wheel bearing is fitted; on 1100 models, two left-hand bearings are fitted. Follow the procedure in Step 16 and drive out the bearing(s). Note that on 1100 models, only the outer bearing may be fitted with a seal.

19 Thoroughly clean the bearing seats with a suitable solvent and inspect the seats for scoring and wear. If a seat is damaged, consult a Yamaha dealer before reassembling the wheel.

20 Install the new bearing into its seat in the right-hand side of the hub, with the marked or sealed side facing outwards. Using a bearing

driver or a socket large enough to contact the outer race of the bearing, drive it in until it's completely seated.

21 On 650 models, install the bearing collar and the spacer. On 1100 models, install bearing spacer.

22 On 650 models, follow the procedure in Step 20 and install the new bearing into the left-hand side of the hub, with the marked or sealed side facing out. On 1100 models, follow the same procedure to install both new bearings into the hub, one at a time. Note that the outer bearing must be fitted with the seal facing out (see illustration).

23 On 1100 models, lubricate the bearing seal with lithium soap-based grease and press them into the right-hand side of the hub, using a bearing driver or a suitable socket. Level the seal with the rim of the hub with a small block of wood. Install the spacer in the seal (see illustration 17.14).

24 Install the wheel (see Section 16). **Note:** *On 1100 models, degrease the brake disc using acetone or brake system cleaner.*

18 Tyres

General information

1 The wire spoked wheels fitted to all models covered in this manual are designed to take tubed tyres fitted with an inner tube; do not fit tubeless tyres to these wheel rims. The 2003-on XVS1100A and XVS1100S models are fitted with cast alloy wheels designed for tubeless tyres.

2 Refer to *Daily (pre-ride) checks* at the beginning of this manual for tyre maintenance and pressures, and to the scheduled checks in Chapter 1 for wheel maintenance.

17.22 Sealed side (arrowed) of outer bearing must face outwards

Fitting new tyres

3 When selecting new tyres, refer to the tyre information at the beginning of this Chapter and in the Owners Manual. Ensure that front and rear tyre types are compatible, and of the correct size and correct speed rating (see illustration). If necessary seek advice from a Yamaha dealer or motorcycle tyre specialist.

4 It is recommended that tyres are fitted by a motorcycle tyre specialist rather than attempted in the home workshop. This is particularly relevant in the case of tubeless tyres because the force required to break the seal between the wheel rim and tyre bead is substantial, and is usually beyond the capabilities of an individual working with normal tyre levers. Additionally, the specialist will be able to balance the wheels after tyre fitting.

5 If a puncture occurs on a tubed tyre, replace the inner tube with a new one rather than attempting a repair. Make sure that the object which caused the puncture is removed from the tire. Note that punctured tubeless tyres can in some cases be repaired; seek the advice of a Yamaha dealer or a motorcycle tyre specialist concerning tyre repairs.

MANUFACTURERS NAME
OR BRAND NAME

LOAD AND PRESSURE
MARKING REQUIREMENT
(NOT APPLICABLE IN U.K.)

PATTERN CODE

ECE TYPE APPROVAL MARK
AND NUMBER

MAX SPEED

LOAD INDEX

SPEED SYMBOL

MANUFACTURERS NAME
OR BRAND NAME

A COMMERCIAL NAME
OR IDENTITY

REAR TYRE
FITMENT

NORTH AMERICAN TYRE
IDENTIFICATION NUMBER

VARIABLE BELT DENSITY
WHERE APPLICABLE

NORTH AMERICAN DEPT. OF
TRANSPORTATION
COMPLIANCE SYMBOL

TYRE CONSTRUCTION
DETAILS (NOT
REQUIRED IN U.K.)

COUNTRY OF MANUFACTURE

BIAS BELTED TYRE SIZE

SPEED SYMBOL

ARROW DENOTING
THE DIRECTION OF
WHEEL ROTATION

THE WORD TUBELESS
WHERE APPLICABLE

TYRE SIZE DESIGNATION

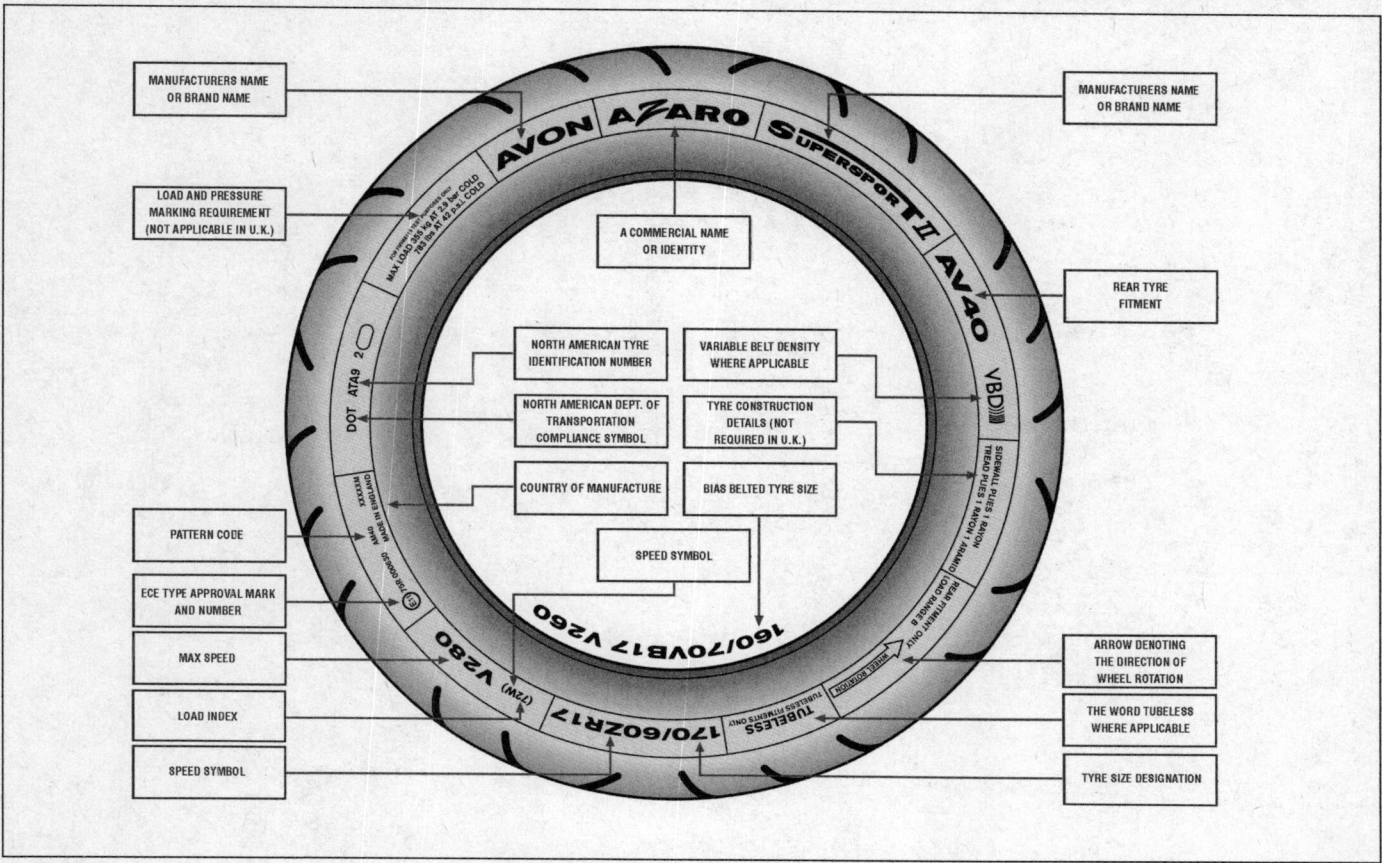

18.3 Common tyre sidewall markings

Notes

Chapter 7
Bodywork

Contents

Degrees of difficulty

Easy, suitable for novice with little experience	**Fairly easy,** suitable for beginner with some experience	**Fairly difficult,** suitable for competent DIY mechanic	**Difficult,** suitable for experienced DIY mechanic	**Very difficult,** suitable for expert DIY or professional

Specifications

Torque settings
Front mudguard mounting bolts . . . . 10 Nm
Rear mudguard mounting bolts (1100 models) . . . . 26 Nm
Rear mudguard bracket mounting bolts (650 models) . . . . 48 Nm
Rear mudguard to bracket bolts (650 models) . . . . 26 Nm

1 General information

1 This Chapter covers the procedures necessary to remove and install the body parts. Since many service and repair operations on these motorcycles require the removal of the body parts, the procedures are grouped here and referred to from other Chapters.
2 In the case of damage to covers and body panels other that those made of steel, it is usually necessary to replace the component with a new (or used) one. The material from which the body panels are made does not lend itself to conventional repair techniques. There are, however, some shops that specialise in 'plastic welding', so it may be worthwhile seeking the advice of one of these specialists before consigning an expensive component to the bin. Aftermarket repair kits are available for small areas of damage.
3 When attempting to remove a cover or body panel, first study it closely, noting any fasteners and associated fittings, to be sure of returning everything to its correct place on installation. Once the evident fasteners have been removed, try to withdraw the panel as described but DO NOT FORCE IT – if it will not release, check that all fasteners have been removed and try again. Where a panel engages another by means of tabs, be careful not to break the tab or its mating slot. Remember that a few moments of patience at this stage will save you a lot of money in replacing a broken component! To remove trim clips, push the centre into the body, then

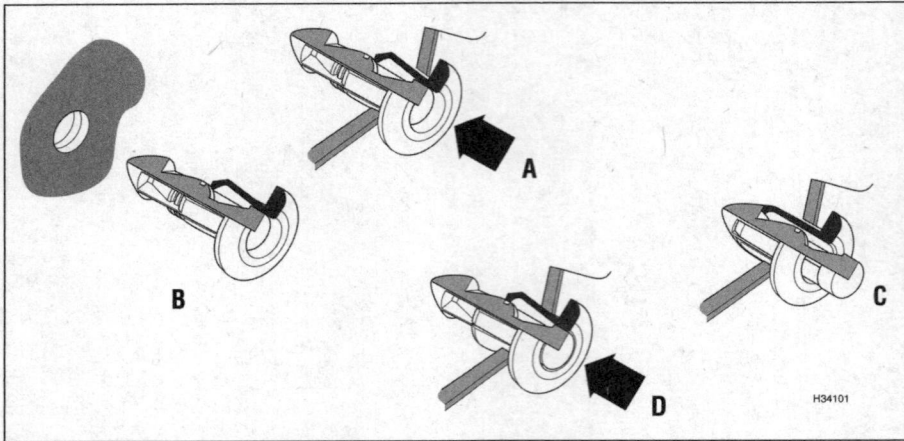

1.3 Trim clip removal and installation

*To remove the trim clip, push its centre pin (A) inwards and withdraw the clip from the panel (B)
To install the trim clip, depress the pawls and push the centre pin outwards so that the clip can
be inserted in the panel (C), then press the centre pin in level with the head of the clip to lock it
in place.*

draw the clip out of the panel **(see
illustration)**.

4 When installing a cover or body panel, first
study it closely, noting any fasteners and
associated fittings removed with it, to be sure
of returning everything to its correct place.
Check that all fasteners are in good condition,
including all trim clips and rubber mounts; any
of these that are faulty must be replaced with
new ones before the panel is reassembled.
Check also that all mounting brackets are

straight, and repair or renew them if
necessary before attempting to install the
panel. To install trim clips, first push the
centre back out so that it protrudes from the
top of the clip. Fit the clip into its hole, then
push the centre in so that it is flush with the
top of the clip.

5 Tighten the fasteners securely, but be
careful not to overtighten any of them or the
panel may break (not always immediately) due
to the uneven stress.

2 Seats

1 Undo the nut or bolt behind the passenger
seat, then lift up the seat and draw it
backwards noting how the tab at the front
locates **(see illustrations)**.
2 To remove the rider's seat, undo the bolts
securing the bracket to the rear mudguard,
then lift up the back of the seat and draw it
backwards noting how the tabs at the front
locate **(see illustrations)**.
3 Installation is the reverse of removal.

3 Toolbox cover

1 Unlock the cover, then carefully pull it
forward to release the tab on the top edge
and the hook on the lower front edge, and lift
it off the bike **(see illustrations)**.
2 Installation is the reverse of removal.
Ensure the cover is correctly installed before
locking it.

4 Battery cover

1 Remove the bolt securing the cover, then

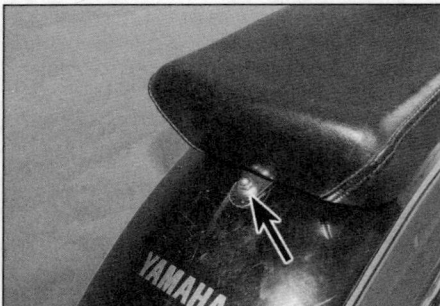

2.1a Undo the nut (arrowed) . . .

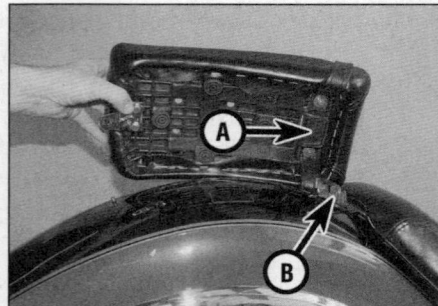

**2.1b . . . then draw back the passenger's
seat – tab (A) locates under bracket (B)**

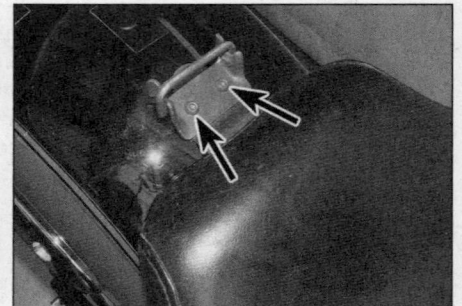

2.2a Undo the bolts (arrowed) . . .

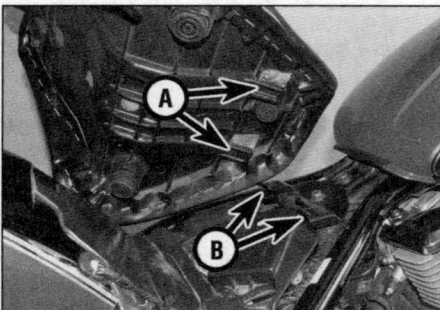

**2.2b . . . then draw back the rider's seat –
tabs (A) locate under bracket (B)**

3.1a Unlock the toolbox cover . . .

**3.1b . . . then release the tab (arrowed) to
remove it**

4.1a Undo the cover bolt – 650 models

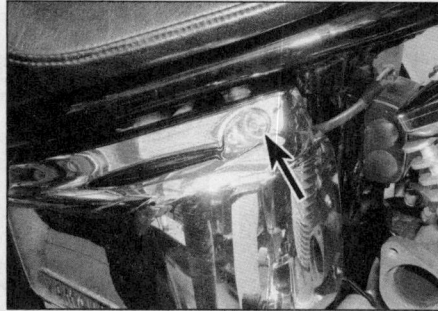

4.1b Undo the cover bolt – 1100 models . . .

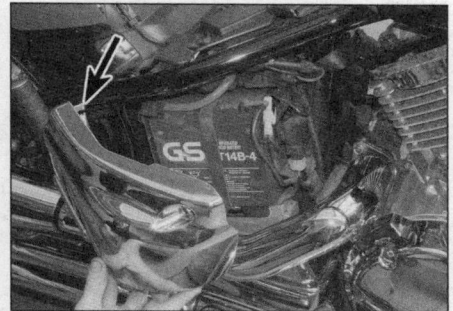

4.1c . . . and lift off the cover, noting the tab (arrowed)

carefully pull it forward to release the tabs and lift it off the bike **(see illustrations)**.

2 Installation is the reverse of removal. Ensure the cover is correctly installed before tightening the bolt.

5 Left-hand frame/transmission cover

1 The cover is secured by four bolts. Identify the bolts by the rubber bushes they pass through in the cover.

2 To remove the cover, undo the bolts and lift the cover off **(see illustrations)**.

3 Installation is the reverse of removal.

6 Right-hand frame cover

1 Remove the exhaust system (see Chapter 3).

2 On 650 models, note the matchmarks on the brake arm and the brake intermediate shaft, then remove the pinch bolt and pull the lever off the shaft **(see illustration)**. Undo the bolts that secure the cover and lift it off **(see illustration)**.

3 On 1100 models, remove the bolt securing

the cover, then carefully pull it forward to release the pegs and lift it off the bike **(see illustrations)**.

4 Installation is the reverse of removal.

7 ICU panel (1100 models)

1 Remove the seats (see Section 2). Disconnect the battery negative (-ve) lead (see Chapter 8).

2 The panel is secured to the frame by three trim clips – follow the procedure in Section 1

5.2a Undo the cover fixings – 1100 model shown . . .

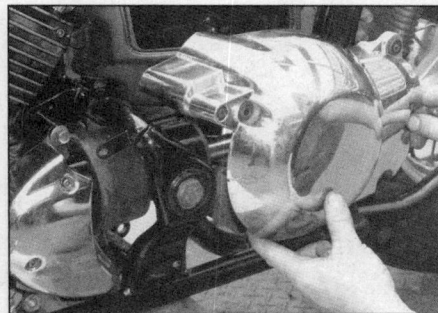

5.2b . . . and lift off the cover – 650 model shown

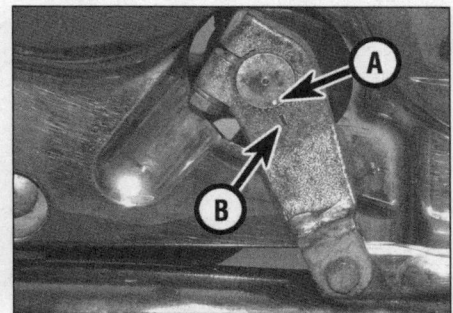

6.2a Note the marks (A) on the shaft and (B) on the brake arm

6.2b Undo the cover bolts (arrowed)

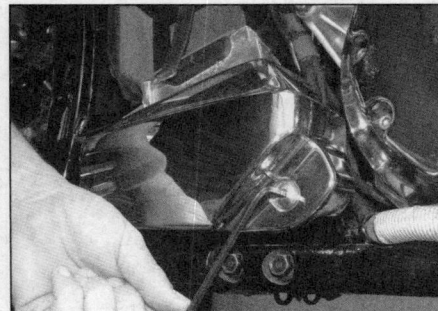

6.3a Remove the bolt . . .

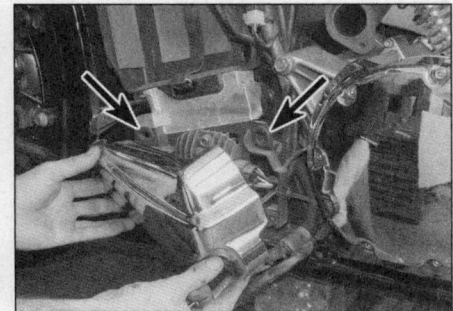

6.3b . . . then pull it off, noting the peg locations (arrowed)

7.2a Remove the trim clips (arrowed) . . .

7.2b . . . then lift up the ICU panel

to remove them, then displace the panel **(see illustrations)**. To remove the panel from the bike, disconnect the ICU wiring connectors.

3 Installation is the reverse of removal.

8 Toolbox and backing panel

1 Remove the toolbox cover (see Section 3).

650 models

2 Undo the two bolts securing the toolbox to the frame, then manoeuvre the toolbox out.
3 Installation is the reverse of removal.

1100 models

4 The toolbox is integral with the left-hand backing panel. To remove the panel, first remove the left-hand frame cover (see Section 5) and the ICU panel (see Section 7). Remove the battery (see Chapter 8).
5 On the left-hand side of the bike, study the location of the components fixed to the backing panel and, if necessary, make a sketch to aid installation.
6 Unclip the wiring loom from the backing panel and pull the wiring connectors out of the cover **(see illustration)**. Trace the wiring from the fuel pump and disconnect it at the connector. Position the wiring loom clear of the panel.

7 Undo the screws securing the fuel hose guide plate and remove the plate **(see illustration)**. Pull the fuel pump off and secure it clear of the panel **(see illustration)**.
8 Unclip the immobiliser wiring from the panel **(see illustration)**.
9 Unclip the fusebox from the panel **(see illustration)**.
10 Unclip the fuel filter from the top of the panel **(see illustration)**.
11 Undo the bolts securing the bracket for the left-hand frame cover and remove the bracket, then undo the bolts securing the left-hand backing panel, noting that one bolt is located on the right-hand side behind the

8.6 Location of the wiring loom connectors

8.7a Undo the screws (arrowed)

8.7b Pull the fuel pump off the tabs (arrowed)

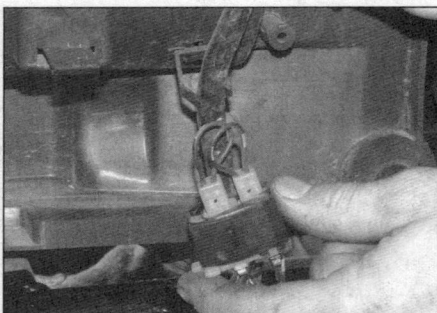

8.8 Unclip the immobiliser wiring

8.9 Unclip the fusebox

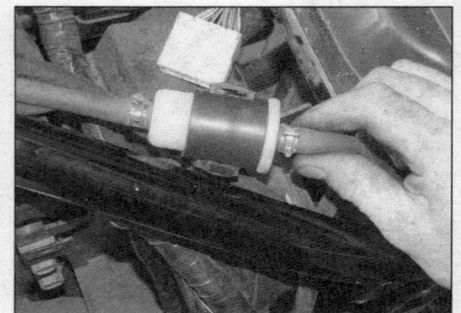

8.10 Unclip the fuel filter

8.11a Undo the bolts and remove the bracket

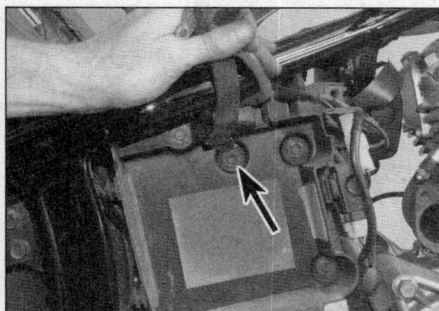
8.11b Note the bolt (arrowed) behind the battery position

8.11c Lift off the backing panel

battery position **(see illustrations)**. Lift off the backing panel **(see illustration)**.
12 Installation is the reverse of removal. Make sure all wires and hoses are correctly routed and connected, and secured by any clips or ties.

9 Battery tray and backing panel

1 Remove the battery cover (see Section 4).
2 Remove the battery (see Chapter 8).
3 Remove the right-hand frame cover (see Section 6).

650 models

4 Lift out the panel at the back of the battery housing **(see illustration)**.

5 Study the location of the components fixed to the backing panel and, if necessary, make a sketch to aid installation **(see illustration)**.
6 Unclip the relay assembly, fusebox, turn signal relay, starter relay and carburettor heater relay from the panel (refer to Chapter 8 for individual component location).
7 Remove the screws securing the ICU to the panel, then disconnect the ICU wiring connectors and lift it off.
8 Undo the bolts securing the backing panel to the frame. Check that all the wiring is clear of the panel, then lift the panel off.
9 Installation is the reverse of removal. Make sure all wires are correctly routed and connected.

1100 models

10 Displace the ICU panel (see Section 7).

11 Unclip the starter relay from the back of the backing panel **(see illustration)**.
12 Disconnect the regulator/rectifier wiring connector **(see illustration)**. Position the regulator/rectifier connector and the alarm wiring loom clear of the panel.
13 Undo the bolts securing the backing panel to the frame, then lift the panel off **(see illustration)**.
14 Installation is the reverse of removal. Make sure all wires are correctly routed and connected.

10 Steering head panels

1 Remove the fuel tank (see Chapter 3).
2 Remove the bolts at the front securing the panels to the steering head **(see illustration)**.

9.4 Lift out the panel

9.5 Study the location of the electrical components fixed to the panel

9.11 Displace the starter relay

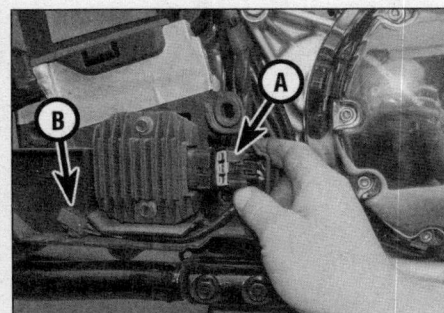
9.12 Regulator/rectifier (A) and alarm (B) wiring connectors

9.13 Lift off the backing panel

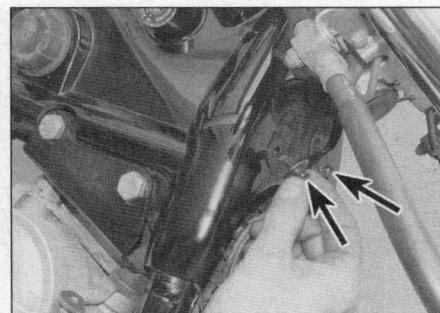
10.2 Remove the bolts (arrowed) . . .

10.3 . . . and the tank rubbers

10.4 Note how the panels lock together on the top edge

11.2 Release the brake hose clips from the front mudguard

3 Pull off the tank mounting rubbers **(see illustration)**.
4 The panels are clipped together on the top edge – ease them apart carefully and lift them off **(see illustration)**.
5 Installation is the reverse of removal. Renew the tank mounting rubbers if they are damaged or deteriorated.

11 Front mudguard

1 Remove the front wheel (see Chapter 6).
2 If not already done, remove the bolt(s) securing the brake hose clip(s) to the mudguard bracket **(see illustration)**.

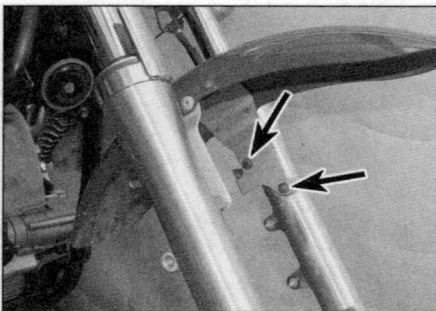

11.3a Undo the bolts (arrowed) . . .

3 Undo the bolts securing the mudguard to the fork sliders and lift the mudguard off **(see illustrations)**.
4 Installation is the reverse of removal. Tighten the mudguard mounting bolts to the torque setting specified at the beginning of this Chapter.

12 Rear mudguard

1 Remove the seats (see Section 2).

650 models

2 Remove the battery cover (see Section 4). Trace the tail light/turn signal light wiring to

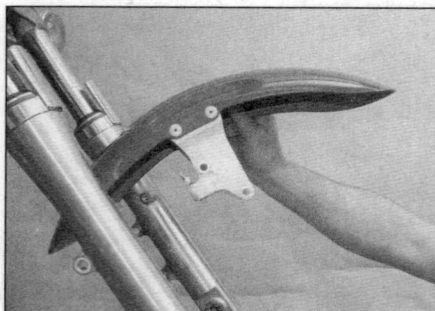

11.3b . . . and lift off the mudguard

the connector and disconnect it **(see illustration)**.
3 Loosen the bolts securing the mudguard brackets to the frame, then support the mudguard and remove the bolts. Lift off the mudguard assembly **(see illustrations)**.
4 To remove the mudguard brackets from the mudguard on XVS650A and S models, undo the bolts securing the brackets and lift them off.
5 To remove the mudguard brackets from the mudguard on XVS650 models, first displace the tail light assembly from the mudguard to access the turn signal wiring connectors (see Chapter 8). Disconnect the turn signal connectors and label the wiring to aid installation. Remove the bolts securing the brackets to the mudguard and lift off the brackets together with the turn signals. Take care not to snag the turn signal wiring as it passes through the hole in the mudguard.
6 If required, the tail light/turn signal assembly on XVS650A and S models can be separated from the mudguard (see Chapter 8).
7 Installation is the reverse of removal. Tighten the mounting bolts to the torque settings specified at the beginning of this Chapter. Check the operation of the brake/tail light and rear turn signals.

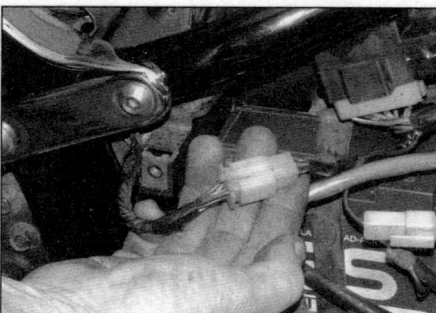

12.2 Disconnect the tail light/turn signal light connector – 650 models

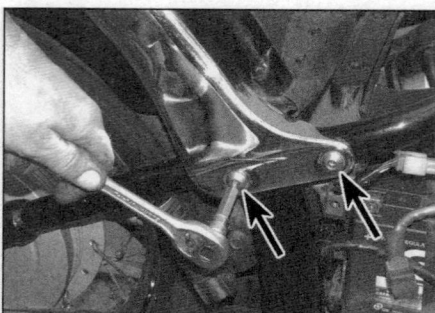

12.3a Mudguard is secured by two bolts (arrowed) on each side

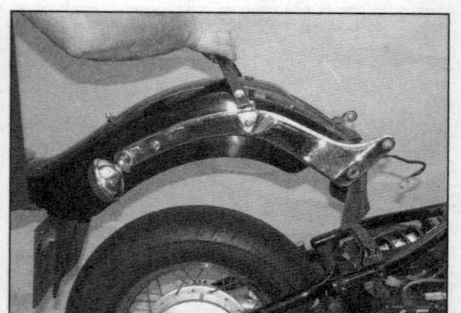

12.3b Lift off the mudguard assembly

12.10 Disconnect the tail light/turn signal light connector – 1100 models

12.11 Remove the mudguard trim clip

12.12 Remove the mudguard bolts and trim

1100 models

8 Disconnect the battery negative (-ve) lead (see Chapter 8).
9 Displace the ICU panel (see Section 7).
10 Trace the tail light/turn signal light wiring to the connector and disconnect it (see illustration).
11 Follow the procedure in Section 1 and remove the trim clip from the centre of the mudguard (see illustration).
12 Undo the bolts securing the mudguard to the bracket and lift off the trim together with

the bolts (see illustration). Note which way round the trim fits and mark it if necessary to aid installation.
13 Lift off the mudguard assembly (see illustration).
14 If required, the tail light/turn signal assembly can be separated from the mudguard (see Chapter 8).
15 Installation is the reverse of removal. Tighten the mudguard mounting bolts to the torque setting specified at the beginning of this Chapter. Check the operation of the brake/tail light and rear turn signals.

13 Mirrors

1 Loosen the locknut on the bottom of the mirror stem, then unscrew the mirror from the bracket – note that the right-hand mirror (attached to the front brake master cylinder) unscrews clockwise (see illustrations).
2 Installation is the reverse of removal. Hold the mirror in the desired position and tighten the locknut securely.

12.13 Lift off the mudguard assembly

13.1a Mirror is secured by locknut (arrowed)

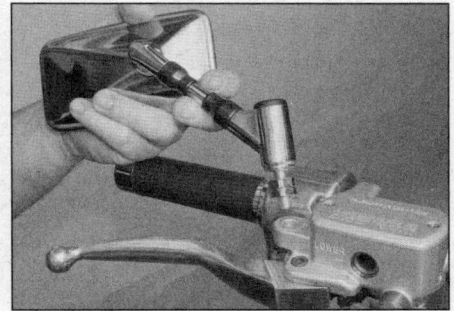
13.1b Right-hand mirror unscrews clockwise

Chapter 8
Electrical system

Contents

Degrees of difficulty

Easy, suitable for novice with little experience	**Fairly easy,** suitable for beginner with some experience	**Fairly difficult,** suitable for competent DIY mechanic	**Difficult,** suitable for experienced DIY mechanic	**Very difficult,** suitable for expert DIY or professional

Specifications

Battery
650 models
  Capacity 12V, 10Ah
  Type GT12B-4
1100 models
  Capacity 12V, 12Ah
  Type GT14B-4
Charge condition (all models)
  Fully charged 12.8V
  Discharged 12.0V
  Charging time . . . . 6.5 hours

Fuses

Main fuse	30A
Headlight fuse	15A
Ignition fuse	10A
Signal circuit fuse	10A
Carburettor heater fuse	15A
Back-up fuse	5A
Park fuse	10A

Bulb specifications (European models)

Headlight	60/55W
Sidelight	4W
Tail/brake lights	5/21W
Turn signals	21W
Speedometer light	1.4W
Oil level warning light (1100 models)	1.7W
Engine warning light	1.7W
Turn signal indicator	
650 models (1997 to 2000)	3W
All other models	1.7W
Neutral indicator	
650 models (1997 to 2000)	3W
All other models	1.7W
High beam indicator	1.7W

Bulb specifications (US models)

Headlight	60/55W
Tail/brake lights	8/27W
Turn signals (650 models)	27W
Front turn signals/running lights (1100 models)	27/8W
Rear turn signals (1100 models)	27W
Speedometer light	1.4W
Oil level warning light (1100 models)	1.7W
Engine warning light	1.7W
Turn signal indicator	1.7W
Neutral indicator	1.7W
High beam indicator	1.7W

Charging system

Alternator stator coil resistance	
650 models	0.50 to 0.62 ohms
1100 models	0.36 to 0.44 ohms
Regulated voltage output	14 volts at 5000 rpm
Regulated voltage output (no load)	14.1 to 14.9 V

Carburettor heater

Resistance	6 to 12 ohms at 20°C

EVAP system

Solenoid resistance	28 to 34 ohms at 20°C

Fuel pump

Resistance	1.6 to 2.2 ohms at 20°C

Starter motor

Brush length	
Standard	12.5 mm
Service limit	
650 models	4.0 mm
1100 models	5.0 mm
Commutator diameter	
Standard	28 mm
Service limit	27 mm
Mica undercut	0.7 mm

Torque specifications

Alternator stator bolts	
650 models	7 Nm
1100 models	10 Nm
Pick-up coil bolts	7 Nm
Starter motor mounting bolts	10 Nm

1 General information

All models have a 12 volt electrical system charged by a three-phase alternator with a separate regulator/rectifier.

The regulator maintains the charging system output within the specified range to prevent overcharging, and the rectifier converts the ac (alternating current) output of the alternator to dc (direct current) to power the lights and other components and to charge the battery. The alternator rotor is mounted on the left-hand end of the crankshaft.

The starting system includes the starter motor, the battery, the starter relay, the engine kill switch and the ignition (main) switch. The starter cut-out relay is part of the safety system which allows the starter motor to operate only if the transmission is in neutral (neutral switch on) or, if the transmission is in gear with the clutch lever pulled into the handlebar and the sidestand up. The starter motor is mounted on the front of the crankcase.

Note: *Keep in mind that electrical parts, once purchased, cannot be returned. To avoid unnecessary expense, make very sure the faulty component has been positively identified before buying a replacement part.*

2 Electrical system fault finding

⚠️ **Warning: To prevent the risk of short circuits, the ignition (main) switch must always be OFF and the battery negative (–ve) terminal should be disconnected before any of the bike's other electrical components are disturbed. Don't forget to reconnect the terminal securely once work** *is finished or if battery power is needed for circuit testing.*

1 A typical electrical circuit consists of an electrical component, the switches, relays, etc. related to that component and the wiring and connectors that link the component to both the battery and the frame. To aid in locating a problem in any electrical circuit, refer to *Wiring Diagrams* at the end of this Chapter.

2 Before tackling any troublesome electrical circuit, first study the wiring diagram (see end of this Chapter) thoroughly to get a complete picture of what makes up that individual circuit. Faults can often be tracked down by noting if other components related to that circuit are operating properly or not. If several components or circuits fail at one time, it may be that the fault lies in the fuse or earth (ground) connection, as several circuits are often routed through the same fuse and earth (ground) connections.

3 Electrical problems often stem from simple causes, such as loose or corroded connections or a blown fuse. Prior to any electrical fault finding, always check the condition of the fuse, wires and connections in the problem circuit visually. Intermittent failures can be especially frustrating, since you cannot always duplicate the failure when it is convenient to do a test. In such situations, it is good practice to clean all connections and terminals in the affected circuit, whether or not they appear to be good, and ensure that the connectors fit together tightly.

4 If testing instruments are going to be used, study the wiring diagram to plan where you will make the necessary connections in order to pinpoint the trouble spot accurately.

5 The basic tools needed for electrical fault finding include a battery and bulb test circuit, a continuity tester, a test light, and jumper wires. A multimeter capable of reading volts, ohms and amps is also very useful as an alternative to the above, and is necessary for performing more extensive tests and checks.

HAYNES HiNT *Refer to Fault Finding Equipment in the Reference section for details of how to use electrical test equipment.*

3 Battery inspection and maintenance

Caution: Be extremely careful when handling or working around the battery. The electrolyte is very caustic and an explosive gas (hydrogen) is given off when the battery is charging.

1 Remove the battery cover (see Chapter 7).

2 Unscrew the negative (–ve) terminal bolt first and disconnect the lead from the battery (see illustration). Lift up the insulating cover to access the positive (+ve) terminal, then unscrew the bolt and disconnect the lead. Release the battery strap and remove the battery from the bike (see illustration).

3 The battery fitted on all models is of the maintenance-free (sealed) type, therefore requiring no specific maintenance. Do not attempt to open the battery as resulting damage will mean it will be unfit for further use. However, the following checks should still be regularly performed.

4 Check that the battery terminals and leads are tight and clean. If corrosion is evident, unscrew the terminal bolts and disconnect the leads from the battery, disconnecting the negative (–ve) terminal first. Clean the terminals and lead ends with a wire brush or penknife and steel wool. Reconnect the leads, connecting the negative (–ve) terminal last, and apply a thin coat of petroleum jelly to the connections to slow further corrosion.

5 The battery case should be kept clean to prevent current leakage, which can discharge the battery over a period of time (especially when it sits unused). Remove the battery from the motorcycle and wash the outside of the

3.2a Disconnect the negative (-ve) terminal (A) first, then the positive (+ve) terminal (B)

3.2b Release the strap and lift out the battery

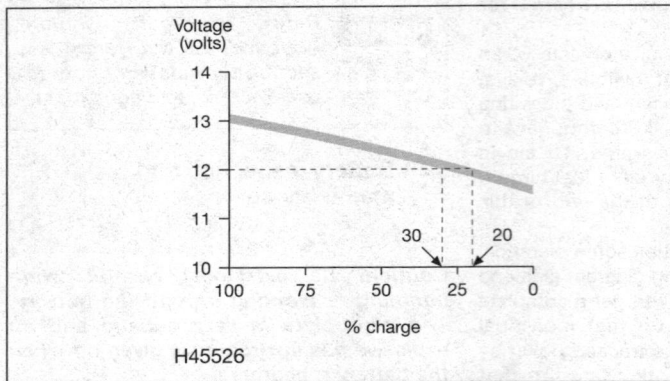

Voltage (volts)

14
13
12
11
10

100 75 50 25 0

% charge

30   20

H45526

3.8 Measure the voltage to assess the condition of the battery from the chart

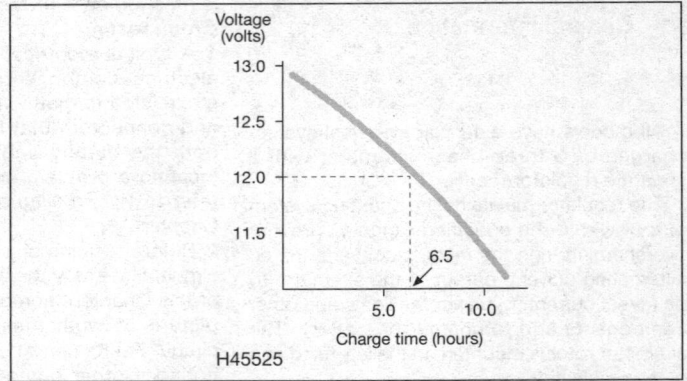

Voltage (volts)

13.0
12.5
12.0
11.5

5.0   10.0

Charge time (hours)

6.5

H45525

4.2 Measure the voltage to determine the charging time required

case with a solution of baking soda and water. Rinse the battery thoroughly, then dry it.

6 Look for cracks in the case and renew the battery if any are found. If acid has been spilled on the frame or battery box, neutralise it with a baking soda and water solution, then dry it thoroughly.

7 If the motorcycle sits unused for long periods of time, disconnect the leads from the battery terminals, negative (–ve) terminal first. Refer to Section 4 and charge the battery once every month to six weeks.

8 The condition of the battery can be assessed by measuring the voltage present at the battery terminals, and comparing the figure against the chart **(see illustration)**. Connect the voltmeter positive (+ve) probe to the battery positive (+ve) terminal, and the negative (–ve) probe to the battery negative (–ve) terminal. When fully charged, there should be 12.8 volts (or more) present. If the voltage falls below 12.0 volts the battery must be removed, disconnecting the negative (–ve) terminal first, and recharged as described in Section 4.

9 On installation, ensure the battery terminals and lead ends are clean, then reconnect the leads, connecting the positive (+ve) terminal first.

10 Install the battery cover (see Chapter 7).

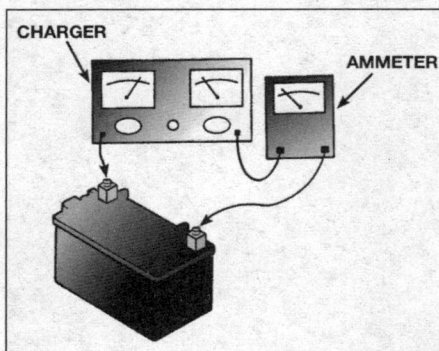

CHARGER

AMMETER

4.4 If the charger has no built-in ammeter, connect one in series as shown. DO NOT connect the ammeter between the battery terminals or it will be ruined

HAYNES HiNT *Battery corrosion can be kept to a minimum by applying a layer of petroleum jelly to the terminals after the cables have been connected.*

4 Battery charging

Caution: Be extremely careful when handling or working around the battery. The electrolyte is very caustic and an explosive gas (hydrogen) is given off when the battery is charging.

1 Ensure the charger is suitable for charging a 12V battery.

2 Remove the battery from the motorcycle (see Section 3). If not already done, refer to Section 3, Step 8, and check the open circuit voltage of the battery. Refer to the chart **(see illustration)** and read off the charging time required according to the voltage reading taken.

3 Connect the charger to the battery BEFORE switching the charger ON. Make sure that the positive (+ve) lead on the charger is connected to the positive (+ve) terminal on the battery, and the negative (–ve) lead is connected to the negative (–ve) terminal. The battery should be charged for the specified time, or until the voltage across the terminals reaches 12.8V (allow the battery to stabilise for 30 minutes after charging, before taking a voltage reading). Exceeding this time can cause the battery to overheat, buckling the plates and rendering it useless.

4 Few owners will have access to an expensive current controlled charger, so if a normal domestic charger is used check that after a possible initial peak, the charge rate falls to a safe level **(see illustration)**. If the battery becomes hot during charging **STOP**.

Further charging will cause damage. Refer to the charge rate and time marked on the battery – normally the charge rate is 1/10 of its ampere-hour capacity, thus a 12 Ah battery would be charged at a rate of 1.2 amps. **Note:** *In emergencies the battery can be charged at a higher rate of around 3.0 amps for a period of 1 hour. However, this is not recommended and the low amp charge is by far the safer method of charging the battery.*

5 If the recharged battery discharges rapidly when left disconnected it is likely that an internal short caused by physical damage or sulphation has occurred. A new battery will be required. A sound battery will tend to lose its charge at about 1% per day.

6 Install the battery (see Section 3).

7 If the motorcycle sits unused for long periods of time, charge the battery once every month to six weeks and leave it disconnected. Alternatively, remove the battery and store it in a cool, dry place.

5 Fuses

1 The electrical system is protected by fuses of different ratings. All except the main fuse are housed in the fusebox. On 650 models, the fusebox is located behind the battery cover **(see illustration)**. On 1100 models, the

5.1a Location of the fusebox – 650 models

5.1b Location of the fusebox – 1100 models

5.2a Location of the main fuse/starter relay – 650 models

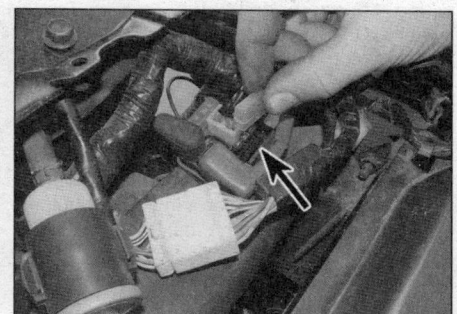

5.2b Location of the main fuse/starter relay – 1100 models

fusebox is located behind the toolbox cover (see illustration).

2 The main fuse is integral with the starter relay. On 650 models, the relay is located behind the battery cover (see illustration). On 1100 models, the relay is located underneath the ICU panel beneath the rider's seat (see illustration).

3 To check the fuses, follow the appropriate procedure in Chapter 7 to access the fusebox or relay. Unclip the fusebox lid or pull the plastic cover off the main fuse (see illustration).

4 The fuses can be removed and checked visually. If you can't pull the fuse out with your fingertips, use a suitable pair of pliers. A blown fuse is easily identified by a break in the element (see illustration), or the fuse can be tested for continuity using an ohmmeter or continuity tester – if there is no continuity, it has blown. Each fuse is clearly marked with its rating and must only be replaced by a fuse of the same rating. Spare fuses are housed in the fusebox, and a spare main fuse is housed in the starter relay. If a spare fuse is used, always replace it with a new one so that a spare of each rating is carried on the bike at all times.

⚠️ Warning: Never put in a fuse of a higher rating or bridge the terminals with any other substitute, however temporary it may be. Serious damage may be done to the circuit, or a fire may start.

5 If a fuse blows, be sure to check the wiring circuit very carefully for evidence of a short-circuit. Look for bare wires and chafed, melted or burned insulation. If the fuse is renewed before the cause is located, the new fuse will blow immediately.

5.3 Unclip the fusebox lid

6 Occasionally a fuse will blow or cause an open-circuit for no obvious reason. Corrosion of the fuse ends and fusebox terminals may occur and cause poor fuse contact. If this happens, remove the corrosion with a penknife or steel wool, then spray the fuse end and terminals with electrical contact cleaner.

6 Lighting system check

Note: If the ignition is switched ON for any checks, remember to switch it OFF again before proceeding further or removing any electrical component from the system.

1 The battery provides power for operation of the headlight, tail light, brake light, turn signals and speedometer lights. If none of the lights operate, always check battery condition before proceeding. Low battery voltage indicates either a faulty battery or a defective charging system. Refer to Section 3 for battery checks and Section 31 for charging system tests. Also, check the condition of the fuses (see Section 5). When checking for a blown filament in a bulb, it is advisable to back up a visual check with a continuity test of the filament as it is not always apparent that a bulb has blown. When testing for continuity, remember that on tail light and turn signal bulbs it is often the metal body of the bulb that is the earth or ground.

Headlight

2 If the headlight fails to work, check the bulb first (see Section 7) and then the headlight fuse. Next disconnect the headlight wiring

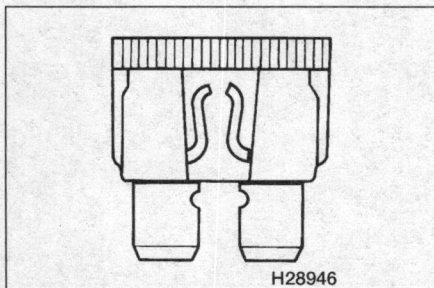

5.4 A blown fuse can be identified by a break in the element

H28946

connector and check for battery voltage on the supply side of the wiring connector with a test light or multimeter. Refer to Wiring Diagrams at the end of this Chapter, then connect the negative probe of the multimeter to earth (ground) and the positive probe to first the high beam connector terminal and then the low beam connector terminal with the ignition (main) switch ON. Where a light switch is fitted, this must be switched ON. Don't forget to select either high or low beam at the handlebar switch while conducting this test.

3 If no voltage is indicated at either terminal, check the wiring between the headlight connector, light switches and the ignition switch, then check the switches themselves. On later models, check the headlight relay.

4 If voltage is indicated, check for continuity between the black wire connector terminal and earth (ground). If there is no continuity, check the earth (ground) circuit for an open or poor connection.

Sidelight (European models)

5 If the sidelight fails to work, check the bulb and the bulb terminals first (see Section 7). Next check for battery voltage at the blue/red wire terminal on the supply side of the sidelight wiring connector, with the ignition (main) switch and, where fitted, the light switch ON.

6 If no voltage is indicated, check the wiring between the sidelight, the light switch (where fitted) and the ignition switch, then check the switches themselves.

7 If voltage is indicated, check for continuity between the wiring connector terminals on the sidelight side of the wiring connector and the corresponding terminals in the bulbholder; no continuity indicates a break in the circuit. If continuity is present, check for continuity between the black wire terminal and earth (ground). If there is no continuity, check the earth (ground) circuit for a broken or poor connection.

Running lights (US models)

Note: On US models, the front turn signals also function as the running lights.

8 If the running light fails to work, check the bulb and the bulb terminals first (see Section 12) and then the headlight fuse. Next check for battery voltage at the blue wire terminal on the supply side of the running light

wiring connector, with the ignition (main) switch ON.

9 If no voltage is indicated, check the wiring between the running light and the ignition switch, then check the switch itself.

10 If voltage is indicated, check for continuity between the wiring connector terminals on the position light side of the wiring connector and the corresponding terminals in the bulbholder; no continuity indicates a break in the circuit. If continuity is present, check for continuity between the black wire terminal and earth (ground). If there is no continuity, check the earth (ground) circuit for a broken or poor connection.

Tail light

11 If the tail light fails to work, check the bulb and the bulb terminals first (see Section 9). Note that on some models, the tail light is protected by the headlight fuse – refer to *Wiring Diagrams* at the end of this Chapter. Next check for battery voltage at the blue/red wire terminal on the supply side of the tail light wiring connector, with the ignition (main) switch and, where fitted, the light switch ON.

12 If no voltage is indicated, check the wiring between the tail light, the light switch (where fitted) and the ignition switch, then check the switches themselves.

13 If voltage is indicated, check for continuity between the wiring connector terminals on the tail light side of the wiring connector and the corresponding terminals in the bulbholder; no continuity indicates a break in the circuit. If continuity is present, check for continuity between the black wire terminal and earth

(ground). If there is no continuity, check the earth (ground) circuit for a broken or poor connection.

Brake light

14 If the brake light fails to work, check the bulb and the bulb terminals first (see Section 9) and then the turn signal system fuse. Next check for battery voltage at the yellow wire terminal on the supply side of the tail light wiring connector, with the ignition (main) switch ON and the brake lever or pedal applied.

15 If no voltage is indicated, check the brake light switches (see Section 11), then the wiring between the tail light unit and the switches.

16 If voltage is indicated, check for continuity between the black wire terminal and earth (ground). If there is no continuity, check the earth (ground) circuit for a broken or poor connection.

Turn signal lights

17 If one light fails to work, check the bulb and the bulb terminals (see Section 12), then the wiring connectors. If none of the turn signals work, first check the turn signal system fuse.

18 If the fuse is good, check the turn signal circuit and relay (see Section 14).

Speedometer lights

19 If the light fails to work, first check the bulb and the bulbholder terminals (see Section 15).

20 If the bulb(s) is OK, check for battery voltage at the blue wire terminal on the supply

side of the wiring connector, with the ignition (main) switch and, where fitted, the light switch ON.

21 If no voltage is indicated, refer to *Wiring Diagrams* at the end of this Chapter and check the lighting circuit.

7   Headlight bulb and sidelight bulb

Note: *The headlight bulb is of the quartz-halogen type. Do not touch the bulb glass as skin acids will shorten the bulb's service life. If the bulb is accidentally touched, it should be wiped carefully when cold with a rag soaked in methylated spirit and dried before fitting.*

⚠ **Warning: Allow the headlight bulb time to cool before removing it if the headlight has just been on.**

Headlight bulb

1 Remove the headlight rim retaining bolts and pull the rim and headlight assembly out of the shell, noting how the tab on the top of the rim locates **(see illustrations)**.

2 Disconnect the wiring connector from the back of the headlight bulb **(see illustration)**. Where fitted, pull back the boot on the sidelight bulbholder and twist the bulbholder anti-clockwise to remove it **(see illustration 7.10a)**.

3 Remove the rubber cover from the back of the headlight bulb, noting how it fits **(see illustration)**.

4 Twist the bulbholder anti-clockwise and remove the bulb **(see illustrations)**.

7.1a Remove the retaining bolts (arrowed) . . .

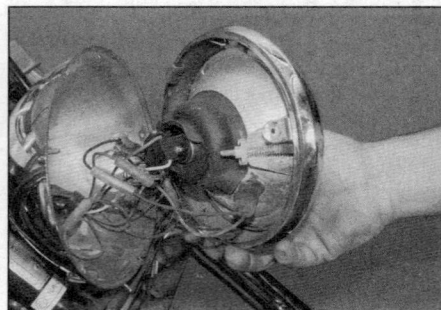
7.1b . . . and pull the assembly out of the shell

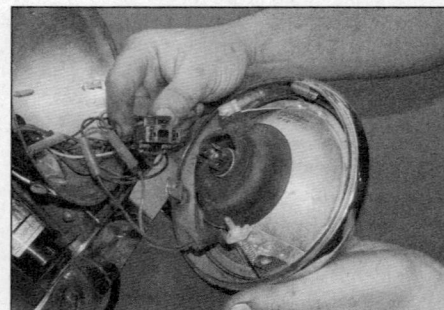
7.2 Pull off the headlight bulb connector

7.3 Remove the rubber cover

7.4a Twist the headlight bulbholder anti-clockwise . . .

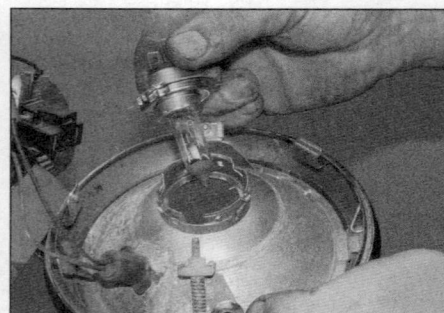
7.4b . . . and remove the bulb

5 Fit the new bulb, bearing in mind the information in the **Note** above. Make sure the tabs on the bulbholder fit correctly in the slots in the reflector housing, then twist the bulb clockwise to secure it in position.

6 Install the rubber cover. Check that the contacts inside the wiring connector are clean and free from corrosion, then connect the wiring connector. Install the sidelight bulbholder into its socket.

7 Fit the headlight assembly into the headlight shell, ensuring the tab on the top of the rim is correctly located in the shell **(see illustration)**. Secure the assembly with the retaining bolts

8 Check the operation of the headlight.

HAYNES HiNT

Always use a paper towel or dry cloth when handling new bulbs to prevent injury if the bulb should break and to increase bulb life.

Sidelight bulb – European models

9 Remove the headlight assembly from the shell and disconnect the headlight wiring connector (see Steps 1 and 2).

10 Pull back the boot on the sidelight bulbholder and twist the bulbholder anti-clockwise to remove it, then push the bulb into the bulbholder and twist it anti-clockwise to remove it **(see illustrations)**.

11 Check that the contacts inside the bulbholder are clean and free from corrosion. Install the new bulb in the bulbholder, then install the bulbholder in its socket. Install the rubber boot.

12 Reconnect the headlight bulb and install the headlight assembly (see Step 7).

13 Check the operation of the sidelight.

---

8 Headlight shell

1 Follow the procedure in Section 7 and remove the headlight assembly from the shell. If required, disconnect the sidelight wiring connectors **(see illustration)**.

2 To remove the headlight shell, first note the arrangement of the wiring inside the shell, then free the wiring from the clip at the back of the shell **(see illustration)**. Disconnect the front turn signal wiring connectors and free the signal wiring from the clips on the headlight bracket **(see illustration)**.

3 Remove the bolts securing the headlight bracket to the bottom yoke and lift off the shell, carefully easing the wiring out of the back of the shell **(see illustration)**.

4 Installation is the reverse of removal. Make that all the wiring is correctly connected and secured. Check the operation of the headlight and sidelight. Check the headlight aim (see Chapter 1).

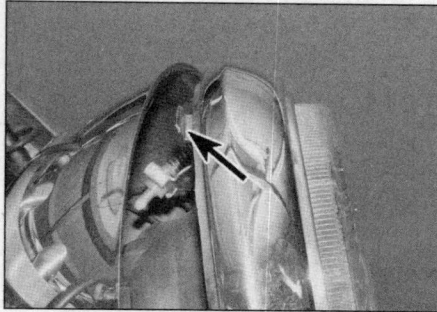

7.7 Ensure the tab (arrowed) is correctly located in the shell

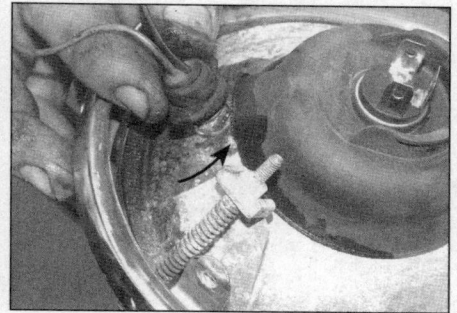

7.10a Twist the sidelight bulbholder anti-clockwise . . .

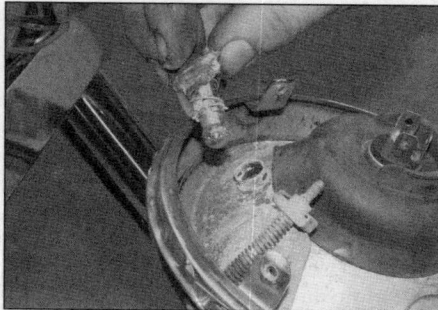

7.10b . . . and remove it from the headlight

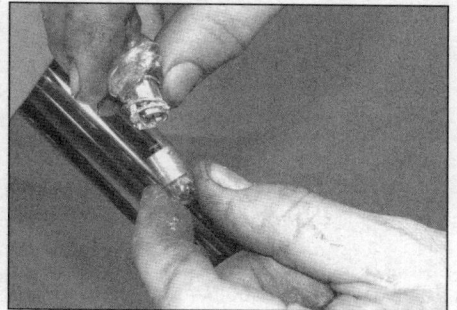

7.10c Push the bulb in and twist it anti-clockwise

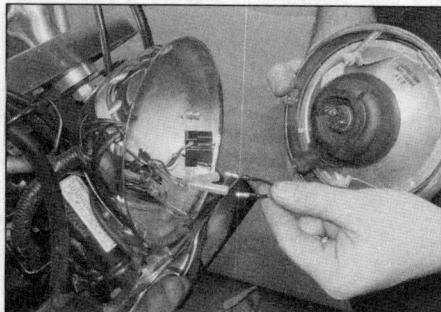

8.1 Disconnect the sidelight wiring connectors

8.2a Free the wiring from the clip (arrowed) inside the shell . . .

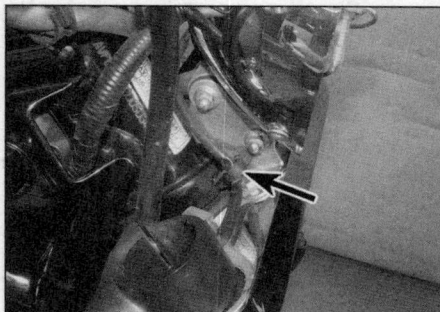

8.2b . . . and from the clips (arrowed) on the bracket

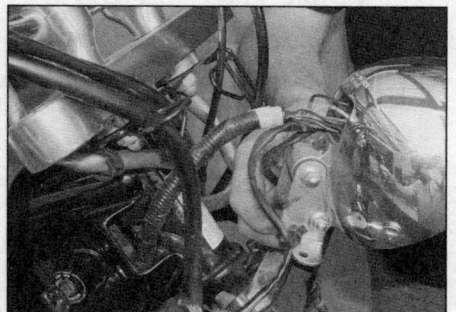

8.3 Ease the wiring out of the shell carefully

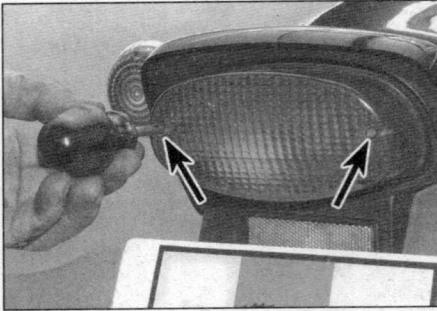

9.1a Remove the tail light lens screws – standard models

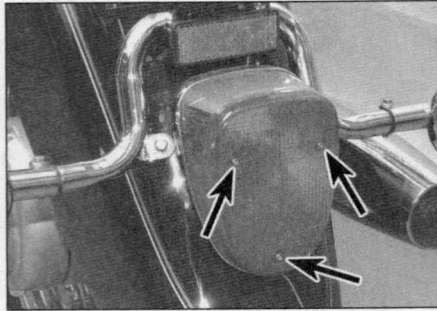

9.1b Remove the tail light lens screws – A and S models

9.2a Remove the bulb – standard models

9.2b Remove the bulb – A and S models

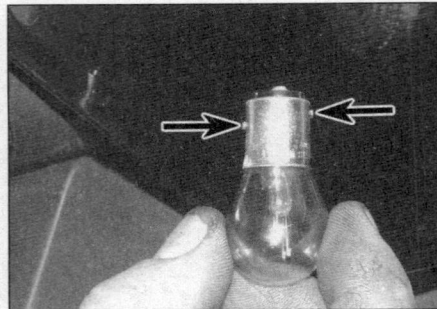

9.3 Note that the pins (arrowed) on the bulb are offset

position of the rubber gasket, grommets and spacers.

3 Disconnect the light unit wiring connector and remove the unit. **Note:** *Some models are fitted with a multi-pin connector, others have individual connectors for each wire. Where individual connectors are fitted, label the wiring to aid installation.*

4 Installation is the reverse of removal. Make that all the wiring is correctly connected. Check the operation of the tail light and the brake light.

11 Brake light switches

9 Brake/tail light bulbs

1 Remove the screws securing the tail light lens and remove the lens, noting how it fits **(see illustrations)**.

2 Push the bulb into the socket and twist it anti-clockwise to remove it **(see illustrations)**.

3 Check that the contacts inside the socket are clean and free from corrosion. Line up the pins on the bulb body with the slots in the socket – the pins on the bulb are offset so it can only be installed one way **(see illustration)**. Push the bulb in and turn it clockwise until it locks into place. **Note:** *It is a good idea to use a paper towel or dry cloth*

when handling the new bulb to prevent injury if the bulb should break and to increase bulb life.

4 Check the condition of the lens sealing gasket and renew it if it is damaged, then install the lens and tighten the screws securely.

5 Check the operation of the brake/tail light.

10 Tail light unit

1 Remove the rear mudguard (see Chapter 7).

2 On the underside of the mudguard, remove the nuts and washers securing the light unit to the mudguard and lift it off **(see illustration)**. On XVS650A and XVS1100A models, note the

Check

Note: *If the ignition is switched ON for any checks, remember to switch it OFF again before proceeding further or removing any electrical component from the system.*

1 Before checking the switches, check the brake light circuit (see Section 6).

2 The front brake light switch is mounted on the underside of the brake master cylinder **(see illustration)**. Disconnect the wiring connectors from the switch **(see illustration)**. Using a continuity tester, connect the probes to the terminals of the switch. With the brake lever at rest, there should be no continuity. With the brake lever applied, there should be continuity. If the switch does not function as described, replace it with a new one.

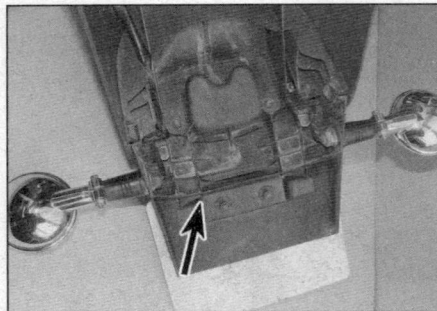

10.2 Tail light unit is secured on the underside of the mudguard – standard models shown

11.2a Location of the front brake light switch

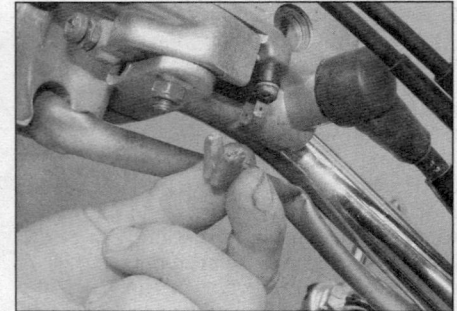

11.2b Disconnect the wiring from the switch terminals

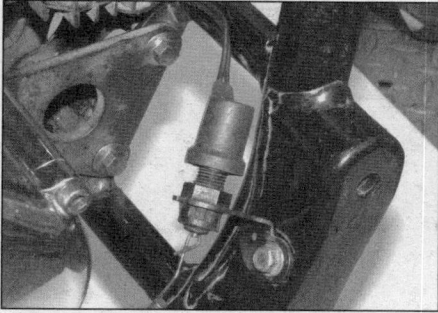

11.3a Location of the rear brake light switch – 650 model

11.3b Disconnect the wiring at the connector – 650 model

11.3c Disconnect the wiring at the connector – 1100 model

3 The rear brake light switch is mounted on the right-hand side of the machine behind the brake pedal **(see illustration)**. Trace the wiring from the switch and disconnect it at the connector **(see illustrations)**. Using a continuity tester, connect the probes to the two terminals on the switch side of the wiring connector. With the brake pedal at rest, there should be no continuity. With the brake pedal applied, there should be continuity. If the switch does not function as described, replace it with a new one.

4 If the switches are good, connect the wiring and check for voltage at the brown wire terminal on the supply side of the connector with the ignition switch ON. If no voltage is indicated, check the wiring between the switch and the ignition (main) switch (see *Wiring Diagrams* at the end of this Chapter).

Renewal

Front brake light switch

5 The switch is mounted on the underside of the brake master cylinder. Disconnect the wiring connectors from the switch **(see illustration 11.2b)**.

6 Remove the screw securing the switch to the bottom of the master cylinder and remove the switch.

7 Installation is the reverse of removal. The switch is not adjustable.

Rear brake light switch

8 On 650 models, the switch is mounted on a bracket behind the brake pedal **(see**

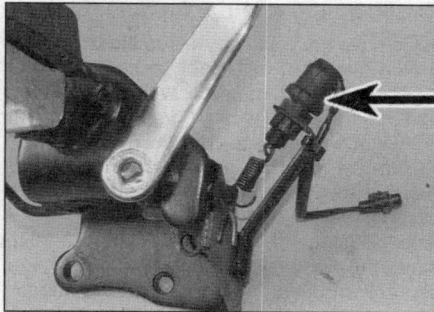

11.8 Location of rear brake light switch – 1100 model

illustration 11.3a). On 1100 models, the switch is mounted on the back of the right-hand footrest bracket **(see illustration)**. Trace the wiring from the switch and disconnect it at the connector. On 650 models, free the wiring from any ties and feed it through to the switch.

9 Detach the lower end of the switch spring from the brake mechanism **(see illustration)**. Loosen the switch locknut, then unscrew the switch from the bracket.

10 Installation is the reverse of removal, noting the following:
- Ensure the switch spring is securely connected to the brake pedal mechanism.
- Ensure the wiring is securely connected.
- On 650 models, secure the wiring with new cable ties.
- Adjust the switch as necessary (see Chapter 1, Section 12).

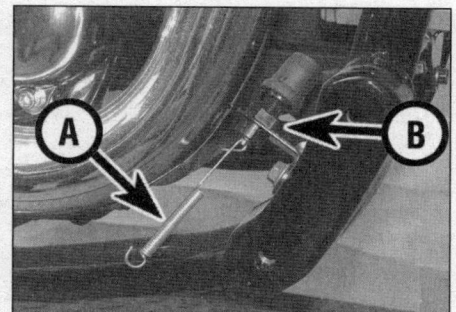

11.9 Disconnect the switch spring (A), then loosen the locknut (B)

12 Turn signal bulbs

Note: *On US models, the front turn signals also function as the running lights – the signal bulbs have twin elements and the pins on the bulb body are offset so it can only be installed one way.*

1 Undo the screws securing the turn signal lens and remove the lens and bezel, noting how they fit **(see illustrations)**.

2 Push the bulb into the socket and twist it anti-clockwise to remove it **(see illustration)**.

3 Check that the contacts inside the socket are clean and free from corrosion. Line up the pins on the bulb body with the slots in the socket, then push the bulb in and turn it clockwise until it locks into place. **Note:** *It is a*

12.1a Undo the screws (arrowed) . . .

12.1b . . . and remove the lens (A) and bezel (B)

12.2 Push the bulb in and twist it anti-clockwise to remove it

12.5 Align the cut-out (arrowed) with the bracket

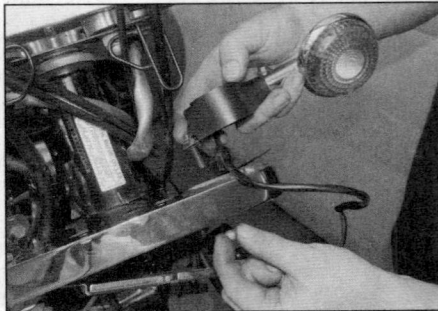

13.3 Remove the assembly from the bottom yoke as described

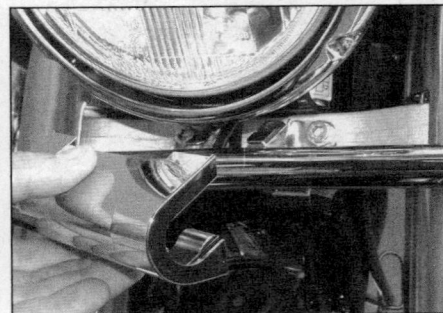

13.5 Unclip the plastic trim

good idea to use a paper towel or dry cloth when handling the new bulb to prevent injury if the bulb should break and to increase bulb life.

4 Check the condition of the lens sealing gasket and renew it if it is damaged.

5 Install the bezel, aligning the cut-out with the mounting bracket, then install the lens aligning the notch at the top with the bezel **(see illustration)**. Tighten the screws securely.

6 Check the operation of the turn signals and running lights, as applicable.

13 Turn signal assemblies

Front

XVS650/1100 standard models

1 Remove the front forks (see Chapter 5).

2 Remove the headlight assembly, then disconnect the turn signal wiring connectors and free the signal wiring from the clips on the headlight bracket (see Section 8)

3 Remove the nut and bolt securing the turn signal assembly to the bottom yoke and lift off the assembly **(see illustration)**.

4 Installation is the reverse of removal. Make sure the wiring is correctly routed and securely connected. Check the operation of the turn signals.

XVS650/1100 A and S models

5 Remove the plastic trim **(see illustration)**.

6 Remove the headlight assembly, then disconnect the turn signal wiring connectors and free the signal wiring from the clips on the headlight bracket (see Section 8).

7 Remove the bolts securing the turn signal bracket to the bottom yoke and lift off the assembly.

8 Installation is the reverse of removal. Make sure the wiring is correctly routed and securely connected. Check the operation of the turn signals.

Rear

XVS650 standard models

9 Remove the rear mudguard, then follow the procedure to remove the mudguard brackets (see Chapter 7).

10 Undo the nut securing the turn signal assembly to the bracket and lift it off.

11 Installation is the reverse of removal. Make sure the wiring is correctly routed and securely connected. Check the operation of the turn signals.

XVS1100 standard models

12 Remove the rear mudguard (see Chapter 7).

13 Remove the tail light unit (see Section 10). Disconnect the turn signal wiring connectors.

14 Remove the screws securing the mud flap to the rear mudguard, then undo the nut securing the turn signal assembly to the flap and lift it off **(see illustration)**.

15 Installation is the reverse of removal. Make sure the wiring is correctly routed and securely connected. Check the operation of the turn signals.

XVS650/1100 A and S models

16 Remove the rear mudguard (see Chapter 7).

17 Remove the tail light unit (see Section 10). Disconnect the turn signal wiring connectors.

18 Remove the rear number plate, then undo the bolts securing the turn signal assembly and lift it off **(see illustration)**.

19 Installation is the reverse of removal. Make sure the wiring is correctly routed and securely connected. Check the operation of the turn signals.

14 Turn signal circuit

Note: *If the ignition is switched ON for any checks, remember to switch it OFF again before proceeding further or removing any electrical component from the system.*

1 Most turn signal problems are the result of a burned-out bulb or corroded socket. This is especially true when the turn signals function properly in one direction, but fail to flash in the other direction. Check the bulbs and the sockets (see Section 12) and the wiring connectors. Also, check the signal system fuse (see Section 5) and the switch (see Section 18).

13.14 Nut (arrowed) secures turn signal to mud flap

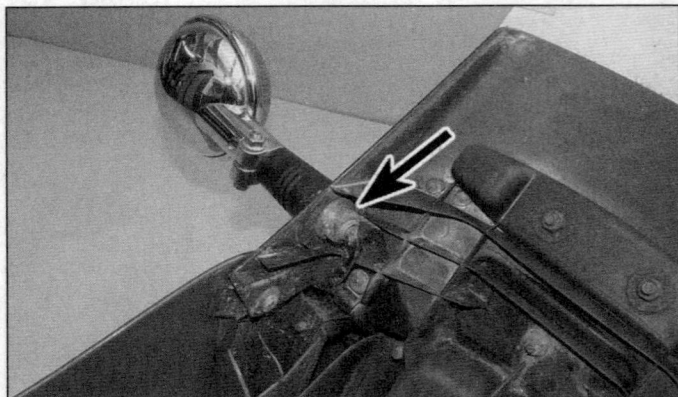

13.18 Bolts (arrowed) secure turn signal assembly

14.3a Location of the turn signal relay – 650 models

14.3b Location of the turn signal relay – 1100 models

2 The battery provides power for operation of the turn signals, so if they do not operate, check the battery voltage. Low battery voltage indicates either a faulty battery or a defective charging system. Refer to Section 3 for battery checks and Section 31 for charging system tests.

3 If the bulbs, sockets, connectors, fuse, switch and battery are good, check the turn signal relay. On 650 models, the relay is located behind the battery cover, above the starter relay **(see illustration)**. On 1100 models, the relay is located behind the steering head – follow the procedure in Chapter 3 to remove the fuel tank and airbox to access the relay **(see illustration)**.

4 Disconnect the relay connector and check for voltage at the brown wire terminal in the connector with the ignition ON. If no voltage is indicated, refer to the appropriate wiring diagram at the end of this Chapter and check the wiring between the relay and the ignition (main) switch for continuity.

5 If voltage is indicated, reconnect the relay, then check for voltage at the brown/white wire terminal in the connector with the ignition ON, and with the signal switch turned to either LEFT or RIGHT.

6 If no voltage is indicated, replace the relay with a new one.

7 If voltage is indicated, check the wiring between the relay, turn signal switch and turn signal lights for continuity.

15 Speedometer, cable (650 models) and sensor (1100 models)

650 models

1 If the speedometer is thought to be faulty, first remove the speedometer cable and check it (see Steps 4 to 7).

2 If the cable is good, raise the front wheel off the ground using an auxiliary stand and turn the wheel slowly in the normal direction of rotation. The cable socket inside the speedometer drive unit should be seen to rotate – if not, remove the front wheel and inspect the drive unit and

the tabbed drive plate in the left-hand side of the hub (see Chapter 6).

3 If the fault seems to be with the speedometer itself, remove the instrument and take it to a Yamaha dealer for assessment (see Steps 9 to 11).

Speedometer cable

4 Unscrew the knurled ring securing the speedometer cable to the drive unit on the left-hand side of the front wheel hub and detach the cable **(see illustration)**.

5 Remove the three bolts securing the speedometer housing to the top of the fuel tank **(see illustration)**.

6 Ease the assembly up – it helps to push the cable up from under the fuel tank – and unscrew the knurled ring securing the cable to the back of the speedometer **(see illustration)**.

7 Note how the cable is routed, then pull it up through the fuel tank and remove it.

8 Installation is the reverse of removal. Make sure the speedometer cable does not snag the wiring harness and does not interfere with the steering. Where applicable, route the cable through the guide on the front mudguard. Ensure the squared ends of the inner cable fit correctly into the back of the speedometer and the drive unit, then tighten the knurled rings on both ends of the cable securely.

Speedometer removal and installation

9 Follow the procedure in Steps 4 to 6, then disconnect the speedometer lights and warning lights wiring connectors **(see illustration)**.

10 Using a very small Phillips screwdriver,

15.4 Unscrew the knurled ring (arrowed) and detach the speedometer cable

15.5 Speedometer housing is secured by three bolts (arrowed)

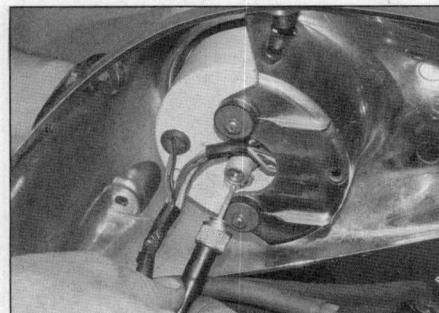

15.6 Detach the cable from the back of the speedometer

15.9 Disconnect the wiring connectors (arrowed)

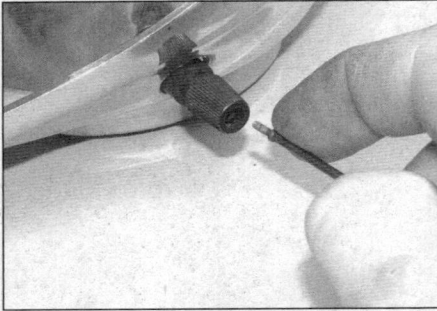

15.10a Undo the screw securing the reset knob . . .

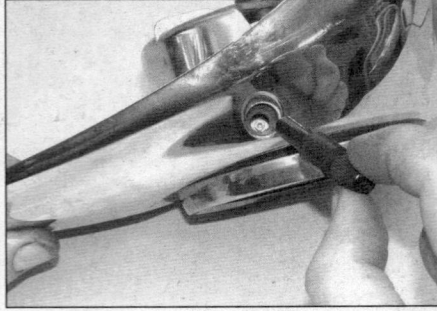

15.10b . . . and pull it off

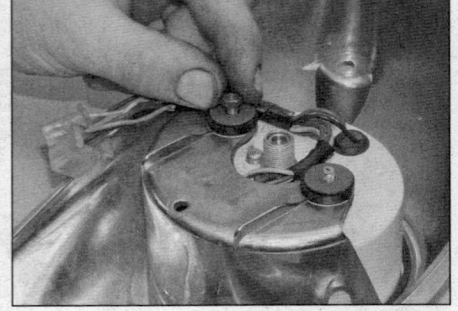

15.11a Remove the nuts and washers . . .

remove the screw securing the trip reset knob and pull it off **(see illustrations)**.

11 Remove the nuts and washers securing the speedometer in the housing, then lift the speedometer out **(see illustrations)**.

12 If required, pull the speedometer light bulbholder out of the case, twisting it gently, then pull the bulb out of the holder **(see illustrations)**. Press the new bulb in carefully and install the holder.

13 Installation is the reverse of removal. Check that the contacts inside the wiring connectors are clean and free from corrosion, then connect them securely.

1100 models

14 The speedometer is controlled electronically by the speed sensor. If the speedometer is thought to be faulty, first check the back-up fuse (see Section 5).

15 If the fuse is good, test the output from the sensor as follows.

16 Support the motorcycle on an auxiliary stand so the rear wheel is off the ground. Make sure the transmission is in neutral.

17 Remove the left-hand frame cover (see Chapter 7). Pull the wiring connectors out of the cover and identify the connector for the speed sensor **(see illustration)**. Note that the sensor is located on the rear of the transmission casing **(see illustration)**.

18 Connect the positive (+ve) probe of a multimeter set to the DC20V scale to the white wire terminal in the connector, and connect the negative (–ve) probe to earth (ground). Turn the ignition ON. Turn the rear wheel in its normal direction of rotation and check the reading on the multimeter – it should be seen to fluctuate between zero and

5 volts as the wheel is turned. If not, replace the speed sensor with a new one.

19 If the multimeter reading is correct, refer to *Wiring Diagrams* at the end of this Chapter and check that the wiring and connectors between the sensor and related electrical components is good. If no fault can be found, have the speedometer and the ICU (see Chapter 4) tested by a Yamaha dealer.

Speedometer removal and installation

20 Remove the seats, then displace the ICU panel to access the speedometer wiring connector (see Chapter 7).

21 Disconnect the speedometer wiring connector **(see illustration)**.

22 Remove the fuel tank (see Chapter 3).

23 Unclip the speedometer wiring from the underside of the tank.

24 Remove the three bolts securing the

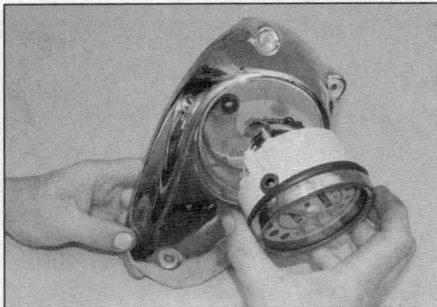

15.11b . . . and lift out the speedometer

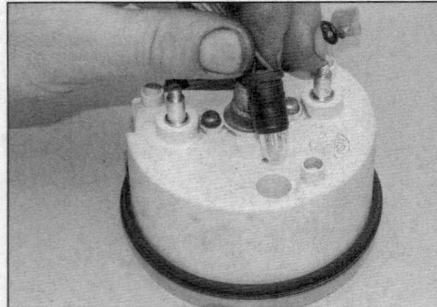

15.12a Pull the bulbholder out of the case . . .

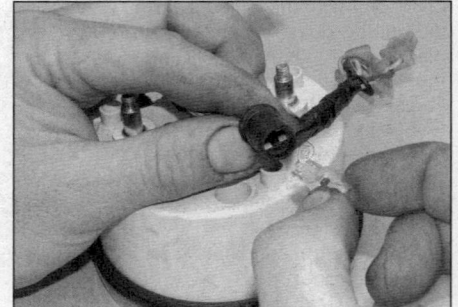

15.12b . . . and pull the bulb out of the holder

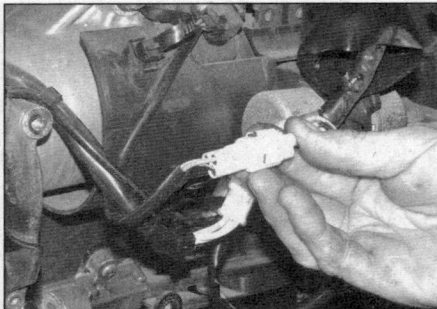

15.17a Pull the speed sensor wiring connector out of the cover

15.17b Location of the speed sensor

15.21 Disconnect the speedometer wiring connector

15.24a Speedometer housing is secured by three bolts (arrowed)

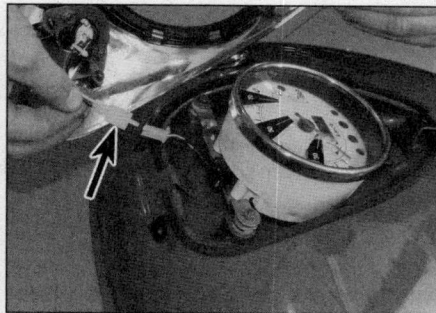

15.24b Disconnect the trip button wiring connector (arrowed)

15.25a Remove the nuts and washers (arrowed) . . .

speedometer housing to the top of the fuel tank, then lift it up and disconnect the trip button wiring connector **(see illustrations)**.

25 Undo the nuts and washers securing the speedometer to the tank, then lift the speedometer out **(see illustrations)**.

26 If required, pull the speedometer light bulbholders out of the case, twisting them gently, then pull the bulbs out of the holders. Press the new bulbs in carefully and install the holders.

27 Installation is the reverse of removal. Don't forget to secure the wiring to the underside of the fuel tank. Check that the contacts inside the wiring connectors are clean and free from corrosion, then connect them securely.

Speedometer sensor

28 To test the sensor, follow the procedure in Steps 14 to 18.

29 To fit a new sensor, first remove the left-hand frame cover (see Chapter 7). Pull the wiring connectors out of the cover and disconnect the speed sensor connector **(see illustration 15.17a)**.

30 Remove the bolt securing the sensor to the transmission casing and lift the sensor out **(see illustration)**.

31 Installation is the reverse of removal. Don't forget to secure the wiring to the underside of the fuel tank. Check that the contacts inside the wiring connectors are clean and free from corrosion, then connect them securely.

16 Warning lights

Note: *Late 650/1100A Europe models are fitted with an immobiliser system, the immobiliser warning light is illuminated by an LED – refer to Chapter 4, Section 9.*

1 The warning and indicator functions – engine warning, neutral, high beam, turn signals, and oil level (1100 models only) – are all illuminated by bulbs located in the back of the speedometer case **(see illustration)**. To access the bulbs, follow the appropriate procedure in Section 15 to remove the speedometer.

2 The engine warning light should come on for 1.4 seconds when the ignition is switched ON as a check of the system, and then go off. If the light begins to flash refer to Chapter 4, Section 6 for more information. If the light does not come on, first check the bulb. If the bulb is good, refer to *Wiring Diagrams* at the end of this Chapter and check the wiring and connectors between the light, the ICU and related electrical components. If no fault can be found, the ICU may be faulty – have it tested by a Yamaha dealer.

3 On 1100 models, the oil level warning light should come on when the ignition (main) switch is turned ON before starting the engine, and then go off as soon as the engine starts. If the light does not come on, first check the

bulb. If the bulb is good, refer to *Wiring Diagrams* at the end of this Chapter and check the wiring and connectors between the light, the relay and the oil level sensor. If no fault can be found, check the relay and the sensor (see Section 24). **Note:** *If the light remains on once the engine has started, STOP the engine immediately and check the oil level – see Daily (pre-ride) checks. If the oil level is correct, check the wiring circuit as described above.*

4 The neutral, high beam and turn signal lights should come on when the function is selected by the appropriate switch. If a light does not come on, refer to *Wiring Diagrams* at the end of this Chapter and check the fuse where relevant. Next, test the bulb. If the bulb is good, refer to *Wiring Diagrams* and check the wiring and connectors between the light and the switch or relevant wiring circuit. Follow the procedure in Section 22 to test the neutral switch.

17 Ignition (main) switch

⚠️ **Warning: To prevent the risk of short circuits, disconnect the battery negative (–ve) lead before making any ignition (main) switch checks.**

1 Remove the fuel tank (see Chapter 3). Remove the steering head panels (see Chapter 7).

15.25b . . . and lift out the speedometer

15.30 Lift the speedometer sensor out of the casing

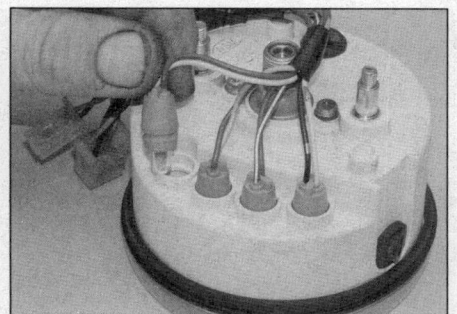

16.1 Location of the warning light bulbs – 650 model shown

17.2 Ignition switch mounting bolts (arrowed)

17.3 Disconnect the switch wiring connectors (arrowed)

2 Undo the bolts securing the switch to the frame **(see illustration)**. Note that on some models, the switch is secured by shear bolts. The heads of the bolts must be tapped around using a suitable punch or drift, or drilled off, before the switch can be removed.

3 Pull the switch out and disconnect the wiring connectors **(see illustration)**.

4 Using a multimeter or a continuity tester, make checks on the switch side of the connector. Check the continuity of the connector terminal pairs (see *Wiring Diagrams* at the end of this Chapter). Continuity should exist between the terminals connected by a solid line on the diagram when the switch key is turned to the indicated position.

5 If the switch fails any of the tests, replace it with a new one. **Note:** *On later Europe 650/1100A models fitted with an immobiliser*

system, if a new ignition (main) switch is fitted, a new ICU will also be required – refer to your Yamaha dealer for details.

6 Installation is the reverse of removal, noting the following:
● Ensure the wiring is securely connected.
● If shear bolts are used to secure the switch, tighten the bolts until their heads shear off.

18 Handlebar switch check

1 Generally speaking, the handlebar switch units are reliable and trouble-free. Most problems, when they do occur, are caused by

dirty or corroded contacts, but wear and breakage of internal parts is a possibility that should not be overlooked. If breakage does occur, the entire switch unit and related wiring harness will have to be replaced with a new one, as individual parts are not available.

2 The switches can be checked for continuity using a multimeter or a continuity tester.

3 Remove the fuel tank (see Chapter 3) and the steering head panels (see Chapter 7) to access the switch wiring connectors. Trace the wiring harness from the switch in question back to its connectors and disconnect it **(see illustrations)**.

4 Check for continuity between the terminals on the switch side of the connector with the switch in the ON and OFF position (i.e. switch OFF – no continuity, switch ON – continuity) – see *Wiring Diagrams* at the end of this Chapter.

5 If the continuity check indicates a problem exists, refer to Section 19, remove the switch and spray the switch contacts with electrical contact cleaner. If they are accessible, the contacts can be scraped clean with a penknife or polished with steel wool **(see illustration)**. If switch components are damaged or broken, it should be obvious when the switch is disassembled.

19 Handlebar switch removal and installation

1 If the switch unit is to be removed from the motorcycle, rather than just displaced from the handlebar, first remove the fuel tank (see Chapter 3) and the steering head panels (see Chapter 7) to access the switch wiring connectors. Trace the wiring harness of the switch in question back to its connectors and disconnect it (see Section 18).

2 Free the wiring from any clips and ties and feed it back to the switch, noting its correct routing.

3 If removing the right-hand switch unit, disconnect the wiring connectors from the brake light switch **(see illustration 11.2b)**. If removing the left-hand switch unit, undo the screws securing the clutch switch to the

18.3a Trace the wiring for the left-hand handlebar switches . . .

18.3b . . . to the connectors behind the steering head

18.3c Trace the wiring for the right-hand handlebar switches . . .

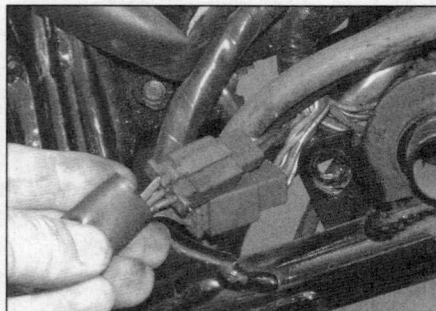

18.3d . . . to the connectors behind the steering head

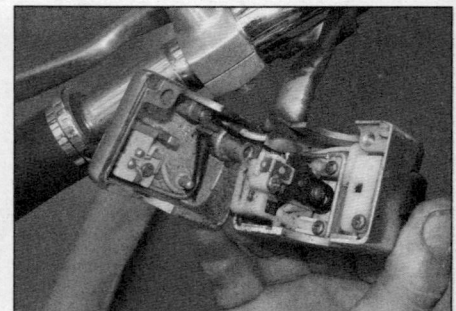

18.5 Ensure the switch contacts are clean and free from corrosion

19.3 Clutch switch is secured by two screws (arrowed)

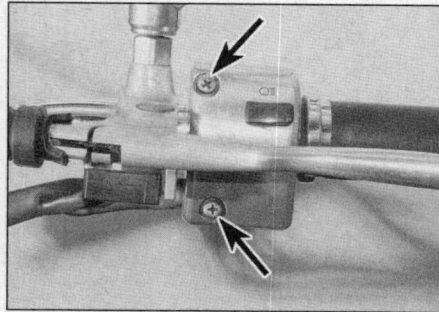

19.4a Switch unit screws (arrowed)

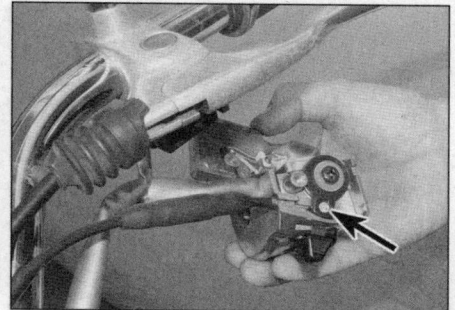

19.4b Location of choke lever on 1100 models

underside of the clutch lever bracket **(see illustration)**.

4 Unscrew the switch unit screws and free the unit from the handlebar by separating the halves **(see illustration)**. On 1100 models, when removing the left-hand switch, disconnect the choke cable from the lever, noting how it fits **(see illustration)**.

5 Installation is the reverse of removal. On 1100 models, refer to Chapter 3 for installation of the choke cable, if required. Make sure the locating pin in the switch unit locates in the hole in the handlebar. Make sure the wiring is securely connected, correctly routed and secured by the clips and ties.

6 Check the operation of the switch.

20 Sidestand switch

Check

1 The sidestand switch is mounted on the sidestand bracket **(see illustration)**. The switch is part of the safety circuit which prevents or stops the engine running if the transmission is in gear whilst the sidestand is down, and prevents the engine from starting if the transmission is in gear unless the sidestand is up and the clutch lever is pulled in. If the switch is thought to be faulty, perform the following checks.

2 Before checking the electrical circuit, check

the main and ignition fuses (see Section 5).

3 On 650 models, to access the wiring connector, remove the fuel tank (see Chapter 3) and the steering head panels (see Chapter 7). On 1100 models, to access the wiring connector, remove the left-hand frame cover (see Chapter 7). Trace the wiring from the switch and disconnect it at the connector **(see illustrations)**.

4 Check the operation of the switch using a multimeter or continuity tester. Connect the meter probes to the terminals on the switch side of the connector. With the sidestand up there should be continuity (zero resistance) between the terminals, and with the stand down there should be no continuity (infinite resistance).

5 If the switch does not perform as expected, it is defective and must be renewed.

6 If the switch is good, check the other

components in the safety circuit and the starter circuit as described in the relevant Sections of this Chapter. If all components are good, check the wiring between the various components (see *Wiring Diagrams* at the end of this Chapter).

Renewal

7 Disconnect the sidestand switch wiring connector (see Step 3). Release the wiring from any ties and feed it back to the switch noting the correct routing.

8 Undo the screws securing the switch to the stand bracket and remove the switch **(see illustration)**.

9 Install the new switch and tighten the screws securely. Ensure the tab on the sidestand depresses the switch plunger when the stand is down **(see illustration)**.

10 Ensure the wiring is correctly routed up to

20.1 Location of the sidestand switch – 1100 models shown

20.3a Location of the switch wiring connector – 650 models shown

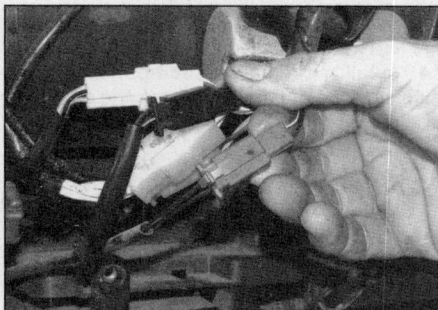

20.3b Location of the switch wiring connector – 1100 models shown

20.8 Sidestand switch mounting screws

20.9 Ensure the tab (arrowed) depresses the switch plunger

21.2 Test for continuity between the clutch switch terminals (arrowed)

22.7a Location of the neutral switch – 650 models

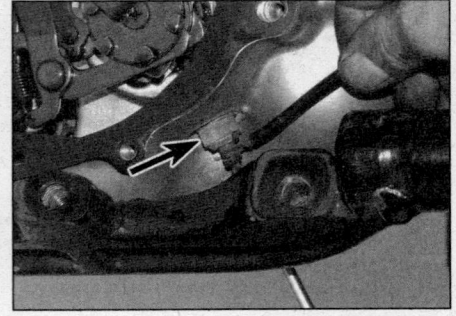

22.7b Location of the neutral switch – 1100 models

the connector and retained by all the necessary clips and ties. Reconnect the wiring connector.

11 Install the remaining components in the reverse order of removal. Check the operation of the switch.

21 Clutch switch

Check

1 The clutch switch is mounted on the underside of the clutch lever bracket **(see illustration 19.3)**. The switch is part of the safety circuit which prevents or stops the engine running if the transmission is in gear whilst the sidestand is down, and prevents the engine from starting if the transmission is in gear unless the sidestand is up and the clutch lever is pulled in. If the switch is thought to be faulty, perform the following check.

2 Connect the probes of a multimeter or a continuity tester to the two switch terminals **(see illustration)**. There should be continuity (zero resistance) with the clutch lever pulled in, and no continuity (infinite resistance) with the clutch lever out.

3 If the switch is good, check the other components in the safety circuit and the starter circuit as described in the relevant Sections of this Chapter. If all components are good, check the wiring between the various components (see *Wiring Diagrams* at the end of this Chapter).

Renewal

4 Remove the fuel tank (see Chapter 3) and the steering head panels (see Chapter 7) to access the switch wiring connector. Trace the wiring harness from the clutch switch back to its connector and disconnect it (see Section 18).

5 Undo the screws securing the switch to the underside of the clutch lever bracket and lift it off. Note the route of the switch wiring harness.

6 Install the new switch and tighten the screws securely.

7 Ensure the wiring is correctly routed up to

the connector and retained by all the necessary clips and ties. Reconnect the wiring connector.

8 Install the remaining components in the reverse order of removal. Check the operation of the switch.

22 Neutral switch

Check

1 If the neutral light fails to come on when the transmission is in neutral and the ignition is switched ON, first check the signal fuse and the bulb (see Section 16).

2 The switch is part of the safety circuit which prevents or stops the engine running if the transmission is in gear whilst the sidestand is down, and prevents the engine from starting if the transmission is in gear unless the sidestand is up and the clutch lever is pulled in. If the switch is thought to be faulty, perform the following checks.

3 On 650 models, to access the neutral switch wiring connector, follow the procedure in Section 15 and disconnect the warning lights wiring connector.

4 On 1100 models, to access the neutral switch wiring connector, follow the procedure in Section 15 and disconnect the speedometer wiring connector.

5 Use a multimeter or continuity tester to check for continuity between the light blue wire terminal on the switch side of the wiring connector and the crankcase. With the transmission in neutral, there should be continuity. If there is no continuity, check for a break in the wire between the connector and the neutral switch.

6 With the transmission in gear, there should be no continuity. If there is continuity when in gear, check that the wire is not earthed (grounded).

7 The switch is located on the lower, left-hand side of the engine. On 650 models, it is behind the middle gear cover **(see illustration)**. On 1100 models, it is below the alternator cover **(see illustration)**. Follow the appropriate procedure in Chapter 2A, Section

5 (650 models), or Chapter 2B, Section 5 (1100 models), to access the switch.

8 If the wire is good, loosen the switch terminal screw and disconnect the wire. With the transmission in neutral, test for continuity between the switch terminal and the crankcase. If there is no continuity, the switch and/or the switch contact on the selector drum is damaged.

9 If the switch is good, check the other components in the safety circuit and the starter circuit as described in the relevant Sections of this Chapter. If all components are good, check the wiring between the various components (see *Wiring Diagrams* at the end of this Chapter).

Renewal

10 Drain the engine oil (see Chapter 1).

11 On 650 models, remove the screws securing the neutral switch in the crankcase and lift it out. Discard any O-ring or gasket as a new one must be fitted. Check that the contact plunger in the end of the selector drum is not damaged or seized (see Chapter 2A, Section 27). Renew any damaged parts as necessary. Install the neutral switch with a new O-ring or gasket and tighten the screws securely.

12 On 1100 models, unscrew the switch from the crankcase and discard the sealing washer as a new one must be used. Check that the contact plunger in the switch is not damaged or seized (see Chapter 2B, Section 27). Renew any damaged parts as necessary. Install the neutral switch with a new sealing washer and tighten it securely.

13 Install the neutral switch wire and tighten the terminal screw securely.

14 Install the remaining components in the reverse order of removal. Check the operation of the switch.

23 Relay assembly

1 The relay assembly is a sealed unit which incorporates the starter circuit cut-out relay and its diodes, and the fuel pump relay. On 650 models, the relay assembly is located on

the rear edge of the battery backing panel – remove the battery cover for access (see Chapter 7). On 1100 models, the relay assembly is located behind the steering head – remove the fuel tank and airbox for access (see Chapter 3).

2 Disconnect the battery negative (-ve) lead, then displace the relay assembly and disconnect the wiring connector (see illustrations). Refer to the wiring diagram for your model at the end of this Chapter, and the appropriate test procedure below. Note: If, after testing, the relay assembly and diodes are good, but the starting system fault still exists, check all other components in the starting circuit (i.e. the neutral switch, sidestand switch, clutch switch, starter switch and starter relay) as described in the relevant Sections of this Chapter. If all components are good, check the wiring between the various components (see Wiring Diagrams at the end of this Chapter).

3 Before refitting the relay assembly, check that the contacts inside the wiring connector are clean and free from corrosion, then connect the relay assembly securely. Install the remaining components in the reverse order of removal.

Starter circuit cut-out relay and diodes

4 The starter circuit cut-out relay is part of the safety circuit which prevents or stops the engine running if the transmission is in gear whilst the sidestand is down, and prevents the engine from starting if the transmission is in gear unless the sidestand is up and the clutch lever is pulled in. In addition, on later Europe 650/1100A models fuel cut-off solenoids are incorporated in the ignition system (see Wiring Diagrams at the end of this Chapter).

Starter circuit relay check

5 To check the operation of the relay, connect a multimeter set to the ohms x 1 scale, or a continuity tester, between the blue and blue/white (black on later Europe models) wire terminals of the relay. There should be no continuity. Now, using a fully charged 12V battery and two suitable jumper wires, connect the battery positive (+ve) terminal to the relay's red/black wire terminal and the

23.2a Disconnect the relay wiring connector – 650 models

23.2b Displace the relay assembly – 1100 models

battery negative (–ve) terminal to the relay's black/yellow wire terminal. With voltage applied, the test equipment should show continuity. If it doesn't, replace the relay assembly with a new one.

Diode check

6 The diodes contained within the relay assembly can be checked by performing a continuity test. Refer to the appropriate wiring diagram at the end of this chapter and connect the meter (set to the ohms function) or continuity tester across the wire terminals for the diode being tested. The diode should show continuity in one direction and no continuity when the meter or tester probes are reversed. If the diode shows the same condition in both directions it should be considered faulty.

7 Early 1100 models have an additional diode located in the wiring loom alongside the speedometer wiring connector. Remove the seats, then displace the ICU panel to access the wiring loom (see Chapter 7). Unwrap the loom sheath to access the diode and pull it out of its connector (see illustrations). Test as described above in Step 8.

Fuel pump relay check and pump resistance check

Fuel pump relay check

8 The pump relay is housed within the relay assembly. Remove the relay assembly as described in Step 2 above.

9 To check the operation of the pump relay, connect a multimeter set to the ohms x 1 scale, or a continuity tester, between the

red/black and blue/black wire terminals of the relay. There should be no continuity. Now, using a fully charged 12V battery and two suitable jumper wires, connect the battery positive (+ve) terminal to the relay's red/black wire terminal and the battery negative (–ve) terminal to the relay's blue/red wire terminal. With voltage applied, the test equipment should show continuity. If it doesn't, replace the relay assembly with a new one.

10 Install the relay assembly as described in Step 3.

Fuel pump resistance check

11 To test the fuel pump's resistance, first remove the left-hand frame cover (see Chapter 7). Pull the wiring connectors out of the cover, then trace the wiring back from the pump and disconnect it at the connector.

12 With the multimeter set to the ohms x 1 scale, connect the positive (+ve) probe to the blue/black wire terminal on the pump side of the connector, and the negative (–ve) probe to the black wire terminal (see illustration). If the reading is not as specified at the beginning of this Chapter, replace the pump with a new one (see Chapter 3).

24 Oil level relay and sensor (1100 models)

1 The oil level warning light should come on when the ignition (main) switch is turned ON before starting the engine, and then go off as soon as the engine starts. If the warning light

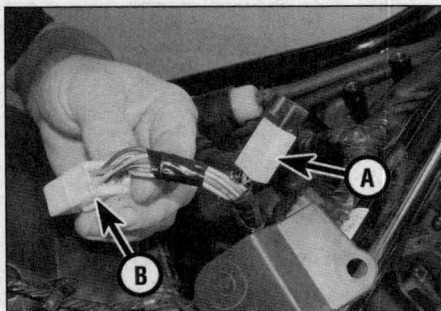
23.7a Location of the separate diode (A) and speedometer wiring connector (B)

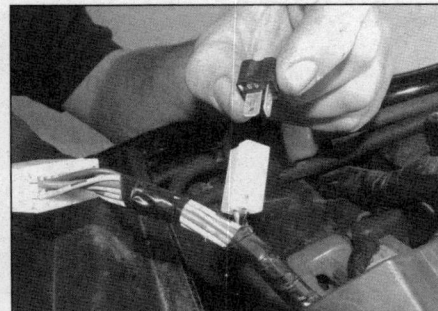
23.7b Pull the diode out of its connector

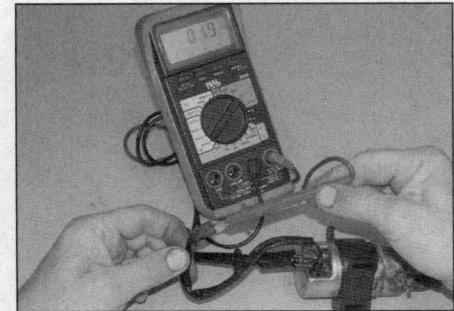
23.12 Checking the fuel pump resistance

24.2 Location of the oil level relay

24.7 Location of the oil level sensor wiring connector (arrowed)

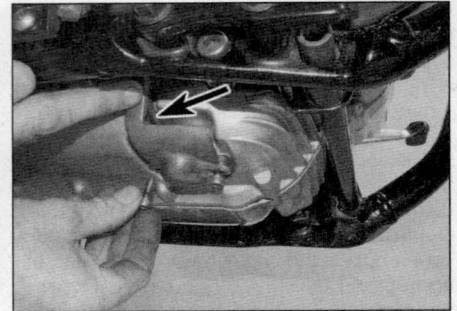

24.8a Remove the mounting bolts – note the route of the wire (arrowed)

does not come on, or remains on once the engine has started, and the bulb, wiring and connectors between the light, the relay and the oil level sensor are good, check the relay and sensor as follows.

Note: *The warning light may flicker during sudden acceleration or deceleration or when riding up or down hill. Note that this is a characteristic of the system and provided the oil level is correct, does not indicate a fault.*

Oil level relay

2 To check the operation of the relay, remove the battery cover (see Chapter 7). The relay is located on the front edge of the battery tray **(see illustration)**. Unclip the relay from its holder and disconnect the relay wiring connector.

3 Connect a multimeter set to the ohms x 1 scale, or a continuity tester, between the black/white and black wire terminals of the relay. There should be no continuity. Now, using a fully-charged 12V battery and two suitable jumper wires, connect the battery positive (+ve) lead to the relay's red/white wire terminal and the negative (–ve) lead to the relay's black/red wire terminal. With voltage applied, the test equipment should show continuity. If it doesn't, replace the relay with a new one.

4 Check that the contacts inside the wiring connector are clean and free from corrosion, then connect the relay securely.

5 Install the remaining components in the reverse order of removal.

Oil level sensor

6 The sensor is located on the underside of the right-hand crankcase. To check the sensor, first drain the engine oil (see Chapter 1).

7 Remove the right-hand frame cover (see Chapter 7), then trace the wire back from the sensor and disconnect it at the single bullet connector **(see illustration)**. Release the wire from any cable ties and feed it back to the sensor noting the correct routing.

8 Unscrew the two bolts securing the sensor to the bottom of the right-hand crankcase and remove the cover, noting the route of the sensor wire **(see illustration)**. Withdraw the sensor, being prepared to catch any residual oil **(see illustration)**. Check the condition of the O-ring and replace it with a new one if it is damaged.

9 Connect one probe of a multimeter set to the ohms x 1 scale, or continuity tester, to the sensor wire and the other probe to the base of the sensor. With the sensor in its normal installed position (wiring at the bottom), there should be continuity. Turn the sensor upside down. There should be no continuity. If either condition does not occur, replace the sensor with a new one.

10 Before installing the sensor, smear the O-ring with lithium soap grease, then fit the sensor into the crankcase. Ensure the wire is correctly routed, then fit the cover and tighten the bolts securely.

11 Feed the wiring to the connector and secure it with the cable ties.

12 Fill the engine with the correct quantity of oil, then check the level (see Chapter 1 and *Daily (pre-ride) checks*).

13 Install the remaining components in the reverse order of removal. Check the operation of the sensor.

25 Horn

1 If the horn doesn't work, first check the signal fuse (see Section 5) and the battery (see Section 3).

2 The horn is mounted on the frame below the steering head – remove the mounting bolt, then disconnect the wiring connectors and lift the horn off **(see illustrations)**.

3 Using two jumper wires, apply battery voltage directly to the terminals on the horn. If the horn sounds, check the switch (see Section 18) and the wiring between the switch and the horn (see *Wiring Diagrams* at the end of this Chapter).

4 If the horn doesn't sound, replace it with a new one.

5 Installation is the reverse of removal. Ensure the wiring connectors are a tight fit on the horn terminals and tighten the mounting bolt securely. Check the operation of the horn.

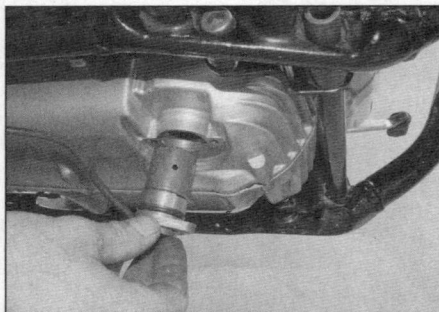

24.8b Withdraw the sensor from the crankcase

25.2a Remove the horn mounting bolt . . .

25.2b . . . and disconnect the wiring from the horn terminals (arrowed)

26.4 Heater relay (arrowed) is mounted on front edge of battery tray on 650 models

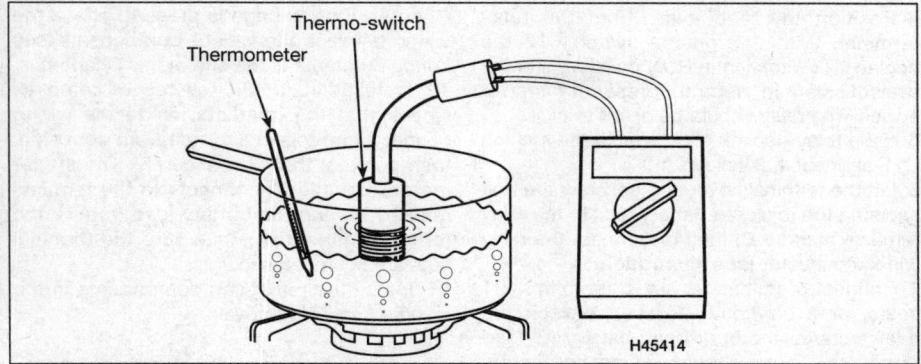

26.8 Set-up for testing the thermo-switch

1 Brown/yellow wire terminal
2 Black/yellow wire terminal
3 Container with water
4 Thermometer

26 Carburettor heater system

1 Both carburettors have two heater units threaded into their bodies (see Chapter 3). The heaters are controlled by a thermo-switch and a heater relay (except later 1100 models), and the system is protected by the heater fuse (see *Wiring Diagrams* at the end of this Chapter).
2 If a failure of the heater system is suspected, first check the heater fuse (see Section 5).
3 If the fuse is good, proceed to check the carburettor heater relay on 650 models and early 1100 models.
4 Trace the wiring from the carburettor heaters to the heater relay and disconnect the relay from its connector.
5 Connect a multimeter set to the ohms x 1 scale, or a continuity tester, between the brown/black and black/yellow wire terminals of the relay. There should be no continuity. Now, using a fully-charged 12V battery and two suitable jumper wires, connect the battery positive (+ve) lead to the relay's brown/yellow wire terminal and the negative (–ve) lead to the relay's light blue wire terminal. With voltage applied, the test equipment should show continuity. If it doesn't, replace the relay with a new one.
6 Check that the contacts inside the wiring connector are clean and free from corrosion, then connect the relay securely.
7 Trace the wiring from the heater relay to the

thermo-switch and disconnect the switch from the wiring loom. Test the switch as follows.
8 Fill a small heatproof container with cold water (below 10°C) and place it on a stove. Connect a multimeter set to the ohms x 1 scale, or a continuity tester, between the two wire terminals of the switch. Using some wire or other support, suspend the switch in the water and place a thermometer in the water so that its bulb is close to the switch (see illustration).
9 Initially, the test equipment should show continuity. Now heat the water very gently – as the temperature rises to around 23°C the switch should open and there should be no continuity. Turn the heat off.
10 Cool the water by adding ice – as the temperature falls to around 12°C the switch should close and there should be continuity.
11 If the teat results are not as stated, replace the thermo-switch with a new one.
12 Check that the contacts inside the wiring connector are clean and free from corrosion, then connect the thermo-switch securely.
13 If the relay and thermo-switch are good, disconnect the individual carburettor heater wiring connectors and check the heater resistance with a multimeter as follows.
14 Connect the positive (+ve) meter probe to the heater wire terminal, and the negative (–ve) probe to the heater body (see illustration). If the reading is not as specified

at the beginning of this Chapter, replace the heater with a new one.
15 When fitting a new carburettor heater, apply a smear of thermo-grease to the threads, then screw it into the carburettor body and tighten it securely. Ensure the wiring connectors are a tight fit on the heater terminals
16 Install the remaining components in the reverse order of removal.

27 EVAP system solenoid (California models)

Note: *Refer to Chapter 1, Section 24 for details of the EVAP system.*
1 To check the solenoid, remove the left-hand frame cover (see Chapter 7). Unclip the solenoid from its holder and disconnect the wiring connector.
2 Connect a multimeter set to the ohms x 1 scale between the brown and black wire terminals of the solenoid.
3 If the reading is not as specified at the beginning of this Chapter, replace the solenoid with a new one.
4 If the solenoid is good, check the wiring between the solenoid and the ignition fuse.

28 Starter relay

1 If the starter circuit is faulty, first check the main fuse and ignition fuse (see Section 5). Next check the starter relay as follows.
2 On 650 models, the relay is located on the front edge of the battery tray – remove the battery cover for access (see Chapter 7). On 1100 models, the relay is located underneath the ICU panel – remove the seats and displace the panel for access (see Chapter 7).
3 Lift the terminal cover and unscrew the bolt securing the thick black starter motor lead to the relay terminal marked M (see illustration).

26.14 Checking carburettor heater resistance

28.3 Disconnect the starter motor lead from terminal M

4 Position the lead away from the relay terminal. With the ignition switch ON, the engine kill switch in the RUN position, and the transmission in neutral, press the starter switch. The relay should be heard to click.

5 If the relay doesn't click, switch the ignition OFF and test it as follows.

6 Lift the terminal cover and unscrew the bolt securing the thick red battery lead to the relay terminal marked B, then disconnect the relay wiring connector (see illustration).

7 Connect a multimeter set to the ohms x 1 scale, or a continuity tester, between the relay's starter motor (M) and battery (B) lead terminals. There should be no continuity. Now, using a fully-charged 12V battery and two suitable jumper wires, connect the battery positive (+ve) terminal to the relay's red/white wire terminal, and the battery negative (–ve) terminal to the relay's blue wire terminal. With voltage applied the relay should be heard to click and the test equipment should show continuity.

8 If the relay does not click when battery voltage is applied and indicates no continuity (infinite resistance) across its terminals, it is faulty and must be replaced with a new one. Remove the relay with its rubber sleeve from its mounting lug.

9 If the relay is good, check for battery voltage at the red/white wire terminal on the loom side of the relay wiring connector when the starter button is pressed with the ignition switched ON. If voltage is present, check the other components in the starter circuit as described in the relevant Sections of this Chapter. If no voltage is present, check the wiring between the various components (see Wiring Diagrams at the end of this Chapter).

10 Installation is the reverse of removal. Check that the contacts inside the wiring connector are clean and free from corrosion, then connect the relay securely. The starter motor lead (black) connects to the terminal marked M, and the battery lead (red) to the terminal marked B. Make sure the terminal nuts are tightened securely.

11 Install the remaining components in the reverse order of removal.

29 Starter motor removal and installation

Removal

1 Disconnect the battery negative (–ve) lead (see Section 3).

2 Pull back the terminal boot, remove the nut securing the lead to the starter motor terminal and disconnect the lead (see illustration).

3 Unscrew the two bolts securing the starter motor and draw the starter motor out of the crankcase and remove it from the machine (see illustrations).

4 Remove the O-ring on the end of the starter motor and discard it, as a new one must be used.

Installation

5 Fit a new O-ring onto the end of the starter motor, making sure it is seated in its groove, and smear it with grease (see illustration).

6 Manoeuvre the motor into position and slide it into the crankcase. Ensure that the starter motor teeth mesh correctly with those of the starter intermediate gear (see illustration). Install the mounting bolts and tighten them to the torque setting specified at the beginning of this Chapter.

7 Connect the lead to the starter motor terminal and secure it with the nut. Make sure the boot is correctly seated over the terminal.

8 Connect the battery negative (–ve) lead.

30 Starter motor overhaul

1 Remove the starter motor (see Section 29).

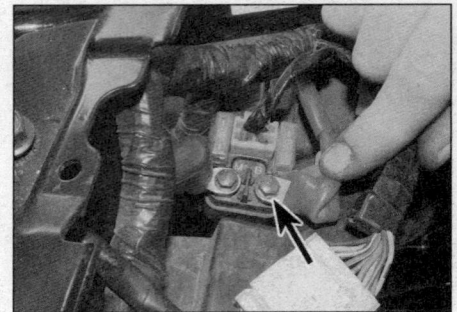
28.6 Disconnect the battery lead from terminal B

29.2 Disconnect the starter motor terminal lead

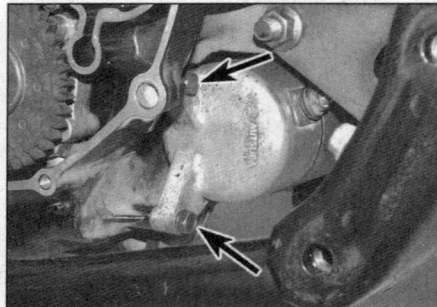
29.3a Undo the starter motor mounting bolts – 650 models shown

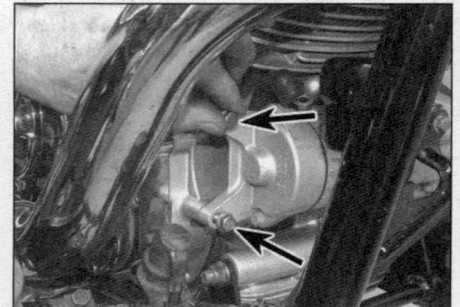
29.3b Undo the starter motor mounting bolts – 1100 models shown

29.3c Withdraw the starter motor from the crankcase

29.5 Fit a new O-ring and smear it with grease

29.6 Location of starter intermediate gear (arrowed)

30.2 Remove the terminal nut, washer and insulating washers

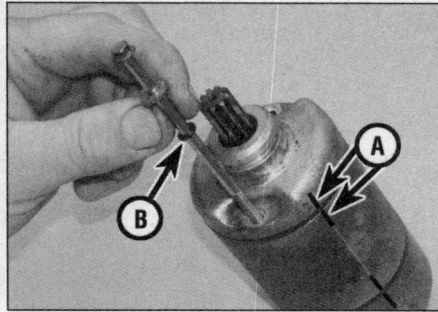

30.3 Note the alignment marks (A) and O-ring (B)

30.4 Remove the front cover

650 models

Disassembly

2 Noting the order in which they are fitted, unscrew the terminal nut and remove it along with its washer and insulating washers **(see illustration)**.

3 Note the alignment marks between the main housing and the front and rear covers, or make your own if they are unclear, then unscrew the two long bolts and remove the bolts and O-rings **(see illustration)**.

4 Remove the front cover from the motor **(see illustration)**.

5 Remove the tabbed washer from inside the cover and slide the insulating washer and shim(s) from the front end of the armature, noting the order in which they are fitted **(see illustrations)**.

6 Remove the main housing and remove the cover O-rings from the housing and discard

them as new ones must be fitted on reassembly **(see illustrations)**.

7 Remove the rear cover and brushplate assembly from the armature commutator **(see illustration)**. Remove the shim(s) from the rear end of the armature shaft **(see illustration)**.

8 Note how the brushplate locates in the rear cover, then lift the brushplate assembly out **(see illustrations)**.

30.5a Remove the tabbed washer – note the oil seal (arrowed) and needle bearing

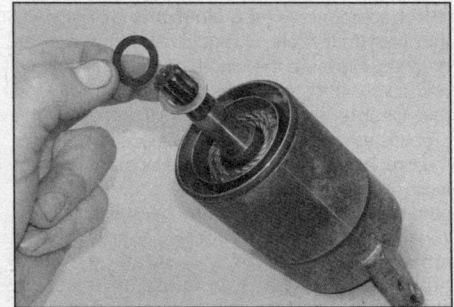

30.5b Remove the insulating washer and shim(s)

30.6a Pull off the main housing . . .

30.6b . . . and remove the cover O-rings

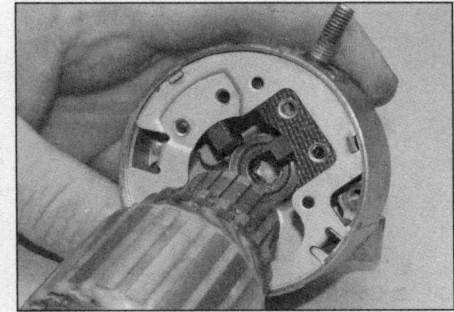

30.7a Pull the rear cover and brushplate off the commutator

30.7b Remove the shim(s) from the armature shaft

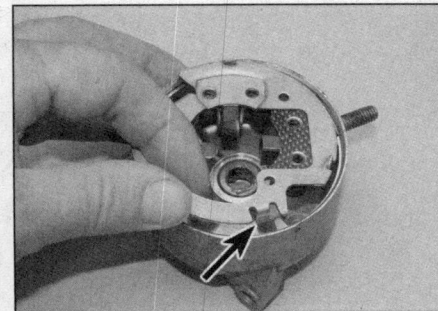

30.8a Note how the brushplate locates in the cover . . .

30.8b . . . then lift it out

30.9 Remove the brushes from their holders

9 Lift the brush springs and slide the brushes out from their holders, noting that one brush is attached to the terminal and the other is attached to the brushplate (see illustration).

Inspection

10 Check the general condition of all the starter motor components (see illustration). The parts that are most likely to require attention are the brushes. Measure the length of the brushes and compare the results to the brush length listed in this Chapter's Specifications. If either of the brushes are worn beyond the service limit, renew the brushplate assembly. If the brushes are not worn excessively, cracked, chipped, or otherwise damaged, they may be re-used.

11 Inspect the commutator bars on the armature for scoring, scratches and discoloration. The commutator can be cleaned and polished with crocus cloth, but

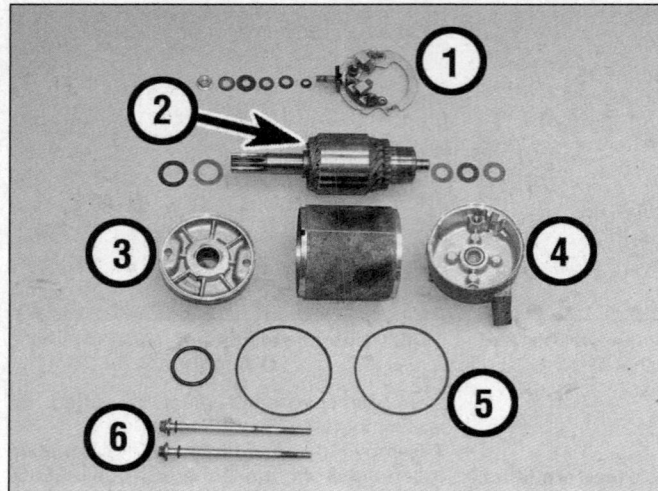

30.10 Starter motor components – 650 models

1 Brushplate and terminal
2 Armature and shims
3 Front cover
4 Rear cover
5 O-rings
6 Assembly bolts

do not use sandpaper or emery paper. After cleaning, wipe away any residue with a cloth soaked in electrical system cleaner or denatured alcohol.

12 Using a multimeter or a continuity tester, check for continuity between the commutator bars (see illustration). Continuity should exist (Yamaha specify zero resistance) between each bar and all of the others.

13 Check for continuity between the commutator bars and the armature shaft (see illustration). There should be no continuity

(infinite resistance – Yamaha specify a resistance of over 1 M-ohm); if the checks indicate otherwise, the armature is defective.

14 Check the depth of the insulating mica undercut between the commutator bars – if it is less than the amount specified at the beginning of this Chapter, scrape the mica away using a suitably shaped hacksaw blade until it is correct (see illustration).

15 Measure the diameter of the commutator and replace the starter motor with a new one if it has worn below the minimum diameter specified (see illustration).

16 Check the starter pinion gear for worn, cracked, chipped and broken teeth. If the gear is damaged or worn, replace the starter motor with a new one – individual components are not available

17 Inspect the end covers for signs of cracks or wear. Check the oil seal and needle bearing in the front cover and the bush in the rear cover for wear and damage (see illustration 30.5a). Inspect the magnets in the main housing and the housing itself for cracks.

18 Inspect the terminal insulating washers and the O-ring and square insulating washer on the terminal for signs of damage, and renew them if necessary. Renew the O-rings on the long assembly bolts.

Reassembly

19 Slide the brushes back into their holders and place the brush spring ends onto the brushes.

20 If removed, fit the square insulating washer and O-ring onto the terminal. Install the terminal and brushplate assembly into the rear cover (see illustration 30.8a).

21 Fit the insulating washers onto the terminal, followed by the plain washer and nut.

22 Slide the shims onto the rear end of the armature shaft (see illustration 30.7b). Lubricate the shaft with a smear of grease, then insert the shaft into the rear cover,

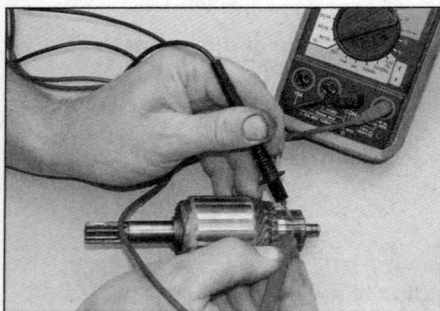

30.12 Continuity should exist between the commutator bars

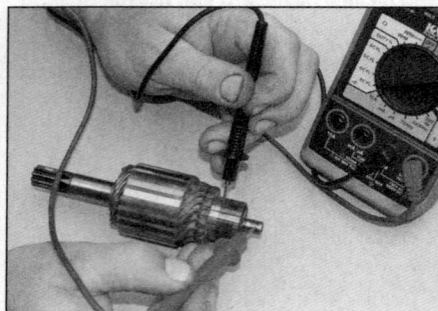

30.13 There should be no continuity between the commutator bars and the armature shaft

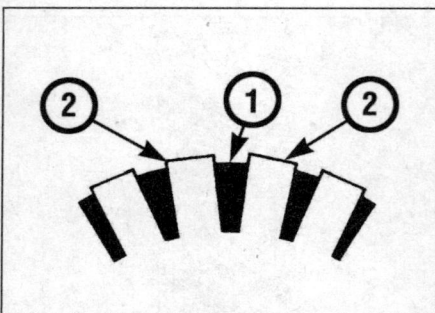

30.14 Cut the Mica (1) is below the commutator bars (2)

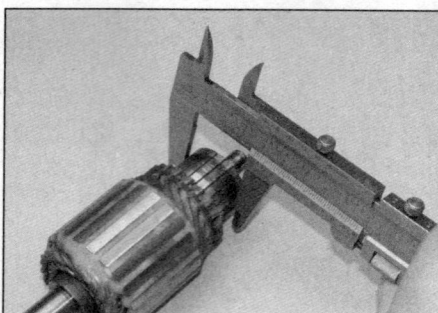

30.15 Measure the diameter of the commutator

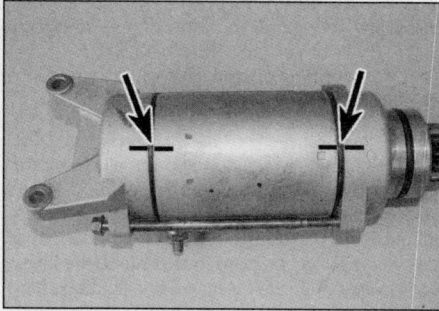

30.27 Note the alignment marks between the main housing and covers

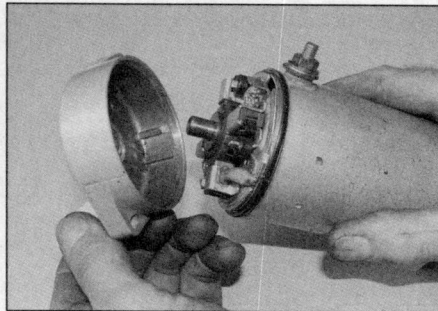

30.28 Lift off the rear cover

30.29 Remove the shims from the end of the shaft (arrowed)

locating the brushes on the commutator as you do, taking care not to damage the brushes **(see illustration 30.7a)**. Check that each brush is securely pressed against the commutator by its spring and is free to move easily in its holder.

23 Fit new O-rings onto the main housing, then fit the housing over the armature and onto the rear cover, aligning the marks made on removal.

24 Slide the shims and then the insulating washer onto the front end of the armature shaft and lubricate the shaft with a smear of grease. Apply a smear of grease to the inside of the front cover oil seal and fit the tabbed washer into the cover, making sure the tabs locate correctly **(see illustrations 30.5b**

and a). Install the cover onto the main housing, aligning the marks made on removal (see Step 3).

25 If fitted, slide a new O-ring onto each of the long bolts. Check that the marks on the rear cover, main housing and front cover are correctly aligned, then install the bolts **(see illustration 30.3)**.

26 Install the starter motor (see Section 29).

1100 models

Disassembly

27 Note the alignment marks between the main housing and the front and rear covers, or make your own if they are unclear, then

unscrew the two long bolts and remove the bolts **(see illustration)**.

28 Remove the rear cover from the motor **(see illustration)**.

29 Remove the shims from the rear end of the armature shaft **(see illustration)**.

30 Carefully lever the brush springs onto the brush holders to release the pressure on the brushes, then pull the terminal brushes (with insulated wires) out of the holders and lift off the brushplate **(see illustrations)**.

31 Remove the rear cover O-ring **(see illustration)**.

32 Remove the main housing and remove the front cover O-ring **(see illustrations)**. Discard the cover O-rings as new ones must be fitted on reassembly.

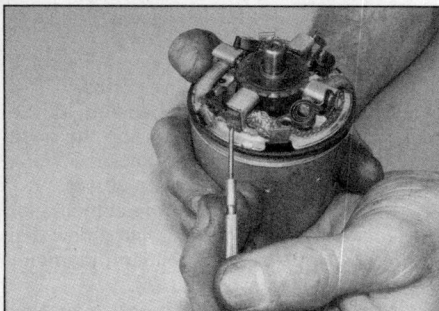

30.30a Lever the springs onto the brush holders . . .

30.30b . . . then pull the terminal brushes out of their holders (arrowed) . . .

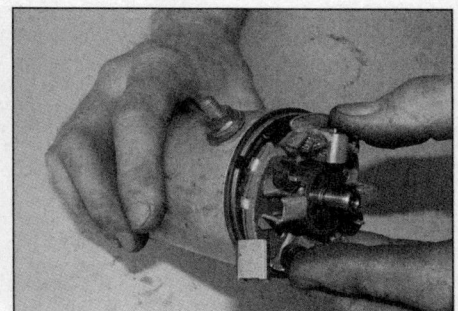

30.30c . . . and lift off the brushplate

30.31 Remove the rear cover O-ring

30.32a Remove the main housing . . .

30.32b . . . and the front cover O-ring

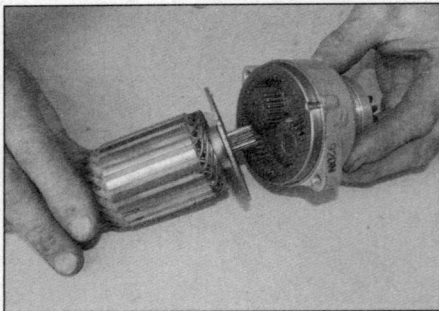

30.33 Pull the armature out of the front cover . . .

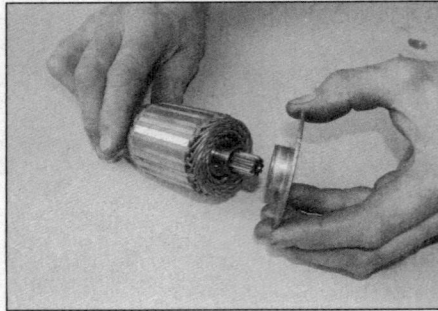

30.34 . . . and lift off the plate

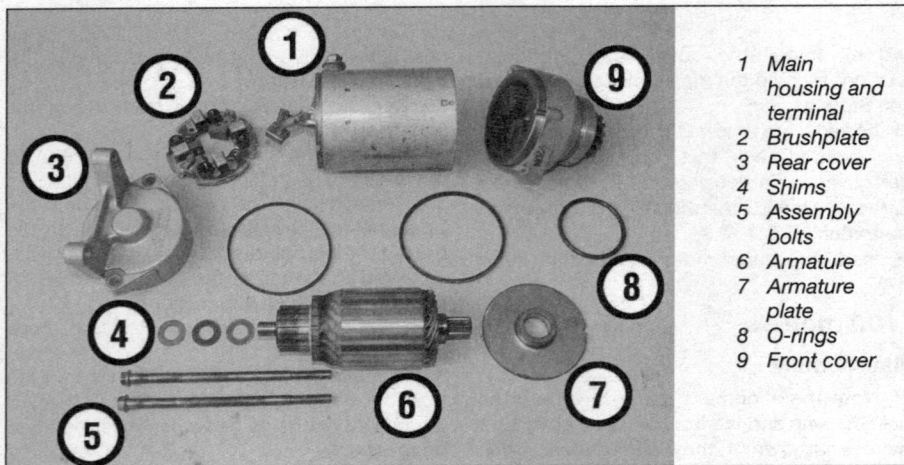

30.35 Starter motor components – 1100 models

1 Main housing and terminal
2 Brushplate
3 Rear cover
4 Shims
5 Assembly bolts
6 Armature
7 Armature plate
8 O-rings
9 Front cover

30.36a Measuring the length of the starter motor brushes

30.36b Terminal assembly (A) and brushplate assembly (B)

30.42a Inspect the starter pinion . . .

30.42b . . . and planetary gears for wear and damage

33 Pull the armature out of the front cover carefully, noting the location of the planetary gears in the cover (see illustration).

34 Lift the plate off the end of the armature (see illustration).

Inspection

35 Check the general condition of all the starter motor components (see illustration).

36 The parts that are most likely to require attention are the brushes. Measure the length of the brushes and compare the results to the brush length listed in this Chapter's Specifications (see illustration). If any of the brushes are worn beyond the service limit, renew the brushplate assembly and terminal assembly at the same time (see illustration). If the brushes are not worn excessively, cracked, chipped, or otherwise damaged, they may be re-used.

37 Inspect the commutator bars on the armature for scoring, scratches and discoloration. The commutator can be cleaned and polished with crocus cloth, but do not use sandpaper or emery paper. After cleaning, wipe away any residue with a cloth soaked in electrical system cleaner or denatured alcohol.

38 Using a multimeter or a continuity tester, check for continuity between the commutator bars (see illustration 30.12). Continuity should exist (Yamaha specify 0.026 to 0.034 ohms) between each bar and all of the others.

39 Check for continuity between the commutator bars and the armature shaft (see illustration 30.13). There should be no continuity (infinite resistance – Yamaha specify a resistance of over 1 M-ohm); if the checks indicate otherwise, the armature is defective.

40 Check the depth of the insulating mica undercut between the commutator bars – if it is less than the amount specified at the beginning of this Chapter, scrape the mica away using a suitably shaped hacksaw blade until it is correct (see illustration 30.14).

41 Measure the diameter of the commutator and replace the starter motor with a new one if it has worn below the minimum diameter specified (see illustration 30.15).

42 Check the starter pinion and planetary gears for worn, cracked, chipped and broken teeth (see illustrations). If any parts are damaged or worn, a new starter motor will have to be fitted as individual components are not available.

43 Inspect the end covers for signs of cracks or wear and inspect the magnets in the main housing and the housing itself for cracks.

44 If removed, inspect the terminal insulating washers for signs of damage, and renew them if necessary. Renew the O-rings on the long bolts.

Reassembly

45 Fit the plate onto the end of the armature and fit the armature into the front cover, ensuring the armature pinion engages with the planetary gears (see illustration 30.33).

46 Fit a new O-ring onto the front cover, then

30.48 Installed brushplate assembly should look like this

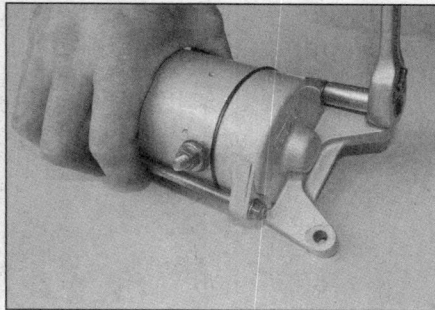

30.50 Tighten the long bolts

install the main housing, aligning the marks made on removal **(see illustrations 30.32b and a)**.

47 Fit a new O-ring onto the main housing **(see illustration 30.31)**.

48 Install the brush plate, ensuring the wires for the terminal brushes are correctly routed through the plate, then fit the terminal brushes into their holders. Ensure the brush springs are located correctly on the ends of the brushes **(see illustration)**.

49 Install the shims on the end of the armature shaft, then install the rear cover, aligning the marks made on removal **(see illustrations 30.29 and 30.28)**.

50 Check that the marks on the rear cover, main housing and front cover are correctly aligned, then install the bolts **(see illustration)**.

51 Install the starter motor (see Section 29).

31 Charging system testing

General information

1 If the performance of the charging system is suspect, the system as a whole should be checked first, followed by testing of the individual components (the alternator and the voltage regulator/rectifier). **Note:** *Before beginning the checks, make sure the battery is*

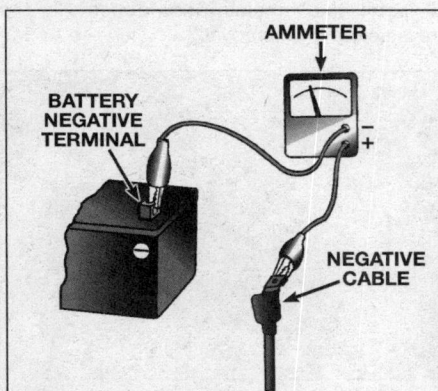

31.6 Checking the charging system leakage rate

fully charged and that all system connections are clean and tight.

2 Checking the output of the charging system and the performance of the various components within the charging system requires the use of a multimeter (with voltage, current and resistance checking facilities).

3 When making the checks, follow the procedures carefully to prevent incorrect connections or short circuits, as irreparable damage to electrical system components may result if short circuits occur.

4 If the charging system of the machine is thought to be faulty, remove the battery cover and perform the following checks.

Leakage test

Caution: Always connect an ammeter in series, never in parallel with the battery, otherwise it will be damaged. Do not turn the ignition ON or operate the starter motor when the ammeter is connected – a sudden surge in current will blow the meter's fuse.

5 Turn the ignition switch OFF and disconnect the lead from the battery negative (–ve) terminal.

6 Set the multimeter to the Amps function and connect its negative (–ve) probe to the battery negative (–ve) terminal, and positive (+ve) probe to the disconnected negative (–ve) lead **(see illustration)**. Always set the meter to a high amps range initially and then bring it down to the mA (milli Amps) range; if there is a high current flow in the circuit it may blow the meter's fuse.

7 No current flow should be indicated. If

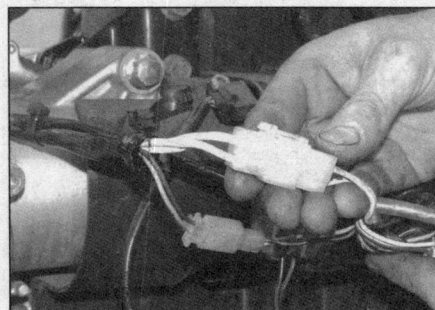

32.3 Disconnect the alternator wiring connector

current leakage is indicated (generally greater than 0.1 mA), there is a short circuit in the wiring, although if an alarm system is fitted its current draw should be taken into account. Using the wiring diagrams at the end of this Chapter, systematically disconnect individual electrical components, checking the meter each time until the source is identified.

8 If no leakage is indicated, disconnect the meter and connect the negative (–ve) lead to the battery, tightening it securely.

Output test

9 Start the engine and warm it up to normal operating temperature.

10 To check the regulated voltage output, allow the engine to idle and connect a multimeter set to the 0 to 20 volts DC scale (voltmeter) across the terminals of the battery, positive (+ve) lead to battery positive (+ve) terminal, negative (–ve) lead to battery negative (–ve) terminal. Slowly increase the engine speed to 5000 rpm and note the reading obtained.

11 Allow the engine to idle again, and turn on the headlight. Slowly increase the engine speed to 5000 rpm again and note the reading obtained.

12 The regulated voltage should be as specified at the beginning of this Chapter at all times. If the voltage is outside these limits, check the alternator, then the regulator/rectifier (see Sections 32 and 33).

32 Alternator

Check

1 Disconnect the battery negative (–ve) lead.

2 On 650 models, remove the fuel tank (see Chapter 4). On 1100 models, remove the left-hand frame cover (see Chapter 7).

3 Trace the wiring back from the alternator cover on the left-hand side of the engine and disconnect it at the connector containing the three white wires **(see illustration)**. Check that the contacts inside the wiring connector are clean and free from corrosion.

4 Using a multimeter set to the ohms x 1 (ohmmeter) scale, measure the resistance between the centre wire and each of the other two on the alternator side of the connector, taking a total of two readings, then check for continuity between each terminal and ground (earth). If the stator coil windings are in good condition the resistance readings should be within the range shown in the Specifications at the beginning of this Chapter and there should be no continuity (infinite resistance) between the terminals and ground (earth). If not, check the fault is not due to damaged wiring between the connector and coils. If the wiring is good, the alternator stator coil assembly is at fault and should be replaced with a new one.

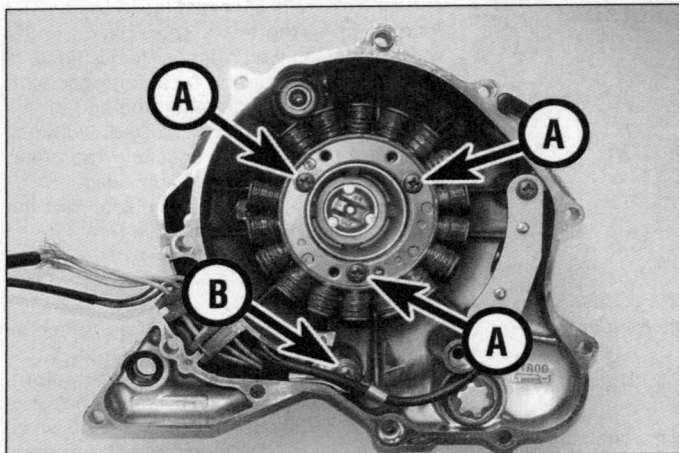

32.8a Location of the alternator stator bolts (A) and wiring clamp (B) – 650 models

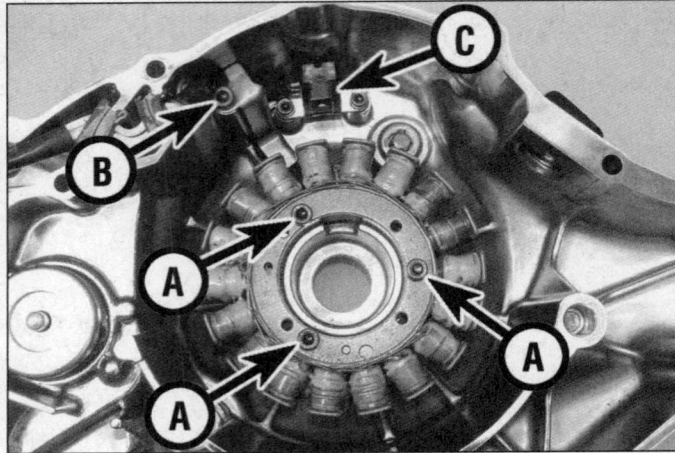

32.8b Location of the alternator stator bolts (A), wiring clamp (B) and pick-up coil (C) – 1100 models

Removal and installation

5 Follow Steps 1 to 3 above. In addition, on 650 models, remove the transmission cover and the middle gear cover (see Chapter 2A).
6 Feed the wiring back to the alternator cover, noting its routing and releasing it from any clips.
7 Disconnect the clutch cable from the bracket on the alternator cover, then remove the alternator cover (see Chapter 2A or 2B as applicable).
8 Unscrew the bolts securing the alternator stator and the wiring clamp to the inside of the cover, then free the wiring grommets from the cutout in the cover and remove the stator (see illustrations). On 1100 models, unscrew the bolts securing the pick-up coil and remove the pick-up coil and stator assembly.
9 To remove the alternator rotor, follow the procedure in Chapter 2A or 2B as applicable.
10 Fit the alternator stator and the wiring grommets into their locations in the cover. On 1100 models, install the pick-up coil and stator assembly. Apply a suitable non-permanent thread locking compound to the fixing bolts and tighten them to the torque setting specified at the beginning of this Chapter. Install the wiring clamp and tighten the clamp bolt securely.

11 If required, follow the procedure in Chapter 2A or 2B as applicable and install the alternator rotor.
12 Follow the procedure in Chapter 2A or 2B as applicable and install alternator cover and clutch cable.
13 Feed the wiring up to the connector, securing it with any clips, and reconnect it.
14 Install the remaining components in the reverse order of removal.

33 Regulator/rectifier

Check

1 Yamaha provides no test specifications for the regulator/rectifier other than the charging system regulated voltage output test (see Section 31). If the regulator/rectifier is suspected of being faulty, first check all other components and the wiring and connectors in the charging circuit, referring to the relevant Sections in this Chapter and to the wiring diagrams at the end.
2 If all other components and the wiring are good, remove the unit (see below) and take it

to a Yamaha dealer for testing. Alternatively, substitute the suspect unit with a known good one and see if the fault is cured.

HAYNES HiNT *Clues to a faulty regulator are constantly blowing bulbs, with brightness varying considerably with engine speed, and battery overheating.*

Removal and installation

3 On 650 models, the regulator/rectifier is mounted to the frame in front of the engine unit (see illustration).
4 On 1100 models, the regulator/rectifier is mounted behind the right-hand frame cover (see illustration). Follow the procedure in Chapter 7 to remove the cover.
5 Unscrew the bolt(s) securing the regulator/rectifier, then disconnect the wiring connector and remove it (see illustration).
6 Install the new unit and tighten its bolts securely. Check that the contacts inside the wiring connector are clean and free from corrosion, then connect the regulator/rectifier securely.
7 Install the remaining components in the reverse order of removal.

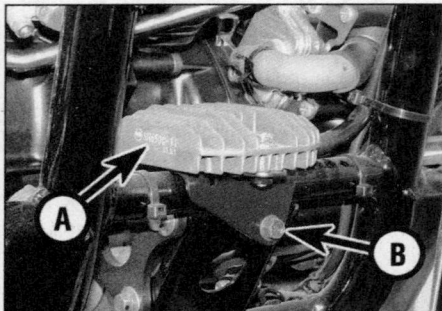

33.3 Location of the regulator/rectifier (A) – 650 models. Note the mounting bolt (B)

33.4 Location of the regulator/rectifier – 1100 models. Note the mounting bolts (arrowed)

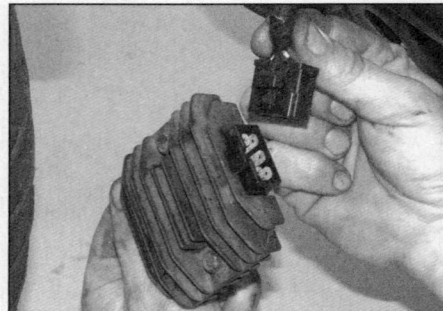

33.5 Regulator/rectifier wiring connector

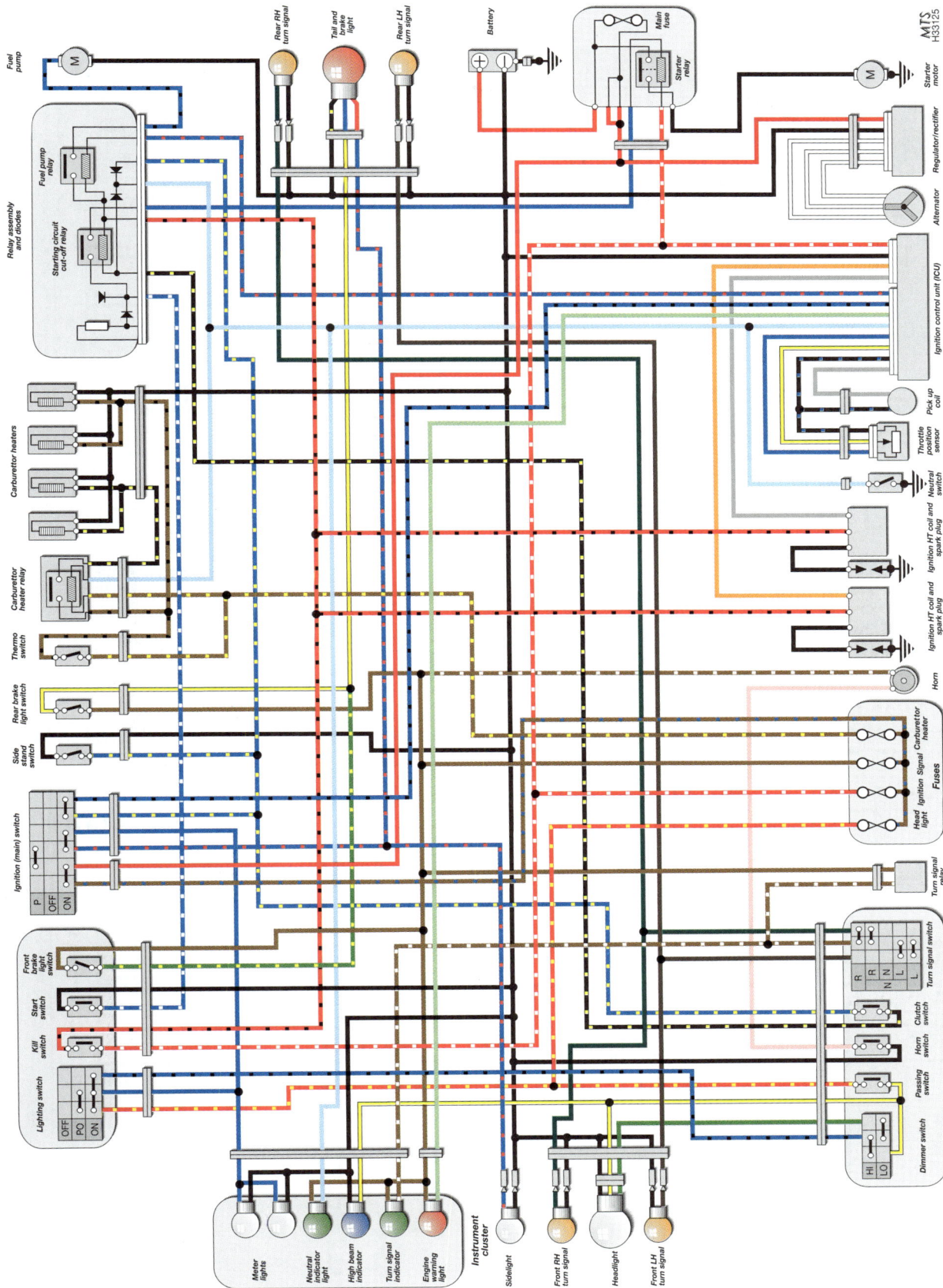

Fuel pump

Rear RH turn signal

Tail and brake light

Rear LH turn signal

Battery

Main fuse

Starter relay

Starter motor

Regulator/rectifier

Alternator

Relay assembly and diodes

Fuel pump relay

Starting circuit cut-off relay

Ignition control unit (ICU)

Pick up coil

Throttle position sensor

Neutral switch

Carburettor heaters

Ignition HT coil and spark plug

Ignition HT coil and spark plug

Carburettor heater relay

Thermo switch

Horn

Rear brake light switch

Carburettor heater

Side stand switch

Ignition Signal

Fuses

Ignition (main) switch

Head light

P
OFF
ON

Turn signal relay

Turn signal switch

R
R
N
L
L

Front brake light switch

Start switch

Clutch switch

Kill switch

Horn switch

Lighting switch

Passing switch

OFF
PO
ON

Dimmer switch

HI
LO

Instrument cluster

Meter lights

Neutral indicator light

High beam indicator

Turn signal indicator

Engine warning light

Sidelight

Front RH turn signal

Headlight

Front LH turn signal

XVS650 and XVS650A 1997 to 2000 (Europe)

MTS
H33125

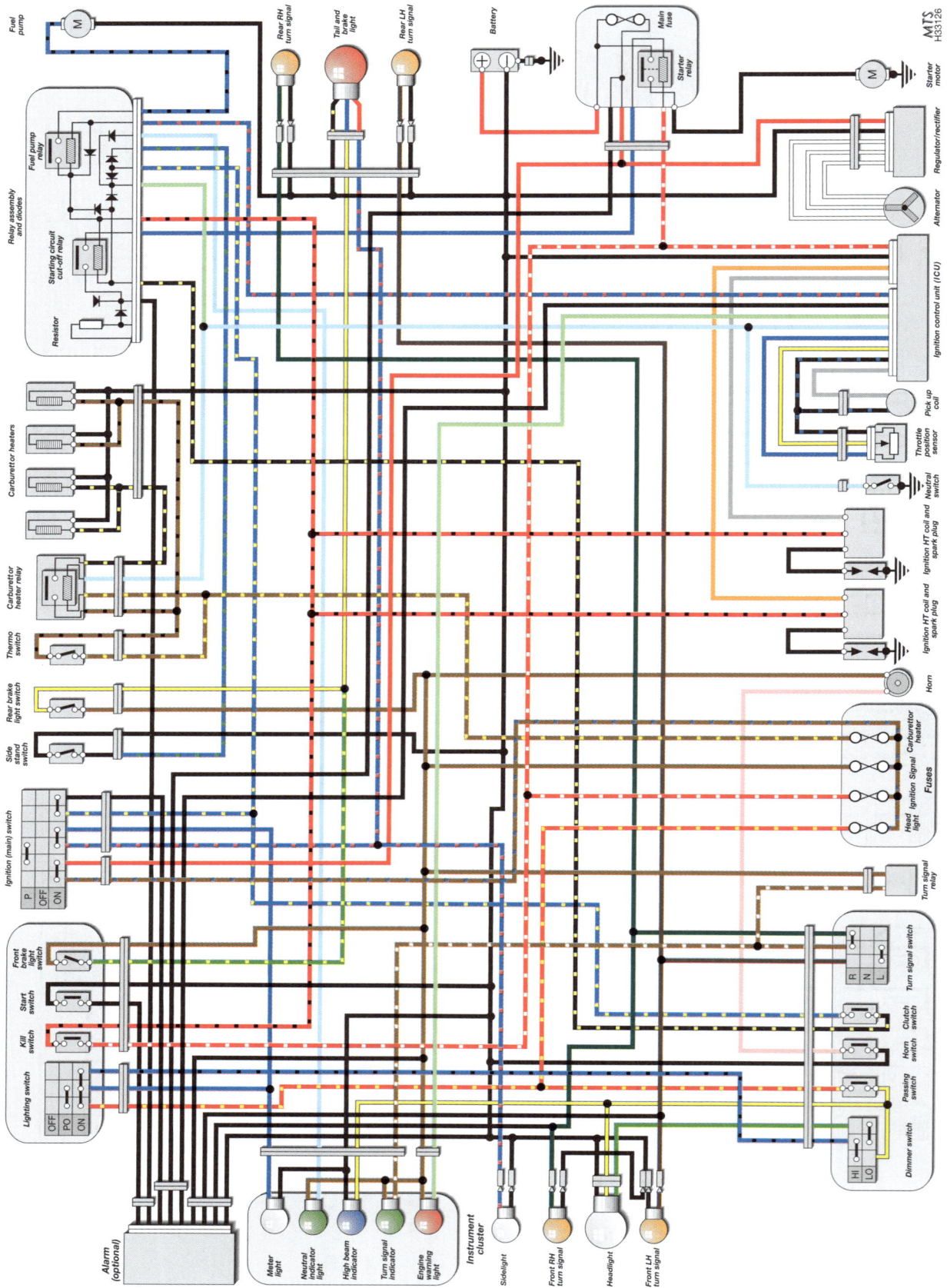

XVS650 2001-on (Europe)

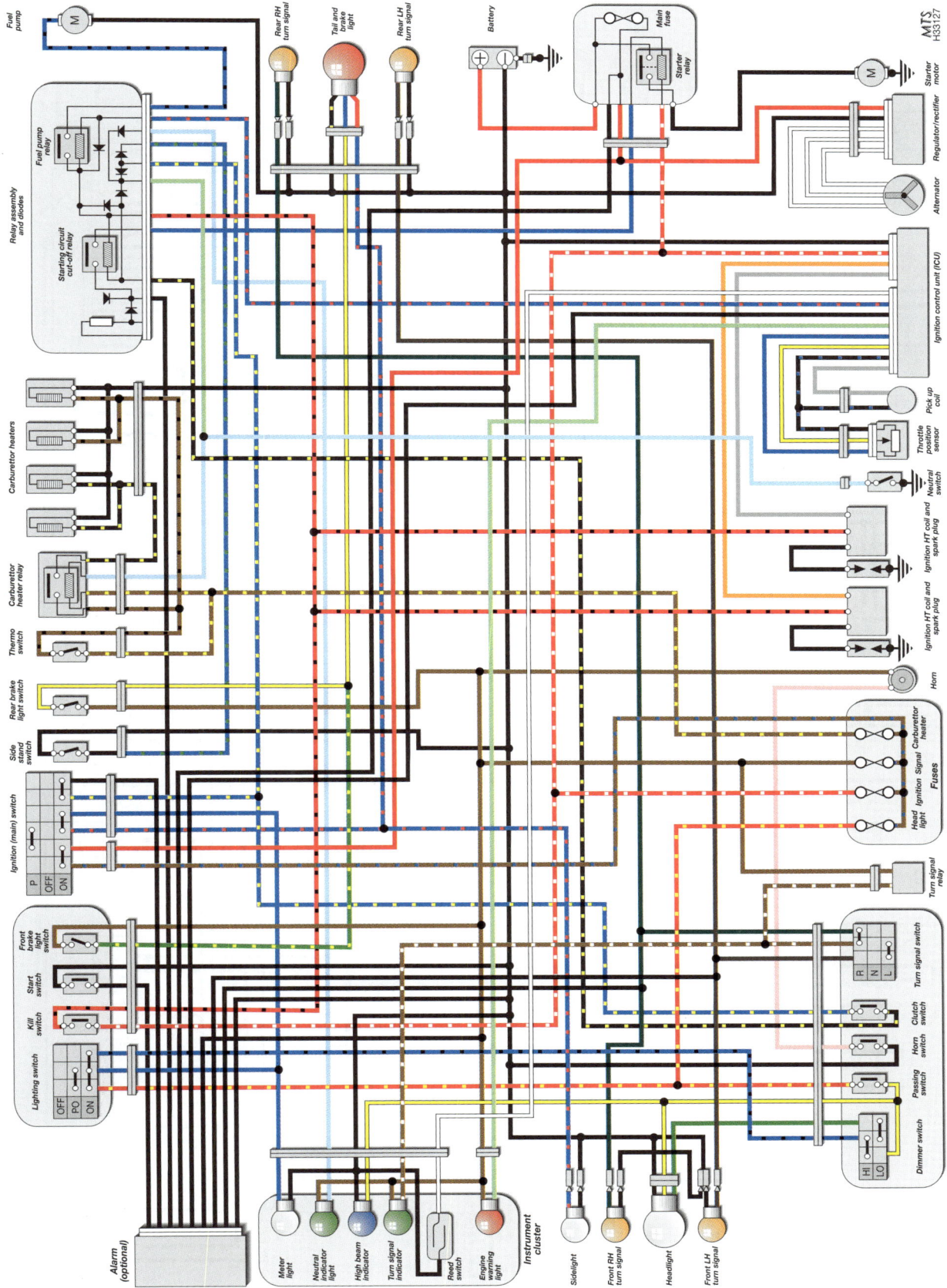

XVS650A 2001 to 2003 (Europe)

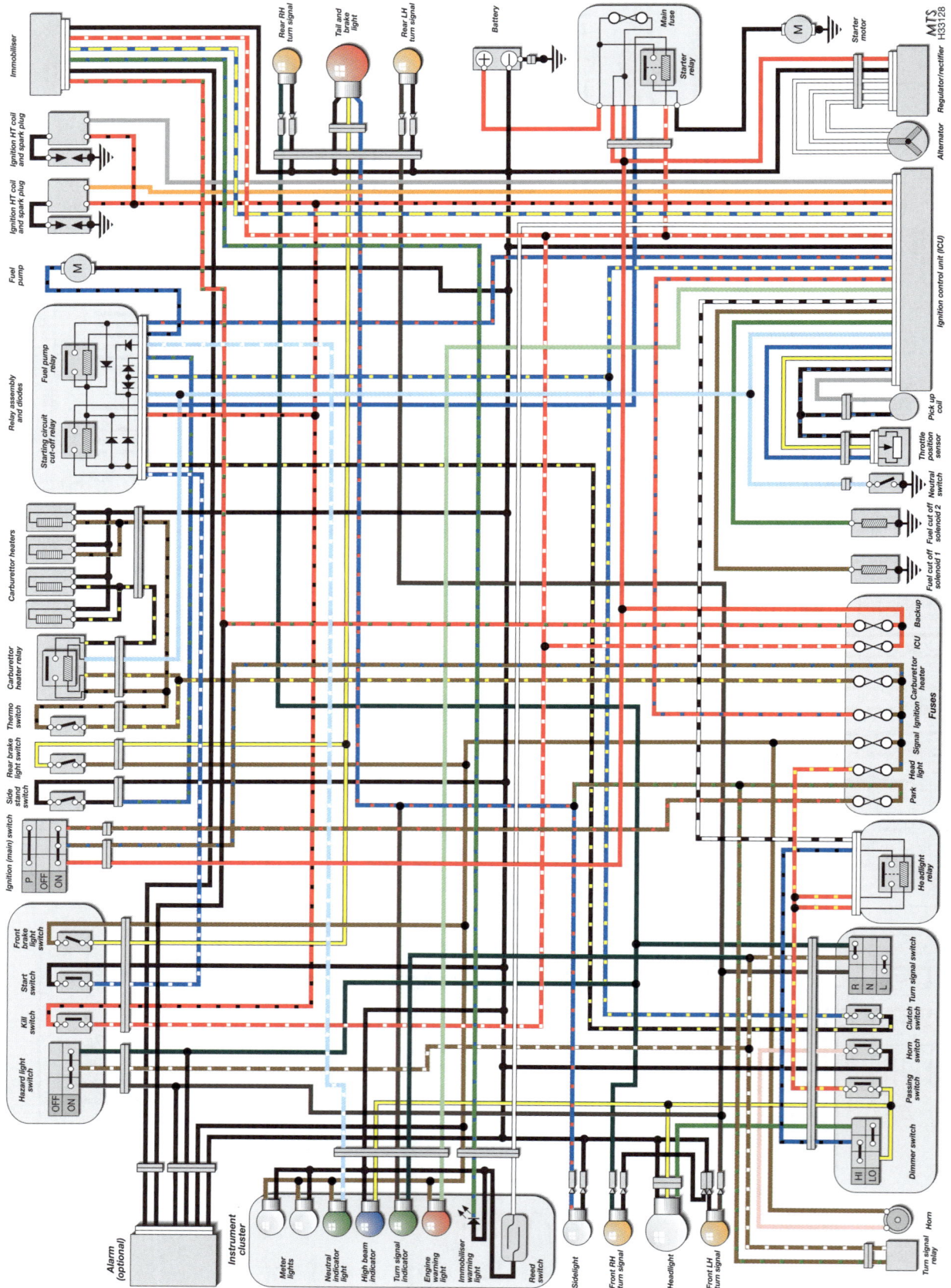

XVS650A 2004-on (Europe)

XVS650 (US models)

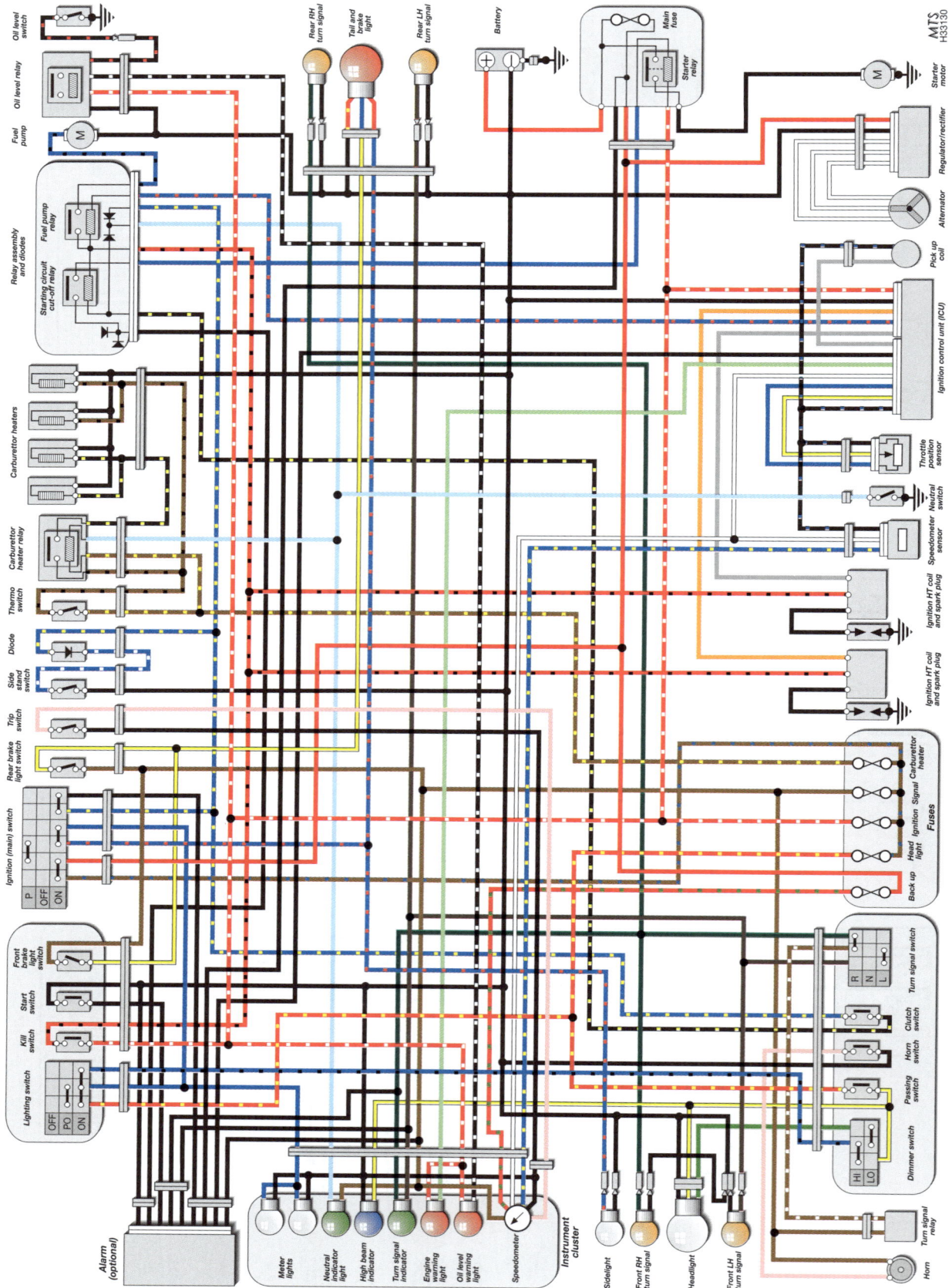

XVS1100 1999-on and XVS1100A 2000 to 2002 (Europe)

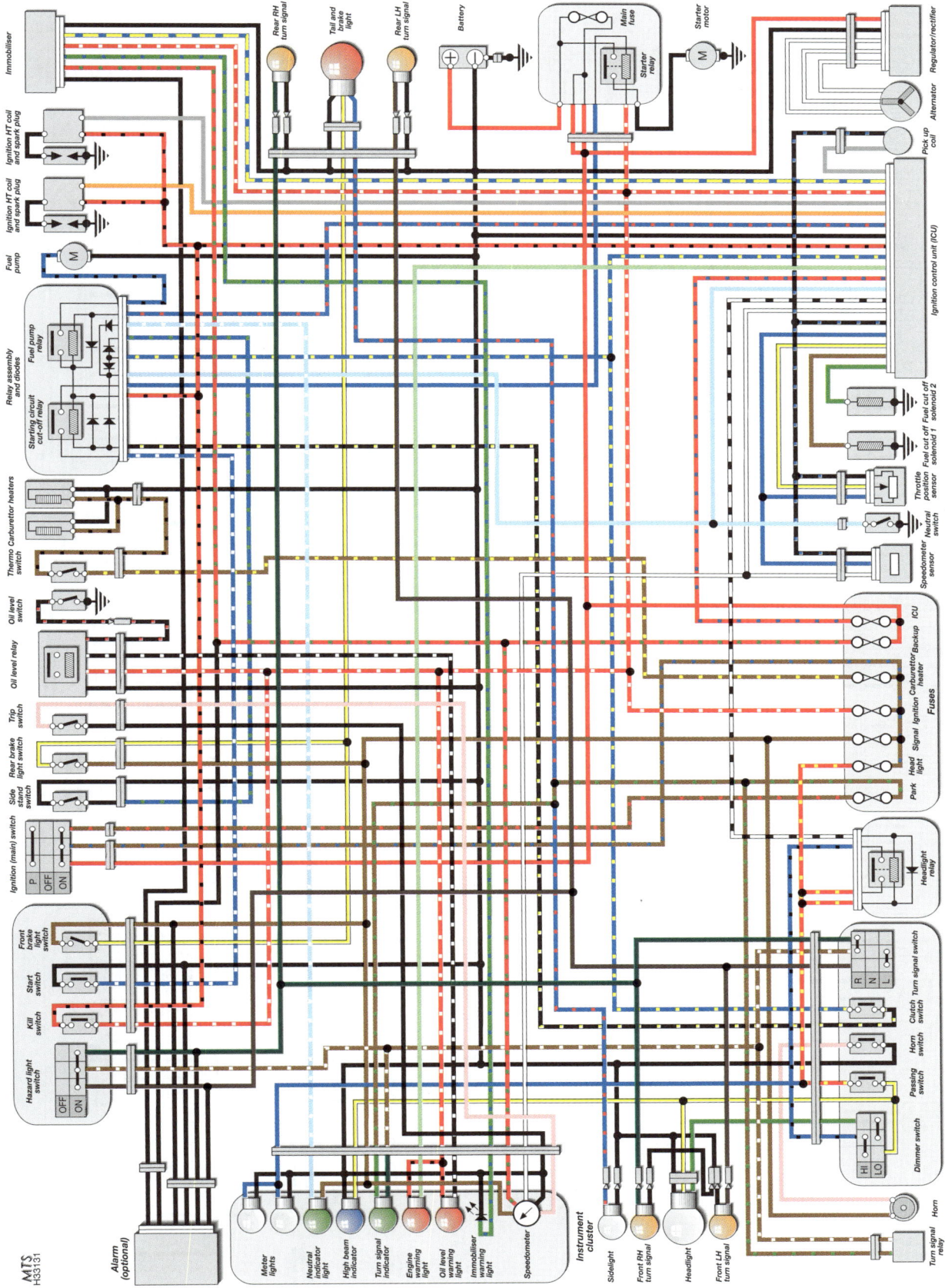

XVS1100A 2003-on (Europe)

MTS
H33131

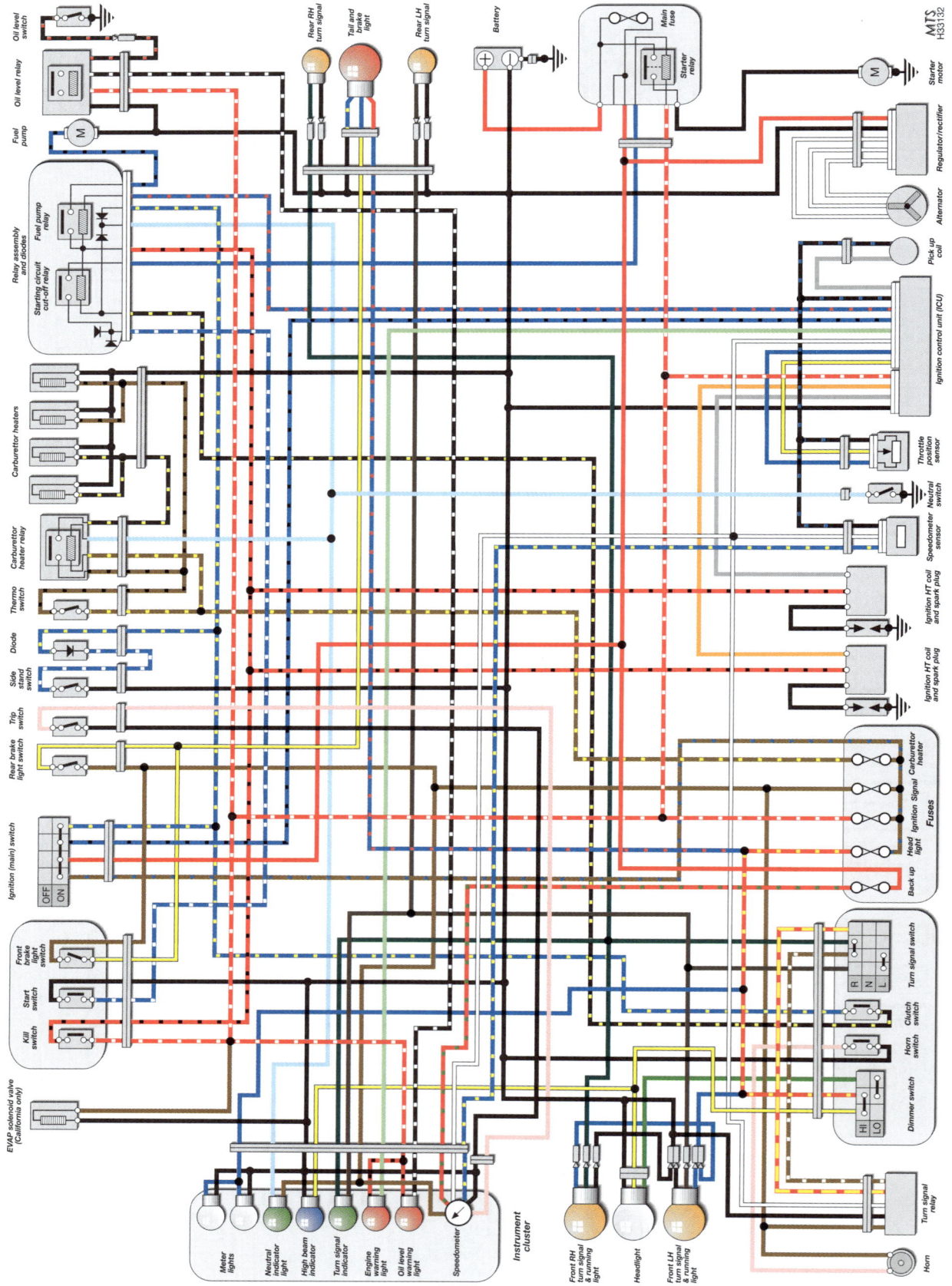

XVS1100 (US models)

Reference

Tools and Workshop Tips

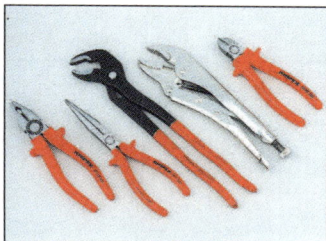

- Building up a tool kit and equipping your workshop ● Using tools ● Understanding bearing, seal, fastener and chain sizes and markings ● Repair techniques

Security

- Locks and chains ● U-locks ● Disc locks ● Alarms and immobilisers ● Security marking systems ● Tips on how to prevent bike theft

Lubricants and fluids

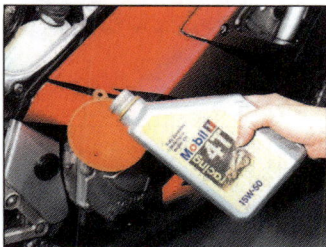

- Engine oils ● Transmission (gear) oils ● Coolant/anti-freeze ● Fork oils and suspension fluids ● Brake/clutch fluids ● Spray lubes, degreasers and solvents

Conversion Factors

34 Nm x 0.738

= 25 lbf ft

- Formulae for conversion of the metric (SI) units used throughout the manual into Imperial measures

MOT Test Checks

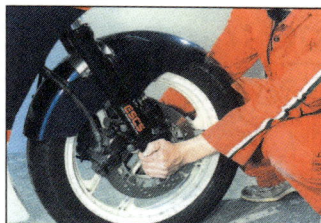

- A guide to the UK MOT test ● Which items are tested ● How to prepare your motorcycle for the test and perform a pre-test check

Storage

- How to prepare your motorcycle for going into storage and protect essential systems ● How to get the motorcycle back on the road

Fault Finding

- Common faults and their likely causes ● How to check engine cylinder compression ● How to make electrical tests and use test meters

Technical Terms Explained

- Component names, technical terms and common abbreviations explained

Index

Buying tools

A toolkit is a fundamental requirement for servicing and repairing a motorcycle. Although there will be an initial expense in building up enough tools for servicing, this will soon be offset by the savings made by doing the job yourself. As experience and confidence grow, additional tools can be added to enable the repair and overhaul of the motorcycle. Many of the specialist tools are expensive and not often used so it may be preferable to hire them, or for a group of friends or motorcycle club to join in the purchase.

As a rule, it is better to buy more expensive, good quality tools. Cheaper tools are likely to wear out faster and need to be renewed more often, nullifying the original saving.

> ⚠ **Warning: To avoid the risk of a poor quality tool breaking in use, causing injury or damage to the component being worked on, always aim to purchase tools which meet the relevant national safety standards.**

The following lists of tools do not represent the manufacturer's service tools, but serve as a guide to help the owner decide which tools are needed for this level of work. In addition, items such as an electric drill, hacksaw, files, soldering iron and a workbench equipped with a vice, may be needed. Although not classed as tools, a selection of bolts, screws, nuts, washers and pieces of tubing always come in useful.

For more information about tools, refer to the Haynes *Motorcycle Workshop Practice TechBook* (Bk. No. 3470).

Manufacturer's service tools

Inevitably certain tasks require the use of a service tool. Where possible an alternative tool or method of approach is recommended, but sometimes there is no option if personal injury or damage to the component is to be avoided. Where required, service tools are referred to in the relevant procedure.

Service tools can usually only be purchased from a motorcycle dealer and are identified by a part number. Some of the commonly-used tools, such as rotor pullers, are available in aftermarket form from mail-order motorcycle tool and accessory suppliers.

Maintenance and minor repair tools

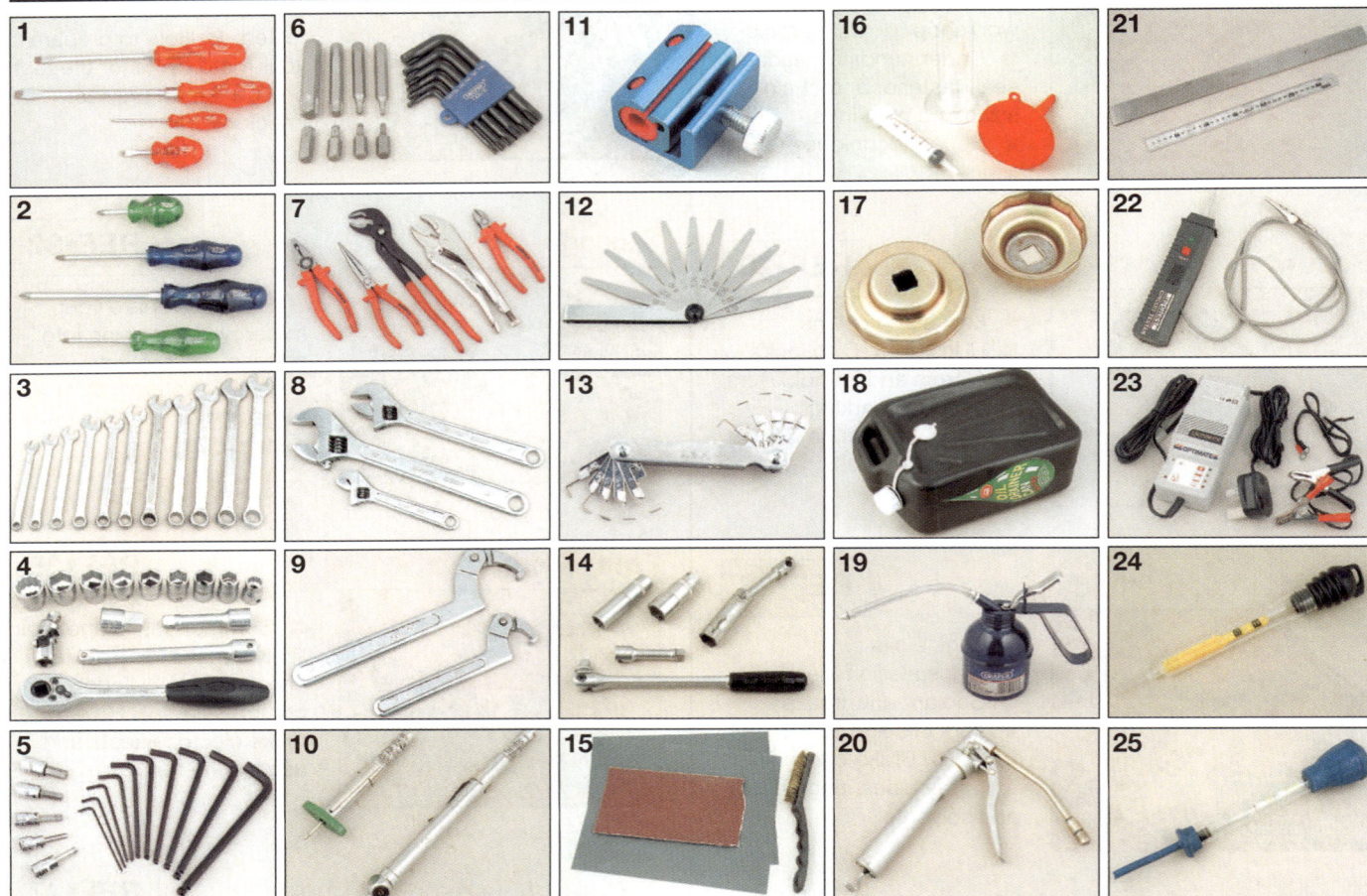

1 Set of flat-bladed screwdrivers
2 Set of Phillips head screwdrivers
3 Combination open-end and ring spanners
4 Socket set (3/8 inch or 1/2 inch drive)
5 Set of Allen keys or bits

6 Set of Torx keys or bits
7 Pliers, cutters and self-locking grips (Mole grips)
8 Adjustable spanners
9 C-spanners
10 Tread depth gauge and tyre pressure gauge

11 Cable oiler clamp
12 Feeler gauges
13 Spark plug gap measuring tool
14 Spark plug spanner or deep plug sockets
15 Wire brush and emery paper

16 Calibrated syringe, measuring vessel and funnel
17 Oil filter adapters
18 Oil drainer can or tray
19 Pump type oil can
20 Grease gun

21 Straight-edge and steel rule
22 Continuity tester
23 Battery charger
24 Hydrometer (for battery specific gravity check)
25 Anti-freeze tester (for liquid-cooled engines)

Repair and overhaul tools

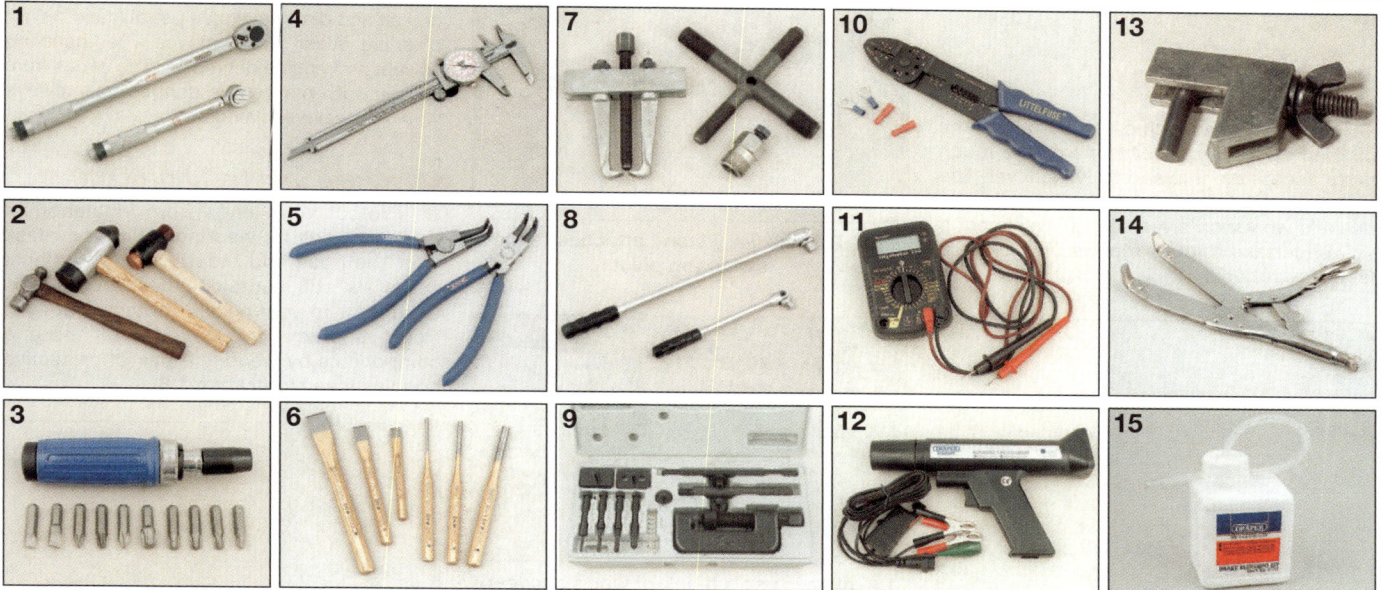

1 Torque wrench
(small and mid-ranges)
2 Conventional, plastic or
soft-faced hammers
3 Impact driver set

4 Vernier gauge
5 Circlip pliers (internal and
external, or combination)
6 Set of cold chisels
and punches

7 Selection of pullers
8 Breaker bars
9 Chain breaking/
riveting tool set

10 Wire stripper and
crimper tool
11 Multimeter (measures
amps, volts and ohms)
12 Stroboscope (for
dynamic timing checks)

13 Hose clamp
(wingnut type shown)
14 Clutch holding tool
15 One-man brake/clutch
bleeder kit

Specialist tools

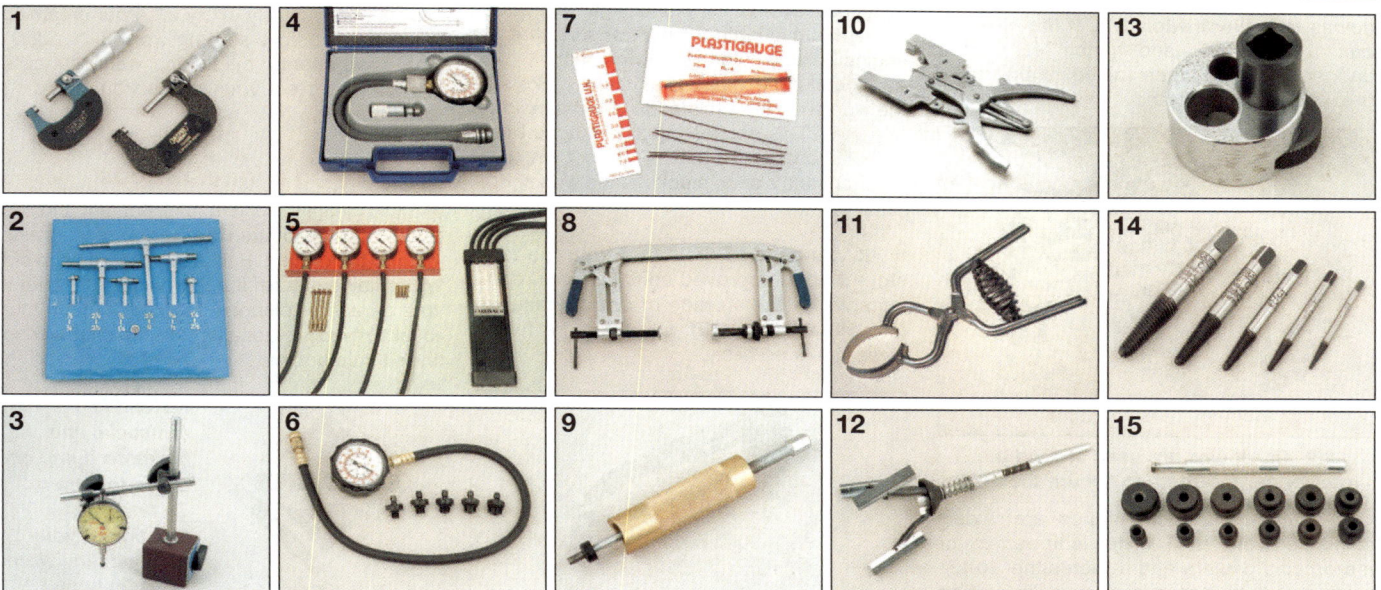

1 Micrometers
(external type)
2 Telescoping gauges
3 Dial gauge

4 Cylinder
compression gauge
5 Vacuum gauges (left) or
manometer (right)
6 Oil pressure gauge

7 Plastigauge kit
8 Valve spring compressor
(4-stroke engines)
9 Piston pin drawbolt tool

10 Piston ring removal and
installation tool
11 Piston ring clamp
12 Cylinder bore hone
(stone type shown)

13 Stud extractor
14 Screw extractor set
15 Bearing driver set

1 Workshop equipment and facilities

The workbench

● Work is made much easier by raising the bike up on a ramp - components are much more accessible if raised to waist level. The hydraulic or pneumatic types seen in the dealer's workshop are a sound investment if you undertake a lot of repairs or overhauls **(see illustration 1.1)**.

1.1 Hydraulic motorcycle ramp

● If raised off ground level, the bike must be supported on the ramp to avoid it falling. Most ramps incorporate a front wheel locating clamp which can be adjusted to suit different diameter wheels. When tightening the clamp, take care not to mark the wheel rim or damage the tyre - use wood blocks on each side to prevent this.
● Secure the bike to the ramp using tie-downs **(see illustration 1.2)**. If the bike has only a sidestand, and hence leans at a dangerous angle when raised, support the bike on an auxiliary stand.

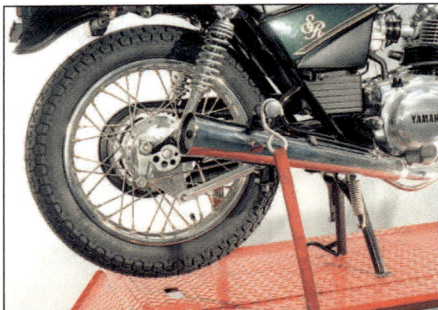

1.2 Tie-downs are used around the passenger footrests to secure the bike

● Auxiliary (paddock) stands are widely available from mail order companies or motorcycle dealers and attach either to the wheel axle or swingarm pivot **(see illustration 1.3)**. If the motorcycle has a centrestand, you can support it under the crankcase to prevent it toppling whilst either wheel is removed **(see illustration 1.4)**.

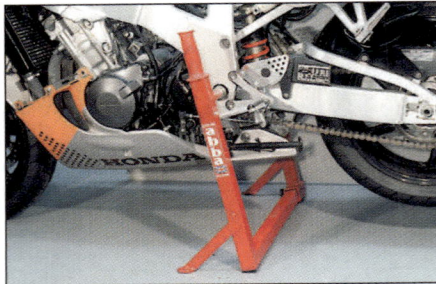

1.3 This auxiliary stand attaches to the swingarm pivot

1.4 Always use a block of wood between the engine and jack head when supporting the engine in this way

Fumes and fire

● Refer to the Safety first! page at the beginning of the manual for full details. Make sure your workshop is equipped with a fire extinguisher suitable for fuel-related fires (Class B fire - flammable liquids) - it is not sufficient to have a water-filled extinguisher.
● Always ensure adequate ventilation is available. Unless an exhaust gas extraction system is available for use, ensure that the engine is run outside of the workshop.
● If working on the fuel system, make sure the workshop is ventilated to avoid a build-up of fumes. This applies equally to fume build-up when charging a battery. Do not smoke or allow anyone else to smoke in the workshop.

Fluids

● If you need to drain fuel from the tank, store it in an approved container marked as suitable for the storage of petrol (gasoline) **(see illustration 1.5)**. Do not store fuel in glass jars or bottles.

1.5 Use an approved can only for storing petrol (gasoline)

● Use proprietary engine degreasers or solvents which have a high flash-point, such as paraffin (kerosene), for cleaning off oil, grease and dirt - never use petrol (gasoline) for cleaning. Wear rubber gloves when handling solvent and engine degreaser. The fumes from certain solvents can be dangerous - always work in a well-ventilated area.

Dust, eye and hand protection

● Protect your lungs from inhalation of dust particles by wearing a filtering mask over the nose and mouth. Many frictional materials still contain asbestos which is dangerous to your health. Protect your eyes from spouts of liquid and sprung components by wearing a pair of protective goggles **(see illustration 1.6)**.

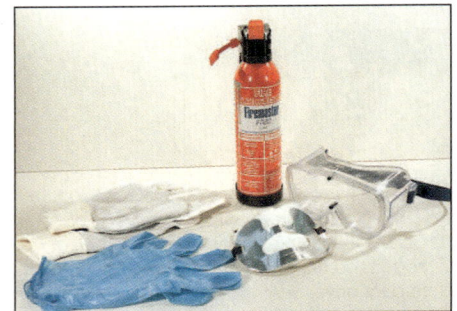

1.6 A fire extinguisher, goggles, mask and protective gloves should be at hand in the workshop

● Protect your hands from contact with solvents, fuel and oils by wearing rubber gloves. Alternatively apply a barrier cream to your hands before starting work. If handling hot components or fluids, wear suitable gloves to protect your hands from scalding and burns.

What to do with old fluids

● Old cleaning solvent, fuel, coolant and oils should not be poured down domestic drains or onto the ground. Package the fluid up in old oil containers, label it accordingly, and take it to a garage or disposal facility. Contact your local authority for location of such sites or ring the oil care hotline.

OIL CARE
FOLLOW THE CODE
OIL BANK LINE
0800 66 33 66
www.oilbankline.org.uk

Note: It is antisocial and illegal to dump oil down the drain. To find the location of your local oil recycling bank, call this number free.

In the USA, note that any oil supplier must accept used oil for recycling.

2 Fasteners -
screws, bolts and nuts

Fastener types and applications

Bolts and screws

● Fastener head types are either of hexagonal, Torx or splined design, with internal and external versions of each type **(see illustrations 2.1 and 2.2)**; splined head fasteners are not in common use on motorcycles. The conventional slotted or Phillips head design is used for certain screws. Bolt or screw length is always measured from the underside of the head to the end of the item **(see illustration 2.11)**.

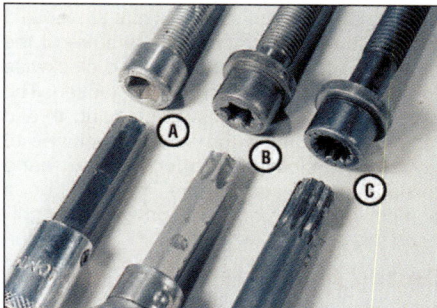

2.1 Internal hexagon/Allen (A), Torx (B) and splined (C) fasteners, with corresponding bits

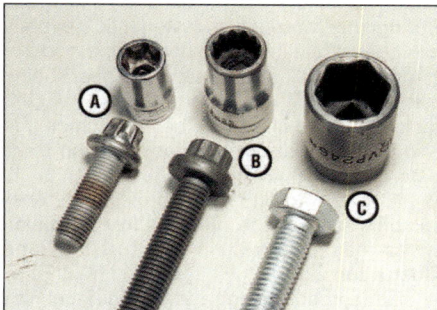

2.2 External Torx (A), splined (B) and hexagon (C) fasteners, with corresponding sockets

● Certain fasteners on the motorcycle have a tensile marking on their heads, the higher the marking the stronger the fastener. High tensile fasteners generally carry a 10 or higher marking. Never replace a high tensile fastener with one of a lower tensile strength.

Washers (see illustration 2.3)

● Plain washers are used between a fastener head and a component to prevent damage to the component or to spread the load when torque is applied. Plain washers can also be used as spacers or shims in certain assemblies. Copper or aluminium plain washers are often used as sealing washers on drain plugs.

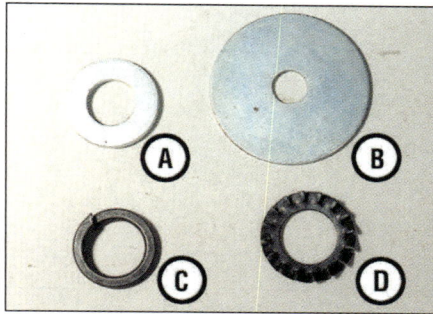

2.3 Plain washer (A), penny washer (B), spring washer (C) and serrated washer (D)

● The split-ring spring washer works by applying axial tension between the fastener head and component. If flattened, it is fatigued and must be renewed. If a plain (flat) washer is used on the fastener, position the spring washer between the fastener and the plain washer.
● Serrated star type washers dig into the fastener and component faces, preventing loosening. They are often used on electrical earth (ground) connections to the frame.
● Cone type washers (sometimes called Belleville) are conical and when tightened apply axial tension between the fastener head and component. They must be installed with the dished side against the component and often carry an OUTSIDE marking on their outer face. If flattened, they are fatigued and must be renewed.
● Tab washers are used to lock plain nuts or bolts on a shaft. A portion of the tab washer is bent up hard against one flat of the nut or bolt to prevent it loosening. Due to the tab washer being deformed in use, a new tab washer should be used every time it is disturbed.
● Wave washers are used to take up endfloat on a shaft. They provide light springing and prevent excessive side-to-side play of a component. Can be found on rocker arm shafts.

Nuts and split pins

● Conventional plain nuts are usually six-sided **(see illustration 2.4)**. They are sized by thread diameter and pitch. High tensile nuts carry a number on one end to denote their tensile strength.

2.4 Plain nut (A), shouldered locknut (B), nylon insert nut (C) and castellated nut (D)

● Self-locking nuts either have a nylon insert, or two spring metal tabs, or a shoulder which is staked into a groove in the shaft - their advantage over conventional plain nuts is a resistance to loosening due to vibration. The nylon insert type can be used a number of times, but must be renewed when the friction of the nylon insert is reduced, ie when the nut spins freely on the shaft. The spring tab type can be reused unless the tabs are damaged. The shouldered type must be renewed every time it is disturbed.
● Split pins (cotter pins) are used to lock a castellated nut to a shaft or to prevent slackening of a plain nut. Common applications are wheel axles and brake torque arms. Because the split pin arms are deformed to lock around the nut a new split pin must always be used on installation - always fit the correct size split pin which will fit snugly in the shaft hole. Make sure the split pin arms are correctly located around the nut **(see illustrations 2.5 and 2.6)**.

2.5 Bend split pin (cotter pin) arms as shown (arrows) to secure a castellated nut

2.6 Bend split pin (cotter pin) arms as shown to secure a plain nut

Caution: If the castellated nut slots do not align with the shaft hole after tightening to the torque setting, tighten the nut until the next slot aligns with the hole - never slacken the nut to align its slot.

● R-pins (shaped like the letter R), or slip pins as they are sometimes called, are sprung and can be reused if they are otherwise in good condition. Always install R-pins with their closed end facing forwards **(see illustration 2.7)**.

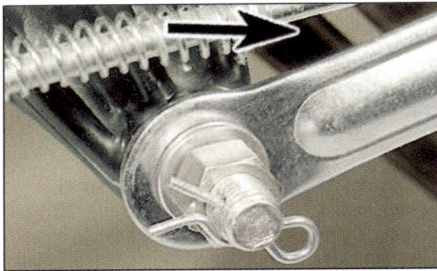

2.7 Correct fitting of R-pin. Arrow indicates forward direction

Circlips (see illustration 2.8)

● Circlips (sometimes called snap-rings) are used to retain components on a shaft or in a housing and have corresponding external or internal ears to permit removal. Parallel-sided (machined) circlips can be installed either way round in their groove, whereas stamped circlips (which have a chamfered edge on one face) must be installed with the chamfer facing away from the direction of thrust load **(see illustration 2.9)**.

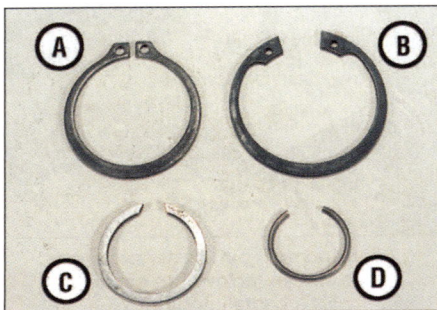

2.8 External stamped circlip (A), internal stamped circlip (B), machined circlip (C) and wire circlip (D)

● Always use circlip pliers to remove and install circlips; expand or compress them just enough to remove them. After installation, rotate the circlip in its groove to ensure it is securely seated. If installing a circlip on a splined shaft, always align its opening with a shaft channel to ensure the circlip ends are well supported and unlikely to catch **(see illustration 2.10)**.

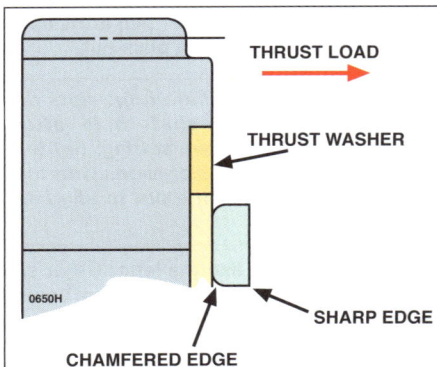

2.9 Correct fitting of a stamped circlip

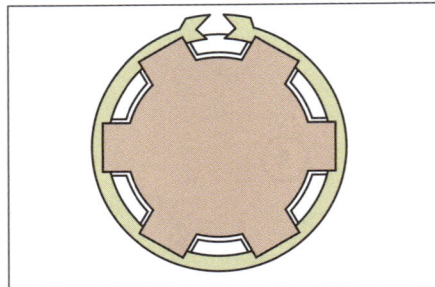

2.10 Align circlip opening with shaft channel

● Circlips can wear due to the thrust of components and become loose in their grooves, with the subsequent danger of becoming dislodged in operation. For this reason, renewal is advised every time a circlip is disturbed.

● Wire circlips are commonly used as piston pin retaining clips. If a removal tang is provided, long-nosed pliers can be used to dislodge them, otherwise careful use of a small flat-bladed screwdriver is necessary. Wire circlips should be renewed every time they are disturbed.

Thread diameter and pitch

● Diameter of a male thread (screw, bolt or stud) is the outside diameter of the threaded portion **(see illustration 2.11)**. Most motorcycle manufacturers use the ISO (International Standards Organisation) metric system expressed in millimetres, eg M6 refers to a 6 mm diameter thread. Sizing is the same for nuts, except that the thread diameter is measured across the valleys of the nut.

● Pitch is the distance between the peaks of the thread **(see illustration 2.11)**. It is expressed in millimetres, thus a common bolt size may be expressed as 6.0 x 1.0 mm (6 mm thread diameter and 1 mm pitch). Generally pitch increases in proportion to thread diameter, although there are always exceptions.

● Thread diameter and pitch are related for conventional fastener applications and the accompanying table can be used as a guide. Additionally, the AF (Across Flats), spanner or socket size dimension of the bolt or nut **(see illustration 2.11)** is linked to thread and pitch specification. Thread pitch can be measured with a thread gauge **(see illustration 2.12)**.

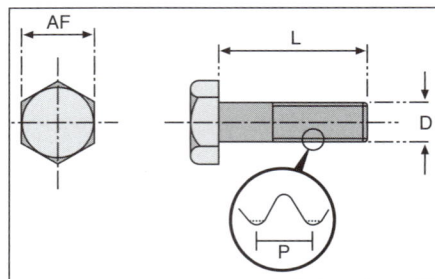

2.11 Fastener length (L), thread diameter (D), thread pitch (P) and head size (AF)

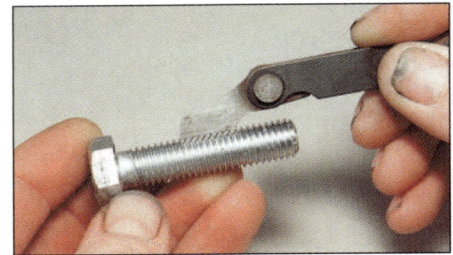

2.12 Using a thread gauge to measure pitch

AF size	Thread diameter x pitch (mm)
8 mm	M5 x 0.8
8 mm	M6 x 1.0
10 mm	M6 x 1.0
12 mm	M8 x 1.25
14 mm	M10 x 1.25
17 mm	M12 x 1.25

● The threads of most fasteners are of the right-hand type, ie they are turned clockwise to tighten and anti-clockwise to loosen. The reverse situation applies to left-hand thread fasteners, which are turned anti-clockwise to tighten and clockwise to loosen. Left-hand threads are used where rotation of a component might loosen a conventional right-hand thread fastener.

Seized fasteners

● Corrosion of external fasteners due to water or reaction between two dissimilar metals can occur over a period of time. It will build up sooner in wet conditions or in countries where salt is used on the roads during the winter. If a fastener is severely corroded it is likely that normal methods of removal will fail and result in its head being ruined. When you attempt removal, the fastener thread should be heard to crack free and unscrew easily - if it doesn't, stop there before damaging something.

● A smart tap on the head of the fastener will often succeed in breaking free corrosion which has occurred in the threads **(see illustration 2.13)**.

● An aerosol penetrating fluid (such as WD-40) applied the night beforehand may work its way down into the thread and ease removal. Depending on the location, you may be able to make up a Plasticine well around the fastener head and fill it with penetrating fluid.

2.13 A sharp tap on the head of a fastener will often break free a corroded thread

● If you are working on an engine internal component, corrosion will most likely not be a problem due to the well lubricated environment. However, components can be very tight and an impact driver is a useful tool in freeing them (see illustration 2.14).

2.14 Using an impact driver to free a fastener

● Where corrosion has occurred between dissimilar metals (eg steel and aluminium alloy), the application of heat to the fastener head will create a disproportionate expansion rate between the two metals and break the seizure caused by the corrosion. Whether heat can be applied depends on the location of the fastener - any surrounding components likely to be damaged must first be removed (see illustration 2.15). Heat can be applied using a paint stripper heat gun or clothes iron, or by immersing the component in boiling water - wear protective gloves to prevent scalding or burns to the hands.

2.15 Using heat to free a seized fastener

● As a last resort, it is possible to use a hammer and cold chisel to work the fastener head unscrewed (see illustration 2.16). This will damage the fastener, but more importantly extreme care must be taken not to damage the surrounding component.

Caution: Remember that the component being secured is generally of more value than the bolt, nut or screw - when the fastener is freed, do not unscrew it with force, instead work the fastener back and forth when resistance is felt to prevent thread damage.

2.16 Using a hammer and chisel to free a seized fastener

Broken fasteners and damaged heads

● If the shank of a broken bolt or screw is accessible you can grip it with self-locking grips. The knurled wheel type stud extractor tool or self-gripping stud puller tool is particularly useful for removing the long studs which screw into the cylinder mouth surface of the crankcase or bolts and screws from which the head has broken off (see illustration 2.17). Studs can also be removed by locking two nuts together on the threaded end of the stud and using a spanner on the lower nut (see illustration 2.18).

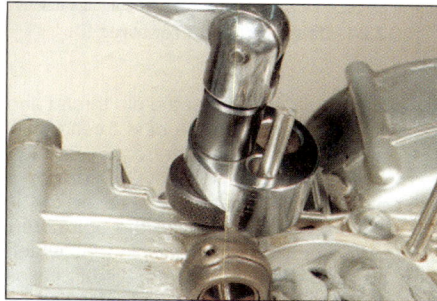

2.17 Using a stud extractor tool to remove a broken crankcase stud

2.18 Two nuts can be locked together to unscrew a stud from a component

● A bolt or screw which has broken off below or level with the casing must be extracted using a screw extractor set. Centre punch the fastener to centralise the drill bit, then drill a hole in the fastener (see illustration 2.19). Select a drill bit which is approximately half to three-quarters the

2.19 When using a screw extractor, first drill a hole in the fastener . . .

diameter of the fastener and drill to a depth which will accommodate the extractor. Use the largest size extractor possible, but avoid leaving too small a wall thickness otherwise the extractor will merely force the fastener walls outwards wedging it in the casing thread.

● If a spiral type extractor is used, thread it anti-clockwise into the fastener. As it is screwed in, it will grip the fastener and unscrew it from the casing (see illustration 2.20).

2.20 . . . then thread the extractor anti-clockwise into the fastener

● If a taper type extractor is used, tap it into the fastener so that it is firmly wedged in place. Unscrew the extractor (anti-clockwise) to draw the fastener out.

> ⚠️ *Warning: Stud extractors are very hard and may break off in the fastener if care is not taken - ask an engineer about spark erosion if this happens.*

● Alternatively, the broken bolt/screw can be drilled out and the hole retapped for an oversize bolt/screw or a diamond-section thread insert. It is essential that the drilling is carried out squarely and to the correct depth, otherwise the casing may be ruined - if in doubt, entrust the work to an engineer.

● Bolts and nuts with rounded corners cause the correct size spanner or socket to slip when force is applied. Of the types of spanner/socket available always use a six-point type rather than an eight or twelve-point type - better grip

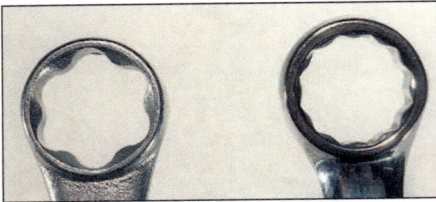

2.21 Comparison of surface drive ring spanner (left) with 12-point type (right)

is obtained. Surface drive spanners grip the middle of the hex flats, rather than the corners, and are thus good in cases of damaged heads **(see illustration 2.21)**.

● Slotted-head or Phillips-head screws are often damaged by the use of the wrong size screwdriver. Allen-head and Torx-head screws are much less likely to sustain damage. If enough of the screw head is exposed you can use a hacksaw to cut a slot in its head and then use a conventional flat-bladed screwdriver to remove it. Alternatively use a hammer and cold chisel to tap the head of the fastener around to slacken it. Always replace damaged fasteners with new ones, preferably Torx or Allen-head type.

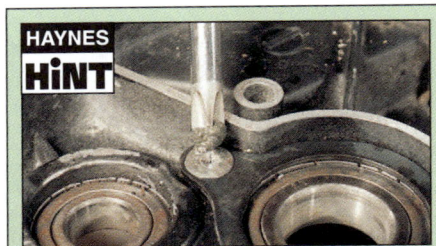

A dab of valve grinding compound between the screw head and screwdriver tip will often give a good grip.

Thread repair

● Threads (particularly those in aluminium alloy components) can be damaged by overtightening, being assembled with dirt in the threads, or from a component working loose and vibrating. Eventually the thread will fail completely, and it will be impossible to tighten the fastener.

● If a thread is damaged or clogged with old locking compound it can be renovated with a thread repair tool (thread chaser) **(see illustrations 2.22 and 2.23)**; special thread

2.22 A thread repair tool being used to correct an internal thread

2.23 A thread repair tool being used to correct an external thread

chasers are available for spark plug hole threads. The tool will not cut a new thread, but clean and true the original thread. Make sure that you use the correct diameter and pitch tool. Similarly, external threads can be cleaned up with a die or a thread restorer file **(see illustration 2.24)**.

2.24 Using a thread restorer file

● It is possible to drill out the old thread and retap the component to the next thread size. This will work where there is enough surrounding material and a new bolt or screw can be obtained. Sometimes, however, this is not possible - such as where the bolt/screw passes through another component which must also be suitably modified, also in cases where a spark plug or oil drain plug cannot be obtained in a larger diameter thread size.

● The diamond-section thread insert (often known by its popular trade name of Heli-Coil) is a simple and effective method of renewing the thread and retaining the original size. A kit can be purchased which contains the tap, insert and installing tool **(see illustration 2.25)**. Drill out the damaged thread with the size drill specified **(see illustration 2.26)**. Carefully retap the thread **(see illustration 2.27)**. Install the

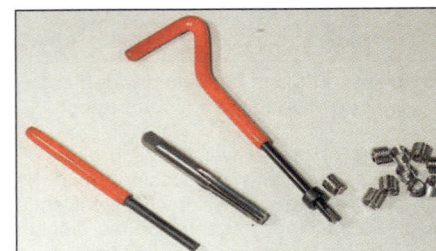

2.25 Obtain a thread insert kit to suit the thread diameter and pitch required

2.26 To install a thread insert, first drill out the original thread . . .

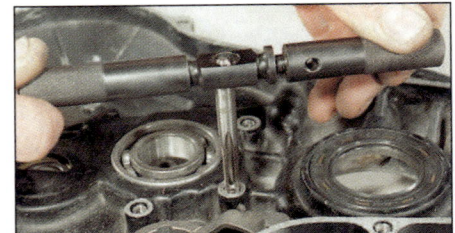

2.27 . . . tap a new thread . . .

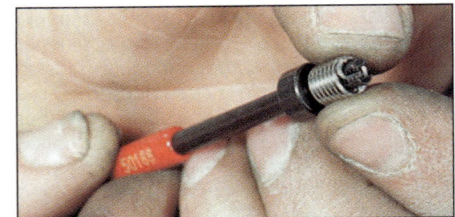

2.28 . . . fit insert on the installing tool . . .

2.29 . . . and thread into the component . . .

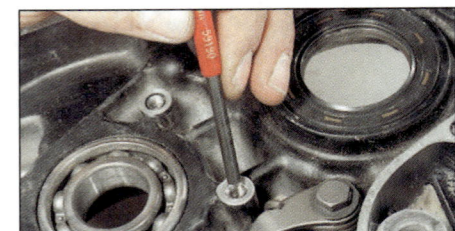

2.30 . . . break off the tang when complete

insert on the installing tool and thread it slowly into place using a light downward pressure **(see illustrations 2.28 and 2.29)**. When positioned between a 1/4 and 1/2 turn below the surface withdraw the installing tool and use the break-off tool to press down on the tang, breaking it off **(see illustration 2.30)**.

● There are epoxy thread repair kits on the market which can rebuild stripped internal threads, although this repair should not be used on high load-bearing components.

Thread locking and sealing compounds

● Locking compounds are used in locations where the fastener is prone to loosening due to vibration or on important safety-related items which might cause loss of control of the motorcycle if they fail. It is also used where important fasteners cannot be secured by other means such as lockwashers or split pins.

● Before applying locking compound, make sure that the threads (internal and external) are clean and dry with all old compound removed. Select a compound to suit the component being secured - a non-permanent general locking and sealing type is suitable for most applications, but a high strength type is needed for permanent fixing of studs in castings. Apply a drop or two of the compound to the first few threads of the fastener, then thread it into place and tighten to the specified torque. Do not apply excessive thread locking compound otherwise the thread may be damaged on subsequent removal.

● Certain fasteners are impregnated with a dry film type coating of locking compound on their threads. Always renew this type of fastener if disturbed.

● Anti-seize compounds, such as copper-based greases, can be applied to protect threads from seizure due to extreme heat and corrosion. A common instance is spark plug threads and exhaust system fasteners.

3 Measuring tools and gauges

Feeler gauges

● Feeler gauges (or blades) are used for measuring small gaps and clearances (see illustration 3.1). They can also be used to measure endfloat (sideplay) of a component on a shaft where access is not possible with a dial gauge.

● Feeler gauge sets should be treated with care and not bent or damaged. They are etched with their size on one face. Keep them clean and very lightly oiled to prevent corrosion build-up.

3.1 Feeler gauges are used for measuring small gaps and clearances - thickness is marked on one face of gauge

● When measuring a clearance, select a gauge which is a light sliding fit between the two components. You may need to use two gauges together to measure the clearance accurately.

Micrometers

● A micrometer is a precision tool capable of measuring to 0.01 or 0.001 of a millimetre. It should always be stored in its case and not in the general toolbox. It must be kept clean and never dropped, otherwise its frame or measuring anvils could be distorted resulting in inaccurate readings.

● External micrometers are used for measuring outside diameters of components and have many more applications than internal micrometers. Micrometers are available in different size ranges, eg 0 to 25 mm, 25 to 50 mm, and upwards in 25 mm steps; some large micrometers have interchangeable anvils to allow a range of measurements to be taken. Generally the largest precision measurement you are likely to take on a motorcycle is the piston diameter.

● Internal micrometers (or bore micrometers) are used for measuring inside diameters, such as valve guides and cylinder bores. Telescoping gauges and small hole gauges are used in conjunction with an external micrometer, whereas the more expensive internal micrometers have their own measuring device.

External micrometer

Note: *The conventional analogue type instrument is described. Although much easier to read, digital micrometers are considerably more expensive.*

● Always check the calibration of the micrometer before use. With the anvils closed (0 to 25 mm type) or set over a test gauge (for

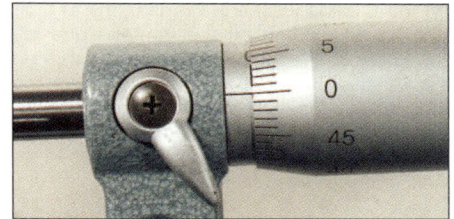

3.2 Check micrometer calibration before use

the larger types) the scale should read zero (see illustration 3.2); make sure that the anvils (and test piece) are clean first. Any discrepancy can be adjusted by referring to the instructions supplied with the tool. Remember that the micrometer is a precision measuring tool - don't force the anvils closed, use the ratchet (4) on the end of the micrometer to close it. In this way, a measured force is always applied.

● To use, first make sure that the item being measured is clean. Place the anvil of the micrometer (1) against the item and use the thimble (2) to bring the spindle (3) lightly into contact with the other side of the item (see illustration 3.3). Don't tighten the thimble down because this will damage the micrometer - instead use the ratchet (4) on the end of the micrometer. The ratchet mechanism applies a measured force preventing damage to the instrument.

● The micrometer is read by referring to the linear scale on the sleeve and the annular scale on the thimble. Read off the sleeve first to obtain the base measurement, then add the fine measurement from the thimble to obtain the overall reading. The linear scale on the sleeve represents the measuring range of the micrometer (eg 0 to 25 mm). The annular scale

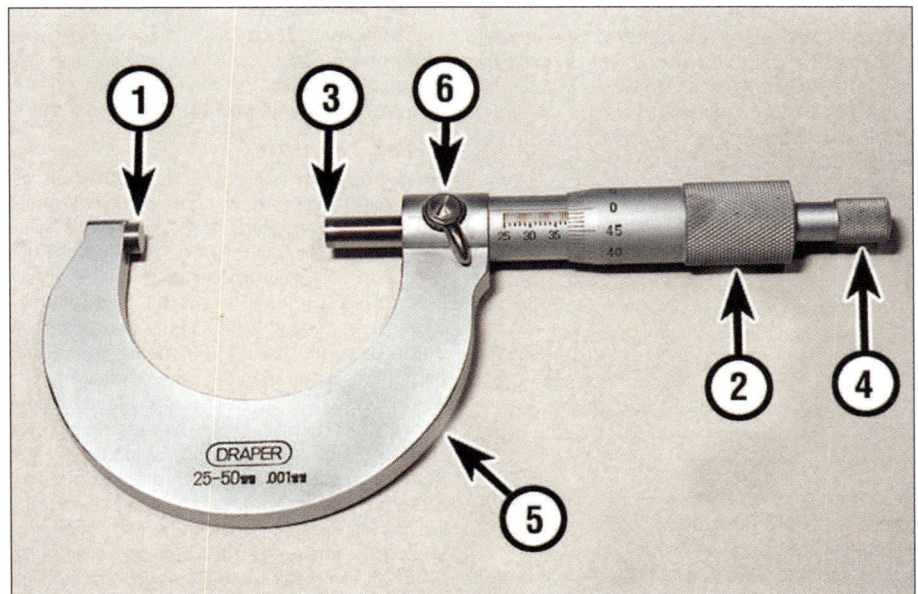

3.3 Micrometer component parts

1	Anvil	3	Spindle	5	Frame
2	Thimble	4	Ratchet	6	Locking lever

on the thimble will be in graduations of 0.01 mm (or as marked on the frame) - one full revolution of the thimble will move 0.5 mm on the linear scale. Take the reading where the datum line on the sleeve intersects the thimble's scale. Always position the eye directly above the scale otherwise an inaccurate reading will result.

In the example shown the item measures 2.95 mm **(see illustration 3.4)**:

Linear scale	2.00 mm
Linear scale	0.50 mm
Annular scale	0.45 mm
Total figure	**2.95 mm**

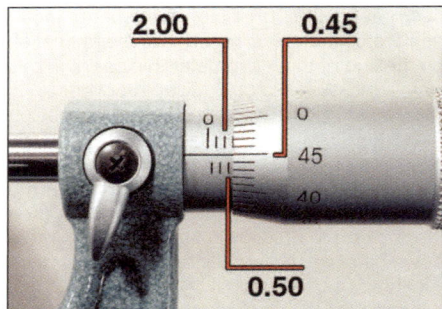

3.5 **Micrometer reading of 46.99 mm on linear and annular scales . . .**

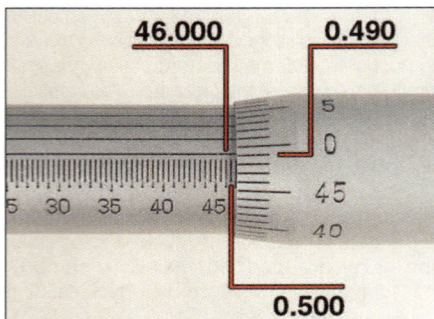

3.7 **Expand the telescoping gauge in the bore, lock its position . . .**

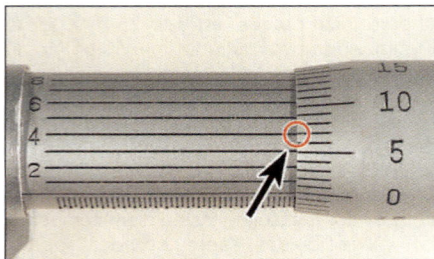

3.4 **Micrometer reading of 2.95 mm**

3.6 **. . . and 0.004 mm on vernier scale**

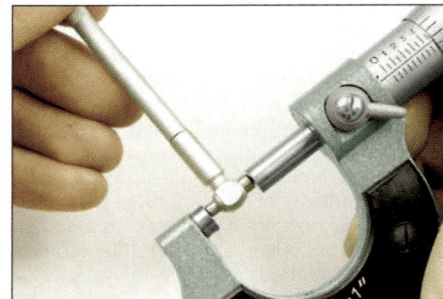

3.8 **. . . then measure the gauge with a micrometer**

Most micrometers have a locking lever (6) on the frame to hold the setting in place, allowing the item to be removed from the micrometer.

● Some micrometers have a vernier scale on their sleeve, providing an even finer measurement to be taken, in 0.001 increments of a millimetre. Take the sleeve and thimble measurement as described above, then check which graduation on the vernier scale aligns with that of the annular scale on the thimble **Note:** *The eye must be perpendicular to the scale when taking the vernier reading - if necessary rotate the body of the micrometer to ensure this.* Multiply the vernier scale figure by 0.001 and add it to the base and fine measurement figures.

In the example shown the item measures 46.994 mm **(see illustrations 3.5 and 3.6)**:

Linear scale (base)	46.000 mm
Linear scale (base)	00.500 mm
Annular scale (fine)	00.490 mm
Vernier scale	00.004 mm
Total figure	**46.994 mm**

Internal micrometer

● Internal micrometers are available for measuring bore diameters, but are expensive and unlikely to be available for home use. It is suggested that a set of telescoping gauges and small hole gauges, both of which must be used with an external micrometer, will suffice for taking internal measurements on a motorcycle.

● Telescoping gauges can be used to measure internal diameters of components. Select a gauge with the correct size range, make sure its ends are clean and insert it into the bore. Expand the gauge, then lock its position and withdraw it from the bore **(see illustration 3.7)**. Measure across the gauge ends with a micrometer **(see illustration 3.8)**.

● Very small diameter bores (such as valve guides) are measured with a small hole gauge. Once adjusted to a slip-fit inside the component, its position is locked and the gauge withdrawn for measurement with a micrometer **(see illustrations 3.9 and 3.10)**.

Vernier caliper

Note: *The conventional linear and dial gauge type instruments are described. Digital types are easier to read, but are far more expensive.*

● The vernier caliper does not provide the precision of a micrometer, but is versatile in being able to measure internal and external diameters. Some types also incorporate a depth gauge. It is ideal for measuring clutch plate friction material and spring free lengths.

● To use the conventional linear scale vernier, slacken off the vernier clamp screws (1) and set its jaws over (2), or inside (3), the item to be measured **(see illustration 3.11)**. Slide the jaw into contact, using the thumbwheel (4) for fine movement of the sliding scale (5) then tighten the clamp screws (1). Read off the main scale (6) where the zero on the sliding scale (5) intersects it, taking the whole number to the left of the zero; this provides the base measurement. View along the sliding scale and select the division which

3.9 **Expand the small hole gauge in the bore, lock its position . . .**

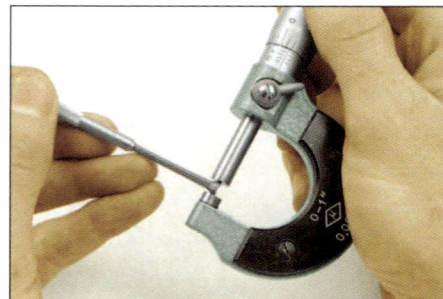

3.10 **. . . then measure the gauge with a micrometer**

lines up exactly with any of the divisions on the main scale, noting that the divisions usually represents 0.02 of a millimetre. Add this fine measurement to the base measurement to obtain the total reading.

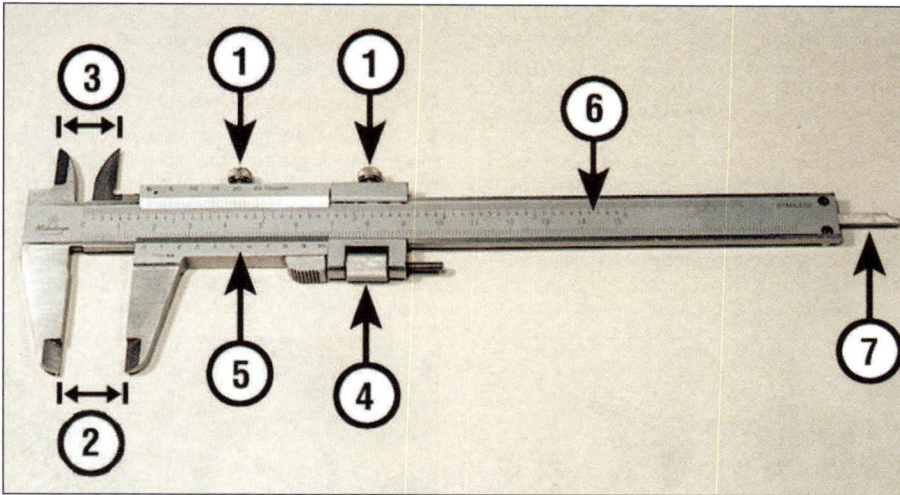

3.11 Vernier component parts (linear gauge)

1	Clamp screws	3	Internal jaws
2	External jaws	4	Thumbwheel

5	Sliding scale
6	Main scale

7 Depth gauge

In the example shown the item measures 55.92 mm **(see illustration 3.12)**:

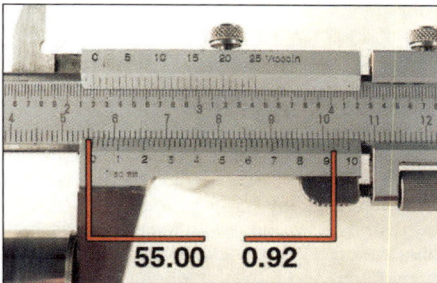

3.12 Vernier gauge reading of 55.92 mm

Base measurement	55.00 mm
Fine measurement	00.92 mm
Total figure	**55.92 mm**

● Some vernier calipers are equipped with a dial gauge for fine measurement. Before use, check that the jaws are clean, then close them fully and check that the dial gauge reads zero. If necessary adjust the gauge ring accordingly. Slacken the vernier clamp screw (1) and set its jaws over (2), or inside (3), the item to be measured **(see illustration 3.13)**. Slide the jaws into contact, using the thumbwheel (4) for fine movement. Read off the main scale (5) where the edge of the sliding scale (6) intersects it, taking the whole number to the left of the zero; this provides the base measurement. Read off the needle position on the dial gauge (7) scale to provide the fine measurement; each division represents 0.05 of a millimetre. Add this fine measurement to the base measurement to obtain the total reading.

In the example shown the item measures 55.95 mm **(see illustration 3.14)**:

Base measurement	55.00 mm
Fine measurement	00.95 mm
Total figure	**55.95 mm**

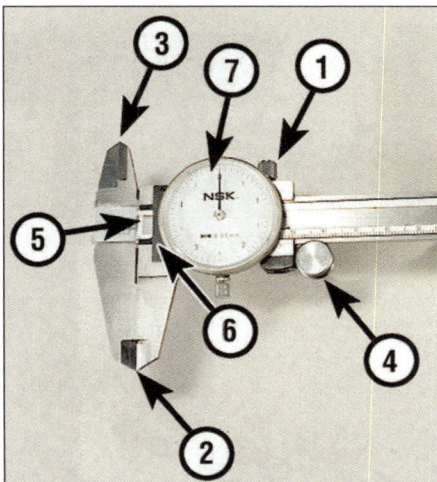

3.13 Vernier component parts (dial gauge)

1	Clamp screw	5	Main scale
2	External jaws	6	Sliding scale
3	Internal jaws	7	Dial gauge
4	Thumbwheel		

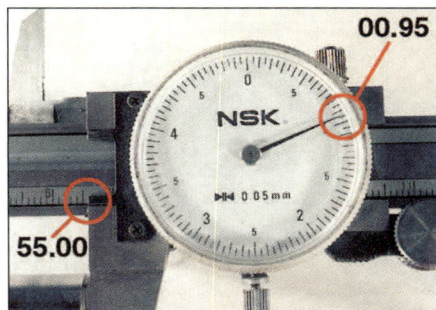

3.14 Vernier gauge reading of 55.95 mm

Plastigauge

● Plastigauge is a plastic material which can be compressed between two surfaces to measure the oil clearance between them. The width of the compressed Plastigauge is measured against a calibrated scale to determine the clearance.

● Common uses of Plastigauge are for measuring the clearance between crankshaft journal and main bearing inserts, between crankshaft journal and big-end bearing inserts, and between camshaft and bearing surfaces. The following example describes big-end oil clearance measurement.

● Handle the Plastigauge material carefully to prevent distortion. Using a sharp knife, cut a length which corresponds with the width of the bearing being measured and place it carefully across the journal so that it is parallel with the shaft **(see illustration 3.15)**. Carefully install both bearing shells and the connecting rod. Without rotating the rod on the journal tighten its bolts or nuts (as applicable) to the specified torque. The connecting rod and bearings are then disassembled and the crushed Plastigauge examined.

3.15 Plastigauge placed across shaft journal

● Using the scale provided in the Plastigauge kit, measure the width of the material to determine the oil clearance **(see illustration 3.16)**. Always remove all traces of Plastigauge after use using your fingernails.

> *Caution: Arriving at the correct clearance demands that the assembly is torqued correctly, according to the settings and sequence (where applicable) provided by the motorcycle manufacturer.*

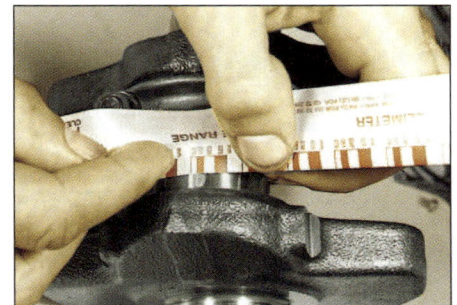

3.16 Measuring the width of the crushed Plastigauge

Dial gauge or DTI (Dial Test Indicator)

● A dial gauge can be used to accurately measure small amounts of movement. Typical uses are measuring shaft runout or shaft endfloat (sideplay) and setting piston position for ignition timing on two-strokes. A dial gauge set usually comes with a range of different probes and adapters and mounting equipment.

● The gauge needle must point to zero when at rest. Rotate the ring around its periphery to zero the gauge.

● Check that the gauge is capable of reading the extent of movement in the work. Most gauges have a small dial set in the face which records whole millimetres of movement as well as the fine scale around the face periphery which is calibrated in 0.01 mm divisions. Read off the small dial first to obtain the base measurement, then add the measurement from the fine scale to obtain the total reading.

In the example shown the gauge reads 1.48 mm **(see illustration 3.17)**:

Base measurement	1.00 mm
Fine measurement	0.48 mm
Total figure	**1.48 mm**

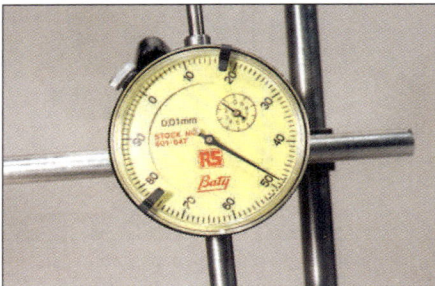

3.17 Dial gauge reading of 1.48 mm

● If measuring shaft runout, the shaft must be supported in vee-blocks and the gauge mounted on a stand perpendicular to the shaft. Rest the tip of the gauge against the centre of the shaft and rotate the shaft slowly whilst watching the gauge reading **(see illustration 3.18)**. Take several measurements along the length of the shaft and record the

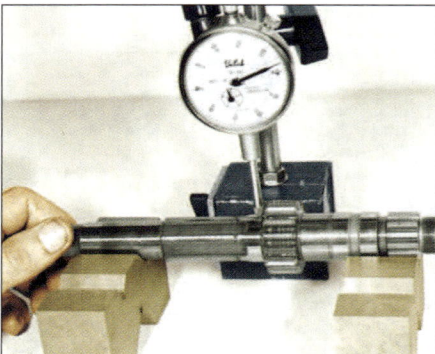

3.18 Using a dial gauge to measure shaft runout

maximum gauge reading as the amount of runout in the shaft. **Note:** *The reading obtained will be total runout at that point - some manufacturers specify that the runout figure is halved to compare with their specified runout limit.*

● Endfloat (sideplay) measurement requires that the gauge is mounted securely to the surrounding component with its probe touching the end of the shaft. Using hand pressure, push and pull on the shaft noting the maximum endfloat recorded on the gauge **(see illustration 3.19)**.

3.19 Using a dial gauge to measure shaft endfloat

● A dial gauge with suitable adapters can be used to determine piston position BTDC on two-stroke engines for the purposes of ignition timing. The gauge, adapter and suitable length probe are installed in the place of the spark plug and the gauge zeroed at TDC. If the piston position is specified as 1.14 mm BTDC, rotate the engine back to 2.00 mm BTDC, then slowly forwards to 1.14 mm BTDC.

Cylinder compression gauges

● A compression gauge is used for measuring cylinder compression. Either the rubber-cone type or the threaded adapter type can be used. The latter is preferred to ensure a perfect seal against the cylinder head. A 0 to 300 psi (0 to 20 Bar) type gauge (for petrol/gasoline engines) will be suitable for motorcycles.

● The spark plug is removed and the gauge either held hard against the cylinder head (cone type) or the gauge adapter screwed into the cylinder head (threaded type) **(see illustration 3.20)**. Cylinder compression is measured with the engine turning over, but not running - carry out the compression test as described in

3.20 Using a rubber-cone type cylinder compression gauge

Fault Finding Equipment. The gauge will hold the reading until manually released.

Oil pressure gauge

● An oil pressure gauge is used for measuring engine oil pressure. Most gauges come with a set of adapters to fit the thread of the take-off point **(see illustration 3.21)**. If the take-off point specified by the motorcycle manufacturer is an external oil pipe union, make sure that the specified replacement union is used to prevent oil starvation.

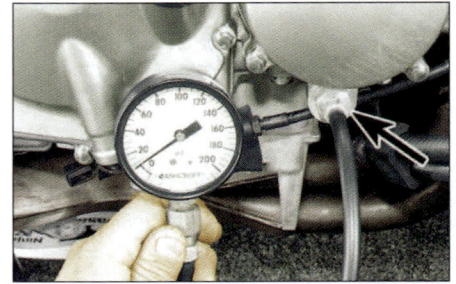

3.21 Oil pressure gauge and take-off point adapter (arrow)

● Oil pressure is measured with the engine running (at a specific rpm) and often the manufacturer will specify pressure limits for a cold and hot engine.

Straight-edge and surface plate

● If checking the gasket face of a component for warpage, place a steel rule or precision straight-edge across the gasket face and measure any gap between the straight-edge and component with feeler gauges **(see illustration 3.22)**. Check diagonally across the component and between mounting holes **(see illustration 3.23)**.

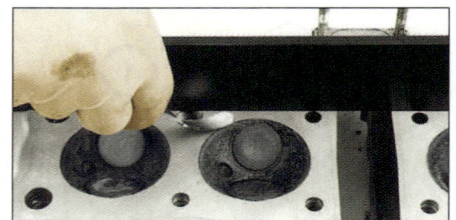

3.22 Use a straight-edge and feeler gauges to check for warpage

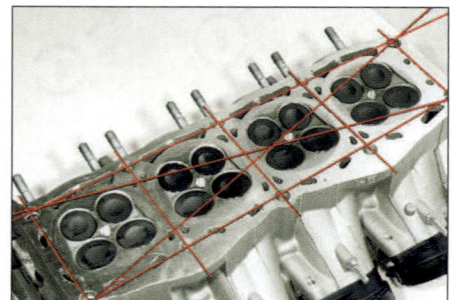

3.23 Check for warpage in these directions

Checking individual components for warpage, such as clutch plain (metal) plates, requires a perfectly flat plate or piece or plate glass and feeler gauges.

4 Torque and leverage

What is torque?

Torque describes the twisting force about a shaft. The amount of torque applied is determined by the distance from the centre of the shaft to the end of the lever and the amount of force being applied to the end of the lever; distance multiplied by force equals torque.

The manufacturer applies a measured torque to a bolt or nut to ensure that it will not slacken in use and to hold two components securely together without movement in the joint. The actual torque setting depends on the thread size, bolt or nut material and the composition of the components being held.

Too little torque may cause the fastener to loosen due to vibration, whereas too much torque will distort the joint faces of the component or cause the fastener to shear off. Always stick to the specified torque setting.

Using a torque wrench

Check the calibration of the torque wrench and make sure it has a suitable range for the job. Torque wrenches are available in Nm (Newton-metres), kgf m (kilograms-force metre), lbf ft (pounds-feet), lbf in (inch-pounds). Do not confuse lbf ft with lbf in.

Adjust the tool to the desired torque on the scale (see illustration 4.1). If your torque wrench is not calibrated in the units specified, carefully convert the figure (see Conversion Factors). A manufacturer sometimes gives a torque setting as a range (8 to 10 Nm) rather than a single figure - in this case set the tool midway between the two settings. The same torque may be expressed as 9 Nm ± 1 Nm. Some torque wrenches have a method of locking the setting so that it isn't inadvertently altered during use.

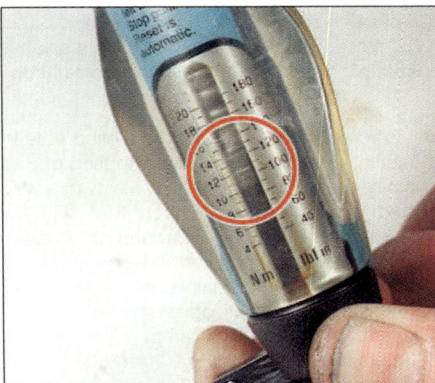

4.1 Set the torque wrench index mark to the setting required, in this case 12 Nm

Install the bolts/nuts in their correct location and secure them lightly. Their threads must be clean and free of any old locking compound. Unless specified the threads and flange should be dry - oiled threads are necessary in certain circumstances and the manufacturer will take this into account in the specified torque figure. Similarly, the manufacturer may also specify the application of thread-locking compound.

Tighten the fasteners in the specified sequence until the torque wrench clicks, indicating that the torque setting has been reached. Apply the torque again to double-check the setting. Where different thread diameter fasteners secure the component, as a rule tighten the larger diameter ones first.

When the torque wrench has been finished with, release the lock (where applicable) and fully back off its setting to zero - do not leave the torque wrench tensioned. Also, do not use a torque wrench for slackening a fastener.

Angle-tightening

Manufacturers often specify a figure in degrees for final tightening of a fastener. This usually follows tightening to a specific torque setting.

A degree disc can be set and attached to the socket (see illustration 4.2) or a protractor can be used to mark the angle of movement on the bolt/nut head and the surrounding casting (see illustration 4.3).

4.2 Angle tightening can be accomplished with a torque-angle gauge . . .

4.3 . . . or by marking the angle on the surrounding component

Loosening sequences

Where more than one bolt/nut secures a component, loosen each fastener evenly a little at a time. In this way, not all the stress of the joint is held by one fastener and the components are not likely to distort.

If a tightening sequence is provided, work in the REVERSE of this, but if not, work from the outside in, in a criss-cross sequence (see illustration 4.4).

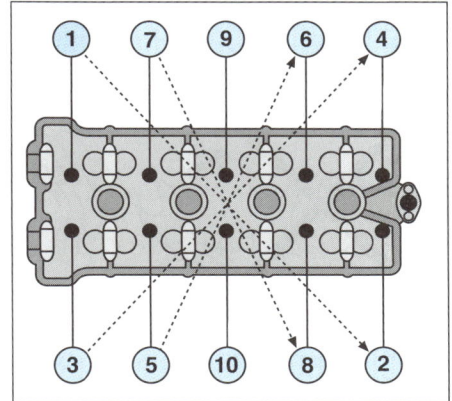

4.4 When slackening, work from the outside inwards

Tightening sequences

If a component is held by more than one fastener it is important that the retaining bolts/nuts are tightened evenly to prevent uneven stress build-up and distortion of sealing faces. This is especially important on high-compression joints such as the cylinder head.

A sequence is usually provided by the manufacturer, either in a diagram or actually marked in the casting. If not, always start in the centre and work outwards in a criss-cross pattern (see illustration 4.5). Start off by securing all bolts/nuts finger-tight, then set the torque wrench and tighten each fastener by a small amount in sequence until the final torque is reached. By following this practice,

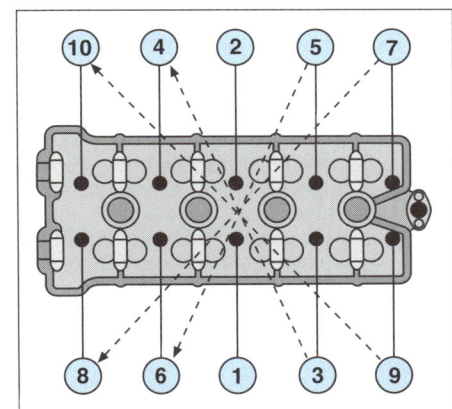

4.5 When tightening, work from the inside outwards

the joint will be held evenly and will not be distorted. Important joints, such as the cylinder head and big-end fasteners often have two- or three-stage torque settings.

Applying leverage

● Use tools at the correct angle. Position a socket wrench or spanner on the bolt/nut so that you pull it towards you when loosening. If this can't be done, push the spanner without curling your fingers around it (see illustration 4.6) - the spanner may slip or the fastener loosen suddenly, resulting in your fingers being crushed against a component.

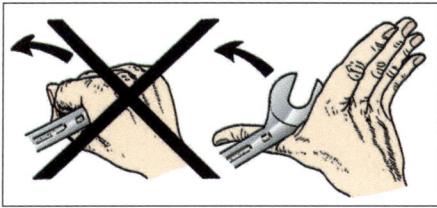

4.6 If you can't pull on the spanner to loosen a fastener, push with your hand open

● Additional leverage is gained by extending the length of the lever. The best way to do this is to use a breaker bar instead of the regular length tool, or to slip a length of tubing over the end of the spanner or socket wrench.
● If additional leverage will not work, the fastener head is either damaged or firmly corroded in place (see Fasteners).

5 Bearings

Bearing removal and installation

Drivers and sockets

● Before removing a bearing, always inspect the casing to see which way it must be driven out - some casings will have retaining plates or a cast step. Also check for any identifying markings on the bearing and if installed to a certain depth, measure this at this stage. Some roller bearings are sealed on one side - take note of the original fitted position.
● Bearings can be driven out of a casing using a bearing driver tool (with the correct size head) or a socket of the correct diameter. Select the driver head or socket so that it contacts the outer race of the bearing, not the balls/rollers or inner race. Always support the casing around the bearing housing with wood blocks, otherwise there is a risk of fracture. The bearing is driven out with a few blows on the driver or socket from a heavy mallet. Unless access is severely restricted (as with wheel bearings), a pin-punch is not recommended unless it is moved around the bearing to keep it square in its housing.

● The same equipment can be used to install bearings. Make sure the bearing housing is supported on wood blocks and line up the bearing in its housing. Fit the bearing as noted on removal - generally they are installed with their marked side facing outwards. Tap the bearing squarely into its housing using a driver or socket which bears only on the bearing's outer race - contact with the bearing balls/rollers or inner race will destroy it (see illustrations 5.1 and 5.2).
● Check that the bearing inner race and balls/rollers rotate freely.

5.1 Using a bearing driver against the bearing's outer race

5.2 Using a large socket against the bearing's outer race

Pullers and slide-hammers

● Where a bearing is pressed on a shaft a puller will be required to extract it (see illustration 5.3). Make sure that the puller clamp or legs fit securely behind the bearing and are unlikely to slip out. If pulling a bearing

5.3 This bearing puller clamps behind the bearing and pressure is applied to the shaft end to draw the bearing off

off a gear shaft for example, you may have to locate the puller behind a gear pinion if there is no access to the race and draw the gear pinion off the shaft as well (see illustration 5.4).

Caution: Ensure that the puller's centre bolt locates securely against the end of the shaft and will not slip when pressure is applied. Also ensure that puller does not damage the shaft end.

5.4 Where no access is available to the rear of the bearing, it is sometimes possible to draw off the adjacent component

● Operate the puller so that its centre bolt exerts pressure on the shaft end and draws the bearing off the shaft.
● When installing the bearing on the shaft, tap only on the bearing's inner race - contact with the balls/rollers or outer race with destroy the bearing. Use a socket or length of tubing as a drift which fits over the shaft end (see illustration 5.5).

5.5 When installing a bearing on a shaft use a piece of tubing which bears only on the bearing's inner race

● Where a bearing locates in a blind hole in a casing, it cannot be driven or pulled out as described above. A slide-hammer with knife-edged bearing puller attachment will be required. The puller attachment passes through the bearing and when tightened expands to fit firmly behind the bearing (see illustration 5.6). By operating the slide-hammer part of the tool the bearing is jarred out of its housing (see illustration 5.7).
● It is possible, if the bearing is of reasonable weight, for it to drop out of its housing if the casing is heated as described opposite. If this

5.6 Expand the bearing puller so that it locks behind the bearing . . .

5.7 . . . attach the slide hammer to the bearing puller

method is attempted, first prepare a work surface which will enable the casing to be tapped face down to help dislodge the bearing - a wood surface is ideal since it will not damage the casing's gasket surface. Wearing protective gloves, tap the heated casing several times against the work surface to dislodge the bearing under its own weight **(see illustration 5.8)**.

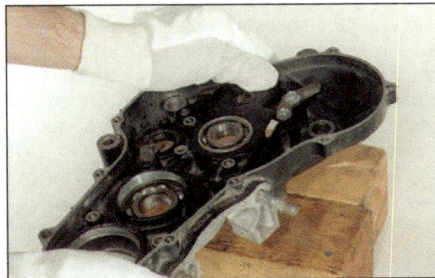

5.8 Tapping a casing face down on wood blocks can often dislodge a bearing

● Bearings can be installed in blind holes using the driver or socket method described above.

Drawbolts

● Where a bearing or bush is set in the eye of a component, such as a suspension linkage arm or connecting rod small-end, removal by drift may damage the component. Furthermore, a rubber bushing in a shock absorber eye cannot successfully be driven out of position. If access is available to a engineering press, the task is straightforward. If not, a drawbolt can be fabricated to extract the bearing or bush.

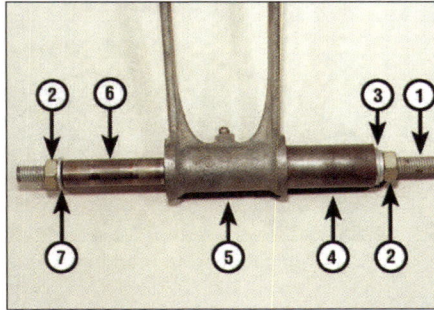

5.9 Drawbolt component parts assembled on a suspension arm

1 Bolt or length of threaded bar
2 Nuts
3 Washer (external diameter greater than tubing internal diameter)
4 Tubing (internal diameter sufficient to accommodate bearing)
5 Suspension arm with bearing
6 Tubing (external diameter slightly smaller than bearing)
7 Washer (external diameter slightly smaller than bearing)

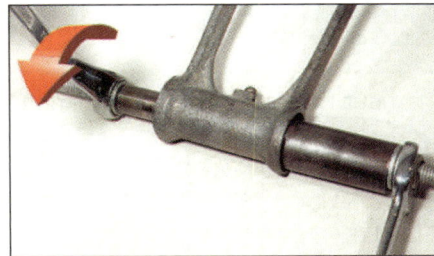

5.10 Drawing the bearing out of the suspension arm

● To extract the bearing/bush you will need a long bolt with nut (or piece of threaded bar with two nuts), a piece of tubing which has an internal diameter larger than the bearing/bush, another piece of tubing which has an external diameter slightly smaller than the bearing/ bush, and a selection of washers **(see illustrations 5.9 and 5.10)**. Note that the pieces of tubing must be of the same length, or longer, than the bearing/bush.
● The same kit (without the pieces of tubing) can be used to draw the new bearing/bush back into place **(see illustration 5.11)**.

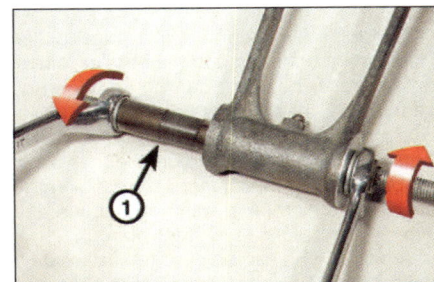

5.11 Installing a new bearing (1) in the suspension arm

Temperature change

● If the bearing's outer race is a tight fit in the casing, the aluminium casing can be heated to release its grip on the bearing. Aluminium will expand at a greater rate than the steel bearing outer race. There are several ways to do this, but avoid any localised extreme heat (such as a blow torch) - aluminium alloy has a low melting point.
● Approved methods of heating a casing are using a domestic oven (heated to 100°C) or immersing the casing in boiling water **(see illustration 5.12)**. Low temperature range localised heat sources such as a paint stripper heat gun or clothes iron can also be used **(see illustration 5.13)**. Alternatively, soak a rag in boiling water, wring it out and wrap it around the bearing housing.

> ⚠ **Warning: All of these methods require care in use to prevent scalding and burns to the hands. Wear protective gloves when handling hot components.**

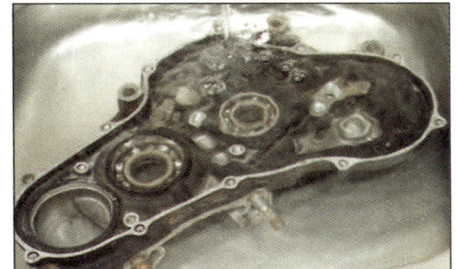

5.12 A casing can be immersed in a sink of boiling water to aid bearing removal

5.13 Using a localised heat source to aid bearing removal

● If heating the whole casing note that plastic components, such as the neutral switch, may suffer - remove them beforehand.
● After heating, remove the bearing as described above. You may find that the expansion is sufficient for the bearing to fall out of the casing under its own weight or with a light tap on the driver or socket.
● If necessary, the casing can be heated to aid bearing installation, and this is sometimes the recommended procedure if the motorcycle manufacturer has designed the housing and bearing fit with this intention.

● Installation of bearings can be eased by placing them in a freezer the night before installation. The steel bearing will contract slightly, allowing easy insertion in its housing. This is often useful when installing steering head outer races in the frame.

Bearing types and markings

● Plain shell bearings, ball bearings, needle roller bearings and tapered roller bearings will all be found on motorcycles (see illustrations 5.14 and 5.15). The ball and roller types are usually caged between an inner and outer race, but uncaged variations may be found.

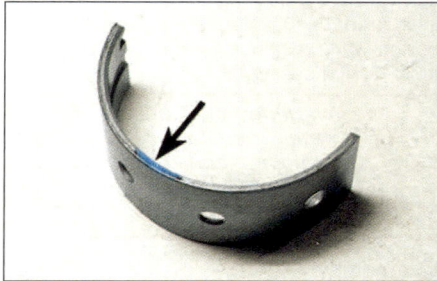

5.14 Shell bearings are either plain or grooved. They are usually identified by colour code (arrow)

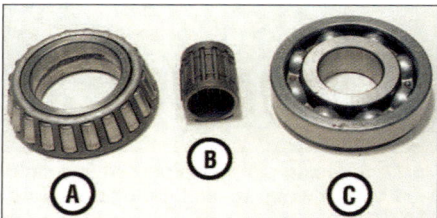

5.15 Tapered roller bearing (A), needle roller bearing (B) and ball journal bearing (C)

● Shell bearings (often called inserts) are usually found at the crankshaft main and connecting rod big-end where they are good at coping with high loads. They are made of a phosphor-bronze material and are impregnated with self-lubricating properties.

● Ball bearings and needle roller bearings consist of a steel inner and outer race with the balls or rollers between the races. They require constant lubrication by oil or grease and are good at coping with axial loads. Taper roller bearings consist of rollers set in a tapered cage set on the inner race; the outer race is separate. They are good at coping with axial loads and prevent movement along the shaft - a typical application is in the steering head.

● Bearing manufacturers produce bearings to ISO size standards and stamp one face of the bearing to indicate its internal and external diameter, load capacity and type (see illustration 5.16).

● Metal bushes are usually of phosphor-bronze material. Rubber bushes are used in suspension mounting eyes. Fibre bushes have also been used in suspension pivots.

5.16 Typical bearing marking

Bearing fault finding

● If a bearing outer race has spun in its housing, the housing material will be damaged. You can use a bearing locking compound to bond the outer race in place if damage is not too severe.

● Shell bearings will fail due to damage of their working surface, as a result of lack of lubrication, corrosion or abrasive particles in the oil (see illustration 5.17). Small particles of dirt in the oil may embed in the bearing material whereas larger particles will score the bearing and shaft journal. If a number of short journeys are made, insufficient heat will be generated to drive off condensation which has built up on the bearings.

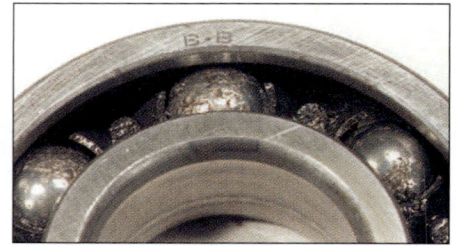

5.17 Typical bearing failures

● Ball and roller bearings will fail due to lack of lubrication or damage to the balls or rollers. Tapered-roller bearings can be damaged by overloading them. Unless the bearing is sealed on both sides, wash it in paraffin (kerosene) to remove all old grease then allow it to dry. Make a visual inspection looking to dented balls or rollers, damaged cages and worn or pitted races (see illustration 5.18).

● A ball bearing can be checked for wear by listening to it when spun. Apply a film of light oil to the bearing and hold it close to the ear - hold the outer race with one hand and spin the inner

5.18 Example of ball journal bearing with damaged balls and cages

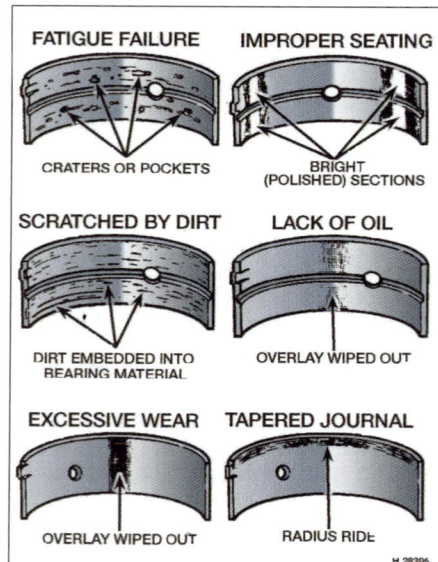

5.19 Hold outer race and listen to inner race when spun

race with the other hand (see illustration 5.19). The bearing should be almost silent when spun; if it grates or rattles it is worn.

6 Oil seals

Oil seal removal and installation

● Oil seals should be renewed every time a component is dismantled. This is because the seal lips will become set to the sealing surface and will not necessarily reseal.

● Oil seals can be prised out of position using a large flat-bladed screwdriver (see illustration 6.1). In the case of crankcase seals, check first that the seal is not lipped on the inside, preventing its removal with the crankcases joined.

6.1 Prise out oil seals with a large flat-bladed screwdriver

● New seals are usually installed with their marked face (containing the seal reference code) outwards and the spring side towards the fluid being retained. In certain cases, such as a two-stroke engine crankshaft seal, a double lipped seal may be used due to there being fluid or gas on each side of the joint.

● Use a bearing driver or socket which bears only on the outer hard edge of the seal to install it in the casing - tapping on the inner edge will damage the sealing lip.

Oil seal types and markings

● Oil seals are usually of the single-lipped type. Double-lipped seals are found where a liquid or gas is on both sides of the joint.
● Oil seals can harden and lose their sealing ability if the motorcycle has been in storage for a long period - renewal is the only solution.
● Oil seal manufacturers also conform to the ISO markings for seal size - these are moulded into the outer face of the seal (see illustration 6.2).

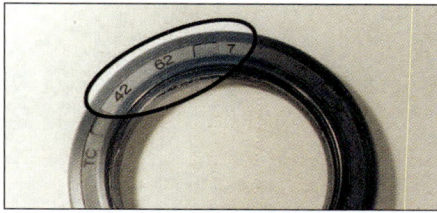

6.2 These oil seal markings indicate inside diameter, outside diameter and seal thickness

7 Gaskets and sealants

Types of gasket and sealant

● Gaskets are used to seal the mating surfaces between components and keep lubricants, fluids, vacuum or pressure contained within the assembly. Aluminium gaskets are sometimes found at the cylinder joints, but most gaskets are paper-based. If the mating surfaces of the components being joined are undamaged the gasket can be installed dry, although a dab of sealant or grease will be useful to hold it in place during assembly.
● RTV (Room Temperature Vulcanising) silicone rubber sealants cure when exposed to moisture in the atmosphere. These sealants are good at filling pits or irregular gasket faces, but will tend to be forced out of the joint under very high torque. They can be used to replace a paper gasket, but first make sure that the width of the paper gasket is not essential to the shimming of internal components. RTV sealants should not be used on components containing petrol (gasoline).
● Non-hardening, semi-hardening and hard setting liquid gasket compounds can be used with a gasket or between a metal-to-metal joint. Select the sealant to suit the application: universal non-hardening sealant can be used on virtually all joints; semi-hardening on joint faces which are rough or damaged; hard setting sealant on joints which require a permanent bond and are subjected to high temperature and pressure. **Note:** *Check first if the paper gasket has a bead of sealant*

impregnated in its surface before applying additional sealant.
● When choosing a sealant, make sure it is suitable for the application, particularly if being applied in a high-temperature area or in the vicinity of fuel. Certain manufacturers produce sealants in either clear, silver or black colours to match the finish of the engine. This has a particular application on motorcycles where much of the engine is exposed.
● Do not over-apply sealant. That which is squeezed out on the outside of the joint can be wiped off, whereas an excess of sealant on the inside can break off and clog oilways.

Breaking a sealed joint

● Age, heat, pressure and the use of hard setting sealant can cause two components to stick together so tightly that they are difficult to separate using finger pressure alone. Do not resort to using levers unless there is a pry point provided for this purpose (see illustration 7.1) or else the gasket surfaces will be damaged.
● Use a soft-faced hammer (see illustration 7.2) or a wood block and conventional hammer to strike the component near the mating surface. Avoid hammering against cast extremities since they may break off. If this method fails, try using a wood wedge between the two components.

> **Caution: If the joint will not separate, double-check that you have removed all the fasteners.**

7.1 If a pry point is provided, apply gently pressure with a flat-bladed screwdriver

7.2 Tap around the joint with a soft-faced mallet if necessary - don't strike cooling fins

Removal of old gasket and sealant

● Paper gaskets will most likely come away complete, leaving only a few traces stuck on

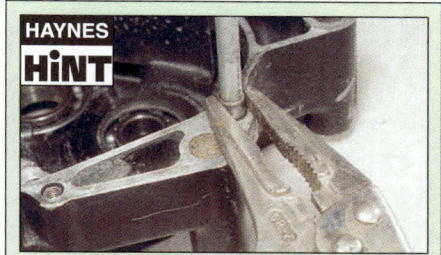

> **Most components have one or two hollow locating dowels between the two gasket faces. If a dowel cannot be removed, do not resort to gripping it with pliers - it will almost certainly be distorted. Install a close-fitting socket or Phillips screwdriver into the dowel and then grip the outer edge of the dowel to free it.**

the sealing faces of the components. It is imperative that all traces are removed to ensure correct sealing of the new gasket.
● Very carefully scrape all traces of gasket away making sure that the sealing surfaces are not gouged or scored by the scraper (see illustrations 7.3, 7.4 and 7.5). Stubborn deposits can be removed by spraying with an aerosol gasket remover. Final preparation of

7.3 Paper gaskets can be scraped off with a gasket scraper tool . . .

7.4 . . . a knife blade . . .

7.5 . . . or a household scraper

7.6 Fine abrasive paper is wrapped around a flat file to clean up the gasket face

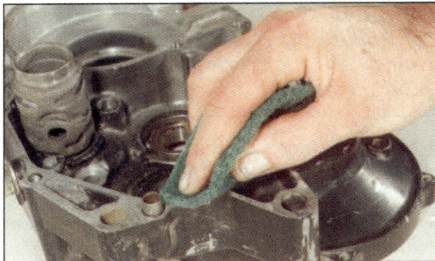

7.7 A kitchen scourer can be used on stubborn deposits

the gasket surface can be made with very fine abrasive paper or a plastic kitchen scourer (see illustrations 7.6 and 7.7).

● Old sealant can be scraped or peeled off components, depending on the type originally used. Note that gasket removal compounds are available to avoid scraping the components clean; make sure the gasket remover suits the type of sealant used.

8 Chains

Breaking and joining final drive chains

● Drive chains for all but small bikes are continuous and do not have a clip-type connecting link. The chain must be broken using a chain breaker tool and the new chain securely riveted together using a new soft rivet-type link. Never use a clip-type connecting link instead of a rivet-type link, except in an emergency. Various chain breaking and riveting tools are available, either as separate tools or combined as illustrated in the accompanying photographs - read the instructions supplied with the tool carefully.

> ⚠️ **Warning: The need to rivet the new link pins correctly cannot be overstressed - loss of control of the motorcycle is very likely to result if the chain breaks in use.**

● Rotate the chain and look for the soft link. The soft link pins look like they have been

8.1 Tighten the chain breaker to push the pin out of the link . . .

8.2 . . . withdraw the pin, remove the tool . . .

8.3 . . . and separate the chain link

deeply centre-punched instead of peened over like all the other pins (see illustration 8.9) and its sideplate may be a different colour. Position the soft link midway between the sprockets and assemble the chain breaker tool over one of the soft link pins (see illustration 8.1). Operate the tool to push the pin out through the chain (see illustration 8.2). On an O-ring chain, remove the O-rings (see illustration 8.3). Carry out the same procedure on the other soft link pin.

> **Caution: Certain soft link pins (particularly on the larger chains) may require their ends to be filed or ground off before they can be pressed out using the tool.**

● Check that you have the correct size and strength (standard or heavy duty) new soft link - do not reuse the old link. Look for the size marking on the chain sideplates (see illustration 8.10).

● Position the chain ends so that they are engaged over the rear sprocket. On an O-ring

8.4 Insert the new soft link, with O-rings, through the chain ends . . .

8.5 . . . install the O-rings over the pin ends . . .

8.6 . . . followed by the sideplate

chain, install a new O-ring over each pin of the link and insert the link through the two chain ends (see illustration 8.4). Install a new O-ring over the end of each pin, followed by the sideplate (with the chain manufacturer's marking facing outwards) (see illustrations 8.5 and 8.6). On an unsealed chain, insert the link through the two chain ends, then install the sideplate with the chain manufacturer's marking facing outwards.

● Note that it may not be possible to install the sideplate using finger pressure alone. If using a joining tool, assemble it so that the plates of the tool clamp the link and press the sideplate over the pins (see illustration 8.7). Otherwise, use two small sockets placed over

8.7 Push the sideplate into position using a clamp

8.8 Assemble the chain riveting tool over one pin at a time and tighten it fully

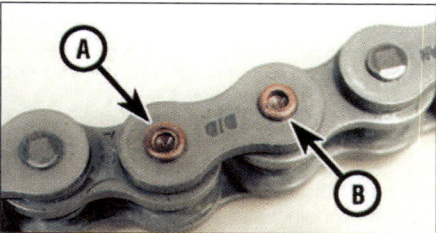

8.9 Pin end correctly riveted (A), pin end unriveted (B)

the rivet ends and two pieces of the wood between a G-clamp. Operate the clamp to press the sideplate over the pins.

● Assemble the joining tool over one pin (following the maker's instructions) and tighten the tool down to spread the pin end securely **(see illustrations 8.8 and 8.9)**. Do the same on the other pin.

> ⚠ **Warning: Check that the pin ends are secure and that there is no danger of the sideplate coming loose. If the pin ends are cracked the soft link must be renewed.**

Final drive chain sizing

● Chains are sized using a three digit number, followed by a suffix to denote the chain type **(see illustration 8.10)**. Chain type is either standard or heavy duty (thicker sideplates), and also unsealed or O-ring/X-ring type.

● The first digit of the number relates to the pitch of the chain, ie the distance from the centre of one pin to the centre of the next pin **(see illustration 8.11)**. Pitch is expressed in eighths of an inch, as follows:

8.10 Typical chain size and type marking

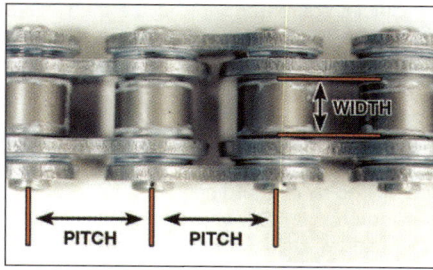

8.11 Chain dimensions

| Sizes commencing with a 4 (eg 428) have a pitch of 1/2 inch (12.7 mm) |
| Sizes commencing with a 5 (eg 520) have a pitch of 5/8 inch (15.9 mm) |
| Sizes commencing with a 6 (eg 630) have a pitch of 3/4 inch (19.1 mm) |

● The second and third digits of the chain size relate to the width of the rollers, again in imperial units, eg the 525 shown has 5/16 inch (7.94 mm) rollers **(see illustration 8.11)**.

9 Hoses

Clamping to prevent flow

● Small-bore flexible hoses can be clamped to prevent fluid flow whilst a component is worked on. Whichever method is used, ensure that the hose material is not permanently distorted or damaged by the clamp.

a) A brake hose clamp available from auto accessory shops **(see illustration 9.1)**.
b) A wingnut type hose clamp **(see illustration 9.2)**.

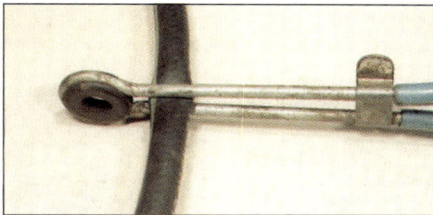

9.1 Hoses can be clamped with an automotive brake hose clamp . . .

9.2 . . . a wingnut type hose clamp . . .

c) Two sockets placed each side of the hose and held with straight-jawed self-locking grips **(see illustration 9.3)**.
d) Thick card each side of the hose held between straight-jawed self-locking grips **(see illustration 9.4)**.

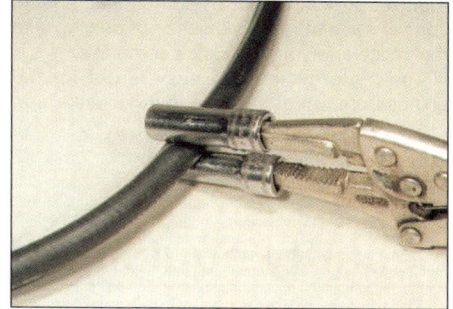

9.3 . . . two sockets and a pair of self-locking grips . . .

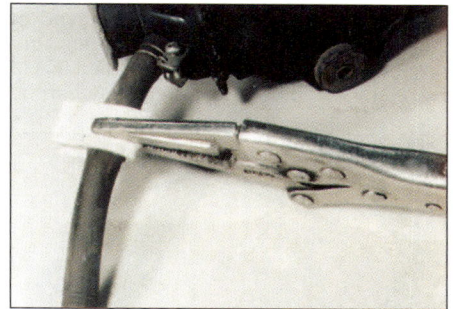

9.4 . . . or thick card and self-locking grips

Freeing and fitting hoses

● Always make sure the hose clamp is moved well clear of the hose end. Grip the hose with your hand and rotate it whilst pulling it off the union. If the hose has hardened due to age and will not move, slit it with a sharp knife and peel its ends off the union **(see illustration 9.5)**.

● Resist the temptation to use grease or soap on the unions to aid installation; although it helps the hose slip over the union it will equally aid the escape of fluid from the joint. It is preferable to soften the hose ends in hot water and wet the inside surface of the hose with water or a fluid which will evaporate.

9.5 Cutting a coolant hose free with a sharp knife

Introduction

In less time than it takes to read this introduction, a thief could steal your motorcycle. Returning only to find your bike has gone is one of the worst feelings in the world. Even if the motorcycle is insured against theft, once you've got over the initial shock, you will have the inconvenience of dealing with the police and your insurance company.

The motorcycle is an easy target for the professional thief and the joyrider alike and

the official figures on motorcycle theft make for depressing reading; on average a motorcycle is stolen every 16 minutes in the UK!

Motorcycle thefts fall into two categories, those stolen 'to order' and those taken by opportunists. The thief stealing to order will be on the look out for a specific make and model and will go to extraordinary lengths to obtain that motorcycle. The opportunist thief on the other hand will look for easy targets which can be stolen with the minimum of effort and risk.

Whilst it is never going to be possible to make your machine 100% secure, it is estimated that around half of all stolen motorcycles are taken by opportunist thieves. Remember that the opportunist thief is always on the look out for the easy option: if there are two similar motorcycles parked side-by-side, they will target the one with the lowest level of security. By taking a few precautions, you can reduce the chances of your motorcycle being stolen.

Security equipment

There are many specialised motorcycle security devices available and the following text summarises their applications and their good and bad points.

Once you have decided on the type of security equipment which best suits your needs, we recommended that you read one of the many equipment tests regularly carried

out by the motorcycle press. These tests compare the products from all the major manufacturers and give impartial ratings on their effectiveness, value-for-money and ease of use.

No one item of security equipment can provide complete protection. It is highly recommended that two or more of the items described below are combined to increase the security of your motorcycle (a lock and chain plus an alarm system is just about ideal). The more security measures fitted to the bike, the less likely it is to be stolen.

Lock and chain

Pros: *Very flexible to use; can be used to secure the motorcycle to almost any immovable object. On some locks and chains, the lock can be used on its own as a disc lock (see below).*

Cons: *Can be very heavy and awkward to carry on the motorcycle, although some types*

will be supplied with a carry bag which can be strapped to the pillion seat.

● Heavy-duty chains and locks are an excellent security measure **(see illustration 1)**. Whenever the motorcycle is parked, use the lock and chain to secure the machine to a solid, immovable object such as a post or railings. This will prevent the machine from being ridden away or being lifted into the back of a van.

● When fitting the chain, always ensure the chain is routed around the motorcycle frame or swingarm **(see illustrations 2 and 3)**. Never merely pass the chain around one of the wheel rims; a thief may unbolt the wheel and lift the rest of the machine into a van, leaving you with just the wheel! Try to avoid having excess chain free, thus making it difficult to use cutting tools, and keep the chain and lock off the ground to prevent thieves attacking it with a cold chisel. Position the lock so that its lock barrel is facing downwards; this will make it harder for the thief to attack the lock mechanism.

Ensure the lock and chain you buy is of good quality and long enough to shackle your bike to a solid object

Pass the chain through the bike's frame, rather than just through a wheel . . .

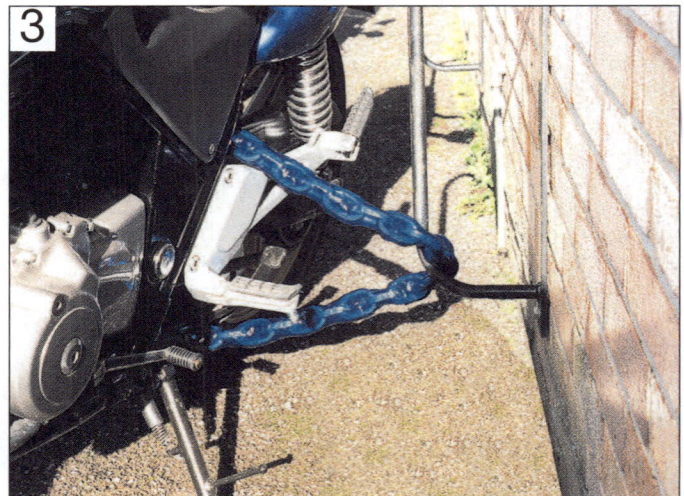

. . . and loop it around a solid object

U-locks

Pros: *Highly effective deterrent which can be used to secure the bike to a post or railings. Most U-locks come with a carrier which allows the lock to be easily carried on the bike.*

Cons: *Not as flexible to use as a lock and chain.*

● These are solid locks which are similar in use to a lock and chain. U-locks are lighter than a lock and chain but not so flexible to use. The length and shape of the lock shackle limit the objects to which the bike can be secured **(see illustration 4)**.

U-locks can be used to secure the bike to a solid object – ensure you purchase one which is long enough

Disc locks

Pros: *Small, light and very easy to carry; most can be stored underneath the seat.*

Cons: *Does not prevent the motorcycle being lifted into a van. Can be very embarrassing if you*

forget to remove the lock before attempting to ride off!

● Disc locks are designed to be attached to the front brake disc. The lock passes through one of the holes in the disc and prevents the wheel rotating by jamming against the fork/brake caliper **(see illustration 5)**. Some are equipped with an alarm siren which sounds if the disc lock is moved; this not only acts as a theft deterrent but also as a handy reminder if you try to move the bike with the lock still fitted.

● Combining the disc lock with a length of cable which can be looped around a post or railings provides an additional measure of security **(see illustration 6)**.

Alarms and immobilisers

Pros: *Once installed it is completely hassle-free to use. If the system is 'Thatcham' or 'Sold Secure-approved', insurance companies may give you a discount.*

Cons: *Can be expensive to buy and complex to install. No system will prevent the motorcycle from being lifted into a van and taken away.*

● Electronic alarms and immobilisers are available to suit a variety of budgets. There are three different types of system available: pure alarms, pure immobilisers, and the more expensive systems which are combined alarm/immobilisers **(see illustration 7)**.

● An alarm system is designed to emit an audible warning if the motorcycle is being tampered with.

● An immobiliser prevents the motorcycle being started and ridden away by disabling its electrical systems.

● When purchasing an alarm/immobiliser system, check the cost of installing the system unless you are able to do it yourself. If the motorcycle is not used regularly, another consideration is the current drain of the system. All alarm/immobiliser systems are powered by the motorcycle's battery; purchasing a system with a very low current drain could prevent the battery losing its charge whilst the motorcycle is not being used.

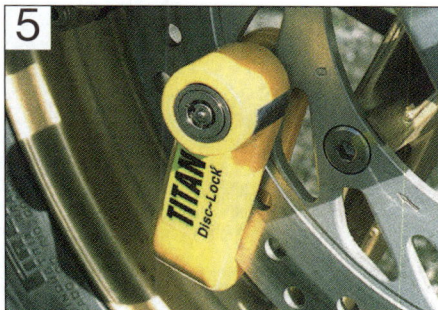

A typical disc lock attached through one of the holes in the disc

A disc lock combined with a security cable provides additional protection

A typical alarm/immobiliser system

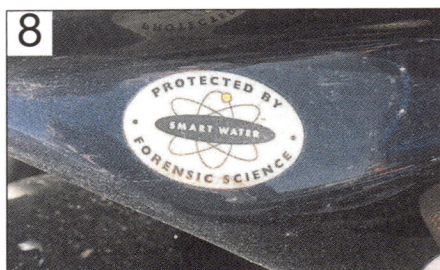

Indelible markings can be applied to most areas of the bike – always apply the manufacturer's sticker to warn off thieves

Chemically-etched code numbers can be applied to main body panels . . .

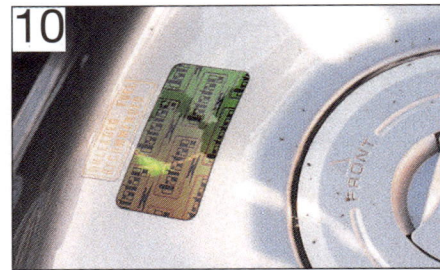

. . . again, always ensure that the kit manufacturer's sticker is applied in a prominent position

Security marking kits

Pros: *Very cheap and effective deterrent. Many insurance companies will give you a discount on your insurance premium if a recognised security marking kit is used on your motorcycle.*

Cons: *Does not prevent the motorcycle being stolen by joyriders.*

● There are many different types of security marking kits available. The idea is to mark as many parts of the motorcycle as possible with a unique security number **(see illustrations 8, 9 and 10)**. A form will be included with the kit to register your personal details and those of the motorcycle with the kit manufacturer. This register is made available to the police to help them trace the rightful owner of any motorcycle or components which they recover should all other forms of identification have been removed. Always apply the warning stickers provided with the kit to deter thieves.

Ground anchors, wheel clamps and security posts

Pros: *An excellent form of security which will deter all but the most determined of thieves.*

Cons: *Awkward to install and can be expensive.*

● Whilst the motorcycle is at home, it is a good idea to attach it securely to the floor or a solid wall, even if it is kept in a securely locked garage. Various types of ground anchors, security posts and wheel clamps are available for this purpose **(see illustration 11)**. These security devices are either bolted to a solid concrete or brick structure or can be cemented into the ground.

Permanent ground anchors provide an excellent level of security when the bike is at home

Security at home

A high percentage of motorcycle thefts are from the owner's home. Here are some things to consider whenever your motorcycle is at home:
✔ Where possible, always keep the motorcycle in a securely locked garage. Never rely solely on the standard lock on the garage door, these are usual hopelessly inadequate. Fit an additional locking mechanism to the door and consider having the garage alarmed. A security light, activated by a movement sensor, is also a good investment.
✔ Always secure the motorcycle to the ground or a wall, even if it is inside a securely locked garage.
✔ Do not regularly leave the motorcycle outside your home, try to keep it out of sight wherever possible. If a garage is not available, fit a motorcycle cover over the bike to disguise its true identity.
✔ It is not uncommon for thieves to follow a motorcyclist home to find out where the bike is kept. They will then return at a later date. Be aware of this whenever you are returning home on your motorcycle. If you suspect you are being followed, do not return home, instead ride to a garage or shop and stop as a precaution.
✔ When selling a motorcycle, do not provide your home address or the location where the bike is normally kept. Arrange to meet the buyer at a location away from your home. Thieves have been known to pose as potential buyers to find out where motorcycles are kept and then return later to steal them.

Security away from the home

As well as fitting security equipment to your motorcycle here are a few general rules to follow whenever you park your motorcycle.
✔ Park in a busy, public place.
✔ Use car parks which incorporate security features, such as CCTV.
✔ At night, park in a well-lit area, preferably directly underneath a street light.
✔ Engage the steering lock.
✔ Secure the motorcycle to a solid, immovable object such as a post or railings with an additional lock. If this is not possible, secure the bike to a friend's motorcycle. Some public parking places provide security loops for motorcycles.
✔ Never leave your helmet or luggage attached to the motorcycle. Take them with you at all times.

Lubricants and fluids

A wide range of lubricants, fluids and cleaning agents is available for motor-cycles. This is a guide as to what is available, its applications and properties.

Four-stroke engine oil

● Engine oil is without doubt the most important component of any four-stroke engine. Modern motorcycle engines place a lot of demands on their oil and choosing the right type is essential. Using an unsuitable oil will lead to an increased rate of engine wear and could result in serious engine damage. Before purchasing oil, always check the recommended oil specification given by the manufacturer. The manufacturer will state a recommended 'type or classification' and also a specific 'viscosity' range for engine oil.

● The oil 'type or classification' is identified by its API (American Petroleum Institute) rating. The API rating will be in the form of two letters, e.g. SG. The S identifies the oil as being suitable for use in a petrol (gasoline) engine (S stands for spark ignition) and the second letter, ranging from A to J, identifies the oil's performance rating. The later this letter, the higher the specification of the oil; for example API SG oil exceeds the requirements of API SF oil. Note: *On some oils there may also be a second rating consisting of another two letters, the first letter being C, e.g. API SF/CD. This rating indicates the oil is also suitable for use in a diesel engines (the C stands for compression ignition) and is thus of no relevance for motorcycle use.*

● The 'viscosity' of the oil is identified by its SAE (Society of Automotive Engineers) rating. All modern engines require multigrade oils and the SAE rating will consist of two numbers, the first followed by a W, e.g.

10W/40. The first number indicates the viscosity rating of the oil at low temperatures (W stands for winter – tested at –20°C) and the second number represents the viscosity of the oil at high temperatures (tested at 100°C). The lower the number, the thinner the oil. For example an oil with an SAE 10W/40 rating will give better cold starting and running than an SAE 15W/40 oil.

● As well as ensuring the 'type' and 'viscosity' of the oil match the recommendations, another consideration to make when buying engine oil is whether to purchase a standard mineral-based oil, a semi-synthetic oil (also known as a synthetic blend or synthetic-based oil) or a fully-synthetic oil. Although all oils will have a similar rating and viscosity, their cost will vary considerably; mineral-based oils are the cheapest, the fully-synthetic oils the most expensive with the semi-synthetic oils falling somewhere in-between. This decision is very much up to the owner, but it should be noted that modern synthetic oils have far better lubricating and cleaning qualities than traditional mineral-based oils and tend to retain these properties for far longer. Bearing in mind the operating conditions inside a modern, high-revving motorcycle engine it is highly recommended that a fully synthetic oil is used. The extra expense at each service could save you money in the long term by preventing premature engine wear.

● As a final note always ensure that the oil is specifically designed for use in motorcycle engines. Engine oils designed primarily for use in car engines sometimes contain additives or friction modifiers which could cause clutch slip on a motorcycle fitted with a wet-clutch.

Two-stroke engine oil

● Modern two-stroke engines, with their high power outputs, place high demands on their oil. If engine seizure is to be avoided it is essential that a high-quality oil is used. Two-stroke oils differ hugely from four-stroke oils. The oil lubricates only the crankshaft and piston(s) (the transmission has its own lubricating oil) and is used on a total-loss basis where it is burnt completely during the combustion process.

● The Japanese have recently introduced a classification system for two-stroke oils, the JASO rating. This rating is in the form of two letters, either FA, FB or FC – FA is the lowest classification and FC the highest. Ensure the oil being used meets or exceeds the recommended rating specified by the manufacturer.

● As well as ensuring the oil rating matches the recommendation, another consideration to make when buying engine oil is whether to purchase a standard mineral-based oil, a semi-synthetic oil (also known as a synthetic blend or synthetic-based oil) or a fully-synthetic oil. The cost of each type of oil varies considerably; mineral-based oils are the cheapest, the fully-synthetic oils the most expensive with the semi-synthetic oils falling somewhere in-between. This decision is very much up to the owner, but it should be noted that modern synthetic oils have far better lubricating properties and burn cleaner than traditional mineral-based oils. It is therefore recommended that a fully synthetic oil is used. The extra expense could save you money in the long term by preventing premature engine wear, engine performance will be improved, carbon deposits and exhaust smoke will be reduced.

● Always ensure that the oil is specifically designed for use in an injector system. Many high quality two-stroke oils are designed for competition use and need to be pre-mixed with fuel. These oils are of a much higher viscosity and are not designed to flow through the injector pumps used on road-going two-stroke motorcycles.

Transmission (gear) oil

● On a two-stroke engine, the transmission and clutch are lubricated by their own separate oil bath which must be changed in accordance with the Maintenance Schedule.
● Although the engine and transmission units of most four-strokes use a common lubrication supply, there are some exceptions where the engine and gearbox have separate oil reservoirs and a dry clutch is used.
● Motorcycle manufacturers will either recommend a monograde transmission oil or a four-stroke multigrade engine oil to lubricate the transmission.
● Transmission oils, or gear oils as they are often called, are designed specifically for use in transmission systems. The viscosity of these oils is represented by an SAE number, but the scale of measurement applied is different to that used to grade engine oils. As a rough guide a SAE90 gear oil will be of the same viscosity as an SAE50 engine oil.

Shaft drive oil

● On models equipped with shaft final drive, the shaft drive gears are will have their own oil supply. The manufacturer will state a recommended 'type or classification' and also a specific 'viscosity' range in the same manner as for four-stroke engine oil.
● Gear oil classification is given by the number which follows the API GL (GL standing for gear lubricant) rating, the higher the number, the higher the specification of the oil, e.g. API GL5 oil is a higher specification than API GL4 oil. Ensure the oil meets or

exceeds the classification specified and is of the correct viscosity. The viscosity of gear oils is also represented by an SAE number but the scale of measurement used is different to that used to grade engine oils. As a rough guide an SAE90 gear oil will be of the same viscosity as an SAE50 engine oil.
● If the use of an EP (Extreme Pressure) gear oil is specified, ensure the oil purchased is suitable.

Fork oil and suspension fluid

● Conventional telescopic front forks are hydraulic and require fork oil to work. To ensure the forks function correctly, the fork oil must be changed in accordance with the Maintenance Schedule.
● Fork oil is available in a variety of viscosities, identified by their SAE rating; fork oil ratings vary from light (SAE 5) to heavy (SAE 30). When purchasing fork oil, ensure the viscosity rating matches that specified by the manufacturer.
● Some lubricant manufacturers also produce a range of high-quality suspension fluids which are very similar to fork oil but are designed mainly for competition use. These fluids may have a different viscosity rating system which is not to be confused with the SAE rating of normal fork oil. Refer to the manufacturer's instructions if in any doubt.

Brake and clutch fluid

● All disc brake systems and some clutch systems are hydraulically operated. To ensure correct operation, the hydraulic fluid must be changed in accordance with the Maintenance Schedule.
● Brake and clutch fluid is classified by its DOT rating with most motorcycle manufacturers specifying DOT 3 or 4 fluid. Both fluid types are glycol-based and can be mixed together without adverse effect; DOT 4 fluid exceeds the requirements of DOT 3

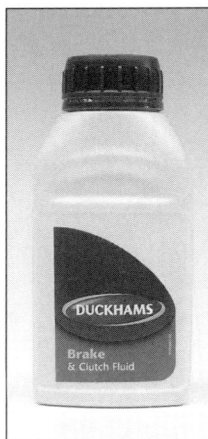

fluid. Although it is safe to use DOT 4 fluid in a system designed for use with DOT 3 fluid, never use DOT 3 fluid in a system which specifies the use of DOT 4 as this will adversely affect the system's performance. The type required for the system will be marked on the fluid reservoir cap.
● Some manufacturers also produce a DOT 5 hydraulic fluid. DOT 5 hydraulic fluid is silicone-based and is not compatible with the glycol-based DOT 3 and 4 fluids. Never mix DOT 5 fluid with DOT 3 or 4 fluid as this will seriously affect the performance of the hydraulic system.

Coolant/antifreeze

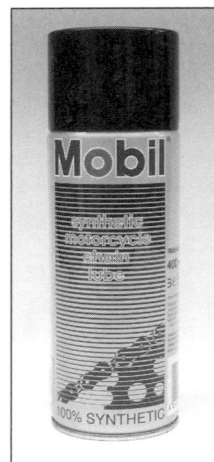

● When purchasing coolant/antifreeze, always ensure it is suitable for use in an aluminium engine and contains corrosion inhibitors to prevent possible blockages of the internal coolant passages of the system. As a general rule, most coolants are designed to be used neat and should not be diluted whereas antifreeze can be mixed with distilled water to provide a coolant solution of the required strength. Refer to the manufacturer's instructions on the bottle.
● Ensure the coolant is changed in accordance with the Maintenance Schedule.

Chain lube

● Chain lube is an aerosol-type spray lubricant specifically designed for use on motorcycle final drive chains. Chain lube has two functions, to minimise friction between the final drive chain and sprockets and to prevent corrosion of the chain. Regular use of a good-quality chain lube will extend the life of the drive chain and sprockets and thus maximise the power being transmitted from the transmission to the rear wheel.
● When using chain lube, always allow some time for the solvents in the lube to evaporate before riding the motorcycle. This will minimise the amount of lube which will

'fling' off from the chain when the motorcycle is used. If the motorcycle is equipped with an 'O-ring' chain, ensure the chain lube is labelled as being suitable for use on 'O-ring' chains.

Degreasers and solvents

● There are many different types of solvents and degreasers available to remove the grime and grease which accumulate around the motorcycle during normal use. Degreasers and solvents are usually available as an aerosol-type spray or as a liquid which you apply with a brush. Always closely follow the manufacturer's instructions and wear eye protection during use. Be aware that many solvents are flammable and may give off noxious fumes; take adequate precautions when using them (see Safety First!).

● For general cleaning, use one of the many solvents or degreasers available from most motorcycle accessory shops. These solvents are usually applied then left for a certain time before being washed off with water.

Brake cleaner is a solvent specifically designed to remove all traces of oil, grease and dust from braking system components. Brake cleaner is designed to evaporate quickly and leaves behind no residue.

Carburettor cleaner is an aerosol-type solvent specifically designed to clear carburettor blockages and break down the hard deposits and gum often found inside carburettors during overhaul.

Contact cleaner is an aerosol-type solvent designed for cleaning electrical components. The cleaner will remove all traces of oil and dirt from components such as switch contacts or fouled spark plugs and then dry, leaving behind no residue.

Gasket remover is an aerosol-type solvent designed for removing stubborn gaskets from engine components during overhaul. Gasket remover will minimise the amount of scraping required to remove the gasket and therefore reduce the risk of damage to the mating surface.

Spray lubricants

● Aerosol-based spray lubricants are widely available and are excellent for lubricating lever pivots and exposed cables and switches. Try to use a lubricant which is of the dry-film type as the fluid evaporates, leaving behind a dry-film of lubricant. Lubricants which leave behind an oily residue will attract dust and dirt which will increase the rate of wear of the cable/lever.

● Most lubricants also act as a moisture dispersant and a penetrating fluid. This means they can also be used to 'dry out' electrical components such as wiring connectors or switches as well as helping to free seized fasteners.

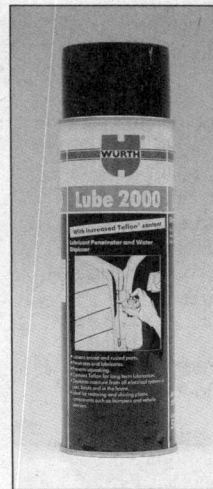

Greases

● Grease is used to lubricate many of the pivot-points. A good-quality multi-purpose grease is suitable for most applications but some manufacturers will specify the use of specialist greases for use on components such as swingarm and suspension linkage bushes. These specialist greases can be purchased from most motorcycle (or car) accessory shops; commonly specified types include molybdenum disulphide grease, lithium-based grease, graphite-based grease, silicone-based grease and high-temperature copper-based grease.

Gasket sealing compounds

● Gasket sealing compounds can be used in conjunction with gaskets, to improve their sealing capabilities, or on their own to seal metal-to-metal joints. Depending on their type, sealing compounds either set hard or stay relatively soft and pliable.

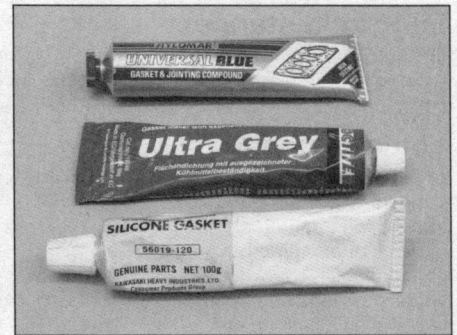

● When purchasing a gasket sealing compound, ensure that it is designed specifically for use on an internal combustion engine. General multi-purpose sealants available from DIY stores may appear visibly similar but they are not designed to withstand the extreme heat or contact with fuel and oil encountered when used on an engine (see 'Tools and Workshop Tips' for further information).

Thread locking compound

● Thread locking compounds are used to secure certain threaded fasteners in position to prevent them from loosening due to vibration. Thread locking compounds can be purchased from most motorcycle (and car) accessory shops. Ensure the threads of the both components are completely clean and dry before sparingly applying the locking compound (see 'Tools and Workshop Tips' for further information).

Fuel additives

● Fuel additives which protect and clean the fuel system components are widely available. These additives are designed to remove all traces of deposits that build up on the carburettors/injectors and prevent wear, helping the fuel system to operate more efficiently. If a fuel additive is being used, check that it is suitable for use with your motorcycle, especially if your motorcycle is equipped with a catalytic converter.

● Octane boosters are also available. These additives are designed to improve the performance of highly-tuned engines being run on normal pump-fuel and are of no real use on standard motorcycles.

Conversion Factors

Length (distance)

Inches (in)	x 25.4	= Millimetres (mm)	x 0.0394 =	Inches (in)
Feet (ft)	x 0.305	= Metres (m)	x 3.281 =	Feet (ft)
Miles	x 1.609	= Kilometres (km)	x 0.621 =	Miles

Volume (capacity)

Cubic inches (cu in; in³)	x 16.387	= Cubic centimetres (cc; cm³)	x 0.061 =	Cubic inches (cu in; in³)
Imperial pints (Imp pt)	x 0.568	= Litres (l)	x 1.76 =	Imperial pints (Imp pt)
Imperial quarts (Imp qt)	x 1.137	= Litres (l)	x 0.88 =	Imperial quarts (Imp qt)
Imperial quarts (Imp qt)	x 1.201	= US quarts (US qt)	x 0.833 =	Imperial quarts (Imp qt)
US quarts (US qt)	x 0.946	= Litres (l)	x 1.057 =	US quarts (US qt)
Imperial gallons (Imp gal)	x 4.546	= Litres (l)	x 0.22 =	Imperial gallons (Imp gal)
Imperial gallons (Imp gal)	x 1.201	= US gallons (US gal)	x 0.833 =	Imperial gallons (Imp gal)
US gallons (US gal)	x 3.785	= Litres (l)	x 0.264 =	US gallons (US gal)

Mass (weight)

Ounces (oz)	x 28.35	= Grams (g)	x 0.035 =	Ounces (oz)
Pounds (lb)	x 0.454	= Kilograms (kg)	x 2.205 =	Pounds (lb)

Force

Ounces-force (ozf; oz)	x 0.278	= Newtons (N)	x 3.6 =	Ounces-force (ozf; oz)
Pounds-force (lbf; lb)	x 4.448	= Newtons (N)	x 0.225 =	Pounds-force (lbf; lb)
Newtons (N)	x 0.1	= Kilograms-force (kgf; kg)	x 9.81 =	Newtons (N)

Pressure

Pounds-force per square inch (psi; lbf/in²; lb/in²)	x 0.070	= Kilograms-force per square centimetre (kgf/cm²; kg/cm²)	x 14.223 =	Pounds-force per square inch (psi; lbf/in²; lb/in²)
Pounds-force per square inch (psi; lbf/in²; lb/in²)	x 0.068	= Atmospheres (atm)	x 14.696 =	Pounds-force per square inch (psi; lbf/in²; lb/in²)
Pounds-force per square inch (psi; lbf/in²; lb/in²)	x 0.069	= Bars	x 14.5 =	Pounds-force per square inch (psi; lbf/in²; lb/in²)
Pounds-force per square inch (psi; lbf/in²; lb/in²)	x 6.895	= Kilopascals (kPa)	x 0.145 =	Pounds-force per square inch (psi; lbf/in²; lb/in²)
Kilopascals (kPa)	x 0.01	= Kilograms-force per square centimetre (kgf/cm²; kg/cm²)	x 98.1 =	Kilopascals (kPa)
Millibar (mbar)	x 100	= Pascals (Pa)	x 0.01 =	Millibar (mbar)
Millibar (mbar)	x 0.0145	= Pounds-force per square inch (psi; lbf/in²; lb/in²)	x 68.947 =	Millibar (mbar)
Millibar (mbar)	x 0.75	= Millimetres of mercury (mmHg)	x 1.333 =	Millibar (mbar)
Millibar (mbar)	x 0.401	= Inches of water (inH₂O)	x 2.491 =	Millibar (mbar)
Millimetres of mercury (mmHg)	x 0.535	= Inches of water (inH₂O)	x 1.868 =	Millimetres of mercury (mmHg)
Inches of water (inH₂O)	x 0.036	= Pounds-force per square inch (psi; lbf/in²; lb/in²)	x 27.68 =	Inches of water (inH₂O)

Torque (moment of force)

Pounds-force inches (lbf in; lb in)	x 1.152	= Kilograms-force centimetre (kgf cm; kg cm)	x 0.868 =	Pounds-force inches (lbf in; lb in)
Pounds-force inches (lbf in; lb in)	x 0.113	= Newton metres (Nm)	x 8.85 =	Pounds-force inches (lbf in; lb in)
Pounds-force inches (lbf in; lb in)	x 0.083	= Pounds-force feet (lbf ft; lb ft)	x 12 =	Pounds-force inches (lbf in; lb in)
Pounds-force feet (lbf ft; lb ft)	x 0.138	= Kilograms-force metres (kgf m; kg m)	x 7.233 =	Pounds-force feet (lbf ft; lb ft)
Pounds-force feet (lbf ft; lb ft)	x 1.356	= Newton metres (Nm)	x 0.738 =	Pounds-force feet (lbf ft; lb ft)
Newton metres (Nm)	x 0.102	= Kilograms-force metres (kgf m; kg m)	x 9.804 =	Newton metres (Nm)

Power

Horsepower (hp)	x 745.7	= Watts (W)	x 0.0013 =	Horsepower (hp)

Velocity (speed)

Miles per hour (miles/hr; mph)	x 1.609	= Kilometres per hour (km/hr; kph)	x 0.621 =	Miles per hour (miles/hr; mph)

Fuel consumption*

Miles per gallon (mpg)	x 0.354	= Kilometres per litre (km/l)	x 2.825 =	Miles per gallon (mpg)

Temperature

Degrees Fahrenheit = (°C x 1.8) + 32   Degrees Celsius (Degrees Centigrade; °C) = (°F - 32) x 0.56

* It is common practice to convert from miles per gallon (mpg) to litres/100 kilometres (l/100km), where mpg x l/100 km = 282

About the MOT Test

In the UK, all vehicles more than three years old are subject to an annual test to ensure that they meet minimum safety requirements. A current test certificate must be issued before a machine can be used on public roads, and is required before a road fund licence can be issued. Riding without a current test certificate will also invalidate your insurance.

For most owners, the MOT test is an annual cause for anxiety, and this is largely due to owners not being sure what needs to be checked prior to submitting the motorcycle for testing. The simple answer is that a fully roadworthy motorcycle will have no difficulty in passing the test.

This is a guide to getting your motorcycle through the MOT test. Obviously it will not be possible to examine the motorcycle to the same standard as the professional MOT tester, particularly in view of the equipment required for some of the checks. However, working through the following procedures will enable you to identify any problem areas before submitting the motorcycle for the test.

It has only been possible to summarise the test requirements here, based on the regulations in force at the time of printing. Test standards are becoming increasingly stringent, although there are some exemptions for older vehicles. More information about the MOT test can be obtained from the TSO publications, *How Safe is your Motorcycle* and *The MOT Inspection Manual for Motorcycle Testing.*

Many of the checks require that one of the wheels is raised off the ground. If the motorcycle doesn't have a centre stand, note that an auxiliary stand will be required. Additionally, the help of an assistant may prove useful.

Certain exceptions apply to machines under 50 cc, machines without a lighting system, and Classic bikes - if in doubt about any of the requirements listed below seek confirmation from an MOT tester prior to submitting the motorcycle for the test.

Check that the frame number is clearly visible.

> **HAYNES HINT**
> *If a component is in borderline condition, the tester has discretion in deciding whether to pass or fail it. If the motorcycle presented is clean and evidently well cared for, the tester may be more inclined to pass a borderline component than if the motorcycle is scruffy and apparently neglected.*

Electrical System

Lights, turn signals, horn and reflector

✔ With the ignition on, check the operation of the following electrical components. **Note:** *The electrical components on certain small-capacity machines are powered by the generator, requiring that the engine is run for this check.*

a) *Headlight and tail light. Check that both illuminate in the low and high beam switch positions.*

b) *Position lights. Check that the front position (or sidelight) and tail light illuminate in this switch position.*

c) *Turn signals. Check that all flash at the correct rate, and that the warning light(s) function correctly. Check that the turn signal switch works correctly.*

d) *Hazard warning system (where fitted). Check that all four turn signals flash in this switch position.*

e) *Brake stop light. Check that the light comes on when the front and rear brakes are independently applied. Models first used on or after 1st April 1986 must have a brake light switch on each brake.*

f) *Horn. Check that the sound is continuous and of reasonable volume.*

✔ Check that there is a red reflector on the rear of the machine, either mounted separately or as part of the tail light lens.

✔ Check the condition of the headlight, tail light and turn signal lenses.

Headlight beam height

✔ The MOT tester will perform a headlight beam height check using specialised beam setting equipment (see illustration 1). This equipment will not be available to the home mechanic, but if you suspect that the headlight is incorrectly set or may have been maladjusted in the past, you can perform a rough test as follows.

✔ Position the bike in a straight line facing a brick wall. The bike must be off its stand, upright and with a rider seated. Measure the height from the ground to the centre of the headlight and mark a horizontal line on the wall at this height. Position the motorcycle 3.8 metres from the wall and draw a vertical line up the wall central to the centreline of the motorcycle. Switch to dipped beam and check that the beam pattern falls slightly lower than the horizontal line and to the left of the vertical line (see illustration 2).

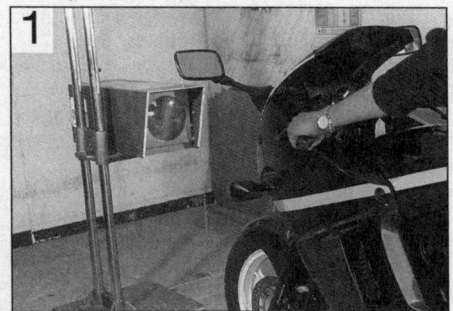

Headlight beam height checking equipment

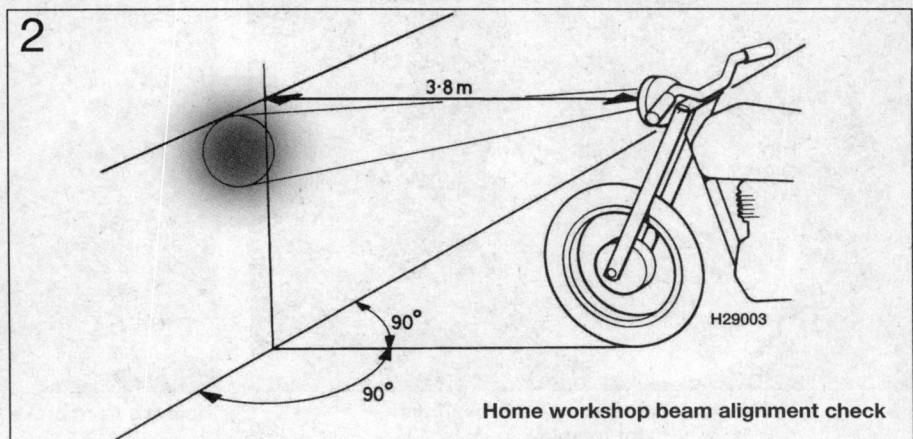

Home workshop beam alignment check

Exhaust System and Final Drive

Exhaust

✔ Check that the exhaust mountings are secure and that the system does not foul any of the rear suspension components.

✔ Start the motorcycle. When the revs are increased, check that the exhaust is neither holed nor leaking from any of its joints. On a linked system, check that the collector box is not leaking due to corrosion.

✔ Note that the exhaust decibel level ("loudness" of the exhaust) is assessed at the discretion of the tester. If the motorcycle was first used on or after 1st January 1985 the silencer must carry the BSAU 193 stamp, or a marking relating to its make and model, or be of OE (original equipment) manufacture. If the silencer is marked NOT FOR ROAD USE, RACING USE ONLY or similar, it will fail the MOT.

Final drive

✔ On chain or belt drive machines, check that the chain/belt is in good condition and does not have excessive slack. Also check that the sprocket is securely mounted on the rear wheel hub. Check that the chain/belt guard is in place.

✔ On shaft drive bikes, check for oil leaking from the drive unit and fouling the rear tyre.

Steering and Suspension

Steering

✔ With the front wheel raised off the ground, rotate the steering from lock to lock. The handlebar or switches must not contact the fuel tank or be close enough to trap the rider's hand. Problems can be caused by damaged lock stops on the lower yoke and frame, or by the fitting of non-standard handlebars.

✔ When performing the lock to lock check, also ensure that the steering moves freely without drag or notchiness. Steering movement can be impaired by poorly routed cables, or by overtight head bearings or worn bearings. The tester will perform a check of the steering head bearing lower race by mounting the front wheel on a surface plate, then performing a lock to lock check with the weight of the machine on the lower bearing (see illustration 3).

✔ Grasp the fork sliders (lower legs) and attempt to push and pull on the forks (see

Front wheel mounted on a surface plate for steering head bearing lower race check

illustration 4). Any play in the steering head bearings will be felt. Note that in extreme cases, wear of the front fork bushes can be misinterpreted for head bearing play.

✔ Check that the handlebars are securely mounted.

✔ Check that the handlebar grip rubbers are secure. They should by bonded to the bar left end and to the throttle cable pulley on the right end.

Front suspension

✔ With the motorcycle off the stand, hold the front brake on and pump the front forks up and down (see illustration 5). Check that they are adequately damped.

Checking the steering head bearings for freeplay

Hold the front brake on and pump the front forks up and down to check operation

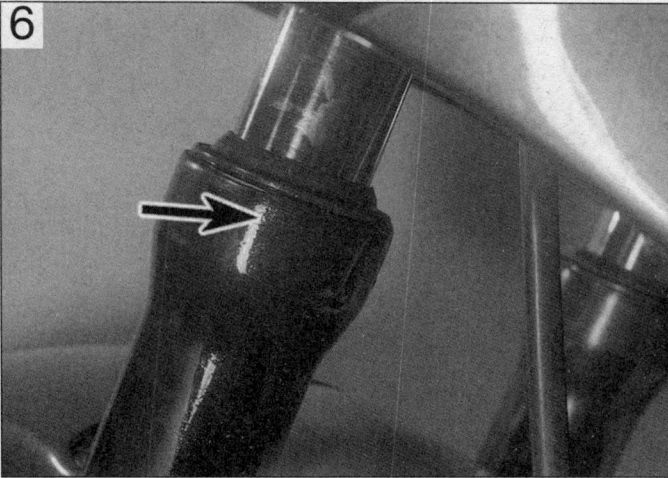
Inspect the area around the fork dust seal for oil leakage (arrow)

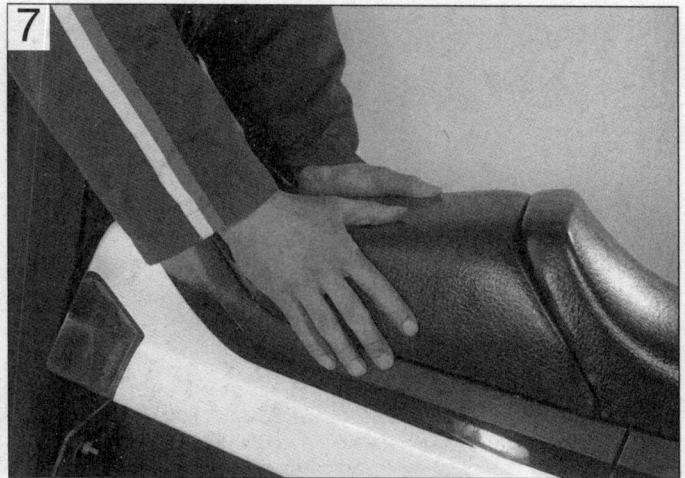
Bounce the rear of the motorcycle to check rear suspension operation

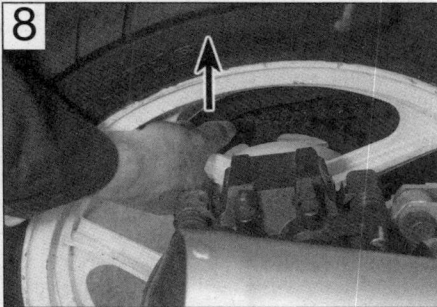
Checking for rear suspension linkage play

leg). On models so equipped, check that there is no oil leaking from the anti-dive units.
✔ On models with swingarm front suspension, check that there is no freeplay in the linkage when moved from side to side.

Rear suspension

✔ With the motorcycle off the stand and an assistant supporting the motorcycle by its handlebars, bounce the rear suspension (see illustration 7). Check that the suspension components do not foul on any of the cycle parts and check that the shock absorber(s) provide adequate damping.
✔ Visually inspect the shock absorber(s) and

check that there is no sign of oil leakage from its damper. This is somewhat restricted on certain single shock models due to the location of the shock absorber.
✔ With the rear wheel raised off the ground, grasp the wheel at the highest point and attempt to pull it up (see illustration 8). Any play in the swingarm pivot or suspension linkage bearings will be felt as movement. Note: Do not confuse play with actual suspension movement. Failure to lubricate suspension linkage bearings can lead to bearing failure (see illustration 9).
✔ With the rear wheel raised off the ground, grasp the swingarm ends and attempt to move the swingarm from side to side and forwards and backwards - any play indicates wear of the swingarm pivot bearings (see illustration 10).

✔ Inspect the area above and around the front fork oil seals (see illustration 6). There should be no sign of oil on the fork tube (stanchion) nor leaking down the slider (lower

Worn suspension linkage pivots (arrows) are usually the cause of play in the rear suspension

Grasp the swingarm at the ends to check for play in its pivot bearings

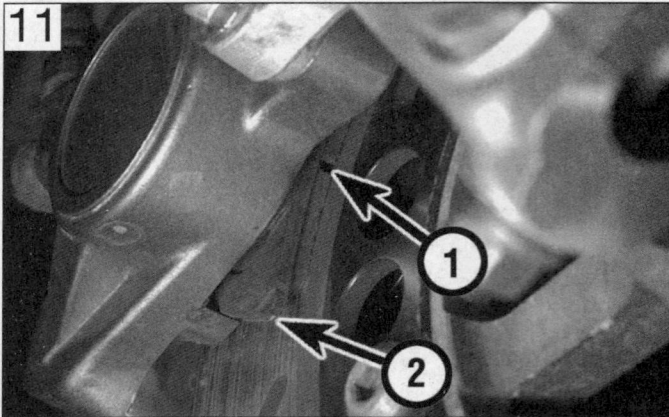

Brake pad wear can usually be viewed without removing the caliper. Most pads have wear indicator grooves (1) and some also have indicator tangs (2)

On drum brakes, check the angle of the operating lever with the brake fully applied. Most drum brakes have a wear indicator pointer and scale.

Brakes, Wheels and Tyres

Brakes

✔ With the wheel raised off the ground, apply the brake then free it off, and check that the wheel is about to revolve freely without brake drag.

✔ On disc brakes, examine the disc itself. Check that it is securely mounted and not cracked.

✔ On disc brakes, view the pad material through the caliper mouth and check that the pads are not worn down beyond the limit **(see illustration 11)**.

✔ On drum brakes, check that when the brake is applied the angle between the operating lever and cable or rod is not too great **(see illustration 12)**. Check also that the operating lever doesn't foul any other components.

✔ On disc brakes, examine the flexible hoses from top to bottom. Have an assistant hold the brake on so that the fluid in the hose is under pressure, and check that there is no sign of fluid leakage, bulges or cracking. If there are any metal brake pipes or unions, check that these are free from corrosion and damage. Where a brake-linked anti-dive system is fitted, check the hoses to the anti-dive in a similar manner.

✔ Check that the rear brake torque arm is secure and that its fasteners are secured by self-locking nuts or castellated nuts with split-pins or R-pins **(see illustration 13)**.

✔ On models with ABS, check that the self-check warning light in the instrument panel works.

✔ The MOT tester will perform a test of the motorcycle's braking efficiency based on a calculation of rider and motorcycle weight. Although this cannot be carried out at home, you can at least ensure that the braking systems are properly maintained. For hydraulic disc brakes, check the fluid level, lever/pedal feel (bleed of air if its spongy) and pad material. For drum brakes, check adjustment, cable or rod operation and shoe lining thickness.

Wheels and tyres

✔ Check the wheel condition. Cast wheels should be free from cracks and if of the built-up design, all fasteners should be secure. Spoked wheels should be checked for broken, corroded, loose or bent spokes.

✔ With the wheel raised off the ground, spin the wheel and visually check that the tyre and wheel run true. Check that the tyre does not foul the suspension or mudguards.

✔ With the wheel raised off the ground, grasp the wheel and attempt to move it about the axle (spindle) **(see illustration 14)**. Any play felt here indicates wheel bearing failure.

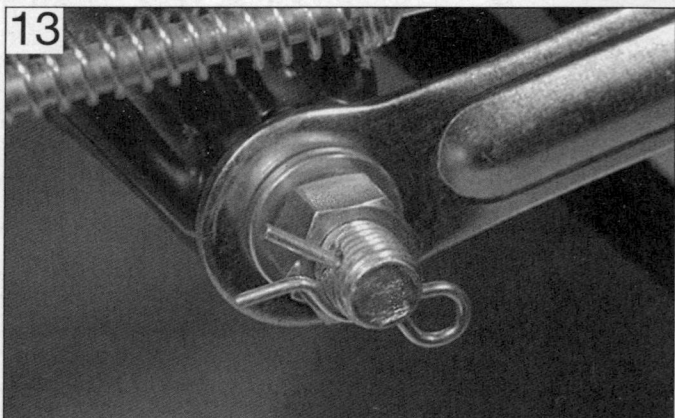

Brake torque arm must be properly secured at both ends

Check for wheel bearing play by trying to move the wheel about the axle (spindle)

Checking the tyre tread depth

Tyre direction of rotation arrow can be found on tyre sidewall

Castellated type wheel axle (spindle) nut must be secured by a split pin or R-pin

Two straightedges are used to check wheel alignment

✔ Check the tyre tread depth, tread condition and sidewall condition **(see illustration 15)**.
✔ Check the tyre type. Front and rear tyre types must be compatible and be suitable for road use. Tyres marked NOT FOR ROAD USE, COMPETITION USE ONLY or similar, will fail the MOT.

✔ If the tyre sidewall carries a direction of rotation arrow, this must be pointing in the direction of normal wheel rotation **(see illustration 16)**.
✔ Check that the wheel axle (spindle) nuts (where applicable) are properly secured. A self-locking nut or castellated nut with a split-pin or R-pin can be used **(see illustration 17)**.
✔ Wheel alignment is checked with the motorcycle off the stand and a rider seated. With the front wheel pointing straight ahead, two perfectly straight lengths of metal or wood and placed against the sidewalls of both tyres **(see illustration 18)**. The gap each side of the front tyre must be equidistant on both sides. Incorrect wheel alignment may be due to a cocked rear wheel (often as the result of poor chain adjustment) or in extreme cases, a bent frame.

General checks and condition

✔ Check the security of all major fasteners, bodypanels, seat, fairings (where fitted) and mudguards.

✔ Check that the rider and pillion footrests, handlebar levers and brake pedal are securely mounted.

✔ Check for corrosion on the frame or any load-bearing components. If severe, this may affect the structure, particularly under stress.

Sidecars

A motorcycle fitted with a sidecar requires additional checks relating to the stability of the machine and security of attachment and swivel joints, plus specific wheel alignment (toe-in) requirements. Additionally, tyre and lighting requirements differ from conventional motorcycle use. Owners are advised to check MOT test requirements with an official test centre.

Preparing for storage

Before you start

If repairs or an overhaul is needed, see that this is carried out now rather than left until you want to ride the bike again.

Give the bike a good wash and scrub all dirt from its underside. Make sure the bike dries completely before preparing for storage.

Engine

● Remove the spark plug(s) and lubricate the cylinder bores with approximately a teaspoon of motor oil using a spout-type oil can **(see illustration 1)**. Reinstall the spark plug(s). Crank the engine over a couple of times to coat the piston rings and bores with oil. If the bike has a kickstart, use this to turn the engine over. If not, flick the kill switch to the OFF position and crank the engine over on the starter **(see illustration 2)**. If the nature on the ignition system prevents the starter operating with the kill switch in the OFF position,

remove the spark plugs and fit them back in their caps; ensure that the plugs are earthed (grounded) against the cylinder head when the starter is operated **(see illustration 3)**.

⚠️ **Warning: It is important that the plugs are earthed (grounded) away from the spark plug holes otherwise there is a risk of atomised fuel from the cylinders igniting.**

HAYNES HINT *On a single cylinder four-stroke engine, you can seal the combustion chamber completely by positioning the piston at TDC on the compression stroke.*

● Drain the carburettor(s) otherwise there is a risk of jets becoming blocked by gum deposits from the fuel **(see illustration 4)**.

● If the bike is going into long-term storage, consider adding a fuel stabiliser to the fuel in the tank. If the tank is drained completely, corrosion of its internal surfaces may occur if left unprotected for a long period. The tank can be treated with a rust preventative especially for this purpose. Alternatively, remove the tank and pour half a litre of motor oil into it, install the filler cap and shake the tank to coat its internals with oil before draining off the excess. The same effect can also be achieved by spraying WD40 or a similar water-dispersant around the inside of the tank via its flexible nozzle.

● Make sure the cooling system contains the correct mix of antifreeze. Antifreeze also contains important corrosion inhibitors.

● The air intakes and exhaust can be sealed off by covering or plugging the openings. Ensure that you do not seal in any condensation; run the engine until it is hot,

Squirt a drop of motor oil into each cylinder

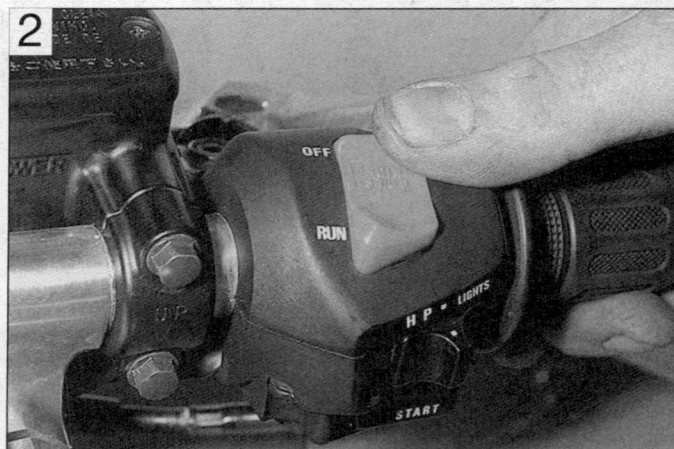

Flick the kill switch to OFF . . .

. . . and ensure that the metal bodies of the plugs (arrows) are earthed against the cylinder head

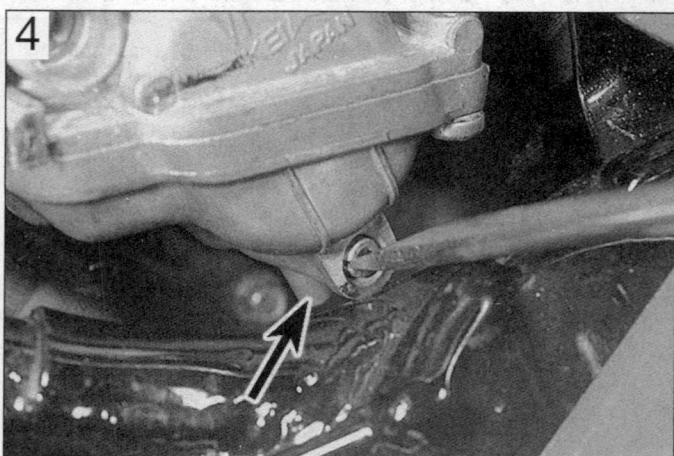

Connect a hose to the carburettor float chamber drain stub (arrow) and unscrew the drain screw

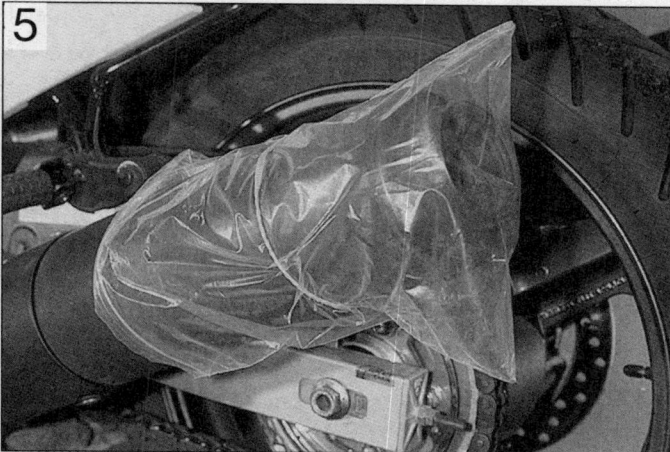

Exhausts can be sealed off with a plastic bag

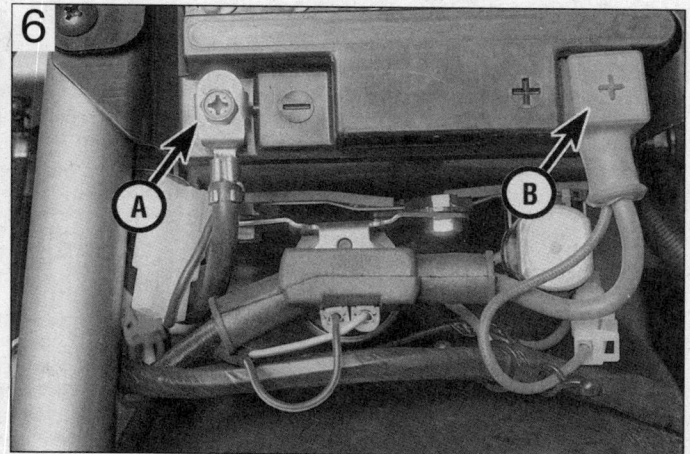

Disconnect the negative lead (A) first, followed by the positive lead (B)

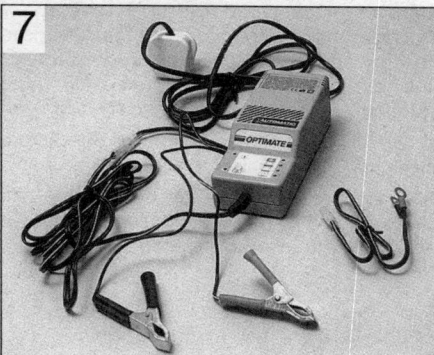

Use a suitable battery charger - this kit also assess battery condition

then switch off and allow to cool. Tape a piece of thick plastic over the silencer end(s) **(see illustration 5)**. Note that some advocate pouring a tablespoon of motor oil into the silencer(s) before sealing them off.

Battery

● Remove it from the bike - in extreme cases of cold the battery may freeze and crack its case **(see illustration 6)**.

● Check the electrolyte level and top up if necessary (conventional refillable batteries). Clean the terminals.
● Store the battery off the motorcycle and away from any sources of fire. Position a wooden block under the battery if it is to sit on the ground.
● Give the battery a trickle charge for a few hours every month **(see illustration 7)**.

Tyres

● Place the bike on its centrestand or an auxiliary stand which will support the motorcycle in an upright position. Position wood blocks under the tyres to keep them off the ground and to provide insulation from damp. If the bike is being put into long-term storage, ideally both tyres should be off the ground; not only will this protect the tyres, but will also ensure that no load is placed on the steering head or wheel bearings.
● Deflate each tyre by 5 to 10 psi, no more or the beads may unseat from the rim, making subsequent inflation difficult on tubeless tyres.

Pivots and controls

● Lubricate all lever, pedal, stand and footrest pivot points. If grease nipples are fitted to the rear suspension components, apply lubricant to the pivots.
● Lubricate all control cables.

Cycle components

● Apply a wax protectant to all painted and plastic components. Wipe off any excess, but don't polish to a shine. Where fitted, clean the screen with soap and water.
● Coat metal parts with Vaseline (petroleum jelly). When applying this to the fork tubes, do not compress the forks otherwise the seals will rot from contact with the Vaseline.
● Apply a vinyl cleaner to the seat.

Storage conditions

● Aim to store the bike in a shed or garage which does not leak and is free from damp.
● Drape an old blanket or bedspread over the bike to protect it from dust and direct contact with sunlight (which will fade paint). This also hides the bike from prying eyes. Beware of tight-fitting plastic covers which may allow condensation to form and settle on the bike.

Getting back on the road

Engine and transmission

● Change the oil and replace the oil filter. If this was done prior to storage, check that the oil hasn't emulsified - a thick whitish substance which occurs through condensation.
● Remove the spark plugs. Using a spout-type oil can, squirt a few drops of oil into the cylinder(s). This will provide initial lubrication as the piston rings and bores comes back into contact. Service the spark plugs, or fit new ones, and install them in the engine.

● Check that the clutch isn't stuck on. The plates can stick together if left standing for some time, preventing clutch operation. Engage a gear and try rocking the bike back and forth with the clutch lever held against the handlebar. If this doesn't work on cable-operated clutches, hold the clutch lever back against the handlebar with a strong elastic band or cable tie for a couple of hours **(see illustration 8)**.
● If the air intakes or silencer end(s) were blocked off, remove the bung or cover used.
● If the fuel tank was coated with a rust

Hold clutch lever back against the handlebar with elastic bands or a cable tie

preventative, oil or a stabiliser added to the fuel, drain and flush the tank and dispose of the fuel sensibly. If no action was taken with the fuel tank prior to storage, it is advised that the old fuel is disposed of since it will go off over a period of time. Refill the fuel tank with fresh fuel.

Frame and running gear

● Oil all pivot points and cables.
● Check the tyre pressures. They will definitely need inflating if pressures were reduced for storage.
● Lubricate the final drive chain (where applicable).
● Remove any protective coating applied to the fork tubes (stanchions) since this may well destroy the fork seals. If the fork tubes weren't protected and have picked up rust spots, remove them with very fine abrasive paper and refinish with metal polish.
● Check that both brakes operate correctly. Apply each brake hard and check that it's not possible to move the motorcycle forwards, then check that the brake frees off again once released. Brake caliper pistons can stick due to corrosion around the piston head, or on the sliding caliper types, due to corrosion of the slider pins. If the brake doesn't free after repeated operation, take the caliper off for examination. Similarly drum brakes can stick due to a seized operating cam, cable or rod linkage.
● If the motorcycle has been in long-term storage, renew the brake fluid and clutch fluid (where applicable).
● Depending on where the bike has been stored, the wiring, cables and hoses may have been nibbled by rodents. Make a visual check and investigate disturbed wiring loom tape.

Battery

● If the battery has been previously removal and given top up charges it can simply be reconnected. Remember to connect the positive cable first and the negative cable last.
● On conventional refillable batteries, if the battery has not received any attention, remove it from the motorcycle and check its electrolyte level. Top up if necessary then charge the battery. If the battery fails to hold a charge and a visual checks show heavy white sulphation of the plates, the battery is probably defective and must be renewed. This is particularly likely if the battery is old. Confirm battery condition with a specific gravity check.
● On sealed (MF) batteries, if the battery has not received any attention, remove it from the motorcycle and charge it according to the information on the battery case - if the battery fails to hold a charge it must be renewed.

Starting procedure

● If a kickstart is fitted, turn the engine over a couple of times with the ignition OFF to distribute oil around the engine. If no kickstart is fitted, flick the engine kill switch OFF and the ignition ON and crank the engine over a couple of times to work oil around the upper cylinder components. If the nature of the ignition system is such that the starter won't work with the kill switch OFF, remove the spark plugs, fit them back into their caps and earth (ground) their bodies on the cylinder head. Reinstall the spark plugs afterwards.
● Switch the kill switch to RUN, operate the choke and start the engine. If the engine won't start don't continue cranking the engine - not only will this flatten the battery, but the starter motor will overheat. Switch the ignition off and try again later. If the engine refuses to start, go through the fault finding procedures in this manual. **Note:** *If the bike has been in storage for a long time, old fuel or a carburettor blockage may be the problem. Gum deposits in carburettors can block jets - if a carburettor cleaner doesn't prove successful the carburettors must be dismantled for cleaning.*

● Once the engine has started, check that the lights, turn signals and horn work properly.

● Treat the bike gently for the first ride and check all fluid levels on completion. Settle the bike back into the maintenance schedule.

This Section provides an easy reference-guide to the more common faults that are likely to afflict your machine. Obviously, the opportunities are almost limitless for faults to occur as a result of obscure failures, and to try and cover all eventualities would require a book. Indeed, a number have been written on the subject.

Successful troubleshooting is not a mysterious 'black art' but the application of a bit of knowledge combined with a systematic and logical approach to the problem. Approach any troubleshooting by first accurately identifying the symptom and then checking through the list of possible causes, starting with the simplest or most obvious and progressing in stages to the most complex.

Take nothing for granted, but above all apply liberal quantities of common sense.

The main symptom of a fault is given in the text as a major heading below which are listed the various systems or areas which may contain the fault. Details of each possible cause for a fault and the remedial action to be taken are given, in brief, in the paragraphs below each heading. Further information should be sought in the relevant Chapter.

1 Engine doesn't start or is difficult to start

- ☐ Starter motor doesn't rotate
- ☐ Starter motor rotates but engine does not turn over
- ☐ Starter works but engine won't turn over (seized)
- ☐ No fuel flow
- ☐ Engine flooded
- ☐ No spark or weak spark
- ☐ Compression low
- ☐ Stalls after starting
- ☐ Rough idle

2 Poor running at low speed

- ☐ Spark weak
- ☐ Fuel/air mixture incorrect
- ☐ Compression low
- ☐ Poor acceleration

3 Poor running or no power at high speed

- ☐ Firing incorrect
- ☐ Fuel/air mixture incorrect
- ☐ Compression low
- ☐ Knocking or pinking
- ☐ Miscellaneous causes

4 Overheating

- ☐ Engine overheats
- ☐ Firing incorrect
- ☐ Fuel/air mixture incorrect
- ☐ Compression too high
- ☐ Engine load excessive
- ☐ Lubrication inadequate
- ☐ Miscellaneous causes

5 Clutch problems

- ☐ Clutch slipping
- ☐ Clutch not disengaging completely

6 Gearchanging problems

- ☐ Doesn't go into gear, or lever doesn't return
- ☐ Jumps out of gear
- ☐ Overselects

7 Abnormal engine noise

- ☐ Knocking or pinking
- ☐ Piston slap or rattling
- ☐ Valve noise
- ☐ Other noise

8 Abnormal driveline noise

- ☐ Clutch noise
- ☐ Transmission noise
- ☐ Final drive noise

9 Abnormal frame and suspension noise

- ☐ Front end noise
- ☐ Shock absorber noise
- ☐ Disc brake noise

10 Excessive exhaust smoke

- ☐ White smoke
- ☐ Black smoke
- ☐ Brown smoke

11 Poor handling or stability

- ☐ Handlebar hard to turn
- ☐ Handlebar shakes or vibrates excessively
- ☐ Handlebar pulls to one side
- ☐ Poor shock absorbing qualities

12 Braking problems

- ☐ Brakes are spongy, don't hold
- ☐ Brake lever pulsates
- ☐ Brakes drag

13 Electrical problems

- ☐ Battery dead or weak
- ☐ Battery overcharged

1 Engine doesn't start or is difficult to start

Starter motor does not rotate

☐ Engine kill switch OFF.
☐ Fuse blown. Check main fuse and ignition circuit fuse (Chapter 8).
☐ Battery voltage low. Check and recharge battery (Chapter 8).
☐ Starter motor defective. Make sure the wiring to the starter is secure. Test starter relay (Chapter 8). If the relay is good, then the fault is in the wiring or motor.
☐ Starter circuit cut-off relay faulty. Check the relay assembly according to the procedure in Chapter 8.
☐ Starter switch not contacting. The contacts could be wet, corroded or dirty. Disassemble and clean the switch (Chapter 8).
☐ Wiring open or shorted. Check all wiring connections and harnesses to make sure that they are dry, tight and not corroded. Also check for broken or frayed wires that can cause a short to earth (ground) (see *Wiring Diagrams*, Chapter 8).
☐ Ignition (main) switch defective. Check the switch according to the procedure in Chapter 8.
☐ Engine kill switch defective. Check for wet, dirty or corroded contacts. Clean or renew the switch as necessary (Chapter 8).
☐ Faulty neutral, sidestand or clutch switch. Check the wiring to each switch and the switch itself according to the procedures in Chapter 8.

Starter motor rotates but engine does not turn over

☐ Starter motor clutch defective. Inspect and repair or renew (Chapter 2A or 2B).
☐ Damaged idler or starter gears. Inspect and renew the damaged parts (Chapter 2A or 2B).

Starter works but engine won't turn over (seized)

☐ Seized engine caused by one or more internally damaged components. Failure due to wear, abuse or lack of lubrication. Damage can include seized valves, rockers, camshafts, pistons, crankshaft, connecting rod bearings, or transmission gears or bearings. Refer to Chapter 2A or 2B for engine disassembly.

No fuel flow

☐ No fuel in tank.
☐ Fuel tank breather hose obstructed.
☐ Tank cap air vent obstructed. Usually caused by dirt or water. Remove it and clean the cap vent hole.
☐ In-line fuel filter clogged. Renew the filter (Chapter 1).
☐ Fuel tap strainer or tap clogged. Remove and clean the tap (Chapter 3).
☐ Electric fuel pump not working. Test it according to the procedure in Chapter 3.
☐ Fuel hose clogged. Remove the fuel hoses and check (Chapter 3).
☐ Carburettor float needle valve clogged. For both of the valves to be clogged, either a very bad batch of fuel with an unusual additive has been used, or some other foreign material has entered the tank. Sometimes after a machine has been stored for many months without running, the fuel turns to a varnish-like liquid and forms deposits on the float needle valves and jets. The carburettors should be removed and overhauled (Chapter 3).
☐ Fuel system shutdown due to ignition system fault – 2003-on 1100 models (Chapter 4).

Engine flooded

☐ Fuel level (carburettor float height) too high. Check and adjust as described in Chapter 3.
☐ Carburettor float needle valve worn or stuck open. A piece of dirt, rust or other debris can cause the needle to seat improperly, causing excess fuel to flow into the float chamber. In this case, the float chamber should be cleaned and the needle and seat inspected. If the needle and seat are worn, then the leaking will persist and the parts should be renewed (Chapter 3).

☐ Starting technique incorrect. Under normal circumstances (i.e., if all the carburettor functions and settings are sound) the machine should start with little or no throttle. When the engine is cold, the choke should be operated and the engine started without opening the throttle. When the engine is at operating temperature, no choke and only a very slight amount of throttle should be necessary. If the engine is flooded, turn the fuel tap OFF and hold the throttle open while cranking the engine. This will allow additional air to reach the cylinders. Remember to turn the fuel tap back ON after the engine starts.

No spark or weak spark

☐ Ignition switch OFF.
☐ Engine kill switch turned to the OFF position.
☐ Battery voltage low. Check and recharge battery as necessary (Chapter 8).
☐ Spark plug(s) dirty, defective or worn out. Locate reason for fouled plug(s) using spark plug condition chart at the back of this manual and follow the plug maintenance procedures in Chapter 1.
☐ Spark plug cap or secondary (HT) wiring faulty. Check condition. Renew either or both components if cracks or deterioration are evident (Chapter 4).
☐ Spark plug cap not making good contact. Make sure that the plug cap fits snugly over the plug end.
☐ Ignition control unit (ICU) defective. Check the unit, referring to Chapter 4 for details.
☐ Pick-up coil defective. Check the pick-up coil, referring to Chapter 4 for details.
☐ Ignition HT coil(s) defective. Check the coils, referring to Chapter 4.
☐ Ignition or kill switch shorted. This is usually caused by water, corrosion, damage or excessive wear. The switches can be disassembled and cleaned with electrical contact cleaner. If cleaning does not help, renew the switches (Chapter 8).
☐ Wiring shorted or broken between:
  Ignition (main) switch and engine kill switch (or blown fuse)
  ICU and engine kill switch
  ICU and ignition HT coils
  Ignition HT coils and plugs
  ICU and pick-up coil
☐ Make sure that all wiring connections are clean, dry and tight. Look for chafed and broken wires (Chapters 4 and 8).

Compression low

☐ Spark plug loose. Remove the plug and inspect the threads. Reinstall and tighten to the specified torque (Chapter 1).
☐ Cylinder head not sufficiently tightened down. If a cylinder head is suspected of being loose, then there's a chance that the gasket or head is damaged if the problem has persisted for any length of time. The head nuts and bolts should be tightened to the specified torque in the correct sequence (Chapter 2A or 2B).
☐ Incorrect valve clearance. This means that the valve is not closing completely and compression pressure is leaking past the valve. Check and adjust the valve clearances (Chapter 1).
☐ Cylinder and/or piston worn. Excessive wear will cause compression pressure to leak past the piston rings. This is usually accompanied by worn rings as well. A top end overhaul is necessary (Chapter 2A or 2B).
☐ Piston rings worn, weak, broken, or sticking. Broken or sticking piston rings usually indicate a lubrication or carburation problem that causes excess carbon deposits to form on the pistons and rings. Top end overhaul is necessary (Chapter 2A or 2B).
☐ Piston ring-to-groove clearance excessive. This is caused by excessive wear of the piston ring lands. Piston renewal is necessary (Chapter 2A or 2B).
☐ Cylinder head gasket damaged. If a head is allowed to become loose, or if excessive carbon build-up on a piston crown and combustion chamber causes extremely high compression, the head

1 Engine doesn't start or is difficult to start (continued)

gasket may leak. Retorquing the head is not always sufficient to restore the seal, so gasket renewal is necessary (Chapter 2A or 2B).

☐ Cylinder head warped. This is caused by overheating or improperly tightened head nuts and bolts. Machine shop resurfacing or head renewal is necessary (Chapter 2A or 2B).

☐ Valve spring broken or weak. Caused by component failure or wear; the springs must be renewed (Chapter 2A or 2B).

☐ Valve not seating properly. This is caused by a bent valve (from over-revving or incorrect valve adjustment), burned valve or seat (incorrect carburation) or an accumulation of carbon deposits on the seat (from carburetion or lubrication problems). The valves must be cleaned and/or renewed and the seats serviced if possible (Chapter 2A or 2B).

Stalls after starting

☐ Improper choke action. Make sure the choke is getting a full stroke and staying in the ON position.

☐ Ignition malfunction. See Chapter 4.

☐ Carburettor malfunction. See Chapter 3.

☐ Fuel contaminated. The fuel can be contaminated with either dirt or water, or can change chemically if the machine is allowed to sit for several months or more. Drain the tank and fuel system (Chapter 3).

☐ Intake air leak. Check for loose carburettor-to-intake joint connections, loose or missing vacuum gauge caps, or loose carburettor covers (Chapter 3).

☐ Engine idle speed incorrect. Turn the adjusting screw until the engine idles at the specified rpm (Chapter 1).

Rough idle

☐ Ignition malfunction (Chapter 4).

☐ Idle speed incorrect (Chapter 1).

☐ Carburettors not synchronised. Adjust carburettors with vacuum gauge or manometer set as described in Chapter 1.

☐ Carburettor malfunction. See Chapter 3.

☐ Fuel contaminated. The fuel can be contaminated with either dirt or water, or can change chemically if the machine is allowed to sit for several months or more. Drain the tank and fuel system (Chapter 3).

☐ Intake air leak. Check for loose carburettor-to-intake joint connections, loose or missing vacuum gauge caps, or loose carburettor covers (Chapter 3).

☐ Air filter element clogged. Clean or renew air filter element (Chapter 1).

2 Poor running at low speed

Spark weak

☐ Battery voltage low. Check and recharge battery (Chapter 8).

☐ Spark plugs fouled, defective or worn out. See Chapter 1 for spark plug maintenance.

☐ Spark plug cap or HT wiring defective. See Chapters 1 and 4 for details on the ignition system.

☐ Spark plug cap not making contact with plug. Make sure it is securely pushed on to the plug.

☐ Incorrect spark plugs. Wrong type, heat range or cap configuration. Check and install correct plugs listed in Chapter 1.

☐ ICU defective. (Chapter 4).

☐ Pick-up coil defective. (Chapter 4).

☐ Ignition HT coil(s) defective (Chapter 4).

Fuel/air mixture incorrect

☐ Air filter element clogged, poorly sealed or missing.

☐ Air filter-to-airbox joint poorly sealed. Look for cracks, holes or loose clamps and renew or repair defective parts.

☐ Pilot screw(s) out of adjustment (Chapter 3).

☐ Pilot jet or air passage clogged. Remove and overhaul the carburettors (Chapter 3).

☐ Air bleed holes clogged. Remove carburettors and clean and blow out all passages (Chapter 3).

☐ Fuel level too high or too low. Adjust the float height (Chapter 3).

☐ Fuel tank air vent obstructed. Make sure that the air vent hose or passage in the filler cap is open.

☐ Carburettor intake joints loose. Check for cracks, breaks or loose clamps or bolts. Repair damaged components or renew seals (Chapter 3).

Compression low

☐ Spark plug loose. Remove the plug and inspect the threads. Reinstall and tighten to the specified torque (Chapter 1).

☐ Cylinder head not sufficiently tightened down. If the cylinder head is suspected of being loose, then there's a chance that the gasket and head are damaged if the problem has persisted for any length of time. The head nuts and bolts should be tightened to the specified torque in the correct sequence (Chapter 2A or 2B).

☐ Incorrect valve clearance. This means that the valve is not closing completely and compression pressure is leaking past the valve. Check and adjust the valve clearances (Chapter 1).

☐ Cylinder and/or piston worn. Excessive wear will cause compression pressure to leak past the piston rings. This is usually accompanied by worn rings as well. A top end overhaul is necessary (Chapter 2A or 2B).

☐ Piston rings worn, weak, broken, or sticking. Broken or sticking piston rings usually indicate a lubrication or carburation problem that causes excess carbon deposits to form on the pistons and rings. Top end overhaul is necessary (Chapter 2A or 2B).

☐ Piston ring-to-groove clearance excessive. This is caused by excessive wear of the piston ring lands. Piston renewal is necessary (Chapter 2A or 2B).

☐ Cylinder head gasket damaged. If a head is allowed to become loose, or if excessive carbon build-up on the piston crown and combustion chamber causes extremely high compression, the head gasket may leak. Retorquing the head is not always sufficient to restore the seal, so gasket renewal is necessary (Chapter 2A or 2B).

☐ Cylinder head warped. This is caused by overheating or improperly tightened head nuts and bolts. Machine shop resurfacing or head renewal is necessary (Chapter 2A or 2B).

☐ Valve spring broken or weak. Caused by component failure or wear; the springs must be renewed (Chapter 2A or 2B).

☐ Valve not seating properly. This is caused by a bent valve (from over-revving or incorrect valve adjustment), burned valve or seat (incorrect carburation) or an accumulation of carbon deposits on the seat (from carburetion or lubrication problems). The valves must be cleaned and/or renewed and the seats serviced if possible (Chapter 2A or 2B).

Poor acceleration

☐ Carburettors leaking or dirty. Overhaul the carburettors (Chapter 3).

☐ Timing not advancing. The pick-up coil or the ICU may be defective. If so, they must be replaced with new ones, as they can't be repaired.

☐ Carburettors not synchronised. Adjust them with a vacuum gauge set or manometer (Chapter 1).

☐ Engine oil viscosity too high. Using a heavier oil than that recommended in Chapter 1 can damage the oil pump or lubrication system and cause drag on the engine.

☐ Brakes dragging. On disc brakes, usually caused by dirt which has entered the brake caliper piston seal, or from a warped disc or bent axle. On drum brakes, usually caused by an incorrectly adjusted brake or dirt inside the brake drum. Check and repair as necessary (Chapter 6).

3 Poor running or no power at high speed

Firing incorrect

☐ Air filter element clogged. Clean or renew filter (Chapter 1).
☐ Spark plugs fouled, defective or worn out. See Chapter 1 for spark plug maintenance.
☐ Spark plug cap or HT wiring defective. See Chapters 1 and 4 for details of the ignition system.
☐ Spark plug cap not making contact with plug. Make sure it is securely pushed on to the plug.
☐ Incorrect spark plugs. Wrong type, heat range or cap configuration. Check and install correct plugs listed in Chapter 1.
☐ ICU defective (Chapter 4).
☐ Ignition HT coil(s) defective (Chapter 4).

Fuel/air mixture incorrect

☐ Air filter element clogged, poorly sealed, or missing.
☐ Air filter-to-airbox joint poorly sealed. Look for cracks, holes or loose clamps, and renew or repair defective parts.
☐ Main jet clogged. Remove and overhaul the carburettors (Chapter 3).
☐ Main jet wrong size. Check the specifications – the standard jetting is for sea level atmospheric pressure and oxygen content.
☐ Throttle shaft-to-carburettor body clearance excessive. Refer to Chapter 3 for inspection procedures.
☐ Air bleed holes clogged. Remove carburettors and clean and blow out all passages (Chapter 3).
☐ Fuel level too high or too low. Adjust the float height (Chapter 3).
☐ Fuel tank air vent obstructed. Make sure the air vent hose or passage in the filler cap is open.
☐ Carburettor intake joints loose. Check for cracks, breaks, or loose clamps or bolts. Repair damaged components or renew seals (Chapter 3).
☐ Fuel tap strainer or tap clogged. Remove the tap and clean it (Chapter 3).
☐ Fuel hose clogged. Remove the fuel hoses and check (Chapter 3).

Compression low

☐ Spark plug loose. Remove the plug and inspect the threads. Reinstall and tighten to the specified torque (Chapter 1).
☐ Cylinder head not sufficiently tightened down. If a cylinder head is suspected of being loose, then there's a chance that the gasket and head are damaged if the problem has persisted for any length of time. The head nuts and bolts should be tightened to the specified torque in the correct sequence (Chapter 2A or 2B).
☐ Incorrect valve clearance. This means that the valve is not closing completely and compression pressure is leaking past the valve. Check and adjust the valve clearances (Chapter 1).
☐ Cylinder and/or piston worn. Excessive wear will cause compression pressure to leak past the piston rings. This is usually accompanied by worn rings as well. A top end overhaul is necessary (Chapter 2A or 2B).
☐ Piston rings worn, weak, broken, or sticking. Broken or sticking piston rings usually indicate a lubrication or carburation problem that causes excess carbon deposits to form on the pistons and rings. Top end overhaul is necessary (Chapter 2A or 2B).

☐ Piston ring-to-groove clearance excessive. This is caused by excessive wear of the piston ring lands. Piston renewal is necessary (Chapter 2A or 2B).
☐ Cylinder head gasket damaged. If a head is allowed to become loose, or if excessive carbon build-up on the piston crown and combustion chamber causes extremely high compression, the head gasket may leak. Retorquing the head is not always sufficient to restore the seal, so gasket renewal is necessary (Chapter 2A or 2B).
☐ Cylinder head warped. This is caused by overheating or improperly tightened head nuts and bolts. Machine shop resurfacing or head renewal is necessary (Chapter 2A or 2B).
☐ Valve spring broken or weak. Caused by component failure or wear; the springs must be renewed (Chapter 2A or 2B).
☐ Valve not seating properly. This is caused by a bent valve (from over-revving or incorrect valve adjustment), burned valve or seat (incorrect carburation) or an accumulation of carbon deposits on the seat (from carburation or lubrication problems). The valves must be cleaned and/or renewed and the seats serviced if possible (Chapter 2A or 2B).

Knocking or pinking

☐ Carbon build-up in combustion chamber. Use of a fuel additive that will dissolve the adhesive bonding the carbon particles to the piston crown and chamber is the easiest way to remove the build-up. Otherwise, the cylinder head will have to be removed and decarbonised (Chapter 2A or 2B).
☐ Incorrect or poor quality fuel. Old or improper grades of fuel can cause detonation. This causes the piston to rattle, thus the knocking or pinking sound. Drain old fuel and always use the recommended fuel grade.
☐ Spark plug heat range incorrect. Uncontrolled detonation indicates the plug heat range is too hot. The plug in effect becomes a glow plug, raising cylinder temperatures. Install the proper heat range plug (Chapter 1).
☐ Improper air/fuel mixture. This will cause the cylinder to run hot, which leads to detonation. Clogged jets or an air leak can cause this imbalance (Chapter 3).

Miscellaneous causes

☐ Throttle valve doesn't open fully. Adjust the cable freeplay (Chapter 1).
☐ Clutch slipping. May be caused by a cable that is improperly adjusted, or loose or worn clutch components. Refer to Chapter 2A or 2B for clutch overhaul procedures.
☐ Ignition timing not advancing (Chapter 4).
☐ Engine oil viscosity too high. Using a heavier oil than the one recommended in Chapter 1 can damage the oil pump or lubrication system and cause drag on the engine.
☐ Brakes dragging. On disc brakes, usually caused by dirt which has entered the brake caliper piston seal, or from a warped disc or bent axle. On drum brakes, usually caused by an incorrectly adjusted brake or dirt inside the brake drum. Check and repair as necessary (Chapter 6).

4 Overheating

Engine overheats

☐ Engine oil level low. Check and add oil (Chapter 1).
☐ Wrong type of oil. If you're not sure what type of oil is in the engine, drain it and fill with the correct type (Chapter 1).
☐ Air leak at carburettor intake joints. Check and tighten or replace seals as necessary (Chapter 3).
☐ Fuel level low. Adjust the float height (Chapter 3).
☐ Worn oil pump or clogged oil passages. Renew pump or clean passages as necessary.
☐ Clogged external oil lines (1100 models). Remove and check for foreign material (see Chapter 2B).
☐ Carbon build-up in combustion chambers. Use of a fuel additive that will dissolve the adhesive bonding the carbon particles to the piston crown and chamber is the easiest way to remove the build-up. Otherwise, the cylinder heads will have to be removed and decarbonised (Chapter 2A or 2B).

Firing incorrect

☐ Spark plug fouled, defective or worn out. See Chapter 1 for spark plug maintenance.
☐ Incorrect spark plug (Chapter 1).
☐ Faulty ignition HT coil(s) (Chapter 4).
☐ ICU defective (Chapter 4).

Fuel/air mixture incorrect

☐ Air filter element clogged, poorly sealed, or missing.
☐ Air filter-to-airbox joint poorly sealed. Look for cracks, holes or loose clamps, and renew or repair defective parts.
☐ Main jet clogged. Remove and overhaul the carburettors (Chapter 3).
☐ Main jet wrong size. Check the specifications – the standard jetting is for sea level atmospheric pressure and oxygen content.
☐ Fuel level too low. Adjust the float height (Chapter 3).
☐ Fuel tank air vent obstructed. Make sure the air vent hose or passage in the filler cap is open.
☐ Carburettor intake joints loose. Check for cracks, breaks, or loose clamps or bolts. Repair damaged components or renew seals (Chapter 3).

Compression too high

☐ Carbon build-up in combustion chambers. Use of a fuel additive that will dissolve the adhesive bonding the carbon particles to the piston crown and chamber is the easiest way to remove the build-up. Otherwise, the cylinder heads will have to be removed and decarbonised (Chapter 2A or 2B).

☐ Incorrectly machined head surface or installation of incorrect gasket during engine assembly.

Engine load excessive

☐ Clutch slipping. Can be caused by damaged, loose or worn clutch components. Refer to Chapter 2A or 2B for overhaul procedures.
☐ Engine oil level too high. The addition of too much oil will cause pressurization of the crankcase and inefficient engine operation. Check Specifications and drain to proper level (Daily (pre-ride) checks).
☐ Engine oil viscosity too high. Using a heavier oil than the one recommended in Chapter 1 can damage the oil pump or lubrication system as well as cause drag on the engine.
☐ Brakes dragging. On disc brakes, usually caused by dirt which has entered the brake caliper piston seal, or from a warped disc or bent axle. On drum brakes, usually caused by an incorrectly adjusted brake or dirt inside the brake drum. Check and repair as necessary (Chapter 6).

Lubrication inadequate

☐ Engine oil level too low. Friction caused by intermittent lack of lubrication or from oil that is overworked can cause overheating. The oil provides an essential cooling function in the engine. Check the oil level (Chapter 1).
☐ Poor quality engine oil or incorrect viscosity or type. Oil is rated not only according to viscosity but also according to type. Some oils are not rated high enough for use in this engine. Check the Specifications section and change to the correct oil (Chapter 1).
☐ Blocked oil filter (Chapter 1).
☐ Camshaft or journals worn causing drop in oil pressure. Inspect cylinder head components (Chapter 2A or 2B). Abnormal wear could be caused by oil starvation at high rpm from low oil level, improper viscosity or type of oil (Chapter 1), or faulty oil pump or pressure relief valve (Chapter 2A or 2B)
☐ Crankshaft and/or bearings worn causing drop in oil pressure. Inspect crankshaft, main and big-end and bearings (Chapter 2A or 2B). Causes as for worn camshaft and journals.

Miscellaneous causes

☐ Modification to exhaust system. Most aftermarket exhaust systems cause the engine to run leaner, which make them run hotter. When installing an accessory exhaust system, always refer to the manufacturers instructions, or check spark plug condition using the chart at the back of this manual and rejet the carburettors.

5 Clutch problems

Clutch slipping

☐ Incorrectly adjusted cable (*Daily (pre-ride) checks*).
☐ Friction plates worn or warped. Overhaul the clutch assembly (Chapter 2A or 2B).
☐ Plain plates worn or warped (Chapter 2A or 2B).
☐ Clutch spring(s) broken or weak. Old or heat-damaged spring(s) (from slipping clutch) should be renew (Chapter 2A or 2B).
☐ Clutch release mechanism defective. Renew any defective parts (Chapter 2A or 2B).
☐ Clutch centre or housing unevenly worn. This causes improper engagement of the plates. Renew the damaged or worn parts (Chapter 2A or 2B).

Clutch not disengaging completely

☐ Clutch cable improperly adjusted (*Daily (pre-ride) checks*).
☐ Clutch plates warped or damaged. This will cause clutch drag, which in turn will cause the machine to creep. Overhaul the clutch assembly (Chapter 2A or 2B).

☐ Sagged or broken spring(s). Check and renew the spring(s) (Chapter 2A or 2B).
☐ Engine oil deteriorated. Old, thin, worn out oil will not provide proper lubrication for the plates, causing the clutch to drag. Change the oil and filter (Chapter 1).
☐ Engine oil viscosity too high. Using a thicker oil than recommended in Chapter 1 can cause the plates to stick together, putting a drag on the engine. Change to the correct viscosity oil (Chapter 1).
☐ Clutch housing seized on shaft. Lack of lubrication, severe wear or damage can cause the housing to seize on the shaft. Overhaul of the clutch, and perhaps transmission, may be necessary to repair the damage (Chapter 2A or 2B).
☐ Clutch release mechanism defective. Worn or damaged release mechanism will fail to apply force to the pressure plate. Overhaul the release mechanism (Chapter 2A or 2B).
☐ Loose clutch centre nut. Causes housing and centre misalignment putting a drag on the engine. Engagement adjustment continually varies. Overhaul the clutch assembly (Chapter 2A or 2B).

6 Gearchanging problems

Doesn't go into gear or lever doesn't return

☐ Clutch not disengaging. See Section 5.
☐ Selector fork(s) worn, bent or seized. Caused by heavy use or lack of lubrication. Overhaul the transmission (Chapter 2A or 2B).
☐ Gear(s) stuck on shaft. Most often caused by a lack of lubrication or excessive wear in transmission bearings and bushings. Overhaul the transmission (Chapter 2A or 2B).
☐ Selector drum worn or binding. Caused by lubrication failure or excessive wear. Renew the cam and bearing (Chapter 2A or 2B).
☐ Gearchange shaft centralising spring weak or broken (Chapter 2A or 2B).
☐ Gearchange linkage broken. Splines stripped out of lever or shaft, caused by allowing the lever to get loose or from dropping the machine. Renew necessary parts (Chapter 2A or 2B).
☐ Gearchange selector arm pawls broken or worn or spring damaged. Poor gear engagement and rotary movement of selector drum results. Renew gearchange shaft assembly (Chapter 2A or 2B).

☐ Stopper arm spring broken. Allows arm to float, causing sporadic gearchange operation. Renew spring (Chapter 2).

Jumps out of gear

☐ Selector fork(s) worn. Overhaul the transmission (Chapter 2A or 2B).
☐ Grooves in selector drum worn. Overhaul the transmission (Chapter 2A or 2B).
☐ Gear dogs or dog slots worn or damaged. The gears should be inspected and renew in pairs (2A or 2B). No attempt should be made to service the worn parts.

Overselects

☐ Pawl spring weak or broken (Chapter 2A or 2B).
☐ Stopper arm spring weak or broken (Chapter 2A or 2B).
☐ Gearchange shaft return spring post broken or distorted (Chapter 2A or 2B).

7 Abnormal engine noise

Knocking or pinking

☐ Carbon build-up in combustion chambers. Use of a fuel additive that will dissolve the adhesive bonding the carbon particles to the piston crown and chamber is the easiest way to remove the build-up. Otherwise, the cylinder heads will have to be removed and decarbonised (Chapter 2A or 2B).
☐ Incorrect or poor quality fuel. Old or improper fuel can cause detonation. This causes the pistons to rattle, thus the knocking or pinking sound. Drain the old fuel and always use the recommended grade fuel (Chapter 1).
☐ Spark plug heat range incorrect. Uncontrolled detonation indicates that the plug heat range is too hot. The plug in effect becomes a glow plug, raising cylinder temperatures. Install the specified heat range plug (Chapter 1).
☐ Incorrect air/fuel mixture. This will cause the cylinders to run hot and lead to detonation. Clogged jets or an air leak can cause this imbalance (Chapter 3).

Piston slap or rattling

☐ Cylinder-to-piston clearance excessive. Inspect and overhaul top-end parts (Chapter 2A or 2B).
☐ Connecting rod bent. Caused by over-revving, trying to start a badly flooded engine or from ingesting a foreign object into the combustion chamber. Replace the damaged parts (Chapter 2A or 2B).
☐ Piston pin or piston pin bore worn or seized from wear or lack of lubrication. Renew damaged parts (Chapter 2A or 2B).
☐ Piston ring(s) worn, broken or sticking. Overhaul the top end (Chapter 2A or 2B).
☐ Piston seizure damage. Usually from lack of lubrication or overheating. Renew the pistons and, where possible, bore the cylinders, as necessary (Chapter 2A or 2B).

☐ Connecting rod small-end or big-end clearance excessive. Caused by excessive wear or lack of lubrication. Renew worn parts.

Valve noise

☐ Incorrect valve clearances. Adjust the clearances (Chapter 1).
☐ Valve spring broken or weak. Check and renew the springs (Chapter 2A or 2B).
☐ Camshaft, bushing or cylinder head worn or damaged. Lack of lubrication at high rpm is usually the cause of damage. Insufficient oil or failure to change the oil at the recommended intervals are the chief causes. Check the oil pump and pressure relief valve (Chapter 2A or 2B).

Other noise

☐ Cylinder head gasket leaking. Head not tightened down correctly or head warped. The head nuts and bolts should be tightened to the specified torque in the correct sequence (Chapter 2A or 2B). Gasket renewal may be necessary or the head may need resurfacing by a machine shop (Chapter 2A or 2B).
☐ Exhaust pipe leaking at cylinder head joint. Caused by improper fit of pipe(s), loose exhaust flange or damaged gasket. Renew the gasket and ensure the exhaust fasteners are tightened evenly and carefully (Chapter 3).
☐ Engine mounting bolts or nuts loose. Tighten all engine mounting bolts and nuts to the specified torque (Chapter 2A or 2B).
☐ Camshaft chain tensioner(s) defective (Chapter 2A or 2B).
☐ Camshaft chain, sprockets or guides worn (Chapter 2A or 2B)).
☐ Crankshaft bearings worn (Chapter 2A or 2B).
☐ Crankshaft runout excessive. Caused by a bent crankshaft (from over-revving) or damage from an upper cylinder component failure (Chapter 2A or 2B).

8 Abnormal driveline noise

Clutch noise

☐ Clutch housing/friction plate clearance excessive (Chapter 2A or 2B).
☐ Loose or damaged clutch pressure plate and/or bolts (Chapter 2A or 2B).

Transmission noise

☐ Engine oil level too low. Causes a howl from transmission. Also affects engine power and clutch operation (Daily (pre-ride) checks).
☐ Bearings worn. Also includes the possibility that the shafts are worn. Overhaul the transmission (Chapter 2A or 2B).

☐ Gears worn or chipped (Chapter 2A or 2B).
☐ Metal chips jammed in gear teeth. Probably pieces from a broken clutch, gear or gearchange mechanism that were picked up by the gears. This will cause early bearing failure (Chapter 2A or 2B).

Final drive noise

☐ Final drive oil level low (Chapter 1).
☐ Final drive gear lash out of adjustment (Chapter 2A or 2B).
☐ Final drive gears or bearings damaged or worn (Chapter 2A or 2B).

9 Abnormal frame and suspension noise

Front end noise

☐ Low oil level or improper viscosity oil in forks. This can sound like spurting and is usually accompanied by irregular fork action (Chapter 5).
☐ Fork spring weak or broken. Makes a clicking or scraping sound. Fork oil, when drained, will have a lot of metal particles in it (Chapter 5).
☐ Steering head bearings loose or damaged. Clicks when braking. Check and adjust or renew as necessary (Chapters 1 and 5).
☐ Fork yokes loose. Make sure all clamp bolts are tightened to the specified torque (Chapter 5).
☐ Fork tube bent. Good possibility if machine has been crashed. Replace tube with a new one (Chapter 5).
☐ Front axle or axle pinch bolt loose. Tighten them to the specified torque (Chapter 6).

Shock absorber noise

☐ Fluid level incorrect. Indicates a leak caused by defective seal. Shock will be covered with oil. Renew shock (Chapter 5).
☐ Defective shock absorber with internal damage. This is in the body of the shock and can't be remedied. The shock must be renewed (Chapter 5).
☐ Bent or damaged shock body. Renew the shock (Chapter 5).
☐ Loose or worn suspension linkage components (1100 models). Check and renew as necessary (Chapter 5).

Brake noise

☐ Squeal caused by dust or dirt on the brake pads. Usually found in combination with glazed pads. Use a clean wire brush to clean off all dust.
☐ Pads glazed. Caused by excessive heat from prolonged use or from contamination. DO NOT use sandpaper, emery cloth, carborundum cloth or any other abrasive to roughen the pad surfaces as abrasives will stay in the pad material and damage the disc. A clean fine wire brush can be used, but pad renewal is recommended as a cure (Chapter 6).
☐ Contamination of brake pads. Oil, grease or brake fluid causing brake to chatter or squeal. The pads must be renewed (Chapter 6).
☐ Disc warped. Can cause a chattering, clicking or intermittent squeal. Usually accompanied by a pulsating lever and uneven braking. Renew the disc (Chapter 6).
☐ Drum brake linings worn or contaminated. Can cause scraping or squealing. Renew the shoes (Chapter 6).
☐ Drum brake linings warped or worn unevenly. Can cause chattering. Renew the shoes (Chapter 6).
☐ Brake drum out of round. Can cause chattering. Renew brake drum (Chapter 6).
☐ Loose or worn wheel bearings. Check and renew as needed (Chapter 6).

10 Excessive exhaust smoke

White smoke

☐ Piston oil ring worn. The ring may be broken or damaged, causing oil from the crankcase to be pulled past the piston into the combustion chamber. Renew the rings (Chapter 2A or 2B).
☐ Cylinders worn, cracked, or scored. Caused by overheating or oil starvation. If worn or scored, the cylinders will have to be rebored (650 models) or renewed (1100 models) and new pistons installed (see Chapter 2A or 2B).
☐ Valve oil seal damaged or worn. Replace oil seals with new ones (Chapter 2A or 2B).
☐ Valve guide worn (Chapter 2A or 2B).
☐ Engine oil level too high, which causes the oil to be forced past the rings. Drain oil to the proper level (Daily (pre-ride) checks).
☐ Head gasket broken between oil return and cylinder. Causes oil to be pulled into the combustion chamber. Renew the head gasket and check the head for warpage (Chapter 2A or 2B).
☐ Abnormal crankcase pressurization, which forces oil past the rings. Clogged breather or hoses usually the cause (Chapter 2A or 2B).

Black smoke

☐ Air filter element clogged. Clean or renew the element (Chapter 1).

☐ Carburettor main jet too large or loose. Compare the jet size to the Specifications (Chapter 3).
☐ Choke stuck ON, causing fuel to be pulled through choke circuit. Check cable operation and choke plungers (Chapter 3).
☐ Fuel level too high. Check and adjust the float height as necessary (Chapter 3).
☐ Float needle valve held off needle seat. Clean the float chambers and fuel line and replace the needles and seats if necessary (Chapter 3).

Brown smoke

☐ Carburettor main jet too small or clogged. Lean condition caused by wrong size main jet or by a restricted orifice. Clean float chambers and jets and compare jet size to Specifications (Chapter 3).
☐ Fuel flow insufficient. Float needle valve stuck closed due to chemical reaction with old fuel. Float level incorrect. Restricted fuel line. Clean line and float chambers and adjust floats if necessary.
☐ Carburettor intake manifolds loose (Chapter 3).
☐ Air filter element poorly sealed or not installed (Chapter 1).

11 Poor handling or stability

Handlebars hard to turn

☐ Steering stem adjuster locknut too tight (Chapter 5).
☐ Bearings damaged. Roughness can be felt as the bars are turned from side-to-side. Renew bearings and races (Chapter 5).
☐ Races dented or worn. Denting results from wear in only one position (e.g., straight ahead), from a collision or from hitting a pothole. Renew races and bearings (Chapter 5).
☐ Steering stem lubrication inadequate. Causes are grease getting hard from age or being washed out by high pressure car washes. Disassemble steering head and regrease the bearings (Chapter 5).
☐ Steering stem bent. Caused by a collision or hitting a pothole. Renew the steering stem. Don't try to straighten the steering stem (Chapter 5).
☐ Front tyre air pressure too low (Daily (pre-ride) checks).

Handlebar shakes or vibrates excessively

☐ Tyres worn or out of balance (Chapter 1 or 6).
☐ Swingarm bearings worn (Chapter 6).
☐ Wheel rim(s) warped or damaged. Inspect wheels for runout (Chapter 6).
☐ Wheel bearings worn. Worn front or rear wheel bearings can cause poor tracking. Worn front bearings will cause wobble (Chapter 6).
☐ Handlebar clamp bolts or bracket nuts loose (Chapter 5).
☐ Steering stem or fork clamps loose. Tighten them to the specified torque (Chapter 5).
☐ Engine mounting bolts loose. Will cause excessive vibration with increased engine rpm (Chapter 2A or 2B).

Handlebar pulls to one side

☐ Frame bent. Definitely suspect this if the machine has been crashed. May or may not be accompanied by cracking near the bend. Renew the frame (Chapter 5).
☐ Wheel out of alignment. Caused by improper location of axle spacers or from bent steering stem or frame (Chapter 5).
☐ Swingarm bent or twisted. Caused by age (metal fatigue) or impact damage. Renew the swingarm (Chapter 5).
☐ Steering stem bent. Caused by impact damage. Renew the steering stem (Chapter 5).
☐ Fork leg bent. Disassemble the forks and renew the damaged parts (Chapter 5).
☐ Fork oil level uneven. Check and add or drain as necessary (Chapter 5).

Poor shock absorbing qualities

☐ Too hard:
 Fork oil level excessive (Chapter 5).
 Fork oil viscosity too high. Use a lighter oil (see the Specifications in Chapter 5).
 Fork tube bent. Causes a harsh, sticking feeling (Chapter 5).
 Fork internal damage (Chapter 5).
 Rear shock shaft or body bent or damaged (Chapter 5).
 Rear shock internal damage.
 Tyre pressure too high (Daily (pre-ride) checks).
☐ Too soft:
 Fork or shock oil insufficient and/or leaking (Chapter 5).
 Fork oil level too low (Chapter 5).
 Fork oil viscosity too light (Chapter 5).
 Fork springs weak or broken (Chapter 5).

12 Braking problems

Front brakes are spongy, don't hold

☐ Air in brake system. Caused by inattention to master cylinder fluid level or by leakage. Locate problem and bleed brakes (Chapter 6).
☐ Pad or disc worn (Chapters 1 and 6).
☐ Brake fluid leak. See paragraph 1.
☐ Contaminated pads. Caused by contact with oil, grease or brake fluid. Renew pads. Clean disc thoroughly with brake cleaner (Chapter 6).
☐ Brake fluid deteriorated. Fluid is old or contaminated. Drain system, replenish with new fluid and bleed the system (Chapter 6).
☐ Master cylinder internal parts worn or damaged causing fluid to bypass (Chapter 6).
☐ Master cylinder bore scratched by foreign material or broken spring. Renew master cylinder (Chapter 6).
☐ Disc warped. Renew disc (Chapter 6).

Brake lever or pedal pulsates

☐ Disc warped. Renew disc (Chapter 6).
☐ Axle bent. Renew axle (Chapter 5).
☐ Brake caliper bolts loose (Chapter 6).

☐ Wheel warped or otherwise damaged (Chapter 6).
☐ Wheel bearings damaged or worn (Chapter 6).
☐ Brake drum out of round. Skim or renew the brake drum (Chapter 6).

Brakes drag

☐ Master cylinder piston seized. Caused by wear or damage to piston or cylinder bore (Chapter 6).
☐ Lever balky or stuck. Check pivot and lubricate (Chapter 6).
☐ Brake caliper binds. Caused by inadequate lubrication or damage to caliper bolts or pin (Chapter 6).
☐ Brake caliper piston seized in bore. Caused by wear or ingestion of dirt past deteriorated seal (Chapter 6).
☐ Brake pad damaged. Pad material separated from backing plate. Usually caused by faulty manufacturing process or from contact with chemicals. Renew pads (Chapter 6).
☐ Pads improperly installed (Chapter 6).
☐ Rear brake pedal freeplay insufficient (Chapter 1).
☐ Rear brake pedal return spring weak. Renew return spring (Chapter 6).
☐ Rear drum brake shoe springs weak. Renew brake shoe springs (Chapter 6).

13 Electrical problems

Battery dead or weak

☐ Battery faulty. Also, broken battery terminal making only occasional contact (Chapter 8).
☐ Battery leads making poor contact (Chapter 8). Renew battery.
☐ Load excessive. Caused by addition of high wattage lights or other electrical accessories.
☐ Ignition (main) switch defective. Switch either earths (grounds) internally or fails to shut off system. Renew the switch (Chapter 8).
☐ Regulator/rectifier defective (Chapter 8).
☐ Alternator stator coil open or shorted (Chapter 8).
☐ Wiring faulty. Wiring earthed (grounded) or connections loose in ignition, charging or lighting circuits (Chapter 8).

Battery overcharged

☐ Regulator/rectifier defective. Overcharging is noticed when battery gets excessively warm or boils over (Chapter 8).
☐ Battery defective. Replace battery with a new one (Chapter 8).
☐ Battery amperage too low, wrong type or size. Install manufacturer's specified amp-hour battery to handle charging load (Chapter 8)

Checking engine compression

● Low compression will result in exhaust smoke, heavy oil consumption, poor starting and poor performance. A compression test will provide useful information about an engine's condition and if performed regularly, can give warning of trouble before any other symptoms become apparent.
● A compression gauge will be required, along with an adapter to suit the spark plug hole thread size. Note that the screw-in type gauge/adapter set up is preferable to the rubber cone type.
● Before carrying out the test, first check the valve clearances as described in Chapter 1.
1 Run the engine until it reaches normal operating temperature, then stop it and remove the spark plug(s), taking care not to scald your hands on the hot components.
2 Install the gauge adapter and compression gauge in No. 1 cylinder spark plug hole (see illustration 1).

Screw the compression gauge adapter into the spark plug hole, then screw the gauge into the adapter

3 On kickstart-equipped motorcycles, make sure the ignition switch is OFF, then open the throttle fully and kick the engine over a couple of times until the gauge reading stabilises.
4 On motorcycles with electric start only, the procedure will differ depending on the nature of the ignition system. Flick the engine kill switch (engine stop switch) to OFF and turn the ignition switch ON; open the throttle fully and crank the engine over on the starter motor for a couple of revolutions until the gauge reading stabilises. If the starter will not operate with the kill switch OFF, turn the ignition switch OFF and refer to the next paragraph.
5 Install the plugs back in their caps/coils and arrange the plug electrodes so that their metal bodies are earthed (grounded) against the cylinder heads; this is essential to prevent damage to the ignition system (see illustration 2). Position the plugs well away from the plug holes otherwise there is a risk of

All spark plugs must be earthed (grounded) against the cylinder head

atomised fuel escaping from the plug holes and igniting. As a safety precaution, cover the cylinder head covers with rag and disconnect the fuel pump wiring connector (see Chapter 4). Turn the ignition switch and kill switch ON, open the throttle fully and crank the engine over on the starter motor for a couple of revolutions until the gauge reading stabilises.
6 After one or two revolutions the pressure should build up to a maximum figure and then stabilise. Take a note of this reading and on multi-cylinder engines repeat the test on the remaining cylinders.
7 The correct pressures are given in Chapter 1 Specifications. If the results fall within the specified range and on multi-cylinder engines all are relatively equal, the engine is in good condition. If there is a marked difference between the readings, or if the readings are lower than specified, inspection of the top-end components will be required.
8 Low compression pressure may be due to worn cylinder bores, pistons or rings, failure of the cylinder head gasket, worn valve seals, or poor valve seating.
9 To distinguish between cylinder/piston wear and valve leakage, pour a small quantity of oil into the bore to temporarily seal the piston rings, then repeat the compression

Bores can be temporarily sealed with a squirt of motor oil

tests (see illustration 3). If the readings show a noticeable increase in pressure this confirms that the cylinder bore, piston, or rings are worn. If, however, no change is indicated, the cylinder head gasket or valves should be examined.
10 High compression pressure indicates excessive carbon build-up in the combustion chamber and on the piston crown. If this is the case the cylinder head should be removed and the deposits removed. Note that excessive carbon build-up is less likely with the used on modern fuels.

Checking battery open-circuit voltage

⚠️ *Warning: The gases produced by the battery are explosive - never smoke or create any sparks in the vicinity of the battery. Never allow the electrolyte to contact your skin or clothing - if it does, wash it off and seek immediate*

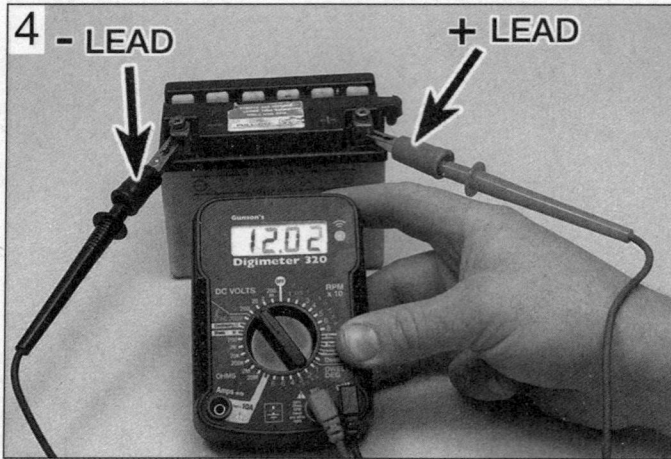

Measuring open-circuit battery voltage

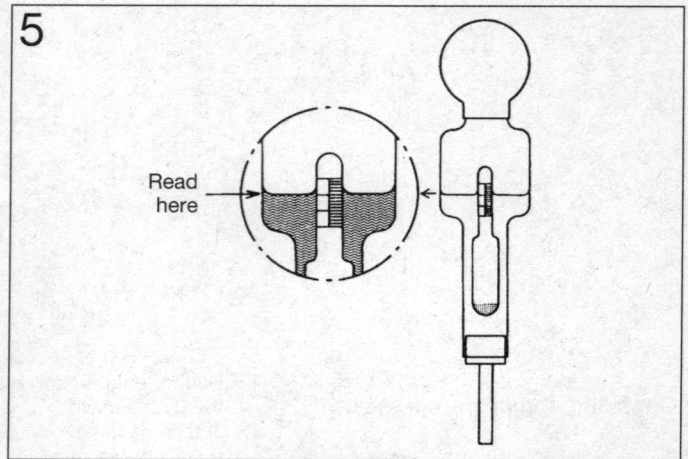

Float-type hydrometer for measuring battery specific gravity

● Before any electrical fault is investigated the battery should be checked.

● You'll need a dc voltmeter or multimeter to check battery voltage. Check that the leads are inserted in the correct terminals on the meter, red lead to positive (+ve), black lead to negative (-ve). Incorrect connections can damage the meter.

● A sound fully-charged 12 volt battery should produce between 12.3 and 12.6 volts across its terminals (12.8 volts for a maintenance-free battery). On machines with a 6 volt battery, voltage should be between 6.1 and 6.3 volts.

1 Set a multimeter to the 0 to 20 volts dc range and connect its probes across the battery terminals. Connect the meter's positive (+ve) probe, usually red, to the battery positive (+ve) terminal, followed by the meter's negative (-ve) probe, usually black, to the battery negative terminal (-ve) **(see illustration 4)**.

2 If battery voltage is low (below 10 volts on a 12 volt battery or below 4 volts on a six volt battery), charge the battery and test the voltage again. If the battery repeatedly goes flat, investigate the motorcycle's charging system.

Checking battery specific gravity (SG)

⚠️ *Warning: The gases produced by the battery are explosive - never smoke or create any sparks in the vicinity of the battery. Never allow the electrolyte to contact your skin or clothing - if it does, wash it off and seek immediate medical attention.*

● The specific gravity check gives an indication of a battery's state of charge.

● A hydrometer is used for measuring specific gravity. Make sure you purchase one which has a small enough hose to insert in the aperture of a motorcycle battery.

● Specific gravity is simply a measure of the electrolyte's density compared with that of water. Water has an SG of 1.000 and fully-charged battery electrolyte is about 26% heavier, at 1.260.

● Specific gravity checks are not possible on maintenance-free batteries. Testing the open-circuit voltage is the only means of determining their state of charge.

1 To measure SG, remove the battery from the motorcycle and remove the first cell cap. Draw

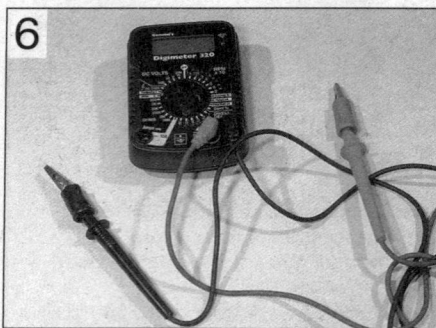

Digital multimeter can be used for all electrical tests

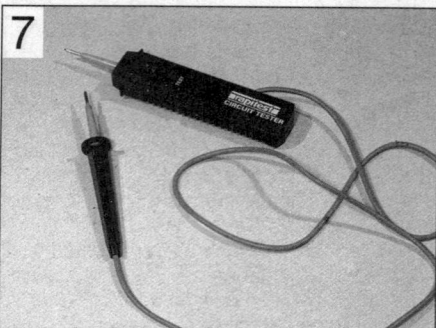

Battery-powered continuity tester

some electrolyte into the hydrometer and note the reading **(see illustration 5)**. Return the electrolyte to the cell and install the cap.

2 The reading should be in the region of 1.260 to 1.280. If SG is below 1.200 the battery needs charging. Note that SG will vary with temperature; it should be measured at 20°C (68°F). Add 0.007 to the reading for every 10°C above 20°C, and subtract 0.007 from the reading for every 10°C below 20°C. Add 0.004 to the reading for every 10°F above 68°F, and subtract 0.004 from the reading for every 10°F below 68°F.

3 When the check is complete, rinse the hydrometer thoroughly with clean water.

Checking for continuity

● The term continuity describes the uninterrupted flow of electricity through an electrical circuit. A continuity check will determine whether an **open-circuit** situation exists.

● Continuity can be checked with an ohmmeter, multimeter, continuity tester or battery and bulb test circuit **(see illustrations 6, 7 and 8)**.

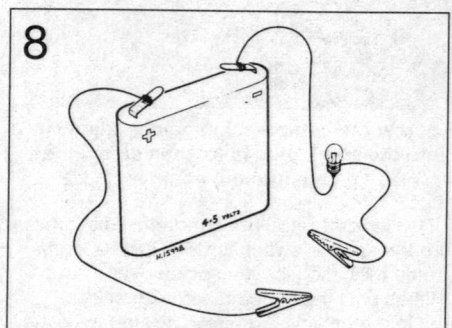

Battery and bulb test circuit

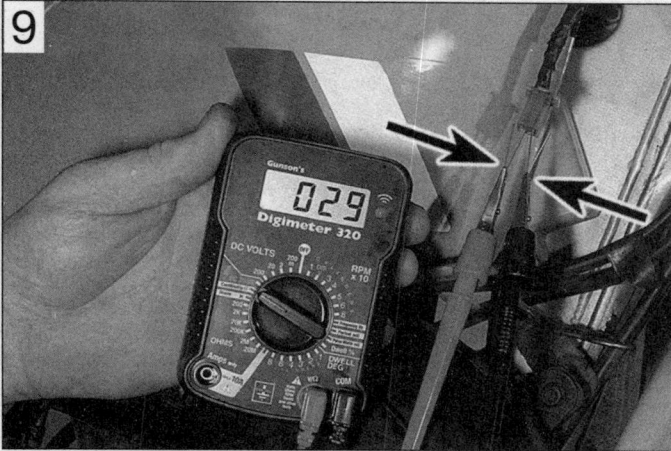

Continuity check of front brake light switch using a meter - note split pins used to access connector terminals

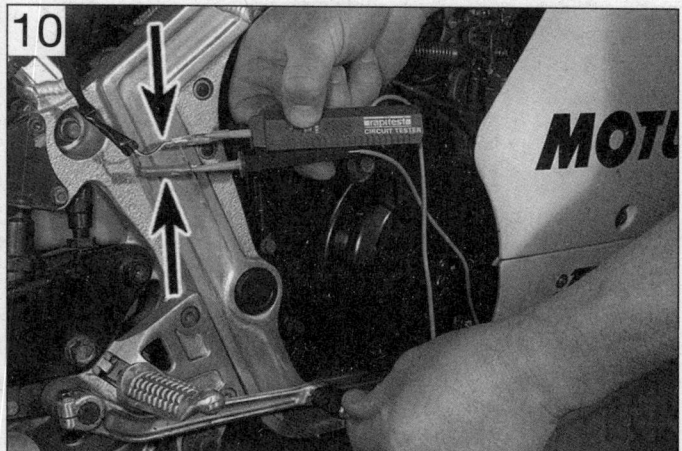

Continuity check of rear brake light switch using a continuity tester

● All of these instruments are self-powered by a battery, therefore the checks are made with the ignition OFF.

● As a safety precaution, always disconnect the battery negative (-ve) lead before making checks, particularly if ignition switch checks are being made.

● If using a meter, select the appropriate ohms scale and check that the meter reads infinity (∞). Touch the meter probes together and check that meter reads zero; where necessary adjust the meter so that it reads zero.

● After using a meter, always switch it OFF to conserve its battery.

Switch checks

1 If a switch is at fault, trace its wiring up to the wiring connectors. Separate the wire connectors and inspect them for security and condition. A build-up of dirt or corrosion here will most likely be the cause of the problem - clean up and apply a water dispersant such as WD40.

2 If using a test meter, set the meter to the ohms x 10 scale and connect its probes across the wires from the switch (see illustration 9). Simple ON/OFF type switches, such as brake light switches, only have two wires whereas combination switches, like the

ignition switch, have many internal links. Study the wiring diagram to ensure that you are connecting across the correct pair of wires. Continuity (low or no measurable resistance - 0 ohms) should be indicated with the switch ON and no continuity (high resistance) with it OFF.

3 Note that the polarity of the test probes doesn't matter for continuity checks, although care should be taken to follow specific test procedures if a diode or solid-state component is being checked.

4 A continuity tester or battery and bulb circuit can be used in the same way. Connect its probes as described above (see illustration 10). The light should come on to indicate continuity in the ON switch position, but should extinguish in the OFF position.

Wiring checks

● Many electrical faults are caused by damaged wiring, often due to incorrect routing or chaffing on frame components.

● Loose, wet or corroded wire connectors can also be the cause of electrical problems, especially in exposed locations.

1 A continuity check can be made on a single length of wire by disconnecting it at each end and connecting a meter or continuity tester

across both ends of the wire (see illustration 11).

2 Continuity (low or no resistance - 0 ohms) should be indicated if the wire is good. If no continuity (high resistance) is shown, suspect a broken wire.

Checking for voltage

● A voltage check can determine whether current is reaching a component.

● Voltage can be checked with a dc voltmeter, multimeter set on the dc volts scale, test light or buzzer (see illustrations 12 and 13). A meter has the advantage of being able to measure actual voltage.

● When using a meter, check that its leads are inserted in the correct terminals on the meter, red to positive (+ve), black to negative (-ve). Incorrect connections can damage the meter.

● A voltmeter (or multimeter set to the dc volts scale) should always be connected in parallel (across the load). Connecting it in series will not harm the meter, but the reading will not be meaningful.

● Voltage checks are made with the ignition ON.

Continuity check of front brake light switch sub-harness

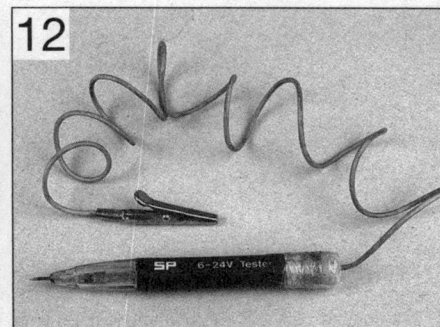

A simple test light can be used for voltage checks

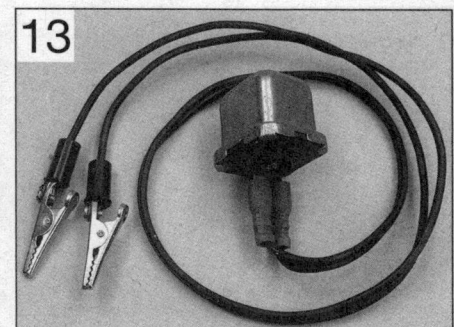

A buzzer is useful for voltage checks

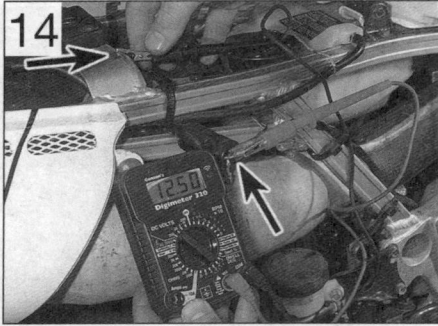

Checking for voltage at the rear brake light power supply wire using a meter . . .

1 First identify the relevant wiring circuit by referring to the wiring diagram at the end of this manual. If other electrical components share the same power supply (ie are fed from the same fuse), take note whether they are working correctly - this is useful information in deciding where to start checking the circuit.

2 If using a meter, check first that the meter leads are plugged into the correct terminals on the meter (see above). Set the meter to the dc volts function, at a range suitable for the battery voltage. Connect the meter red probe (+ve) to the power supply wire and the black probe to a good metal earth (ground) on the motorcycle's frame or directly to the battery negative (-ve) terminal **(see illustration 14)**. Battery voltage should be shown on the meter

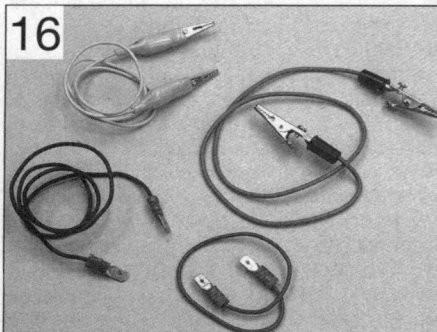

A selection of jumper wires for making earth (ground) checks

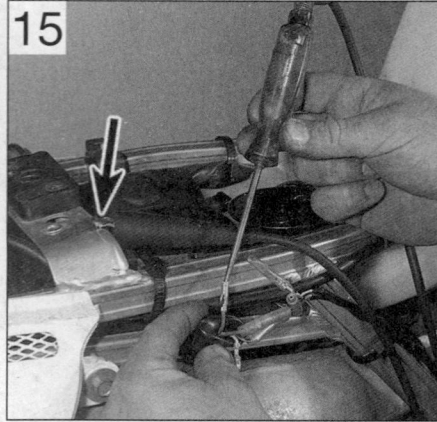

. . . or a test light - note the earth connection to the frame (arrow)

with the ignition switched ON.

3 If using a test light or buzzer, connect its positive (+ve) probe to the power supply terminal and its negative (-ve) probe to a good earth (ground) on the motorcycle's frame or directly to the battery negative (-ve) terminal **(see illustration 15)**. With the ignition ON, the test light should illuminate or the buzzer sound.

4 If no voltage is indicated, work back towards the fuse continuing to check for voltage. When you reach a point where there is voltage, you know the problem lies between that point and your last check point.

Checking the earth (ground)

● Earth connections are made either directly to the engine or frame (such as sensors, neutral switch etc. which only have a positive feed) or by a separate wire into the earth circuit of the wiring harness. Alternatively a short earth wire is sometimes run directly from the component to the motorcycle's frame.

● Corrosion is often the cause of a poor earth connection.

● If total failure is experienced, check the security of the main earth lead from the

negative (-ve) terminal of the battery and also the main earth (ground) point on the wiring harness. If corroded, dismantle the connection and clean all surfaces back to bare metal.

1 To check the earth on a component, use an insulated jumper wire to temporarily bypass its earth connection **(see illustration 16)**. Connect one end of the jumper wire between the earth terminal or metal body of the component and the other end to the motorcycle's frame.

2 If the circuit works with the jumper wire installed, the original earth circuit is faulty. Check the wiring for open-circuits or poor connections. Clean up direct earth connections, removing all traces of corrosion and remake the joint. Apply petroleum jelly to the joint to prevent future corrosion.

Tracing a short-circuit

● A short-circuit occurs where current shorts to earth (ground) bypassing the circuit components. This usually results in a blown fuse.

● A short-circuit is most likely to occur where the insulation has worn through due to wiring chafing on a component, allowing a direct path to earth (ground) on the frame.

1 Remove any bodypanels necessary to access the circuit wiring.

2 Check that all electrical switches in the circuit are OFF, then remove the circuit fuse and connect a test light, buzzer or voltmeter (set to the dc scale) across the fuse terminals. No voltage should be shown.

3 Move the wiring from side to side whilst observing the test light or meter. When the test light comes on, buzzer sounds or meter shows voltage, you have found the cause of the short. It will usually shown up as damaged or burned insulation.

4 Note that the same test can be performed on each component in the circuit, even the switch.

A

ABS (Anti-lock braking system) A system, usually electronically controlled, that senses incipient wheel lockup during braking and relieves hydraulic pressure at wheel which is about to skid.

Aftermarket Components suitable for the motorcycle, but not produced by the motorcycle manufacturer.

Allen key A hexagonal wrench which fits into a recessed hexagonal hole.

Alternating current (ac) Current produced by an alternator. Requires converting to direct current by a rectifier for charging purposes.

Alternator Converts mechanical energy from the engine into electrical energy to charge the battery and power the electrical system.

Ampere (amp) A unit of measurement for the flow of electrical current. Current = Volts ÷ Ohms.

Ampere-hour (Ah) Measure of battery capacity.

Angle-tightening A torque expressed in degrees. Often follows a conventional tightening torque for cylinder head or main bearing fasteners **(see illustration)**.

Angle-tightening cylinder head bolts

Antifreeze A substance (usually ethylene glycol) mixed with water, and added to the cooling system, to prevent freezing of the coolant in winter. Antifreeze also contains chemicals to inhibit corrosion and the formation of rust and other deposits that would tend to clog the radiator and coolant passages and reduce cooling efficiency.

Anti-dive System attached to the fork lower leg (slider) to prevent fork dive when braking hard.

Anti-seize compound A coating that reduces the risk of seizing on fasteners that are subjected to high temperatures, such as exhaust clamp bolts and nuts.

API American Petroleum Institute. A quality standard for 4-stroke motor oils.

Asbestos A natural fibrous mineral with great heat resistance, commonly used in the composition of brake friction materials. Asbestos is a health hazard and the dust created by brake systems should never be inhaled or ingested.

ATF Automatic Transmission Fluid. Often used in front forks.

ATU Automatic Timing Unit. Mechanical device for advancing the ignition timing on early engines.

ATV All Terrain Vehicle. Often called a Quad.

Axial play Side-to-side movement.

Axle A shaft on which a wheel revolves. Also known as a spindle.

B

Backlash The amount of movement between meshed components when one component is held still. Usually applies to gear teeth.

Ball bearing A bearing consisting of a hardened inner and outer race with hardened steel balls between the two races.

Bearings Used between two working surfaces to prevent wear of the components and a build-up of heat. Four types of bearing are commonly used on motorcycles: plain shell bearings, ball bearings, tapered roller bearings and needle roller bearings.

Bevel gears Used to turn the drive through 90°. Typical applications are shaft final drive and camshaft drive **(see illustration)**.

Bevel gears are used to turn the drive through 90°

BHP Brake Horsepower. The British measurement for engine power output. Power output is now usually expressed in kilowatts (kW).

Bias-belted tyre Similar construction to radial tyre, but with outer belt running at an angle to the wheel rim.

Big-end bearing The bearing in the end of the connecting rod that's attached to the crankshaft.

Bleeding The process of removing air from an hydraulic system via a bleed nipple or bleed screw.

Bottom-end A description of an engine's crankcase components and all components contained there-in.

BTDC Before Top Dead Centre in terms of piston position. Ignition timing is often expressed in terms of degrees or millimetres BTDC.

Bush A cylindrical metal or rubber component used between two moving parts.

Burr Rough edge left on a component after machining or as a result of excessive wear.

C

Cam chain The chain which takes drive from the crankshaft to the camshaft(s).

Canister The main component in an evaporative emission control system (California market only); contains activated charcoal granules to trap vapours from the fuel system rather than allowing them to vent to the atmosphere.

Castellated Resembling the parapets along the top of a castle wall. For example, a castellated wheel axle or spindle nut.

Catalytic converter A device in the exhaust system of some machines which converts certain pollutants in the exhaust gases into less harmful substances.

Charging system Description of the components which charge the battery, ie the alternator, rectifer and regulator.

Circlip A ring-shaped clip used to prevent endwise movement of cylindrical parts and shafts. An internal circlip is installed in a groove in a housing; an external circlip fits into a groove on the outside of a cylindrical piece such as a shaft. Also known as a snap-ring.

Clearance The amount of space between two parts. For example, between a piston and a cylinder, between a bearing and a journal, etc.

Coil spring A spiral of elastic steel found in various sizes throughout a vehicle, for example as a springing medium in the suspension and in the valve train.

Compression Reduction in volume, and increase in pressure and temperature, of a gas, caused by squeezing it into a smaller space.

Compression damping Controls the speed the suspension compresses when hitting a bump.

Compression ratio The relationship between cylinder volume when the piston is at top dead centre and cylinder volume when the piston is at bottom dead centre.

Continuity The uninterrupted path in the flow of electricity. Little or no measurable resistance.

Continuity tester Self-powered bleeper or test light which indicates continuity.

Cp Candlepower. Bulb rating commonly found on US motorcycles.

Crossply tyre Tyre plies arranged in a criss-cross pattern. Usually four or six plies used, hence 4PR or 6PR in tyre size codes.

Cush drive Rubber damper segments fitted between the rear wheel and final drive sprocket to absorb transmission shocks **(see illustration)**.

Cush drive rubbers dampen out transmission shocks

D

Degree disc Calibrated disc for measuring piston position. Expressed in degrees.

Dial gauge Clock-type gauge with adapters for measuring runout and piston position. Expressed in mm or inches.

Diaphragm The rubber membrane in a master cylinder or carburettor which seals the upper chamber.

Diaphragm spring A single sprung plate often used in clutches.

Direct current (dc) Current produced by a dc generator.

Decarbonisation The process of removing carbon deposits - typically from the combustion chamber, valves and exhaust port/system.

Detonation Destructive and damaging explosion of fuel/air mixture in combustion chamber instead of controlled burning.

Diode An electrical valve which only allows current to flow in one direction. Commonly used in rectifiers and starter interlock systems.

Disc valve (or rotary valve) A induction system used on some two-stroke engines.

Double-overhead camshaft (DOHC) An engine that uses two overhead camshafts, one for the intake valves and one for the exhaust valves.

Drivebelt A toothed belt used to transmit drive to the rear wheel on some motorcycles. A drivebelt has also been used to drive the camshafts. Drivebelts are usually made of Kevlar.

Driveshaft Any shaft used to transmit motion. Commonly used when referring to the final driveshaft on shaft drive motorcycles.

E

Earth return The return path of an electrical circuit, utilising the motorcycle's frame.

ECU (Electronic Control Unit) A computer which controls (for instance) an ignition system, or an anti-lock braking system.

EGO Exhaust Gas Oxygen sensor. Sometimes called a Lambda sensor.

Electrolyte The fluid in a lead-acid battery.

EMS (Engine Management System) A computer controlled system which manages the fuel injection and the ignition systems in an integrated fashion.

Endfloat The amount of lengthways movement between two parts. As applied to a crankshaft, the distance that the crankshaft can move side-to-side in the crankcase.

Endless chain A chain having no joining link. Common use for cam chains and final drive chains.

EP (Extreme Pressure) Oil type used in locations where high loads are applied, such as between gear teeth.

Evaporative emission control system Describes a charcoal filled canister which stores fuel vapours from the tank rather than allowing them to vent to the atmosphere. Usually only fitted to California models and referred to as an EVAP system.

Expansion chamber Section of two-stroke engine exhaust system so designed to improve engine efficiency and boost power.

F

Feeler blade or gauge A thin strip or blade of hardened steel, ground to an exact thickness, used to check or measure clearances between parts.

Final drive Description of the drive from the transmission to the rear wheel. Usually by chain or shaft, but sometimes by belt.

Firing order The order in which the engine cylinders fire, or deliver their power strokes, beginning with the number one cylinder.

Flooding Term used to describe a high fuel level in the carburettor float chambers, leading to fuel overflow. Also refers to excess fuel in the combustion chamber due to incorrect starting technique.

Free length The no-load state of a component when measured. Clutch, valve and fork spring lengths are measured at rest, without any preload.

Freeplay The amount of travel before any action takes place. The looseness in a linkage, or an assembly of parts, between the initial application of force and actual movement. For example, the distance the rear brake pedal moves before the rear brake is actuated.

Fuel injection The fuel/air mixture is metered electronically and directed into the engine intake ports (indirect injection) or into the cylinders (direct injection). Sensors supply information on engine speed and conditions.

Fuel/air mixture The charge of fuel and air going into the engine. See **Stoichiometric ratio**.

Fuse An electrical device which protects a circuit against accidental overload. The typical fuse contains a soft piece of metal which is calibrated to melt at a predetermined current flow (expressed as amps) and break the circuit.

G

Gap The distance the spark must travel in jumping from the centre electrode to the side electrode in a spark plug. Also refers to the distance between the ignition rotor and the pickup coil in an electronic ignition system.

Gasket Any thin, soft material - usually cork, cardboard, asbestos or soft metal - installed between two metal surfaces to ensure a good seal. For instance, the cylinder head gasket seals the joint between the block and the cylinder head.

Gauge An instrument panel display used to monitor engine conditions. A gauge with a movable pointer on a dial or a fixed scale is an analogue gauge. A gauge with a numerical readout is called a digital gauge.

Gear ratios The drive ratio of a pair of gears in a gearbox, calculated on their number of teeth.

Glaze-busting see **Honing**

Grinding Process for renovating the valve face and valve seat contact area in the cylinder head.

Gudgeon pin The shaft which connects the connecting rod small-end with the piston. Often called a piston pin or wrist pin.

H

Helical gears Gear teeth are slightly curved and produce less gear noise that straight-cut gears. Often used for primary drives.

Installing a Helicoil thread insert in a cylinder head

Helicoil A thread insert repair system. Commonly used as a repair for stripped spark plug threads **(see illustration)**.

Honing A process used to break down the glaze on a cylinder bore (also called glaze-busting). Can also be carried out to roughen a rebored cylinder to aid ring bedding-in.

HT (High Tension) Description of the electrical circuit from the secondary winding of the ignition coil to the spark plug.

Hydraulic A liquid filled system used to transmit pressure from one component to another. Common uses on motorcycles are brakes and clutches.

Hydrometer An instrument for measuring the specific gravity of a lead-acid battery.

Hygroscopic Water absorbing. In motorcycle applications, braking efficiency will be reduced if DOT 3 or 4 hydraulic fluid absorbs water from the air - care must be taken to keep new brake fluid in tightly sealed containers.

I

lbf ft Pounds-force feet. An imperial unit of torque. Sometimes written as ft-lbs.

lbf in Pound-force inch. An imperial unit of torque, applied to components where a very low torque is required. Sometimes written as in-lbs.

IC Abbreviation for Integrated Circuit.

Ignition advance Means of increasing the timing of the spark at higher engine speeds. Done by mechanical means (ATU) on early engines or electronically by the ignition control unit on later engines.

Ignition timing The moment at which the spark plug fires, expressed in the number of crankshaft degrees before the piston reaches the top of its stroke, or in the number of millimetres before the piston reaches the top of its stroke.

Infinity (∞) Description of an open-circuit electrical state, where no continuity exists.

Inverted forks (upside down forks) The sliders or lower legs are held in the yokes and the fork tubes or stanchions are connected to the wheel axle (spindle). Less unsprung weight and stiffer construction than conventional forks.

J

JASO Quality standard for 2-stroke oils.

Joule The unit of electrical energy.

Journal The bearing surface of a shaft.

K

Kickstart Mechanical means of turning the engine over for starting purposes. Only usually fitted to mopeds, small capacity motorcycles and off-road motorcycles.

Kill switch Handebar-mounted switch for emergency ignition cut-out. Cuts the ignition circuit on all models, and additionally prevent starter motor operation on others.

km Symbol for kilometre.

kmh Abbreviation for kilometres per hour.

L

Lambda (λ) sensor A sensor fitted in the exhaust system to measure the exhaust gas oxygen content (excess air factor).

Lapping see **Grinding**.

LCD Abbreviation for Liquid Crystal Display.

LED Abbreviation for Light Emitting Diode.

Liner A steel cylinder liner inserted in a aluminium alloy cylinder block.

Locknut A nut used to lock an adjustment nut, or other threaded component, in place.

Lockstops The lugs on the lower triple clamp (yoke) which abut those on the frame, preventing handlebar-to-fuel tank contact.

Lockwasher A form of washer designed to prevent an attaching nut from working loose.

LT Low Tension Description of the electrical circuit from the power supply to the primary winding of the ignition coil.

M

Main bearings The bearings between the crankshaft and crankcase.

Maintenance-free (MF) battery A sealed battery which cannot be topped up.

Manometer Mercury-filled calibrated tubes used to measure intake tract vacuum. Used to synchronise carburettors on multi-cylinder engines.

Micrometer A precision measuring instrument that measures component outside diameters **(see illustration)**.

Tappet shims are measured with a micrometer

MON (Motor Octane Number) A measure of a fuel's resistance to knock.

Monograde oil An oil with a single viscosity, eg SAE80W.

Monoshock A single suspension unit linking the swingarm or suspension linkage to the frame.

mph Abbreviation for miles per hour.

Multigrade oil Having a wide viscosity range (eg 10W40). The W stands for Winter, thus the viscosity ranges from SAE10 when cold to SAE40 when hot.

Multimeter An electrical test instrument with the capability to measure voltage, current and resistance. Some meters also incorporate a continuity tester and buzzer.

N

Needle roller bearing Inner race of caged needle rollers and hardened outer race. Examples of uncaged needle rollers can be found on some engines. Commonly used in rear suspension applications and in two-stroke engines.

Nm Newton metres.

NOx Oxides of Nitrogen. A common toxic pollutant emitted by petrol engines at higher temperatures.

O

Octane The measure of a fuel's resistance to knock.

OE (Original Equipment) Relates to components fitted to a motorcycle as standard or replacement parts supplied by the motorcycle manufacturer.

Ohm The unit of electrical resistance. Ohms = Volts ÷ Current.

Ohmmeter An instrument for measuring electrical resistance.

Oil cooler System for diverting engine oil outside of the engine to a radiator for cooling purposes.

Oil injection A system of two-stroke engine lubrication where oil is pump-fed to the engine in accordance with throttle position.

Open-circuit An electrical condition where there is a break in the flow of electricity - no continuity (high resistance).

O-ring A type of sealing ring made of a special rubber-like material; in use, the O-ring is compressed into a groove to provide the sealing action.

Oversize (OS) Term used for piston and ring size options fitted to a rebored cylinder.

Overhead cam (sohc) engine An engine with single camshaft located on top of the cylinder head.

Overhead valve (ohv) engine An engine with the valves located in the cylinder head, but with the camshaft located in the engine block or crankcase.

Oxygen sensor A device installed in the exhaust system which senses the oxygen content in the exhaust and converts this information into an electric current. Also called a Lambda sensor.

P

Plastigauge A thin strip of plastic thread, available in different sizes, used for measuring clearances. For example, a strip of Plastigauge is laid across a bearing journal. The parts are assembled and dismantled; the width of the crushed strip indicates the clearance between journal and bearing.

Polarity Either negative or positive earth (ground), determined by which battery lead is connected to the frame (earth return). Modern motorcycles are usually negative earth.

Pre-ignition A situation where the fuel/air mixture ignites before the spark plug fires. Often due to a hot spot in the combustion chamber caused by carbon build-up. Engine has a tendency to 'run-on'.

Pre-load (suspension) The amount a spring is compressed when in the unloaded state. Preload can be applied by gas, spacer or mechanical adjuster.

Premix The method of engine lubrication on older two-stroke engines. Engine oil is mixed with the petrol in the fuel tank in a specific ratio. The fuel/oil mix is sometimes referred to as "petroil".

Primary drive Description of the drive from the crankshaft to the clutch. Usually by gear or chain.

PS Pfedestärke - a German interpretation of BHP.

PSI Pounds-force per square inch. Imperial measurement of tyre pressure and cylinder pressure measurement.

PTFE Polytetrafluroethylene. A low friction substance.

Pulse secondary air injection system A process of promoting the burning of excess fuel present in the exhaust gases by routing fresh air into the exhaust ports.

Q

Quartz halogen bulb Tungsten filament surrounded by a halogen gas. Typically used for the headlight **(see illustration)**.

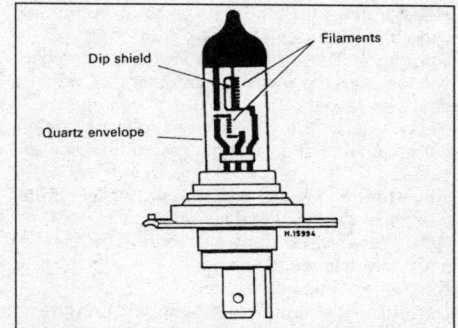

Quartz halogen headlight bulb construction

R

Rack-and-pinion A pinion gear on the end of a shaft that mates with a rack (think of a geared wheel opened up and laid flat). Sometimes used in clutch operating systems.

Radial play Up and down movement about a shaft.

Radial ply tyres Tyre plies run across the tyre (from bead to bead) and around the circumference of the tyre. Less resistant to tread distortion than other tyre types.

Radiator A liquid-to-air heat transfer device designed to reduce the temperature of the coolant in a liquid cooled engine.

Rake A feature of steering geometry - the angle of the steering head in relation to the vertical **(see illustration)**.

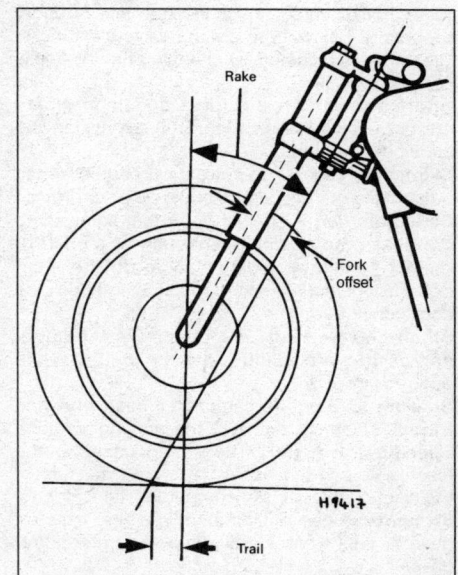

Steering geometry

Rebore Providing a new working surface to the cylinder bore by boring out the old surface. Necessitates the use of oversize piston and rings.

Rebound damping A means of controlling the oscillation of a suspension unit spring after it has been compressed. Resists the spring's natural tendency to bounce back after being compressed.

Rectifier Device for converting the ac output of an alternator into dc for battery charging.

Reed valve An induction system commonly used on two-stroke engines.

Regulator Device for maintaining the charging voltage from the generator or alternator within a specified range.

Relay A electrical device used to switch heavy current on and off by using a low current auxiliary circuit.

Resistance Measured in ohms. An electrical component's ability to pass electrical current.

RON (Research Octane Number) A measure of a fuel's resistance to knock.

rpm revolutions per minute.

Runout The amount of wobble (in-and-out movement) of a wheel or shaft as it's rotated. The amount a shaft rotates 'out-of-true'. The out-of-round condition of a rotating part.

S

SAE (Society of Automotive Engineers) A standard for the viscosity of a fluid.

Sealant A liquid or paste used to prevent leakage at a joint. Sometimes used in conjunction with a gasket.

Service limit Term for the point where a component is no longer useable and must be renewed.

Shaft drive A method of transmitting drive from the transmission to the rear wheel.

Shell bearings Plain bearings consisting of two shell halves. Most often used as big-end and main bearings in a four-stroke engine. Often called bearing inserts.

Shim Thin spacer, commonly used to adjust the clearance or relative positions between two parts. For example, shims inserted into or under tappets or followers to control valve clearances. Clearance is adjusted by changing the thickness of the shim.

Short-circuit An electrical condition where current shorts to earth (ground) bypassing the circuit components.

Skimming Process to correct warpage or repair a damaged surface, eg on brake discs or drums.

Slide-hammer A special puller that screws into or hooks onto a component such as a shaft or bearing; a heavy sliding handle on the shaft bottoms against the end of the shaft to knock the component free.

Small-end bearing The bearing in the upper end of the connecting rod at its joint with the gudgeon pin.

Spalling Damage to camshaft lobes or bearing journals shown as pitting of the working surface.

Specific gravity (SG) The state of charge of the electrolyte in a lead-acid battery. A measure of the electrolyte's density compared with water.

Straight-cut gears Common type gear used on gearbox shafts and for oil pump and water pump drives.

Stanchion The inner sliding part of the front forks, held by the yokes. Often called a fork tube.

Stoichiometric ratio The optimum chemical air/fuel ratio for a petrol engine, said to be 14.7 parts of air to 1 part of fuel.

Sulphuric acid The liquid (electrolyte) used in a lead-acid battery. Poisonous and extremely corrosive.

Surface grinding (lapping) Process to correct a warped gasket face, commonly used on cylinder heads.

T

Tapered-roller bearing Tapered inner race of caged needle rollers and separate tapered outer race. Examples of taper roller bearings can be found on steering heads.

Tappet A cylindrical component which transmits motion from the cam to the valve stem, either directly or via a pushrod and rocker arm. Also called a cam follower.

TCS Traction Control System. An electronically-controlled system which senses wheel spin and reduces engine speed accordingly.

TDC Top Dead Centre denotes that the piston is at its highest point in the cylinder.

Thread-locking compound Solution applied to fastener threads to prevent slackening. Select type to suit application.

Thrust washer A washer positioned between two moving components on a shaft. For example, between gear pinions on gearshaft.

Timing chain See **Cam Chain.**

Timing light Stroboscopic lamp for carrying out ignition timing checks with the engine running.

Top-end A description of an engine's cylinder block, head and valve gear components.

Torque Turning or twisting force about a shaft.

Torque setting A prescribed tightness specified by the motorcycle manufacturer to ensure that the bolt or nut is secured correctly. Undertightening can result in the bolt or nut coming loose or a surface not being sealed. Overtightening can result in stripped threads, distortion or damage to the component being retained.

Torx key A six-point wrench.

Tracer A stripe of a second colour applied to a wire insulator to distinguish that wire from another one with the same colour insulator. For example, Br/W is often used to denote a brown insulator with a white tracer.

Trail A feature of steering geometry. Distance from the steering head axis to the tyre's central contact point.

Triple clamps The cast components which extend from the steering head and support the fork stanchions or tubes. Often called fork yokes.

Turbocharger A centrifugal device, driven by exhaust gases, that pressurises the intake air. Normally used to increase the power output from a given engine displacement.

TWI Abbreviation for Tyre Wear Indicator. Indicates the location of the tread depth indicator bars on tyres.

U

Universal joint or U-joint (UJ) A double-pivoted connection for transmitting power from a driving to a driven shaft through an angle. Typically found in shaft drive assemblies.

Unsprung weight Anything not supported by the bike's suspension (ie the wheel, tyres, brakes, final drive and bottom (moving) part of the suspension).

V

Vacuum gauges Clock-type gauges for measuring intake tract vacuum. Used for carburettor synchronisation on multi-cylinder engines.

Valve A device through which the flow of liquid, gas or vacuum may be stopped, started or regulated by a moveable part that opens, shuts or partially obstructs one or more ports or passageways. The intake and exhaust valves in the cylinder head are of the poppet type.

Valve clearance The clearance between the valve tip (the end of the valve stem) and the rocker arm or tappet/follower. The valve clearance is measured when the valve is closed. The correct clearance is important - if too small the valve won't close fully and will burn out, whereas if too large noisy operation will result.

Valve lift The amount a valve is lifted off its seat by the camshaft lobe.

Valve timing The exact setting for the opening and closing of the valves in relation to piston position.

Vernier caliper A precision measuring instrument that measures inside and outside dimensions. Not quite as accurate as a micrometer, but more convenient.

VIN Vehicle Identification Number. Term for the bike's engine and frame numbers.

Viscosity The thickness of a liquid or its resistance to flow.

Volt A unit for expressing electrical "pressure" in a circuit. Volts = current x ohms.

W

Water pump A mechanically-driven device for moving coolant around the engine.

Watt A unit for expressing electrical power. Watts = volts x current.

Wear limit see **Service limit**

Wet liner A liquid-cooled engine design where the pistons run in liners which are directly surrounded by coolant **(see illustration)**.

Wet liner arrangement

Wheelbase Distance from the centre of the front wheel to the centre of the rear wheel.

Wiring harness or loom Describes the electrical wires running the length of the motorcycle and enclosed in tape or plastic sheathing. Wiring coming off the main harness is usually referred to as a sub harness.

Woodruff key A key of semi-circular or square section used to locate a gear to a shaft. Often used to locate the alternator rotor on the crankshaft.

Wrist pin Another name for gudgeon or piston pin.

M

Main bearings – 2A•39, 2B•39
Maintenance schedule – 1•6
Middle driven gear – 2A•33, 2B•32
Mirrors – 7•7
MOT test checks – REF•27 *et seq*
Mudguards – 7•6

N

Neutral switch – 8•16

O

Oil (engine) – 0•13, 1•2, 1•3, 1•7
Oil (final drive) – 1•2, 1•3, 1•13, 1•22
Oil (front forks) – 5•1, 1•23
Oil level relay and sensor – 8•17
Oil pressure relief valve – 2A•30, 2B•36
Oil pump – 2A•30, 2B•21
Oil strainer – 2A•31, 2B•23

P

Parts – 1•2
Piston rings – 2A•20, 2B•15
Pistons – 2A•18, 2B•15
Primary drive gears – 2A•25, 2B•25

R

Rear brake (650 models)
    check – 1•16
    drum and shoes – 6•14
Rear brake (1100 models)
    caliper – 6•10
    disc – 6•11
    master cylinder – 6•11,
    pads – 1•15, 6•9
Rear suspension
    check – 1•19
    linkage (1100 models) – 5•16
    shock absorber – 5•15
Rear wheel – 6•17
Regulator/rectifier – 8•26
Relay
    assembly – 8•16
    carburettor heater – 8•19
    fuel pump – 8•17
    oil level – 8•18
    starter – 8•19
    starter cut-out – 8•17
    turn signal – 8•9
Rings (piston) – 2A•20, 2B•15
Rocker arms – 2A•11, 2B•13

S

Safety – 0•12
Seats – 7•2
Security – REF•20 *et seq*
Selector drum and forks – 2A•40, 2B•40
Servicing – 1•1 *et seq*
Sidelight – 8•5, 8•6
Sidestand – 1•13, 5•6
Sidestand switch – 8•15
Spark plugs – 1•2, 1•3, 1•12
Speedometer and speed sensor – 8•11
Starter clutch and gears – 2A•21, 2B•25
Starter cut-out relay – 8•17
Starter motor – 8•20
Starter relay – 8•19
Steering
    head bearings – 1•17, 5•14
    head panels – 7•5
    stem – 5•13
Storage – REF•32 *et seq*
Suspension
    adjustment – 1•19
    checks – 1•18
    front forks – 1•23, 5•8, 5•9
    rear shock absorber – 5•15
    rear shock linkage (1100 models) – 5•16
Swingarm – 5•17, 5•19

T

Tensioner (cam chain) – 2A•8, 2B•9
Throttle cables – 1•14, 3•17
Throttle position sensor – 3•2, 4•1, 4•4
Tools and workshop tips – REF•2 *et seq*
Toolbox cover – 7•2, 7•4
Torque settings – 1•2, 1•3, 2A•3, 2B•3, 3•2, 4•1, 5•2, 6•2, 7•1, 8•2
Transmission – 2A•3, 2A•42, 2B•1, 2B•42
Turn signals – 8•9
Tyres
    checks and pressures – 0•16
    fitting – 6•22
    sizes – 6•1

V

Valve clearances – 1•9, 1•12
Valve overhaul – 2A•13, 2B•14

W

Warning lights – 8•13
Weights – 0•11
Wheel
    alignment – 6•15
    bearings – 1•19, 6•21
    inspection and repair – 6•15
    removal and installation – 6•19
Wiring diagrams – 8•27 *et seq*

Preserving Our Motoring Heritage

< The Model J Duesenberg Derham Tourster. Only eight of these magnificent cars were ever built – this is the only example to be found outside the United States of America

Almost every car you've ever loved, loathed or desired is gathered under one roof at the Haynes Motor Museum. Over 300 immaculately presented cars and motorbikes represent every aspect of our motoring heritage, from elegant reminders of bygone days, such as the superb Model J Duesenberg to curiosities like the bug-eyed BMW Isetta. There are also many old friends and flames. Perhaps you remember the 1959 Ford Popular that you did your courting in? The magnificent 'Red Collection' is a spectacle of classic sports cars including AC, Alfa Romeo, Austin Healey, Ferrari, Lamborghini, Maserati, MG, Riley, Porsche and Triumph.

A Perfect Day Out

Each and every vehicle at the Haynes Motor Museum has played its part in the history and culture of Motoring. Today, they make a wonderful spectacle and a great day out for all the family. Bring the kids, bring Mum and Dad, but above all bring your camera to capture those golden memories for ever. You will also find an impressive array of motoring memorabilia, a comfortable 70 seat video cinema and one of the most extensive transport book shops in Britain. The Pit Stop Cafe serves everything from a cup of tea to wholesome, home-made meals or, if you prefer, you can enjoy the large picnic area nestled in the beautiful rural surroundings of Somerset.

> John Haynes O.B.E., Founder and Chairman of the museum at the wheel of a Haynes Light 12.

< The 1936 490cc sohc-engined International Norton – well known for its racing success

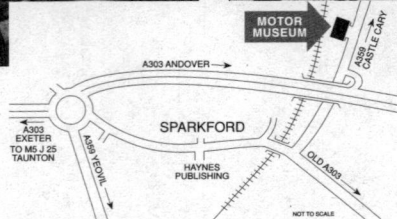

The Museum is situated on the A359 Yeovil to Frome road at Sparkford, just off the A303 in Somerset. It is about 40 miles south of Bristol, and 25 minutes drive from the M5 intersection at Taunton.

Open 9.30am - 5.30pm (10.00am - 4.00pm Winter) 7 days a week, *except Christmas Day, Boxing Day and New Years Day*

Special rates available for schools, coach parties and outings   Charitable Trust No. 292048